CHILTON'S
REPAIR & TUNE-UP GUIDE
JEEP® CJ
1945 to
1981

**CJ-2A • CJ-3A • CJ-3B • CJ-5
CJ-6 • CJ-7 • Scrambler**

Managing Editor KERRY A. FREEMAN, S.A.E.
Senior Editor RICHARD J. RIVELE, S.A.E.
Editor RICHARD J. RIVELE, S.A.E.

President WILLIAM A. BARBOUR
Executive Vice President JAMES A. MIADES
Vice President and General Manager JOHN P. KUSHNERICK

CHILTON BOOK COMPANY
Radnor, Pennsylvania
19089

SAFETY NOTICE

Proper service and repair procedures are vital to the safe, reliable operation of all motor vehicles, as well as the personal safety of those performing repairs. This book outlines procedures for servicing and repairing vehicles using safe, effective methods. The procedures contain many NOTES, CAUTIONS and WARNINGS which should be followed along with standard safety procedures to eliminate the possibility of personal injury or improper service which could damage the vehicle or compromise its safety.

It is important to note that repair procedures and techniques, tools and parts for servicing motor vehicles, as well as the skill and experience of the individual performing the work vary widely. It is not possible to anticipate all of the conceivable ways or conditions under which vehicles may be serviced, or to provide cautions as to all of the possible hazards that may result. Standard and accepted safety precautions and equipment should be used when handling toxic or flammable fluids, and safety goggles or other protection should be used during cutting, grinding, chiseling, prying, or any other process that can cause material removal or projectiles.

Some procedures require the use of tools specially designed for a specific purpose. Before substituting another tool or procedure, you must be completely satisfied that neither your personal safety, nor the performance of the vehicle will be endangered.

Although information in this guide is based on industry sources and is as complete as possible at the time of publication, the possibility exists that the manufacturer made later changes which could not be included here. While striving for total accuracy, Chilton Book Company cannot assume responsibility for any errors, changes, or omissions that may occur in the compilation of this data. .

PART NUMBERS

Part numbers listed in this reference are not recommendations by Chilton for any product by brand name. They are references that can be used with interchange manuals and aftermarket supplier catalogs to locate each brand supplier's discrete part number.

ACKNOWLEDGMENTS

The Chilton Book Company expresses its appreciation to the Jeep Corporation, A Division of American Motors Corporation, Detroit, Michigan for their generous assistance in the preparation of this book.

Copyright © 1981 by Chilton Book Company
All Rights Reserved
Published in Radnor, Pa., by Chilton Book Company
and simultaneously in Ontario, Canada
by Nelson Canada, Limited

Manufactured in the United States of America
1234567890   0987654321

Chilton's Repair & Tune-Up Guide: Jeep® CJ 1945–81
ISBN 0-8019-7136-5 pbk.
Library of Congress Catalog Card No. 81-66637

CONTENTS

Quick Reference Specifications For Your Vehicle

Fill in this chart with the most commonly used specifications for your vehicle. Specifications can be found in Chapters 1 through 3 or on the tune-up decal under the hood of the vehicle.

 **Tune-Up**

Firing Order_____

Spark Plugs:

    Type_____ _____

    Gap (in.)_____

Point Gap (in.)_____

Dwell Angle (°)_____

Ignition Timing (°)_____

    Vacuum (Connected/Disconnected)_____

Valve Clearance (in.)

    Intake_____   Exhaust_____

Capacities

Engine Oil (qts)

    With Filter Change_____

    Without Filter Change_____

Cooling System (qts)_____

Manual Transmission (pts)_____

    Type_____

Automatic Transmission (pts)_____

    Type_____

Front Differential (pts)_____

    Type_____

Rear Differential (pts)_____

    Type_____

Transfer Case (pts)_____

    Type_____

FREQUENTLY REPLACED PARTS

Use these spaces to record the part numbers of frequently replaced parts.

PCV VALVE

Manufacturer_____

Part No._____

OIL FILTER

Manufacturer_____

Part No._____

AIR FILTER

Manufacturer_____

Part No._____

General Information and Maintenance

HOW TO USE THIS BOOK

Chilton's Repair & Tune-Up Guide for the Jeep CJ® is intended to teach you more about the inner workings of your Jeep and save you money on its upkeep. The first two chapters will be used the most, since they contain maintenance and tune-up information and procedures. The following chapters concern themselves with the more complex systems of your Jeep. Operating systems from engine through brakes are covered to the extent that we feel the average do-it-yourselfer should get involved. This book will not explain such things as rebuilding the differential for the simple reason that the expertise required and the investment in special tools make this task uneconomical. We will tell you how to change your own brake pads and shoes, replace points and plugs, and many more jobs that will save you money, give you personal satisfaction and help you avoid problems.

A secondary purpose of this book is as a reference for owners who want to understand their Jeep and/or their mechanics better. In this case, no tools at all are required.

Before removing any parts, read through the entire procedure. This will give you the overall view of what tools and supplies will be required.

The sections begin with a brief discussion of the system and what it involves, followed by adjustments, maintenance, removal and installation procedures, and repair or overhaul procedures. When repair is not considered feasible, we tell you how to remove the part and then how to install the new or rebuilt replacement. In this way, you at least save the labor costs. Backyard repair of such components as the alternator is just not practical.

Two basic mechanic's rules should be mentioned here. One, whenever the left side of the Jeep or engine is referred to, it is meant to specify the driver's side of the Jeep. Conversely, the right side of the Jeep means the passenger's side. Secondly, most screws and bolts are removed by turning counterclockwise, and tightened by turning clockwise. Safety is always the most important rule. Constantly be aware of the dangers involved in working on an automobile and take the proper precautions. Use jackstands when working under a raised vehicle. Don't smoke or allow an exposed flame to come near the battery or any part of the fuel system. Always use the proper tool and use it correctly; bruised knuckles and skinned fingers aren't a mechanic's standard equipment. Always take your time and have patience; Once you have some experience, working on your Jeep will become an enjoyable hobby.

TOOLS AND EQUIPMENT

It would be impossible to catalog each and every tool that you may need to perform all the operations included in this book. It would also not be wise for the amateur to rush out and buy an expensive set of tools on the theory that he may need one of them at some time. The best approach is to proceed slowly, gathering together a good quality set of those tools that are used most frequently. Don't be misled by the low cost of bargain tools. It is far better to spend a little more for quality, name brand tools. Forged wrenches, 10 or 12 point sockets and finetooth ratchets are by far preferable to their less expensive counterparts. As any good mechanic can tell you, there are few worse experiences than trying to work on a truck with bad tools. Your monetary savings will be far outweighed by frustration and mangled knuckles.

Begin accumulating those tools that are used most frequently; those associated with routine maintenance and tune-up. In addition to the normal assortment of screwdrivers and pliers, you should have the following tools for routine maintenance jobs:

1. SAE wrenches, sockets and combination open end/box end wrenches;
2. Jackstands—for support;
3. Oil filter wrench;
4. Oil filler spout or funnel;
5. Grease gun—for chassis lubrication;
6. Hydrometer—for checking the battery;
7. A low flat pan for draining oil;
8. Lots of rags for wiping up the inevitable mess.

In addition to the above items, there are several others that are not absolutely necessary, but are handy to have around. These include oil drying compound, a transmission funnel, and the usual supply of lubricants, antifreeze and fluids, although these can be purchased as needed. This is a basic list for routine maintenance, but only your personal needs can accurately determine your list of tools.

The second list of tools is for tune-ups. While the tools involved here are slightly more sophisticated, they need not be outrageously expensive. There are several inexpensive tach/dwell meters on the market that are every bit as good for the average mechanic as a $100.00 professional model. Just be sure that it goes to at least 1200–1500 rpm on the tach sacle, and that it works on 4, 6,

and 8 cylinder engines. A basic list of tune-up equipment could include:

1. Tach/dwellmeter;
2. Spark plug wrench;
3. Timing light (preferably a DC light that works from the truck's battery);
4. A set of flat feeler gauges;
5. A set of round wire spark plug gauges.

In addition to these basic tools, there are several other tools and gauges you may find useful. These include:

1. A compression gauge. The screw-in type is slower to use, but eliminates the possibility of a faulty reading due to escaping pressure.
2. A manifold vacuum gauge;
3. A test light;
4. An induction meter. This is used for determining whether or not there is current in a wire. These are handy for use if a wire is broken somewhere in a wiring harness. As a final note, you will probably find a torque wrench necessary for all but the most basic work. The beam type models are perfectly adequate, although the newer click type are more precise.

Special Tools

Normally, the use of special factory tools is avoided for repair procedures, since these are not readily available for the do-it-yourself mechanic. When it is possible to perform the job with more commonly available tools, it will be pointed out, but occasionally, a special tool was designed to perform a specific function and should be used. Before substituting another tool, you should be convinced that neither your safety nor the performance of the vehicle will be compromised.

Some special tools are available commercially from major tool manufacturers. Others for your Jeep can be purchased from your dealer or from Owatonna Tool Co., Owatonna, Minnesota 55060, and the Kent-Moore Corp. 1501 S. Jackson St., Jackson, MI 49203.

SERVICING YOUR JEEP SAFELY

It is virtually impossible to anticipate all of the hazards involved with automotive maintenance and service but care and common sense will prevent most accidents.

The rules of safety for mechanics range

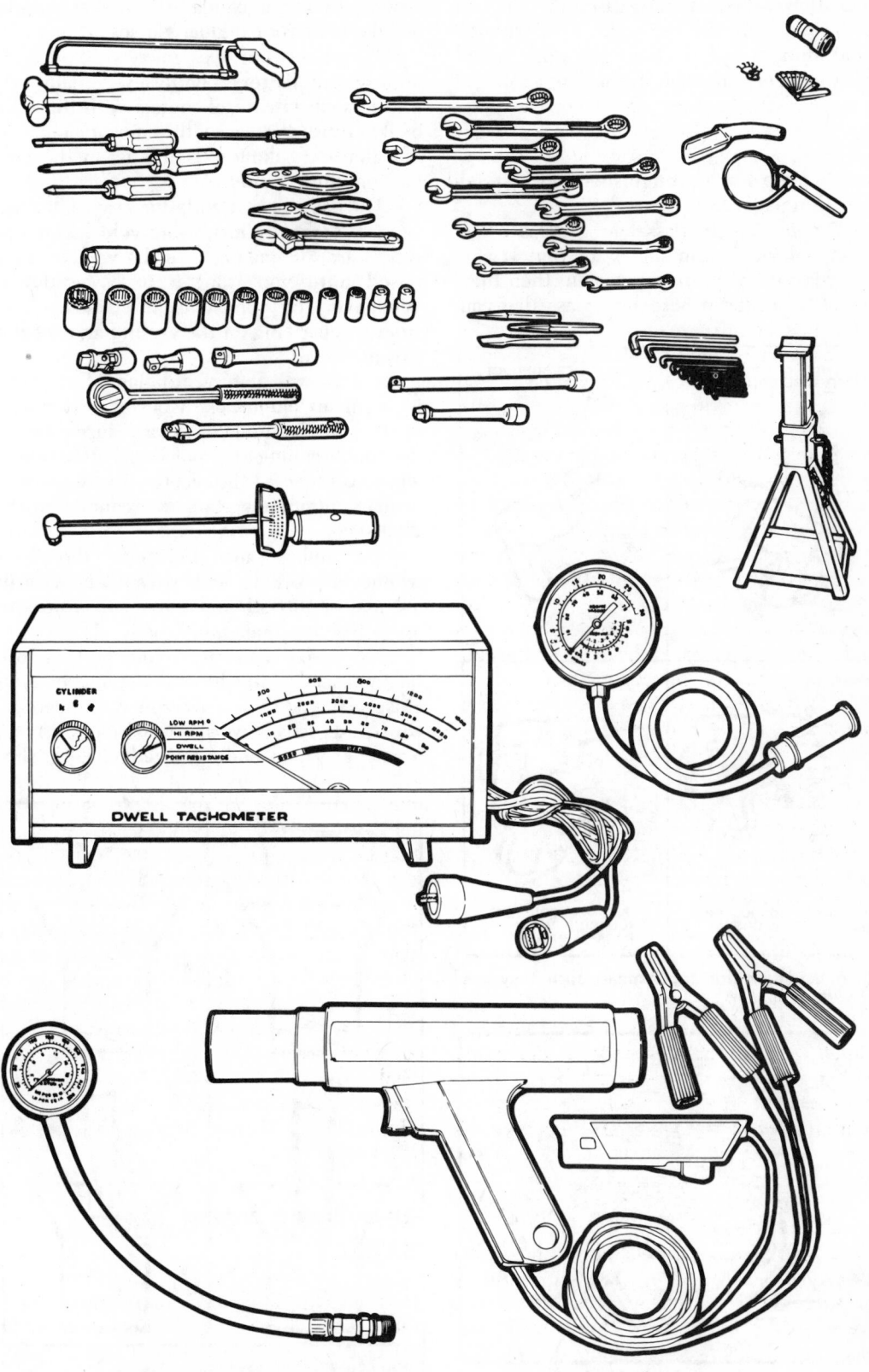

This basic collection of hand tools will handle most of your automotive needs

from "don't smoke around gasoline," to "use the proper tool for the job." The trick to avoid injuries is to develop safe work habits and take every possible precaution.

Do's

• Do keep a fire extinguisher and first aid kit within easy reach.

• Do wear safety glasses or goggles when cutting, drilling, grinding or prying. If you wear glasses for the sake of vision, then they should be made of hardened glass that can serve also as safety glasses, or wear safety goggles over your regular glasses.

• Do shield your eyes whenever you work around the battery. Batteries contain sulphuric acid; in case of contact with the eyes or skin, flush the area with water or a mixture of water and baking soda and get medical attention immediately.

• Do use safety stands for any under-car service. Jacks are for raising vehicles; safety stands are for making sure the vehicle stays raised until you want it to come down. Whenever the vehicle is raised, block the wheels remaining on the ground and set the parking brake.

• Do use adequate ventilation when working with any chemicals. Asbestos dust resulting from brake lining wear can cause cancer.

• Do disconnect the negative battery cable when working on the electrical system. The primary ignition system can contain up to 40,000 volts.

• Do follow manufacturer's directions whenever working with potentially hazardous materials. Both brake fluid and antifreeze are poisonous if taken internally.

• Do properly maintain your tools. Loose hammerheads, mushroomed punches and chisels, frayed or poorly grounded electrical cords, excessively worn screwdrivers, spread wrenches (open end), cracked sockets, slip-

TWO-WIRE CONDUCTOR THIRD WIRE GROUNDING THE CASE

THREE-WIRE CONDUCTOR GROUNDING THRU A CIRCUIT

THREE-WIRE CONDUCTOR ONE WIRE TO A GROUND

THREE-WIRE CONDUCTOR GROUNDING THRU AN ADAPTER PLUG

When using electric tools make sure they are properly grounded

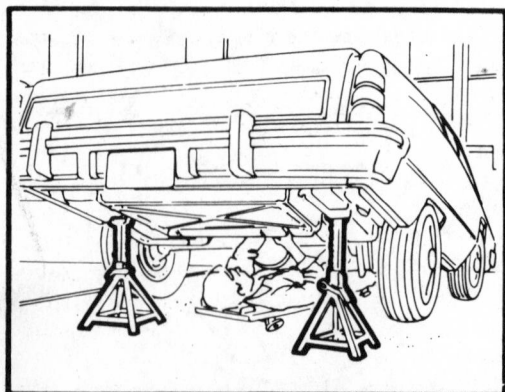

Always use jackstands when working under the truck

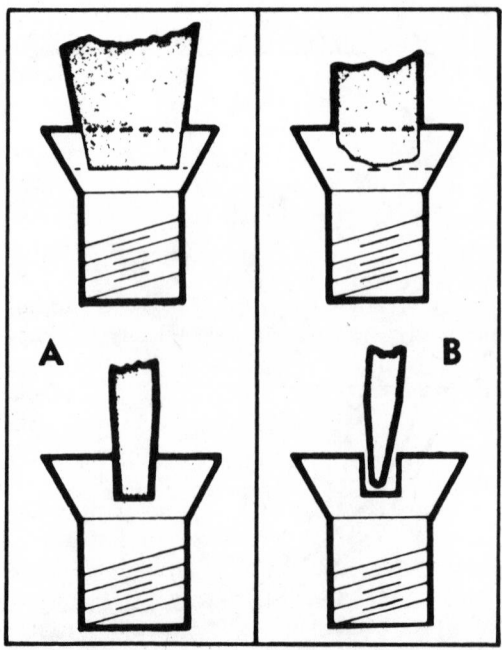

Keep screwdriver tips in good shape. They should fit the slot as shown in "A". If they look like those in "B", they need grinding or replacing

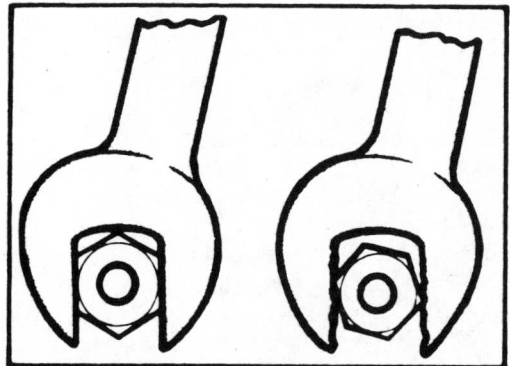

When you're using an open end wrench, use the correct size and position it properly on the flats of the nut or bolt

ping ratchets, or faulty droplight sockets can cause accidents.

• Do use the proper size and type of tool for the job being done.

• Do when possible, pull on a wrench handle rather than push on it, and adjust your stance to prevent a fall.

• Do be sure that adjustable wrenches are tightly adjusted on the nut or bolt and pulled so that the face is on the side of the fixed jaw.

• Do select a wrench or socket that fits the nut or bolt. The wrench or socket should sit straight, not cocked.

• Do strike squarely with a hammer to avoid glancing blows.

• Do set the parking brake and block the drive wheels if the work requires that the engine be running.

Dont's

• Don't run an engine in a garage or anywhere else without proper ventilation—EVER! Carbon monoxide is poisonous; it is absorbed by the body 400 times faster than oxygen; it takes a long time to leave the human body and you can build up a deadly supply of it in your system by simply breathing in a little every day. You may not realize you are slowly poisoning yourself. Always use power vents, windows, fans or open the garage doors.

• Don't work around moving parts while wearing a necktie or other loose clothing. Short sleeves are much safer than long, loose sleeves. Hard-toed shoes with neoprene soles protect your toes and give a better grip on slippery surfaces. Jewelry such as watches, fancy belt buckles, beads or body adornment of any kind is not safe working

around a car. Long hair should be hidden under a hat or cap.

• Don't use pockets for toolboxes. A fall or bump can drive a screwdriver deep into your body. Even a wiping cloth hanging from the back pocket can wrap around a spinning shaft or fan.

• Don't smoke when working around gasoline, cleaning solvent or other flammable material.

• Don't smoke when working around the battery. When the battery is being charged, it gives off explosive hydrogen gas.

• Don't use gasoline to wash your hands; there are excellent soaps available. Gasoline may contain lead, and lead can enter the body through a cut, accumulating in the body until you are very ill. Gasoline also removes all the natural oils from the skin so that bone dry hands will suck up oil and grease.

• Don't service the air conditioning system unless you are equipped with the necessary tools and training. The refrigerant, R-12, is extremely cold and when exposed to the air, will instantly freeze any surface it comes in contact with, including your eyes. Although the refrigerant is normally non-toxic, R-12 becomes a deadly poisonous gas in the presence of an open flame. One good whiff of the vapors from burning refrigerant can be fatal.

HISTORY AND MODEL IDENTIFICATION

The first "Jeep," as we know it today, was the Model MB Military. It was produced from 1941 through 1945. The distinguishing characteristics were an L head, four-cylinder engine, no tailgate, a 6 volt (6 V) electrical system, split windshield, rear-mounted spare tire, and a timing chain.

The next model was the CJ-2A. It was made from 1945 to 1949 and was the first Jeep made available directly to the public. This is the civilian version of the MB Military. The letters CJ stand for Civilian Jeep. The distinguishing characteristics of this model are the L head, four-cylinder engine, split windshield, and 6 V electrical system. The civilian version differs from the Model MB Military in that the spare tire is mounted on the side of the vehicle and there is a tailgate.

The CJ-3A was brought out in 1948. The only outward difference between this model and the CJ-2A is that the CJ-3A has a one-

1941–45 MB military

1945–49 CJ-2A

1948–53 CJ-3A

1950–51 MC-M38 military

1951–68 MD-M38A1 military

1953–64 CJ-3B

1955–69 CJ-5

1970–81 CJ-5

CJ-6

1976—81 CJ-7

1981 Jeep Scrambler

piece windshield. This model was produced until 1953.

The military services received a new model Jeep in 1950; the Model MC-M38 Military. This Jeep had a 24 V electrical system, a four-cylinder L head engine, no tailgate, brush guards over tfhe headlights, a one-piece windshield, and a rear-mounted spare tire. This model was produced only until 1951.

In 1951 the Model MD-M38A1 Military replaced the Model MC-M38 Military. The newer model had rounded front fenders and was made until 1968.

A new civilian Jeep, the Model CJ-3B, was introduced in 1953. It can be distinguished by its high flat hood but also had a four-cylinder, F head engine, side-mounted spare tire, one-piece windshield, tailgate, angular fenders (like all of the earlier models), and a 6 V or 12 V electrical system. The CJ-3B was made until 1964.

The CJ-5, a civilian version of the MD-M38A1 was released in 1955. It had a tailgate, a 6 V or 12 V electrical system, and rounded fenders. Two engines were offered for the first time in the Universal series with this introduction. The traditional four-cylinder F head was offered as well as the V6 Buick engine. The V6 was available from 1965 to 1971. The CJ-5's spare is usually mounted on the side. In 1972 the wheelbase of the CJ-5 was lengthened from 81 to 84 in. to accomodate the larger American Motors engines.

A longer version of the CJ-5 was also introduced in 1955. This was the CJ-6 with a wheelbase of 101 in. It was, identical to the CJ-5 except for the longer wheelbase. The CJ-6 also had its wheelbase elongated (to 104 in.) in 1972 to accommodate the larger American Motors engines.

For the 1976 model year, the CJ-6 was discontinued in the U.S. and Canada, although still exported. A new model, the CJ-7, featuring an optional one-piece removable plastic hardtop, automatic transmission, steel side doors with roll-up windows and the full-time 4WD system, Quadra-Trac,® was introduced. The CJ-7 has a wheelbase of 93.5 in.

In mid-year 1981 Jeep introduced its newest model, the Scrambler. Designed for rugged dependability and good fuel economy, the Scrambler is both a work and recreational vehicle. The standard engine is a GM built 151 cid 4-cylinder with an American Motors 6-258 as an option. A manual 4-speed transmission is standard with automatic as an option. The standard transfer case is the 2-speed Dana 300.

SERIAL NUMBER IDENTIFICATION

Vehicle

1945–70

The vehicle serial number is located on a metal plate mounted on the firewall under the hood. It is on the left side on CJ-5, and CJ-6 models and on the right on CJ-3B models. Identification of a specific vehicle requires a prefix plus a serial number. The following chart identifies the Jeep model by the serial number prefix.

1945–70 Model Identification by Serial Number

Model	Prefix	Serial Number
CJ-2A	no prefix	5 or 6 digit S/N*
CJ-3A	no prefix	5 digit S/N
	451-GB1	5 digit S/N
	452-GB1	5 digit S/N
	453-GB1	5 digit S/N
CJ-3B	453-GB2	5 digit S/N
	454-GB2	5 digit S/N
	57348	5 digit S/N
	8105	5 digit S/N
CJ-5	57548	5 or 6 digit S/N
	8305	5 digit S/N
CJ-5A	8322	5 digit S/N
CJ-6	57648	5 digit S/N
	8405	5 digit S/N
CJ-6A	8422	5 digit S/N

*S/N Serial Number

Any prefix that is not given here indicates that yours is a special vehicle with differences that are not covered in this book.

1971–81

When American Motors Corporation took over the Jeep Corporation, the numbering system was changed to the American Motors

13-digit alpha-numerical Vehicle Identification Number (VIN).

This number is stamped on a metal plate on the left side of the firewall.

Engine

The CJ-2A was equipped with a 4-cylinder L head engine. All CJ-3A, CJ-3B, CJ-5, and CJ-6 Jeeps came with the F head, four-cylinder engine as standard equipment until 1965 when the V6 engine was made available as an option. The engine serial number on the F and L head is located on the water pump boss at the front of the engine. It consists of a five- or six-digit number. The engine code prefix for the Willys, four-cylinder engine is "4J."

The engine number for the V6 engine is located on the right side of the engine, on the crankcase, just below the head. The code is "KLH."

The American Motors engine code is, of course, found on the identification plate on the firewall. The second location is on the engine itself, on a machined surface of the block between number two and three spark plugs on the six-cylinder engines. On the 304 cu in. V8, the number is located on a tag attached to the right valve cover. (For further identification, the displacement is cast into the side of the block.) The letter in the code identifies the engine by displacement (cu in.), carburetor type, and compression ratio.

In 1980, a General Motors 151 cid, 4-cylinder engine became standard equipment on all CJ models. A three character code is stamped into the left rear top corner of the block. Additionally, engines built for sale in Georgia and Tennessee have a non-repeating number stamped into the left rear block flange.

It is sometimes necessary to machine oversized or undersized clearances for cylinder blocks and crankshafts. If your engine is equipped with oversized or undersized parts, it is necessary to order parts that will match the old parts. To find out if your engine is one with odd-sized parts, check the engine number. If it is followed by a letter or a series of letters, odd part sizes are involved. This applies to all Jeeps. The following chart explains just what the letters indicate on engines in Jeeps made through 1971:

• Letter A (10001-A) indicates 0.010 in. undersized main and connecting rod bearings.

• Letter B (10001-B) indicates 0.010 in. oversized cylinder bore.

• Letters AB (10001AB) indicates the combination of the above specifications.

• Letter C (10001C) indicates 0.002 in. undersized piston pin.

• Letter D (10001D) indicates 0.010 in. undersized main bearing journals.

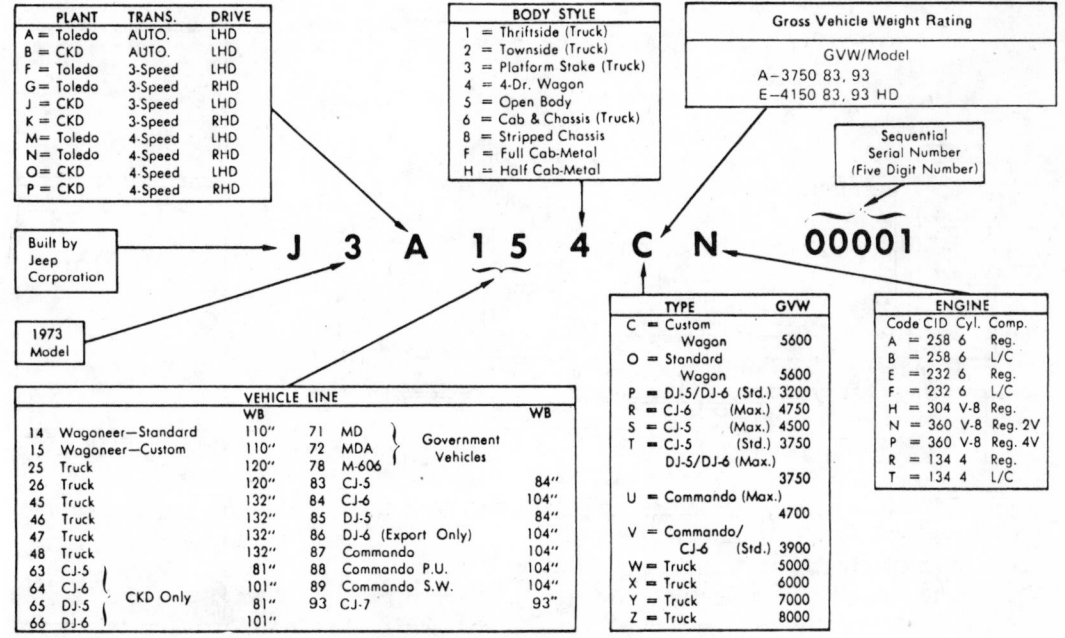

Serial number system for 1971-74

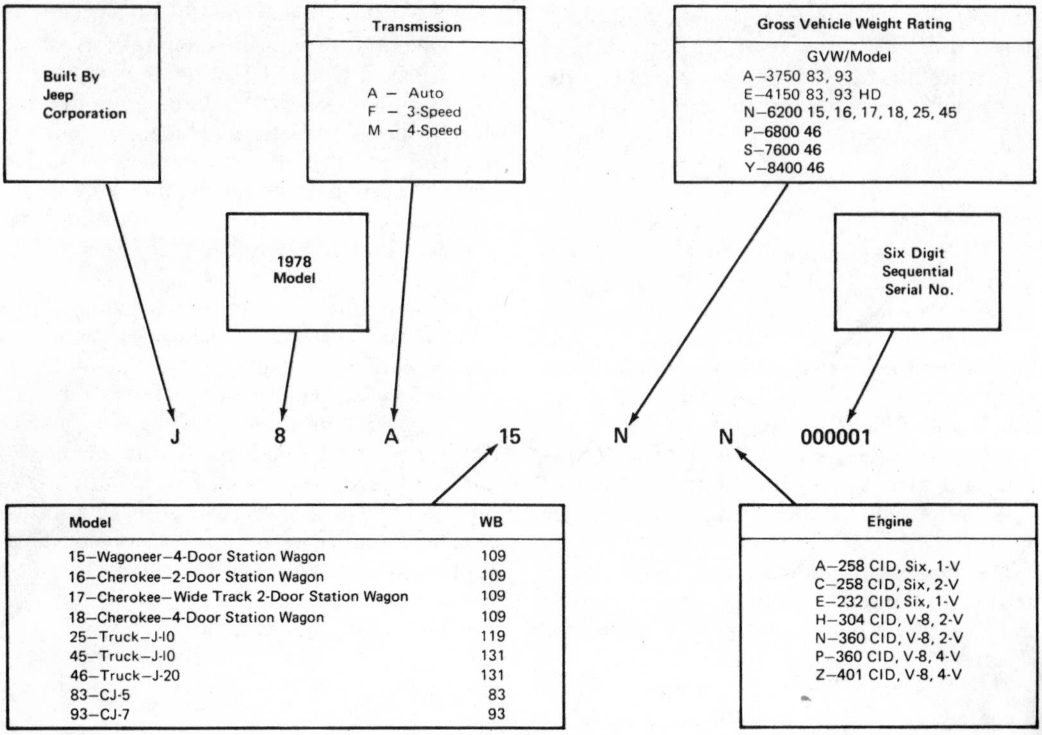

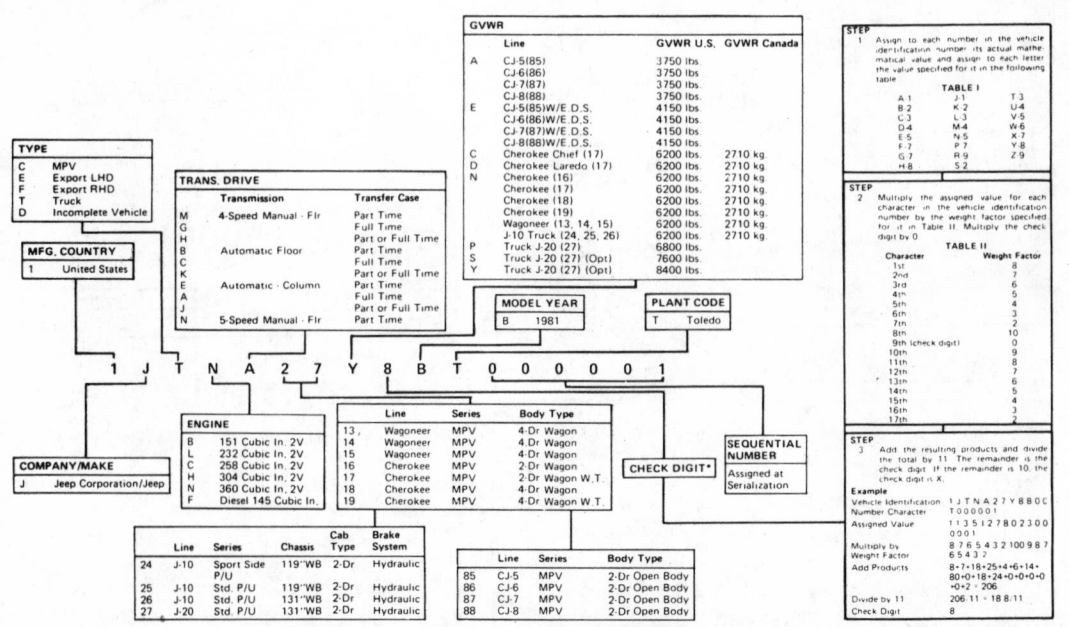

Built By Jeep Corporation		

Transmission

A — Auto
F — 3-Speed
M — 4-Speed

Gross Vehicle Weight Rating

GVW/Model
A–3750 83, 93
E–4150 83, 93 HD
N–6200 15, 16, 17, 18, 25, 45
P–6800 46
S–7600 46
Y–8400 46

1978 Model

Six Digit Sequential Serial No.

J   8   A   15   N   N   000001

Model	WB
15—Wagoneer—4-Door Station Wagon	109
16—Cherokee—2-Door Station Wagon	109
17—Cherokee—Wide Track 2-Door Station Wagon	109
18—Cherokee—4-Door Station Wagon	109
25—Truck—J-I0	119
45—Truck—J-I0	131
46—Truck—J-20	131
83—CJ-5	83
93—CJ-7	93

Engine
A—258 CID, Six, 1-V
C—258 CID, Six, 2-V
E—232 CID, Six, 1-V
H—304 CID, V-8, 2-V
N—360 CID, V-8, 2-V
P—360 CID, V-8, 4-V
Z—401 CID, V-8, 4-V

Serial number code system for 1975–80

GVWR

Line		GVWR U.S.	GVWR Canada
A	CJ-5 (85)	3750 lbs.	
	CJ-6 (86)	3750 lbs.	
	CJ-7 (87)	3750 lbs.	
	CJ-8 (88)	3750 lbs.	
E	CJ-5 (85) W/E.D.S.	4150 lbs.	
	CJ-6 (86) W/E.D.S.	4150 lbs.	
	CJ-7 (87) W/E.D.S.	4150 lbs.	
	CJ-8 (88) W/E.D.S.	4150 lbs.	
C	Cherokee Chief (17)	6200 lbs.	2710 kg.
D	Cherokee Laredo (17)	6200 lbs.	2710 kg.
N	Cherokee (16)	6200 lbs.	2710 kg.
	Cherokee (17)	6200 lbs.	2710 kg.
	Cherokee (18)	6200 lbs.	2710 kg.
	Cherokee (19)	6200 lbs.	2710 kg.
	Wagoneer (13, 14, 15)	6200 lbs.	2710 kg.
	J-10 Truck (24, 25, 26)	6200 lbs.	2710 kg.
P	Truck J-20 (27)	6800 lbs.	
S	Truck J-20 (27) (Opt)	7600 lbs.	
Y	Truck J-20 (27) (Opt)	8400 lbs.	

TYPE

C	MPV
E	Export LHD
F	Export RHD
T	Truck
D	Incomplete Vehicle

MFG. COUNTRY

1	United States

TRANS. DRIVE

	Transmission	Transfer Case
M	4-Speed Manual - Flr	Part Time
G		Full Time
H		Part or Full Time
B	Automatic Floor	Part Time
C		Full Time
K	Automatic - Column	Part or Full Time
E		Full Time
A		Full Time
J		Part or Full Time
N	5-Speed Manual - Flr	Part Time

MODEL YEAR

B	1981

PLANT CODE

T	Toledo

1   J   T   N   A   2   7   Y   8   B   T   0   0   0   0   0   1

COMPANY/MAKE

J	Jeep Corporation/Jeep

ENGINE

B	151 Cubic In. 2V
L	232 Cubic In. 2V
C	258 Cubic In. 2V
H	304 Cubic In. 2V
N	360 Cubic In. 2V
F	Diesel 145 Cubic In.

Line	Series	Body Type
13	Wagoneer	MPV	4-Dr Wagon
14	Wagoneer	MPV	4-Dr Wagon
15	Wagoneer	MPV	4-Dr Wagon
16	Cherokee	MPV	2-Dr Wagon
17	Cherokee	MPV	2-Dr Wagon W.T.
18	Cherokee	MPV	4-Dr Wagon
19	Cherokee	MPV	4-Dr Wagon W.T.

	Line	Series	Chassis	Cab Type	Brake System
24	J-10	Sport Side P/U	119"WB	2-Dr	Hydraulic
25	J-10	Std. P/U	119"WB	2-Dr	Hydraulic
26	J-10	Std. P/U	131"WB	2-Dr	Hydraulic
27	J-20	Std. P/U	131"WB	2-Dr	Hydraulic

	Line	Series	Body Type
85	CJ-5	MPV	2-Dr Open Body
86	CJ-6	MPV	2-Dr Open Body
87	CJ-7	MPV	2-Dr Open Body
88	CJ-8	MPV	2-Dr Open Body

CHECK DIGIT*

SEQUENTIAL NUMBER
Assigned at Serialization

STEP 1 Assign to each number in the vehicle identification number its actual mathematical value and assign to each letter the value specified for it in the following table.

TABLE I

A 1	J 1	T 3
B 2	K 2	U 4
C 3	L 3	V 5
D 4	M 4	W 6
E 5	N 5	X 7
F 7	P 7	Y 8
G 7	R 9	Z 9
H 8	S 2	

STEP 2 Multiply the assigned value for each character in the vehicle identification number by the weight factor specified for it in Table II. Multiply the check digit by 0.

TABLE II

Character	Weight Factor
1st	8
2nd	7
3rd	6
4th	5
5th	4
6th	3
7th	2
8th	10
9th (check digit)	0
10th	9
11th	8
12th	7
13th	6
14th	5
15th	4
16th	3
17th	2

STEP 3 Add the resulting products and divide the total by 11. The remainder is the check digit. If the remainder is 10, the check digit is X.

Example

Vehicle Identification	1 J T N A 2 7 Y 8 B 0 C
Number Character	T 0 0 0 0 0 1
Assigned Value	1 1 3 5 1 2 7 8 0 2 3 0 0
	0 0 0 1
Multiply by	8 7 6 5 4 3 2 1 0 0 9 8 7
Weight Factor	6 5 4 3 2
Add Products	8+7+18+25+4+6+14+
	80+0+18+24+0+0+0+0
	+0+2 = 206
Divide by 11	206 11 - 18 8 11
Check Digit	8

1981 VIN explanation

CJ-5, CJ-6, CJ-7 and Scrambler serial number plate

4-134 engine serial number

CJ-2A, CJ-3A, CJ-3B serial number plate

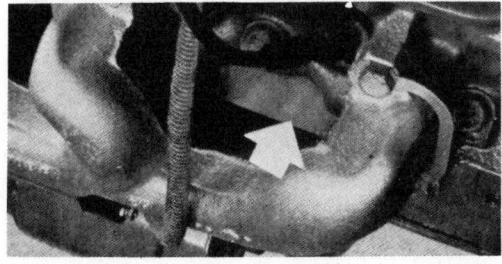

V6 engine serial number

Inline six engine serial number

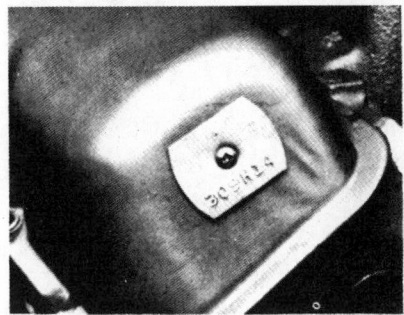

V8 engine serial number

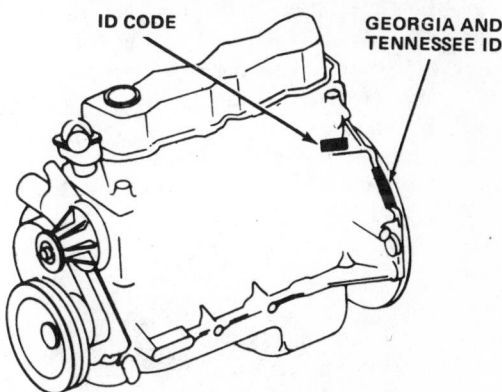

1980–81 4-151 engine ID number locations

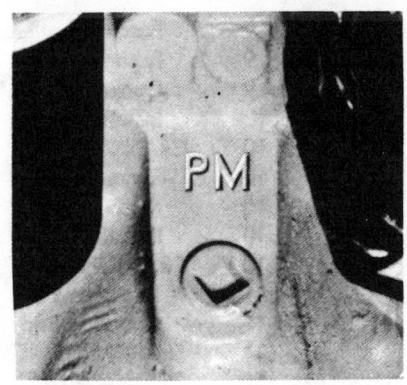

The parts size letter code is on the boss directly above the oil filter on inline sixes

• Letter E (10001E) indicates 0.010 in. undersized connecting rod bearing journals.

Before you replace any of these parts, refer to this chart so the proper tolerances and clearances may be maintained and the right replacement parts may be obtained.

The code for 1972 and later vehicles with American Motors engines is as follows:

• Letter B indicates 0.010 in. oversized cylinder bore.

• Letter M indicates 0.010 in. undersized main bearings.

• Letter P indicates 0.010 in. undersized connecting rod bearings.

• Letters PM indicates a combination of the above specification for P and M.

• Letter C indicates 0.010 in. oversized camshaft block bores.

The parts size code is located on the boss directly above the oil filter on the straight sixes and on the tag adjacent to the engine number on V8s.

Transmission Identification

There is a tag attached to the transmission case that identifies the manufacturer and model of the transmission. It is necessary to have the information on this tag before ordering parts. When reassembling the transmission, be sure that this tag is replaced on the transmission case so identification can be made in the future.

In some cases, the transmission identification number may be embossed on the transmission housing.

ROUTINE MAINTENANCE

See the Maintenance Intervals Chart in this chapter for the recommended maintenance intervals for the components covered here.

Air Cleaner
OIL BATH TYPE

To service the oil bath type air cleaner on the L or F head, four-cylinder engine, first unscrew the oil cup clamp and remove the oil cup from the cleaner body. Remove the oil from the cup and scrape out all the dirt inside, on the bottom. Wash the cup with a safe solvent. Refill the oil cup and replace it on the air cleaner body. Use the same viscosity of oil as you use in the engine crankcase.

To service the air cleaner body (less the oil cup), loosen the hose clamp and remove the hose from the cleaner. Detach the breather hose from the fitting on the cleaner. Remove the two wing nuts and lift the cleaner from the vehicle. Agitate the cleaner body thoroughly in a cleaning solution to clean the filtering element and then dry the element with compressed air. Reinstall the air cleaner body and replace the oil cup. The air cleaner should be serviced every 2,000 miles.

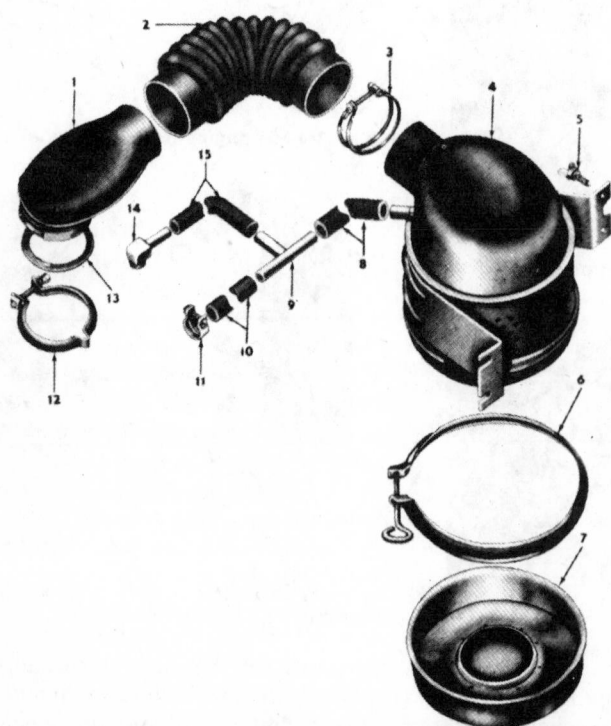

1. Horn
2. Flexible connector
3. Hose clamp
4. Body
5. Wing screw
6. Clamp
7. Oil cup
8. Hose
9. Hose tee
10. Hose
11. Hose clamp
12. Clamp
13. Gasket
14. Elbow
15. Hose

L- and F-head oil bath air cleaner

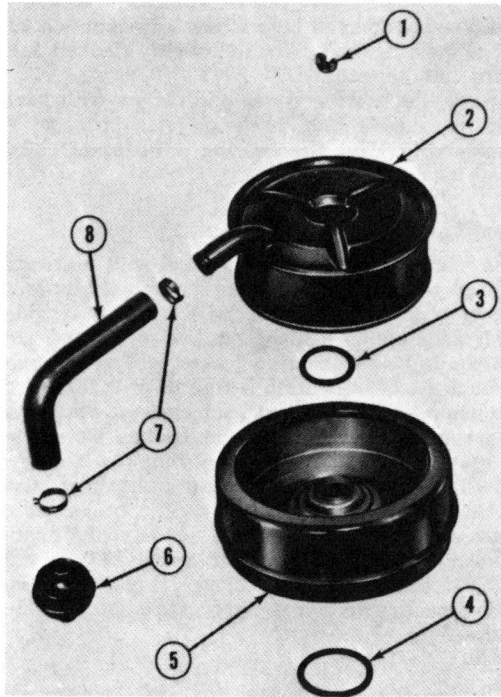

1. Wing nut   5. Oil cup
2. Cover   6. Breather
3. Rubber gasket   7. Clamps
4. Cork gasket   8. Vent tube

V6 oil bath air cleaner

To service the oil bath type air cleaner on V6 engines, first remove the air cleaner from the engine by unscrewing the wing nut on top of the air cleaner. Remove the oil cup from the body of the air cleaner and remove all of the oil from the oil cup. Remove all of the dirt from the inside of the oil cup with a safe solvent. Wash the filter element in solvent, air dry it, and then fill the oil cup to the indicated level with clean oil. Assemble the air cleaner element to the oil cup, making sure that the gasket is in place between the two pieces. Mount the air cleaner assembly in the carburetor, making sure that the gasket between the air cleaner and the carburetor is in place and making a good seal. Secure the air cleaner to the carburetor with the wing nut.

PAPER ELEMENT TYPE

Remove the wing nut or hex nuts on top of the cover. On 4-151 and V8s, remove the cover and lift out the element. On sixes, detach the rubber hose from the engine rocker arm (valve) cover and set the cover aside, being careful not to damage the large diameter hose or hoses to the air cleaner inlet.

POLYURETHANE ELEMENT   PAPER CARTRIDGE

Polyurethane and paper element air cleaner

If the filter element has a foam wrapper, remove the wrapper and wash it in detergent or a safe solvent. Squeeze and blot dry. Wet the wrapper in engine oil and squeeze it tightly in an absorbent towel or rag to remove the excess.

Clean the dirt from the paper element by rapping it gently against a flat surface. Replace the element as necessary.

Clean the housing and the cover. Replace the oiled wrapper, if any, on the element and reinstall the element in the housing, placing it 180° from its original position.

NOTE: *The oiled foam wrapper element is a factory option for some years; it should be available through Jeep parts. There are also aftermarket variations on this, both dry and oiled.*

PCV Valve

The PCV valve, which is the heart of the positive crankcase ventilation system, should be free of dirt and residue and in working order. As long as the valve is kept clean and is not showing signs of becoming damaged or gummed up, it should work properly. When the valve cannot be cleaned sufficiently or becomes sticky and will not operate freely, it should be replaced.

The PCV filter, which is located at the air filter housing on some six-cylinder models, should be checked along with the PCV valve. Just blow out the screen with compressed air in the reverse direction of the normal air flow. Check to see that the screen forms a good seal around the edges of the air cleaner housing so no dirt can pass. If the screen is torn or clogged, or if it is seated improperly and cannot be repaired, replace it.

On 4-151 and V8 engines, the air being drawn into the PCV system passes through a polyurethane foam filter located in the oil filler cap. The filler cap is vented only by a hose connected to the air cleaner. The foam

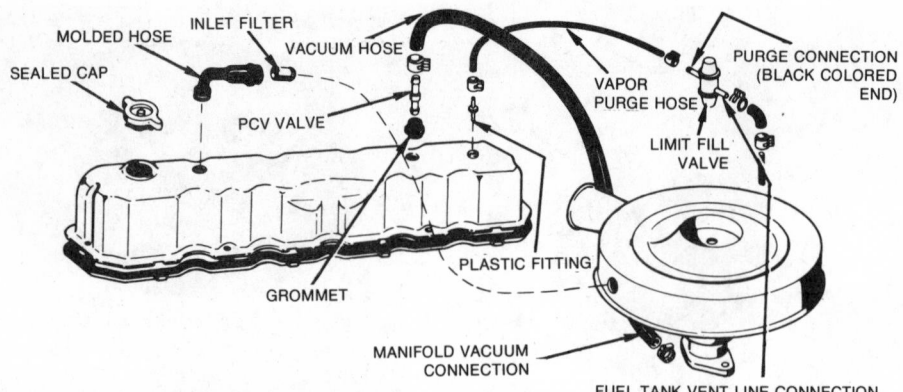

Typical 6-232, 258 PCV system; 1980–81 models don't have the purge hose. The 4-151 system is similar

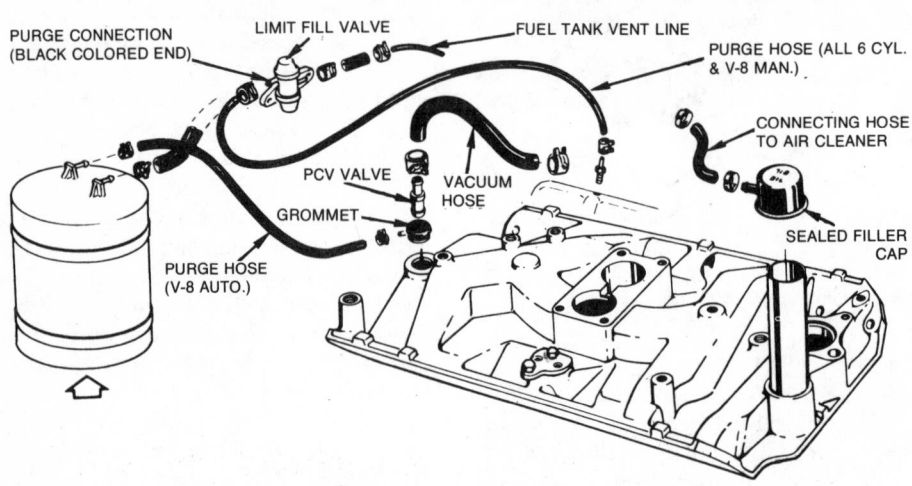

Typical V8 PCV system

PCV system air filter

filter in the oilfiller cap should be cleaned with safe solvent.

The PCV valve is in the right rocker arm (valve) cover on the V6, in the intake mani-fold on the four, in the intake manifold behind the carburetor on the V8; and in the rocker arm cover on the inline sixes.

Heat Riser

The heat riser is a thermostatically operated valve in the exhaust manifold. It closes when the engine is cold, to direct hot exhaust gases to the intake manifold, in order to preheat the incoming fuel/air mixture. If it sticks closed, the result will be a rough idle after the engine warms up. If it sticks open, there will be frequent stalling during warmup, especially in cold and damp weather.

On the V6 and V8, the valve is between the exhaust manifold and the exhaust pipe; on the inline sixes, it is an integral part of the exhaust manifold. The heat riser counter-weight should move freely. If it sticks, apply Jeep Heat Valve Lubricant or something similar (engine cool) to the ends of the shaft.

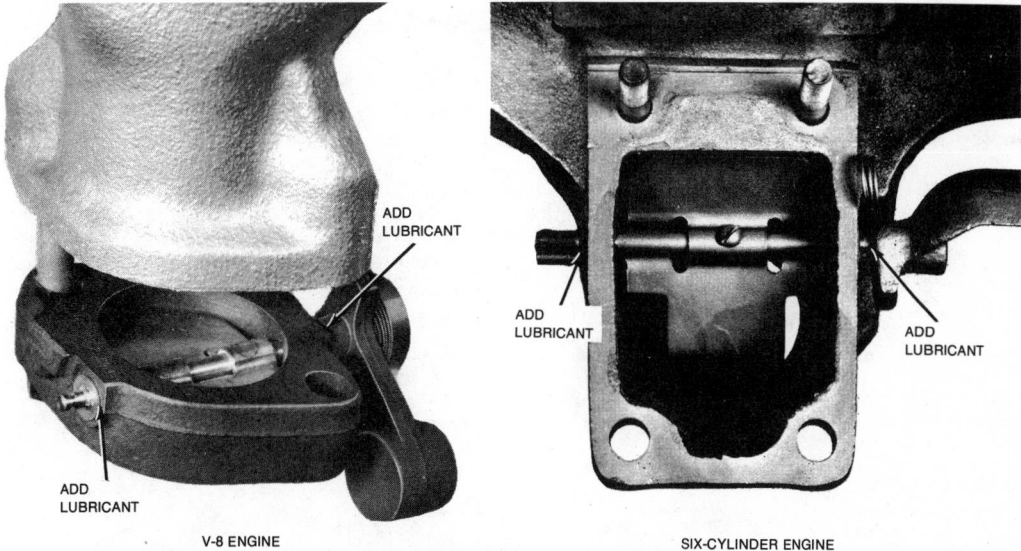

ADD LUBRICANT

ADD LUBRICANT

ADD LUBRICANT

ADD LUBRICANT

V-8 ENGINE

SIX-CYLINDER ENGINE

Heat riser lubrication points (shown detached)

Sometimes rapping the end of the shaft sharply with a hammer (engine hot) will break it loose. If this fails, parts must be removed for repair or replacement.

Belt Tension Adjustment

Any engine V-belt is correctly tensioned when the longest span of belt between pulleys can be depressed about ½ in. in the middle with moderate thumb pressure. To adjust, loosen the accessory's slotted adjusting bracket bolt. If the hinge bolt is very tight, it may have to be loosened, too.

CAUTION: *Be careful not to overtighten belts; this will damage bearings, particularly in air or water pumps and alternators.*

Air Conditioning System Check

The sight glass for checking refrigerant charge is on top of the receiver/dryer, just behind the right side of the radiator.

CAUTION: *Do not attempt to charge or discharge the refrigerant system unless you are thoroughly familiar with its operation and the hazards involved in service. The compressed refrigerant expands and evaporates into the atmosphere at a temperature of −21.7° F. This will freeze any surface that it contacts, including your eyes. Refrigerant-12 also decomposes into a poisonous gas in the presence of flame.*

1. Start the engine and run it at a fast idle.
2. Set the controls for maximum cold with the blower on high.
3. If there are bubbles at the sight glass, the system is low on charge. If there are no bubbles, the system is either fully charged or empty.
4. Feel the high and low pressure lines at the compressor. The high pressure (outlet) line should be warm and the low pressure (inlet) line should be cool. If you can't notice any difference, the system is empty or nearly so.

Even though there is a temperature difference, the system could be overcharged. Disconnect the compressor clutch wire. If the refrigerant in the sight glass remains clear for more than 45 seconds before foaming and then settling, there is an overcharge. If the refrigerant foams, then settles in less than 45 seconds the system is properly charged. If no bubbles at all appear, the system must be empty.

Fluid Level Checks
ENGINE OIL

Make sure that your vehicle is on a level surface to ensure an accurate reading. Then, raise the hood, position the hold-up rod, and measure the oil with the dipstick which is on the left side of four-cylinder and V8 engines and on the right of six-cylinder engines. Add oil through the filler pipe on the right side of

HOW TO SPOT WORN V-BELTS

V-Belts are vital to efficient engine operation—they drive the fan, water pump and other accessories. They require little maintenance (occasional tightening) but they will not last forever. Slipping or failure of the V-belt will lead to overheating. If your V-belt looks like any of these, it should be replaced.

Cracking or weathering

This belt has deep cracks, which cause it to flex. Too much flexing leads to heat build-up and premature failure. These cracks can be caused by using the belt on a pulley that is too small. Notched belts are available for small diameter pulleys.

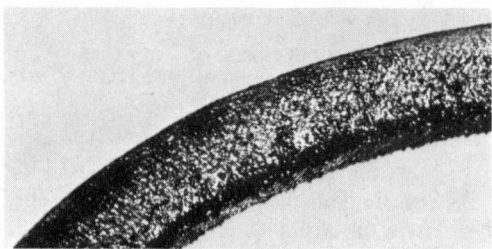

Softening (grease and oil)

Oil and grease on a belt can cause the belt's rubber compounds to soften and separate from the reinforcing cords that hold the belt together. The belt will first slip, then finally fail altogether.

Glazing

Glazing is caused by a belt that is slipping. A slipping belt can cause a run-down battery, erratic power steering, overheating or poor accessory performance. The more the belt slips, the more glazing will be built up on the surface of the belt. The more the belt is glazed, the more it will slip. If the glazing is light, tighten the belt.

Worn cover

The cover of this belt is worn off and is peeling away. The reinforcing cords will begin to wear and the belt will shortly break. When the belt cover wears in spots or has a rough jagged appearance, check the pulley grooves for roughness.

Separation

This belt is on the verge of breaking and leaving you stranded. The layers of the belt are separating and the reinforcing cords are exposed. It's just a matter of time before it breaks completely.

F head engines, through the valve cover filler hole on six-cylinder engines, and through the filler pipe at the front of the engine on V8s.

If the oil is below the ADD mark, add a quart of oil, then recheck the level. If the level is still not reading full, add only a half of a quart at a time, until the dipstick reads FULL. Do not overfill the engine. When you check the oil, make sure that you allow sufficient time for all of the oil to drain back into the crankcase after stopping the engine. A minute or so should be enough time.

MANUAL TRANSMISSION

The level of lubricant in the transmission should be maintained at the filler hole on all manual transmissions. This hole is on the right side. When you check the level in the transmission, make sure that the vehicle is level so that you get a true reading. When you remove the filler plug, lubricant should run out of the hole. Replace the plug quickly for a minimum loss of lubricant. If lubricant does not run out of the hole when the plug is removed, lubricant should be added until it does. Replace the plug as soon as the lubricant reaches the level of the hole.

AUTOMATIC TRANSMISSION

The fluid level in automatic transmissions is checked with a dipstick in the filler pipe at the right rear of the engine. The fluid level should be maintained between the ADD and FULL marks on the end of the dipstick with the automatic transmission fluid at normal operating temperatures. To raise the level from the ADD mark to the FULL mark, requires the addition of one pint of fluid. The

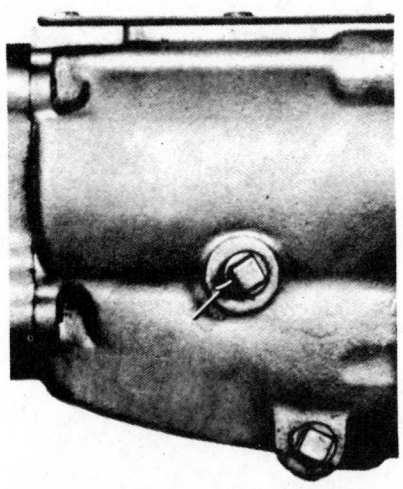

Transmission filler (arrow) and drain plugs

fluid level with the fluid at room temperature (75° F) should be approximately ¼ in. below the ADD mark.

NOTE: *In checking the automatic transmission fluid, insert the dipstick in the filler tube with the markings toward the center of the vehicle. Also, remember that the FULL mark on the dipstick is calibrated for normal operating temperature. This temperature is obtained only after at least 15 miles of expressway driving or the equivalent of city driving.*

1. With the transmission in Park, the engine running at idle speed, the foot brake applied and the vehicle resting on level ground, move the transmission gear selector through each of the gear positions, including Reverse, allowing time for the transmission to engage. Return the shift selector to the Park position and apply the parking brake. Do not turn the engine off, but leave it running at idle speed.

2. Clean all dirt from around the transmission dipstick cap and the end of the filler tube.

3. Pull the dipstick out of the tube, wipe it off with a clean cloth, and push it back into the tube all the way, making sure that it seats completely.

4. Pull the dipstick out of the tube again and read the level of the fluid on the stick. The level should be between the ADD and FULL marks. If fluid must be added, add enough fluid through the tube to raise the level to between the ADD and FULL marks. Do not overfill the transmission because this will cause foaming and loss of fluid through the vent.

NOTE: *Use only Dexron® or Dexron II® transmission fluid.*

BRAKE MASTER CYLINDER

On models through 1971, the master cylinder is located under the floor. To check the level of the brake fluid remove the floor plate. Clean the area of all dirt so that, when you remove the cover, no dirt will fall in and contaminate the brake fluid. Dirt in the hydraulic system could score the inside of the master cylinder or wheel cylinders and cause leakage or brake failure. Unscrew the lid of the master cylinder with a wrench. The fluid level should be within ½ in. from the top of the reservoir chamber. Use only heavy-duty brake fluid and keep it away from any other fluids or vapors that could contaminate it.

On 1972 and later Jeeps, the master cylin-

HOW TO SPOT BAD HOSES

Both the upper and lower radiator hoses are called upon to perform difficult jobs in an inhospitable environment. They are subject to nearly 18 psi at under hood temperatures often over 280°F., and must circulate nearly 7500 gallons of coolant an hour—3 good reasons to have good hoses.

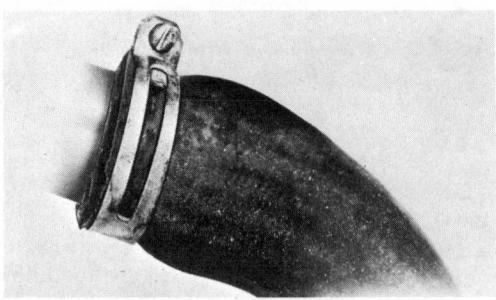

Swollen hose

A good test for any hose is to feel it for soft or spongy spots. Frequently these will appear as swollen areas of the hose. The most likely cause is oil soaking. This hose could burst at any time, when hot or under pressure.

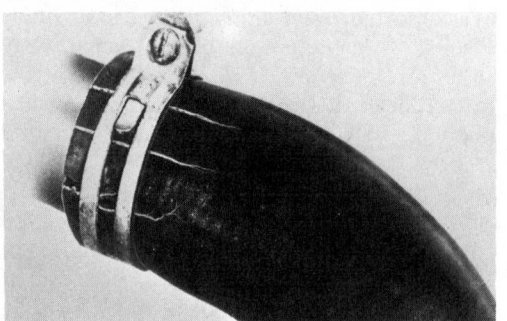

Cracked hose

Cracked hoses can usually be seen but feel the hoses to be sure they have not hardened; a prime cause of cracking. This hose has cracked down to the reinforcing cords and could split at any of the cracks.

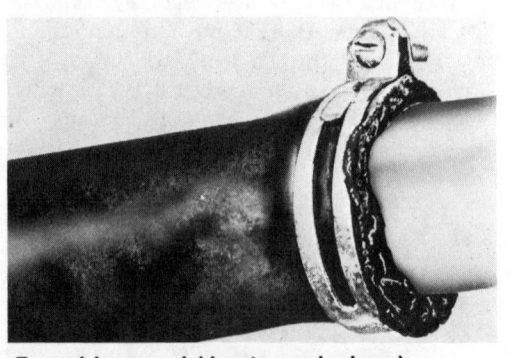

Frayed hose end (due to weak clamp)

Weakened clamps frequently are the cause of hose and cooling system failure. The connection between the pipe and hose has deteriorated enough to allow coolant to escape when the engine is hot.

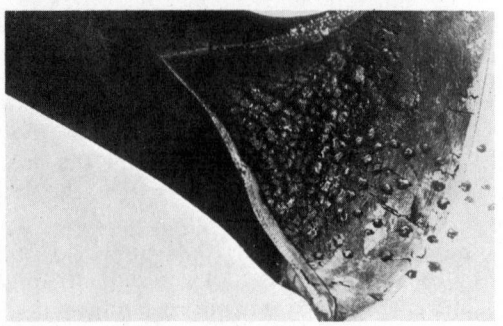

Debris in cooling system

Debris, rust and scale in the cooling system can cause the inside of a hose to weaken. This can usually be felt on the outside of the hose as soft or thinner areas.

1972 and later master cylinder location

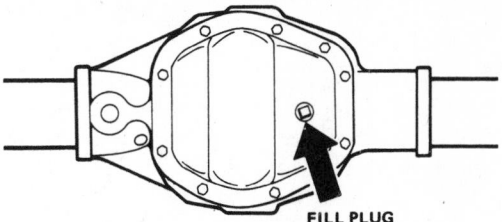

Typical front axle fill plug location

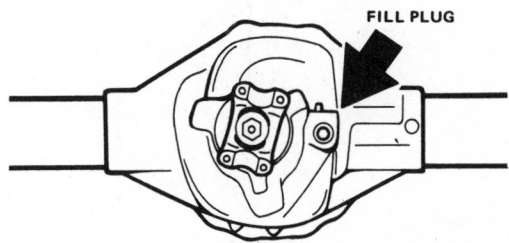

Typical rear axle fill plug location

der is located under the hood, on the left side of the firewall. To check the fluid, use a screwdriver to pry off the retaining clip from the lid of the reservoir. The fluid level should be within ¼ in. of the top of the reservoir.

If the master cylinder is less than half-full, there is probably a leak somewhere in the hydraulic system. Investigate the problem before driving the vehicle.

COOLANT

The coolant level should be maintained about ½ in. below the filler neck of the radiator with L and F head engines.

On the American Motors and GM engines (4, 6, and V8), the coolant level should be maintained 1½ to 2 in. below the bottom of the filler cap when the engine is cold. Since operating temperatures reach as high as 205° F for the four and six, and 190° F for the V8s, coolant could be forced out of the radiator if it is filled too high. The radiator coolant level should be checked regularly, such as every time you fill the vehicle with gas. Never open the radiator cap of an engine that hasn't had sufficient time to cool or the pressure can blow off the cap and send out a spray of scalding water.

AXLES

The plug is located in the differential cover, except on 1976 and later rear axles, which have it on the left front of the housing. A ⅜ in. Allen wrench is needed to remove the 1976 and later rear axle filler plug. The level should be up to the filler hole. When you remove the filler plug, the oil should start to

run out. If it does not, replenish the supply until it does.

MANUAL STEERING GEAR

Through 1971

There is a fill plug on top of the steering gear box. The correct lubricant is SAE 80 gear oil.

1972 and Later

These models use a steering box which is packed with grease. There is normally no need to add lubricant; however, the cover bolt opposite the adjuster may be removed for filling.

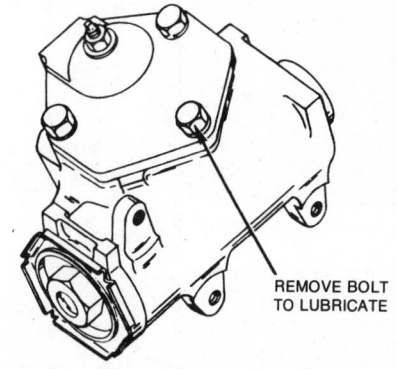

1972–81 manual steering gear filler hole

POWER STEERING RESERVOIR

The level of the fluid should be at the correct point on the dipstick attached to the inside of the lid of the power steering pump. Replenish the supply with DEXRON® automatic transmission fluid.

Capacities

Model	Engine Displacement Cu. In.	Engine Crankcase* (Qts)	Transmission (Pts)			Transfer Case (Pts)		Drive Axle (Pts)		Fuel Tank (Gal)	Cooling System (Qts)		
			3-sp	4-sp	Automatic	Manual	Automatic	Front	Rear		With A/C	Without A/C	HD
CJ-2A	4-134	5.0	3.5	—	—	3.5	—	2.5	2.75	10.5	12.0	—	—
CJ-3A	4-134	5.0	3.5	—	—	3.5	—	2.5	2.75	10.5	12.0	—	—
CJ-3B	4-134	5.0	3.0	—	—	3.5	—	2.5	2.5	10.5	12.0	—	—
CJ-5	4-134	5.0	3.0	6.75	—	3.5	—	2.5	2.5	10.5	12.0	—	—
	4-151	3.0	—	3.0	8.5③	4.0	—	2.5	4.8	14.8	7.8	7.8	—
	6-225	4.0	3.0	6.75	—	3.5	—	2.5	2.5	10.5	10.0	—	—
	6-232	5.0	2.5①	6.5	—	3.25	—	2.5②	2.5②	16.0	10.5	—	12.0
	6-258	5.0	2.5⑤	④	8.5③⑥	⑦	—	2.5②	2.5②	16.0⑧	10.5	—	12.0
	8-304	5.0	2.75⑤	④	8.5③⑥	⑦	—	2.5②	2.5②	16.0⑧	14.0	—	15.5
CJ-6	4-134	5.0	3.0	6.75	—	3.5	—	2.5	2.5	10.5	12.0	—	—
	6-225	4.0	3.0	6.75	—	3.5	—	2.5	2.5	10.5	10.0	—	—

6–232	5.0	2.5①	6.5	—	3.25	—	2.5	2.5	16.0	10.5	—
6–258	5.0	2.5①	—	—	3.25	—	2.5	2.5	16.0	10.5	—
8–304	5.0	2.75	—	—	3.25	—	2.5	2.5	16.0	10.5	—	12.0
CJ-7 4–151	3.0	—	3.0	8.5③	4.0	—	2.5	4.8	14.8	7.8	7.8	9.0
6–232	5.0	2.8	—	—	3.2	—	2.5	4.8	16.0⑧	10.5	—
6–258	5.0	2.8	④	8.5③⑥	3.25	3.5⑨	2.5	4.8	16.0⑧	10.5	12.0	—
8–304	5.0	2.8	—	8.5③⑥	3.25	3.5⑨	2.5	4.8	16.0⑧	13.0	14.5	—
Scrambler 4–151	3.0	—	3.0	8.5③	4.0	—	2.5	4.8	16.0	7.8	7.8	—
6–258	5.0	—	3.0	8.5③	4.0	—	2.5	4.8	16.0	10.5	12.0	—

*Includes filter
① 1976 and later: 3.0
② Dana 44: 3.0
   AMC rear: 1970–79, 4.0; 1980–81, 4.8
③ 17.0 after overhaul
④ T-18: 6.5
   SR-4: 3.0
   T-176: 3.5
⑤ 1976 and later: 3.1
⑥ 1972–79: 10.0 drain; 22.0 overhaul
⑦ 1972–79: 3.25
   1980–81: 4.0
⑧ 1980–81: 14.8
⑨ With reduction unit: 4.5

PART-TIME TRANSFER CASE

The transfer case should be checked in the same manner as the manual transmission. The level should be up to the filler hole. Use the same viscosity oil as in the transmission. The filler hole is on the right side. Check the oil level at the top hole; the bottom one is for draining.

QUADRA-TRAC FULL-TIME TRANSFER CASE

Fluid levels in the Quadra-Trac transfer case and low range reduction unit, if so equipped, should be checked at the same time. The lubricant levels are checked at the filler plug holes. The filler plug holes are located on the rear side of the transfer case assembly, just below center in the middle of the case housing and to the right of center of the reduction unit housing. The lubricant should be level with each filler plug hole. If not, replenish with Quadra-Trac lubricant.

BATTERY ELECTROLYTE

The correct level should be at the bottom of the well inside each cell opening. The surface of the electrolyte should appear distorted, not flat. Only colorless, odorless, preferably distilled, water should be added. It is a good idea to add the water with a squeeze bulb to avoid splashing and spills. If water is frequently needed, the most likely cause is overcharging, caused by voltage regulator problems. If any acid should escape, it can be neutralized with a baking soda and water solution.

CAUTIONS: *Avoid sparks and smoking around the battery; it gives off explosive hydrogen gas. If you get acid on your skin or eyes, rinse it off immediately with lots of water. See a doctor if it got in your eyes. In winter, add water only before driving to prevent the battery from freezing and cracking.*
NOTE: *Original equipment batteries with the ganged caps are often chronically wet on top, causing a lot of corrosion in the battery tray. The problem is insufficient venting. Solve it by removing the caps and drilling a tiny vent hole for each cell through the top of the cap.*

STEERING KNUCKLE

The axle shaft universal joints on models through 1971 are located in the steering knuckle and are bathed in oil as they turn. To

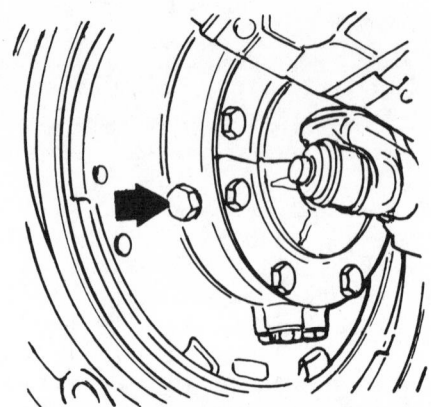

1945–71 front axle steering knuckle fill plug

check the fluid level in the steering knuckle, remove the filler plug from the inside of the knuckle. The fluid should be at the level of the hole. If it is not, replenish the supply. Examine the knuckle for leaks if the level is abnormally low. A leak should be readily visible.

NOTE *This does not apply to 1972 and later models.*

Recommended Lubricants

Component	Lubricant
Manual Transmission	80W-90, GL-4 gear oil
Automatic Transmission	Dexron® or Dexron II® fluid
Part-Time Transfer Case	80W-90, GL-4 or GL-5 gear oil
Quadra-Trac Full-Time Transfer Case	Quadra-Trac® lubricant
Axles (differentials)	80W-90, GL-5 gear oil
Trac-Lok Limited Slip Axles	80W-90, GL-5 limited slip differential lubricant
Steering Box	SAE 80 gear oil through 1971, lithium base grease starting 1972
Steering Knuckles (used through 1971)	SAE 140, GL-3 gear oil
Power Steering	Dexron® or Dexron II® fluid

Tires and Wheels

Some late models have the recommended tire pressures listed on a sticker inside the glovebox door. In general, pressures of 20–24 psi are suitable for highway use with moderate loads and original equipment tires (load range B). Pressures should be checked before driving, since they can increase as much as 6 psi due to heat. It is a good idea to have an accurate gauge and to check pressures weekly. Not all gauges on service station air pumps are to be trusted. In general, truck-type tires require higher pressures and flotation-type tires, lower pressures.

When you buy new tires, give some thought to these points, especially if you are switching to larger tires or to another profile series (50, 60, 70, 78):

1. All four tires should be the same. Four wheel drive requires that all tires be the same size, type, and tread pattern to provide even traction on loose surfaces, to prevent driveline bind when conventional part-time four wheel drive is used, and to prevent excessive wear on the center differential with full time four wheel drive.

2. The wheels must be the correct width for the tire. Tire dealers have charts of tire and rim compatibility. A mismatch can cause sloppy handling and rapid tread wear. The old rule of thumb is that the tread width should match the rim width (inside bead to inside bead) within an inch. For radial tires, the rim width should be 80% or less of the tire (not tread) width.

3. The height (mounted diameter) of the new tires can greatly change speedometer accuracy, engine speed at a given road speed, fuel mileage, acceleration, and ground clearance. Tire makers furnish full measurement specifications. Speedometer drive gears are available from Jeep parts for correction.

NOTE: *Dimensions of tires marked the same size may vary significantly, even among tires from the same maker.*

4. The spare tire should be usable, at least for low speed operation, with the new tires. You will probably have to remove the side mounted spare for clearance. This is especially true on 1972 and later models, since they have a wider tread and minimal tire-to-spare clearance.

5. There shouldn't be any body interference when loaded, on bumps, or in turning.

The only sure way to avoid problems with these points is to stick to tire and wheel sizes available as factory options.

TIRE ROTATION

Tire rotation is recommended to obtain maximum tread wear. The pattern you use depends on personal preference, and whether or not you have a usable spare. Radial tires should not be cross-switched; they last longer if their direction of rotation is not changed. Truck type tires sometimes have directional tread indicated by arrows on the sidewalls; The arrow shows the direction of rotation. They will wear very rapidly if reversed. Studded snow tires will lose their studs if their rotation direction is reversed.

NOTE: *Mark the wheel position or direction of rotation on radial, or studded snow tires before removing them.*

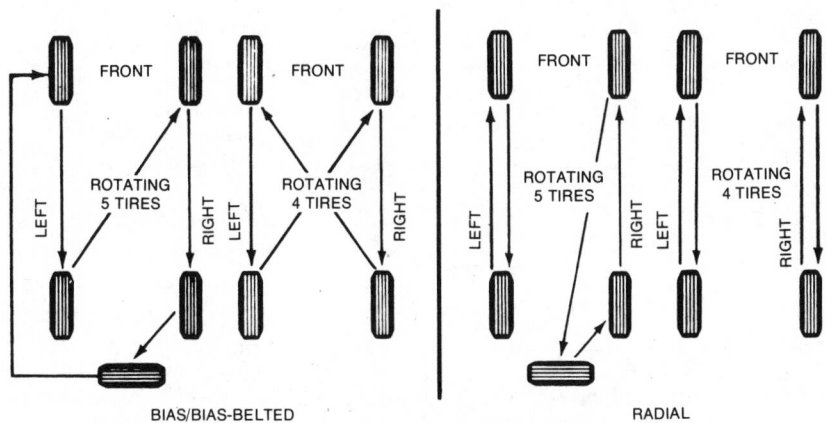

Tire rotation patterns

Maintenance Intervals Chart

Interval	Item	Service
1945–69		
Every 2000 miles	4-134 change oil and filter	See oil viscosity chart
	Complete chassis lube	EP grease
	Steering gear	Check level
	Manual trans.	Check level
	Transfer case	Check level
	Differentials	Check levels
	4-134 distributor oiler, wick and cam	A few drops of engine oil
	4-134 air cleaner	Clean and refill
Every 6000 miles	Air cleaner V6	Clean and refill
	V6 change oil and filter	See oil viscosity chart
Every 12,000 miles	Steering knuckles	Change lubricant
	Front wheel bearings	Repack—EP grease
	Manual trans.	Change fluid
	Transfer case	Change fluid
	Differentials	Change fluid
	Speedometer cable	Lubricate—graphite grease
1970–73		
Every 6000 miles or 6 mos.	Crankcase	Change oil and filter
Every 6000 miles	Complete chassis lube	EP chassis grease
	Manual trans.	Check
	Transfer case	Check
	Steering gear	Check
	Master cyl.	Check
	Differentials	Check
	Tires	Rotate
Every 12,000 miles	Fuel filter	Replace
	PCV valve	Replace
	Oil filter cap	Clean
	Drive belts	Adjust
	Air cleaner—dry type	Replace
	Air cleaner—oil bath	Clean and refill—engine oil
	Distributor cam lubricator	Rotate
	Timing and dwell	Check
	Heat riser	Lubricate
	PCV filter-6 cyl.	Clean
	Points, condenser, roter	Replace
	Spark plugs	Replace
Every 30,000 miles	Manual trans.	Change fluid
	Transfer case	Change fluid
	Differentials	Change fluid
	Steering knuckle housing	Change lubricant
1974–76		
Every 5000 miles or 5 mos.	Crankcase	Change oil and filter
Every 5000 miles	Manual trans.	Check
	Transfer case	Check
	Differentials	Check
	Steering gear	Check
	Power steering	Check
	Master cyl.	Check
	Radiator coolant	Check

Maintenance Intervals Chart (cont.)

Interval	Item	Service
1974–76 Every 5000 miles	Complete chassis lube Point type distributor Point type ignition Heat riser	EP chassis grease Change points, condenser, rotor Change spark plugs Lubricate
Every 10,000 miles	Drive shaft splines	Lubricate
Every 15,000 miles	Air cleaner Coil and plug wires Distributor cap and rotor Drive belts Oil filler cap EGR valve port Fuel filter Canister filter Timing and dwell PCV filter PCV valve	Replace Replace Replace Adjust Clean Clean Replace Replace Check Clean Replace
Every 25,000 miles	Automatic trans.	Change fluid and filter
Every 30,000 miles	Manual trans. Model 20 transfer case Differentials	Change fluid Change fluid Change fluid
1977–81 Every 5000 miles	Crankcase Complete chassis lube Coolant Master cyl. Steering gear Power steering reservoir Trans., man. or auto Manual transfer case Quadra-Trac transfer case Differentials Drive belts Catalytic converter	Change oil and filter EP chassis grease Check Check Check Check Check Check Check Check Adjust Check for bulging or heat damage
Every 25,000 miles	Coolant	Change
Every 30,000 miles	Plug and coil wires Spark plugs Air cleaner Timing V8 oil filler cap Idle speed and mixture Manual trans. Manual transfer case Quadra-Trac transfer case Differentials Front wheel bearings	Inspect and replace if necessary Replace Replace Check and adjust Clean Adjust Drain and refill Drain and refill Drain and refill Drain and refill Repack—EP chassis lube

NOTE: *When vehicle is subjected to severe use, cut the intervals in half.*

Fuel Filter Replacement

4-134

Most of these engines have a fuel pump with a bowl containing a replaceable filter element. Some have only a mesh strainer in the fuel pump.

4-151, INLINE SIX, V6, AND V8

All these engines have a throwaway cartridge filter in the line between the fuel pump and the carburetor. To replace it:

1. Remove the air cleaner as necessary.
2. Put an absorbent rag under the filter to catch spillage.
3. Remove the hose clamps.
4. Remove the filter and short attaching hoses.
5. Remove the hoses if they are to be reused.

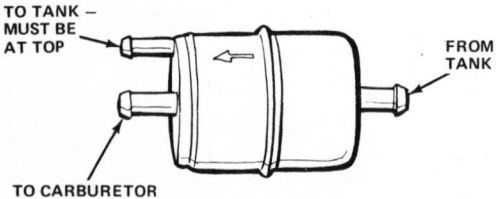

Correct fuel filter installation on all 1975 V8 and all 1976 and later engines

Lowest Air Temperature Anticipated	Multiviscosity Engine Oil
Above 40°F	SAE 10W-30, 40, 50 or 20W-40, 50
Above 32°F	SAE 10W-30 or 10W-40
Above 0°F	SAE 10W-30 or 10W-40
Below 0°F	SAE 5W-20 or 5W-30
	Single-Viscosity Engine Oil
Above 40°F	SAE 30 or 40
Above 32°F	SAE 20W-20
Above 0°F	SAE 20
Below 0°F	SAE 10W

6. Assemble the new filter and hoses.
NOTE: *The original equipment wire hose clamps should be replaced with screw type band clamps for the best results.*
7. 1975 V8 and all 1976 and later filters have two outlets; the extra one is to return fuel vapors and bubbles to the tank so as to

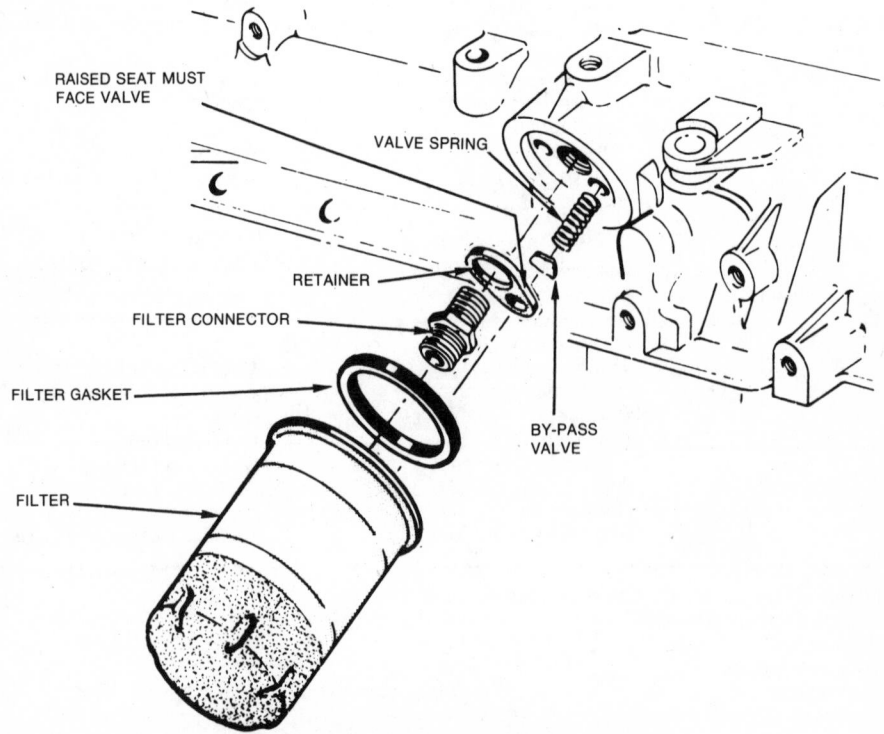

Spin-on oil filter used on inline sixes and V8

prevent vapor lock. The tank line outlet must be up.

8. Install the filter, tighten the clamps, start the engine, and check for leaks. Discard the rag and old filter safely.

LUBRICATION

Fuel and Oil Recommendations

Fuel

All models through 1974 are designed to use a regular grade of gasoline. All 1975 and later models must use unleaded gasoline.

Engine Oil

Only SE or SF labeled oils should be used. You can find the SE or SF marking either on the top or on the side of the container; the viscosity rating should be in the same place. Select the viscosity rating to be used by your type of driving and the temperature range anticipated before the next oil change.

The multi-viscosity oils offer the advantage of being adaptable to temperature extremes. They allow easy starts at low temperatures, yet still give good protection at high speeds and warm temperatures.

Lubricant Changes

Engine Oil

Before draining the oil, make sure that the engine is at operating temperature. Hot oil will hold more impurities in suspension and will flow better, removing more oil and dirt.

Drain the oil into a suitable receptacle. After the drain plug is loosened, unscrew the plug with your fingers, using a rag to shield your fingers from the heat. Push in on the plug as you unscrew it so you can feel when all of the screw threads are out of the hole. You can then remove the plug quickly with the minimum amount of oil running down your arm. You will also have the plug in your hand and not in the bottom of a pan of hot oil.

Engine Oil Filter

Change the oil filter every time you change the oil. The engine should be at operating temperature. On the older L head and F head four-cylinder Jeeps, the oil filter is located on the right side forward part of the engine. To change the element, remove the bolt, remove the lid, and remove and discard the element. Clean out the cup with a clean, dry cloth and flushing oil or clean, light-viscosity engine oil. Clean the lid in the same manner and remove and discard the old gas-

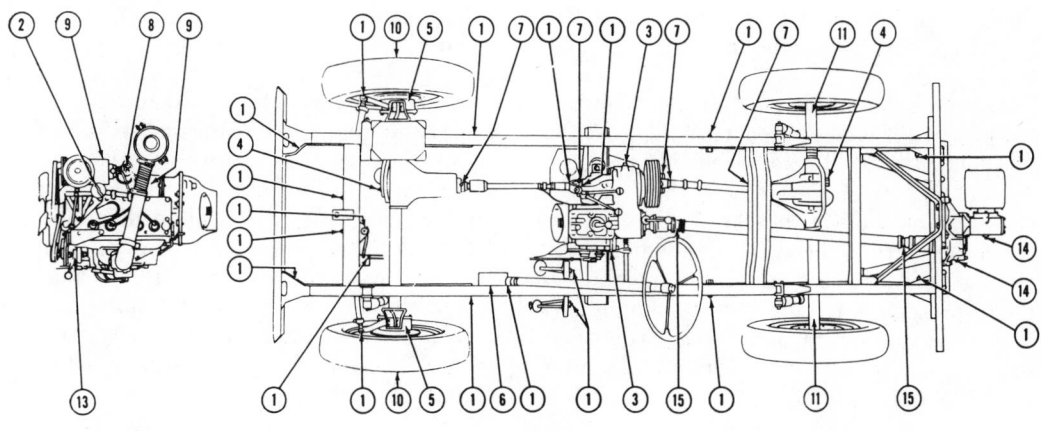

1. Chassis bearings
2. Engine
3. Transmission and transfer case
4. Differentials
5. Front axle U-joints
6. Steering gear
7. Drive shaft U-joints
8. Distributor:
   Oiler
   Wick
   Pivot
   Cam
9. Generator and starter
10. Front wheel bearings
11. Rear wheel bearings
13. Governor
14. Power Take-off (PTO)
15. PTO U-joints

CJ-2A and CJ-3A lubrication chart

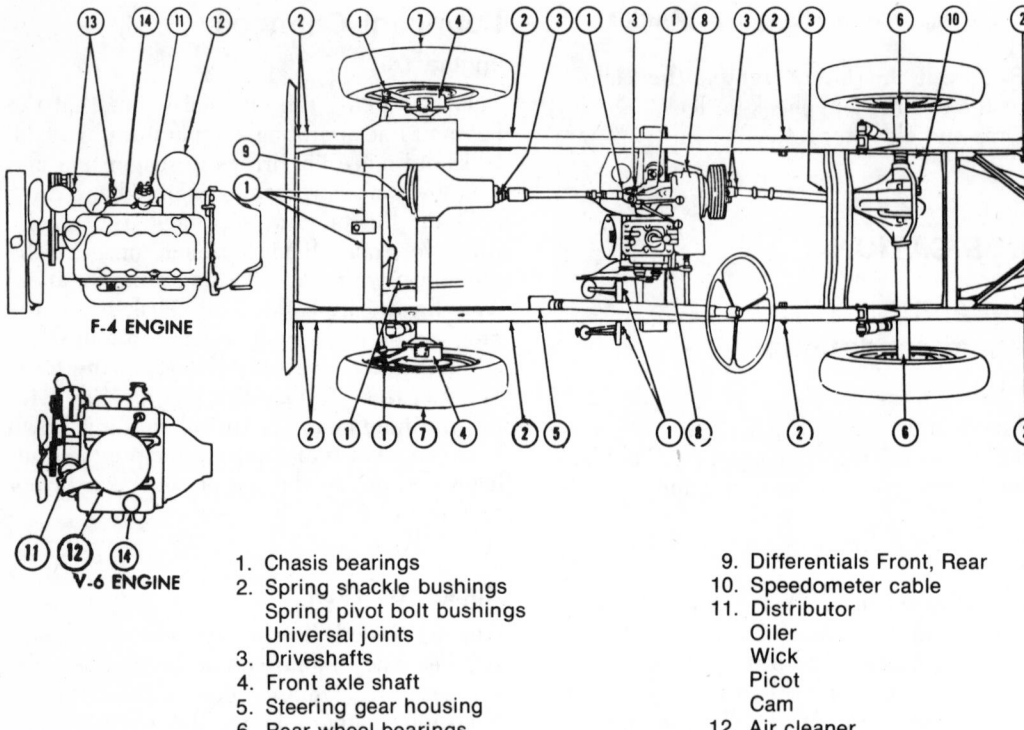

F-4 ENGINE

V-6 ENGINE

1. Chasis bearings
2. Spring shackle bushings
   Spring pivot bolt bushings
   Universal joints
3. Driveshafts
4. Front axle shaft
5. Steering gear housing
6. Rear wheel bearings
7. Front wheel bearings
8. 3 Speed transmission and transfer case
   4 Speed transmission and transfer case[1]
9. Differentials Front, Rear
10. Speedometer cable
11. Distributor
    Oiler
    Wick
    Picot
    Cam
12. Air cleaner
13. Generator
14. Engine

CJ-3B, CJ-5, CJ-6 lubrication chart through 1971

ket. Replace it with a new one. Do not use a solvent that could get into the oil and dilute it. Place the new filter element in the cup. Place the lid on the cup and the bolt down through the center. Tighten the bolt to 10–15 ft. lbs. Start the engine and look for leaks. If a leak does develop, turn off the engine and remove the oil filter lid. Inspect the gasket to see if it is seated properly. Adjust the gasket if needed. Replace the lid, start the engine, and check for leaks. If the leak persists, tighten the bolt further.

On the newer F head, GM 4-cylinder, V6, straight six, and V8 engines, the oil filter is the spin-on type. On the F head engines, the filter is in the same place as the former cartridge type filter. On the V6 engine, the filter is on the right side of the engine just below the alternator. On the straight six engines, the filter is located on the lower, center right side of the engine. On the GM 4-cylinder and V8 engines, the filter is located on the lower, front right side of the engine.

To replace the filter, you will need an oil filter wrench. Loosen the filter with the filter wrench. With a rag wrapped around the fil-

ter, unscrew the filter from the oil pump housing. Be careful of hot oil that might run down the side of the filter, especially on the straight sixes and V8s. On the F head, four-cylinder engines, the filter is mounted with the open side facing downward so you won't have to worry about oil running down on your hand. Make sure that you have a pan under the filter before you start to remove it from the engine so you won't make a mess and, if some of the hot oil does happen to get on you, you will have a place to dump the filter in a hurry. Wipe the base of the mounting plate with a clean, dry cloth. When you install the new filter, smear a small amount of oil on the gasket with your finger, just enough to coat the entire surface where it comes in contact with the mounting plate. When you tighten the filter, turn it only a quarter of a turn after it comes in contact with the mounting plate.

Manual Transmission

Remove the drain plug which is at the bottom of the transmission or else on the side near the bottom. Allow all the lubricant to

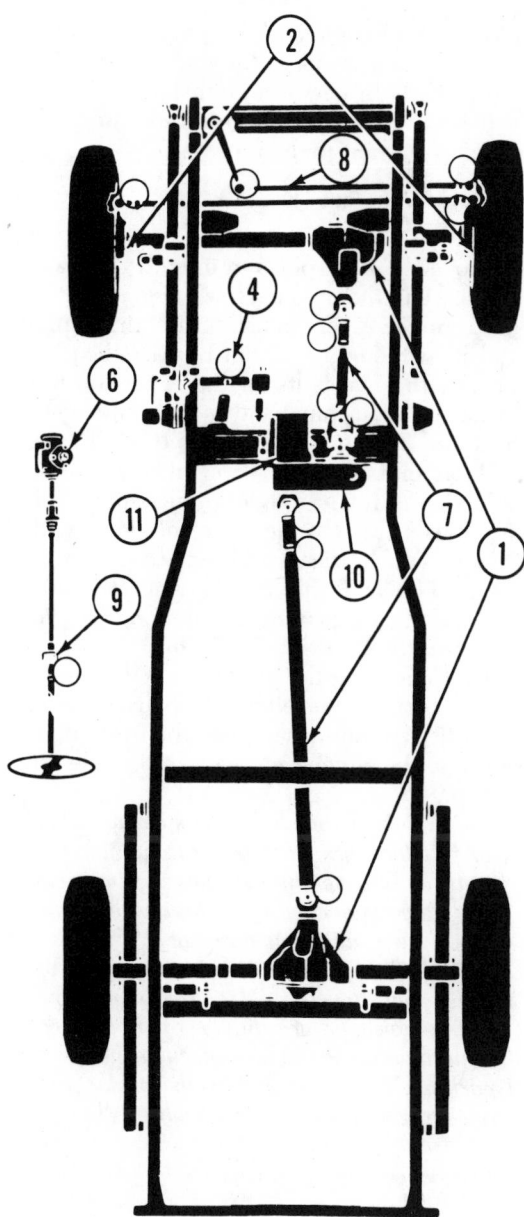

run out before replacing the plug. Replace the oil with the correct oil, usually SAE 80 or SAE 90 gear lubricant.

Automatic Transmission

If, when the transmission fluid level is checked, the fluid is noticed to be discolored from a clear red to brown, has a burned smell, or contains water; it should be changed immediately.

1. Drive the vehicle for at least 20 minutes at expressway speeds or the equivalent to raise the temperature of the fluid to its normal operating range.

2. Drain the automatic transmission fluid into an appropriate container before it has cooled. The fluid is drained by loosening the transmission pan and allowing the fluid to run out around the edges. It is best to loosen only one corner of the pan and allow most of the fluid to drain out.

3. Remove the remaining pan screws, and remove the pan and pan gasket.

4. Remove the strainer and discard it.

5. Remove the O-ring seal from the pick-up pipe and discard it.

6. Install a new O-ring seal on the pick-up pipe and install the new strainer and pipe assembly.

7. Thoroughly clean the bottom pan and position a new gasket on the pan mating surface.

8. Install the pan and tighten the attaching screws to 10–13 ft. lbs.

9. Pour about 5 qts. of Dexron® or Dexron® II automatic transmission fluid down the dipstick tube. Make sure that the funnel, container, hose, or any other item used to assist in filling the transmission is clean.

10. Start the engine with the transmission in Park. Do NOT race it. Allow the engine to idle for a few minutes.

11. After the engine has been running for

○ LUBRICATION POINTS

1. Differentials
2. Front wheel bearings
3. Not used
4. Clutch lever and linkage
5. Not used
6. Manual steering gear
7. Driveshafts
8. Steering linkage
9. Steering shaft U-joint
10. Transfer case
11. Transmission

1972 and later lubrication chart

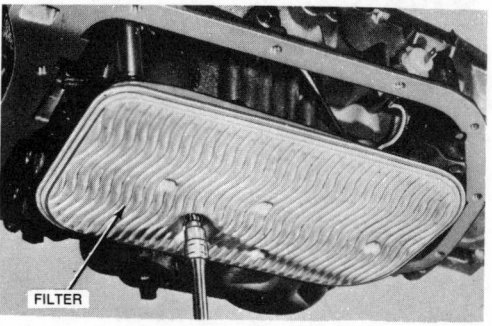

FILTER

Removing automatic transmission filter

a few minutes, move the selector lever through all of the gears.

12. With the selector lever in Park, check the transmission fluid level and adjust as necessary. Remember the transmission fluid must be warm when at the Full mark.

NOTE: *On some 1977–79 models, fluid may overflow through the filler pipe, or vent tube. If this condition occurs:*

1. Insert a length of stiff wire into the vent tube. If the tube is restricted, clean or replace it.

2. If the tube is not restricted, make sure that the fluid level is correct. If the fluid level is correct perform a road test. If the fluid overflows during the road test,

3. Raise and support the vehicle on jack stands.

4. Loosen the vacuum modulator adapter retaining bolt. Pull the modulator outward about ½ to 1 inch. Drain off about 1 pint of fluid. Seat the modulator and tighten the attaching bolt. Lower the vehicle and road test. Check the fluid level and file a new mark on the dipstick for the new fill level.

Front and Rear Axle

Remove the oil by loosening the differential housing cover or by using a suction gun. Refill the axle housings with gear oil until the lubricant level meets the fill hole.

Part-Time Transfer Case

The transfer case is to be serviced at the same time and in the same manner as the transmission. It has its own drain plug which should be opened. Don't rely on the transmission drain plug to completely drain the transfer case. The transfer case and the transmission are not interconnected in Jeeps with four-speed transmissions as they are in some vehicles with three-speed transmissions. You will have to remove the transfer case drain plug if you want to drain it.

Quadra-Trac Full-Time 4WD Transfer Case

Remove the filler plugs from both the transfer case and the optional low-range reduction unit. Remove the transfer case drain plug and allow the unit to drain. Replace the plug. Loosen the five bolts on the reduction unit (it has no drain plug) and pull it out slightly to drain. Tighten the bolts to 10–20 ft. lbs. Add one pint of Quadra-Trac lubricant to the reduction unit and install the filler plug. Fill the transfer case to the filler hole level with Quadra-Trac lubricant and replace the plug.

CAUTION: *Don't overtighten the filler and drain plugs in the aluminum case; the correct torque is 10–25 ft. lb.*

After changing the fluid, it may be necessary to drive the vehicle in figures 8s for about fifteen minutes to work the fresh lubricant into the clutches in the transfer case differential.

CAUTION: *Don't hold the steering wheel on full lock for more than about five seconds at a time during these maneuvers. The power steering fluid can overheat and cause pump and gear damage.*

NOTE: *The Quadra-Trac in some Jeep vehicles may develop a low frequency, pulsating noise or grating or rasping which sometimes occurs in low speed cornering or parking. This is caused by the brake cones releasing suddenly after sticking. The con-*

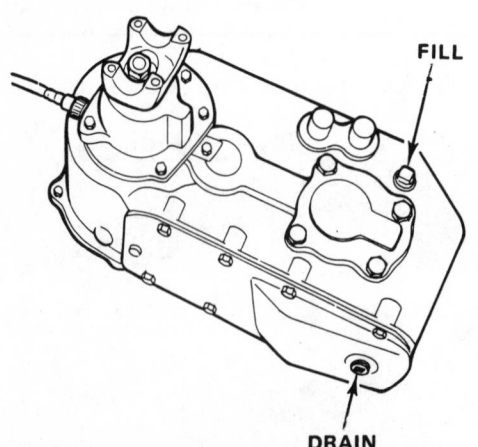

FILL

DRAIN

Dana 300 transfer case drain and fill plugs

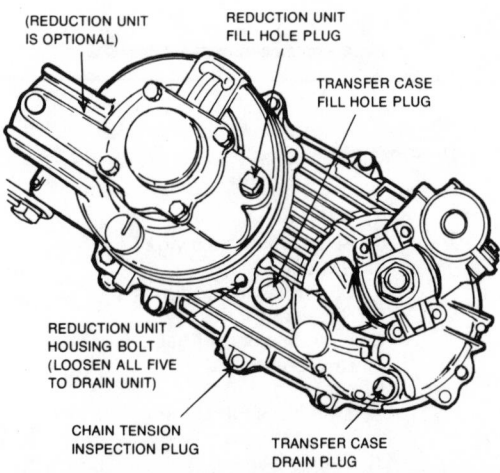

(REDUCTION UNIT IS OPTIONAL)

REDUCTION UNIT FILL HOLE PLUG

TRANSFER CASE FILL HOLE PLUG

REDUCTION UNIT HOUSING BOLT (LOOSEN ALL FIVE TO DRAIN UNIT)

CHAIN TENSION INSPECTION PLUG

TRANSFER CASE DRAIN PLUG

Quadra-Trac transfer case and low range reduction unit drain and fill plugs

dition is known as stick-slip. As a remedy, AMC/Jeep has introduced a new lubricant, part number 8130444, which must be used in a drain and refill procedure. However, this new lubricant is especially prone to water contamination, so a new vent kit must be installed. The kit is part number 8130445. On vehicles that do not exhibit this problem, the original lubricant, part number 5358652 may be used. Directions for installing the vent kit are supplied with the kit.

Front Wheel Bearing Lubrication and Adjustment

The front wheel bearings should be cleaned, inspected, and repacked at the recommended intervals and anytime after they have been submerged in water for any length of time.

NOTE: *Sodium based grease is not compatible with lithium based grease. Read the package labels and be careful not to mix the two types. If there is any doubt as to the type of grease used, completely clean the old grease from the bearing and hub before replacing.*

1. Raise the front of the vehicle and place jackstands under the axle.
2. Remove the wheel.
3. Remove the front hub grease cap and driving hub snap-ring. On models equipped with locking hubs, remove the retainer knob hub ring, actuator knob, snap-ring, outer clutch retaining ring and actuating cam body.
4. Remove the splined driving hub and the pressure spring. This may require slight prying with a screwdriver.

5. Remove the wheel bearing locknut, lockring and adjusting nut.
6. On vehicles with drum brakes, remove the hub and drum assembly. This may require that the brake adjusting wheel be backed off a few turns. The outer wheel bearing and spring retainer will come off with the hub.
7. On vehicles with disc brakes, remove the caliper and suspend it out of the way by hanging it from a suspension or frame member with a length of wire. Do not disconnect the brake hose, and be careful to avoid stretching the hose. Remove the rotor and hub assembly. The outer wheel bearing and spring will come off with the hub.
8. Carefully drive out the inner bearing and seal from the hub, using a wood block.
9. Inspect the bearing races for excessive wear, pitting or grooves. If they are cracked or grooved, or if pitting and excess wear is present, drive them out with a drift or punch.
10. Check the bearing for excess wear, pitting or cracks, or excess looseness.

NOTE: *If it is necessary to replace either the bearing or the race, replace both. Never replace just a bearing or a race. If just one is replaced, premature failure of the new part will result.*

11. If the old parts are retained, thoroughly clean them in a safe solvent and allow them to dry on a clean towel. Never spin them with compressed air.
12. On vehicles with drum brakes, cover the spindle with a cloth and thoroughly brush all dirt from the brakes. Never blow the dirt off the brakes; asbestos fibers have been found to be a cancer causing agent.

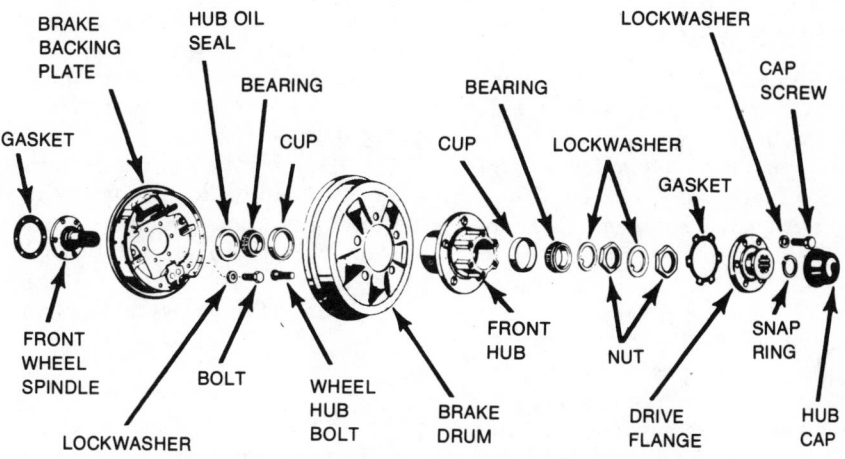

Typical front wheel bearing details, drum brakes shown

13. Remove the cloth and thoroughly clean the spindle.

14. Thoroughly clean the inside of the hub.

15. Pack the inside of the hub with EP wheel bearing grease. Add grease to the hub until it is flush with the inside diameter of the bearing cup.

16. Pack the bearing with the same grease. A wheel bearing packer is best for this operation. If one is not available, place a large amount of grease in the palm of your hand and slide the edge of the bearing cage through the grease to pick up as much as possible, then work the grease in as best you can with your fingers.

17. If a new race is being installed, very carefully drive it into position until it bottoms all around, using a brass drift. Be careful to avoid scratching the surface.

18. Place the inner bearing in the race and install a new grease seal.

19. Place the hub assembly into the spindle and install the outer bearing. Install the wheel bearing nut and torque it to 50 ft. lb. while turning the wheel back and forth to seat the bearings. Back off the nut about ⅓ turn.

20. Install the lockwasher with the inner tab aligned with the keyway in the spindle and turn the inner wheel bearing adjusting nut until the peg engages the nearest hole in the lockwasher.

21. Install the outer locknut and torque it to 50 ft. lb.

22. Install the pressure spring, drive flange, snap ring and hub cap.

23. Install the caliper over the rotor.

Locking Hub Service

Jeep vehicles through 1979 were not factory-equipped with locking hubs. Locking hubs were a dealer-installed option or installed by the owner after purchase. Beginning in 1980, factory-installed hubs were offered. These hubs are designated model 243 by AMC/Jeep.

1945–79

The following is a general service procedure that should apply to all types.

Locking hubs should be lubricated at least once a year and as soon as possible if running for extended periods submerged in water. The same type of grease should be used in the locking hubs as is used on the wheel bearings. EP lithium based chassis lube is preferred.

1. Remove the lock-out screws and washers.

2. Remove the hub ring and knob.

3. Remove the internal snap-ring from the groove in the hub.

4. Remove the cam body ring and clutch retainer from the hub and disassemble the parts.

5. Remove the axle shaft snap-ring. It may be necessary to push in on the gear and pull out on the axle with a bolt to make the snap-ring removal easier.

6. Remove the drive gear and clutch gear. A slight rocking of the hub may make them slide out easier.

7. Remove the coil spring and spring retainer.

8. Clean all the components in a safe solvent. Wipe out the hub with a clean cloth.

9. Grease the inside of the hub liberally.

10. Install the spring retainer ring with the undercut area facing inwards. Be sure it seats against the bearing.

11. Install the coil spring with the large end going in first.

12. Install the axle shaft sleeve and ring and the inner clutch ring with the teeth of both components meshed together in a locked position. It may be necessary to rock the hub to mesh the splines of the axle with those of the axle shaft sleeve and ring. Keep the two gears locked in position.

13. Install the axle shaft snap-ring. Push in on the gear and pull out on the axle with a bolt to allow the snap-ring to go into the groove.

14. Install the actuating cam body ring into the outer clutch retaining ring and install them in the hub.

15. Install the internal snap-ring.

16. Apply a small amount of Lubriplate® grease to the ears of the cam.

17. Assemble the knob in the hub ring and assemble them to the axle with the knob in the locked position. Tighten the screws and washers evenly and alternately, making sure the retainer ring is not cocked in the hub.

18. Torque the screws to 40 in. lb.

1980–81
Model 243

1. Remove the bolts and lockwashers attaching the hub body to the axle.

2. Remove the hub body and discard the gasket.

CAUTION: *Do not turn the hub control dial after removal.*

3. Remove the retaining ring from the axle shaft.

4. Remove the hub clutch and bearing assembly.

5. Clean and inspect all parts.

6. Lubricate all parts with chassis lubricant. DO NOT PACK THE HUB WITH GREASE!

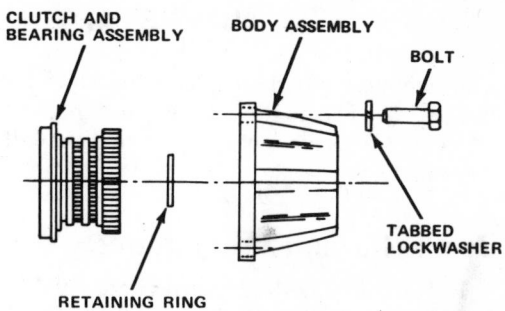

M243 hub removal and installation

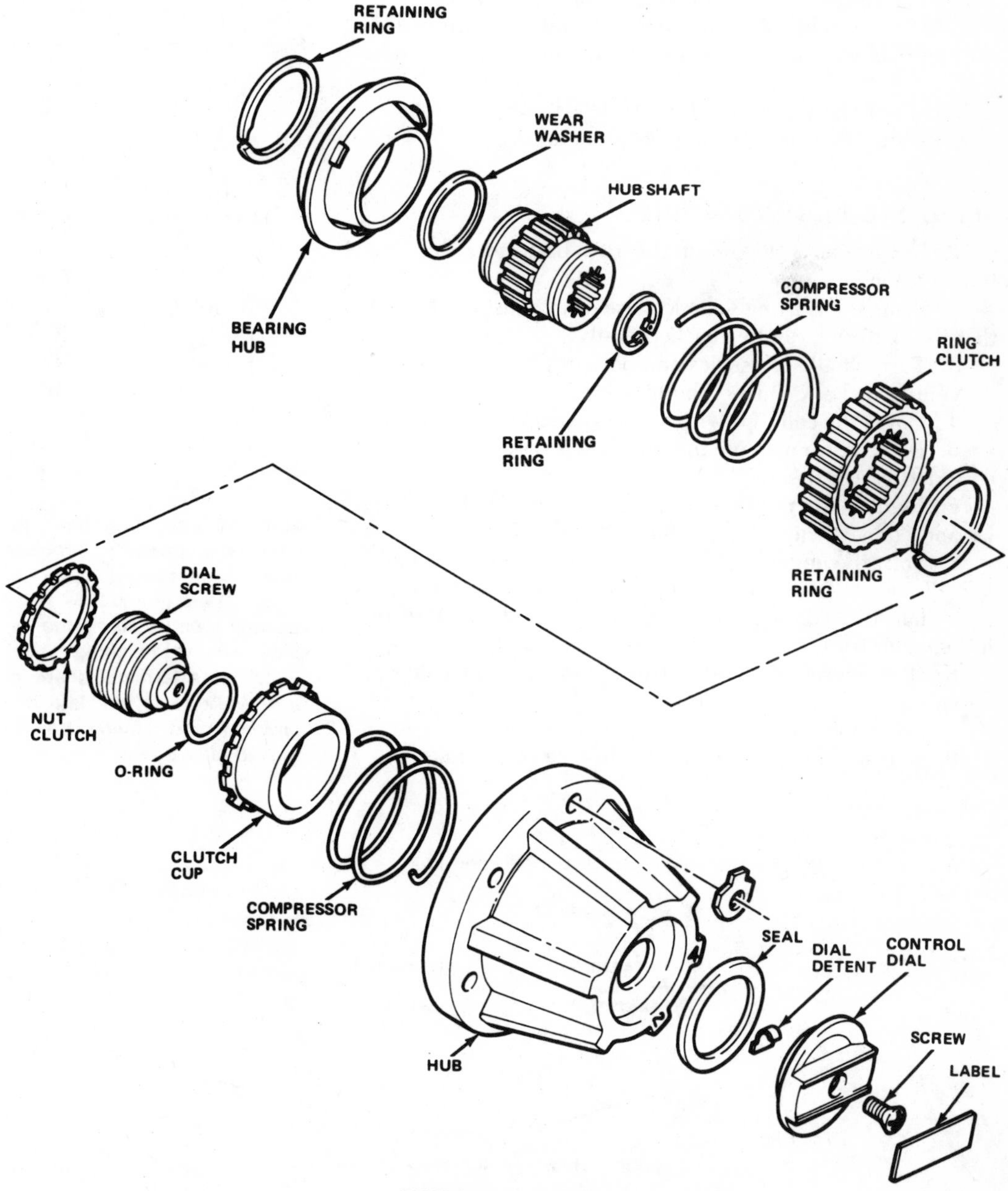

RETAINING RING

WEAR WASHER

HUB SHAFT

COMPRESSOR SPRING

RING CLUTCH

BEARING HUB

RETAINING RING

RETAINING RING

DIAL SCREW

NUT CLUTCH

O-RING

CLUTCH CUP

COMPRESSOR SPRING

HUB

SEAL

DIAL DETENT

CONTROL DIAL

SCREW

LABEL

M243 front drive hub

JUMP STARTING A DEAD BATTERY

The chemical reaction in a battery produces explosive hydrogen gas. This is the safe way to jump start a dead battery, reducing the chances of an accidental spark that could cause an explosion.

CAUTION: *All CJ-2A, CJ-3A and early CJ-3B, CJ-5 and CJ-6 have 6-volt systems. Never jump a 6v system with a 12v system!*

Jump Starting Precautions

1. Be sure both batteries are of the same voltage.
2. Be sure both batteries are of the same polarity (have the same grounded terminal).
3. Be sure the vehicles are not touching.
4. Be sure the vent cap holes are not obstructed.
5. Do not smoke or allow sparks around the battery.
6. In cold weather, check for frozen electrolyte in the battery.
7. Do not allow electrolyte on your skin or clothing.
8. Be sure the electrolyte is not frozen.

Jump Starting Procedure

1. Determine voltages of the two batteries; they must be the same.
2. Bring the starting vehicle close (they must not touch) so that the batteries can be reached easily.
3. Turn off all accessories and both engines. Put both cars in Neutral or Park and set the handbrake.
4. Cover the cell caps with a rag—do not cover terminals.
5. If the terminals on the run-down battery are heavily corroded, clean them.
6. Identify the positive and negative posts on both batteries and connect the cables in the order shown.
7. Start the engine of the starting vehicle and run it at fast idle. Try to start the car with the dead battery. Crank it for no more than 10 seconds at a time and let it cool off for 20 seconds in between tries.
8. If it doesn't start in 3 tries, there is something else wrong.
9. Disconnect the cables in the reverse order.
10. Replace the cell covers and dispose of the rags.

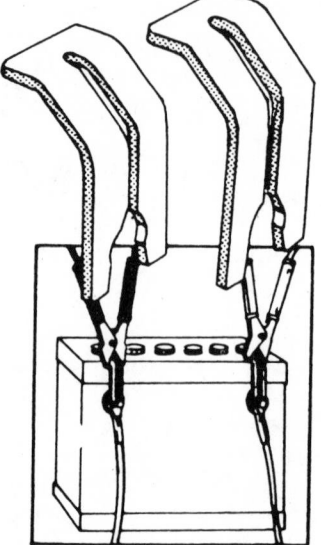

Side terminal batteries occasionally pose a problem when connecting jumper cables. There frequently isn't enough room to clamp the cables without touching sheet metal. Side terminal adaptors are available to alleviate this problem and should be removed after use

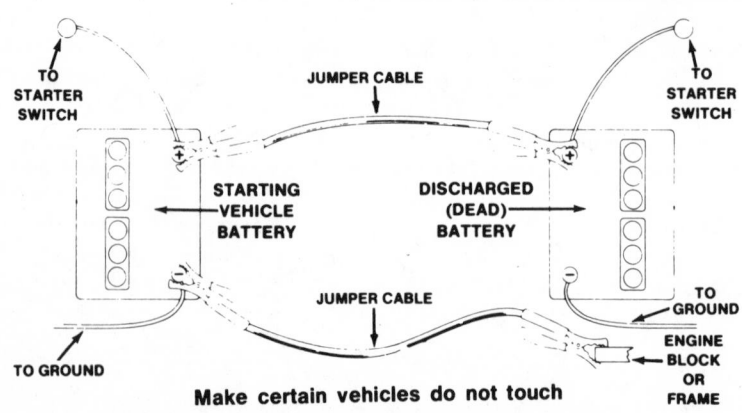

Make certain vehicles do not touch

This hook-up for negative ground cars only

7. Install in reverse of removal. Torque the retaining nuts to 30 ft. lb.

Pushing and Towing

To push-start your vehicle, (*manual transmission only*) follow the procedures below. Check to make sure that the bumpers of both vehicles are aligned so neither will be damaged. Be sure that all electrical system components are turned off (headlights, heater blower, etc.). Turn on the ignition switch. Place the shift lever in second or third and push in the clutch pedal. At about 15 mph, signal the driver of the pushing vehicle to fall back, depress the accelerator pedal, and release the clutch pedal slowly. The engine should start.

When you are doing the pushing or pulling, make sure that the two bumpers match so you won't damage the vehicle you are to push. Another good idea is to put an old tire in between the two vehicles. If the bumpers don't match, perhaps you should tow the other vehicle. Try to keep your Jeep right up against the other vehicle while you are pushing. If the two vehicles do separate, stop and start over again instead of trying to catch up and ramming the other vehicle. Also try, as much as possible, to avoid riding or slipping the clutch.

If you have to tow the other vehicle, make sure that the tow chain or rope is sufficiently long and strong, and that it is attached securely to both vehicles at a strong place. Attach the chain at a point on the frame or as close to it as possible. Once again, go slowly and tell the other driver to do the same. Warn the other driver not to allow too much slack in the line when he gains traction and can move under his own power. Otherwise he may run over the tow line and damage both vehicles.

If your Jeep must be towed, follow these guidelines:

1. A Jeep with a manual transmission can be towed with either all four wheels or either axle on the ground for any distance at a safe speed with both the transmission and transfer case in Neutral.

2. To tow a Jeep with an automatic transmission and Quadra-Trac, the driveshaft to the axle(s) remaining on the ground must be disconnected. Be sure to index mark the driveshafts and yoke flanges for alignment upon assembly. Also, the driveshafts must be tied securely up out of the way or removed completely while the vehicle is being towed.

3. A Jeep equipped with an automatic transmission and Quadra-Trac with the optional low range reduction unit can be towed with all four wheels on the ground without disconnecting the driveshafts. Place the transmission shift lever in Park, the low range reduction unit shift lever in Neutral, and the emergency drive control knob in the Normal position. If the emergency drive system was engaged when the engine was shut down, it will have to be restarted and the emergency drive control knob turned to the Normal position to disengage the system since the control mechanism is vacuum-operated.

CAUTION: *Never tow the Jeep with the emergency drive system engaged or the reduction unit in low range.*

In all cases, unnecessary wear and tear can be avoided by disconnecting the driveshafts at the differentials and either tying them up out of the way or removing them altogether. Be sure to index mark the driveshafts and yoke flanges for proper alignment during assembly. If the Jeep is equipped with free-running front hubs (manual transmission only), there is no need to remove the front driveshaft, simply disengage the hubs.

Jacking and Hoisting

Scissors jacks or hydraulic jacks are recommended for the Jeep CJ. To change a tire, place the jack beneath the spring plate, under the axle, near the wheel to be changed.

Make sure that you are on level ground, that the transmission is in Reverse or Park, the parking brake is set, and the tire diagonally opposite to the one to be changed is blocked. Loosen the lug nuts before you jack the wheel to be changed completely free of the ground.

If you use a hoist, make sure that the pads of the hoist are located in such a way as to lift on the Jeep's frame and not on a shock absorber mount, floor boards, oil pan, or any other part that cannot support the full weight of the vehicle.

Tune-Up

2

TUNE-UP PROCEDURES

Spark Plugs

Spark plugs ignite the air and fuel mixture in the cylinder as the piston reaches the top of the compression stroke. The controlled explosion that results forces the piston down, turning the crankshaft and the rest of the drive train.

The average life of a spark plug is dependent on a number of factors: the mechanical condition of the engine; the type of fuel; driving conditions; and the driver.

When you remove the spark plugs, check their condition. They are a good indicator of the condition of the engine.

A small deposit of light tan or gray material on a spark plug that has been used for any period of time is to be considered normal. Additives in unleaded fuels may give a number of unusual color indications; for instance, MMT (a manganese anti-knock compound) will cause rust red deposits.

The gap between the center electrode and the side or ground electrode can be expected to increase not more than 0.001 in. every 1,000 miles under normal conditions.

When a spark plug is functioning normally or, more accurately, when the plug is installed in an engine that is functioning properly, the plugs can be taken out, cleaned, re-gapped, and reinstalled in the engine without doing the engine any harm.

When, and if, a plug fouls and begins to misfire, you will have to investigate, correct the cause of the fouling, and either clean or replace the plug.

There are several reasons why a spark plug will foul and you can learn which reason by just looking at the plug. A few of the most common reasons for plug fouling, and a description of the fouled plug's appearance, is listed in the "Color Insert" section which also offers solutions to the problems.

Distributor Wiring Sequences and Firing Orders

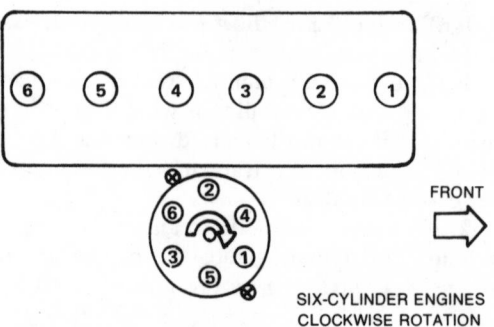

SIX-CYLINDER ENGINES
CLOCKWISE ROTATION
1-5-3-6-2-4

Inline six cylinder engines through 1974 (point-type ignition)

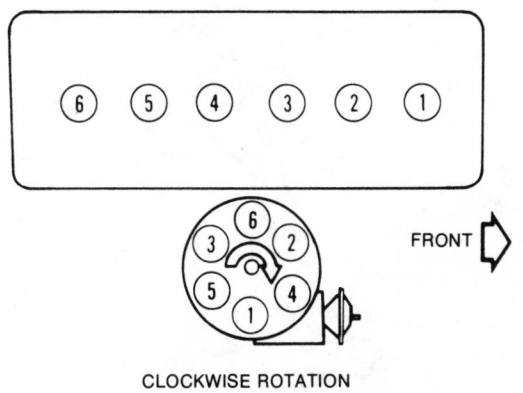

CLOCKWISE ROTATION
1-5-3-6-2-4

SIX-CYLINDER ENGINES

Inline six cylinder engines starting 1975 (electronic ignition)

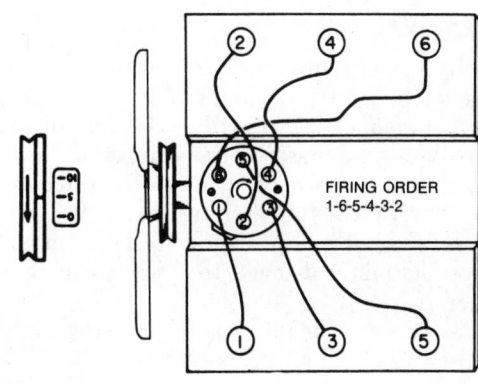

FIRING ORDER
1-6-5-4-3-2

V6

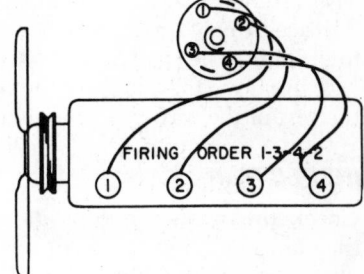

TDC 6
ADV 5

FIRING ORDER 1-3-4-2

4-134

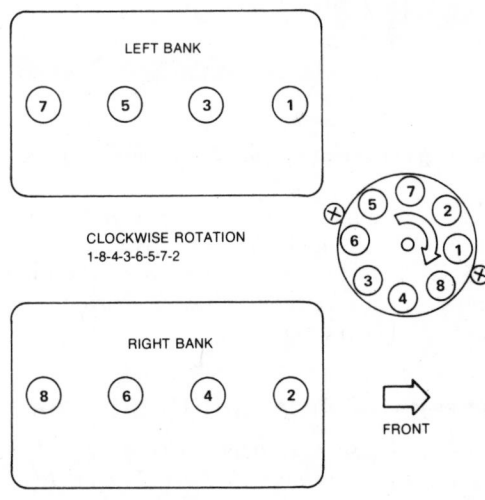

LEFT BANK

CLOCKWISE ROTATION
1-8-4-3-6-5-7-2

RIGHT BANK

FRONT

V-8 ENGINES

V8 engines through 1974 (point-type ignition)

1980—81 4-151

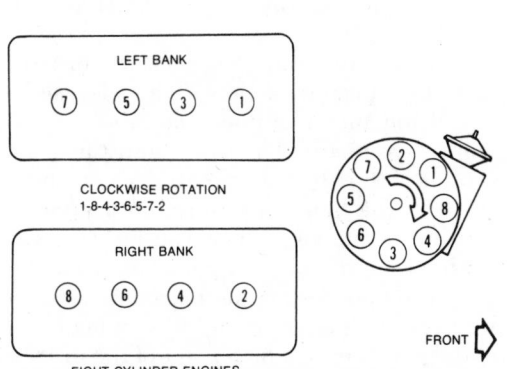

LEFT BANK

CLOCKWISE ROTATION
1-8-4-3-6-5-7-2

RIGHT BANK

FRONT

EIGHT CYLINDER ENGINES

V8 engines starting 1975 (electronic ignition)

Firing positions on 4-134 distributor

REMOVAL

1. Number the wires so you won't cross them when you replace them.

2. Remove the wire from the end of the spark plug by grasping the wire by the rubber boot. If the boot sticks to the plug, remove it by twisting and pulling at the same time. Do not pull the wire itself or you will most certainly damage the delicate carbon core.

3. Use a $^{13}/_{16}$ in. spark plug socket to loosen all of the plugs about two turns.

4. If compressed air is available, blow off the area around the spark plug holes. Otherwise, use a rag or a brush to clean the area. Be careful not to allow any foreign material to drop into the spark plug holes.

5. Remove the plugs by unscrewing them the rest of the way from the engine.

INSPECTION

Check the plugs for deposits and wear. If they are not going to be replaced, clean the plugs thoroughly. Remember that any kind of deposit will decrease the efficiency of the plug. Plugs can be cleaned on a spark plug cleaning machine, which can sometimes be found in service stations, or you can do an acceptable job of cleaning with a stiff brush.

Check spark plug gap before installation. The ground electrode must be parallel to the center electrode and the specified size wire gauge should pass through the gap with a slight drag. If the electrodes are worn, it is possible to file them level.

INSTALLATION

1. Insert the plugs in the spark plug hole and tighten them hand-tight. Take care not to cross-thread them.

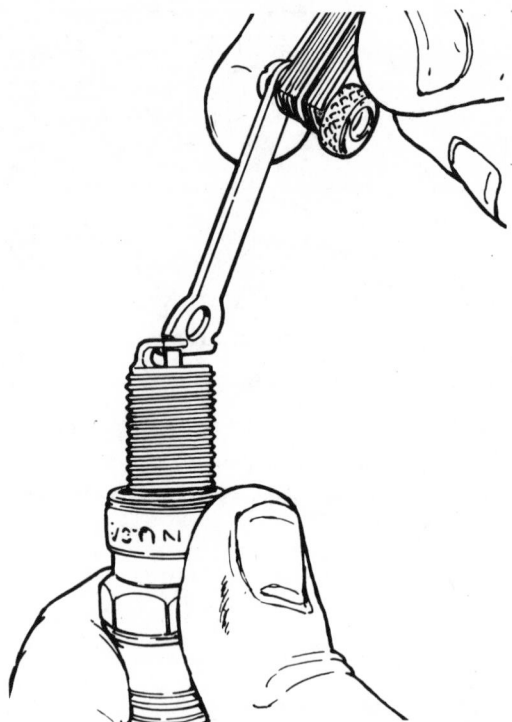

Bending side electrode to adjust spark plug gap

2. Tighten the plugs firmly. The correct torque for all engines is 28 ft. lbs.

3. Install the spark plug wires on their plugs. Make sure that each wire is firmly connected to each plug.

Breaker Points and Condenser

Note: *These components are not used in electronic ignition systems (1975 and later).*

When you replace a set of points, always replace the condenser at the same time.

When you change the point gap or the dwell, you will also have changed the ignition timing. So, if the point gap or dwell is changed, the ignition timing must be adjusted.

There are two ways to check the breaker point gap; it can be done with a feeler gauge or a dwell meter. Either way you set the points, you are basically adjusting the amount of time that the points remain closed or open. The time is measured in degrees of distributor rotation. When you measure the gap between the breaker points with a feeler gauge, you are setting the maximum amount the points will open when the rubbing block on the points is on a high point of the distributor cam. When you adjust the points with a dwell meter, you are adjusting the number of

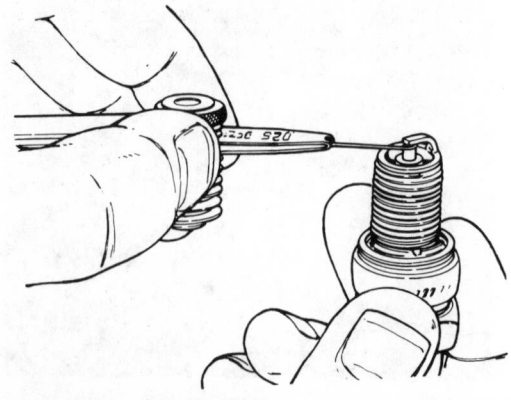

Checking spark plug gap

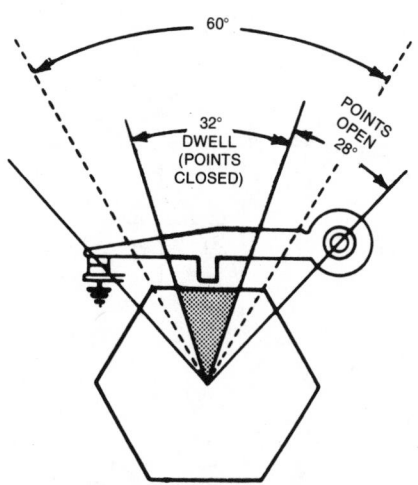

Point dwell diagram for inline sixes

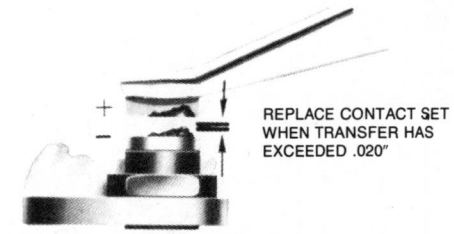

REPLACE CONTACT SET
WHEN TRANSFER HAS
EXCEEDED .020"

Contact point material transfer

degrees that the points will remain closed before they start to open as a high point of the distributor cam approaches the rubbing block.

INSPECTION OF THE POINTS

1. Disconnect the high-tension wire from the top of the distributor and the coil, and unsnap the distributor retaining caps.

2. Remove the distributor cap by prying off the spring clips on the L or F-head, or depressing and turning the hold-down screws on the side of the cap on all other engines.

3. Remove the rotor from the distributor shaft by pulling it straight up. On the 304 cu in. V8 and 225 cu in. V6, the rotor is attached to the distributor shaft by screws. Remove the screws to remove the rotor. Examine the condition of the rotor. If it is cracked or the metal tip is excessively worn or burned, it should be replaced.

4. Pry open the contact points with a screwdriver and check the condition of the contacts. If they are excessively worn, burned, or pitted, they should be replaced.

5. If the points are in good condition, adjust them, and replace the rotor and the distributor cap. If the points need to be replaced, follow the replacement procedure below.

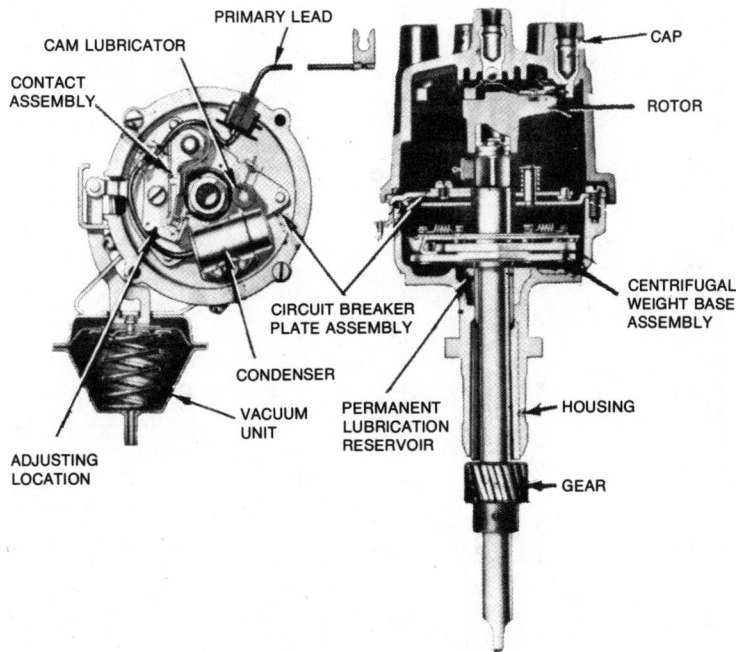

Inline six distributor cutaway

Tune-Up Specifications

Years Engine	Spark Plugs		Distributor		*Ignition Timing (deg)		Intake Valve Opens (deg)	Fuel Pump Press (psi)	*Idle Speed (rpm)		Valve Clearance (in.)	
	Type	Gap (in.)	Dwell (deg)	Gap (in.)	Man Trans	Auto Trans			Man Trans	Auto Trans	Intake	Exhaust
1945–52, 4–134	J-8	.030	42①	.020②	5B	—	9B	3.0	600	—	.016	.016
1953–71, 4–134	J-8	.030	42①	.020②	5B	—	9B	3.0	600	—	.018	.016
1980–81, 4–151	R44TSX	.060	Electronic		10B	12B	33B	6.5–8.0	900	700	Hyd	Hyd
1965–71, V6–225	44S	.035	30	.016	5B	—	24B	5.0	550	—	Hyd	Hyd
1972, 6–232	N-12Y	.035	32	.016	5B	—	12½B	4–5	675	—	Hyd	Hyd
1973, 6–232	N-12Y	.035	32	.016	5B	—	12½B	4–5	700	—	Hyd	Hyd
1974, '6–232	N-12Y	.035	32	.016	5B	—	12½B	4–5	600	—	Hyd	Hyd
1975, 6–232	N-12Y	.035	Electronic		5B	—	12½B	4–5	700	—	Hyd	Hyd
1976, 6–232	N-12Y	.035	Electronic		8B	—	12½B	4–5	600	—	Hyd	Hyd

Year, Engine	Spark Plug	Gap	Dwell	Point Gap								
1977, 6-232	N-12Y	.035	Electronic		5B, 10B(Alt)	—	12B	4-5	850, 600(Alt)	—	Hyd	Hyd
1978, 6-232	N-13L	.035	Electronic		5B, 10B(Alt)	—	12B	4-5	850, 600(Alt)	—	Hyd	Hyd
1972-73, 6-258	N-12Y	.035	32	.016	3B	—	12½B	4-5	700	—	Hyd	Hyd
1974, 6-258	N-12Y	.035	32	.016	3B	—	12½B	4-5	600	—	Hyd	Hyd
1975, 6-258	N-12Y	.035	Electronic		3B	—	12½B	4-5	600	—	Hyd	Hyd
1976, 6-258	N-12Y	.035	Electronic		6B	8B	12B	4-5	600	550(700)	Hyd	Hyd
1977, 6-258	N-12Y	.035	Electronic		3B(6B), 10B(Alt)	8B, 10B(Alt)	12B	4-5	850, 600(Alt)	550(700)	Hyd	Hyd
1978, 6-258	N-13L	.035	Electronic		3B(8B), 10B(Alt)	8B, 10B(Alt)	12B	4-5	850, 600(Alt)	550	Hyd	Hyd
1979, 6-258	N-13L	.035	Electronic		6B	4B	14½B	4-5	700	600	Hyd	Hyd
1980, 6-258	N-14LY	.035	Electronic		8B(6B)	10B(8B)	14½B	4-5	700	600	Hyd	Hyd
1981, 6-258	RFN-14LY	.035	Electronic		8B(4B)	8B(6B)	14½B	4-5	650	550	Hyd	Hyd
1972-74, 8-304	N-12Y	.035	32	.016	5B	—	14¾B	5-6½	750	—	Hyd	Hyd

Tune-Up Specifications (cont.)

Years Engine	Spark Plugs		Distributor		*Ignition Timing (deg)		Intake Valve Opens (deg)	Fuel Pump Press (psi)	*Idle Speed (rpm)		Valve Clearance (in.)	
	Type	Gap (in.)	Dwell (deg)	Gap (in.)	Man Trans	Auto Trans			Man Trans	Auto Trans	Intake	Exhaust
1975, 8–304	N-12Y	.035	Electronic		5B	—	14¾B	5–6½	750	—	Hyd	Hyd
1976, 8–304	N-12Y	.035	Electronic		5B	10B	14¾B	5–6½	750	700	Hyd	Hyd
1977–78, 8–304	N-12Y	.035	Electronic		5B	10B (5B)	14¾B	5–6½	750	700	Hyd	Hyd
1979, 8–304	N-12Y	.035	Electronic		5B	8B	14¾B	5–6½	700 (750)	600	Hyd	Hyd
1980, 8–304	N-12Y	.035	Electronic		8B(5B)	12B(10B)	14¾B	5–6½	700	600	Hyd	Hyd
1981, 8–304	N-12Y	.035	Electronic		8B 12B(Alt)	10B	14¾B	5–6½	600 700(Alt)	600	Hyd	Hyd

* Figures in parentheses are for California Alt. High Altitude Certified engine
① Delco: 25–34
② Delco: .022
NOTE: The underhood specifications sticker often reflects tune-up specifications changes made in production. Sticker figures must be used if they disagree with those in this chart.

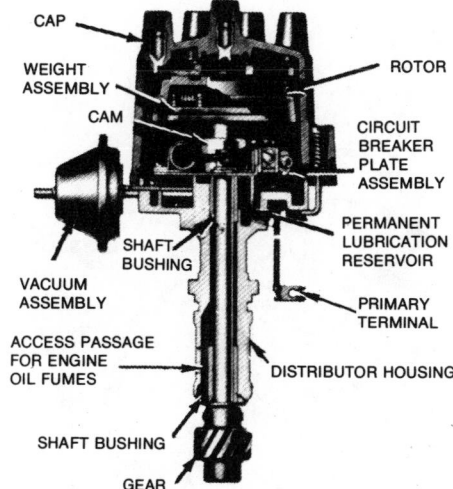

V8 distributor cutaway

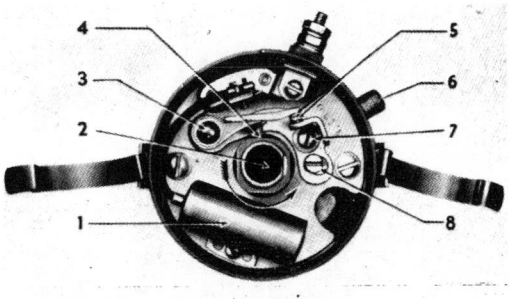

1. Condenser
2. Lubricating wick
3. Breaker arm pivot
4. Distributor camshaft
5. Contacts of the point assembly
6. Oiler
7. Adjustment lockscrew
8. Adjusting screw

4-134 distributor

REPLACEMENT OF THE BREAKER POINTS AND CONDENSER

NOTE: *Most 1945–71 vehicles were equipped with Autolite ignition systems. However, beginning in 1954, some were equipped with Delco systems. Never interchange parts during replacement.*

1. Remove the coil high-tension wire from the top of the distributor cap. Remove the distributor cap from the distributor and place it out of the way. Remove the rotor from the distributor shaft.

2. Remove the dust cover that is in the top of the distributor on some models, covering the points. It is pressed in handtight.

3. Loosen the screw that holds the condenser lead to the body of the breaker points. Remove the condenser from the points.

4. Remove the screw that holds and grounds the condenser to the distributor body. Remove the condenser from the distributor and discard it.

5. Remove the points assembly attaching screws and adjustment lockscrews. A screwdriver with a holding mechanism will come in handy here so you don't drop a screw into the distributor and have to remove the entire distributor just to retrieve it.

6. Remove the points by lifting them straight up off the locating dowel on the plate. Wipe off the cam and apply new cam lubricant. Discard the old set of points.

7. Slip the new set of points onto the locating dowel and install the screws that hold the assembly onto the plate. Do not tighten them all the way.

8. Attach the new condenser to the plate with the ground screw.

9. Attach the condenser lead to the points at the proper place. On American Motors engines, and the V6, the primary wire from the coil must now be attached to the points also. Make sure that the connectors for these two wires do not touch the body of the distributor; they will short out the primary circuit of the ignition if they do.

10. Apply a small amount of cam lubricant to the shaft where the rubbing block of the points touches.

ADJUSTMENT OF THE BREAKER POINTS WITH A FEELER GAUGE

1. If the contact points of the assembly are not parallel, bend the stationary contact so they make contact across the entire surface of the contacts. Bend only the bracket part of the point assembly—not the contact surface.

2. Turn the engine until the rubbing block of the points is on one of the high points of the distributor cam. You can do this by either turning the ignition switch to the start position and releasing it quickly or by using a wrench on the bolt that holds the crankshaft pulley to the crankshaft.

3. Place the correct size feeler gauge between the contacts. Make sure it is parallel with the contact surfaces.

4. With your free hand, insert a screwdriver into the notch provided for adjustment or into the eccentric adjusting screw, and then twist the screwdriver to either increase or decrease the gap to the proper setting. V6 and V8 engines have to be adjusted at the adjusting screw with an allen wrench.

5. Tighten the adjustment lockscrew and

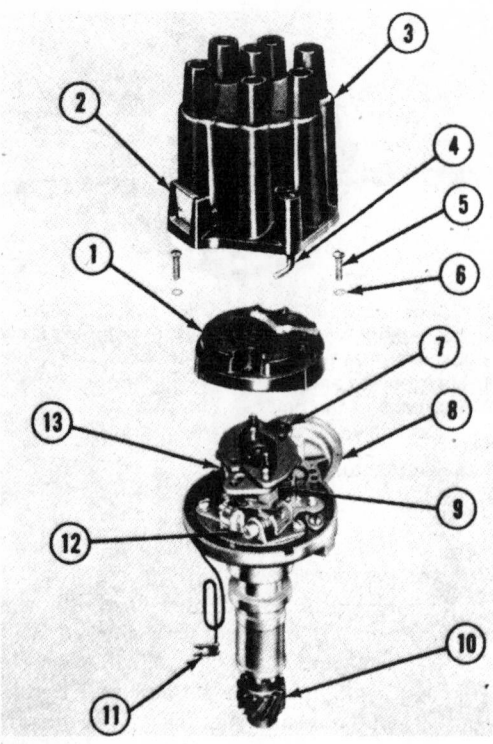

1. Rotor
2. Point dwell adjustment window
3. Distributor cap
4. Cap latch
5. Rotor mounting screw
6. Lockwasher
7. Advance mechanism
8. Vacuum advance unit
9. Distributor camshaft
10. Drive gear
11. Primary lead
12. Points assembly
13. Condenser

V6 distributor

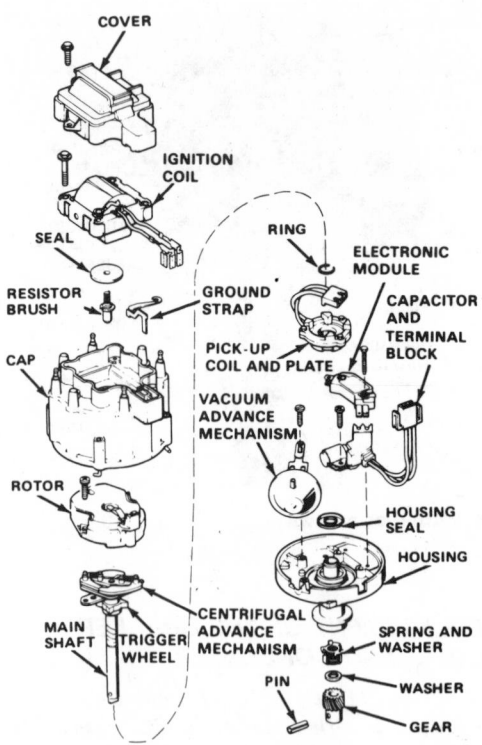

Exploded view of the HEI distributor

recheck the contact gap to make sure that it didn't change when the lockscrew was tightened.

6. Replace the rotor, distributor cap, and the high-tension wire that connects the top of the distributor and the coil. Make sure that the rotor is firmly seated all the way onto the distributor shaft and that the tab of the rotor is aligned with the notch in the shaft. Align the tab in the base of the distributor cap with the notch in the distributor body. Make sure that the cap is firmly seated on the distributor and that the retainers are in place. Make sure that the end of the high-tension wire is firmly placed in the top of the distributor and the coil.

ADJUSTMENT OF THE BREAKER POINTS WITH A DWELL METER

NOTE: *Some early models have 6v ignition systems. Make sure your dwell meter has a 6v capability.*

1. Adjust the points with a feeler gauge as described above.

2. Connect the dwell meter to the ignition circuit as according to the manufacturer's instructions. One lead of the meter is to be connected to a ground and the other lead is to be connected to the distributor post on the coil. An adapter is usually provided for this purpose.

3. If the dwell meter has a set line on it, adjust the meter to zero the indicator.

4. Start the engine.

NOTE: *Be careful when working on any vehicle while the engine is running. Make sure that the transmission is in neutral and that the parking brake is on. Keep hands, clothing, tools, and the wires of the test instruments clear of the rotating fan blades.*

5. Observe the reading on the dwell meter. If the meter does not have a scale for four-cylinder engines, multiply the eight-cylinder reading by two. If the reading is within the specified range, turn off the engine and remove the dwell meter.

6. If the reading is above the specified range, the breaker point gap is too small. If the reading is below the specified range, the gap is too large. In either case, the engine

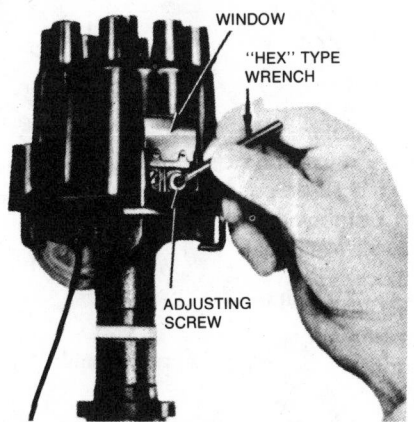

8-304 point gap and dwell adjustment

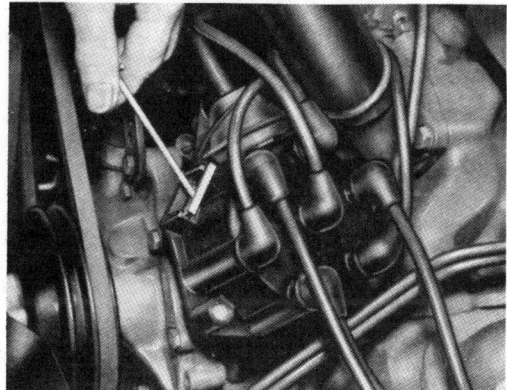

Point gap and dwell adjustment on V6

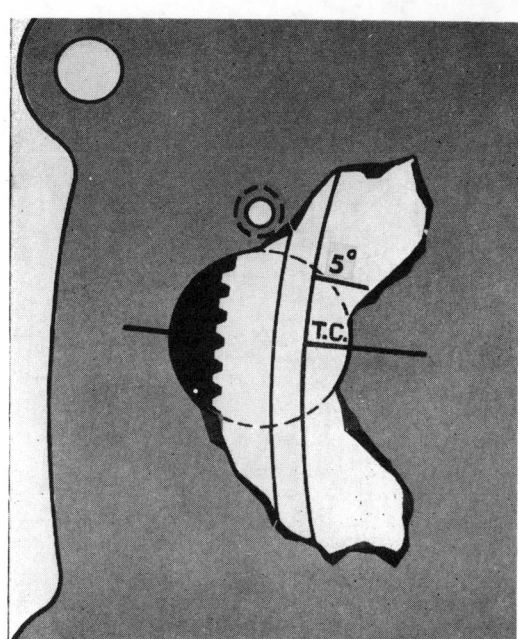

Timing marks on CJ-2A and early CJ-3A flywheel

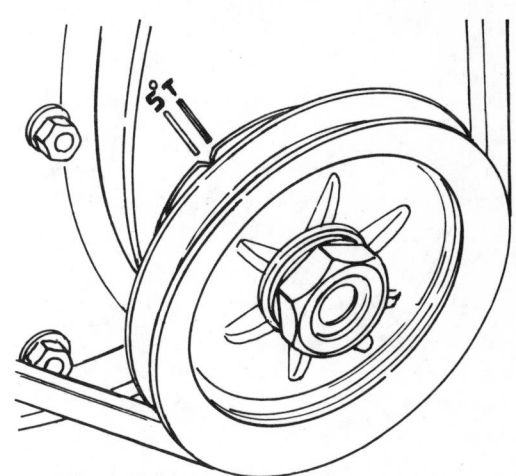

4-134 timing marks

must be stopped and the gap adjusted in the manner previously covered.

NOTE: *On the V6 engine and V8 engines, it is possible to adjust the dwell while the engine is running.*

Start the engine and check the reading on the dwell meter. When the correct reading is obtained, disconnect the dwell meter.

7. Check the adjustment of the ignition timing.

Ignition Timing

Ignition timing is the measurement, in degrees of crankshaft rotation, of the point at which the spark plugs fire in each of the cylinders. It is measured in degrees before or after Top Dead Center (TDC) of the compression stroke. Ignition timing is controlled by turning the distributor in the engine.

Ideally, the air-fuel mixture in the cylinder will be ignited by the spark plug just as the piston passes TDC of the compression stroke. If this happens, this piston will be beginning the power stroke just as the compressed and ignited air-fuel mixture starts to expand. The expansion of the air-fuel mixture then forces the piston down on the power stroke and turns the crankshaft.

Because it takes a fraction of a second for the spark plug to ignite the gases in the cylinder, the spark plug must fire a little before the piston reaches TDC. Otherwise, the mixture will not be completely ignited as the piston passes TDC and the full benefit of the explosion will not be used by the engine. The

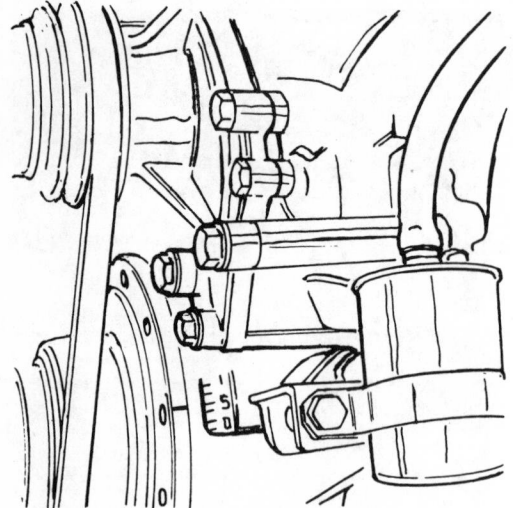

V6-225 timing marks

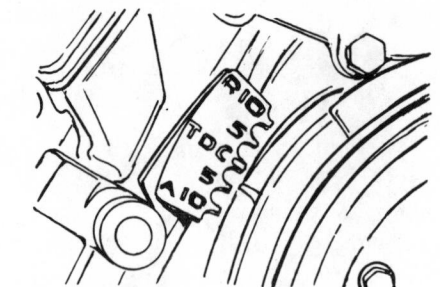

8-304 timing marks

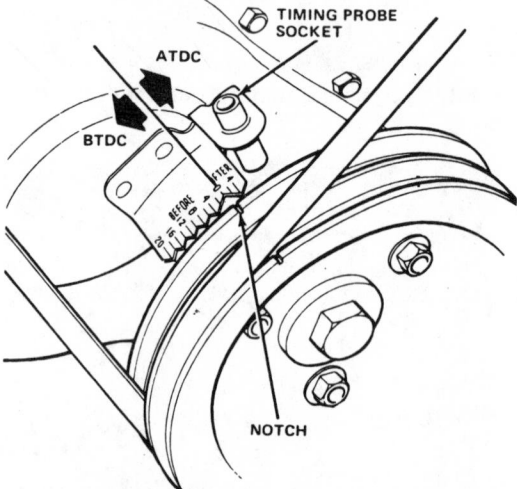

4-151 timing marks

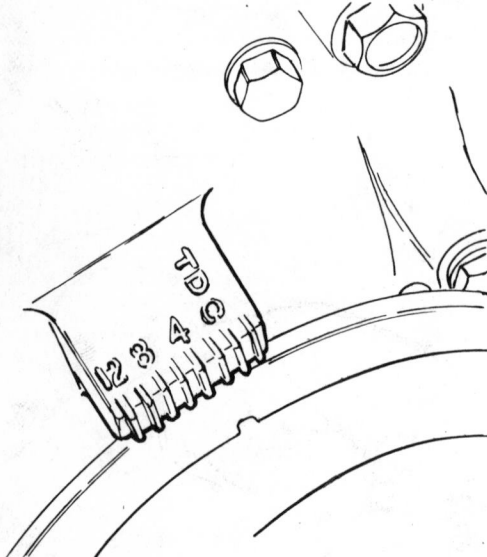

6-232, 258 timing marks with point type ignition

timing measurement is given in degrees of crankshaft rotation before the piston reaches TDC (BTDC). If the setting for the ignition timing is 5° BTDC, the spark plug must fire 5° before that piston reaches TDC. This only holds true, however, when the engine is at idle speed.

As the engine speed increases, the pistons go faster. The spark plugs have to ignite the fuel even sooner if it is to be completely ignited when the piston reaches TDC. To do this, the distributor has a means to advance the timing of the spark as the engine speed increases. In some Jeeps that were made before 1972, the advancing of the spark in the

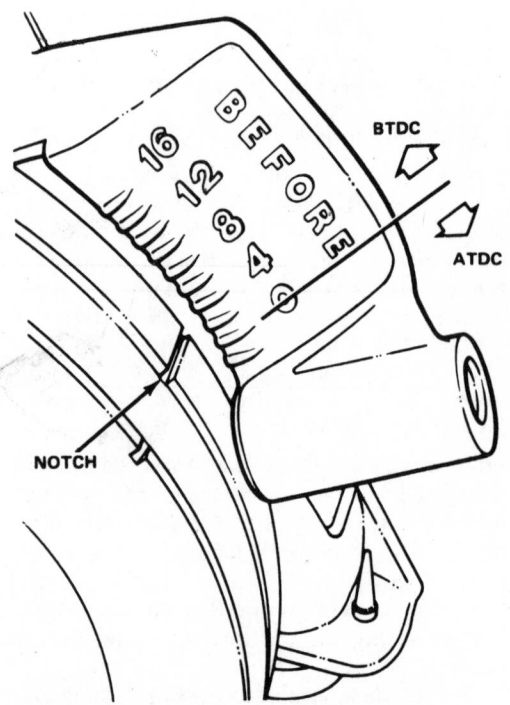

6-258 timing marks with electronic ignition

distributor was accomplished by weights alone. Others have a vacuum diaphragm to assist the weights. It is necessary to disconnect the vacuum line to the distributor when the engine is being timed.

If the ignition is set too far advanced (BTDC), the ignition and expansion of the fuel in the cylinder will occur too soon and tend to force the piston down while it is still traveling up. This causes engine ping. If the engine is too far retarded after TDC (ATDC), the piston will have already passed TDC and started on its way down when the fuel is ignited. This will cause the piston to be forced down for only a portion of its travel. This will result in poor engine performance and lack of power.

The timing is best checked with a timing light. This device is connected in series with the no. 1 spark plug. The current that fires the spark plug also causes the light to flash.

When the engine is running, the timing light is aimed at the crankshaft pulley, and the marks on the timing gear.

NOTE: *The following procedure applies to both point-type and breakerless electronic systems.*

IGNITION TIMING ADJUSTMENT

NOTE: *Some early engines have 6v ignition systems. Make sure your tach/dwell and timing light have 6v capability.*

1. Locate the timing marks on the pulley and on the front of the engine, or on the flywheel on CJ-2A and early CJ-3A engines.

2. Clean off the timing marks so you can see them.

3. Mark the timing marks with a piece of chalk or white paint. Mark the one on the engine that will indicate correct timing when it is aligned with the mark on the pulley or flywheel.

4. Attach a tachometer to the engine.

5. Attach a timing light according to the manufacturer's instructions. If the timing light has three wires, one is attached to the no. 1 spark plug lead with an adapter. The other two are connected to the battery. The red one goes to the positive side of the battery and the black one to the negative terminal.

6. Disconnect the vacuum line to the distributor at the distributor. Plug the end of the hose.

7. Check to make sure that all of the wires clear the fan and then start the engine.

8. If there is an idle speed solenoid, disconnect it.

9. Aim the timing light at the timing marks. If the marks that you put on the pulley and the engine are aligned, the timing is correct. Turn off the engine and remove the tachometer and the timing light. If the marks are not in alignment, proceed to the following steps.

10. Turn off the engine.

11. Loosen the distributor lockbolt just enough so that the distributor can be turned with a little effort.

12. Start the engine. Keep the cords of the timing light clear of the fan.

13. With the timing light aimed at the pulley and the marks on the engine, turn the distributor in the director of rotor rotation to retard the spark, and in the opposite direction of rotor rotation to advance the spark. Line up the marks on the pulley and the engine.

14. When the marks are aligned, tighten the distributor lockbolt and recheck the timing with the timing light to make sure that the distributor did not move when you tightened the distributor lockbolt.

15. Turn off the engine and remove the timing light.

NOTE: *On CJ-3A models beginning with engine #130859, a 4½ inch starter motor was used. To use the larger starter, it was necessary to increase the width of the cylinder block flange, partially covering the flywheel hole. This makes it impossible to use the hole for timing purposes. In this event, use the timing marks on the crank-*

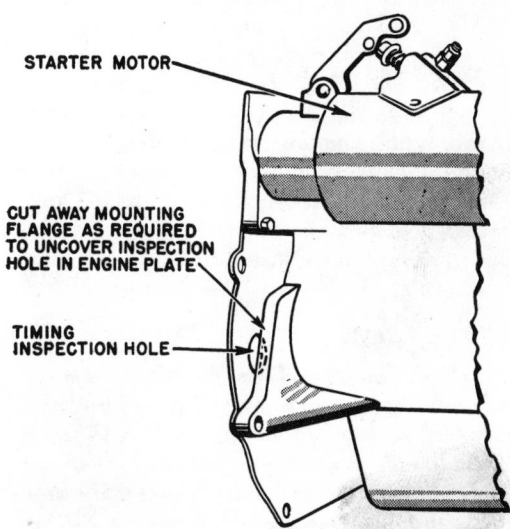

STARTER MOTOR

CUT AWAY MOUNTING FLANGE AS REQUIRED TO UNCOVER INSPECTION HOLE IN ENGINE PLATE

TIMING INSPECTION HOLE

Covered timing hole on CJ-3A engines

shaft pulley. If a replacement block is installed with the later design in a vehicle originally equipped with the earlier design timing marks, it will be necessary to cut away enough of the flange to allow a view of the timing marks, as no other timing marks exist on these early engines.

Valve Lash Adjustment

Valve lash determines how far the valves enter into the cylinder and how long they stay open and closed.

If the valve clearance is too large, part of the lift of the camshaft will be used in removing the excessive clearance. The valve will, consequently, not be opening as far as it should. This condition has two effects; the valve train components will emit a tapping sound as they take up the excessive clearance and the engine will perform poorly.

If the valve clearance is too small, the intake valves and the exhaust valves will open too far and they will not fully seat on the cylinder head when they close. When a valve seats itself on the cylinder head, it does two things; it seals the combustion chamber so that none of the gases in the cylinder escape and it cools itself by transferring some of the heat it absorbs from the combustion in the cylinder to the cylinder head and to the engine's cooling system. If the valve clearance is too small, the engine will run poorly because of the gases escaping from the combustion chamber. The valves will also become overheated and will warp, since they cannot transfer heat unless they are touching the valve seat in the cylinder head.

NOTE: *While all valve adjustments must be made as accurately as possible, it is better to have the valve adjustment slightly loose than slightly tight, as burned valves may result from overly tight adjustments.*

The only Jeep engine on which the valve lash can be adjusted is the 134 cu. in. four-cylinder. The rest all use hydraulic lifters which require no adjustment.

4-134 ENGINE

NOTE: *The L-head has all the valves in the block. Adjustment procedure is the same for all valves. Rotor-type exhaust valves were not original equipment, however some repair kits did supply these. In those cases, follow the specifications for F-head engines.*

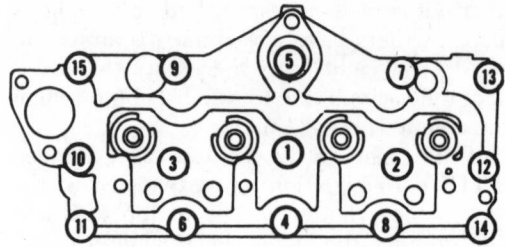

F-head cylinder head torque sequence; L-head is similar

NOTE: *The engine must be cold when the valves are adjusted.*

1. On the F-head, remove the valve cover. Check all the cylinder head bolts to make sure they are tightened to the correct torque specifications.

2. Remove the side valve spring cover.

3. Turn the engine until the lifter for the front intake valve is down as far as it will go. The lifter should be resting on the center of the heel (back) of the cam lobe for that valve. You can observe the position of the lifter by looking through the side valve spring cover opening. Put the correct size feeler gauge between the rocker arm and the valve stem. There should be a very slight drag on the feeler gauge when it is pulled through the gap. If there is a slight drag, the valve is at the correct setting. If the feeler gauge cannot pass between the rocker arm and the valve stem, the gap between them is too small and must be increased. If the gauge can be

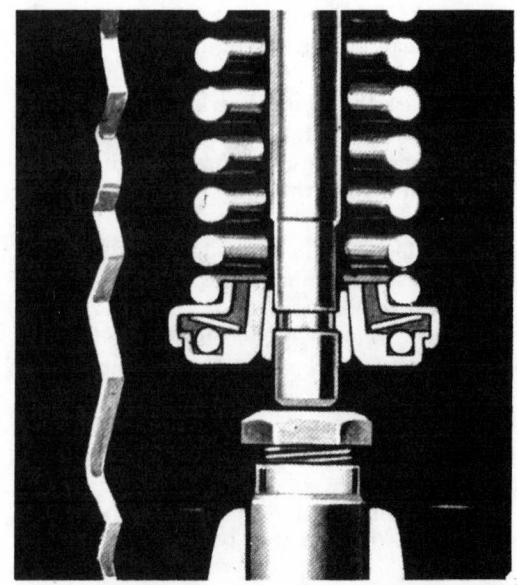

L-head intake and exhaust valve adjustment; F-head exhaust valve adjustment screw

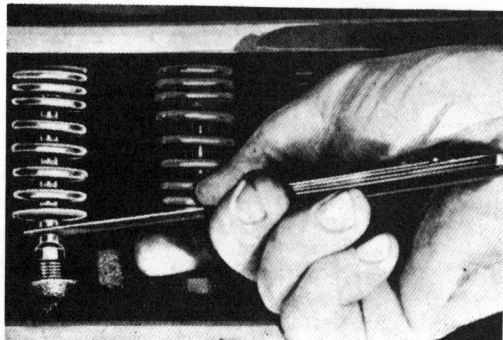

L- and F-head exhaust valve adjustment

passed through the gap without any drag, the gap is too large and must be decreased. Loosen the locknut on the top of the rocker arm (pushrod side) by turning it counterclockwise.

Turn the adjusting screw clockwise to lessen the gap and counterclockwise to increase the gap. When the gap is correct, turn the locknut clockwise to lock the adjusting screw. Follow this procedure for all of the intake valves, making sure that the lifter is all the way down for each adjustment.

4. Turn the engine so that the first exhaust valve is completely closed and the lifter that operates that particular valve is all of the way down and on the heel of the cam lobe that operates it.

5. Insert the correct size feeler gauge between the valve stem of the exhaust valve and the adjusting screw. This is done through the side of the engine in the space that is exposed when the side valve spring cover is removed. If there is a slight drag on the feeler gauge, you can assume that the gap is correct. If there is too much drag or not enough, turn the adjusting screw clockwise to increase the gap and counterclockwise to decrease the gap.

6. When all of the valves have been adjusted to the proper clearance, replace the covers with new gaskets.

Carburetor

This section contains only tune-up adjustment procedures for carburetors. Descriptions, adjustments, and overhaul procedures for carburetors can be found in the "Fuel System" section of this book.

When the engine in your Jeep is running, the air-fuel mixture from the carburetor is being drawn into the engine by a partial vacuum which is created by the movement of the pistons downward on the intake stroke. The amount of air-fuel mixture that enters into the engine is controlled by the throttle plate(s) in the bottom of the carburetor. When the engine is not running the throttle plate(s) is closed, completely blocking off the bottom of the carburetor from the inside of the engine. The throttle plates are connected by the throttle linkage to the accelerator pedal in the passenger compartment of the Jeep. When you depress the pedal, you open the throttle plates in the carburetor to admit more air-fuel mixture to the engine.

When the engine is not running, the throttle plates are closed. When the engine is idling, it is necessary to have the throttle plates open slightly. To prevent having to hold your foot on the pedal when the engine is idling, an idle speed adjusting screw was added to the carburetor linkage.

The idle adjusting screw contacts a lever (throttle lever) on the outside of the carburetor. When the screw is turned, it either opens or closes the throttle plates of the carburetor, raising or lowering the idle speed of the engine. This screw is called the curb idle adjusting screw.

1. Curb idle speed adjusting screw
2. Idle mixture adjusting screw

Carter YF938D carburetor used on CJ-3B models. The adjustment points on CJ-2A and CJ-3A models are similar

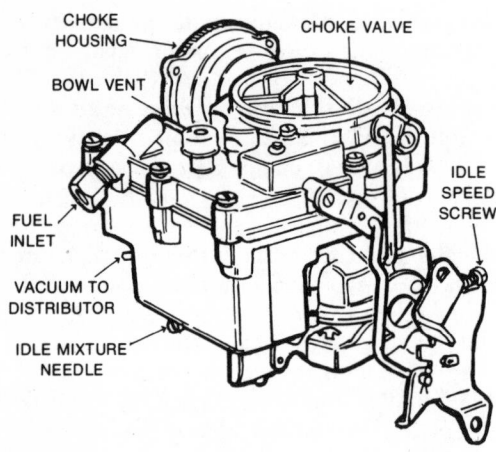

Rochester 2GC carburetor adjustment points

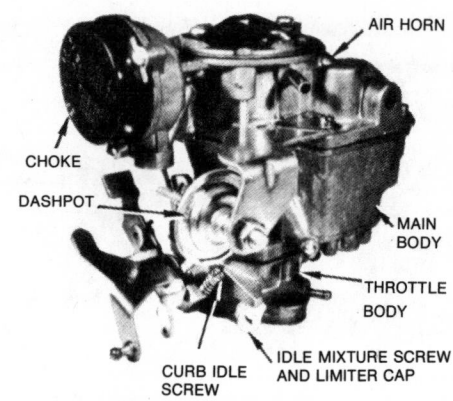

Carter YF on inline sixes

IDLE SPEED ADJUSTMENT—THROUGH 1971

1. Start the engine and run it until it reaches operating temperature.

2. If it hasn't already been done, check and adjust the ignition timing. After you have set the timing, turn off the engine.

3. Attach a tachometer to the engine.

4. Remove the air cleaner. Turn on the headlights to high beam.

5. Start the engine and check the idle speed on the tachometer. If the reading on the tachometer is correct, turn off the engine and remove the tachometer. If it is not correct, proceed to the following step.

6. Turn the idle speed adjusting screw at the bottom of the carburetor with a screwdriver—clockwise to increase the idle speed and counterclockwise to decrease it.

MIXTURE ADJUSTMENT—THROUGH 1971

The idle mixture screw is located at the very bottom of the carburetor.

1. Turn the screw until it is all the way in. Do not force the screw in any further because it is very easy to damage the needle valve and its seat by screwing the adjusting screw in too tightly.

2. Turn the screw out ¾–1¾ turns. This should be the normal adjustment setting. For a richer mixture, turn the screw in. The ideal setting for the mixture adjustment screw results in the maximum engine rpm.

IDLE SPEED AND MIXTURE ADJUSTMENT—1972

Use the "lean best idle" procedure to adjust the idle speed and mixture on 1972 engines.

1. Start engine and allow it to reach normal operating temperature. If engine is equipped with air pump, disconnect by-pass valve air inlet hose.

2. Adjust the idle speed to specified rpm by turning either the idle adjustment screw or throttle stop solenoid.

NOTE: *If idle adjustment procedure is not completed within 3 minutes, run engine at 2,000 rpm for 1 minute to stabilize engine temperature.*

3. Turn mixture screw(s) counterclockwise (richer) until loss of rpm is noticed, then turn mixture screw(s) clockwise (leaner), past original starting point, counting the number of turns of the screw(s).

4. Continue turning mixture screw(s) clockwise until engine loses rpm due to an overly lean mixture.

5. Return the screw(s) to the midpoint between the two extremes and the highest rpm reading.

6. Turn the mixture adjusting screw(s) clockwise (leaner) to the point where engine rpm just begins to drop, then counterclockwise the minimum amount to obtain the previously established highest rpm. This is the "lean best idle."

NOTE: *This procedure should first be attempted with limiter caps installed on the mixture adjustment screw(s). If a satisfactory idle cannot be obtained with the caps in place, then carefully remove them by threading a sheet metal screw into the center of the cap and make the adjustment as outlined above. Once the "lean best idle" has been established, install service limiter caps with the tabs positioned against the full rich stops.*

IDLE SPEED AND MIXTURE ADJUSTMENT—1973–80

The procedure for adjusting the idle speed and mixture is called the lean drop procedure and is made with the engine operating at normal operating temperature and the air cleaner in place as follows:

1. Turn the mixture screws to the full rich position with the tabs on limiters against stops. Note position of screw head slot inside limiter cap slots.

2. Remove idle limiter caps.

3. Remove limiter caps by threading a sheet metal screw in center of cap and turning clockwise. Discard limiter caps.

4. Reset adjustment screws to same position noted before limiter caps were removed.

5. Start engine and allow it to reach normal operating temperature.

6. Adjust idle speed to 30 rpm above the specified rpm. See "Tune-Up Specifications" chart.

    a. On 6 cylinder engines with throttle stop solenoid, turn solenoid in or out to obtain specified rpm;

    b. On V8 engines with throttle stop solenoid, turn hex screw on throttle stop solenoid carriage to obtain specified rpm. This is done with solenoid wire connected;

    c. Tighten solenoid locknut, if so equipped;

    d. Disconnect solenoid wire and adjust curb idle speed screw to obtain idle speed of 500 rpm;

    e. Reconnect solenoid wire.

7. Starting from full rich stop position, as was determined before limiter caps were removed, turn mixture adjusting screws clockwise (leaner) until a loss of engine speed is noticed.

8. Turn screws counterclockwise (richer) until the highest rpm reading is obtained at lean best idle setting. The lean best idle setting is on the lean side of the highest rpm setting without changing rpm.

9. If the idle speed changed more than 30 rpm during the mixture adjustment procedure, reset the idle speed to 30 rpm above the specified rpm with idle speed adjusting screw or the throttle stop solenoid and repeat the mixture adjustment.

10. Install new limiter caps over mixture adjusting screws with tabs positioned against full rich stops. Be careful not to disturb idle mixture setting while installing caps.

IDLE SPEED ADJUSTMENT—1981

Idle mixture screws on these carburetors are sealed with plugs or dowel pins. A mixture adjustment must be undertaken ONLY when the carburetor is overhauled, the throttle body replaced, or the engine does not meet required emission standards. Since expensive testing equipment is needed to properly

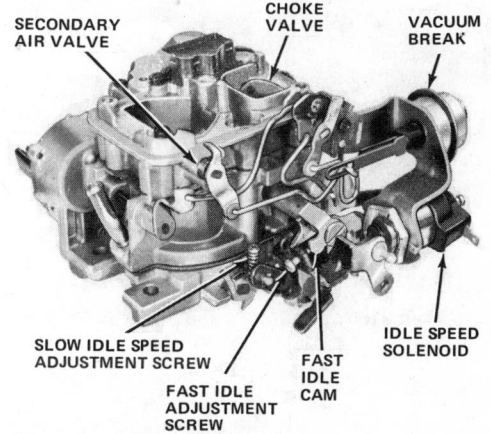

Rochester 2SE and E2SE carburetor adjustment points

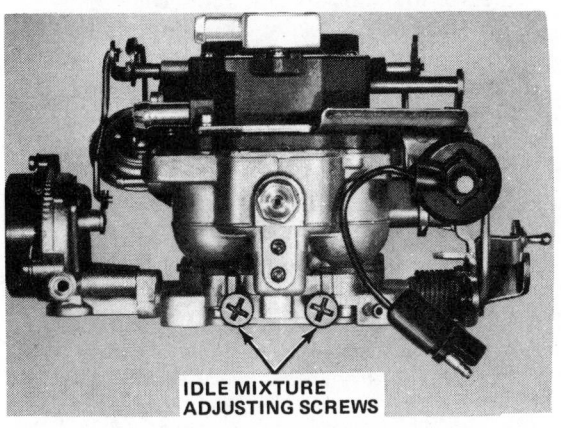

IDLE MIXTURE ADJUSTING SCREWS

Carter BBD carburetor used on 1980 6-258

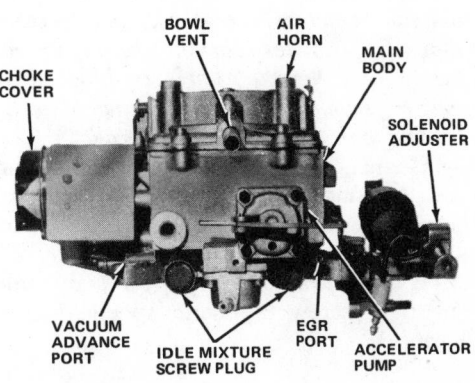

Motorcraft 2100 carburetor used on 1979 8-304

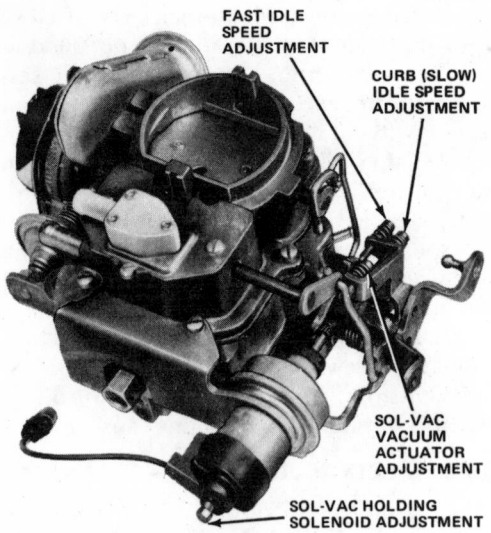

Carter BBD carburetor used on 1981 6-258

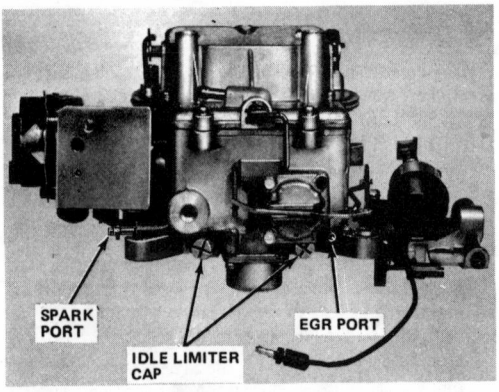

Motorcraft 2150 carburetor used on 1980–81 8-304

set the mixture, only the idle speed adjusting procedure is given below.

NOTE: *The adjustment is made with the manual transmission in neutral and the automatic in drive. Therefore, make certain that the vehicles parking brake is set firmly, and that the wheels are blocked. It may be a good idea to have someone in the vehicle with their foot on the brake.*

1. Connect tachometer, start engine and warm to normal operating temperature. Choke and intake manifold heater (six-cylinder engine only) must be off.

2. If not within OK range, turn curb idle adjustment screw to obtain specified curb idle rpm.

3. For six-cylinder engine (BBD carburetor):

a. Disconnect vacuum hose from vacuum actuator and holding solenoid wire connector. Adjust curb (slow) idle speed adjustment screw to obtain specified curb (slow) idle rpm if not within OK range. Refer to Emission Control Information label, and Tune-Up Specifications.

b. Apply direct source of vacuum to vacuum actuator.

c. Turn vacuum actuator adjustment screw on throttle lever until specified rpm is obtained (900 rpm for manual transmissions, and 800 rpm for automatic transmissions).

d. Disconnect manifold vacuum source from vacuum actuator.

e. With jumper wire apply battery voltage (12V) to energize holding solenoid. Turn A/C on, if equipped.

NOTE: *Throttle must be opened manually to allow Sol-Vac throttle positioner to be extended.*

f. With Sol-Vac throttle positioner extended, idle speed should be 650± 70 rpm for automatic transmission equipped vehicles and 750± 70 rpm for manual transmission equipped vehicles.

g. If idle speed is not within tolerance, adjust Sol-Vac (hex-head adjustment screw) to obtain specified rpm.

h. Remove jumper wire from Sol-Vac holding solenoid wire connector.

i. Connect Sol-Vac holding solenoid wire connector.

j. Connect original hose to vacuum actuator.

4. For four- and eight-cylinder engines (2SE, E2SE or 2150 carburetor, turn nut on solenoid plunger or hex screw on solenoid carriage to obtain specified idle rpm.

a. Tighten locknut, if equipped.

b. Disconnect solenoid wire connector and adjust curb idle screw to obtain 500 rpm idle speed.

c. Connect solenoid wire connector.

d. If model 2150 carburetor (eight-cylinder engine, is equipped with dashpot. With throttle at curb idle position, fully depress dashpot stem and measure clearance between stem and throttle lever. Clearance should be 0.032 inch (0.813 mm). Adjust by loosening locknut and turning dashpot.

Engine and Engine Rebuilding

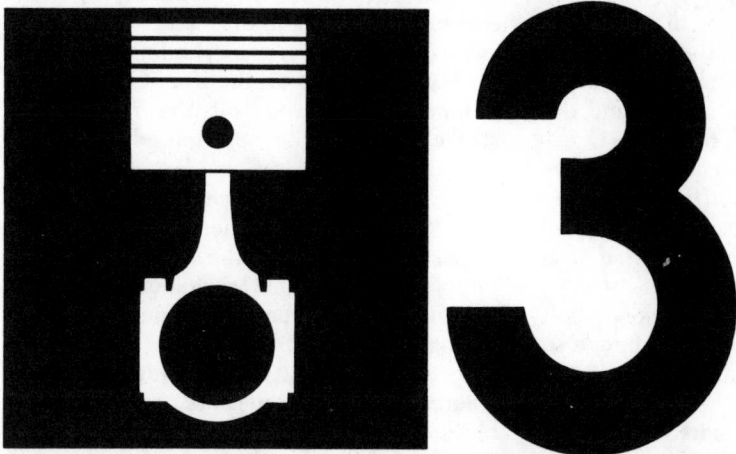

ENGINE ELECTRICAL

Distributor

REMOVAL

To remove the distributor assembly, follow the procedure below.

1. Disconnect the ignition switch battery wire and the tachometer connector, if equipped. Detach the distributor cap retainers and set the cap aside, leaving the high tension wires in place. You may have to detach the wires at the spark plugs. For diagrams of firing orders and distributor wiring, refer to the tune-up and troubleshooting chapter.

2. Remove the primary lead from the terminal post at the side of the distributor. Detach the wire connector with electronic ignition.

NOTE: *The wire connector for the 1978–81 electronic ignition distributor will contain special conductive grease. Do not remove it. The same grease will also be found on the metal parts of the rotor, for radio interference suppression. Do not remove it, even if it looks charred.*

3. Disconnect the vacuum tube if there is one.

4. Unlatch the two or four distributor cap retaining cap.

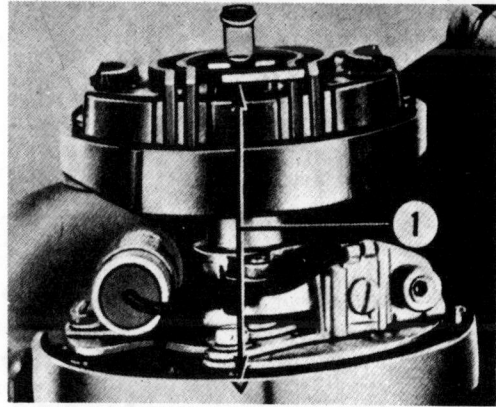

Scribe a mark on the distributor to show the rotor location before removing the distributor

5. Note the position of the rotor in relation to the base. Scribe a mark on the base of the distributor and on the engine block to facilitate reinstallation. Align the marks with the direction the metal tip of the rotor is pointing.

6. Remove the screw that holds the distributor to the engine.

7. Lift the distributor assembly from the engine.

INSTALLATION

1. Turn the distributor shaft until the rotor tip points in the direction of the No. 1

plug wire terminal in the distributor cap. Turn the rotor ⅛ turn counterclockwise. The rotor should turn back to the No. 1 position on installation. Insert the distributor shaft and assembly into the engine. Line up the mark on the distributor and the one on the engine with the metal tip of the rotor. Make sure that the vacuum advance diaphragm is pointed in the same direction as it was pointed originally. This will be done automatically if the marks on the engine and the distributor are lined up with the rotor.

NOTE: *On the V6 and F-Head, the distributor shaft fits into a slot in the end of the oil pump shaft. Therefore, the rotor won't turn when the distributor is pressed into place.*

2. Install the distributor hold-down bolt and clamp. Leave the screw loose enough so that you can move the distributor with heavy hand pressure.

3. Connect the primary wire to the distributor side of the coil. Install the distributor cap on the distributor housing. Secure the distributor cap with the spring clips or the screw type retainers, whichever is used.

4. Install the spark plug wires. Make sure that the wires are pressed all of the way into the top of the distributor cap and firmly onto the spark plugs.

NOTE: *Design of the V6 engine requires a special form of distributor cam. The distributor may be serviced in the regular way and should cause no more problems than any other distributor, if the firing plan is thoroughly understood. The distributor cam is not ground to standard six cylinder indexing intervals. This particular form requires that the original pattern of spark plug wiring be used. The engine will not run in balance if number one spark plug wire is inserted into number six distributor cap tower, even though each wire in the firing sequence is advanced to the next distributor tower. There is a difference between the firing intervals of each succeeding cylinder through the 720° engine cycle.*

5. Adjust the point dwell and set the ignition timing. Refer to the tune-up section.

If the engine has been turned while the distributor was removed, or if the marks were not drawn, it will be necessary to initially time the engine. Follow the procedure below.

INSTALLATION, ENGINE DISTURBED

1. It is necessary to place the no. 1 cylinder in the firing position to correctly install the distributor. To locate this position, some engines have marks placed on the flywheel while other engines have marks placed on the timing gear covers and crankshaft pulleys. The flywheel marks may be viewed through a covered opening directly in back of the starting motor by loosening the hole cover and sliding it to one side.

2. Remove the no. 1 cylinder spark plug. Turn the engine until the piston in no. 1 cylinder is moving up on the compression stroke. This can be determined by placing your thumb over the spark plug hole and feeling the air being forced out of the cylinder. Stop turning F-head engines when either the 5° mark on the flywheel is in the middle of the flywheel inspection opening, or the marks on the crankshaft pulley and the timing gear cover are in alignment.

3. Oil the distributor housing lightly where the distributor bears on the cylinder block.

4. Install the distributor so that the rotor, which is mounted on the shaft, points toward the no. 1 spark plug terminal tower position when the cap is installed. Of course you won't be able to see the direction in which the rotor is pointing if the cap is on the distributor. Lay the cap on the top of the distributor and make a mark on the side of the distributor housing just below the no. 1 spark plug terminal. Make sure the rotor points toward that mark when you install the distributor.

5. When the distributor shaft has reached the bottom of the hole, move the rotor back and forth slightly until the driving lug on the end of the shaft enters the slot, which is cut in the end of the oil pump gear on the F-Head, or when the drive gears of the distributor and cam mesh on the other engines, and until the distributor assembly slides down into place.

On models that have a gear on the end of the distributor shaft and a gear on the end of the oil pump drive, these gears have to mesh with the same teeth as originally installed when the distributor is inserted into the engine. Once again, the marks that were placed on the engine and the base of the distributor housing come into play. If the distributor shaft gear and the oil pump drive gear are but one tooth off from what they are supposed to be, the engine will not run correctly.

6. When the distributor is correctly installed, the breaker points should be in such a position that they are just ready to break contact with each other. This is accomplished

by rotating the distributor body after it has been installed in the engine. Once again, line up the marks that you made before the distributor was removed from the engine.

7. Install the distributor hold-down screw and the hold-down bracket. Be sure that the models that have vacuum advance units are free to turn in the mounting socket. Note that the vacuum advance control of some distributors is connected directly to the place on which the points are mounted. When this is the case, the plate must be free to turn rather than the distributor body.

8. Install the spark plug into the no. 1 spark plug hole and continue from step 3 of the distributor installation procedure.

NOTE: *A CJ-5 and CJ-6 F-head distributor (IAD 4041) is identical to the distributor of the CJ-3B (IAD 4008A) except for the hold-down arm. The CJ-5 and CJ-6 distributor was issued to replace the distributor originally installed in the CJ-3B. It is necessary to remove the oil pump in order to install the newer distributor in the CJ-3B. Place the distributor in the correct timing position and install the hold-down screw. Engage the distributor drive and carefully mesh the gears without disturbing the correct timing position of the distributor, and then replace the oil pump.*

Alternator and Generator

All Jeeps through 1964 had DC generators. In 1965, alternators were installed on the Tuxedo Park versions of the CJ-5 and CJ-6. These models were known respectively as

1. Auxiliary terminal
2. Output terminal
3. Auxiliary terminal
4. Field terminal
5. Ground terminal
6. Ground terminal

Motorola alternator used through 1971

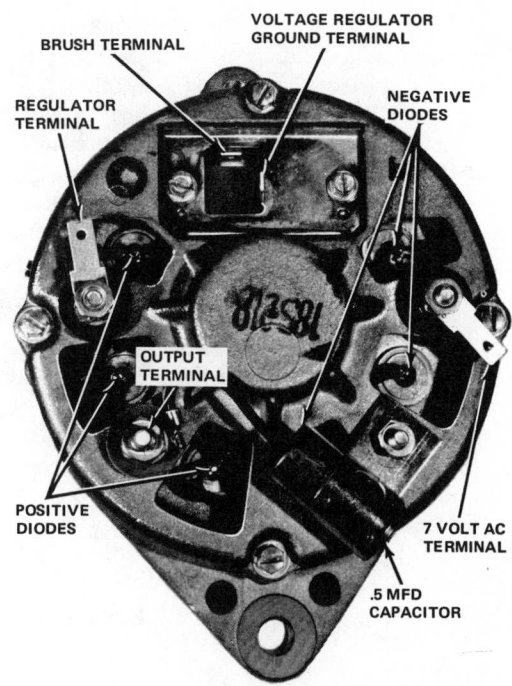

1972-75 Prestolite alternator

the CJ-5A and CJ-6A. Starting 1966, all Jeeps came with alternators.

An alternator differs from a conventional DC shunt generator in that the armature is stationary, and is called the stator, while the field rotates and is called the rotor. The higher current values in the alternator's stator are conducted to the external circuit through fixed leads and connections, rather than through a rotating commutator and brushes as in a DC generator. This eliminates a major point of maintenance.

The alternator employs a three-phase stator winding. The rotor consists of a field coil encased between six-poled, interleaved sections, producing a twelve-pole magnetic field with alternating north and south poles. By rotating the rotor inside the stator, an alternating current is induced in the stator windings. This alternating current is changed to direct current by diodes and is routed out of the alternator through the output terminal. Diode rectifiers act as one-way electrical valves. Half of the diodes have a negative polarity and are grounded. The other half of the diodes have a positive polarity and are connected to the output terminal.

Since the diodes have a high resistance to the flow of current in one direction, and a low resistance in the opposite direction, they are connected in a manner which allows current to flow from the alternator to the battery in the low-resistance direction.

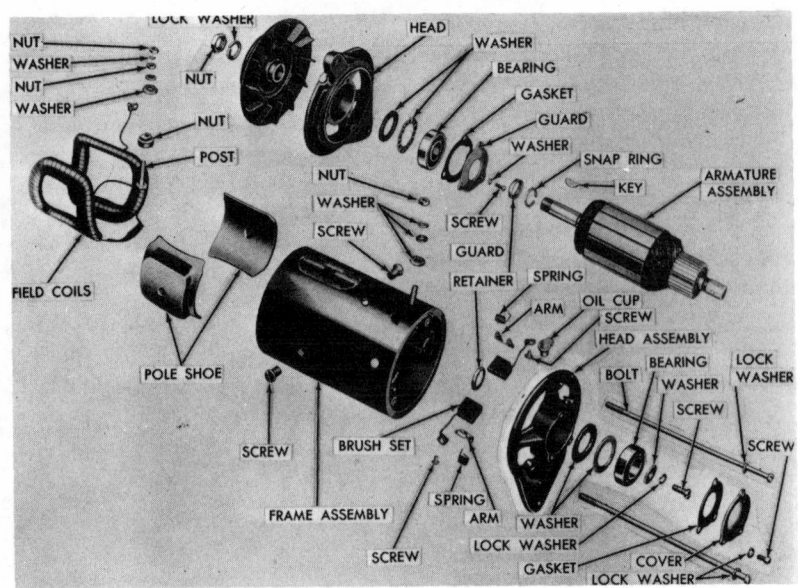

Exploded view of the generator

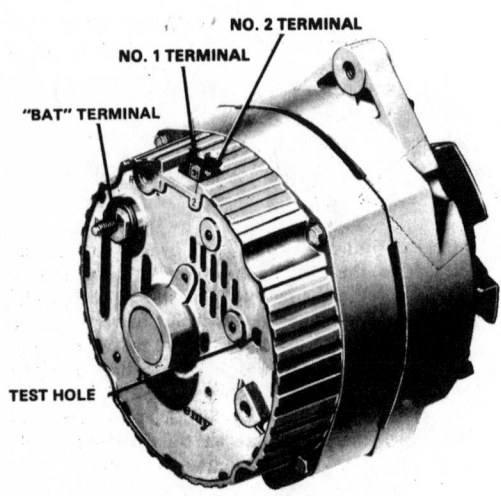

1976–81 Delcotron alternator

The high resistance in the other direction prevents the flow of current from the battery to the alternator. Because of this feature, there is no need for a circuit breaker between the alternator and the battery.

Residual magnetism in the rotor field poles is minimal. The starting field current must, therefore, be supplied by the battery. It is connected to the field winding through the ignition switch and the charge indicator lamp or ammeter.

As in the DC shunt generator, the alternator voltage is regulated by varying the field current. This is accomplished electronically in the transistorized voltage regulator. No current regulator is required because all alternators have self-limiting current characteristics.

An alternator is better than a conventional, DC shunt generator because it is lighter and more compact, because it is designed to supply the battery and accessory circuits through a wide range of engine speeds, and because it eliminates the necessary maintenance of replacing brushes and servicing commutators.

The transistorized voltage regulator is an electronic switching device. It senses the voltage at the auxiliary terminal of the alternator and supplies the necessary field current for maintaining the system voltage at the output terminal. The output current is determined by the battery electrical load—such as operating the headlights or heater blower.

The transistorized voltage regulator is a sealed unit that has no adjustments and must be replaced as a complete unit when it ceases to operate.

ALTERNATOR PRECAUTIONS

To prevent damage to the alternator and regulator, the following precautionary measures must be taken when working with the electrical system.

1. Never reverse battery connections. Always check the battery polarity visually. This is to be done before any connections are made to be sure that all of the connections

correspond to the battery ground polarity of the Jeep.

2. Booster batteries for starting must be connected properly. Make sure that the positive cable of the booster battery is connected to the positive terminal of the battery that is getting the boost. This applies to both negative and ground cables.

3. Disconnect the battery cables before using a fast charger; the charger has a tendency to force current through the diodes in the opposite direction for which they were designed. This burns out the diodes.

4. Never use a fast charger as a booster for starting the vehicle.

5. Never disconnect the voltage regulator while the engine is running.

6. Do not ground the alternator output terminal.

7. Do not operate the alternator on an open circuit with the field energized.

8. Do not attempt to polarize an alternator.

REMOVAL AND INSTALLATION

1. Remove all of the electrical connections from the alternator or generator. Label all of the wires so that you can install them correctly.

2. Remove all of the attaching nuts, bolts and washers noting different sized threads or nuts and bolts that go in certain holes.

3. Remove the alternator carefully.

4. To install, reverse the above procedure.

BELT TENSION ADJUSTMENT

The fan belt drives the generator/alternator and the water pump. If it is too loose, it will slip and the generator/alternator will not be able to produce the rated current. If the belt is too loose, the water pump would not be driven and the engine could overheat. Check the tension of the fan belt by pushing your thumb down on the longest span of belt midway between the pulleys. If the belt flexes more than ½ in., it should be tightened. Loosen the bolt on the adjusting bracket and pivot bolt and move the alternator or generator away from the engine to tighten the belt. Do not apply pressure to the rear of the cast aluminum housing of an alternator; it might break. Tighten the adjusting bolts when the proper tension is reached.

Regulator

The voltage regulators that are used with alternators are transistorized and cannot be serviced. If the voltage regulator is not operating properly, it must be replaced.

The voltage regulators that are used with shunt type generators are serviceable and can be adjusted. These regulators have three units: the circuit breaker, the voltage regulator and the current-limiting regulator. Each has a separate function.

VOLTAGE REGULATOR

The function of the voltage regulator unit is to hold the generated voltage at a predetermined value as long as the circuit values allow the voltage to build to the operating load.

The electromagnet of the voltage regulator unit has a winding of many turns of fine wire and is connected across the charging circuit so that the system voltage controls the amount of magnetism.

The contacts of the voltage regulator unit are connected in the generator field circuit so that the field circuit is completed through the contacts when they are closed and through a resistor when the contacts are opened.

When the voltage rises to a predetermined amount, there is sufficient magnetism created by the regulator winding to pull the armature down. This opens the contacts and inserts resistance in the field circuit of the generator, thus reducing the field current. The generated voltage immediately drops, reducing the pull on the armature to the point where the spring closes the contacts. The output again rises and the cycle is repeated.

These cycles occur at sufficiently high frequencies to hold the generated voltage at a constant level and they will continue as long as the voltage of the circuit is high enough to keep the voltage regulator unit in operation. When there is a current load that is great enough to lower the battery voltage below the operating voltage of the voltage regulating unit, the contacts will remain closed and the generator will maintain a charging rate that is limited by its speed and capacity output.

CURRENT-LIMITING REGULATOR

The function of the current-limiting regulator is to limit the output of the generator to its maximum safe output.

The electromagnet of the current regulator

unit consists of a winding of heavy wire connected in a series with the generator output. When the generator output reaches a predetermined level, the current in the winding produces enough magnetism to overcome spring tension and pull the armature down. This opens the contacts and inserts resistance in the field circuit of the generator. With the field current reduced by the resistance, the generator output falls and there is no longer sufficient magnetism to hold the contacts open. As soon as the spring closes the contacts, the output rises and the cyle is repeated. These cycles occur at a high enough frequency to limit the output to a minimum fluctuation.

VOLTAGE TESTS AND ADJUSTMENTS

Circuit Breaker

The circuit breaker is the unit with the heavy wire windings and is located on the end of the unit.

Connect an ammeter in series with the regulator B (battery) terminal and the lead that is removed from that terminal. Connect a voltmeter from the regulator A (armature) terminal to the regulator base.

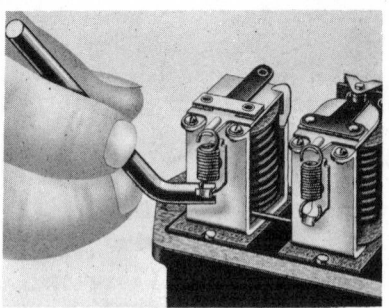

Bending the spring hanger to adjust the voltage on an Autolite regulator

Adjusting the air gap on the voltage unit in the Autolite regulator

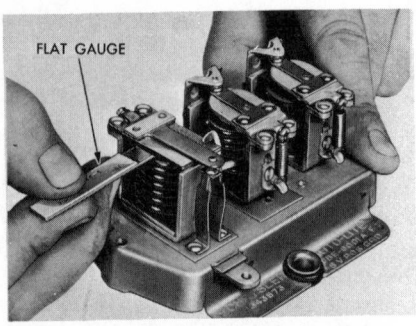

Adjusting the air gap on an Autolite regulator

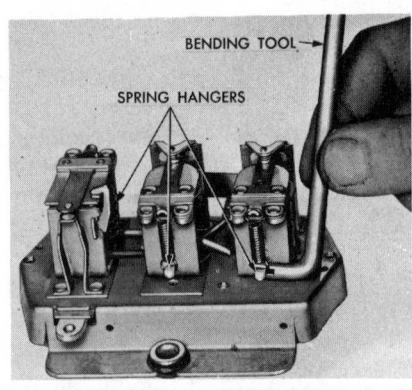

Adjusting the voltage unit setting in the Autolite regulator

Adjusting the point gap on an Autolite regulator

Disconnect the field lead from the regulator F terminal and insert a variable resistance between the lead and the regulator terminal.

Run the generator at about 1,000 generator rpm. Insert all of the resistance in the field circuit. Slowly reduce the resistance, noting the voltage reading just before the change caused by the closing of the circuit breaker. Increase the charging rate to the figure specified for the regulator being tested, then reduce the charging rate by inserting resistance into the field circuit. Note the

Cleaning the Autolite regulator current regulator points

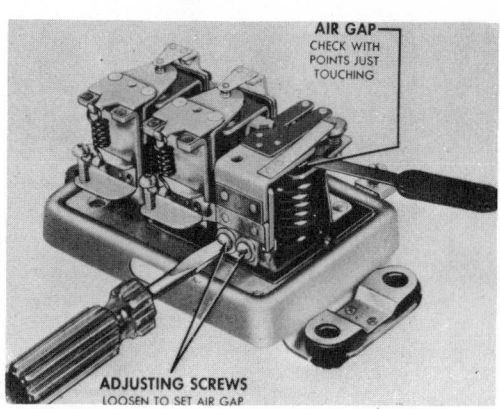

Measuring the cutout air gap on the Delco regulator

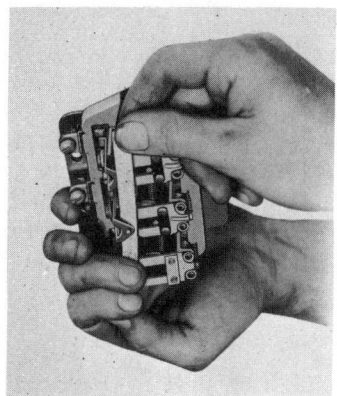

Using tape to clean the current regulator points on an Autolite regulator

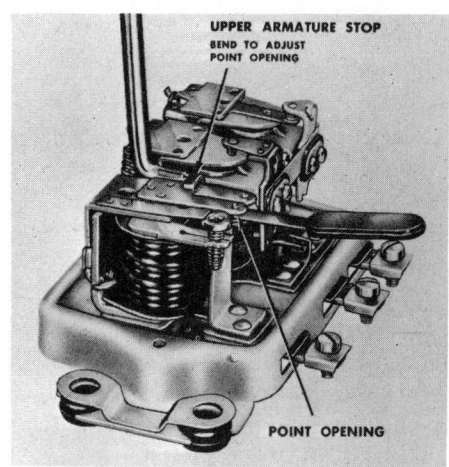

Adjusting the cutout point opening on the Delco regulator

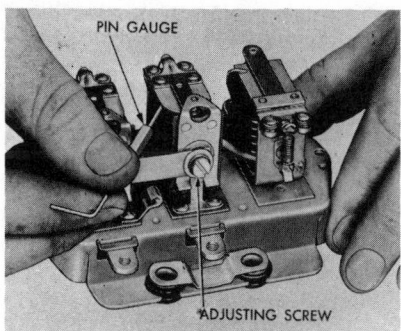

Adjusting the current regulator air gap on the Autolite regulator

charging rate just before the circuit breaker opens and the ammeter reading drops to zero. The closing voltage and the opening voltage or current should be within the limits specified.

To adjust the closing voltage, change the armature spring tension by bending the hanger at the lower end of the spring. Increase the spring tension to raise the closing voltage or decrease the tension to lower the voltage.

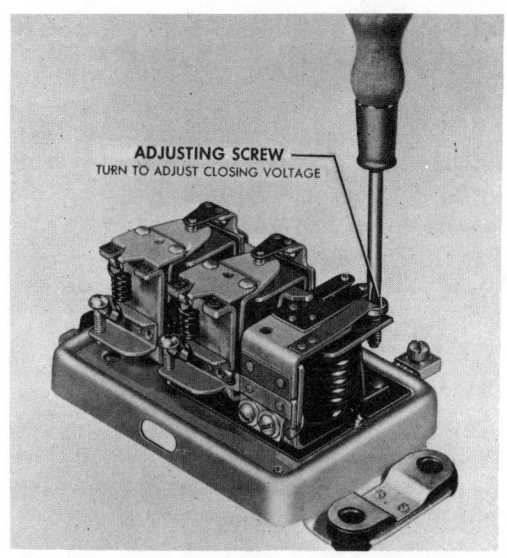

Adjusting the cutout closing voltage on the Delco regulator

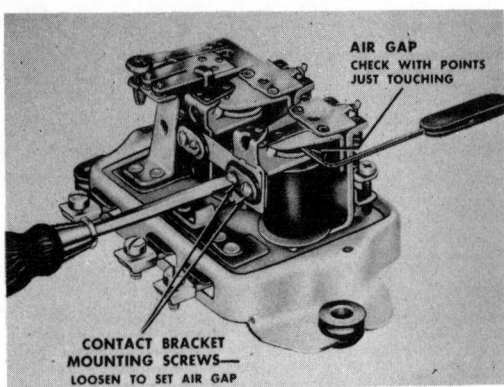

Adjusting the voltage unit air gap on Delco regulators

Adjusting the voltage unit setting on Delco regulators

To adjust the opening voltage, raise or lower the stationary contact, keeping the contacts perfectly aligned. Increasing the contact gap lowers the opening voltage. Change the contact gap by expanding or contracting the stationary contact bracket, keeping the contacts aligned. Do not adjust the gap between the contacts to less than the specified minimum.

Voltage Regulator

The voltage regulator unit is the one with the fine wire winding. Connect the ammeter as noted above and connect the voltmeter from the regulator B terminal to the regulator base. Remove the variable resistance from the field circuit.

Run the generator at one-half maximum

output for 15 minutes to make sure the regulator is at normal temperature. Have the cover on the unit during this warm-up period and also when taking the readings.

Stop the engine, then bring it to approximately 2,500 generator rpm. Adjust the amperage to one-half of the maximum output by turning on lights or accessories and then note the voltmeter reading. This reading should be within the limits specified for the voltage regulator. To adjust the operating voltage, change the armature spring tension by bending the hanger at the lower end of the armature spring. After each adjustment, stop the engine and then restart it. Bring it up to speed and adjust the current before taking a reading. The clicks of the opening and closing of the contacts should be regular and clear without irregularities. If the tone is not clear and regular, remove the regulator cover and inspect the contacts. The contacts should be flat and not burned excessively, and should be aligned to make full face contact. Refer to the section on cleaning the contacts if necessary.

Current Regulator

The current regulator is the unit in the middle of the unit with the heavy wire winding.

Connect the regulator and instruments as described above for the voltage regulator and run the generator at approximately 3,000 generator rpm. Turn on lights and accessories so the generator must charge at its maximum rate. The ammeter should show a reading within the specified limits. To adjust the opening amperage, change the armature spring tension by bending the hanger at the lower end of the armature spring. Stop the engine after each adjustment and then restart it. Bring the engine to speed and take an ammeter reading. Keep the cover on the unit when taking the readings.

The clicks of the points closing and opening should be clear in tone and regular in frequency without irregularities or misses. If this is not the case, the contacts will have to be serviced.

Contacts

The contacts should be inspected on all three of the units inside the cover of the voltage regulator. The contacts will become grayed and slightly worn during normal use. If the contacts are burned or dirty, or if they are not smooth or aligned properly, they should be adjusted and cleaned. File the contacts smooth. Just file enough so that there is a smooth surface presented to each contact. It is not necessary to file out every trace of pitting. After filing, dampen a clean cloth with carbon tetrachloride and pull the cloth between the contacts of each of the three units. Repeat with a clean dry cloth.

NOTE: *Keep in mind that after filing the points, the gap might have been changed enough to affect the performance of the three units. Check the three units and perform the adjustments. It might be a good idea to examine the contacts before making any adjustments. If the contacts need to be serviced, do it before adjusting spring tensions, etc.*

REMOVAL AND INSTALLATION

If the voltage regulator still does not function properly, after all of the checks and adjustments, replace the entire unit. Follow the procedure below.

1. Remove all of the electrical connections. Label them as you remove them so you can replace them in the correct order on the replacement unit.

2. Remove all of the hold-down screws and then remove the unit from the vehicle.

3. Install the new voltage regulator using the hold-down screws from the old one, or new ones if they are provided with the replacement regulator. Tighten down the hold-down screws.

4. Connect the armature lead to the armature terminal of the voltage regulator.

5. Connect the battery lead to the battery terminal of the voltage regulator.

6. Momentarily touch the field lead to the battery terminal of the voltage regulator. This polarizes the generator and voltage regulator so they have the same polarization as the rest of the electrical system. This has to be done every time all of the leads are disconnected from the generator voltage regulator.

7. Connect the field lead to the field terminal of the voltage regulator.

Starter Motor

The starter on the L and F-head four-cylinder engines can be removed from the top of the engine. The starter motor on all other engines must be removed from beneath the vehicle.

REMOVAL AND INSTALLATION

1. Disconnect the battery and solenoid leads from the starter. Mark them so you can replace them in the correct position when the starter is to be installed.

2. Remove all of the attachment bolts that attach the starter to the bellhousing.

3. Lift the starter from the engine.

4. Install the starter in the reverse order of the above.

STARTER DRIVE REPLACEMENT
Autolite

1. Remove the cover of the starter drive's actuating lever arm. Remove the thru-bolts, starter drive gear housing, and the return spring of the drive gear's actuating lever.

2. Remove the pivot pin which retains the starter gear actuating lever and remove the lever and armature.

3. Remove the stop-ring retainer. Remove and discard the stop-ring which holds the drive gear to the armature shaft and then remove the drive gear assembly.

To install the unit:

1. Lightly Lubriplate® the armature shaft splines and install the starter drive gear assembly on the shaft. Install a new stop-ring and stop-ring retainer.

2. Position the starter drive gear actuating lever to the frame and starter drive assembly. Install the pivot pin.

3. Fill the starter drive gear housing one-quarter full of grease.

4. Position the drive actuating lever return spring and the drive gear housing to the frame, then install and tighten the thru-bolts. Be sure that the stop-ring retainer is properly seated in the drive housing.

Delco-Remy

1. Remove the thru-bolts.

2. Remove the starter drive housing.

3. Slide the two-piece thrust collar off the end of the armature shaft.

4. Slide a standard ½ in. pipe coupling, or other spacer, onto the shaft so the end of the coupling butts against the edge of the retainer.

5. Tap the end of the coupling with a hammer, driving the retainer toward the armature end of the snap-ring.

6. Remove the snap-ring from its groove in the shaft with pliers. Slide the retainer and the starter drive from the armature.

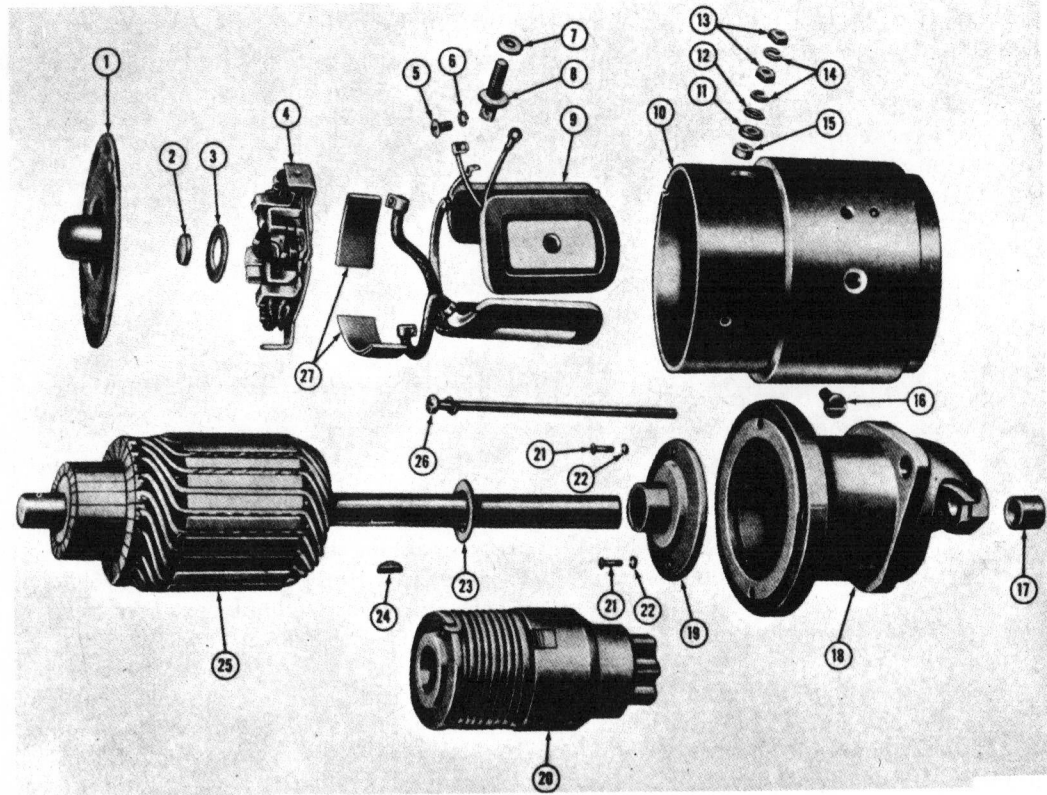

1. End Plate
2. Plug
3. Thrust washer
4. Brush plate assembly
5. Screw
6. Lockwasher
7. Insulating washer
8. Terminal
9. Field coil and pole shoe set
10. Frame
11. Insulating washer
12. Washer
13. Nut
14. Lockwasher
15. Insulating bushing
16. Pole shoe screw
17. Sleeve bearing
18. Drive end frame
19. Intermediate bearing
20. Bendix drive
21. Screw
22. Lockwasher
23. Thrust washer
24. Key
25. Armature
26. Thru-bolt
27. Insulator

4-134 starter

To install the unit:

1. Lubricate the drive end of the shaft with silicone lubricant.

2. Slide the drive gear assembly onto the shaft, with the gear facing outward.

3. Slide the retainer onto the shaft with the cupped surface facing away from the gear.

4. Stand the whole starter assembly on a block of wood with the snap-ring positioned on the upper end of the shaft. Drive the snap-ring down with a small block of wood and a hammer. Slide the snap-ring into its groove.

5. Install the thrust collar onto the shaft with the shoulder next to the snap-ring.

6. With the retainer on one side of the snap-ring and the thrust collar on the other side, squeeze them together with a pair of pliers until the ring seats in the retainer. On models without a thrust collar, use a washer. Remember to remove the washer before installing the starter in the engine.

Prestolite

1. Slide the thrust collar off the armature shaft.

2. Using a standard ½ in. pipe connector, drive the snap-ring retainer off the shaft.

3. Remove the snap-ring from the groove, and then remove the drive assembly.

To install the unit:

1. Lubricate the drive end and splines with Lubriplate®.

2. Install the clutch assembly onto the shaft.

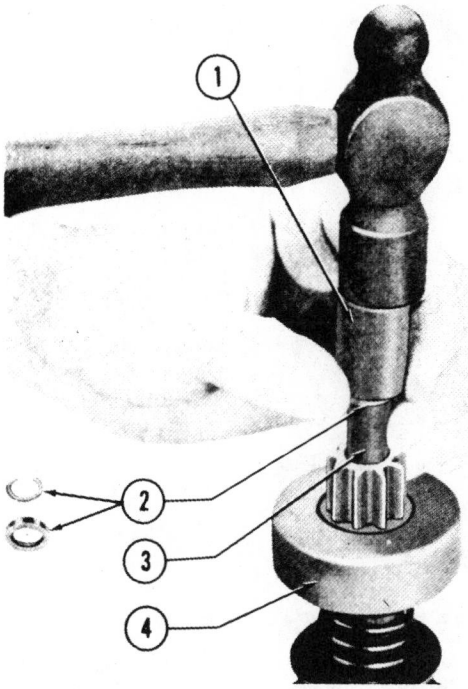

1. ½ in. pipe coupling
2. Snap ring and retainer
3. Armature shaft
4. Drive assembly

Removing the starter drive assembly from the armature shaft

3. Install the snap-ring retainer with the cupped surface facing toward the end of the shaft.

4. Install the snap-ring into the groove. Use a new snap-ring if necessary.

5. Install the thrust collar onto the shaft with the shoulder against the snap-ring.

6. Force the retainer over the snap-ring in the same manner as was used for the Delco-Remy starters.

SOLENOID OR RELAY REPLACEMENT
Autolite

On the early CJ-2A, CJ-3A, CJ-3B, CJ-5, and CJ-6 with Autolite starters, there were no solenoids or relays to activate the starter drive. The starter drive activated itself by the centrifugal force of the starter motor and deactivated itself in the normal way (by the centrifugal force of the engine's flywheel).

Autolite starters were installed with solenoids mounted on the starter housing beginning in 1960.

To remove the solenoid from the starter, remove all of the leads to the solenoid, remove the connecting lever, and remove the attaching bolts that hold the solenoid assem-

1. 'R' terminal contact
2. Switch terminal
3. Grommet
4. Plunger
5. Solenoid
6. Return spring
7. Shift lever
8. Bushing
9. Pinion stop
10. Overrunning clutch
11. Field coil
12. Armature
13. Bushing
14. Insulated brush holders
15. Brush spring
16. Grounded brush holder
17. Brush

V6 starter

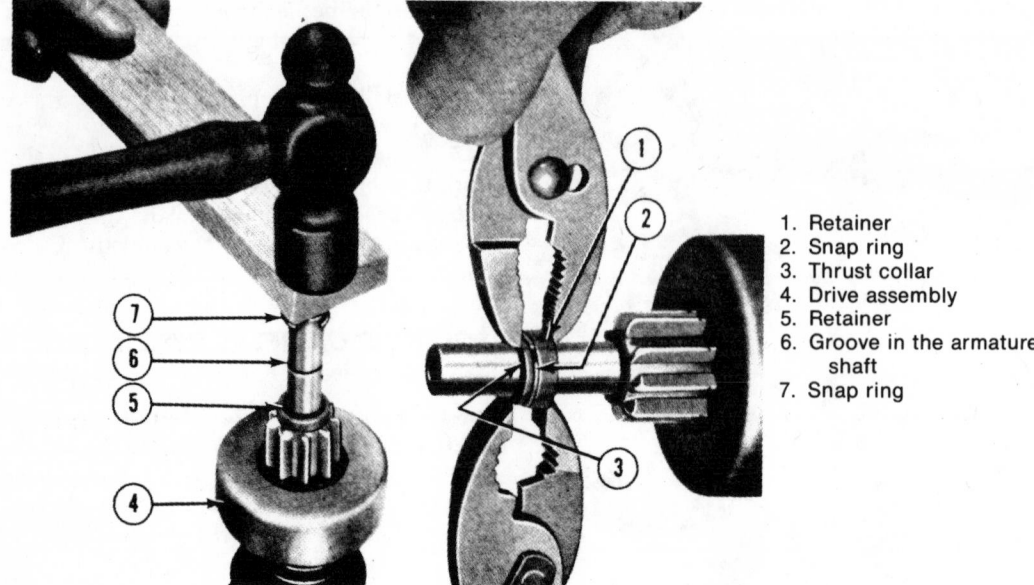

1. Retainer
2. Snap ring
3. Thrust collar
4. Drive assembly
5. Retainer
6. Groove in the armature shaft
7. Snap ring

Installing the pinion stop retainer and thrust collar on the armature shaft

bly to the starter housing. Remove the solenoid assembly from the starter housing.

To install the solenoid assembly, reverse the above procedure.

Delco-Remy

Remove the leads from the solenoid. Remove the drive housing of the starter motor. Remove the shift lever pin and bolt from the shift lever. Remove the attaching bolts that hold the solenoid assembly to the housing of the starter motor. Remove the starter solenoid from the starter housing. To install the solenoid, reverse the above procedure.

Prestolite

Remove the leads to the solenoid assembly. Remove the attaching bolts that hold the so-

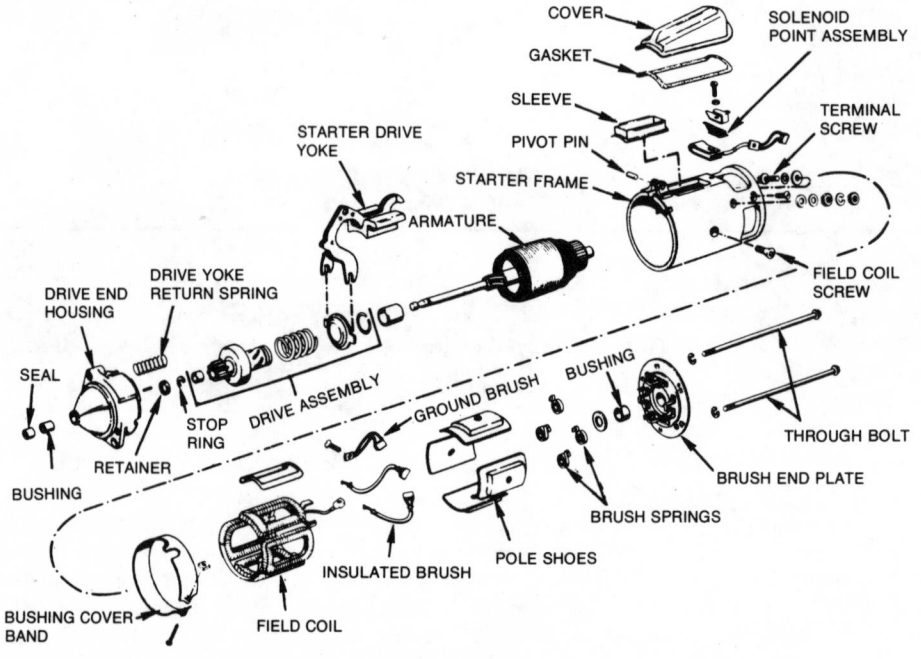

1972-81 starter

Generator and Regulator Specifications

Make	Model No.	Output (amps)	Brush Spring Tension (oz)	Model No.	Regulated Voltage	Regulated Amperage	Cutout Relay Closing Voltage
Generators—6 Volt				*Regulators—6 Volt*			
Autolite	GDZ 4817 GDZ 6001	35	35–53	VRP-6003 VRP-4007 VBO-4601	7.1–7.3	49	6.3–6.8
	GGW 4801 GGW 7404	45	35–53 18–36	VBO-4601C	7.1–7.3	49	6.3–6.8
Delco-Remy	1102811	45	28	1972063	6.9–7.4	42–47	5.9–6.7
Generators—12 Volts				*Regulators—12 Volt*			
Autolite	GJP 7202 GJP 7402A GJC 7002	35 30	18–36	VBO4201E4A VRX 6009	14.3	36	12.6–13.6
Delco-Remy	1102096	36	28	1972029	13.8–14.8	30	11.8–13.5
Prestolite	GJP 7402A	35	18–36	R-2-K-1 ①	14.2–14.6	35	—

① Motorola transistorized regulator

lenoid to the starter housing. Remove the bolt from the shift lever. Remove the solenoid assembly from the starter housing. Reverse the procedure for installation.

Battery

REMOVAL AND INSTALLATION

Remove the hold-down screws from the battery box. Loosen the nuts that secure the cable ends to the battery terminals. Lift the battery cables from the terminals with a twisting motion.

If there is a battery cable puller available, make use of it. Lift the battery from the vehicle.

Before installing the battery in the vehicle, make sure that the battery terminals are clean and free from corrosion. Use a battery terminal cleaner on the terminals and on the inside of the battery cable ends. If a cleaner is not available, use heavy sandpaper to remove the corrosion. A mixture of baking soda and water will neutralize any acid. Place the battery in the vehicle. Install the cables onto the terminals. Tighten the nuts on the cable

ends. Smear a light coating of grease on the cable ends and the tops of the terminals. This will prevent buildup of oxidized acid on the terminals and the cable ends. Install and tighten the nuts of the battery box.

ENGINE MECHANICAL

Design

L-HEAD 4-CYLINDER

The Model L4-134 engine is an L-head four-cylinder engine. The cylinder block and crankcase are cast integrally. Both intake and exhaust valves are mounted in the cylinder block with through water jacketing to provide effective cooling. The valves are operated by conventional valve tappets.

The engine is equipped with a fully counterbalanced crankshaft supported by three main bearings. To better control balance, the counterweights are independently forged and permanently attached to the crankshaft with dowels and capscrews that are tack-welded. Crankshaft end play is adjusted by

Battery and Starter Specifications

Engine	Battery Ampere* Hour Capacity	Volts	Terminal Grounded	Make	Starters Lock Test Amps	Volts	Torque (ft. lbs.)	No-Load Test Amps	Volts	RPM	Brush Spring Tension (oz)
L and F-head 134	100	6	Neg	Autolite	335	2	6④	65	5	4300	42–53
F-head 134	50	12	Neg	Autolite	170①	4	1.5②	50	10	4400③	31–47
L and F-head 134	100	6	Neg	Delco-Remy	600	3	15	60	3	6000	24
F-head 134	50	12	Neg	Delco-Remy	435	5.8	10.5	75	10.3	6900	35
F-head 134	50	12	Neg	Prestolite	405	—	9	50	10	5300	32–40
151	50	12	Neg	Delco-Remy	—	—	—	70	11	11900	32–40
V6	50	12	Neg	Delco-Remy	—	—	—	75	10.6	6200	32–40
232, 258, 304	50④	12	Neg	Autolite	600	3.4	13.0	65⑤	12	9250	40

① 280 amps with model MDU 7004 starter
② 6.2 ft. lbs. with the model MDU 7004 starter
③ 5300 rpms with the model MDU 7004 starter
④ 60 and 70 amp battery optional
⑤ 1980–81 77
*Starting 1978, battery ratings are given in reserve capacity expressed in minutes, rather than ampere hours. The standard equipment has a rating of 75 minutes, with 95, 110, and 135 optional.

Alternator and Regulator Specifications

Year	Alternator					Regulator	
	Manufacturer	Engine No. Cyl. (cu in.)	Field Current @ 12V (amps)	Output (amps)		Manufacturer	Volts @ 75°F
1965–74	Motorola	6—232, 258 8—304	1.8–2.5	37		Motorola	13.75–14.2
	Motorola	F-Head	1.2–1.7	35		Motorola	14.2–14.6
	Motorola	V6—225	1.2–1.7	35		Motorola	14.2–14.6
1975	Motorola	all V8	1.8–2.5	37①		Motorola	12.7–15.3
	Delco-Remy	all 6	4.0–5.0	37②		Delco-Remy	12.0–15.5
1976	Motorcraft	all V8	2.5–3.0	40③		Motorcraft	13.1–14.8
	Delco-Remy	all 6	4.0–5.0	37④		Delco-Remy	12.0–15.5
1977	Motorcraft	all V8	2.5–3.0	40③		Motorcraft	13.1–14.8
	Delco-Remy	all 6	4.0–5.0	37④		Delco-Remy	12.0–15.5
1978–79	Delco-Remy	all	4.0–5.0	37④		Delco-Remy	12.0–15.5
1980–81	Delco-Remy	all	4.0–5.0	42④		Delco-Remy	12.0–15.5

① Optional: 51 and 62 amp
② Optional: 55 and 63 amp
③ Optional: 60 amp
④ Optional: 63 amp

shims placed between the crankshaft thrust washer and the shoulder on the crankshaft.

Aluminum pistons, forged steel connecting rods, and replaceable main and connecting rod bearings are used in this engine. The camshaft on current production engines is gear driven from the crankshaft (chain driven on early production engines).

The water pump is mounted on the front of the cylinder block, and is belt driven by the crankshaft. Circulation of the coolant is controlled by a thermostat installed in the water outlet which is mounted on top of the cylinder head.

The engine is pressure lubricated. An oil pump, gear driven by the camshaft, is mounted externally on the left side of the crankcase. The pump forces the lubricant through oil channels and drilled passages in the crankshaft to efficiently lubricate the main and connecting rod bearings. Lubricant

is also force fed to the camshaft bearings and timing gears. Cylinder walls and piston pins are lubricated from spurt holes in the "follow" side of the connecting rods.

The carburetor is mounted on top of the intake manifold. The intake and exhaust manifolds are mounted on the left side of the cylinder block. A thermostatically controlled valve in the exhaust manifold controls the temperature of fuel-air mixture in the intake manifold.

F-HEAD 4 CYLINDER

The F-head, four-cylinder engine is of a combination valve-in-head and valve-in-block construction. The intake valves are mounted in the head and are operated by pushrods through rocker arms. The intake manifold is cast as an integral part of the cylinder head and is completely water-jacketed. This type of construction transfers heat from the cool-

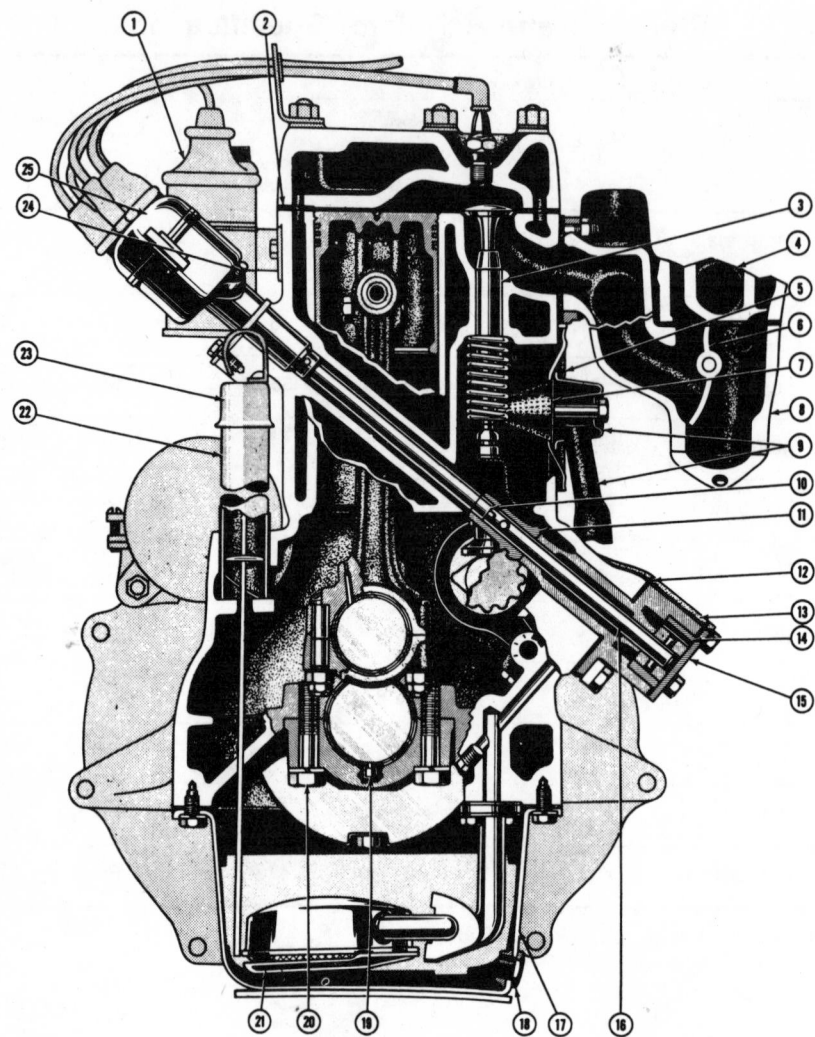

1. Ignition coil
2. Cylinder head gasket
3. Exhaust valve guide
4. Intake manifold
5. Valve spring cover
6. Heat control valve
7. Crankcase ventilator gasket
8. Exhaust manifold
9. Crankcase ventilator
10. Distributor shaft friction spring
11. Oil pump driven gear
12. Oil pump gasket
13. Oil pump
14. Oil pump rotor
15. Oil pump cover
16. Oil relief plunger
17. Relief plunger spring
18. Relief valve shim
19. Relief plunger spring retainer
20. Oil pump shaft
21. Oil pan
22. Drain plug
23. Oil float support
24. Crankshaft bearing dowel
25. Bearing screw
26. Oil float
27. Oil filler tube
28. Oil filler cap & level indicator
29. Distributor oiler
30. Distributor

4-134 L-head cutaway view

ing system to the intake passages and assists in vaporizing the fuel when the engine is cold. Therefore, there is no heat control valve (heat riser) needed in the exhaust manifold.

The exhaust valves are mounted in the block with thorough water jacketing to provide effective cooling of the valves.

The engine is pressure-lubricated. An oil pump which is driven by the camshaft forces the lubricant through oil channels and drilled passages in the crankshaft to efficiently lubricate the main and connecting rod bearings. Lubricant is also force-fed to the camshaft bearings, rocker arms, and timing gears. Cylinder walls and piston pins are lubricated from spurt holes in the 'follow' side of the connecting rods.

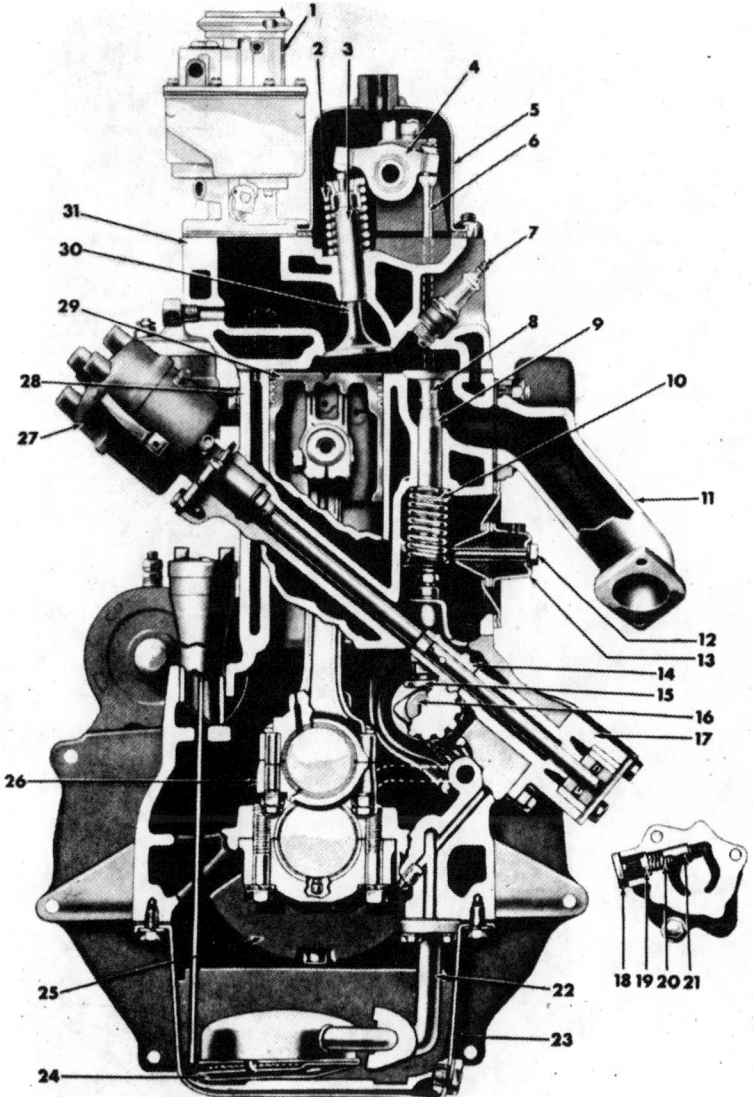

1. Carburetor
2. Intake valve spring
3. Intake valve stem
    guide
4. Rocker arm
5. Rocker arm cover
6. Intake valve pushrod
7. Spark plug
8. Exhaust valve
9. Exhaust valve stem
    guide
10. Exhaust valve spring
11. Exhaust manifold
12. Valve spring cover
    screw
13. Crankcase ventilator
14. Oil pump drive gear
15. Exhaust valve tappet
16. Camshaft
17. Oil pump
18. Oil pump relief spring
    retainer
19. Oil pump relief
    plunger gasket
20. Oil plunger relief
    spring
21. Oil pump relief
    plunger
22. Oil float support
23. Oil pan
24. Oil float
25. Crankshaft
26. Connecting rod
27. Distributor
28. Piston and pin
29. Cylinder block
30. Intake valve
31. Cylinder head

F-head engine cutaway from the front

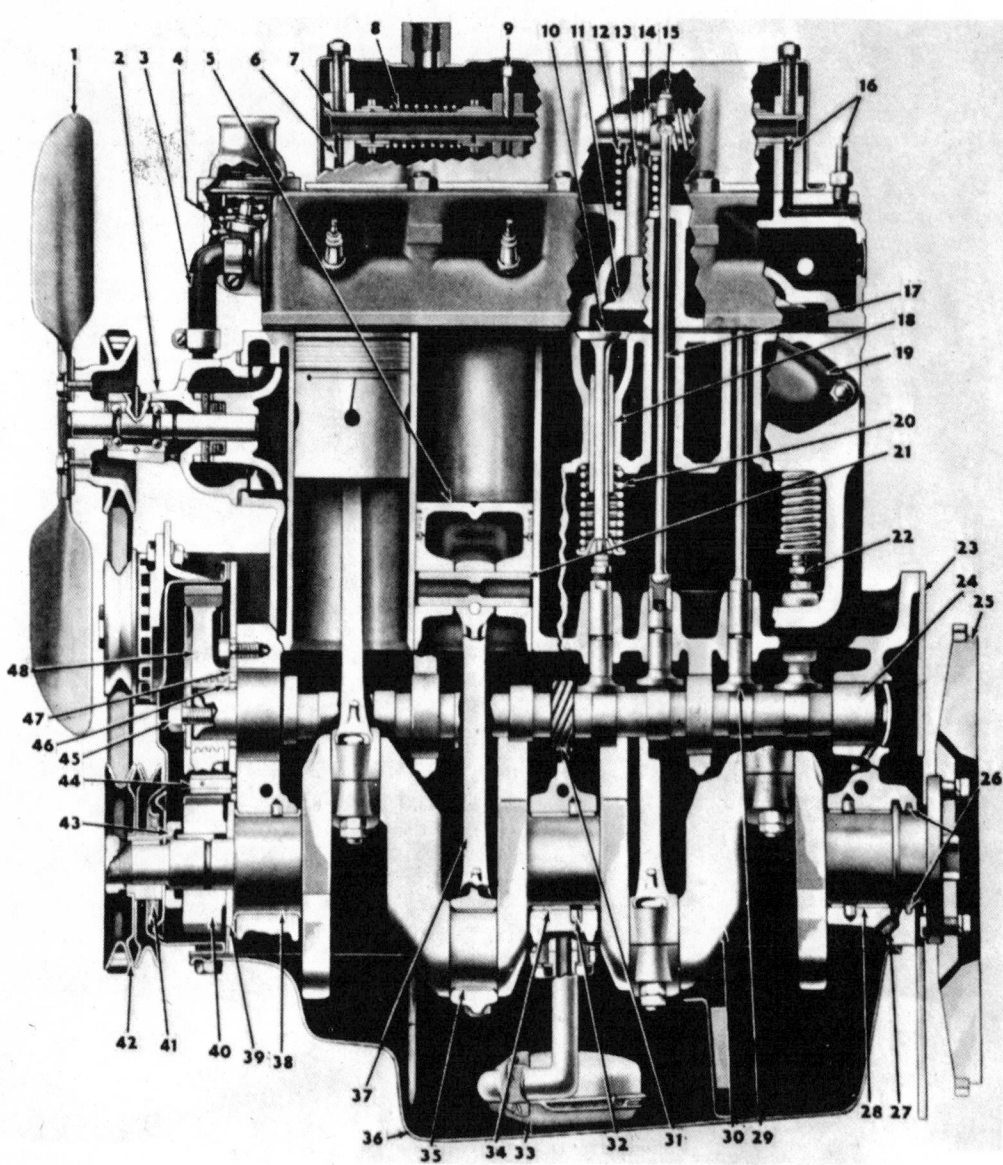

1. Fan assembly
2. Water pump assembly
3. Water bypass tube
4. Thermostat
5. Piston
6. Oil return tube
7. Rocker arm shaft
8. Rocker arm shaft spring
9. Rocker arm shaft lock screw
10. Exhaust valve
11. Intake valve
12. Intake valve spring
13. Intake valve guide
14. Rocker arm
15. Adjusting screw
16. Oil inlet tube
17. Push rod
18. Exhaust valve guide
19. Exhaust manifold
20. Exhaust valve spring
21. Piston pin
22. Valve tappet adjusting screw
23. Engine rear support plate
24. Camshaft
25. Flywheel
26. Rear bearing oil seal
27. Oil return channel
28. Rear main bearing shell
29. Tappet
30. Crankshaft
31. Oil pump drive gear
32. Main bearing dowel
33. Oil float assembly
34. Center main bearing shell
35. Connecting rod bearing
36. Oil pan
37. Connecting rod
38. Front main bearing shell
39. Front engine plate
40. Crankshaft gear
41. Crankshaft front end seal
42. Fan and generator pully
43. Crankshaft gear spacer
44. Timing gear oil jet
45. Camshaft gear screw
46. Camshaft thrust plate spacer
47. Camshaft thrust plate
48. Camshaft gear

F-head engine cutaway from the side

General Engine Specifications

Engine Year	Carburetor Type	Horsepower at rpm	Torque (ft. lb.) at rpm	Bore x Stroke	Ratio Compression	Cranking Compression Pressure	Oil Pressure (psi) at 2000 rpm
4–134, 1945–52	1 bbl	60 @ 4000	105 @ 2000	3.125 x 3.375	7.0:1	115–145	35
4–134, 1953–67	1 bbl	75 @ 4000	114 @ 2000	3.125 x 4.375	7.4:1	115–145	35
4–134, 1968–71	1 bbl	75 @ 4000	114 @ 2000	3.125 x 4.375	6.7:1	100–125	35
4–151, 1980–81	2 bbl	90 @ 4400	128 @ 2400	4.000 x 3.000	8.24:1	140	38
V6–225, 1965–71	2 bbl	160 @ 4200	235 @ 2400	3.750 x 3.400	9.0:1	150–180	33
6–232, 1972–75	1 bbl	100 @ 3600	185 @ 1800	3.750 x 3.500	8.0:1	140 Minimum	50
6–232, 1976–78	1 bbl	90 @ 3050	170 @ 2000	3.750 x 3.500	8.0:1	140 Minimum	50
6–258, 1972–75	1 bbl	110 @ 3500	195 @ 2000	3.750 x 3.895	8.0:1	150 Minimum	50
6–258, 1976–78	1 bbl	95 @ 3050	180 @ 2100	3.750 x 3.895	8.0:1	120–150	50
6–258, 1979–81	2 bbl	114 @ 3600	196 @ 2000	3.750 x 3.895	8.0:1	120–150	50
V8–304, 1972–75	2 bbl	150 @ 4200	245 @ 2500	3.750 x 3.440	8.4:1	150 Minimum	50
V8–304, 1976–81	2 bbl	120 @ 3200	220 @ 2200	3.750 x 3.440	8.4:1	120–150	50

The circulation of the coolant is controlled by a thermostat in the water outlet elbow which is cast as part of the cylinder head.

The engine is equipped with a fully counterbalanced crankshaft that is supported by three main bearings. The counterweights of the crankshaft are independently forged and are permanently attached to the crankshaft with dowels and cap screws that are tack-welded. Crankshaft end-play is adjusted by placing shims between the crankshaft thrust washer and the shoulder on the crankshaft.

The pistons have an extra groove directly above the top ring which acts as a heat dam or insulator.

The engine has a compression ratio ranging from 6.3:1 to 7.8:1; this permits the use of regular octane gas. The displacement of the F-head engine is 134.2 cu in.

4-151

The 151 cid General Motors-built, overhead valve, four cylinder engine has a cross-flow cylinder head, five main crankshaft bearings, hydraulic lifters, conventional ball socket rocker arms, exceptionally long pushrods, a

Torque Specifications
All figures given in foot pounds (ft. lbs.)

Engine	Cyl Head	Conn Rod	Main Bearing	Crankshaft Damper	Flywheel	Manifold	
						Intake	Exhaust
4–134	60–70	35–45	65–75	65–75	35–41	29–35①	29–35
4–151	95	30	65	160	55	Bolt:40 Nut:30	Bolt:40 Nut:30
V6–225	65–85	30–40	80–110	140 min	50–65	45–55	14–20
6–232	105	28	80③	55	105	43	25
6–258	105②	33	80	80	105	23	23
V8–304	110	28	100	55	105	43	25

① F-head has no intake manifold
② 1981:85
③ 1981:65

Piston and Ring Specifications
All measurements given in inches (in.).

Engine	Ring Gap			Ring Side Clearance			Piston Clearance *
	#1 Compression	#2 Compression	Oil Control	#1 Compression	#2 Compression	Oil Control	
4–134	.007–.017	.007–.017	.007–.017	.002–.004	.0015–.0035	.001–.00255	.0025–.0045
4–151	.0027–.0033	.009–.019	.015–.055	.0025–.0033	.0025–.0033	.0025–.0033	.0025–.0033
V6–225	.010–.020	.010–.020	.015–.035	.002–.0035	.003–.005	.0015–.0085	.0005–.0011
6–232	.010–.020	.010–.020	.015–.055	.0015–.003	.0015–.003	.001–.008	.0009–.0017
6–258	.010–.020	.010–.020	.015–.055	.0015–.003	.0015–.003	.001–.008	.0009–.0017
V8–304	.010–.020	.010–.020	.010–.025	.0015–.0035	.0015–.003	.0011–.008	.0010–.0018

*Measured at the top of the skirt.

gear driven camshaft and a coolant heated aluminum intake manifold.

V6

The V6 engine has a displacement of 225 cu in. and a compression ratio of 9.0:1 which permits the use of regular octane gas.

It has two banks of three cylinders each which are opposed to one another at a 90° angle. The left bank of cylinders, as viewed from the driver's seat, is set forward of the right bank so that the connecting rods of opposite pairs of pistons and rods can be attached to the same crankpin.

The crankshaft counterbalance weights are cast as an integral part of the crankshaft. All

Crankshaft and Connecting Rod Specifications
All measurements given in inches (in.)

Engine	Crankshaft					Connecting Rod	
	Main Bearing Journal Dia	Main Bearing Oil Clearance	Shaft End Play	Thrust on No.	Journal Dia	Oil Clearance	Side Clearance
4–134	2.3331–2.3341	.0003–.0029	.004–.006	1	1.9375–1.9383	.0001–.0019	.004–.010
4–151	2.2988	.0005–.0022	.0035–.0085	5	1.8690	.0007–.0027	.006–.022
V6–225	2.4995	.0005–.0021	.004–.008	2	2.0000	.0020–.0023	.006–.014
6–232	2.4986–2.5001	.0010–.0020	.0015–.0065	3	2.0934–2.0955	.0010–.0020	.005–.014
6–258	2.4986–2.5001	.0010–.0020①	.0015–.0065⑤	3	2.0934–2.0955	.0010–.0020②	.005–.014
V8–304	2.7474–2.7489③	.0010–.0020④	.003–.008⑥	3	2.0934–2.0955	.0010–.0020	.006–.018

① 1974–79: .0010–.0030 (.0025 preferred)
② 1974–76: .0010–.0030 (.0025 preferred)
　　1977–81: .0010–.0025 (.0015–.0020 preferred)
③ #5: 2.7464–2.7479
④ #5: .0020–.0030
⑤ 1981: #1: .0005–.0026
　　2, 3, 4, 5, 6: .0005–.0030
　　7: .0011–.0035
⑥ 1981: #1: .0010–.0030
　　#5: .0020–.0040

Valve Specifications

Engine	Seat Angle (deg)	Face Angle (deg)	Spring Test Pressure (lbs @ in.)	Spring Installed Height (in.)	Stem-to-Guide Clearance (in.)		Stem Diameter (in.)	
					Intake	Exhaust	Intake	Exhaust
4–134 L-Head	45	45	120 @ 1.750	2.109	.0007–.0022	.0025–.0045	.3730	.3715
4–134 F-Head	45	45	153 @ 1.400 ①	1.660 ⑦	.0007–.0022	.0025–.0045	.3733–.3738	.3710–.3720
4–151	46	45	176 @ 1.250	1.660	.0010–.0027	.0010–.0027	.3422	.3422
V6–225	45	45	168 @ 1.260	1.640	.0012–.0032	.0015–.0035 ②	.3415–.3427	.3402–.3412 ②
6–232	③	④	195 @ 1.475	1.786 ⑧	.0010–.0030	.0010–.0030	.3715–.3725	.3715–.3725
6–258	③	④	195 @ 1.475 ⑨	1.786	.0010–.0030	.0010–.0030	.3715–.3725	.3715–.3725
V8–304	③	④	218 @ 1.359	1.786	.0010–.0030	.0010–.0030	.3715–.3725	.3715–.3725

① Exhaust: 120 @ 1.750
② Measured at the top
③ Intake: 30; exhaust: 44.5
④ Intake: 29; exhaust: 44
⑤ Not used
⑥ Not used
⑦ Exhaust: 2.109
⑧ 1966–70: 1.8125
⑨ 2 bbl: 204 @ 1.386

Camshaft Specifications

Engine	Journal Diameter					Bearing Clearance	Lobe Lift		Camshaft End Play
	1	2	3	4	5		Intake	Exhaust	
4–134 L-Head	2.1860–2.1855	2.1225–2.1215	2.0600–2.0590	1.6230–1.6225	—	.0010–.0025	.3510	.3510	.004–.007
4–134 F-Head	2.1860–2.1855	2.1225–2.1215	2.0600–2.0590	1.6230–1.6225	—	.0010–.0025	.2600	.3510	.004–.007
4–151	1.8690	1.8690	1.8690	—	—	.0007–.0027	.3980	.3980	.0015–.0050
V6–225	1.7550–1.7560	1.7250–1.7260	1.6950–1.6960	1.6650–1.6660	—	.0015–.0040	NA	NA	NA
6–232, 6–258	2.0290–2.0300	2.0190–2.0200	2.0090–2.0100	1.9990–2.0000	—	.0010–.0030	.2540	.2540	0
8–304	2.1195–2.1205	2.0895–2.0905	2.0595–2.0605	2.0295–2.0305	1.9995–2.0005	.0010–.0030	.2660	.2660	0

of the crankshaft bearings are identical in diameter, except for no. 2 bearing which is the thrust bearing; it is larger than the rest.

The cast-iron heads are interchangeable.

The camshaft, which is located above the crankshaft—between the two banks, operates hydraulic valve lifters. The rocker arms are not adjustable.

232, 258 SIXES

The American Motors six-cylinder engines are inline sixes with overhead intake and exhaust valves. The valves are operated by paired bridged pivot rocker arms in 1973 and 1975–79 models. The rockers are mounted on a common shaft in most 1972 and 1974 models. None of the rocker arms are adjustable. The 232 was last used in the 1978 model year.

304 V8

The 304 V8 has two banks of four cylinders each which are opposed to each other at a 90° angle. The camshaft is located above the crankshaft, between the two banks. It operates the valves through the use of hydraulic lifters, pushrods, and separately mounted rocker arms on 1972 models. The rocker arms are mounted in pairs on bridged pivots on 1973–79 models.

A two-barrel carburetor is used.

Engine Removal and Installation

L-HEAD

1. Drain the cooling system by opening the drain cocks on the bottom of the radiator and the lower right side of the block.
2. Disconnect the battery.
3. Remove the upper and lower radiator hoses and the heater hoses.
4. Remove the four bolts securing the fan hub and blades.
5. Remove the four radiator attaching screws and lift out the radiator.
6. Disconnect the fuel line and the windshield wiper hose at the fuel pump.
7. Remove the air cleaner from the carburetor.
8. Disconnect the choke and throttle controls.
9. Disconnect the cables at the starter and remove the starter.
10. Disconnect the generator wires.
11. Disconnect the wires from the coil, oil pressure sender and temperature sender.

12. Disconnect the exhaust pipe from the manifold.
13. Place a jack under the crankshaft pulley, disconnect and remove the two front engine supports, and slightly lower the engine. This will allow access to the two top bolts on the bell housing.
14. Install a lifting sling and shop crane on the engine and take up all slack.
15. Unbolt the engine from the bell housing.
16. Pull the engine forward or roll the vehicle backwards until the clutch clears the bell housing. Then, lift the engine up and out of the vehicle.
17. Installation is the reverse of removal.

F-HEAD

1. Drain the cooling system by opening the draincocks at the bottom of the radiator and the lower right side of the cylinder block.
2. Disconnect the battery at the positive terminal to avoid the possibility of a short circuit.
3. Remove the air cleaner horn from the carburetor and disconnect the breather hose at the oil filler pipe.
4. Disconnect the carburetor choke and throttle controls by loosening the clamp bolts and setscrews.
5. Disconnect the fuel tank-to-fuel pump line at the fuel pump by unscrewing the connecting nut.
6. Plug the fuel line to prevent leakage. Disconnect the windshield wiper vacuum hose at the fuel pump.
7. Remove the radiator stay bar on the CJ-3B.
8. Remove the upper and lower radiator hoses. Remove the heater hoses, if so equipped, from the water pump and the rear of the cylinder head.
9. Remove the fan hub and fan blades.
10. Remove the four radiator attaching screws and remove the radiator and shroud as one unit.
11. Remove the starter motor cables and remove the starter motor.
12. Disconnect the wires from the alternator or the generator. Disconnect the ignition primary wire at the ignition coil.
13. Disconnect the oil pressure and temperature sending unit wires at the units.
14. Disconnect the exhaust pipe at the exhaust manifold by removing the stud nuts.
15. Remove the spark plug wires from the cable bracket that is mounted to the rocker

arm cover. Remove the cable bracket by removing the stud nuts.

16. Remove the rocker arm cover by removing the attaching stud nuts.

17. Attach a lifting bracket to the engine using the head bolts. Be sure that the bolts selected will hold the engine with the weight balanced. Attach the lifting bracket to a boom hoist, or other lifting device, and take up all of the slack.

18. Remove the two nuts and bolts from each front engine support. Disconnect the engine ground strap. Remove the engine supports. Lower the engine slightly to permit access to the two top bolts on the flywheel housing.

19. Remove the bolts that attach the flywheel housing to the engine.

20. Pull the engine forward, or roll the vehicle backward, until the clutch clears the flywheel housing. Lift the engine from the vehicle.

21. To install the engine, reverse the above procedure.

51

1. Disconnect the battery.
2. Remove the air cleaner.
3. Jack up the vehicle and support it on jackstands.
4. Disconnect the exhaust pipe from the manifold.
5. Disconnect the oxygen sensor.
6. Disconnect the wires from the starter.
7. Unbolt the starter and remove it from the vehicle.
8. Disconnect the wires from the distributor and oil pressure sending unit.
9. Remove the engine mount nuts.
10. On vehicles with manual transmission, remove the clutch slave cylinder and flywheel inspection plate.
11. Remove the clutch or converter housing-to-engine bolts.
12. On vehicle with automatic transmission, disconnect the converter from the drive plate.
13. Lower the vehicle.
14. Support the transmission with a jack.
15. Tag all hoses at the carburetor and remove them.
16. Disconnect the mixture control solenoid wire from the carburetor. (not all vehicle have these)
17. Disconnect the wires from the alternator.

18. Disconnect the throttle cable from the bracket and the carburetor.

19. Disconnect the choke and solenoid wires at the carburetor.

20. Disconnect the temperature sender wire.

21. Drain the radiator at the drain cock, then remove the lower hose.

22. Remove the upper radiator hose and the heater hoses.

23. Remove the fan shroud, and radiator.

24. Remove the power steering hoses at the pump.

25. Attach a shop crane to the engine and lift it out of the vehicle.

NOTE: *The manual transmission may have to be raised slightly to allow a smooth separation.*

26. Installation is the reverse of removal. Observe the following torque values:

• Clutch/converter housing-to-engine: 35 ft. lb.

• Clutch slave cylinder: 18 ft. lb.

• Engine mount nuts: 34 ft. lb.

Starter mounting bolts: 27 ft. lb.

Starter bracket nut: 40 in. lb.

• Exhaust pipe-to-manifold nuts: 35 ft. lb.

V6

1. Remove the hood.
2. Disconnect the battery ground cable from the engine and the battery.
3. Remove the air cleaner.
4. Drain the coolant from the radiator and engine.
5. Disconnect the alternator wiring harness from the connector at the regulator.
6. Disconnect the upper and lower radiator hoses from the engine.
7. Remove the right and left radiator support bars.
8. Remove the radiator from the vehicle.
9. Disconnect the engine wiring harnesses from the connectors which are located on the firewall.
10. Disconnect the battery cable and wiring from the engine starter assembly.
11. Remove the starter assembly from the engine.
12. Disconnect the engine fuel hoses from the fuel lines at the right frame rails.
13. Plug the fuel lines.
14. Disconnect the throttle linkage and the choke cable from the carburetor and remove the cable support bracket that is mounted on the engine.

15. Disconnect the exhaust pipes from the right and left sides of the engine.

16. Place a jack under the transmission and support the weight of the transmission.

17. Remove the bolts that secure the engine to the front motor mounts.

18. Attach a suitable sling to the engine lifting eyes and, using a hoist, lift the engine just enough to support its weight.

19. Remove the bolts that secure the engine to the flywheel housing.

20. Raise the engine slightly and slide the engine forward to remove the transmission main shaft from the clutch plate splines.

NOTE: *The engine and the transmission must be raised slightly to release the spline from the clutch plate while sliding the engine forward.*

21. When the engine is free of the transmission shaft, raise the engine and remove it from the vehicle.

22. To install the engine, reverse the procedure given above.

232 and 258 Sixes, 304 V8

1. Remove the air cleaner.

2. Drain the cooling system.

3. Disconnect the upper and lower radiator hoses.

4. If equipped with an automatic transmission, disconnect the cooler lines from the radiator.

5. Remove the radiator and the fan.

6. If so equipped, remove the power steering pump and the drive belt, and place the unit aside. Do not remove the power steering hoses. Remove the battery and tray if equipped with the V8 (1972–75).

Note: *If the vehicle has air conditioning, detach and set aside the air conditioning compressor. If this isn't possible, the system will have to be professionally discharged and then recharged after the engine is installed.*

7. Disconnect all wires, lines, linkage, and hoses that are connected to the engine. Remove the oil filter on the Sixes.

8. Remove both of the engine front support cushion-to-frame retaining nuts.

9. Disconnect the exhaust pipe, or pipes if equipped with the V8, at the support bracket and exhaust manifold.

10. Support the weight of the engine with a lifting device.

11. Remove the front support cushion and bracket assemblies from the engine.

12. Remove the transfer case shift lever boot and the transmission access cover.

13. If equipped with an automatic transmission, remove the upper bolts securing the transmission bellhousing to the engine. If equipped with a manual transmission, remove the upper bolts that secure the clutch housing to the engine.

14. Remove the starter motor.

15. If the vehicle is equipped with an automatic transmission:

a. Remove the engine to transmission adapter plate inspection covers;

b. Mark the assembled position of the converter and flex plate and remove the converter-to-flex plate retaining screws;

c. Remove the remaining bolts securing the transmission bellhousing to the engine.

16. If equipped with a manual transmission, remove the lower cover of the clutch housing and the remaining bolts that secure the clutch housing to the engine.

17. Support the transmission with a floor jack.

18. Attach a suitable sling to the engine and using a hoist, lift the engine upward and forward at the same time, removing it from the vehicle.

19. Install the engine by reversing the above procedure.

Observe the following torque values:

• Clutch housing spacer-to-block bolts: 12 ft. lb.

• Clutch housing-to-block bottom bolts: 43 ft. lb.

• Clutch housing-to-block top bolts: 27 ft. lb.

• Exhaust pipe-to-manifold bolts: 20 ft. lb.

• Engine mount nuts: 35 ft. lb.

Rocker Shafts and Rocker Studs
REMOVAL AND INSTALLATION
F-Head

Remove the rocker arm cover attaching bolts and remove the rocker arm cover. Remove the nuts from the rocker arm shaft support studs. Remove the intake valve pushrods from the engine. Install in the reverse order. Tighten the rocker arm retaining bolts to 30–3 ft. lbs.

4-151

1. Remove the rocker arm cover.

2. Remove the rocker arm capscrew and ball.

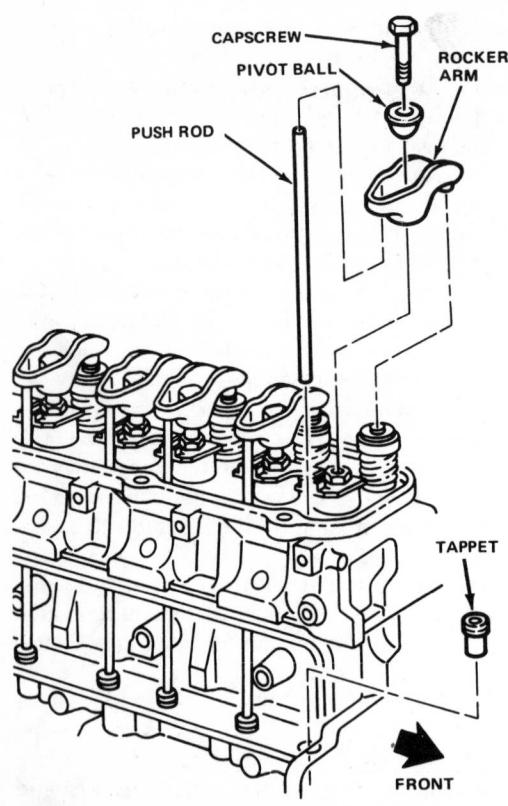

4-151 rocker arm and pushrod removal and installation

3. Remove the rocker arm.

4. Installation is the reverse of removal. Torque the capscrew to 20 ft. lb. DO NOT OVERTORQUE!

V6

Remove the crankcase ventilator valve from the right side valve cover. Remove the four attaching bolts from the right and left side valve covers and remove both of the valve covers.

Unscrew, but do not remove, the bolts that attach the rocker arm assemblies to the cylinder heads. Remove the rocker arm assemblies, with the bolts in place, from the cylinder heads. Mark each of the pushrods so that they can be installed in their original positions. Remove the pushrods. Install in the reverse order. Tighten the bolts to 30 ft. lbs., a little at a time.

1972 and 1974 232, 258 Sixes

Remove the valve cover by removing the six valve cover attaching screws. Loosen, but do not remove, the six bolts that attach the rocker arm assembly to the cylinder head. Lift the whole rocker arm assembly off the

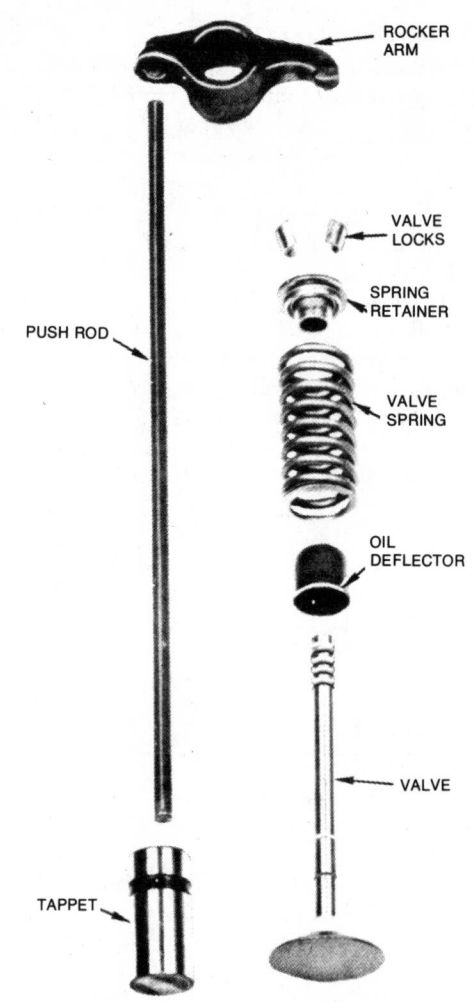

1972 and 1974 six cylinder engine valve train

head with the bolts in place. Identify each of the pushrods so that they can be replaced in their original positions. Remove the pushrods. Install in reverse order. Tighten the bolts, working evenly, from the center outward. Tighten to 22 ft. lbs.

1973, 1975–81 232, 258 Sixes and 1973–81 304 V8

On these engines the rocker arms pivot on a bridged pivot that is secured with two capscrews. The bridged pivots maintain proper rocker arm-to-valve tip alignment.

1. Remove the rocker cover and gasket.

2. Remove the two capscrews at each bridged pivot, backing off each capscrew one turn at a time to avoid breaking the bridge.

3. Remove each bridged pivot and corresponding pair of rocker arms and place them

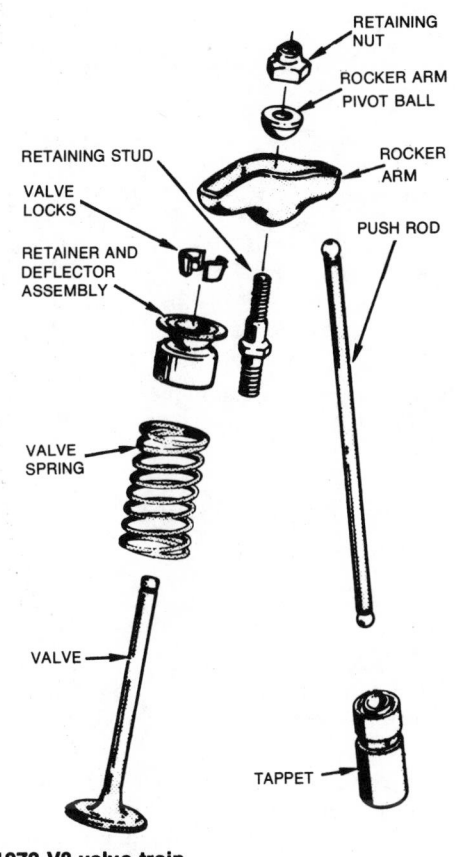

1972 V8 valve train

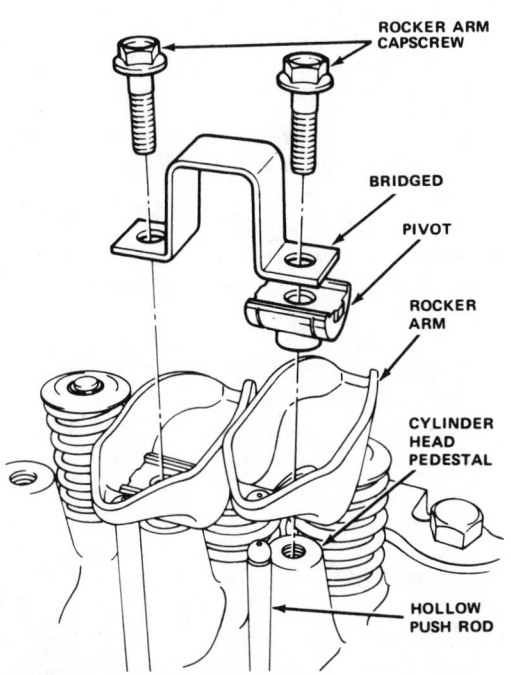

Bridged pivot type rocker arms

on a clean surface in the same order as they are removed.

NOTE: *Bridged pivots, capscrews, rockers, and pushrods must all be reinstalled in their original positions.*

4. Clean all the parts in a suitable solvent and use compressed air to blow out the oil passages in the pushrods and the rocker arms. Replace any excessively worn parts.

5. Install rocker arms, pushrods and bridged pivots in the same positions from which they were removed.

NOTE: *Be sure that the bottom end of each pushrod is centered in the plunger cap of each hydraulic valve tappet.*

6. Install the capscrews and tighten them one turn at a time, alternating between the two screws on each bridge. Tighten the capscrews to 21 ft. lbs. on the Sixes and 10 ft. lbs. on the 304 V8.

7. Install the rocker cover(s) with new gasket(s).

1972 304 V8

The 1972 304 V8 has each rocker arm individually mounted on a separate stud. Each rocker assembly consists of the following: a rocker arm retaining stud, a rocker arm pivot ball, a rocker arm, and a retaining nut which screws onto the rocker arm retaining stud. Each assembly is removed and installed separately. To remove, unscrew the rocker retaining nut from the stud and lift off the rocker arm and its pivot ball. To remove the stud from the block use a wrench. Label the pushrods so that they can be installed in their original positions and remove them from the block.

When installing the rocker arm retaining studs, use caution not to cross thread them. They are designed to cause an interference fit. Lubricate the studs with high pressure grease before installing them in the head. Install the rocker arm assemblies in the reverse order of removal. Tighten the rocker arm retaining nuts to 23 ft. lbs.

Cylinder Head
REMOVAL AND INSTALLATION

It is important to note that each engine has its own head bolt tightening sequence and torque. Incorrect tightening procedure may cause head warpage and compression loss. Correct sequence and torque for each engine model is shown in this chapter.

L-Head

1. Remove the spark plugs.
2. Remove the temperature sending unit.
3. Remove the head nuts.
4. Lift the head from the block.

NOTE: *Do not use a sharp instrument such as a chisel or screwdriver to break the head from the block. If the head sticks, screw lifting hooks into the #1 and 4 spark plug holes.*

5. Install the head, using a new gasket. Make sure the head and block surfaces are clean. Torque the head to 60–70 ft. lb.

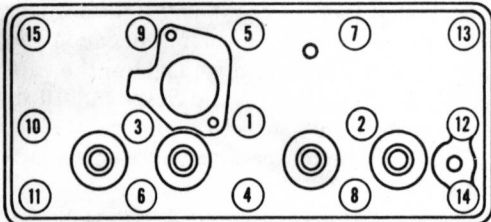

4-134 L-head cylinder head bolt tightening sequence

F-Head

1. Drain the coolant.
2. Remove the upper radiator hose.
3. Remove the carburetor.
4. On early engines remove the by-pass hose on the front of the cylinder head.
5. Remove the rocker arm cover.
6. Remove the rocker arm attaching stud nuts and rocker arm shaft assembly.
7. Remove the cylinder head bolts. One of the bolts is located below the carburetor mounting, inside the intake manifold.
8. Lift off the cylinder head.
9. Reverse the procedure to install the cylinder head. Tighten the head bolts first to 40 ft. lbs. then to the specified torque in the correct sequence.

F-head cylinder head torque sequence

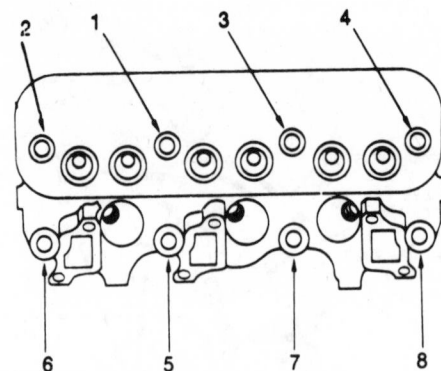

V6-225 cylinder head torque sequence

V6

1. Remove the intake manifold.
2. Remove the rocker cover.
3. Remove the exhaust pipes at the flanges.
4. Remove the alternator in order to remove the right head.
5. Remove the dipstick and power steering pump, if so equipped, in order to remove the left head.
6. Remove the valve cover and the rocker assemblies. Mark these parts so that they can be re-installed in exactly the same positions.
7. Unbolt the head bolts and lift off the cylinder head(s). It is very important that the inside of the engine be protected from dirt. The hydraulic lifters are particularly susceptible to being damaged by dirt.
8. To install, use the reverse procedure.

4-151 and 232, 258 Sixes

NOTE: *The 151 rocker cover is sealed with RTV silicone gasket material. Do not use a conventional Gasket.*

1. Drain the cooling system and disconnect the hoses at the thermostat housing.
2. Remove the cylinder head cover (valve cover), the gasket, the rocker arm assembly, and the pushrods.

NOTE: *The push rods must be replaced in their original positions.*

3. Remove the intake and exhaust manifold from the cylinder head.
4. Disconnect the spark plug wires and remove the spark plugs to avoid damaging them.
5. Disconnect the temperature sending unit wire, ignition coil and bracket assembly and battery ground cable from the engine.
6. Remove the cylinder head bolts, the cylinder head and gasket from the block.

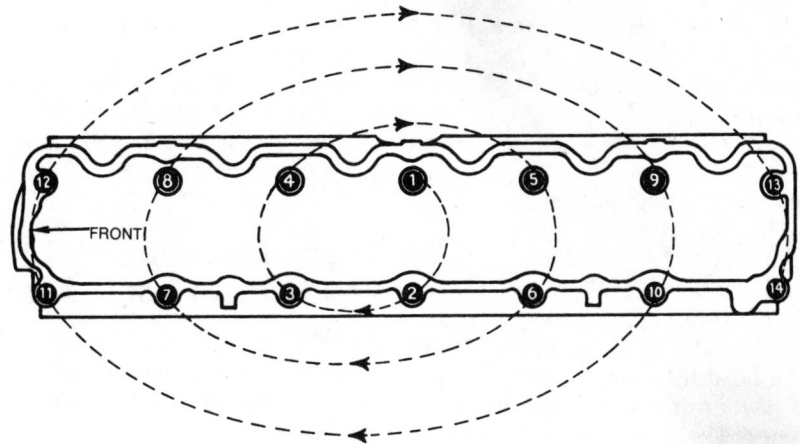

Inline six cylinder head torque sequence

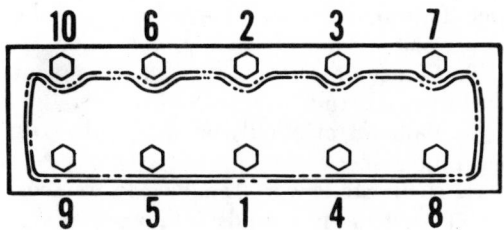

4-151 cylinder head torque sequence

7. To install reverse the procedure. Tighten the headbolts to the specified torque, in the proper sequence.

304 V8

1. Drain the cooling system and cylinder block.

2. When removing the right cylinder head, it may be necessary to remove the heater core housing from the firewall.

3. Remove the valve cover(s) and gasket(s).

4. Remove the rocker arm assemblies and the push rods.

NOTE: *The valve train components must be replaced in their original positions.*

5. Remove the spark plugs to avoid damaging them.

6. Remove the intake manifold with the carburetor still attached.

7. Remove the exhaust pipes at the flange of the exhaust manifold. When replacing the exhaust pipes it is advisable to install new gaskets at the flange.

8. Loosen all of the drive belts.

9. Disconnect the battery ground cable and alternator bracket from the right cylinder head.

10. Disconnect the air pump and power steering pump brackets from the left cylinder head.

11. Remove the cylinder head bolts and lift the head(s) from the cylinder block.

12. Remove the cylinder head gasket from the head or the block.

13. To install, reverse the above procedure.

NOTE: *Apply an even coat of sealing compound to both sides of the new head gasket only. Wire brush the cylinder head bolts,*

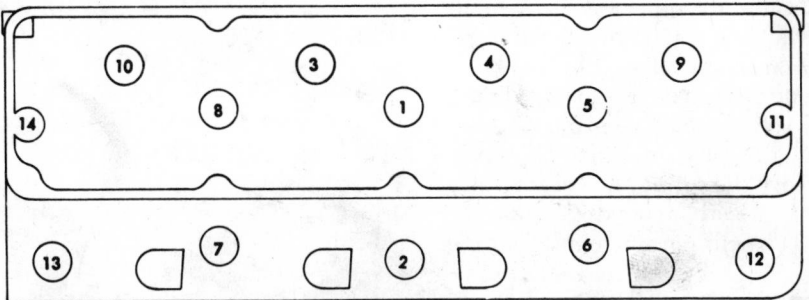

V8 cylinder head torque sequence

then lightly oil them prior to installation. First, tighten all bolts to 80 ft. lbs. then tighten to the specified torque. Follow the correct sequence.

OVERHAUL

See the engine rebuilding section.

L and F Head Engines

In the L-head engine, all of the valves are in the block. In the F-head, the intake valve are in the head; the exhaust in the block. After removing the head from the cylinder block, remove the valves from the cylinder head on F-head engines. These valves are the intake valves, and are removed in the following manner:

1. Depress the valve spring with a valve spring tool.
2. Remove the valve spring retainer locks.
3. Remove the rubber O-ring from the top of the valve.
4. Remove the valve spring retainer and the valve spring from the head.
5. Remove the valve from the head.
6. Replace the valves by reversing the above procedure.

NOTE: *All of the valves must be replaced in their original positions. Even though the F-head exhaust valves and all of the L-head valves are located in the block of the engine and not the head the procedure for removing them will be given here.*

1. Remove the attaching bolts from the side valve spring cover. Remove the side valve spring cover and gasket.
2. Use rags to block off the three holes in the exhaust chamber to prevent the valve retaining locks from falling into the crankcase, should they be accidentally dropped.
3. Using a valve spring compressor, compress the valve springs only on those valves which are in the closed position (valve seated against the head). Remove the valve spring retainer locks, the retainer, and the exhaust valve spring. Close the other valves by rotating the camshaft and repeat the above operation for the remaining valves.
4. Lift all of the valves from the cylinder block. If the valve cannot be removed from the block, pull the valve upward as far as possible and remove the spring. Lower the valve and remove any carbon deposits from the valve stem. This will permit removal of the valve.
5. Install by reversing the above procedure.

NOTE: *All of the valves must be replaced in their original positions. Do not get the exhaust and intake valve springs mixed. They are not interchangeable.*

Refer to the engine rebuilding section for further servicing of the cylinder head and its components.

Intake Manifold

REMOVAL AND INSTALLATION

L-Head

The intake and exhaust manifolds are bolted together and are easiest removed as an assembly.

1. On models so equipped, remove the crankcase ventilator tube which runs from the ventilator valve mounted in the intake manifold to an elbow mounted on the valve cover plate.
2. Remove the seven nuts from the manifold-to-block studs.
3. Pull the manifolds off the studs. Discard the gasket.
4. If the studs were removed for replacement, coat the new studs with a sealer such as Permatex® No. 2, prior to installation.
5. Place a new gasket in position on the studs and carefully slide the manifolds on. Torque to 29–35 ft. lb. in a circular pattern from the ends toward the center.

F-Head

On the F-head engine the intake manifold is cast as an integral part of the head.

4-151

1. Remove battery negative cable.
2. Remove air cleaner and PCV valve hose.

WARNING: *DO NOT remove block drain*

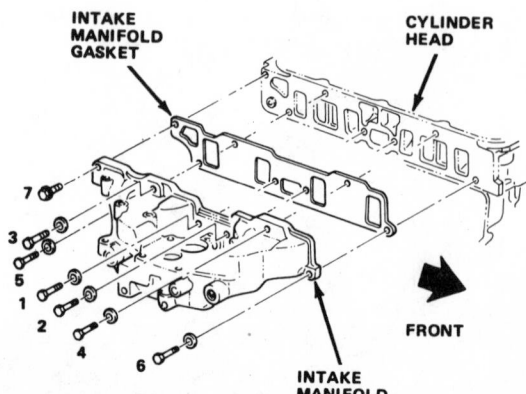

4-151 intake manifold bolt tightening sequence

plugs or loosen radiator draincock with system hot and under pressure because serious burns from coolant can occur.

3. Drain cooling system.

NOTE: *DO NOT WASTE reusable coolant. If solution is clean, drain into a clean container for reuse.*

4. Tag and remove vacuum hoses (ensure distributor vacuum advance hose is removed).

5. Disconnect fuel pipe and electrical wire connections from carburetor.

6. Disconnect carburetor throttle linkage. Remove carburetor and carburetor spacer.

7. Remove bellcrank and throttle linkage brackets and move to one side for clearance.

8. Remove heater hose at intake manifold.

9. Remove alternator. Note position of spacers for installation.

10. Remove manifold-to-cylinder head bolts and remove manifold.

11. Position replacement gasket and install replacement manifold on cylinder head. Start all bolts.

12. Tighten all bolts with 37 foot-pounds torque.

13. Connect heater hose to intake manifold.

14. Install bellcrank and throttle linkage brackets.

15. Connect carburetor throttle linkage to brackets and bellcrank.

16. Install carburetor spacer and tighten bolts with 15 foot-pounds torque.

17. Install carburetor and gasket. Tighten nuts with 15 foot-pounds torque.

18. Install fuel pipe and electrical wire connections. Install vacuum hoses.

19. Install battery negative cable.

WARNING: *Use extreme caution when engine is operating. Do not stand in direct line with fan. Do not put hands near pulleys, belts or fan. Do not wear loose clothing.*

20. Refill cooling system. Start engine and inspect for leaks.

21. Install air cleaner and PCV valve hose.

V6

1. Drain the cooling system.

2. Disconnect the crankcase vent hose, distributor vacuum hose, and the fuel line from the carburetor.

3. Disconnect the two distributor leads from the coil.

4. Disconnect the wire from the temperature sending unit.

5. Remove the ten cap bolts that hold the intake manifold to the cylinder head. They *must* be replaced in their original location.

6. Remove the intake manifold assembly and gasket from the engine.

7. Reverse the above procedure for installation. Tighten the bolts to the correct torque, and in the proper sequence.

232, 258 Sixes

The intake manifold and exhaust manifold are mounted externally on the left side of the engine and are attached to the cylinder head. The intake and exhaust manifolds are removed as a unit. On some engines, an exhaust gas recirculation valve is mounted on the side of the intake manifold.

1. Remove the air cleaner and carburetor.

2. Disconnect the accelerator cable from the accelerator bellcrank.

3. Disconnect the PCV vacuum hose from the intake manifold.

4. Disconnect the distributor vacuum hose and electrical wires at the TCS solenoid vacuum valve.

5. Remove the TCS solenoid vacuum valve and bracket from the intake manifold. In some cases it might not be necessary to remove the TCS unit.

6. If so equipped, disconnect the EGR valve vacuum hoses.

7. Remove the power steering mounting bracket and pump and set it aside without disconnecting the hoses.

8. Remove the EGR valve, if so equipped.

9. Disconnect the exhaust pipe from the manifold flange. Disconnect the spark CTO hoses and remove the oxygen sensor.

10. Remove the manifold attaching bolts, nuts and clamps.

11. Separate the intake manifold and exhaust manifold from the engine as an assembly. Discard the gasket.

12. If either manifold is to be replaced, they should be separated at the heat riser area.

13. Clean the mating surfaces of the manifolds and the cylinder head before replacing the manifolds. Replace them in reverse order of the above procedure with a new gasket. Tighten the bolts and nuts to the specified torque in the proper sequence.

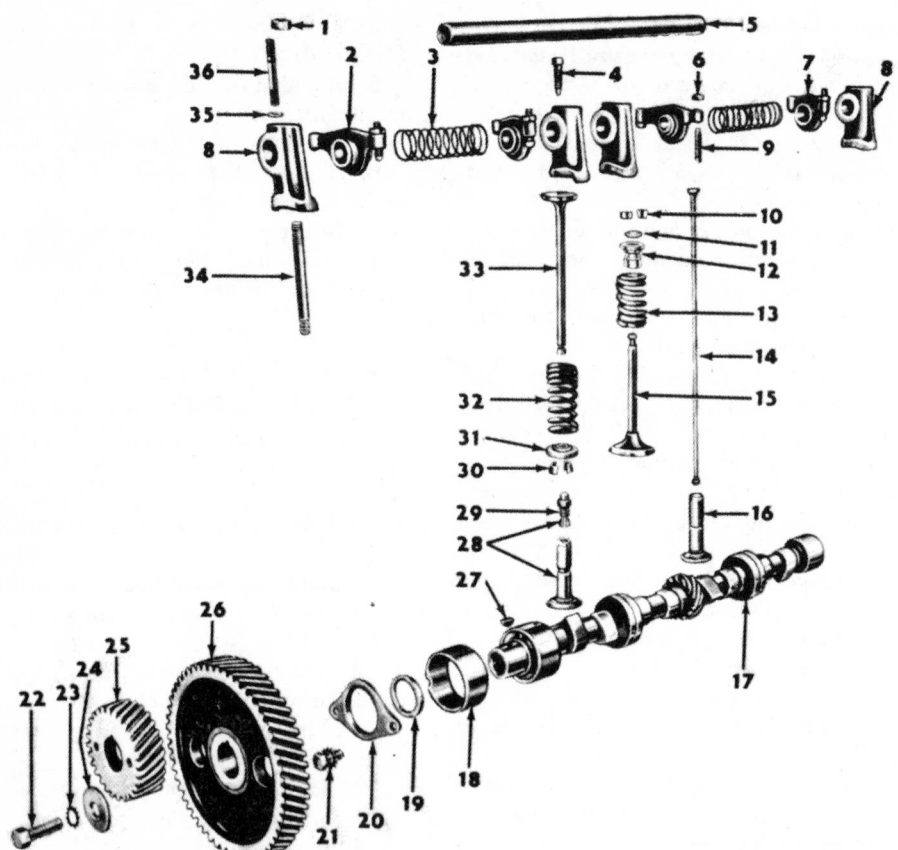

1. Nut
2. Left rocker arm
3. Rocker arm shaft spring
4. Rocker shaft lock screw
5. Rocker shaft
6. Nut
7. Right rocker arm
8. Rocker arm shaft bracket
9. Intake valve tappet adjusting screw
10. Intake valve upper retainer lock
11. Oil seal
12. Intake valve spring upper retainer
13. Intake valve spring
14. Intake valve push rod
15. Intake valve
16. Intake valve tappet
17. Camshaft
18. Camshaft front bearing
19. Camshaft thrust plate spacer
20. Camshaft thrust plate
21. Bolt and lock washer
22. Bolt
23. Lockwasher
24. Camshaft gear washer
25. Crankshaft gear
26. Camshaft gear
27. Woodruff key No. 9
28. Exhaust valve tappet
29. Tappet adjusting screw
30. Spring retainer lock
31. Roto cap assembly
32. Exhaust valve spring
33. Exhaust valve
34. Rocker shaft support stud
35. Washer
36. Rocker arm cover stud

F-head valve train

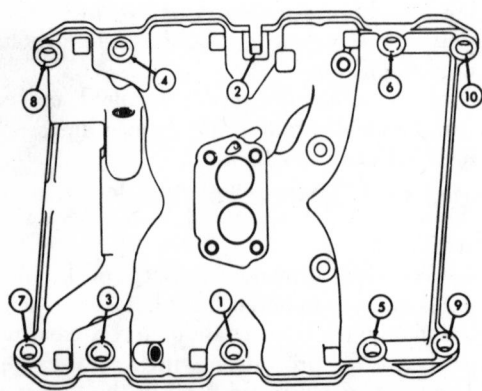

V6 intake manifold torque sequence

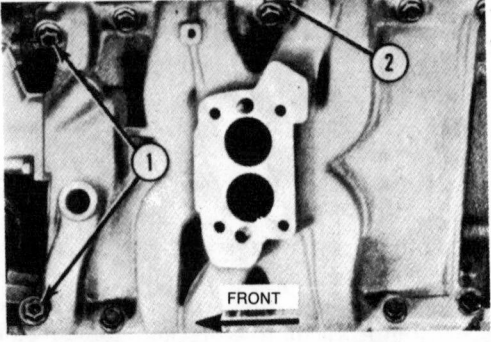

1. Long bolt   2. Open bolt

Replace the bolts in their original locations on the V6 intake manifold

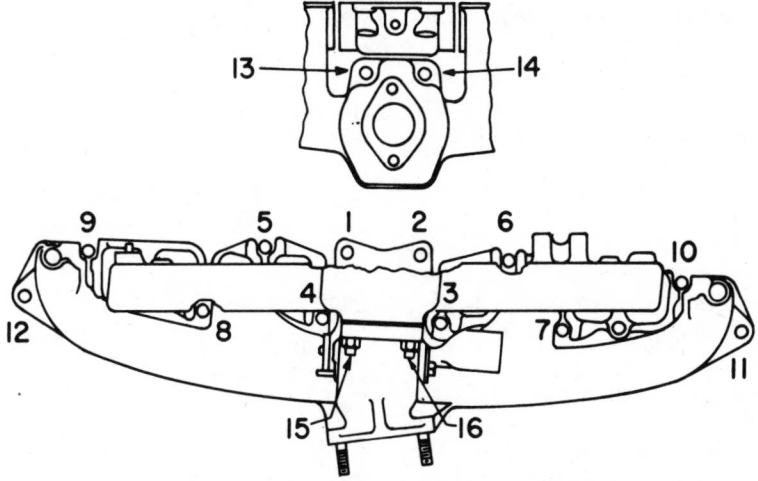

Inline six intake manifold torque sequence

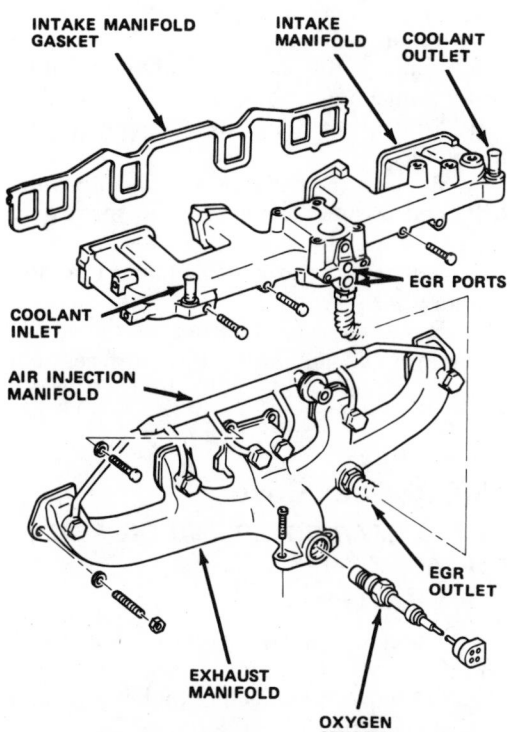

Intake and exhaust manifolds on 6-258 engines with oxygen sensor

304 V8

1. Drain the coolant from the radiator.

2. Remove the air cleaner assembly.

3. Disconnect the spark plug wires. Remove the spark plug wire brackets from the valve covers, and the bypass valve bracket.

4. Disconnect the upper radiator hose and the by-pass hose from the intake manifold. Disconnect the heater hose from the rear of the manifold.

5. Disconnect the ignition coil bracket and lay the coil aside.

6. Disconnect the TCS solenoid vacuum valve from the right side valve cover.

7. Disconnect all lines, hoses, linkages and wires from the carburetor and intake manifold and TCS components as required.

8. Disconnect the air delivery hoses at the air distribution manifolds.

9. Disconnect the air pump diverter valve and lay the valve and the bracket assembly, including the hoses, forward of the engine.

10. Remove the intake manifold after removing the cap bolts that hold it in place. Remove and discard the side gaskets and the end seals.

11. Clean the mating surfaces of the intake manifold and the cylinder head before replacing the intake manifold. Use new gaskets and tighten the cap bolts to the correct torque. Install in reverse order of the above procedure.

NOTE: *There is no specified tightening sequence for this intake manifold. Start at the center bolts and work outward.*

Exhaust Manifolds

REMOVAL AND INSTALLATION

L-Head

See Intake Manifolds.

F-Head

1. Remove the air delivery hose from the air injection tube assembly if the engine is so equipped. If not, proceed to step two.

2. Remove the five nuts from the manifold studs.

3. Pull the manifold from the mounting studs. Be careful not to damage the air injection tubes if the engine is equipped with an air pump.

4. Remove the gaskets from the cylinder block.

5. If the exhaust manifold is to be replaced it will be necessary to remove the air injection tubes from the exhaust manifold. The application of heat may be necessary to aid removal.

6. Use new gaskets when replacing the exhaust manifold. Make sure that the mating surfaces of both the exhaust manifold and the cylinder head are clean. Tighten the attaching nuts to the correct torque specification. Replace in reverse order of the above procedure.

4-151

1. Remove air cleaner and heated air tube.

2. Remove engine oil dipstick tube attaching bolt.

3. Remove oxygen sensor, if equipped.

4. Raise vehicle and disconnect exhaust pipe from manifold. Lower vehicle.

5. Remove exhaust manifold bolts and remove manifold and gasket.

6. Install replacement gasket and exhaust manifold on cylinder head. Tighten all bolts to 39 foot-pounds torque.

7. Install dipstick tube attaching bolt.

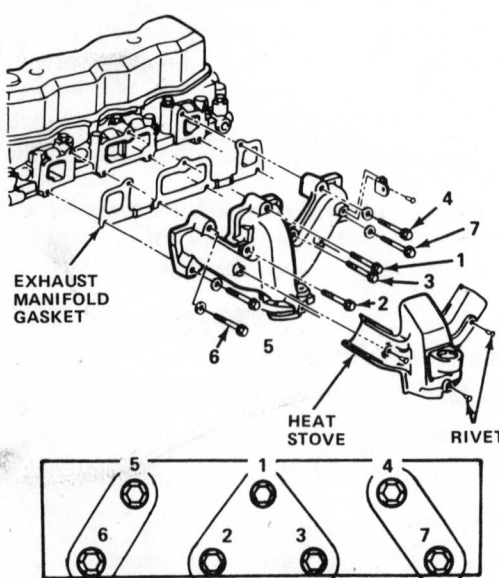

4-151 exhaust manifold bolt tightening sequence

V6

1. Remove the five attaching screws, one nut, and exhaust manifold from the side of the cylinder head.

2. Use a new gasket when replacing the exhaust manifolds. Make sure that the mating surfaces of the manifold and the cylinder head are clean. Tighten the manifold nuts and bolts to the correct torque.

232, 258 Sixes

The intake and exhaust manifolds of the 232 and 258 cu in. Sixes must be removed together. See the procedure for removing and installing the intake manifold.

304 V8

1. Disconnect the spark plug wires.

2. Disconnect the air delivery hose at the distribution manifold.

3. Remove the air distribution manifold and the injection trubes.

4. Disconnect the exhaust pipe at the manifold.

5. Remove the exhaust manifold attaching bolts and washers along with the spark plug shields.

6. Separate the exhaust manifold from the cylinder head.

7. Install in reverse order of the above procedure. Clean the mating surfaces and tighten the attaching bolts to the correct torque.

Timing Gear Cover

TIMING GEAR COVER AND OIL SEAL REPLACEMENT

L and F-Head

1. Remove the drive belts and crankshaft pulley.

2. Remove the attaching bolts, nuts and lock washers that hold the timing gear cover to the engine.

3. Remove the timing gear cover.

4. Remove the timing pointer.

5. Remove the timing gear cover gasket.

6. Remove and discard the crankshaft oil seal from the timing gear cover.

7. Replace in reverse order of the above procedure. Replace the crankshaft oil seal. Use a new timing gear cover gasket.

4-151

1. Disconnect the battery ground.

2. Remove the crankshaft pulley hub.

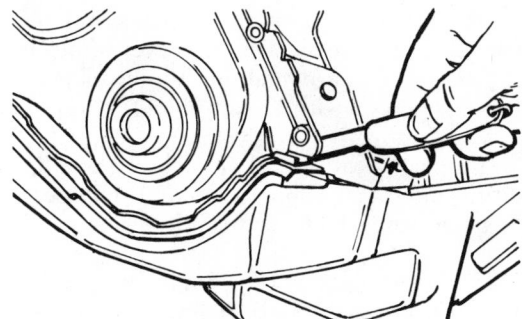

Cutting the pan gasket on 4-151 engines

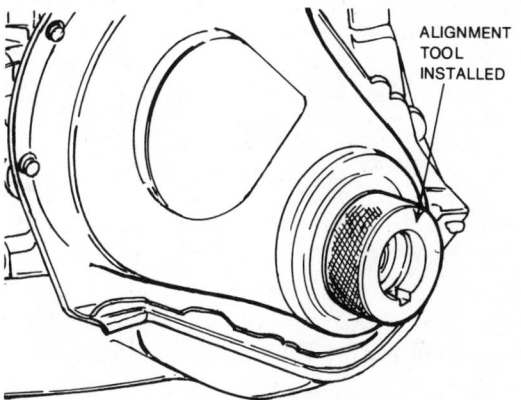

Timing case cover alignment tool installed on 4-151 engines

3. Remove the alternator bracket.

4. Remove the fan and radiator shroud.

5. Remove the oil pan-to-timing case cover bolts.

6. Pull the cover forward just enough to allow cutting the oil pan front seal flush with the block on both sides of the cover. Use a sharp knife or razor.

7. Remove the front cover.

8. Clean the gasket surface on the block and cover.

9. Cut the tabs from the new oil pan front seal.

10. Install the seal on the cover, pressing the tips into the holes provided in the cover.

11. Coat a new gasket with sealer and place on the cover.

12. Apply a ⅛ inch bead of RTV sealant to the joint formed at the oil pan and block.

13. Install an aligning tool such as tool J-23042 in the timing case cover seal.

NOTE: *It is important that an aligning tool*

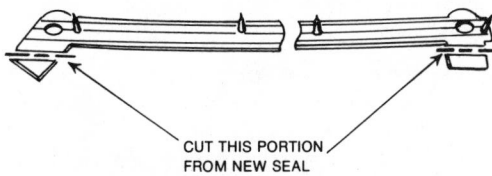

CUT THIS PORTION FROM NEW SEAL

4-151 oil pan seal modification

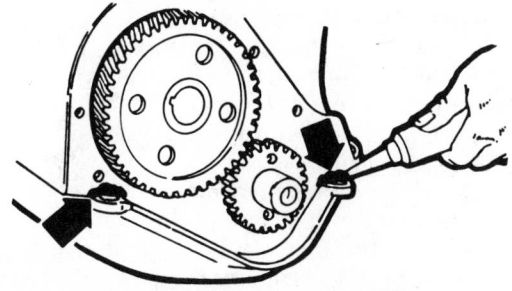

Applying RTV sealant on 4-151 engines

is used to avoid seal damage and to ensure a tight, even seal fit.

14. Position the cover on the block and partially tighten the two oil pan-to-cover bolts.

15. Install the remaining bolts, and tighten all bolts to 45 in. lb.

16. Install all other parts in reverse order of removal. Torque the fan assembly bolts to 18 ft. lb.

V6

1. Remove the water pump and crankshaft pulley.

2. Remove the two bolts that attach the oil pan to the timing chain cover.

3. Remove the five bolts that attach the timing chain cover to the engine block.

4. Remove the cover and gasket.

5. Remove the crankshaft front oil seal.

6. From the rear of the timing chain cover, coil new packing around the crankshaft hole in the cover so that the ends of the packing are at the top. Drive in the new packing with a punch. It will be necessary to ream out the hole to obtain clearance for the crankshaft vibration damper hub.

232, 258 Sixes

COVER REMOVED

1. Remove the drive belts, engine fan and hub assembly, the accessory pulley, and vibration damper.

2. Remove the oil pan to timing chain cover screws and the screws that attach the cover to the block.

3. Raise the timing chain cover just high enough to detach the retaining nibs of the oil pan neoprene seal from the bottom side of the cover. This must be done to prevent pull-

CUT HERE

CUT HERE

Trim the timing gear cover gasket as indicated before installation on inline sixes

ing the seal end tabs away from the tongues of the oil pan gaskets which would cause a leak.

4. Remove the timing chain cover and gasket from the engine.

5. Use a razor blade to cut off the oil pan seal end tabs flush with the front face of the cylinder block and remove the seal. Clean the timing chain cover, oil pan, and cylinder block surfaces.

6. Apply seal compound (Perfect Seal, or equivalent) to both sides of replacement timing case cover gasket and position gasket on cylinder block.

7. Cut end tabs off replacement oil pan gasket corresponding to pieces cut off original gasket. Cement these pieces on oil pan.

8. Coat oil pan seal end tabs generously with Permatex No. 2, or equivalent, and position seal on timing case cover.

9. Position timing case cover on engine. Place Timing Case Cover Alignment Tool and Seal Installer J-22248 in crankshaft opening of cover.

10. Install cover-to-block screws and oil pan-to-cover screws. Tighten cover-to-block screws with 5 foot-pounds torque and oil pan-to-cover screws with 11 foot-pounds torque.

11. Remove cover aligning tool and position replacement oil seal on tool with seal lip facing outward. Apply light film of Perfect Seal, or equivalent, on outside diameter of seal.

12. Insert draw screw from Tool J-9163 into seal installing tool. Tighten nut against tool until tool contacts cover.

13. Remove tools and apply light film of engine oil to seal lip.

14. Install vibration damper and tighten retaining screw with 80 foot-pounds torque.

15. Install damper pulley. Tighten capscrews with 20 foot-pounds torque.

16. Install engine fan and hub assembly.

17. Install drive belt(s).

COVER INSTALLED

1. Remove drive belts.
2. Remove vibration damper pulley.
3. Remove vibration damper.
4. Remove oil seal with Tool J-9256.

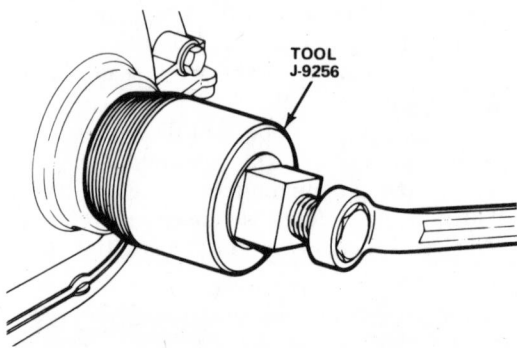

TOOL
J-9256

6-258 timing case cover oil seal removal

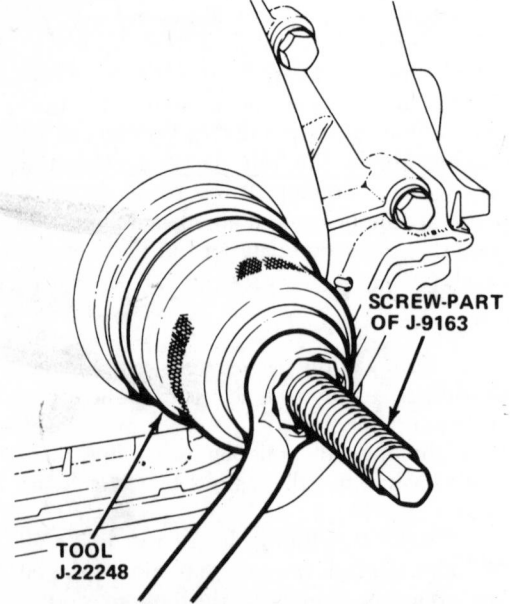

SCREW-PART
OF J-9163

TOOL
J-22248

Timing case oil seal installation, 6-258 engines

5. Position replacement oil seal on Timing Case Cover Alignment Tool and Seal Installer J-22248 with seal lip facing outward. Apply light film of Perfect Seal, or equivalent, to outside diameter of seal.

6. Insert draw screw from Tool J-9163 into seal installing tool. Tighten nut against tool until tool contacts cover.

7. Remove tools. Apply light film of engine oil to seal lip.

8. Install vibration damper and tighten retaining bolt with 80 foot-pounds torque.

9. Install damper pulley. Tighten capscrews with 20 foot-pounds torque.

10. Install drive belt(s).

304 V8

1. Remove the negative battery cable.

2. Drain the cooling system and disconnect the radiator hoses and by-pass hose.

3. Remove all of the drive belts and the fan and spacer assembly.

4. Remove the alternator and the front portion of the alternator bracket as an assembly.

5. Disconnect the heater hose.

6. Remove the power steering pump, and/or the air pump, and the mounting bracket as an assembly. Do not disconnect the power steering hoses.

7. Remove the distributor cap and note the position of the rotor. Remove the distributor. (See the Engine Electrical Section.)

8. Remove the fuel pump.

9. Remove the vibration damper and pulley.

10. Remove the two front oil pan bolts and the bolts which secure the timing chain cover to the engine block.

NOTE: *The timing gear cover retaining bolts vary in length and must be installed in the same locations from which they were removed.*

11. Remove the cover by pulling forward until it is free of the locating dowel pins.

12. Clean the gasket surface of the cover and the engine block.

13. Pry out the original seal from inside the timing chain cover and clean the seal bore.

14. Drive the new seal into place from the inside with a block of wood until it contacts the outer flange of the cover.

15. Apply a light film of motor oil to the lips of the new seal.

16. Before reinstalling the timing gear

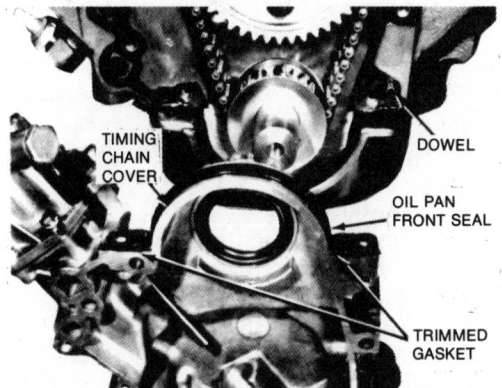

Trim the timing gear cover gasket as indicated before installation on the V8

cover, remove the lower locating dowel pin from the engine block. The pin is required for correct alignment of the cover and must either be reused or a replacement dowel pin installed after the cover is in position.

17. Cut both sides of the oil pan gasket flush with the engine block with a razor blade.

18. Trim a new gasket to correspond to the amount cut off at the oil pan.

19. Apply sealer to both sides of the new gasket and install the gasket on the timing case cover.

20. Install the new front oil pan seal.

21. Align the tongues of the new oil pan gasket pieces with the oil pan seal and cement them into place on the cover.

22. Apply a bead of sealer to the cutoff edges of the original oil pan gaskets.

23. Place the timing case cover into position and install the front oil pan bolts. Tighten the bolts slowly and evenly until the cover aligns with the upper locating dowel.

24. Install the lower dowel through the cover and drive it into the corresponding hole in the engine block.

25. Install the cover retaining bolts in the same locations from which they were removed. Tighten to 25 ft. lbs.

26. Assemble the remaining components in the reverse order of removal.

Timing Chain or Gears and Tensioner

REMOVAL AND INSTALLATION

L-Head in CJ-2A Models Before Engine #175402

1. Remove the timing chain cover.

2. Pull the sprockets forward alternately and evenly until they are free.

3. On installation, align the timing marks on the sprockets. Check the end float between the crankshaft sprocket and the thrust plate. Clearance should be .004–.008 in. Camshaft gear-to-thrust plate clearance is .003–.0055 in. Both clearances are adjustable by shim packs. Check, also, the running clearances between the gears. Proper clearance is 0–.002 in.

4. Adjust the valve timing.

L-head After Engine #175402 and All F-head

1. Remove the timing gear cover.

2. Use a puller to remove both the crank-

Timing gear alignment on 4-134 engines before engine #175402

4-134 timing gear alignment for engines after #175402

shaft and the camshaft gear from the engine after removing all attaching nuts and bolts.

3. Remove the Woodruff keys.

Installation is as follows:

1. Install the Woodruff key in the longer of the two keyways on the front end of the crankshaft.

2. Install the crankshaft timing gear on the front end of the crankshaft with the timing mark facing away from the cylinder block.

3. Align the keyway in the gear with the Woodruff key and then drive or press the gear onto the crankshaft firmly against the thrust washer.

4. Turn the camshaft or the crankshaft as

necessary so that the timing marks on the two gears will be together after the camshaft gear is installed.

5. Install the Woodruff key in the keyway on the front of the camshaft.

6. Start the large timing gear on the camshaft with the timing mark facing out.

NOTE: *Do not drive the gear onto the camshaft as the camshaft may drive the plug out of the rear of the engine and cause an oil leak.*

7. Install the camshaft retaining screw and torque it to 30–40 ft. lbs. This will draw the gear onto the camshaft as the screw is tightened. Standard running tolerance between the timing gears is 0.000 to 0.002 in. Adjust the valve timing.

4-151

NOTE: *Removal of the camshaft gear requires a special adapter #J-971 and the use of a press. Camshaft removal is necessary.*

1. Place the adapter on the press and place the camshaft through the opening.

2. Press the shaft out of the gear using a socket or other suitable tool.

CAUTION: *The thrust plate must be in position so that the woodruff key does not damage the gear when the shaft is pressed out.*

3. To install the gear firmly support the shaft at the back of the front journal in an arbor press using press plate adapters J-21474-13 or J-21795-1.

4. Place the gear spacer ring and thrust plate over the end of the shaft, and install the woodruff key in the shaft keyway.

5. Install the camshaft gear and press it onto the shaft until it bottoms against the

1. Puller   2. Camshaft gear

Pulling the 4-134 valve timing gears for engines after #175402

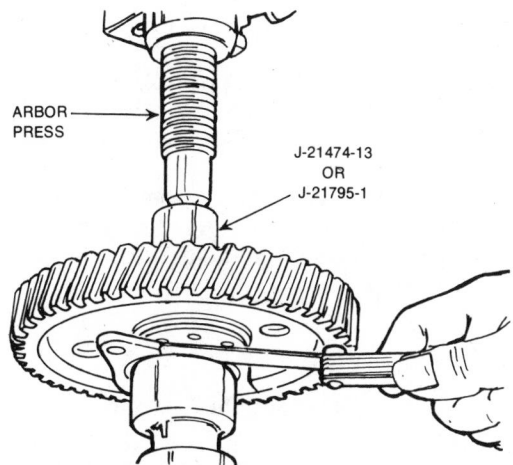

Installing 4-151 camshaft timing gear and measuring thrust plate end clearance

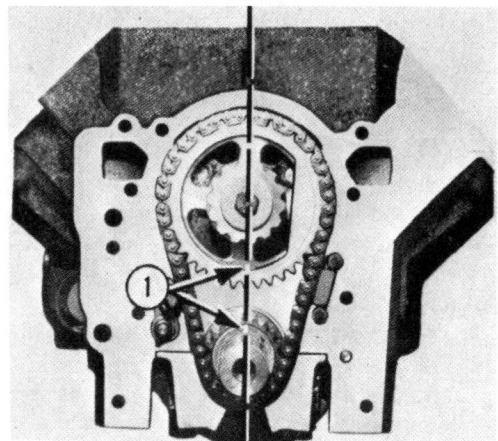

V6 valve timing sprocket alignment

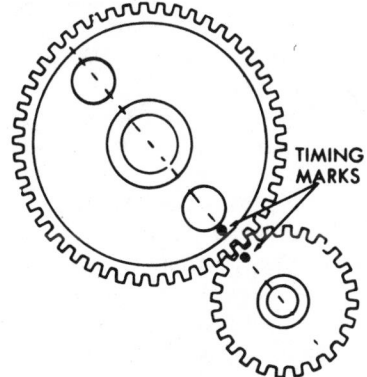

4-151 timing mark alignment

gear spacer ring. The end clearance of the thrust plate should be .0015″ to .0050″. If less than .0015″, the spacer ring should be replaced. If more than .0050″, the thrust plate should be replaced.

V6

1. Remove the timing chain cover.
2. Make sure that the timing marks on the crankshaft and the camshaft sprockets are aligned. This will make installing the parts easier.
NOTE: *It is not necessary to remove the timing chain dampers (tensioners) unless they are worn or damaged and require replacement.*
3. Remove the front crankshaft oil slinger.
4. Remove the bolt and the special washer that hold the camshaft distributor drive gear and fuel pump eccentric at the forward end of the camshaft. Remove the eccentric and the gear from the camshaft.

5. Alternately pry forward the camshaft sprocket and then the crankshaft sprocket until the camshaft sprocket is pried from the camshaft.
6. Remove the camshaft sprocket, sprocket key, and timing chain from the engine.
7. Pry the crankshaft sprocket from the crankshaft.
Install as follows:
1. If the engine has not been disturbed proceed to step Number 4 for installation procedures.
2. If the engine has been disturbed turn the crankshaft so that number one piston is at top dead center.
3. Temporarily install the sprocket key and the camshaft sprocket on the camshaft. Turn the camshaft so that the index mark of the sprocket is downward. Remove the key and sprocket from the camshaft.
4. Assemble the timing chain and sprockets. Install the keys, sprockets, and chain assembly on the camshaft and crankshaft so that the index marks of both the sprockets are aligned.
NOTE: *It will be necessary to hold the spring loaded timing chain damper out of the way while installing the timing chain and sprocket assembly.*
5. Install the front oil slinger on the crankshaft with the inside diameter against the sprocket (concave side toward the front of the engine).
6. Install the fuel pump eccentric on the camshaft and the key, with the oil groove of the eccentric forward.
7. Install the distributor drive gear on the camshaft. Secure the gear and eccentric to

the camshaft with the retaining washer and bolt.

8. Torque the bolt to 40–55 ft. lbs.

232, 258 Sixes

1. Remove the drive belts, engine fan and hub assembly, accessory pulley, vibration damper and timing chain cover.

2. Remove the oil seal from the timing chain cover.

3. Remove the camshaft sprocket retaining bolt and washer.

4. Rotate the crankshaft until the timing mark on the crankshaft sprocket is closest to and in a center line with the timing pointer of the camshaft sprocket.

5. Remove the crankshaft sprocket, camshaft sprocket and timing chain as an assembly. Disassemble the chain and sprockets.

Installation is as follows:

1. Assemble the timing chain, crankshaft sprocket and camshaft sprocket with the timing marks aligned.

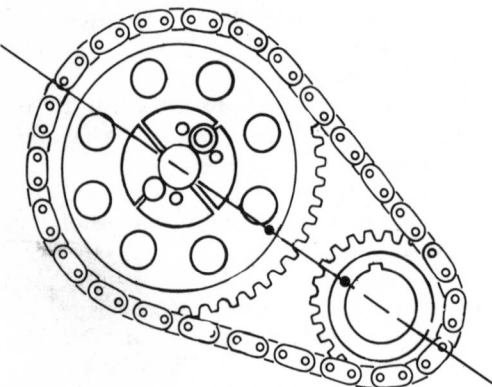

Timing gear alignment on the 6-232, 258

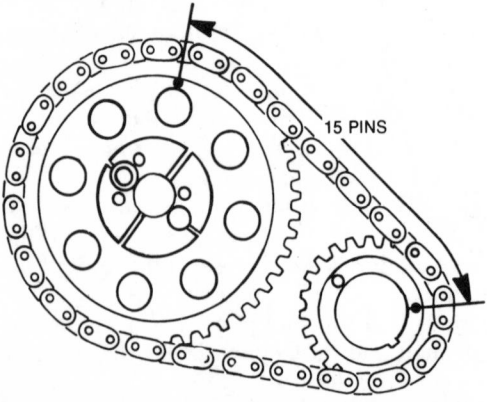

Correct timing chain installation verification, 6-232, 258

2. Install the assembly to the crankshaft and the camshaft.

3. Install the camshaft sprocket retaining bolt and washer and tighten to 45–55 ft. lbs.

4. Install the timing chain cover and a new oil seal.

5. Install the vibration damper, accessory pulley, engine fan and hub assembly and drive belts. Tighten the belts to the proper tension.

304 V8

1. Remove the timing chain cover and gasket.

2. Remove the crankshaft oil slinger.

3. Remove the camshaft sprocket retaining bolt and washer, distributor drive gear and fuel pump eccentric.

4. Rotate the crankshaft until the timing mark on the crankshaft sprocket is adjacent to, and on a center line with, the timing mark on the camshaft sprocket.

5. Remove the crankshaft sprocket, camshaft sprocket and timing chain as an assembly.

6. Clean all of the gasket surfaces.

Installation is as follows:

1. Assemble the timing chain, crankshaft sprocket and camshaft sprocket with the timing marks on both sprockets aligned.

2. Install the assembly to the crankshaft and the camshaft.

3. Install the fuel pump eccentric, distrib-

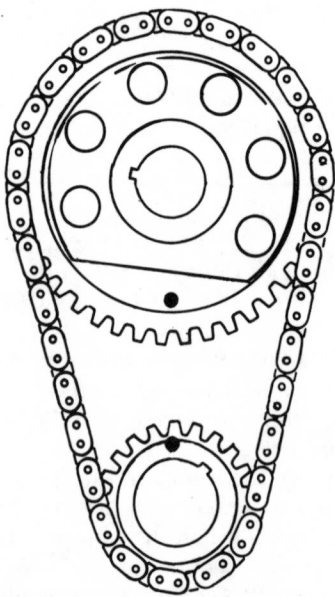

Timing gear alignment on 8-304 engines

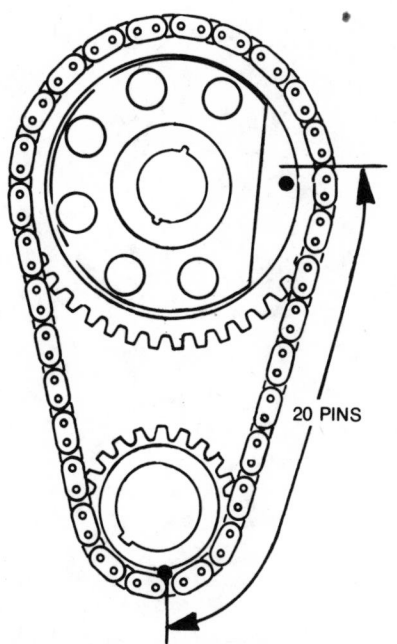

Correct timing chain installation verification, 8-304

utor drive gear, washer and retaining bolt. Tighten the bolt to 25–35 ft. lbs.

4. Install the crankshaft oil slinger.

5. Install the timing chain cover using a new gasket and oil seal.

NOTE: *In mid-year 1979, a new timing chain, camshaft sprocket and crankshaft sprocket were phased into production on all 8-304 engines. These are offered as replacement parts for older engines. When installing any one of these parts on an older engine, all three parts must be installed. None of the new parts is useable in conjunction with the older parts. They must be installed as a set. To determine the necessity for a replacement of an older chain, perform the following deflection test:*

1. Remove the timing case cover.

2. Rotate the sprockets until all slack is removed from the right side of the chain.

3. Locate the dowel on the lower left side of the engine and measure up ¾ in. Make a mark.

4. Measure across the chain with a straightedge from the mark to a point at the bottom of the camshaft sprocket.

5. Grab the chain at the point where the straightedge crosses it. Push the chain left (inward) as far as it will go. Make a mark on the block at this point. Push the chain to the right as far as it will go. Make another mark. Measure between the two marks. Total deflection should not exceed ⅞ in.

6. Replace the chain and sprockets if deflection is not within specifications.

7. Replace the timing case cover.

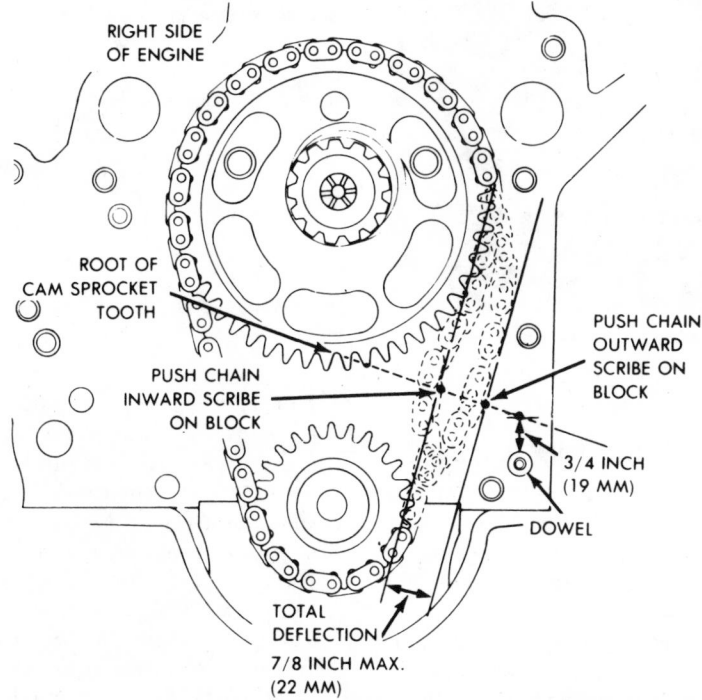

Measuring timing chain deflection on 8-304 engines

Valve Timing

4-134 BEFORE SERIAL NUMBER 175402 (CHAIN-DRIVEN)

1. Turn the crankshaft so that Nos. 1 & 4 piston are at TDC as indicated by the TC mark on the flywheel seen through the timing hole in the right side of the flywheel housing.

2. Place the camshaft sprocket on the shaft and turn the shaft until the punch mark on the rim of the sprocket faces the punchmark on the crankshaft sprocket.

3. Remove the camshaft sprocket and install the sprocket and timing chain. Timing is correct when a line drawn through the sprocket centers, intersects the timing marks on both sprockets.

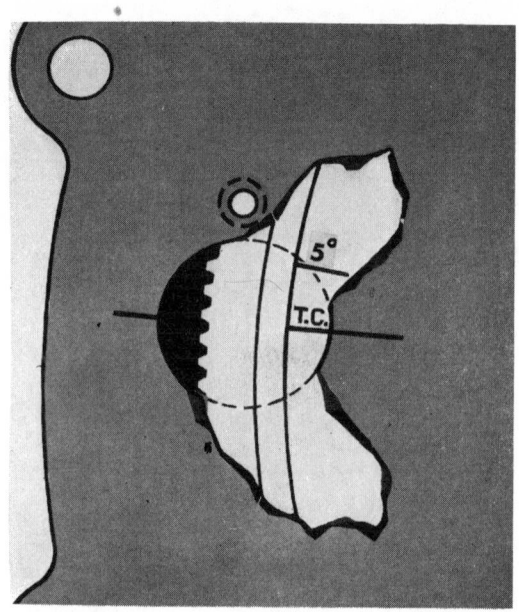

Flywheel timing marks on CJ-2A engines after engine #175402

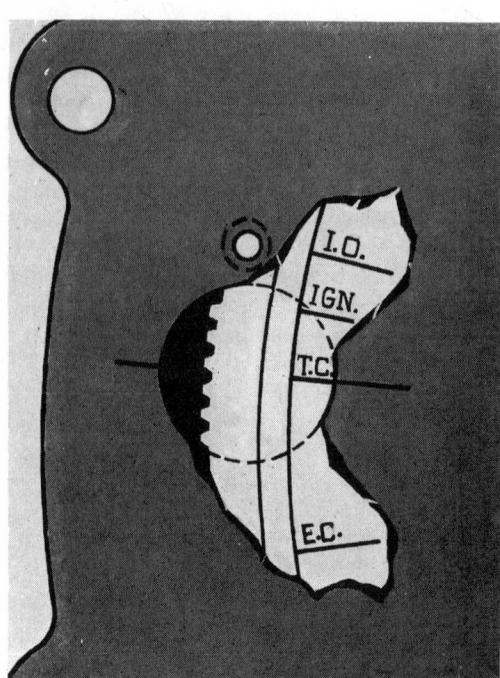

Flywheel timing marks on CJ-2A engines before engine #175402

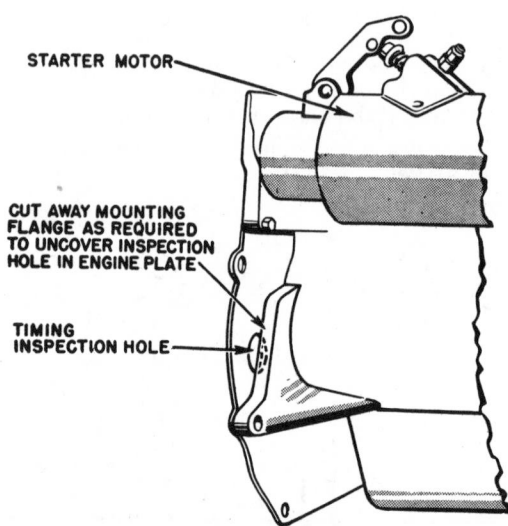

Uncovering timing inspection hole on CJ-3A engines

4-134 AFTER SERIAL NUMBER 175402 (GEAR-DRIVEN)

1. Install the timing gears with the marks aligned as shown.

2. Set the intake valve clearance to .020 in. on the #1 cylinder.

3. Rotate the crankshaft until the #1 cylinder intake valve is ready to open as indicated by the IO mark on the flywheel. The mark should be centered in the hole.

NOTE: *Some later models do not have an IO mark. TC and 5° are the only marks. On these engines, the intake valve opens at 9° BTC. To estimate valve opening, measure the distance between TC and 5° and measure about that distance further on.*

NOTE: *On CJ-3A models beginning with engine #130859, a 4½ inch starter motor was used. To use the larger starter, it was necessary to increase the width of the cylinder block flange, partially covering the flywheel hole. This makes it impossible to use the hole for timing purposes. In this event, use the timing marks on the crankshaft pulley. If a replacement block is installed with the later design in a vehicle originally equipped with the earlier design timing marks, it will be necessary to cut away enough of the flange to allow a view of the timing marks, as no other timing marks exist on these early engines.*

Camshaft
REMOVAL AND INSTALLATION
L and F-Head

1. Remove the engine.
2. Remove the exhaust manifold.
3. Remove the oil pump and the distributor.
4. Remove the crankshaft pulley.
5. Remove the cylinder head.
6. Remove the exhaust valves.
7. Remove the timing gear cover and the crankshaft and camshaft timing gears.
8. Remove the front end plate.
9. Push the intake and exhaust valve lifters into the cylinder block as far as possible so that the ends of the lifters are not in contact with the camshaft.
10. Secure each tappet in the raised position by installing a clip-type clothes pin on the shank of each tappet or tie them up in the valve chamber.
11. Remove the camshaft thrust plate attaching screws. Remove the camshaft thrust plate and spacer.
12. Pull the camshaft forward out of the cylinder block being careful to prevent damage to the camshaft bearing surfaces.
13. Install in the reverse order of the above procedure.

4-151

1. Remove air cleaner.
2. Drain cooling system.
NOTE: *Do not waste reusable coolant. If solution is clean, drain coolant into a clean container for reuse. It may be necessary to attach a flexible hose to the drains to route the coolant to the container.*
3. Remove timing gear cover.
4. Disconnect radiator hoses at radiator. Remove radiator.
5. Remove two camshaft thrust plate screws through holes in camshaft gear.
6. Remove tappets.
7. Remove distributor, oil pump drive and fuel pump.

Removing 4-151 camshaft thrust plate screws

8. Remove camshaft and gear assembly by pulling out through front of block. Support shaft carefully when removing to prevent damaging camshaft bearings.
9. Thoroughly coat camshaft journals with high quality engine oil supplement such as STP or its equivalent.
10. Install camshaft assembly in engine block. Use care to prevent damaging bearings or camshaft.
11. Turn crankshaft and camshaft so that valve timing marks on gear teeth are aligned. Engine is now in number four cylinder firing position. Install camshaft thrust plate-to-block screws and tighten with 75 inch-pounds torque.
12. Install timing gear cover and gasket.
13. Line up keyway in hub with key on crankshaft and slide hub onto shaft. Install center bolt and tighten with 160 foot-pounds torque.
14. Install valve tappets, push rods, push rod cover, oil pump shaft and gear assembly and fuel pump. Install distributor according to following procedure.
   a. Turn crankshaft 360 degrees to firing position of number one cylinder (number one exhaust and intake valve tappets both on base circle (heel) of camshaft and timing notch on vibration damper indexed with top dead center mark [TDC] on timing degree scale).
   b. Install distributor and align shaft so that rotor arm points toward number one cylinder spark plug contact.
15. Install rocker arms and pivot balls over push rods. With tappets on base circle (heel) of camshaft, tighten rocker arm capscrews with 20 foot-pounds torque. Do not over-tighten.
16. Install cylinder head cover.

17. Install intake manifold.

18. Install radiator and lower radiator hose.

19. Install belt, fan and shroud. Tighten fan bolts with 18 foot-pounds torque. Install upper radiator hose. Tighten belts.

V6

1. Remove the engine.

2. Remove the intake manifold and carburetor assembly.

3. Remove the distributor.

4. Remove the fuel pump.

5. Remove the alternator, drive belts, cooling fan, fan pulley, and water pump.

6. Remove the crankshaft pulley and the vibration damper.

7. Remove the oil pump.

8. Remove the timing chain cover.

9. Remove the timing chain and the camshaft sprocket, along with the distributor drive gear and the fuel pump eccentric.

10. Remove the rocker arm assemblies.

NOTE: *The pushrods need not be removed. But if they are, be sure that they are replaced in their original positions.*

11. Lift the tappets up so that they are not in contact with the camshaft. Use wire clips or clip-type clothes pins to hold the tappets up.

12. Carefully guide the camshaft forward out of the engine. Avoid marring the bearing surfaces.

13. Install in reverse order of the above procedure.

232, 258 Sixes

1. Drain the cooling system and remove the radiator. With air conditioning, remove the condenser and receiver assembly as a unit, without disconnecting any lines or discharging the system.

2. Remove the valve cover and gasket, the rocker assemblies, pushrods, cylinder head and gasket and the lifters.

NOTE: *The valve train components must be replaced in their original locations.*

3. Remove the drive belts, cooling fan, fan hub assembly, vibration damper and the timing chain cover.

4. Remove the fuel pump and distributor assembly, including the spark plug wires.

5. Rotate the crankshaft until the timing mark of the crankshaft sprocket is adjacent to, and on a center line with, the timing mark of the camshaft sprocket.

6. Remove the crankshaft sprocket, cam-

shaft sprocket, and the timing chain as an assembly.

7. Remove the front bumper or grille as required and carefully slide out the camshaft.

8. Install in reverse order of the above procedures.

304 V8

1. Disconnect the battery cables.

2. Drain the radiator and both banks of the block. Remove the lower hose at the radiator, the by-pass hose at the pump, the thermostat housing and the radiator. With air conditioning, remove the condenser and receiver assembly as a unit, without disconnecting any lines or discharging the system.

3. Remove the distributor, all wires, and the coil from the manifold.

4. Remove the intake manifold as an assembly.

5. Remove the valve covers, rocker arms and pushrods.

6. Remove the lifters.

NOTE: *The valve train components must be replaced in their original locations.*

7. Remove the cooling fan and hub assembly, fuel pump, and heater hose at the water pump.

8. Remove the alternator and bracket as an assembly. Just move it aside, do not disconnect the wiring.

9. Remove the crankshaft pulley and the damper. Remove the lower radiator hose at the water pump.

10. Remove the timing chain cover.

11. Remove the distributor-oil pump drive gear, fuel pump eccentric, sprockets and the timing chain.

12. Remove the grille.

13. Remove the camshaft carefully by sliding it forward out of the engine.

14. Install by reversing the above procedure.

Crankshaft

REMOVAL AND INSTALLATION

4-134 L and F-Head

1. Remove the engine from the vehicle.

2. Remove the fan, hub, timing cover, pulleys and timing gears from the engine.

3. Slide the thrust washers and adjusting shims from the front end of the crankshaft. Be careful to avoid losing or mismatching the washers and shims!

4. Remove the oil pan and pickup.

5. Pull the two pieces of the rear main cap packing out from the sides of the cap.

6. Note the match marks on the bearing caps and remove the nuts and washers from the cap dowels.

7. Using a pry bar under the ends of each main cap, carefully lift the caps off the dowels. Take great care to avoid damage to the caps or dowels, as bent dowels must be replaced.

8. Note the match marks on the connecting rod caps and remove the bearing caps from the rods.

9. Lift the crankshaft from the block.

10. Lubricate all bearing surfaces generously with clean engine oil.

11. Install the crankshaft and bearing caps. If new bearings are installed, check their fit with Plastigage.

12. Torque all caps to the values shown in the torque specifications chart.

13. Install all other parts in reverse order of removal.

4-151

1. Remove the engine and mount it on a work stand.

2. Remove the spark plugs.

3. Remove the fan and pulley.

4. Remove the vibration damper and hub.

5. Remove the oil pan and oil pump.

6. Remove the timing case cover.

7. Remove the crankshaft timing gear.

8. Remove the connecting rod bearing caps. Mark each for reassembly.

9. Remove the main bearing caps, marking each for reassembly.

10. Remove the crankshaft.

11. Installation is the reverse of removal. Note the following points:

    a. Oil all parts with clean engine oil.

    b. After installing the crankshaft, install the main and rod bearing caps loosely and strike both ends of the crankshaft with a rubber mallet, first the front, then the rear, to center the thrust bearing.

    c. Tighten all bearing caps to the values shown in the torque chart. If new bearings are used, check the clearances with Plastigage.

    d. Make sure timing marks are aligned in timing gears.

V6-225

1. Remove the engine and mount it on a work stand.

2. Remove the flywheel.

3. Remove the fan and hub.

4. Remove the crankshaft pulley and vibration damper.

5. Remove the timing chain and sprocket.

6. Remove the oil pan, and pickup.

7. Remove the connecting rod caps, marking them for reassembly.

8. Mark the main bearing caps.

9. Remove the two bolts from the cap and carefully lift it off with the aid of a pry bar. Similarly remove the next two caps.

10. To remove the last cap, a special tool, main bearing bolt remover W-323 is necessary.

11. Lift the crankshaft from the block.

12. Use new rear main oil seals, and install the crankshaft. Oil all bearing surfaces with clean engine oil.

13. Install all bearing caps loosely, and pry the crankshaft back and forth several times to seat the thrust bearing.

14. If new bearings are used, check the clearances with Plastigage.

15. Install all parts in reverse of removal. Observe the torque values in the torque chart.

6-232, 258 and 8-304

1. Remove the engine from the vehicle and mount it on a work stand.

2. Drain the oil.

3. Remove the flywheel or torque converter, match marking the pieces for installation.

4. Remove all drive belts.

5. Remove the fan and hub assembly.

6. Remove the crankshaft pulley and vibration damper.

7. Remove the timing case cover.

8. Remove the oil pan.

9. Remove the oil pump and pickup.

10. Remove the rod bearing caps, marking them for installation.

11. Remove the main bearing caps, marking them for installation.

12. Lift out the crankshaft.

13. Installation is the reverse of removal. Coat all moving parts with clean engine oil. Observe all torque values listed in the torque chart.

NOTE: *A replacement oil pickup tube must be used. Do not attempt to install the original. Make sure the plastic button is inserted in the bottom of the pickup screen. Always use a new rear main seal. If new bearings are installed, check clearances with Plastigage.*

Pistons and Connecting Rods

REMOVAL AND INSTALLATION

NOTE: *If there is a notch on top of the piston or an F mark anywhere on the piston, it must face to the front of the engine.*

L and F-Head

The pistons and connecting rods can be removed from the engine with the engine in the vehicle. Refer to the engine rebuilding section for the proper procedure. The connecting rod identifying number must be toward the camshaft side of the block. Mark all pistons and rods so that they can be replaced in their original positions.

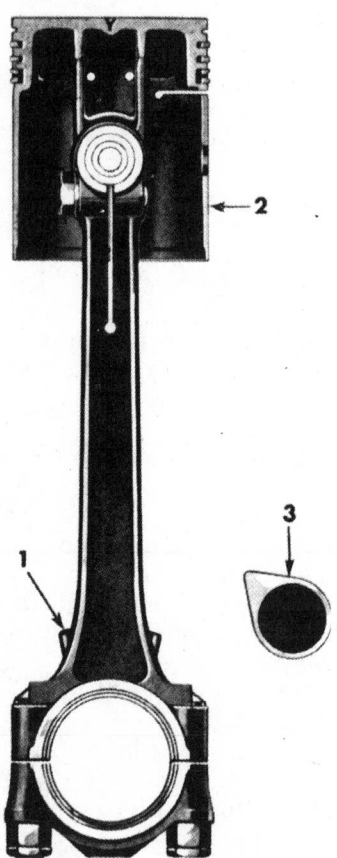

1. Oil spray hole
2. Piston skirt T-slot
3. Relative position of camshaft

4-134 piston and rod assembly

4-151

The letter F, or the notches in the edge of the piston, goes toward the front of the engine.

On the 151 4 cylinder engine the notch on the connecting rod should be opposite the notch on the piston.

V6

Use connecting rod bolt guides on the bolts to hold the upper half of the bearing shell in place when removing the bearing caps and bearings from the lower half of the connecting rods.

Place the notch on the pistons forward and the oil spurt hole in the bottom of the connecting rod facing up.

232, 258 Sixes and 304 V8

The connecting rods and caps are stamped with the number of the cylinder to which they belong. Replace them in their original positions.

The numbered sides and squirt hole must face the camshaft when assembled in the Sixes. The numbered sides must face out on the 304 V8.

NOTCHES TOWARD
FRONT OF ENGINE

BOSS ON ROD TOWARD
REAR OF ENGINE

CHAMFERED CORNERS
TOWARD FRONT OF ENGINE

LEFT NO. 1-3-5

V6-225 left bank piston and rod assembly

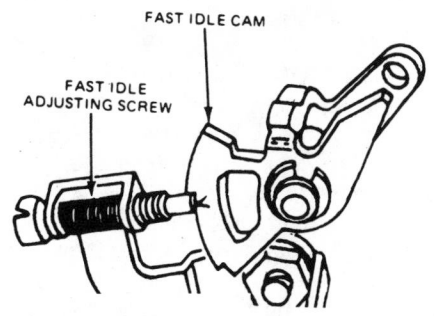

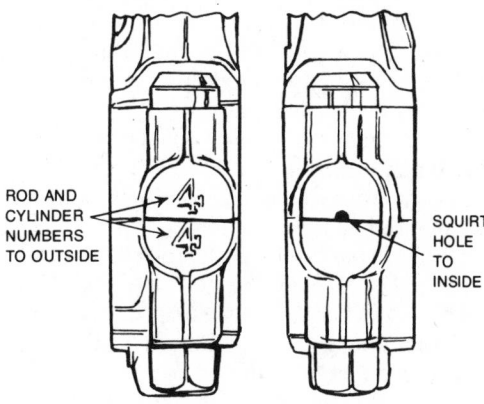

4-151 rod number and squirt hole

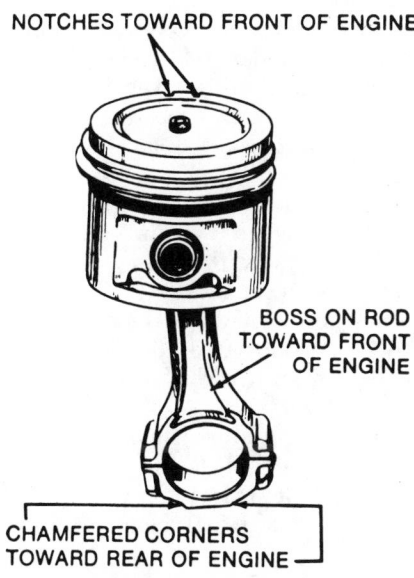

V6-225 right bank piston and rod assembly

ENGINE LUBRICATION

Oil Pan

REMOVAL AND INSTALLATION •
L-Head, F-Head, V6

To remove the oil pan on these engines, remove the oil pan attaching bolts and remove the oil pan. Clean all of the attaching surfaces and install new gaskets.

4-151

1. Disconnect the battery ground.
2. Raise the vehicle and support it on jackstands.
3. Drain the oil.
4. Remove the starter.
5. Unbolt and remove the oil pan.
6. Clean all gasket surfaces, and remove all sludge and deposits from the pan.
7. Install the rear pan gasket in the main bearing cap and apply a small amount of RTV sealant in the depressions where the pan gasket contacts the block.
8. Position the gasket on the pan. Apply a ⅛ x ¼ inch bead of RTV sealant at the split lines of the front and side gaskets.
9. Position the pan on the block carefully to avoid gasket misalignment. Install the bolts and tighten them to 45 in. lb.
10. Install the starter. Tighten the bolts to 17 ft. lb.; the nut to 40 in. lb.
11. Connect the starter cables, lower the vehicle, fill the crankcase and run the engine to operating temperature, checking for leaks.

232, 258 Sixes and 304 V8

1. Raise the vehicle and drain the engine oil.

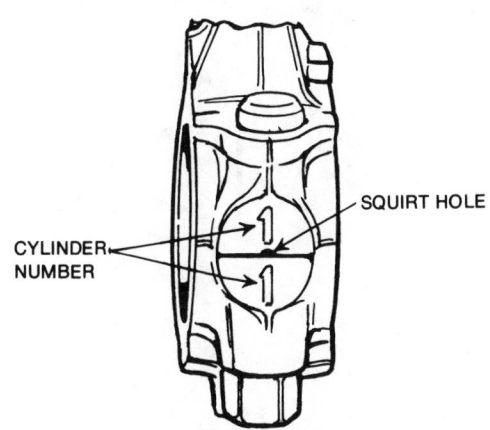

6-232, 258 connecting rod numbering

2. Remove the starter motor.

3. Place a jack under the transmission bell housing. Disconnect the engine right support cushion bracket from the block and raise the engine to allow sufficient clearance for oil pan removal.

4. Remove the oil pan attaching bolts and remove the oil pan.

5. Remove the oil pan front and rear neoprene oil seals and the side gaskets. Thoroughly clean the gasket surfaces of the oil pan and the engine block. Remove all of the sludge and dirt from the oil pan sump.

6. Apply a generous amount of RTV silicone to the end tabs of a new oil pan front seal and install the seal to the timing case cover.

7. Cement new oil pan side gaskets into position on the engine block and apply a generous amount of RTV silicone to the side gasket contacting surface of the seal end tabs.

8. Install the seal in the recess of the rear main bearing cap, making sure that it is fully seated.

9. Coat the oil pan contacting surface of the front and rear oil pan seals with engine oil.

10. Install the oil pan and assemble the engine mount in the reverse order of removal.

Rear Main Oil Seal

REPLACEMENT

4-134 L and F-Head

NOTE: *On early L-head engines, the rear bearing is sealed by a wick packing. This packing is installed in a groove machined into the rear main bearing cap. On later L-head and all F-head engines, a steel-backed lip seal is used. This seal can be used to replace the older wick seal, and can be replaced without removing the crankshaft.*

The following steps apply to wick type seals:

1. Remove the engine from the vehicle.

2. Remove the timing chain cover and crankshaft timing gear.

3. Remove the oil pan and pickup unit.

4. Slide the thrust washers and adjusting shims off the front end of the crankshaft.

5. Move the two pieces of the rear main cap packing away from the sides of the cap.

6. Note the numbers of the main caps and block for position when installing.

7. Unbolt and remove the main bearing caps.

CAUTION: *Take great care in removing the caps. Lift them evenly and avoid binding on the dowels. If you suspect that any of the dowels were bent during removal, replace them.*

8. Unbolt and remove the connecting rod caps, taking care to note their position for installation.

9. Lift out the crankshaft.

10. Remove the rear main seal wicking from the grooves.

11. If a steel-backed lip type seal is being used to replace the older style wicking, go on to the next procedure for later L-head and all F-head engines. If a wick type seal is being used, clean the seal grooves, and insert the seal in the grooves with your fingers.

12. Using a round piece of wood, roll the seal tightly into the groove starting at one end and working toward the center, then the other end toward the center.

13. A small portion of the packing will protrude above the surface of the cap. This should be cut off flush with the cap at each end.

The following procedure should be used for later L-head and all F-head engines with steel-backed lip type seals:

1. Raise and support the vehicle on jackstands.

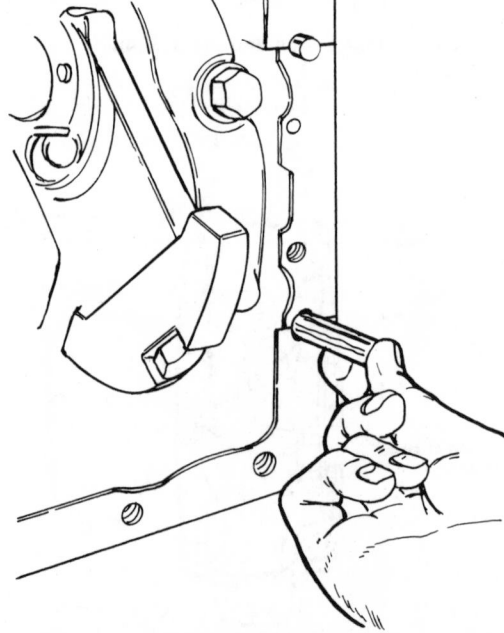

Late L-head and all F-head rear bearing cap packing

2. Remove the oil pan.

3. Remove the rear main bearing cap.

4. Using a center punch, drive the upper seal out of its groove just far enough to grasp it with a pliers, and pull it the rest of the way.

5. Apply a light film of chassis grease to the lower seal and install it in the cap.

6. Install the rubber packings in the upper crankcase half. The packings are of a predetermined length to allow about ¼ inch protrusion. This protrusion is necessary for a positive seal. DO NOT TRIM THESE SEALS!

7. Apply a small amount of RTV sealant to both sides and face of the bearing cap and install it.

8. Torque the cap to the figure shown in the torque specifications chart.

9. Install all parts in reverse of removal.

6-225

NOTE: *For removal of both upper and lower seals, the crankshaft must be removed from the engine. Crankshaft removal is easiest with the engine out of the vehicle.*

1. Remove engine.

2. Remove the timing case and gears, and any spacers and shims from the front of the crankshaft.

3. Remove the oil pan and oil pickup.

4. Note the mating of crankshaft and main caps. Match mark them with an indelible inker.

5. Unbolt the #1 main bearing cap. Using a pry bar, carefully lift the cap from the dowels. Take great care to avoid damaging the dowels. Any bent dowels must be replaced.

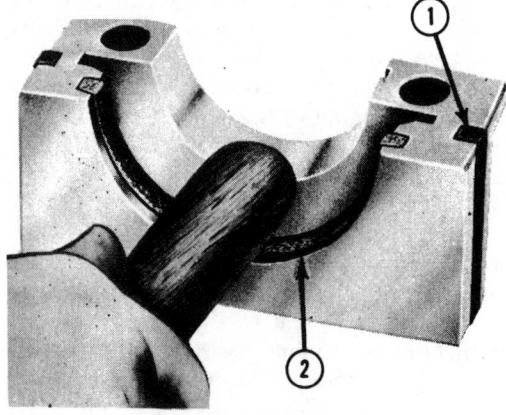

1. Neoprene seal
2. Fabric seal

Installing the V6-225 crankshaft rear oil seal

6. In the same manner, remove the next two caps.

7. To remove the rear cap, rear main bearing bolt remover, special tool W-323 or its equivalent must be used.

8. Match mark the connecting rod caps and remove them.

9. Lift out the crankshaft.

10. Remove the braided seal from the inner groove of the cap and the neoprene seals from the outer grooves.

11. Using a center punch, drive the block seal out just far enough to grasp with a pliers and pull out.

12. Dip a new block seal in engine oil and force it into place in the block.

13. Insert the new braided cap seal into the groove in the cap and coat it with engine oil.

14. Cut the ends of the braided seals flush with the cap and block surfaces.

15. The new neoprene seals are installed after the cap is torqued in place. These seals are supposed to project about $1/16$ inch above the cap. DO NOT CUT THESE SEALS FLUSH WITH THE CAP! Before installation, dip the neoprene seals in kerosene for about 1–2 minutes. After installation squirt some more kerosene on the protruding ends of the seals. Then, peen the ends of the seals with a hammer to make sure of a tight seal at the upper parting line between the cap and block.

16. Installation of the crankshaft and remaining parts is the reverse of removal. Torque the main cap bolts evenly, one side then the other, a little at a time until the torque value is reached.

NOTE: *Whenever the second cap is removed, the thrust surfaces must be aligned. To do this, pry the crankshaft back and forth several times throughout its end travel with the cap bolts of the second main cap only finger tight.*

4-151

NOTE: *The seal is a one piece unit that can be removed and installed without removing the oil pan or crankshaft.*

1. Raise and support the vehicle on jackstands.

2. Remove the transmission and transfer case as an assembly.

3. Disconnect and remove the starter.

4. On manual transmission vehicles, remove the flywheel inspection plate, and clutch slave cylinder.

5. Remove the flywheel or drive plate housing.

6. On manual transmission, remove the clutch assembly by backing out the bolts evenly around the pressure plate.

7. Remove the flywheel or drive plate. It is a good idea to match mark the flywheel location for assembly.

8. Using a small-bladed screwdriver, pry the rear seal out from around the crankshaft hub. Be careful to avoid damaging the seating groove or hub.

9. With a light hammer, tap the seal into position with the lip facing the front of the engine. Assemble all other parts in reverse order, using the procedures found in this book.

6-232, 258, 8-304

This seal is a two-piece neoprene type with a single lip.

1. Raise and support the vehicle on jackstands.

2. Remove the oil pan.

3. Remove the rear main bearing cap and discard the lower seal.

4. Loosen all remaining main bearing caps.

5. Using a center punch, carefully drive the upper half of the seal out of the block just far enough to grasp with a pliers and pull out.

6. Remove the oil pan front and rear seals and the side gaskets.

7. Clean all gasket surfaces.

8. Wipe clean the sealing surface of the crankshaft and coat it lightly with engine oil.

9. Coat the lip of the upper seal with engine oil and install it in the block. The lip faces forward.

10. Coat both end tabs of the lower seal with RTV silicone sealer. Do not get any RTV sealer on the seal lip.

11. Coat the outer curved surface of the seal with liquid soap. Coat the seal lip with engine oil.

12. Install the seal into the cap, pressing firmly.

13. Coat both chamfered edges of the cap with RTV sealer.

CAUTION: *Do not allow any RTV sealer to get on the mating surfaces of the cap or block as this will affect bearing clearance.*

14. Install the rear main cap.

15. Tighten all main bearing cap bolts gradually to 80 ft. lb.

16. Replace the oil pan.

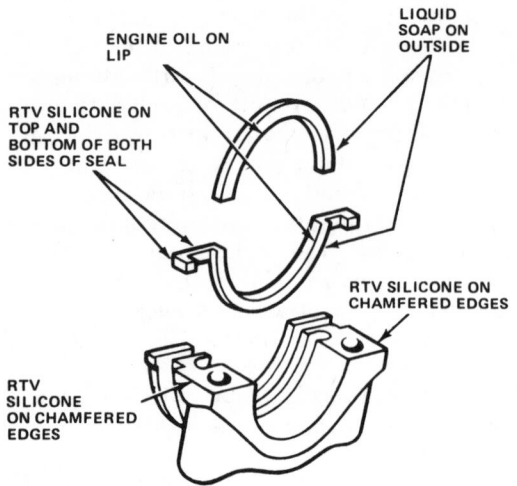

6-232, 258 and 8-304 rear main oil seal installation

Oil Pump

REMOVAL AND INSTALLATION

L and F-head

1. Set number one piston at TDC in order to reinstall the oil pump without disturbing the ignition timing.

2. Remove the distributor cover and note the position of the rotor. Keep the rotor in that position when the oil pump is installed.

3. Remove the cap screws and lockwashers that attach the oil pump to the cylinder block. Carefully slide the oil pump and its driveshaft out of the cylinder block.

The oil pump is driven by the camshaft by means of a spiral gear. The distributor in turn is driven by the oil pump by means of a tongue on the end of the distributor shaft which engages a slot in the end of the oil pump shaft. Because the tongue and the slot are both machined off center, the two shafts can be meshed in only one position. Since the position of the distributor shaft determines the timing of the engine, and is controlled by the oil pump shaft, the position of the oil pump shaft with respect to the camshaft is important.

If only the oil pump has been removed, install it so that the slot in the end of the shaft lines up with the tip of the distributor shaft and allows that shaft to slip into it without disturbing the original position of the distributor. If the engine has been disturbed or both the distributor and the oil pump have been removed, follow the procedure given below.

1. Turn the crankshaft to align the timing

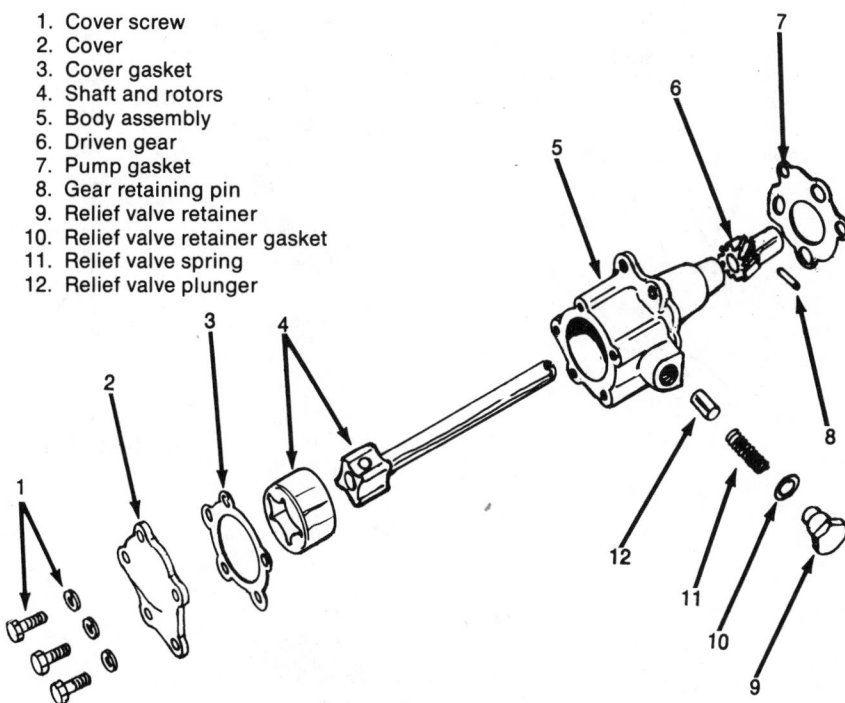

1. Cover screw
2. Cover
3. Cover gasket
4. Shaft and rotors
5. Body assembly
6. Driven gear
7. Pump gasket
8. Gear retaining pin
9. Relief valve retainer
10. Relief valve retainer gasket
11. Relief valve spring
12. Relief valve plunger

Oil pump used on late L-head and all F-head engines

marks on the crankshaft and camshaft timing gears.

2. Install the oil pump gasket on the pump.

3. With the wider side of the slot on top, start the oil pump drive shaft into the opening in the cylinder keeping the mounting holes in the body of the pump in alignment with the holes in the cylinder block.

4. Insert a long blade screwdriver into the distributor shaft opening in the side of the cylinder block and engage the slot in the oil pump shaft. Turn the shaft so that the slot is positioned at what would be roughly the ninethirty position on a clock face.

5. Remove the screwdriver and observe the position of the slot in the end of the oil pump shaft to make certain it is properly positioned.

6. Replace the screwdriver and, while turning the screwdriver clockwise to guide the oil pump driveshaft gear into engagement with the camshaft gear, press against the oil pump to force it into position.

7. Remove the screwdriver and again observe the position of the slot. If installation was properly made, the slot will be in a position roughly equivalent to the eleven o'clock position on the face of a clock, with the wider side of the slot still on the top. If the slot is improperly positioned, remove the oil pump and repeat the operation.

8. Coat the threads of the capscrews with gasket cement and secure the oil pump in place.

V6

1. Remove the oil filter.

2. Disconnect the wire from the oil pressure indicator switch in the filter by-pass valve cap.

3. Remove the screws that attach the oil pump cover assembly to the timing chain cover.

4. Remove the cover assembly and slide out the oil pump.

5. Install in reverse order of the above procedure.

4-151, 232, 258 Sixes

1. Drain the oil and remove the oil pan.

2. Remove the oil pump retaining screws and separate the oil pump and gasket from the engine block.

NOTE: *On 6-cyl. engines, do not disturb the position of the oil pick-up tube and screen assembly in the pump body. If the tube is moved within the pump body, a new assembly must be installed to assure an airtight seal.*

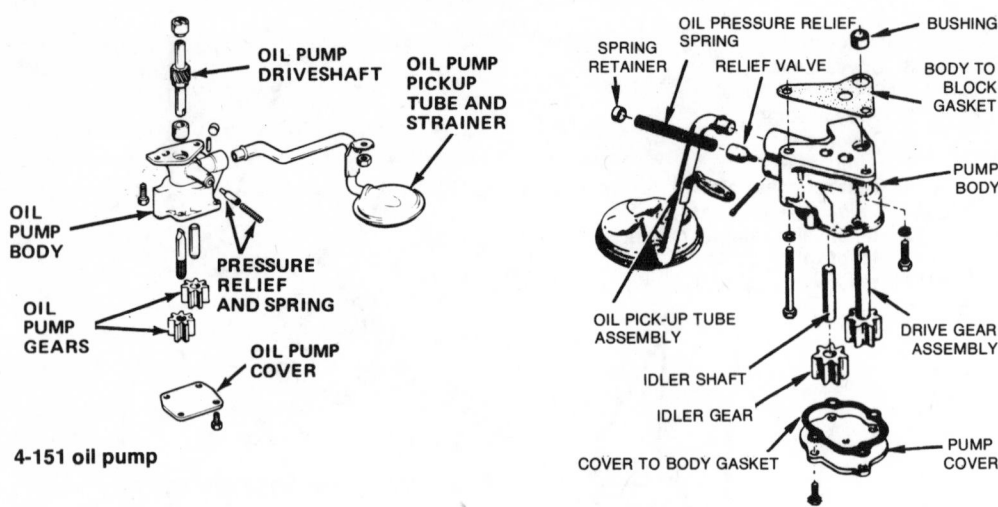

4-151 oil pump

Inline six oil pump

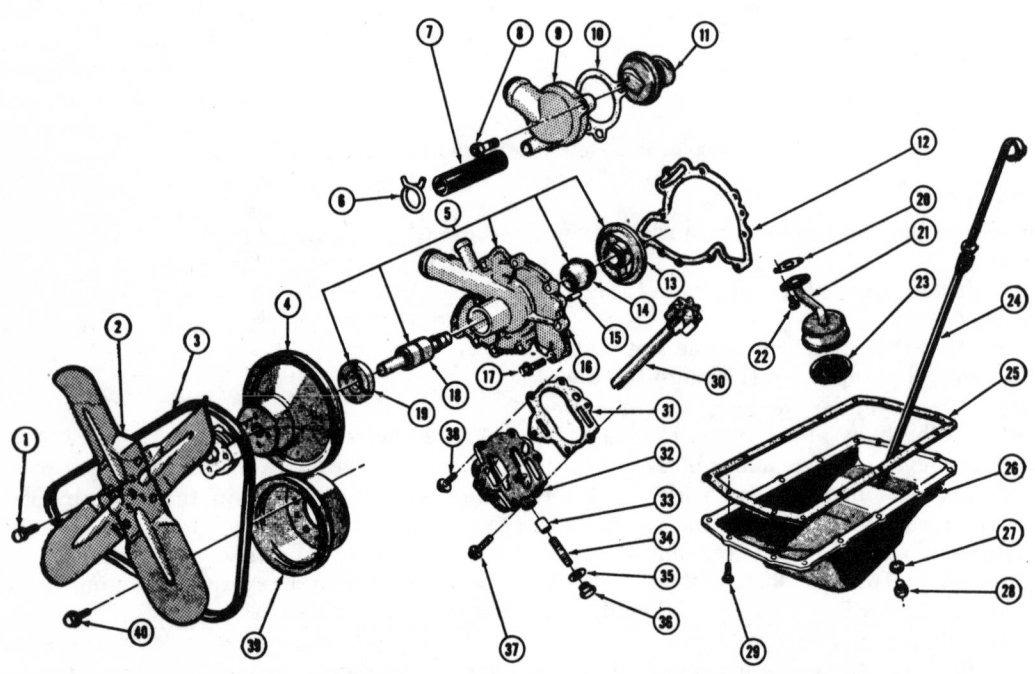

1. Bolt and lock washer
2. Fan assembly
3. Fan and alternator belt
4. Fan driven pulley
5. Water pump assembly
6. Hose clamp
7. Thermostat by-pass hose
8. Hex head bolt
9. Water outlet elbow
10. Water outlet elbow gasket
11. Thermostat
12. Water pump gasket
13. Impeller and insert, water pump

14. Water pump seal
15. Dowel pin
16. Water pump cover
17. Bolt
18. Water pump shaft and bearing
19. Fan hub
20. Oil suction pipe gasket
21. Oil suction housing, pipe and flange
22. Bolt
23. Oil pump screen
24. Oil dipstick
25. Oil pan gasket
26. Oil pan assembly

27. Drain plug gasket
28. Drain plug
29. Screw and lockwasher
30. Oil pump shaft and gear
31. Oil pump cover gasket
32. Valve by-pass and cover assembly
33. Oil pressure valve
34. Valve by-pass spring
35. Oil pressure valve cap gasket
36. Oil pressure valve cap
37. Screw
38. Screw
39. Fan driving pulley
40. Hex head bolt

V6 lubrication and cooling components

3. Install in reverse order of the above procedure.

304 V8

Remove the retaining screws and separate the oil pump cover, gasket and oil filter as an assembly from the pump body (timing chain cover). Install in reverse order with a new filter and gasket.

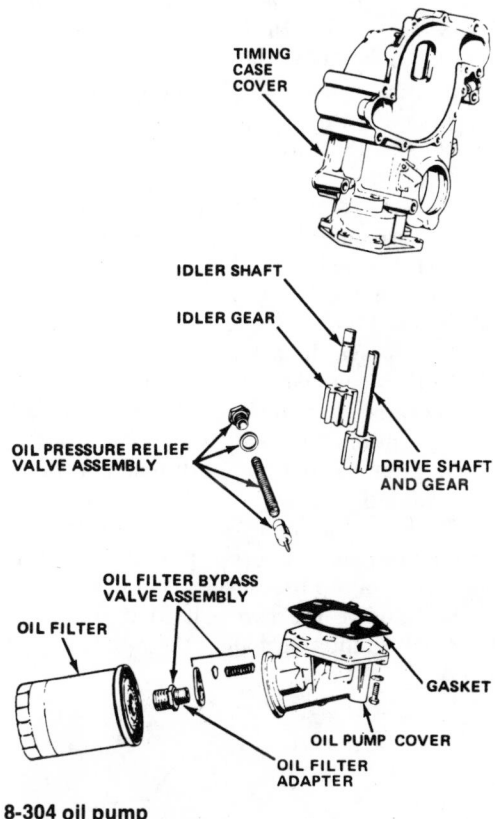

8-304 oil pump

ENGINE COOLING

The satisfactory performance of any water cooled engine is controlled to a great extent by the proper operation of the cooling system. The engine block is fully water jacketed to prevent distortion of the cylinder walls. Directed cooling and water holes in the cylinder head cause water to flow past the valve seats, which are one of the hottest parts of any engine, and carry the heat away from the valves and seats.

The minimum temperature of the coolant is controlled by a thermostat mounted in the outlet passage of the engine. When the coolant temperature is below the temperature rating of the thermostat, the thermostat remains closed and the coolant is directed through the radiator-by-pass hose to the water pump. If the coolant temperature is too high, the thermostat opens and coolant flow is directed to the top of the radiator. The radiator dissipates the excess engine heat before the coolant is recirculated through the engine.

The cooling system is pressurized and the operating pressure is regulated by the rating of the radiator cap which contains a relief valve.

Radiator
REMOVAL AND INSTALLATION

1. Drain the radiator by opening the drain cock and removing the radiator pressure cap.
2. Remove the upper and lowqer hose clamps and hoses at the radiator.
3. Disconnect the automatic transmission oil cooler lines at the radiator, if so equipped. Remove the radiator shroud from the radiator, if so equipped.
4. Remove all attaching screws that secure the radiator to the radiator body support.
5. Remove the radiator.
6. Replace in reverse order of the above procedure.

Thermostat
REMOVAL AND INSTALLATION

The thermostat is located in the water outlet housing at the front or on top of the engine. On the V6 and the 304 V8 the water outlet housing is located in the front of the intake manifold.

To remove the thermostats from all of these engines, first drain the cooling system. It is not necessary to disconnect or remove any of the hoses. Remove the two attaching screws and lift the housing from the engine. Remove the thermostat and the gasket. To install, place the thermostat in the housing with the spring inside the engine. Install a new gasket with a small amount of sealing compound applied to both sides. Install the water outlet and tighten the attaching bolts to 30 ft. lbs. Refill the cooling system.

Water Pump
REMOVAL AND INSTALLATION
4-134 L and F-Head

1. Disconnect the hoses at the pump. Remove the fan belt.

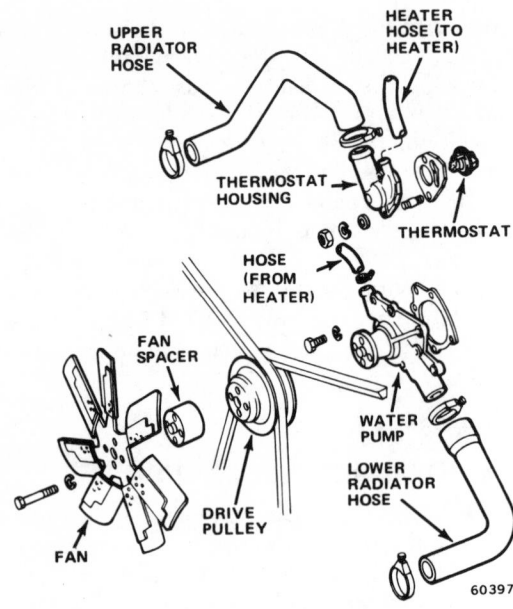

Six-Cylinder Cooling System

2. Unbolt the fan and hub assembly.

3. Unbolt and remove the pump.

4. Installation is the reverse of removal. Torque the pump bolts to 17 ft. lb. Always use a new gasket coated with sealer.

4-151

1. Remove the fan belt.

2. Remove the fan and hub assembly.

3. Disconnect the hoses at the pump.

4. Unbolt and remove the pump.

5. Installation is the reverse of removal. Always use a new gasket coated with sealer. Torque the water pump bolts to 25 ft. lb. Tighten the fan and hub bolts to 18 ft. lb.

V6-225

1. Disconnect all hoses at the pump.

2. Remove the drive belts.

3. Remove the fan and hub assembly.

4. Unbolt and remove the water pump along with the alternator adjustment bracket.

5. Installation is the reverse of removal. Always use a new gasket coated with sealer. Torque the water pump bolts to 6–8 ft. lb.

6-232, 258

1. Disconnect all hoses at the pump.

2. Remove the drive belts.

3. Remove the fan shroud attaching screws.

4. Unbolt the fan and fan drive assembly and remove along with the shroud. On some

models it may be easier to turn the shroud ½ turn.

5. Unbolt and remove the pump.

CAUTION: *Engines built for sale in California having a single, serpentine drive belt and viscous fan drive, have a reverse rotating pum and drive. These components are identified by the word REVERSE stamped on the drive cover and inner side of the fan, and REV cast into the water pump body. Never interchange standard rotating parts with these.*

6. Installation is the reverse of removal. Always use a new gasket coated with sealer. Torque the water pump bolts to 13 ft. lb.; the fan bolts to 18 ft. lb.

8-304

1. Disconnect all hoses at the pump.

2. Loosen all drive belts.

3. Remove the shroud, but reinsert one bolt to hold the radiator.

4. Remove the fan and hub.

5. If the vehicle is equipped with A/C install a double nut on the compressor bracket-to-water pump stud and remove the stud.

6. Remove, but do not disconnect the alternator and bracket.

7. If so equipped, remove the nuts that attach the power steering pump to the rear half of the pump bracket.

8. Remove the two bolts that attach the front half to the rear half of the bracket.

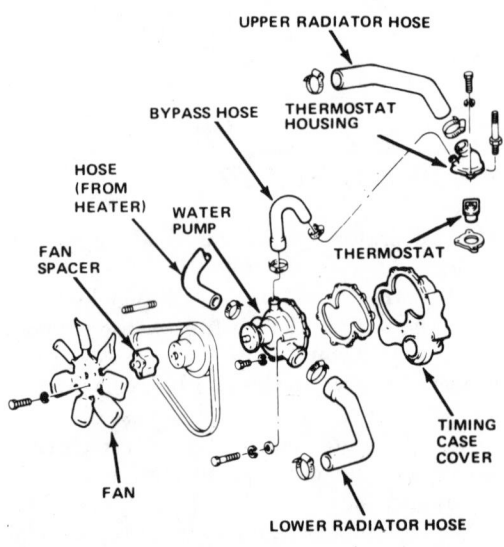

Eight-Cylinder Cooling System

9. Remove the remaining upper screw from the inner air pump support bracket, loosen the lower bolt and drop the bracket away from the power steering front bracket.

10. Remove the front half of the power steering bracket from the water pump mounting stud.

11. Unbolt and remove the water pump.

12. Installation is the reverse of removal. Always use a new gasket coated with sealer. Torque the pump-to timing case bolts to 48 in. lb. and the pump-to-block bolts to 25 ft. lb. Torque the power steering pulley nut to 60 ft. lb.

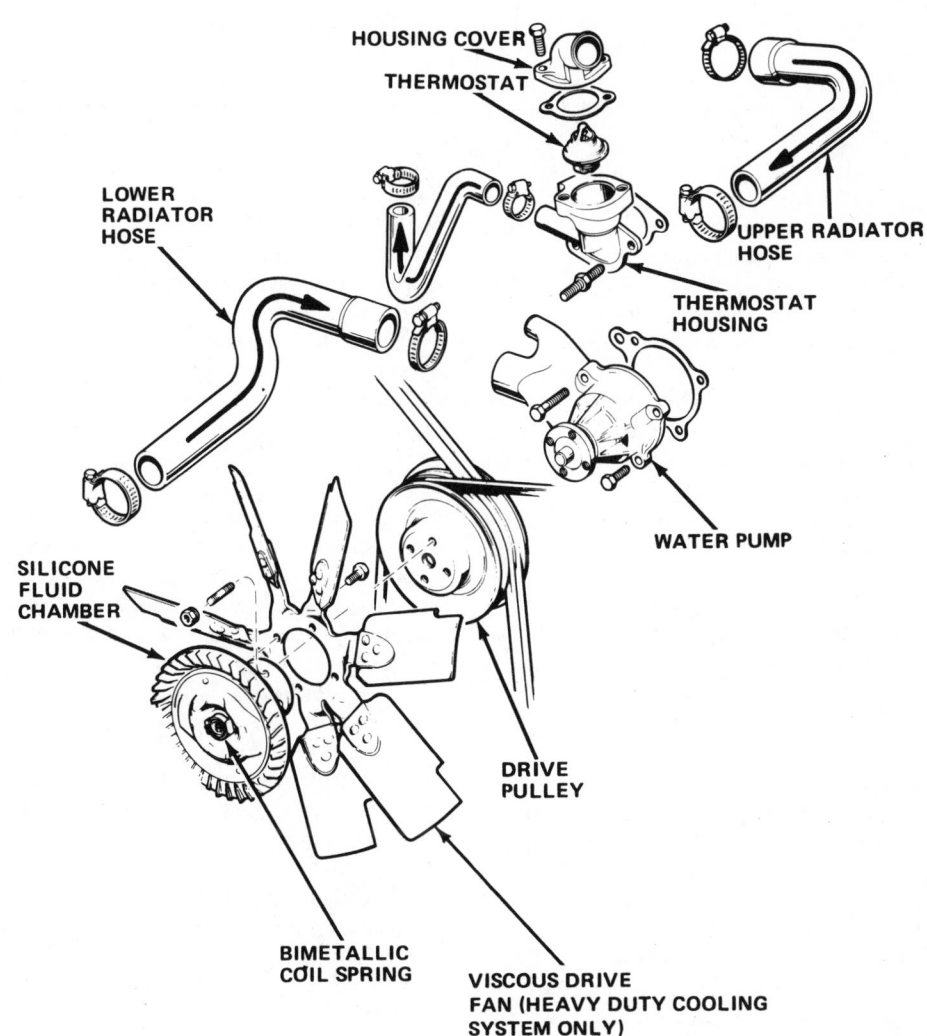

4-151 water pump and related components

ENGINE REBUILDING

Most procedures involved in rebuilding an engine are fairly standard, regardless of the type of engine involved. This section is a guide accepted rebuilding procedures. Examples of standard rebuilding practices are illustrated and should be used along with specific details concerning your particular engine, found earlier in this chapter.

The procedures given here are those used by any competent rebuilder. Obviously some of the procedures cannot be performed by the do-it-yourself mechanic, but are provided so that you will be familiar with the services that should be offered by rebuilding or machine shops. As an example, in most instances, it is more profitable for the home mechanic to remove the cylinder heads, buy the necessary parts (new valves, seals, keepers, keys, etc.) and deliver these to a machine shop for the necessary work. In this way you will save the money to remove and install the cylinder head and the mark-up on parts.

On the other hand, most of the work involved in rebuilding the lower end is well within the scope of the do-it-yourself mechanic. Only work such as hot-tanking, actually boring the block or Magnafluxing (invisible crack detection) need be sent to a machine shop.

Tools

The tools required for basic engine rebuilding should, with a few exceptions, be those included in a mechanic's tool kit. An accurate torque wrench, and a dial indicator (reading in thousandths) mounted on a universal base should be available. Special tools, where required, are available from the major tool suppliers. The services of a competent automotive machine shop must also be readily available.

Precautions

Aluminum has become increasingly popular for use in engines, due to its low weight and excellent heat transfer characteristics. The following precautions must be observed when handling aluminum (or any other) engine parts:

—Never hot-tank aluminum parts.
—Remove all aluminum parts (identification tags, etc.) from engine parts before hot-tanking (otherwise they will be removed during the process).

—Always coat threads lightly with engine oil or anti-seize compounds before installation, to prevent seizure.
—Never over-torque bolts or spark plugs in aluminum threads. Should stripping occur, threads can be restored using any of a number of thread repair kits available (see next section).

Inspection Techniques

Magnaflux and Zyglo are inspection techniques used to locate material flaws, such as stress cracks. Magnaflux is a magnetic process, applicable only to ferrous materials. The Zyglo process coats the matrial with a fluorescent dye penetrant, and any material may be tested using Zyglo. Specific checks of suspected surface cracks may be made at lower cost and more readily using spot check dye. The dye is sprayed onto the suspected area, wiped off, and the area is then sprayed with a developer. Cracks then will show up brightly.

Overhaul

The section is divided into two parts. The first, Cylinder Head Reconditioning, assumes that the cylinder head is removed from the engine, all manifolds are removed, and the cylinder head is on a workbench. The camshaft should be removed from overhead cam cylinder heads. The second section, Cylinder Block Reconditioning, covers the block, pistons, connecting rods and crankshaft. It is assumed that the engine is mounted on a work stand, and the cylinder head and all accessories are removed.

Procedures are identified as follows:

Unmarked—Basic procedures that must be performed in order to successfully complete the rebuilding process.

Starred (*)—Procedures that should be performed to ensure maximum performance and engine life.

Double starred (**)—Procedures that may be performed to increase engine performance and reliability.

When assembling the engine, any parts that will be in frictional contact must be prelubricated, to provide protection on initial start-up. Any product specifically formulated for this purpose may be used. NOTE: *Do not use engine oil.* Where semi-permanent (locked but removable) installation of bolts or nuts is desired, threads should be cleaned and located with Loctite® or a similar product (non-hardening).

Repairing Damaged Threads

Several methods of repairing damaged threads are available. Heli-Coil® (shown here), Keenserts® and Microdot® are among the most widely used. All involve basically the same principle—drilling out stripped threads, tapping the hole and installing a pre-wound insert—making welding, plugging and oversize fasteners unnecessary.

Two types of thread repair inserts are usually supplied—a standard type for most Inch Coarse, Inch Fine, Metric Coarse and Metric Fine thread sizes and a spark plug type to fit most spark plug port sizes. Consult the individual manufacturer's catalog to determine exact applications. Typical thread repair kits will contain a selection of pre-wound threaded inserts, a tap (corresponding to the outside diameter threads of the insert) and an installation tool. Spark plug inserts usually differ because they require a tap equipped with pilot threads and a combined reamer/tap section. Most manufacturers also supply blister-packed thread repair inserts separately in addition to a master kit containing a variety of taps and inserts plus installation tools.

Before effecting a repair to a threaded hole, remove any snapped, broken or damaged bolts or studs. Penetrating oil can be used to free frozen threads; the offending item can be removed with locking pliers or with a screw or stud extractor. After the hole is clear, the thread can be repaired, as follows:

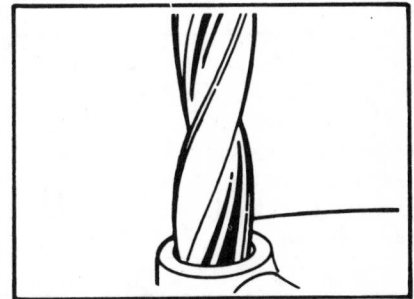

Drill out the damaged threads with specified drill. Drill completely through the hole or to the bottom of a blind hole

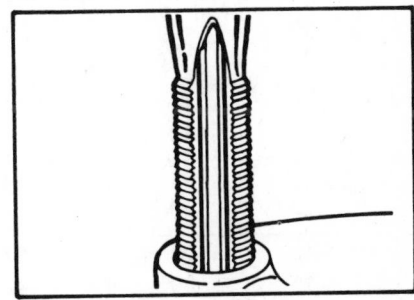

With the tap supplied, tap the hole to receive the thread insert. Keep the tap well oiled and back it out frequently to avoid clogging the threads

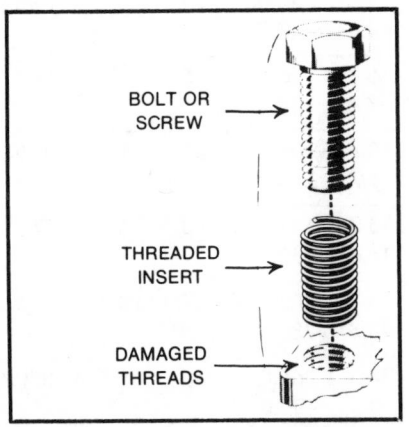

Damaged bolt holes can be repaired with thread repair inserts

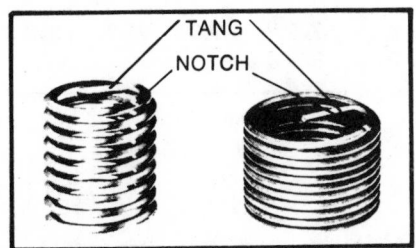

Standard thread repair insert (left) and spark plug thread insert (right)

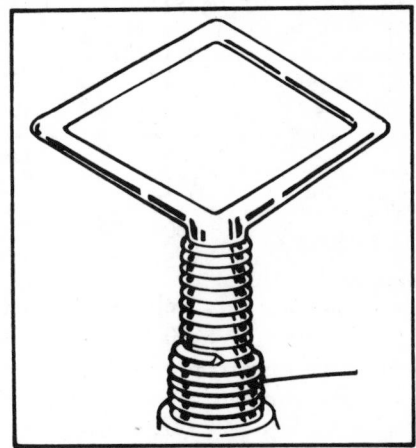

Screw the threaded insert onto the installation tool until the tang engages the slot. Screw the insert into the tapped hole until it is ¼–½ turn below the top surface. After installation break off the tang with a hammer and punch

Standard Torque Specifications and Fastener Markings

The Newton-metre has been designated the world standard for measuring torque and will gradually replace the foot-pound and kilogram-meter. In the absence of specific torques, the following chart can be used as a guide to the maximum safe torque of a particular size/grade of fastener.

- There is no torque difference for fine or coarse threads.
- Torque values are based on clean, dry threads. Reduce the value by 10% if threads are oiled prior to assembly.
- The torque required for aluminum components or fasteners is considerably less.

U. S. BOLTS

SAE Grade Number	1 or 2			5			6 or 7		

Bolt Markings

Manufacturer's marks may vary—number of lines always 2 less than the grade number.

Usage	Frequent			Frequent			Infrequent		
Bolt Size (inches)—(Thread)	Maximum Torque			Maximum Torque			Maximum Torque		
	Ft-Lb	kgm	Nm	Ft-Lb	kgm	Nm	Ft-Lb	kgm	Nm
¼—20	5	0.7	6.8	8	1.1	10.8	10	1.4	13.5
—28	6	0.8	8.1	10	1.4	13.6			
⁵⁄₁₆—18	11	1.5	14.9	17	2.3	23.0	19	2.6	25.8
—24	13	1.8	17.6	19	2.6	25.7			
⅜—16	18	2.5	24.4	31	4.3	42.0	34	4.7	46.0
—24	20	2.75	27.1	35	4.8	47.5			
⁷⁄₁₆—14	28	3.8	37.0	49	6.8	66.4	55	7.6	74.5
—20	30	4.2	40.7	55	7.6	74.5			
½—13	39	5.4	52.8	75	10.4	101.7	85	11.75	115.2
—20	41	5.7	55.6	85	11.7	115.2			
⁹⁄₁₆—12	51	7.0	69.2	110	15.2	149.1	120	16.6	162.7
—18	55	7.6	74.5	120	16.6	162.7			
⅝—11	83	11.5	112.5	150	20.7	203.3	167	23.0	226.5
—18	95	13.1	128.8	170	23.5	230.5			
¾—10	105	14.5	142.3	270	37.3	366.0	280	38.7	379.6
—16	115	15.9	155.9	295	40.8	400.0			
⅞—9	160	22.1	216.9	395	54.6	535.5	440	60.9	596.5
—14	175	24.2	237.2	435	60.1	589.7			
1—8	236	32.5	318.6	590	81.6	799.9	660	91.3	894.8
—14	250	34.6	338.9	660	91.3	849.8			

METRIC BOLTS

NOTE: *Metric bolts are marked with a number indicating the relative strength of the bolt. These numbers have nothing to do with size.*

Description	Torque ft-lbs (Nm)			
Thread size x pitch (mm)	Head mark—4		Head mark—7	
6 x 1.0	2.2–2.9	(3.0–3.9)	3.6–5.8	(4.9–7.8)
8 x 1.25	5.8–8.7	(7.9–12)	9.4–14	(13–19)
10 x 1.25	12–17	(16–23)	20–29	(27–39)
12 x 1.25	21–32	(29–43)	35–53	(47–72)
14 x 1.5	35–52	(48–70)	57–85	(77–110)
16 x 1.5	51–77	(67–100)	90–120	(130–160)
18 x 1.5	74–110	(100–150)	130–170	(180–230)
20 x 1.5	110–140	(150–190)	190–240	(160–320)
22 x 1.5	150–190	(200–260)	250–320	(340–430)
24 x 1.5	190–240	(260–320)	310–410	(420–550)

NOTE: *This engine rebuilding section is a guide to accepted rebuilding procedures. Typical examples of standard rebuilding procedures are illustrated. Use these procedures along with the detailed instructions earlier in this chapter, concerning your particular engine.*

Cylinder Head Reconditioning

Procedure	Method
Remove the cylinder head:	See the engine service procedures earlier in this chapter for details concerning specific engines.
Identify the valves:	Invert the cylinder head, and number the valve faces front to rear, using a permanent felt-tip marker.
Remove the rocker arms:	Remove the rocker arms with shaft(s) or balls and nuts. Wire the sets of rockers, balls and nuts together, and identify according to the corresponding valve.
Remove the valves and springs:	Using an appropriate valve spring compressor (depending on the configuration of the cylinder head), compress the valve springs. Lift out the keepers with needlenose pliers, release the compressor, and remove the valve, spring, and spring retainer. See the engine service procedures earlier in this chapter for details concerning specific engines.
Check the valve stem-to-guide clearance: 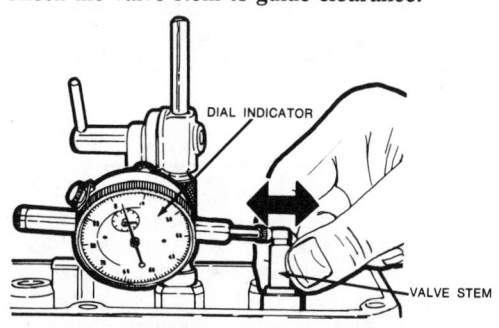 **Check the valve stem-to-guide clearance**	Clean the valve stem with lacquer thinner or a similar solvent to remove all gum and varnish. Clean the valve guides using solvent and an expanding wire-type valve guide cleaner. Mount a dial indicator so that the stem is at 90° to the valve stem, as close to the valve guide as possible. Move the valve off its seat, and measure the valve guide-to-stem clearance by rocking the stem back and forth to actuate the dial indicator. Measure the valve stems using a micrometer, and compare to specifications, to determine whether stem or guide wear is responsible for excessive clearance. NOTE: *Consult the Specifications tables earlier in this chapter.*

Cylinder Head Reconditioning

Procedure	Method
De-carbon the cylinder head and valves: 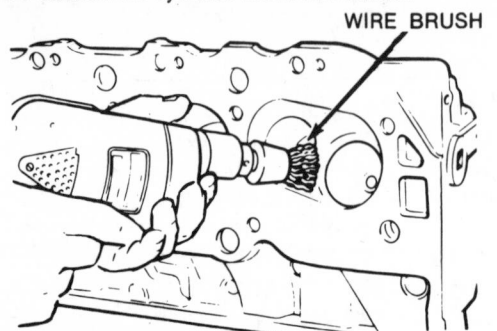WIRE BRUSH **Remove the carbon from the cylinder head with a wire brush and electric drill**	Chip carbon away from the valve heads, combustion chambers, and ports, using a chisel made of hardwood. Remove the remaining deposits with a stiff wire brush. **NOTE:** *Be sure that the deposits are actually removed, rather than burnished.*
Hot-tank the cylinder head (cast iron heads only): **CAUTION:** *Do not hot-tank aluminum parts.*	Have the cylinder head hot-tanked to remove grease, corrosion, and scale from the water passages. **NOTE:** *In the case of overhead cam cylinder heads, consult the operator to determine whether the camshaft bearings will be damaged by the caustic solution.*
Degrease the remaining cylinder head parts:	Clean the remaining cylinder head parts in an engine cleaning solvent. Do not remove the protective coating from the springs.
Check the cylinder head for warpage: 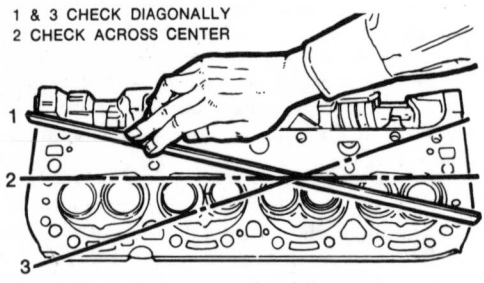1 & 3 CHECK DIAGONALLY 2 CHECK ACROSS CENTER **Check the cylinder head for warpage**	Place a straight-edge across the gasket surface of the cylinder head. Using feeler gauges, determine the clearance at the center of the straight-edge. If warpage exceeds .003″ in a 6″ span, or .006″ over the total length, the cylinder head must be resurfaced. **NOTE:** *If warpage exceeds the manufacturer's maximum tolerance for material removal, the cylinder head must be replaced.* When milling the cylinder heads of V-type engines, the intake manifold mounting position is altered, and must be corrected by milling the manifold flange a proportionate amount.
*Knurl the valve guides: 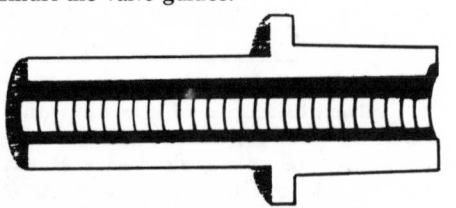 **Cut-away view of a knurled valve guide**	*Valve guides which are not excessively worn or distorted may, in some cases, be knurled rather than replaced. Knurling is a process in which metal is displaced and raised, thereby reducing clearance. Knurling also provides excellent oil control. The possibility of knurling rather than replacing valve guides should be discussed with a machinist.
Replace the valve guides: **NOTE:** *Valve guides should only be replaced if damaged or if an oversize valve stem is not available.*	See the engine service procedures earlier in this chapter for details concerning specific engines. Depending on the type of cylinder head, valve guides may be pressed, hammered, or shrunk in. In cases where the guides are shrunk into the head, replacement should be left to an equipped machine shop. In other

Cylinder Head Reconditioning

Procedure	Method

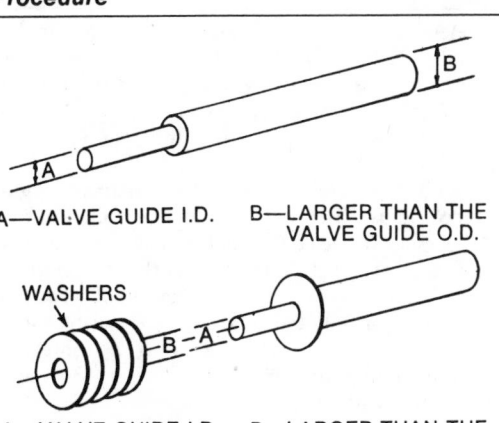

A—VALVE GUIDE I.D.   B—LARGER THAN THE
                        VALVE GUIDE O.D.

WASHERS

A—VALVE GUIDE I.D.   B—LARGER THAN THE
                        VALVE GUIDE O.D.

Valve guide installation tool using washers for installation

cases, the guides are replaced using a stepped drift (see illustration). Determine the height above the boss that the guide must extend, and obtain a stack of washers, their I.D. similar to the guide's O.D., of that height. Place the stack of washers on the guide, and insert the guide into the boss.

NOTE: *Valve guides are often tapered or beveled for installation.* Using the stepped installation tool (see illustration), press or tap the guides into position. Ream the guides according to the size of the valve stem.

Replace valve seat inserts:

Replacement of valve seat inserts which are worn beyond resurfacing or broken, if feasible, must be done by a machine shop.

Resurface (grind) the valve face:

FOR DIMENSIONS,
REFER TO
SPECIFICATIONS

CHECK FOR
BENT STEM

DIAMETER

VALVE FACE ANGLE

1/32″ MINIMUM   THIS LINE
                  PARALLEL WITH
                  VALVE HEAD

Critical valve dimensions

Using a valve grinder, resurface the valves according to specifications given earlier in this chapter.

CAUTION: *Valve face angle is not always identical to valve seat angle.* A minimum margin of $1/32″$ should remain after grinding the valve. The valve stem top should also be squared and resurfaced, by placing the stem in the V-block of the grinder, and turning it while pressing lightly against the grinding wheel.

NOTE: *Do not grind sodium filled exhaust valves on a machine. These should be hand lapped.*

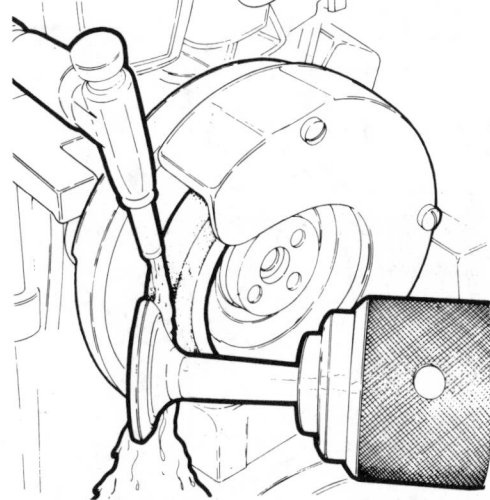

Valve grinding by machine

Cylinder Head Reconditioning

Procedure	Method
Resurface the valve seats using reamers of grinder: 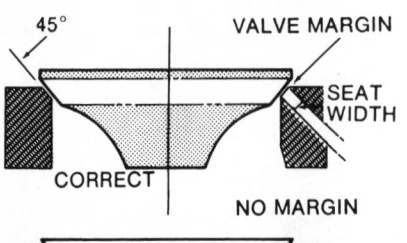 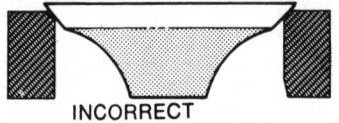 Valve seat width and centering 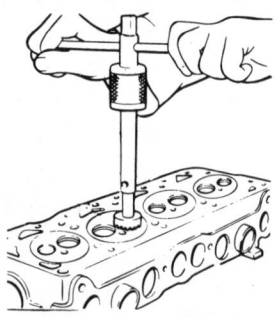 **Reaming the valve seat with a hand reamer**	Select a reamer of the correct seat angle, slightly larger than the diameter of the valve seat, and assemble it with a pilot of the correct size. Install the pilot into the valve guide, and using steady pressure, turn the reamer clockwise. **CAUTION:** *Do not turn the reamer counterclockwise.* Remove only as much material as necessary to clean the seat. Check the concentricity of the seat (following). If the dye method is not used, coat the valve face with Prussian blue dye, install and rotate it on the valve seat. Using the dye marked area as a centering guide, center and narrow the valve seat to specifications with correction cutters. **NOTE:** *When no specifications are available, minimum seat width for exhaust valves should be $^{5}/_{64}''$, intake valves $^{1}/_{16}''$.* After making correction cuts, check the position of the valve seat on the valve face using Prussian blue dye.
	To resurface the seat with a power grinder, select a pilot of the correct size and coarse stone of the proper angle. Lubricate the pilot and move the stone on and off the valve seat at 2 cycles per second, until all flaws are gone. Finish the seat with a fine stone. If necessary the seat can be corrected or narrowed using correction stones.
Check the valve seat concentricity:  **Check the valve seat concentricity with a dial gauge**	Coat the valve face with Prussian blue dye, install the valve, and rotate it on the valve seat. If the entire seat becomes coated, and the valve is known to be concentric, the seat is concentric.
	*Install the dial gauge pilot into the guide, and rest of the arm on the valve seat. Zero the gauge, and rotate the arm around the seat. Run-out should not exceed .002''.

Cylinder Head Reconditioning

Procedure	Method

*Lap the valves:
NOTE: *Valve lapping is done to ensure efficient sealing of resurfaced valves and seats.*

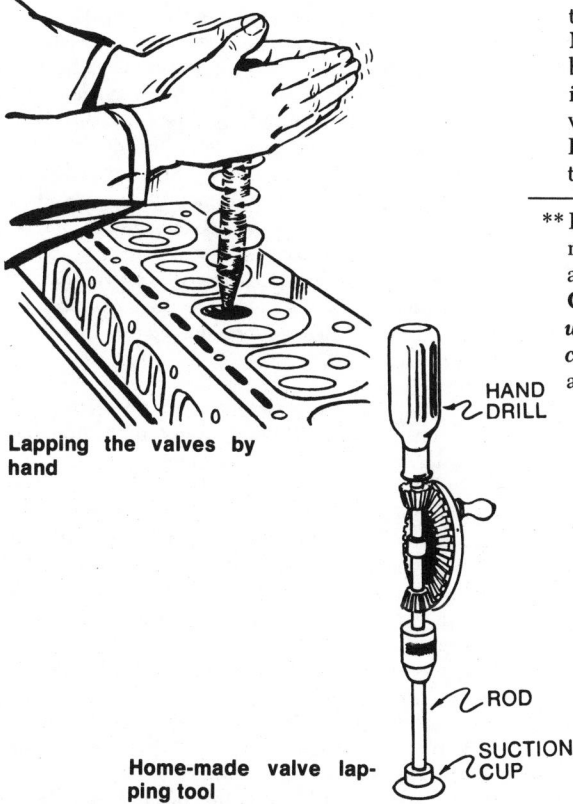

Lapping the valves by hand

Home-made valve lapping tool

Invert the cylinder head, lightly lubricate the valve stems, and install the valves in the head as numbered. Coat valve seats with fine grinding compound, and attach the lapping tool suction cup to a valve head.
NOTE: *Moisten the suction cup.* Rotate the tool between the palms, changing position and lifting the tool often to prevent grooving. Lap the valve until a smooth, polished seat is evident. Remove the valve and tool, and rinse away all traces of grinding compound.

**Fasten a suction cup to a piece of drill rod, and mount the rod in a hand drill. Proceed as above, using the hand drill as a lapping tool.
CAUTION: *Due to the higher speeds involved when using the hand drill, care must be exercised to avoid grooving the seat.* Lift the tool and change direction of rotation often.

HAND DRILL

ROD

SUCTION CUP

Check the valve springs:

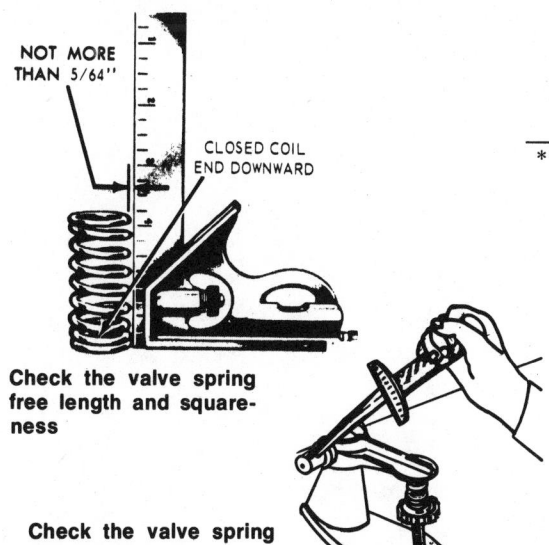

NOT MORE THAN 5/64"

CLOSED COIL END DOWNWARD

Check the valve spring free length and squareness

Check the valve spring test pressure

Place the spring on a flat surface next to a square. Measure the height of the spring, and rotate it against the edge of the square to measure distortion. If spring height varies (by comparison) by more than $1/16''$ or if distortion exceeds $1/16''$, replace the spring.

**In addition to evaluating the spring as above, test the spring pressure at the installed and compressed (installed height minus valve lift) height using a valve spring tester. Springs used on small displacement engines (up to 3 liters) should be ∓ 1 lb of all other springs in either position. A tolerance of ∓ 5 lbs is permissible on larger engines.

Cylinder Head Reconditioning

Procedure	Method
*Install valve stem seals: 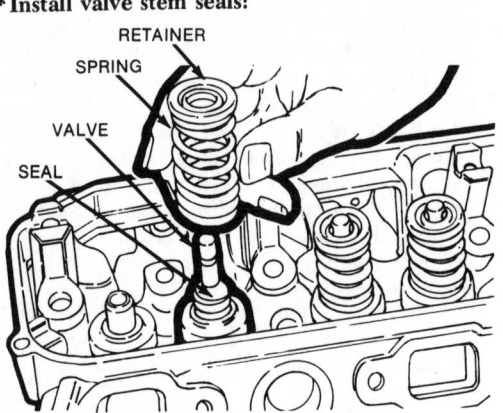 **Install valve stem seals**	*Due to the pressure differential that exists at the ends of the intake valve guides (atmospheric pressure above, manifold vacuum below), oil is drawn through the valve guides into the intake port. This has been alleviated somewhat since the addition of positive crankcase ventilation, which lowers the pressure above the guides. Several types of valve stem seals are available to reduce blow-by. Certain seals simply slip over the stem and guide boss, while others require that the boss be machined. Recently, Teflon guide seals have become popular. Consult a parts supplier or machinist concerning availability and suggested usages. **NOTE:** *When installing seals, ensure that a small amount of oil is able to pass the seal to lubricate the valve guides; otherwise, excessive wear may result.*
Install the valves:	See the engine service procedures earlier in this chapter for details concerning specific engines. Lubricate the valve stems, and install the valves in the cylinder head as numbered. Lubricate and position the seals (if used) and the valve springs. Install the spring retainers, compress the springs, and insert the keys using needlenose pliers or a tool designed for this purpose. **NOTE:** *Retain the keys with wheel bearing grease during installation.*
Check valve spring installed height: 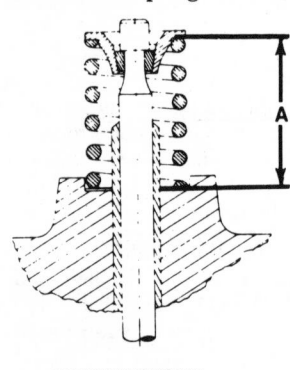 **Valve spring installed height (A)**  **Measure the valve spring installed height (A) with a modified steel rule**	Measure the distance between the spring pad the lower edge of the spring retainer, and compare to specifications. If the installed height is incorrect, add shim washers between the spring pad and the spring. **CAUTION:** *Use only washers designed for this purpose.*

Cylinder Head Reconditioning

Procedure	Method
Inspect the rocker arms, balls, studs, and nuts: 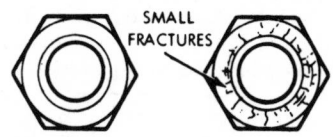 **Stress cracks in the rocker nuts**	Visually inspect the rocker arms, balls, studs, and nuts for cracks, galling, burning, scoring, or wear. If all parts are intact, liberally lubricate the rocker arms and balls, and install them on the cylinder head. If wear is noted on a rocker arm at the point of valve contact, grind it smooth and square, removing as little material as possible. Replace the rocker arm if excessively worn. If a rocker stud shows signs of wear, it must be replaced (see below). If a rocker nut shows stress cracks, replace it. If an exhaust ball is galled or burned, substitute the intake ball from the same cylinder (if it is intact), and install a new intake ball. **NOTE:** *Avoid using new rocker balls on exhaust valves.*
Replace rocker studs: 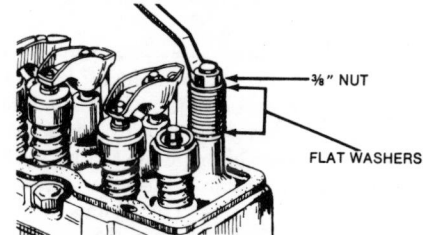 **Extracting a pressed-in rocker stud** 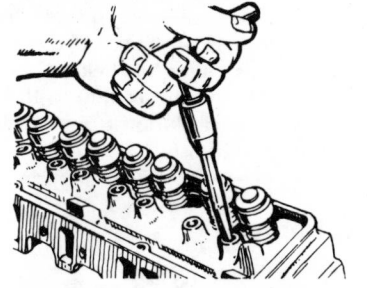 **Ream the stud bore for oversize rocker studs**	In order to remove a threaded stud, lock two nuts on the stud, and unscrew the stud using the lower nut. Coat the lower threads of the new stud with Loctite, and install. Two alternative methods are available for replacing pressed in studs. Remove the damaged stud using a stack of washers and a nut (see ilustration). In the first, the boss is reamed .005–.006″ oversize, and an oversize stud pressed in. Control the stud extension over the boss using washers, in the same manner as valve guides. Before installing the stud, coat it with white lead and grease. To retain the stud more positively drill a hole through the stud and boss, and install a roll pin. In the second method, the boss is tapped, and a threaded stud installed.
Inspect the rocker shaft(s) and rocker arms: 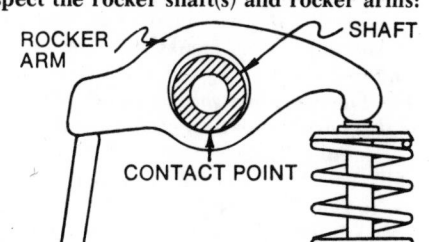 **Check the rocker arm-to-rocker shaft contact area**	Remove the rocker arms, springs and washers from rocker shaft. **NOTE:** *Lay out parts in the order as they are removed.* Inspect rocker arms for pitting or wear on the valve contact point, or excessive bushing wear. Bushings need only be replaced if wear is excessive, because the rocker arm normally contacts the shaft at one point only. Grind the valve contact point of rocker arm smooth if necessary, removing as little material as possible. If excessive material must be removed to smooth and square the arm, it should be replaced. Clean out all oil holes and passages in rocker shaft. If shaft is grooved or worn, replace it. Lubricate and assemble the rocker shaft.

Cylinder Head Reconditioning

Procedure	Method
Inspect the pushrods:	Remove the pushrods, and, if hollow, clean out the oil passages using fine wire. Roll each pushrod over a piece of clean glass. If a distinct clicking sound is heard as the pushrod rolls, the rod is bent, and must be replaced.
	*The length of all pushrods must be equal. Measure the length of the pushrods, compare to specifications, and replace as necessary.
*Inspect the valve lifters: 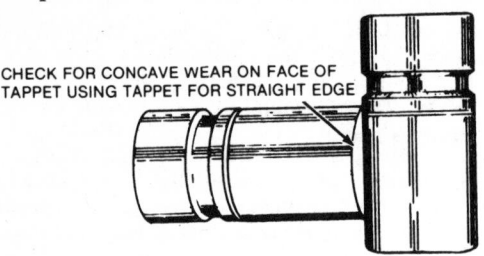 CHECK FOR CONCAVE WEAR ON FACE OF TAPPET USING TAPPET FOR STRAIGHT EDGE **Check the lifter face for squareness**	Remove lifters from their bores, and remove gum and varnish, using solvent. Clean walls of lifter bores. Check lifters for concave wear as illustrated. If face is worn concave, replace lifter, and carefully inspect the camshaft. Lightly lubricate lifter and insert it into its bore. If play is excessive, an oversize lifter must be installed (where possible). Consult a machinist concerning feasibility. If play is satisfactory, remove, lubricate, and reinstall the lifter.
*Testing hydraulic lifter leak down:	Submerge lifter in a container of kerosene. Chuck a used pushrod or its equivalent into a drill press. Position container of kerosene so pushrod acts on the lifter plunger. Pump lifter with the drill press, until resistance increases. Pump several more times to bleed any air out of lifter. Apply very firm, constant pressure to the lifter, and observe rate at which fluid bleeds out of lifter. If the fluid bleeds very quickly (less than 15 seconds), lifter is defective. If the time exceeds 60 seconds, lifter is sticking. In either case, recondition or replace lifter. If lifter is operating properly (leak down time 15–60 seconds), lubricate and install it.

Cylinder Block Reconditioning

Procedure	Method
Checking the main bearing clearance: 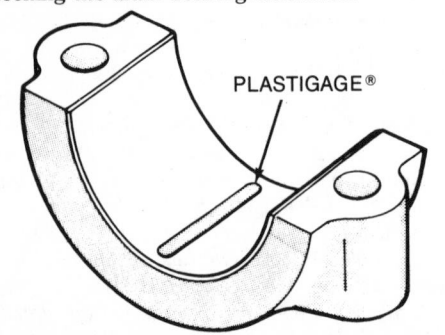 PLASTIGAGE® **Plastigage® installed on the lower bearing shell**	Invert engine, and remove cap from the bearing to be checked. Using a clean, dry rag, thoroughly clean all oil from crankshaft journal and bearing insert. NOTE: *Plastigage® is soluble in oil; therefore, oil on the journal or bearing could result in erroneous readings.* Place a piece of Plastigage along the full length of journal, reinstall cap, and torque to specifications. NOTE: **Specifications are given in the engine specifications earlier in this chapter.** Remove bearing cap, and determine bearing clearance by comparing width of Plastigage to the scale on Plastigage envelope. Journal taper is determined by comparing width of the Plas-

Cylinder Block Reconditioning

Procedure	Method

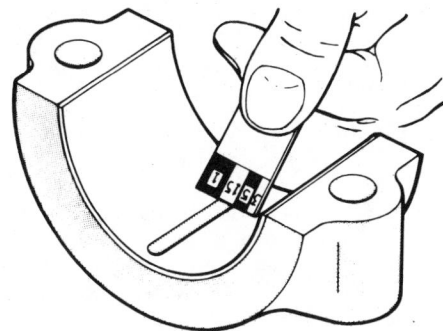

Measure Plastigage® to determine main bearing clearance

tigage strip near its ends. Rotate crankshaft 90° and retest, to determine journal eccentricity. **NOTE:** *Do not rotate crankshaft with Plastigage installed.* If bearing insert and journal appear intact, and are within tolerances, no further main bearing service is required. If bearing or journal appear defective, cause of failure should be determined before replacement.

* Remove crankshaft from block (see below). Measure the main bearing journals at each end twice (90° apart) using a micrometer, to determine diameter, journal taper and eccentricity. If journals are within tolerances, reinstall bearing caps at their specified torque. Using a telescope gauge and micrometer, measure bearing I.D. parallel to piston axis and at 30° on each side of piston axis. Subtract journal O.D. for bearing I.D. to determine oil clearance. If crankshaft journals appear defective, or do not meet tolerances, there is no need to measure bearings; for the crankshaft will require grinding and/or undersize bearings will be required. If bearing appears defective, cause for failure should be determined prior to replacement.

Check the connecting rod bearing clearance:

Connecting rod bearing clearance is checked in the same manner as main bearing clearance, using Plastigage. Before removing the crankshaft, connecting rod side clearance also should be measured and recorded.

* Checking connecting rod bearing clearance, using a micrometer, is identical to checking main bearing clearance. If no other service is required, the piston and rod assemblies need not be removed.

Remove the crankshaft:

Using a punch, mark the corresponding main bearing caps and saddles according to position (i.e., one punch on the front main cap and saddle, two on the second, three on the third, etc.). Using number stamps, identify the corresponding connecting rods and caps, according to cylinder (if no numbers are present). Remove the main and connecting rod caps, and place

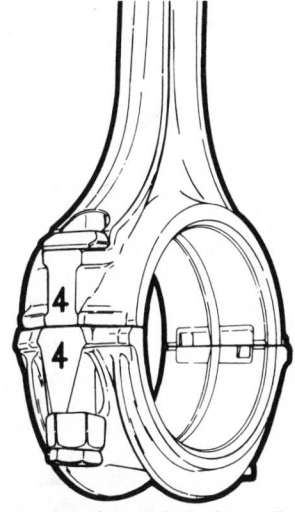

Match the connecting rod to the cylinder with a number stamp

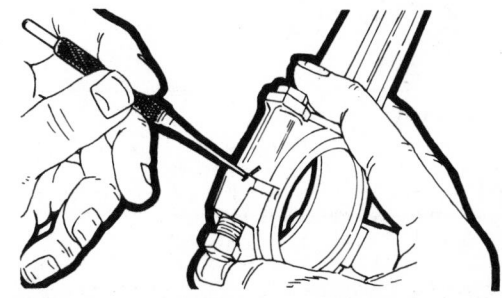

Match the connecting rod and cap with scribe marks

Cylinder Block Reconditioning

Procedure	Method
	sleeves of plastic tubing or vacuum hose over the connecting rod bolts, to protect the journals as the crankshaft is removed. Lift the crankshaft out of the block.
Remove the ridge from the top of the cylinder: RIDGE CAUSED BY CYLINDER WEAR CYLINDER WALL TOP OF PISTON **Cylinder bore ridge**	In order to facilitate removal of the piston and connecting rod, the ridge at the top of the cylinder (unworn area; see illustration) must be removed. Place the piston at the bottom of the bore, and cover it with a rag. Cut the ridge away using a ridge reamer, exercising extreme care to avoid cutting too deeply. Remove the rag, and remove cuttings that remain on the piston. **CAUTION:** *If the ridge is not removed, and new rings are installed, damage to rings will result.*
Remove the piston and connecting rod: **Push the piston out with a hammer handle**	Invert the engine, and push the pistons and connecting rods out of the cylinders. If necessary, tap the connecting rod boss with a wooden hammer handle, to force the piston out. **CAUTION:** *Do not attempt to force the piston past the cylinder ridge* (see above).
Service the crankshaft:	Ensure that all oil holes and passages in the crankshaft are open and free of sludge. If necessary, have the crankshaft ground to the largest possible undersize.
	** Have the crankshaft Magnafluxed, to locate stress cracks. Consult a machinist concerning additional service procedures, such as surface hardening (e.g., nitriding, Tuftriding) to improve wear characteristics, cross drilling and chamfering the oil holes to improve lubrication, and balancing.
Removing freeze plugs:	Drill a small hole in the middle of the freeze plugs. Thread a large sheet metal screw into the hole and remove the plug with a slide hammer.
Remove the oil gallery plugs:	Threaded plugs should be removed using an appropriate (usually square) wrench. To remove soft, pressed in plugs, drill a hole in the plug, and thread in a sheet metal screw. Pull the plug out by the screw using pliers.

Cylinder Block Reconditioning

Procedure	Method
Hot-tank the block: NOTE: *Do not hot-tank aluminum parts.*	Have the block hot-tanked to remove grease, corrosion, and scale from the water jackets. **NOTE:** *Consult the operator to determine whether the camshaft bearings will be damaged during the hot-tank process.*
Check the block for cracks:	Visually inspect the block for cracks or chips. The most common locations are as follows: Adjacent to freeze plugs. Between the cylinders and water jackets. Adjacent to the main bearing saddles. At the extreme bottom of the cylinders. Check only suspected cracks using spot check dye (see introduction). If a crack is located, consult a machinist concerning possible repairs.
	** Magnaflux the block to locate hidden cracks. If cracks are located, consult a machinist about feasibility of repair.
Install the oil gallery plugs and freeze plugs:	Coat freeze plugs with sealer and tap into position using a piece of pipe, slightly smaller than the plug, as a driver. To ensure retention, stake the edges of the plugs. Coat threaded oil gallery plugs with sealer and install. Drive replacement soft plugs into block using a large drift as a driver.
	* Rather than reinstalling lead plugs, drill and tap the holes, and install threaded plugs.
Check the bore diameter and surface: 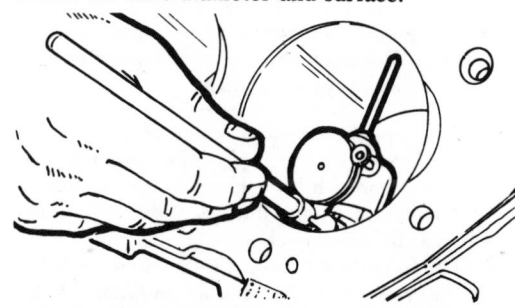 **Measure the cylinder bore with a dial gauge**	Visually inspect the cylinder bores for roughness, scoring, or scuffing. If evident, the cylinder bore must be bored or honed oversize to eliminate imperfections, and the smallest possible oversize piston used. The new pistons should be given to the machinist with the block, so that the cylinders can be bored or honed exactly to the piston size (plus clearance). If no flaws are evident, measure the bore diameter using a telescope gauge and micrometer, or dial gauge, parallel and perpendicular to the engine centerline, at the top (below the ridge) and bottom of the bore. Subtract the bottom measurements from the top to determine taper, and the parallel to

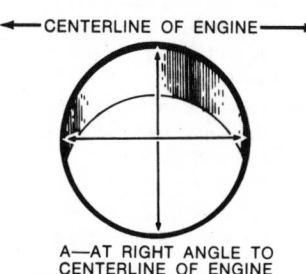

A—AT RIGHT ANGLE TO CENTERLINE OF ENGINE
B—PARALLEL TO CENTERLINE OF ENGINE

Cylinder bore measuring points

Measure the cylinder bore with a telescope gauge

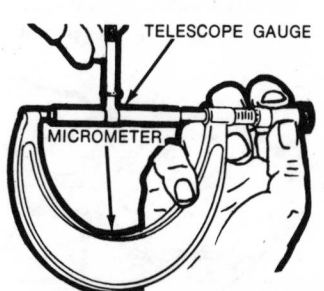

Measure the telescope gauge with a micrometer to determine the cylinder bore

Cylinder Block Reconditioning

Procedure	Method
	the centerline measurements from the perpendicular measurements to determine eccentricity. If the measurements are not within specifications, the cylinder must be bored or honed, and an oversize piston installed. If the measurements are within specifications the cylinder may be used as is, with only finish honing (see below). **NOTE:** *Prior to submitting the block for boring, perform the following operation(s).*
Check the cylinder block bearing alignment: 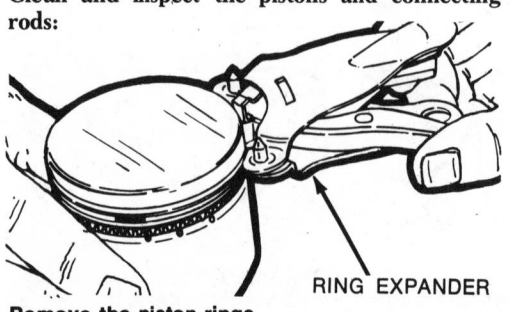 Check the main bearing saddle alignment	Remove the upper bearing inserts. Place a straightedge in the bearing saddles along the centerline of the crankshaft. If clearance exists between the straightedge and the center saddle, the block must be alignbored.
*Check the deck height:**	The deck height is the distance from the crankshaft centerline to the block deck. To measure, invert the engine, and install the crankshaft, retaining it with the center main cap. Measure the distance from the crankshaft journal to the block deck, parallel to the cylinder centerline. Measure the diameter of the end (front and rear) main journals, parallel to the centerline of the cylinders, divide the diameter in half, and subtract it from the previous measurement. The results of the front and rear measurements should be identical. If the difference exceeds .005″, the deck height should be corrected. **NOTE:** *Block deck height and warpage should be corrected at the same time.*
Check the block deck for warpage:	Using a straightedge and feeler gauges, check the block deck for warpage in the same manner that the cylinder head is checked (see Cylinder Head Reconditioning). If warpage exceeds specifications, have the deck resurfaced. **NOTE:** *In certain cases a specification for total material removal (cylinder head and block deck) is provided. This specification must not be exceeded.*
Clean and inspect the pistons and connecting rods: RING EXPANDER Remove the piston rings	Using a ring expander, remove the rings from the piston. Remove the retaining rings (if so equipped) and remove piston pin. **NOTE:** *If the piston pin must be pressed out, determine the proper method and use the proper tools; otherwise the piston will distort.* Clean the ring grooves using an appropriate tool, exercising care to avoid cutting too deeply. Thoroughly clean all carbon and varnish from the piston with solvent. **CAUTION:** *Do not use a wire brush or caustic solvent on pistons.* Inspect the pistons for scuffing, scoring, cracks, pitting, or excessive ring

Cylinder Block Reconditioning

Procedure	Method

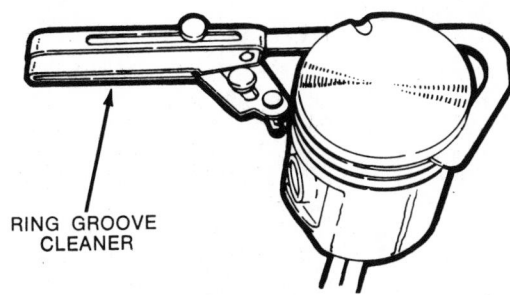

RING GROOVE
CLEANER

Clean the piston ring grooves

groove wear. If wear is evident, the piston must be replaced. Check the connecting rod length by measuring the rod from the inside of the large end to the inside of the small end using calipers (see illustration). All connecting rods should be equal length. Replace any rod that differs from the others in the engine.

* Have the connecting rod alignment checked in an alignment fixture by a machinist. Replace any twisted or bent rods.

* Magnaflux the connecting rods to locate stress cracks. If cracks are found, replace the connecting rod.

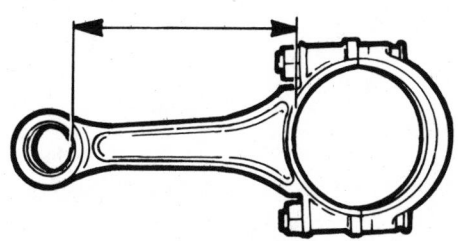

Check the connecting rod length (arrow)

Fit the pistons to the cylinders:

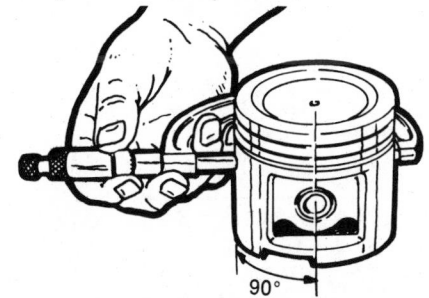

90°

Measure the piston prior to fitting

Using a telescope gauge and micrometer, or a dial gauge, measure the cylinder bore diameter perpendicular to the piston pin, 2½″ below the deck. Measure the piston perpendicular to its pin on the skirt. The difference between the two measurements is the piston clearance. If the clearance is within specifications or slightly below (after boring or honing), finish honing is all that is required. If the clearance is excessive, try to obtain a slightly larger piston to bring clearance within specifications. Where this is not possible, obtain the first oversize piston, and hone (or if necessary, bore) the cylinder to size.

Assemble the pistons and connecting rods:

Install the piston pin lock-rings (if used)

Inspect piston pin, connecting rod small end bushing, and piston bore for galling, scoring, or excessive wear. If evident, replace defective part(s). Measure the I.D. of the piston boss and connecting rod small end, and the O.D. of the piston pin. If within specifications, assemble piston pin and rod.
CAUTION: *If piston pin must be pressed in, determine the proper method and use the proper tools; otherwise the piston will distort.*
    Install the lock rings; ensure that they seat properly. If the parts are not within specifications, determine the service method for the type of engine. In some cases, piston and pin are serviced as an assembly when either is defective. Others specify reaming the piston and connecting rods for an oversize pin. If the connecting rod bushing is worn, it may in many cases be replaced. Reaming the piston and replacing the rod bushing are machine shop operations.

Cylinder Block Reconditioning

Procedure	*Method*

Clean and inspect the camshaft:

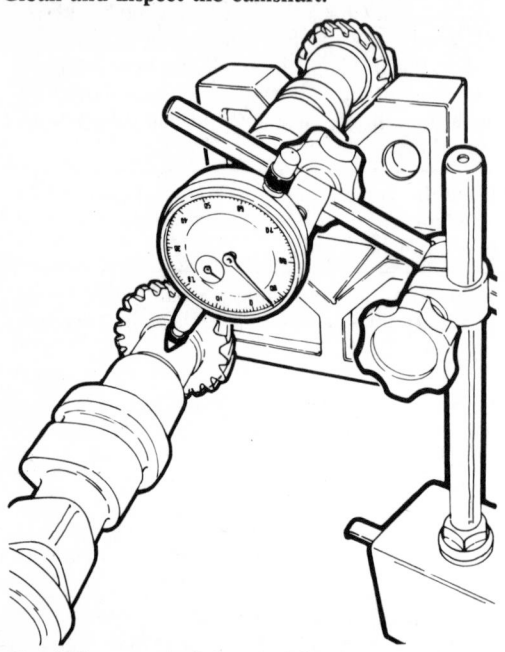

Degrease the camshaft, using solvent, and clean out all oil holes. Visually inspect cam lobes and bearing journals for excessive wear. If a lobe is questionable, check all lobes as indicated below. If a journal or lobe is worn, the camshaft must be regrounded or replaced.

NOTE: *If a journal is worn, there is a good chance that the bushings are worn.* If lobes and journals appear intact, place the front and rear journals in V-blocks, and rest a dial indicator on the center journal. Rotate the camshaft to check straightness. If deviation exceeds .001", replace the camshaft.

* Check the camshaft lobes with a micrometer, by measuring the lobes from the nose to base and again at 90° (see illustration). The lift is determined by subtracting the second measurement from the first. If all exhaust lobes and all intake lobes are not identical, the camshaft must be reground or replaced.

Check the camshaft for straightness

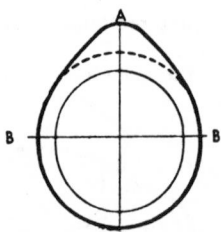

Camshaft lobe measurement

Replace the camshaft bearings:

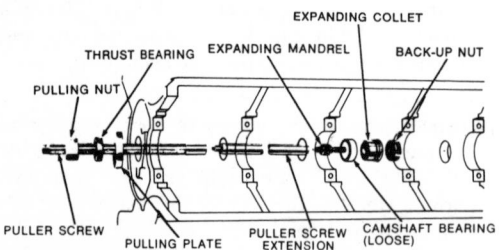

Camshaft bearing removal and installation tool (OHV engines only)

If excessive wear is indicated, or if the engine is being completely rebuilt, camshaft bearings should be replaced as follows: Drive the camshaft rear plug from the block. Assemble the removal puller with its shoulder on the bearing to be removed. Gradually tighten the puller nut until bearing is removed. Remove remaining bearings, leaving the front and rear for last. To remove front and rear bearings, reverse position of the tool, so as to pull the bearings in toward the center of the block. Leave the tool in this position, pilot the new front and rear bearings on the installer, and pull them into position: Return the tool to its original position and pull remaining bearings into position.

NOTE: *Ensure that oil holes align when installing bearings.* Replace camshaft rear plug, and stake it into position to aid retention.

Finish hone the cylinders:

Chuck a flexible drive hone into a power drill, and insert it into the cylinder. Start the hone, and remove it up and down in the cylinder at a rate which will produce approximately a 60° cross-hatch pattern.

NOTE: *Do not extend the hone below the cylinder bore.* After developing the pattern, remove

Cylinder Block Reconditioning

Procedure	Method

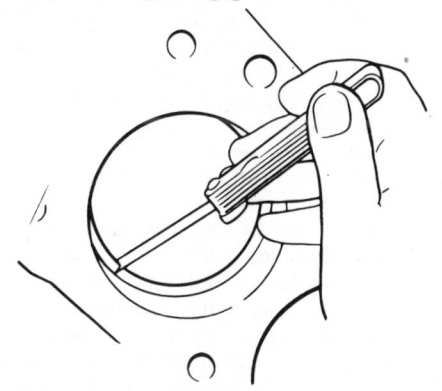

CROSS HATCH PATTERN

50°-60°

Cylinder bore after honing

the hone and recheck piston fit. Wash the cylinders with a detergent and water solution to remove abrasive dust, dry, and wipe several times with a rag soaked in engine oil.

Check piston ring end-gap:

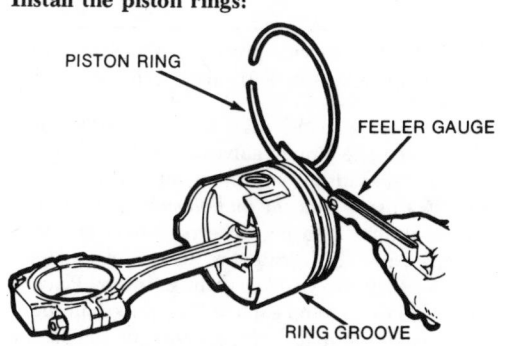

Check the piston ring end gap

Compress the piston rings to be used in a cylinder, one at a time, into that cylinder, and press them approximately 1″ below the deck with an inverted piston. Using feeler gauges, measure the ring end-gap, and compare to specifications. Pull the ring out of the cylinder and file the ends with a fine file to obtain proper clearance.
CAUTION: *If inadequate ring end-gap is utilized, ring breakage will result.*

Install the piston rings:

PISTON RING

FEELER GAUGE

RING GROOVE

Check the piston ring side clearance

Inspect the ring grooves in the piston for excessive wear or taper. If necessary, recut the groove(s) for use with an overwidth ring or a standard ring and spacer. If the groove is worn uniformly, overwidth rings, or standard rings and spacers may be installed without recutting. Roll the outside of the ring around the groove to check for burrs or deposits. If any are found, remove with a fine file. Hold the ring in the groove, and measure side clearance. If necessary, correct as indicated above.
NOTE: *Always install any additional spacers above the piston ring.*
   The ring groove must be deep enough to allow the ring to seat below the lands (see illustration). In many cases, a "go-no-go" depth gauge will be provided with the piston rings. Shallow grooves may be corrected by recutting, while deep grooves require some type of filler or expander

Cylinder Block Reconditioning

Procedure	Method
	behind the piston. Consult the piston ring supplier concerning the suggested method. Install the rings on the piston, lowest ring first, using a ring expander. NOTE: *Position the rings as specified by the manufacturer.* Consult the engine service procedures earlier in this chapter for details concerning specific engines.
Install the camshaft:	Liberally lubricate the camshaft lobes and journals, and install the camshaft. CAUTION: *Exercise extreme care to avoid damaging the bearings when inserting the camshaft.* Install and tighten the camshaft thrust plate retaining bolts.
	See the engine service procedures earlier in this chapter for details concerning specific engines.
Check camshaft end-play (OHV engines only): Check the camshaft end-play with a feeler gauge DIAL INDICATOR CAMSHAFT Check the camshaft end-play with a dial indicator	Using feeler gauges, determine whether the clearance between the camshaft boss (or gear) and backing plate is within specifications. Install shims behind the thrust plate, or reposition the camshaft gear and retest endplay. In some cases, adjustment is by replacing the thrust plate. See the engine service procedures earlier in this chapter for details concerning specific engines. *Mount a dial indicator stand so that the stem of the dial indicator rests on the nose of the camshaft, parallel to the camshaft axis. Push the camshaft as far in as possible and zero the gauge. Move the camshaft outward to determine the amount of camshaft endplay. If the endplay is not within tolerance, install shims behind the thrust plate, or reposition the camshaft gear and retest. See the engine service procedures earlier in this chapter for details concerning specific engines.
Install the rear main seal:	See the engine service procedures earlier in this chapter for details concerning specific engines.
Install the crankshaft: 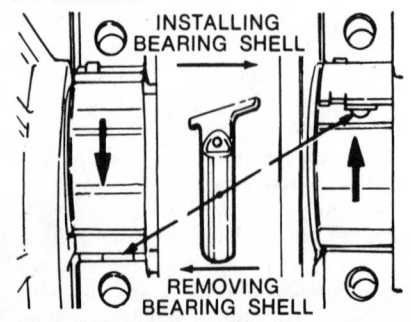 INSTALLING BEARING SHELL REMOVING BEARING SHELL Remove or install the upper bearing insert using a roll-out pin	Thoroughly clean the main bearing saddles and caps. Place the upper halves of the bearing inserts on the saddles and press into position. NOTE: *Ensure that the oil holes align.* Press the corresponding bearing inserts into the main bearing caps. Lubricate the upper main bearings, and lay the crankshaft in position. Place a strip of Plastigage on each of the crankshaft journals, install the main caps, and torque to specifications. Remove the main caps, and compare the Plastigage to the scale on the Plastigage envelope. If clearances are within tolerances, remove the Plastigage, turn the crankshaft 90°, wipe off all oil and retest. If all clearances are correct,

Cylinder Block Reconditioning

Procedure	**Method**

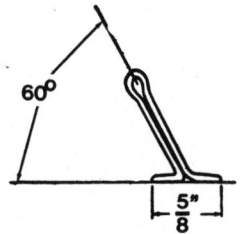

Home-made bearing roll-out pin

remove all Plastigage, thoroughly lubricate the main caps and bearing journals, and install the main caps. If clearances are not within tolerance, the upper bearing inserts may be removed, without removing the crankshaft, using a bearing roll out pin (see illustration). Roll in a bearing that will provide proper clearance, and retest. Torque all main caps, excluding the thrust bearing cap, to specifications. Tighten the thrust bearing cap finger tight. To properly align the thrust bearing, pry the crankshaft the extent of its axial travel several times, the last movement held toward the front of the engine, and torque the thrust bearing cap to specifications. Determine the crankshaft end-play (see below), and bring within tolerance with thrust washers.

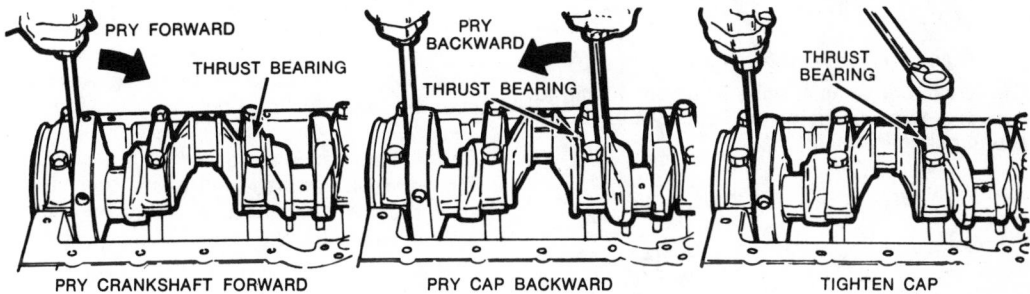

Aligning the thrust bearing

Measure crankshaft end-play:

Mount a dial indicator stand on the front of the block, with the dial indicator stem resting on the nose of the crankshaft, parallel to the crankshaft axis. Pry the crankshaft the extent of its travel rearward, and zero the indicator. Pry the crankshaft forward and record crankshaft end-play. **NOTE:** *Crankshaft end-play also may be measured at the thrust bearing, using feeler gauges (see illustration).*

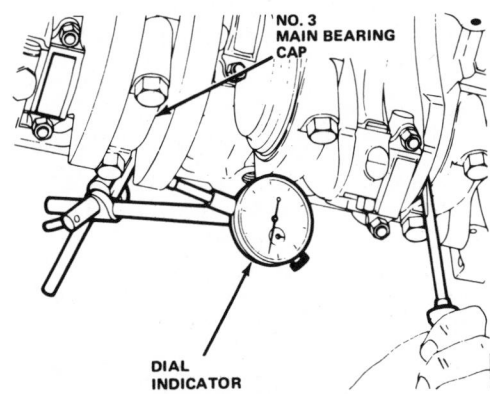

Check the crankshaft end-play with a dial indicator

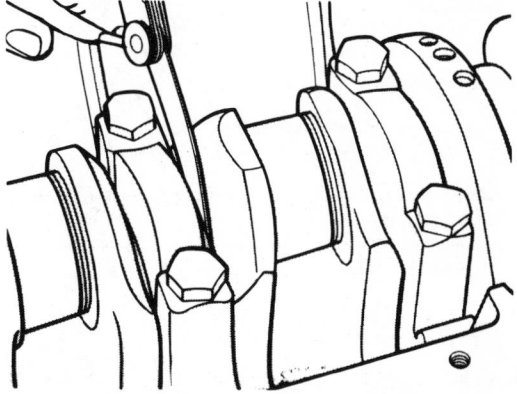

Check the crankshaft end-play with a feeler gauge

Cylinder Block Reconditioning

Procedure	*Method*
Install the pistons:	Press the upper connecting rod bearing halves into the connecting rods, and the lower halves into the connecting rod caps. Position the piston ring gaps according to specifications (see car section), and lubricate the pistons. Install a ring compresser on a piston, and press two long (8″) pieces of plastic tubing over the rod bolts. Using the tubes as a guide, press the pistons into the bores and onto the crankshaft with a wooden hammer handle. After seating the rod on the crankshaft journal, remove the tubes and install the cap finger tight. Install the remaining pistons in the same manner. Invert the engine and check the bearing clearance at two points (90° apart) on each journal with Plastigage.

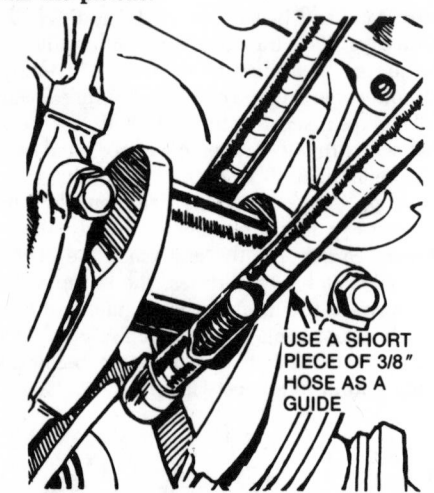

USE A SHORT PIECE OF 3/8″ HOSE AS A GUIDE

Use lengths of vacuum hose or rubber tubing to protect the crankshaft journals and cylinder walls during piston installation

NOTE: *Do not turn the crankshaft with Plastigage installed.* If clearance is within tolerances, remove *all* Plastigage, thoroughly lubricate the journals, and torque the rod caps to specifications. If clearance is not within specifications, install different thickness bearing inserts and recheck.

CAUTION: *Never shim or file the connecting rods or caps.* Always install plastic tube sleeves over the rod bolts when the caps are not installed, to protect the crankshaft journals.

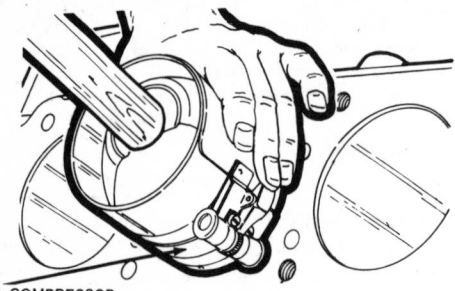

RING COMPRESSOR

Install the piston using a ring compressor

| Check connecting rod side clearance: | Determine the clearance between the sides of the connecting rods and the crankshaft using feeler gauges. If clearance is below the minimum tolerance, the rod may be machined to provide adequate clearance. If clearance is excessive, substitute an unworn rod, and recheck. If clearance is still outside specifications, the crankshaft must be welded and reground, or replaced. |

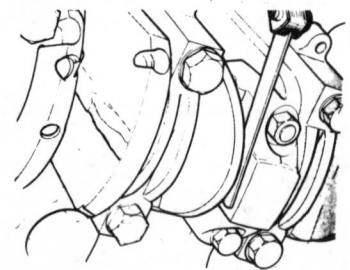

Check the connecting rod side clearance with a feeler gauge

| Inspect the timing chain (or belt): | Visually inspect the timing chain for broken or loose links, and replace the chain if any are found. If the chain will flex sideways, it must be replaced. Install the timing chain as specified. Be sure the timing belt is not stretched, frayed or broken.
NOTE: *If the original timing chain is to be reused, install it in its original position.* |

Cylinder Block Reconditioning

Procedure	Method
Check timing gear backlash and runout (OHV engines):	Mount a dial indicator with its stem resting on a tooth of the camshaft gear (as illustrated). Rotate the gear until all slack is removed, and zero the indicator. Rotate the gear in the opposite direction until slack is removed, and record gear backlash. Mount the indicator with its stem resting on the edge of the camshaft gear, parallel to the axis of the camshaft. Zero the indicator, and turn the camshaft gear one full turn, recording the runout. If either backlash or runout exceed specifications, replace the worn gear(s).

Check the camshaft gear backlash

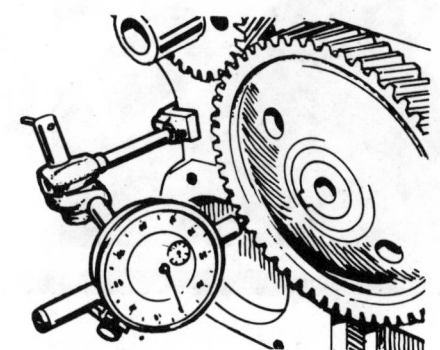

Check the camshaft gear run-out

Completing the Rebuilding Process

Follow the above procedures, complete the rebuilding process as follows:

Fill the oil pump with oil, to prevent cavitating (sucking air) on initial engine start up. Install the oil pump and the pickup tube on the engine. Coat the oil pan gasket as necessary, and install the gasket and the oil pan. Mount the flywheel and the crankshaft vibration damper or pulley on the crankshaft. NOTE: *Always use new bolts when installing the flywheel*. Inspect the clutch shaft pilot bushing in the crankshaft. If the bushing is excessively worn, remove it with an expanding puller and a slide hammer, and tap a new bushing into place.

Position the engine, cylinder head side up. Lubricate the lifters, and install them into their bores. Install the cylinder head, and torque it as specified. Insert the pushrods and install the rocker shaft(s) or position the rocker arms on the pushrods. Adjust the valves.

Install the intake and exhaust manifolds, the carburetor(s), the distributor and spark plugs. Adjust the point gap and the static ignition timing. Mount all accessories and install the engine in the car. Fill the radiator with coolant, and the crankcase with high quality engine oil.

Break-in Procedure

Start the engine, and allow it to run at low speed for a few minutes, while checking for leaks. Stop the engine, check the oil level, and fill as necessary. Restart the engine, and fill the cooling system to capacity. Check the point dwell angle and adjust the ignition timing and the valves. Run the engine at low to medium speed (800–2500 rpm) for approximately ½ hour, and retorque the cylinder head bolts. Road test the car, and check again for leaks.

Follow the manufacturer's recommended engine break-in procedure and maintenance schedule for new engines.

Emission Controls and Fuel System

EMISSION CONTROLS

There are three types of automotive pollutants; crankcase fumes, exhaust gases and gasoline evaporation. The equipment that is used to limit these pollutants is commonly called emission control equipment.

PCV System

The crankcase emission control equipment consists of a positive crankcase ventilation valve (PCV), a closed or open oil filler cap and hoses to connect this equipment.

When the engine is running, a small portion of the gases which are formed in the combustion chamber during combustion leak by the piston rings and enter the crankcase. Since these gases are under pressure they tend to escape from the crankcase and enter into the atmosphere. If these gases were allowed to remain in the crankcase for any length of time, they would contaminate the engine oil and cause sludge to build up. If the gases are allowed to escape into the atmosphere, they would pollute the air, as they contain unburned hydrocarbons. The crankcase emission control equipment recycles these gases back into the engine combustion chamber where they are burned.

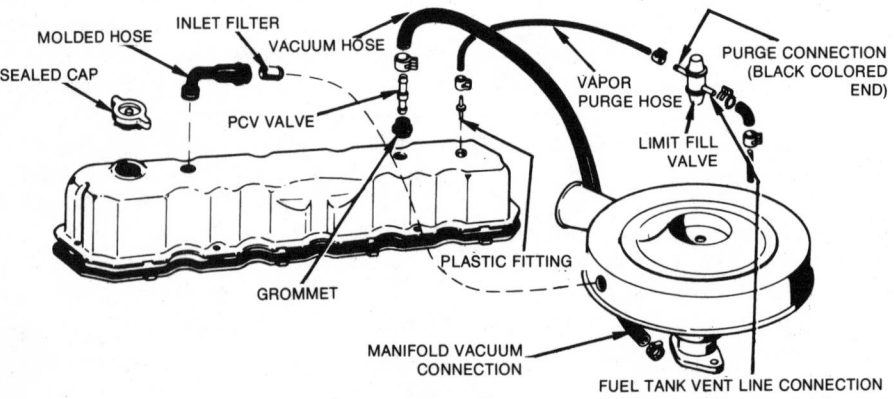

Typical PCV system

Crankcase gases are recycled in the following manner: while the engine is running, clean filtered air is drawn into the crankcase either directly through the oil filler cap, or through the carburetor air filter and then through a hose leading to the oil filler cap. As the air passes through the crankcase it picks up the combustion gases and carries them out of the crankcase, up through the PCV valve and into the intake manifold. After they enter the intake manifold they are drawn into the combustion chamber where they are burned.

The most critical component in the system is the PCV valve. This vacuum controlled valve regulates the amount of gases which are recycled into the combustion chamber. At low engine speeds the valve is partially closed, limiting the flow of gases into the intake manifold. As engine speed increases, the valve opens to admit greater quantities of the gases into the intake manifold. If the valve should become blocked or plugged, the gases will be prevented from escaping from the crankcases by the normal route. Since these gases are under pressure, they will find their own way out of the crankcase. This alternate route is usually a weak oil seal or gasket in the engine. As the gas escapes by the gasket, it also creates an oil leak. Besides causing oil leaks, a cloged PCV valve also allows these gases to remain in the crankcase for an extended period of time, promoting the formation of sludge in the engine.

The above explanation and the troubleshooting procedure which follows applies to all engines equipped with PCV systems.

TROUBLESHOOTING

With the engine running, pull the PCV valve and hose from the engine. Block off the end of the valve with your finger. The engine speed should drop at least 50 rpm when the end of the valve is blocked. If the engine speed does not drop at least 50 rpm, then the valve is defective and should be replaced. Shake the valve; if it rattles it probably isn't clogged.

REMOVAL AND INSTALLATION

1. Pull the PCV valve and hose from the engine.
2. Remove the PCV valve from the hose. Inspect the inside of the PCV valve hose. If it is dirty, disconnect it from the intake manifold and clean it.

To install, proceed as follows:

1. If the PCV valve hose was removed, connect it to the intake manifold.
2. Connect the PCV valve to its hose.
3. Install the PCV valve on the engine.

Air Injection System

All of the engines used in Jeeps except the L-134 and the 4-151 at some point incorporated the air injection system for controlling the emission of exhaust gases into the atmosphere. Since this type of emission control system is common to all of the engines, it will be explained here.

The exhaust emission control air injection system consists of a belt driven air pump which directs compressed air through connecting hoses to a steel distribution manifold into stainless steel injection tubes in the exhaust port adjacent to each exhaust valve. The air, with its normal oxygen content, reacts with the hot, but incompletely burned exhaust gases and permits further combustion in the exhaust port or manifold.

AIR PUMP

The air injection pump is a positive displacement vane type which is permanently lubricated and requires little periodic maintenance. The only serviceable parts on the air pump are the filter, exhaust tube, and relief valve. The relief valve relieves the air flow when the pump pressure reaches a preset level. This occurs at high engine rpm. This serves to prevent damage to the pump and to limit maximum exhaust manifold temperatures.

NOTE: *On 1974–79 models the relief valve assembly is incorporated in the diverter*

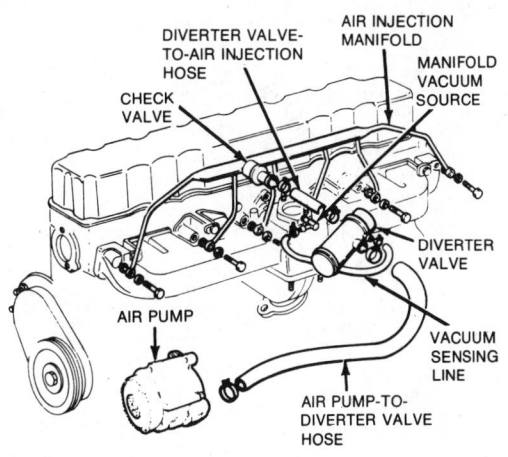

Typical air pump system

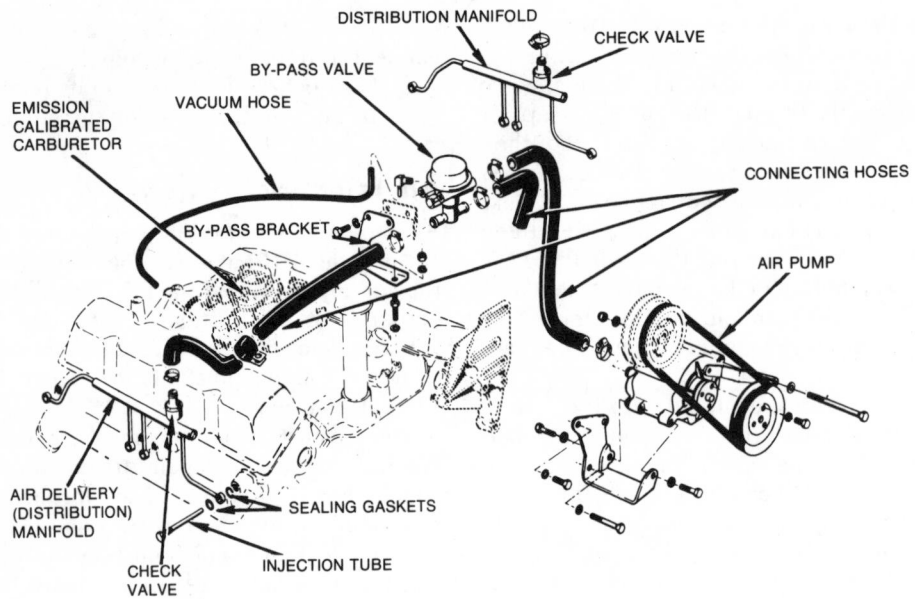

Typical V8 air pump system

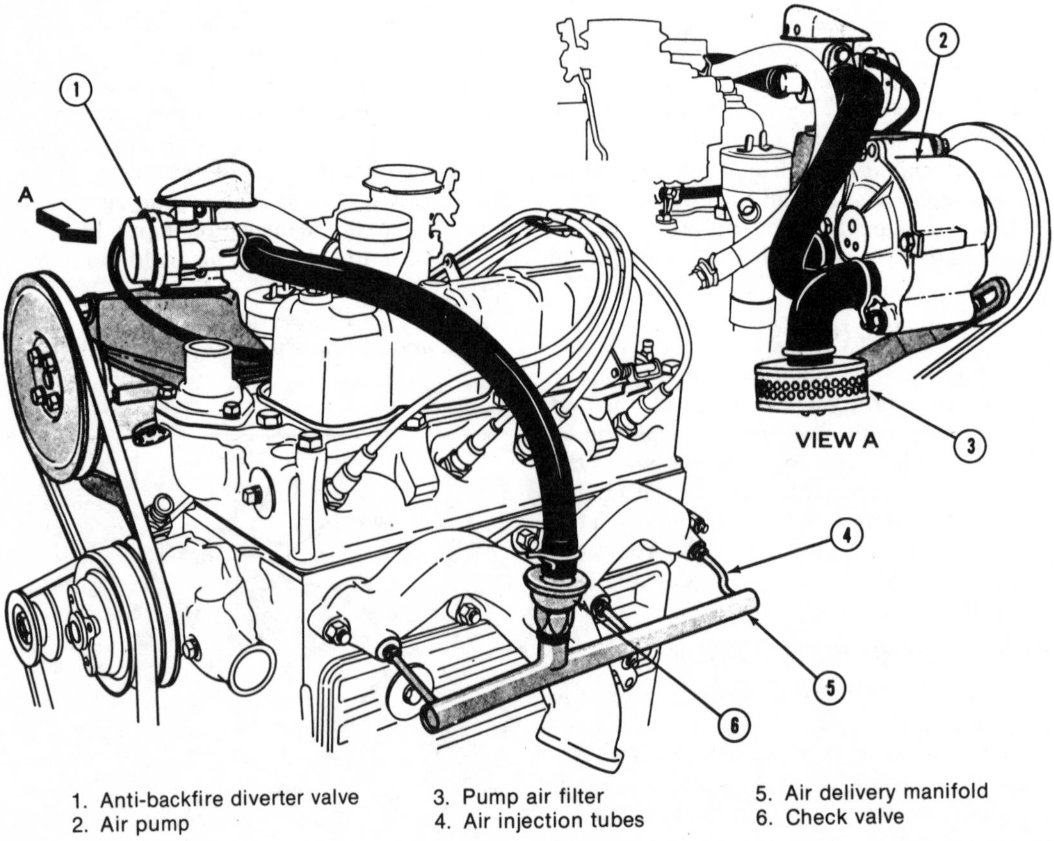

1. Anti-backfire diverter valve
2. Air pump
3. Pump air filter
4. Air injection tubes
5. Air delivery manifold
6. Check valve

F-head air pump system

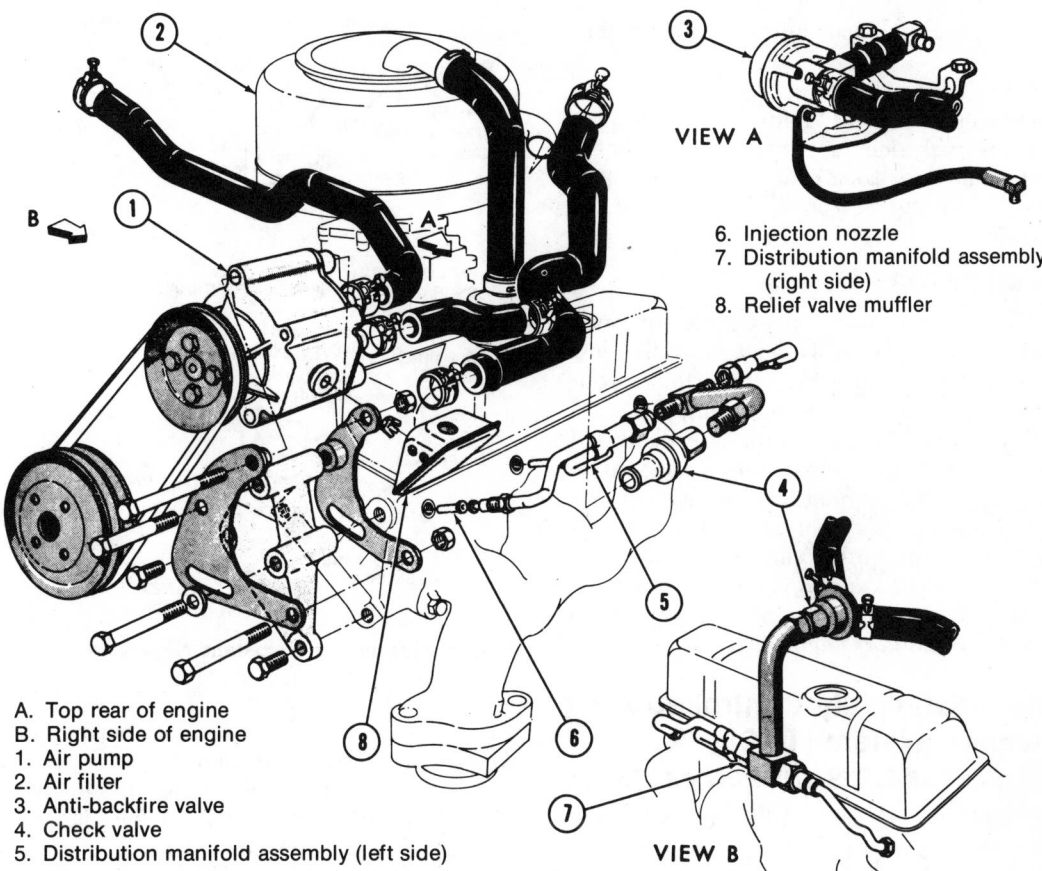

VIEW A

6. Injection nozzle
7. Distribution manifold assembly (right side)
8. Relief valve muffler

A. Top rear of engine
B. Right side of engine
1. Air pump
2. Air filter
3. Anti-backfire valve
4. Check valve
5. Distribution manifold assembly (left side)

VIEW B

V6 air pump system

valve. If the relief valve is believed to be defective, the diverter valve assembly must be replaced.

PUMP AIR FILTER

The air filter attached to the pump (all except American Motors engines), is a replaceable element type. The filter should be replaced every 12,000 miles under normal conditions and sooner under off-road use. Some models draw their air supply through the carburetor air filter.

The air pump on American Motors engines is equipped with a centrifugal fan type air filter. This filter fan requires no servicing aside from replacement if damaged.

AIR DELIVERY MANIFOLD

The air delivery manifold distributes the air from the pump to each of the air delivery tubes in a uniform manner. A check valve is integral with the air delivery manifold. Its function is to prevent the reverse flow of exhaust gases to the pump should the pump fail. The reverse flow would damage the air pump and connecting hose.

AIR INJECTION TUBES

The air injection tubes are inserted into the exhaust ports. The tubes project into the exhaust ports, directing air into the vicinity of the exhaust valve.

ANTI-BACKFIRE VALVE

The anti-backfire diverter valve prevents engine backfire by briefly interrupting the air being injected into the exhaust manifold during periods of deceleration or rapid throttle closure. On the F-head and all of the American Motors engines the valve opens when a sudden increase in manifold vacuum overcomes the diaphragm spring tension. With the valve in the open position the air flow is directed to the atmosphere.

On the V6, the anti-backfire valve is what is commonly called a gulp valve. During rapid deceleration the valve is opened by the sudden high vacuum condition in the intake manifold and gulps air into the intake manifold.

Both of these valves prevent backfiring in the exhaust manifold. Both valves also prevent an over rich fuel mixture from being burned in the exhaust manifold, which would cause backfiring and possible damage to the engine.

CARBURETOR

The carburetors used on engines equipped with emission controls have specific flow characteristics that differ from the carburetors used on vehicles not equipped with such devices. The carburetors are identified by number. The correct carburetor should be used when replacement is necessary.

A carburetor dashpot is used on the F-head to control throttle closing speed.

NOTE: *All of the components discussed in the following paragraphs apply only to American Motors engines.*

Thermostatically Controlled Air Cleaner System (TAC)
232 AND 258 SIXES THROUGH 1977

The TAC system applied to the AMC sixes consists of a two-piece heat shroud positioned on the exhaust manifold, a hot air hose, and an air duct and valve assembly located in the air cleaner snorkel.

The air duct and valve assembly incorporates an air valve, a thermostat mechanism, and a spring.

The temperature of the air entering the air cleaner is thermostatically regulated by the air duct and valve assembly. Cold air is supplied from the engine compartment and hot air from the shrouded exhaust manifold.

The thermostat unit in the air duct is exposed to incoming air on the air filter side of the air valve. The spring-loaded air valve is connected to the thermostat unit through linkage. The spring holds the valve in the

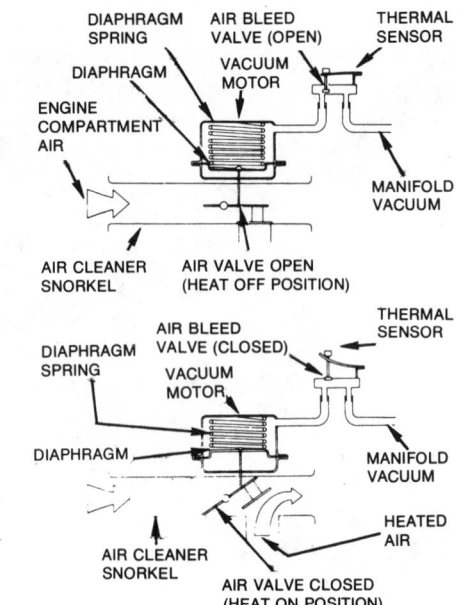

Vacuum controlled thermostatic air cleaner

closed (heat on) position until the thermostat overcomes the spring tension.

While the engine is warming up and the air temperature entering the air duct is less than 105°F, the thermostat is in the retracted position and the air valve is held in the closed (heat on) position.

As the temperature of the air passing over the thermostat unit rises, the thermostat starts to open and pulls the air valve down, closing off the heated air intake and opening the cool air intake, allowing cooler engine compartment air to enter the air cleaner.

When the temperature of the air reaches 130°F, the air valve is completely open to engine compartment air.

4-151, 304 V8, 1978–81 SIXES

This system consists of a heat shroud which is integral with the right side exhaust manifold, a hot air hose and a special air cleaner

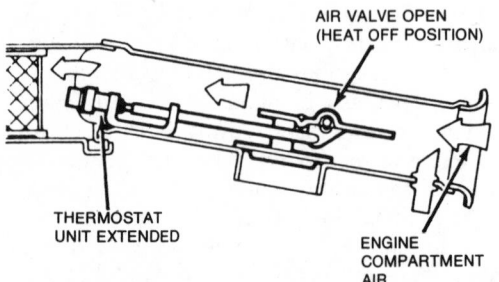
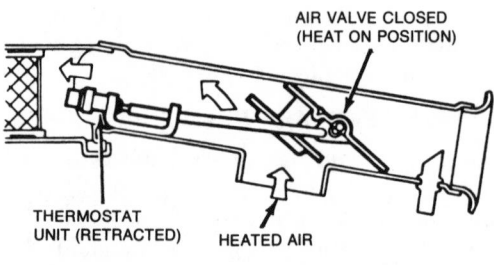

Non-vacuum thermostatically controlled air cleaner

assembly equipped with a thermal sensor and a vacuum motor and air valve assembly.

The thermal sensor incorporates an air bleed valve which regulates the amount of vacuum applied to the vacuum motor, controlling the air valve position to supply either heated air from the exhaust manifold or air from the engine compartment.

During the warm-up period when underhood temperatures are low, the air bleed valve is closed and sufficient vacuum is applied to the vacuum motor to hold the air valve in the closed (heat on) position.

As the temperature of the air entering the air cleaner approaches approximately 115°F, the air bleed valve opens to decrease the amount of vacuum applied to the vacuum motor. The diaphragm spring in the vacuum motor then moves the air valve into the open (heat off) position, allowing only underhood air to enter the air cleaner.

The air valve in the air cleaner will also open, regardless of airtemperature, during heavy acceleration to obtain maximum air flow through the air cleaner.

Transmission Controlled Spark System

The purpose of this system is to reduce the emission of oxides of nitrogen by lowering the peak combustion pressure and temperature during the power stroke.

The system incorporates the following components:

AMBIENT TEMPERATURE OVERRIDE SWITCH (1973 ONLY)

This switch, located at the firewall, senses ambient temperatures and completes the

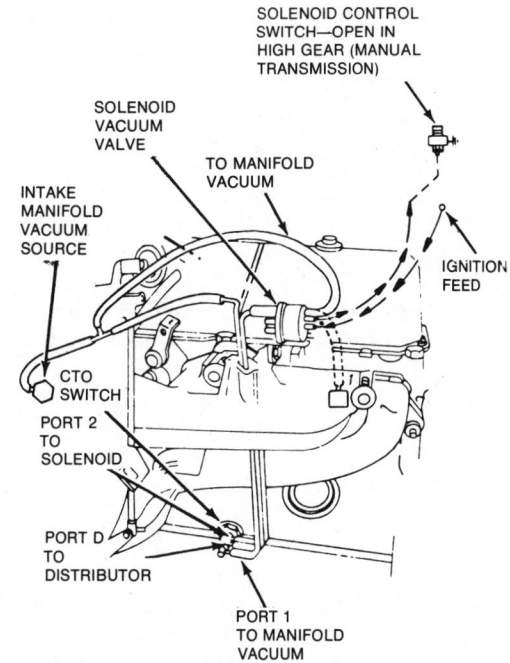

Inline six TCS system

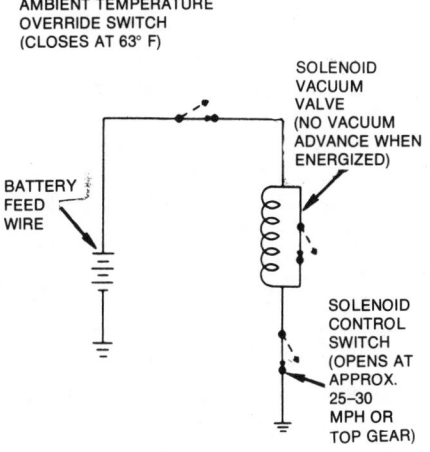

TCS electrical diagram

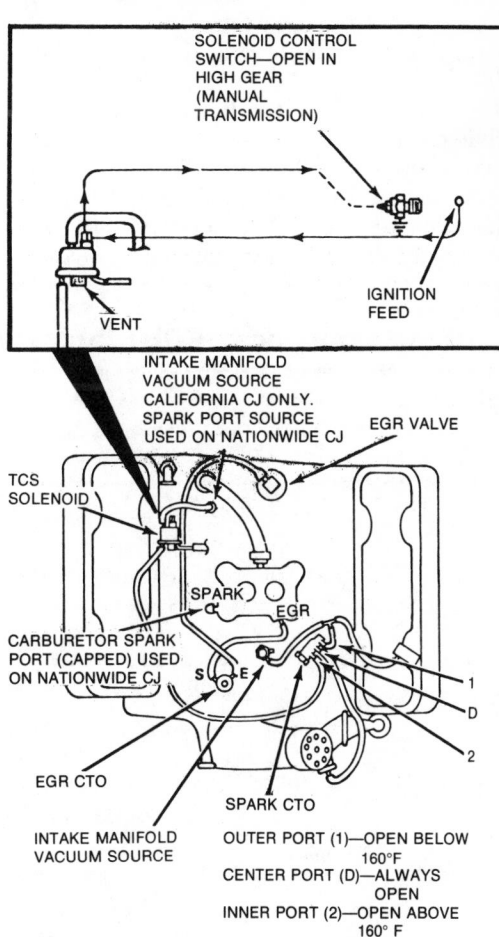

V8 TCS system

electrical circuit from the battery to the solenoid vacuum valve when ambient temperatures are above 63°F.

SOLENOID VACUUM VALVE

This valve is attached to the ignition coil bracket at the right side of the engine (1973 V8 engines), right rear intake manifold (1974–80 V8), or to a bracket at the rear of the intake manifold (Sixes). When the valve is energized, carburetor vacuum is blocked off and the distributor vacuum line is vented to the atmosphere through a port in the valve, resulting in no vacuum advance. When the valve is de-energized, vacuum is applied to the distributor resulting in normal vacuum advance.

SOLENOID CONTROL SWITCH

This switch is located on the transmission on vehicles with manual transmissions. It opens or closes in relation to speed and gear range. When the transmission is in high gear, the switch opens and breaks the ground circuit to the solenoid vacuum valve. In lower gear ranges the switch closes and completes the ground circuit to the solenoid vacuum valve. The switch is operated by the transmission shifter shaft.

On vehicles equipped with an automatic transmission, the switch is located along the speedometer cable on the firewall. The switch is operated by speedometer cable rpm. At about 32 to 36 mph the switch will open the electrical ground circuit to the solenoid vacuum valve.

NOTE: *On 1976–80 models, the switch closes at a lower speed (22–28 mph) on deceleration.*

COOLANT TEMPERATURE OVERRIDE SWITCH

The switch reacts to coolant temperatures to route either intake manifold or carburetor vacuum to the distributor vacuum advance diaphragm.

When the coolant temperature is below 160°F, intake manifold vacuum is applied through a hose connection to the distributor advance diaphragm, resulting in full vacuum advance.

When the coolant temperature is above 160°F, intake manifold vacuum is blocked off and carburetor vacuum is then applied through the solenoid vacuum valve to the distributor advance diaphragm, resulting in decreased vacuum advance.

NOTE: *Some vehicles made for California, intake manifold vacuum routed through the TCS solenoid is applied to the distributor when the coolant temperature is above 160°F.*

The relationship between distributor vacuum advance and the operation of the TCS system and coolant temperature override switch can be determined by referring to the Emission

Emission Control Distributor Vacuum Application Chart, 1973

Manual Transmission Gear		Ambient (Air) Temperature	Coolant Temperature	Vacuum Applied to the Distributor
3 Speed	4 Speed			
1–2	1–2–3	Below 63°F	Below 160°F	Manifold
1–2	1–2–3	Below 63°F	Above 160°F	Carburetor
1–2	1–2–3	Above 63°F	Above 160°F	None
1–2	1–2–3	Above 63°F	Below 160°F	Manifold
3	4	Below 63°F	Below 160°F	Manifold
3	4	Below 63°F	Above 160°F	Carburetor
3	4	Above 63°F	Above 160°F	Carburetor
3	4	Above 63°F	Below 160°F	Manifold

Emission Control Distributor Vacuum Application Chart, 1974–80

Transmission Gear			Coolant Temperature	Vacuum Source
3 Speed	4 Speed	Automatic		
1–2	1–2–3	Below 32–36 mph	Below 160°F	Manifold
1–2	1–2–3	Below 32–36 mph	Above 160°F	Through the Solenoid Vacuum Valve
3	4	Above 32–36 mph	Below 160°F	Manifold
3	4	Above 32–36 mph	Above 160°F	No Vacuum

Control Distributor Vacuum Application Chart.

Exhaust Gas Recirculation (EGR) System

The EGR system consists of a diaphragm actuated flow control valve (EGR valve), coolant temperature override switch (EGR CTO), an exhaust backpressure sensor low temperature vacuum signal modulator (1973 only), high temperature vacuum signal modulator (1973 only), and connecting hoses. In 1980, a Thermal Vacuum Switch, located in the air cleaner, was added to control the vacuum signal between the EGR & CTO.

The purpose of the EGR system is to limit the formation of oxides of nitrogen by diluting the fresh air intake charge with a metered amount of exhaust gas, thereby reducing the

peak temperatures of the burning gases in the combustion chambers.

EGR VALVE

The EGR valve is mounted on a machined surface at the rear of the intake manifold on V8 engines and on the side of the intake manifold on the Sixes. When a backpressure sensor is used, the EGR valve is mounted on a spacer which is an integral part of the backpressure sensor.

The valve is held in a normally closed position by a coil spring located above the diaphragm. A special fitting is provided at the carburetor to route ported (above the throttle plates) vacuum through the CTO and a TVS or BPS (when used), and the high and low temperature sensors (used in 1973 only), and hose connections to a fitting located above the diaphragm on the valve. A passage in the intake manifold directs exhaust gas from the exhaust crossover passage on V8s and from near the heat riser on the Sixes, to the EGR

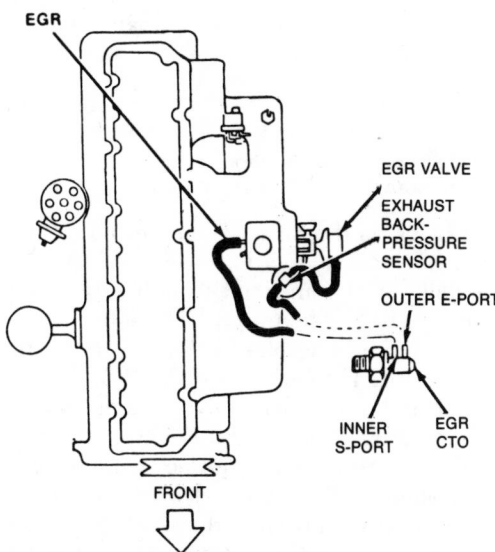

1974–79 six cylinder EGR system

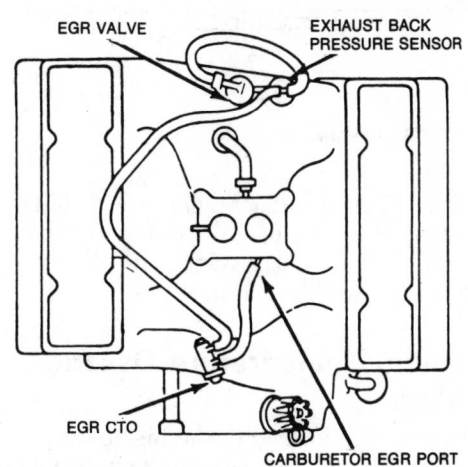

1974-79 8-304 EGR system

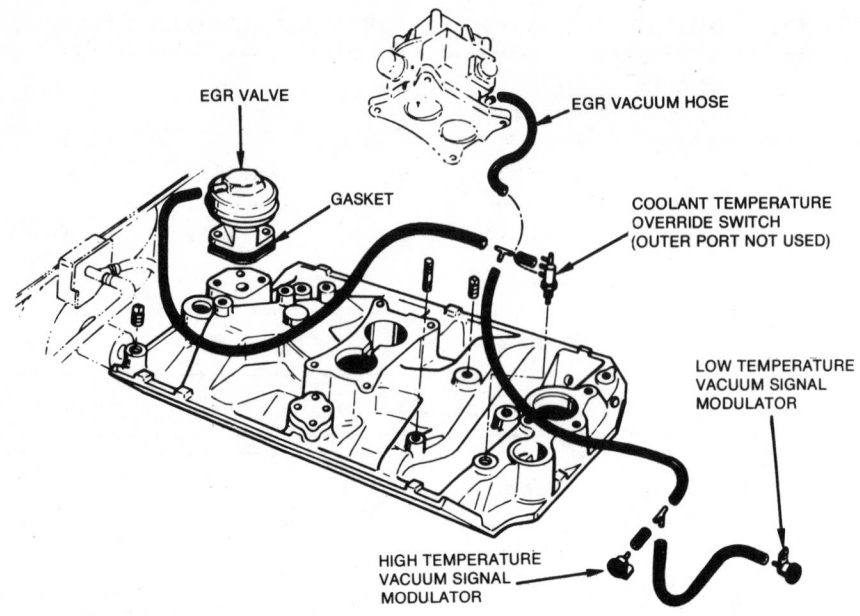

1973 V8 EGR system. The modulator isn't used on later models

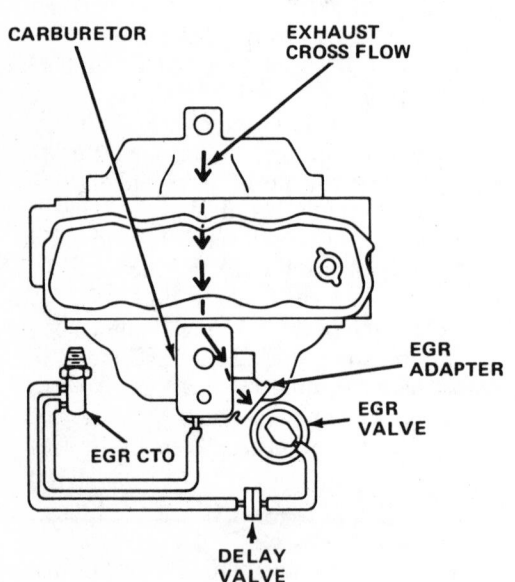

4-151 EGR system

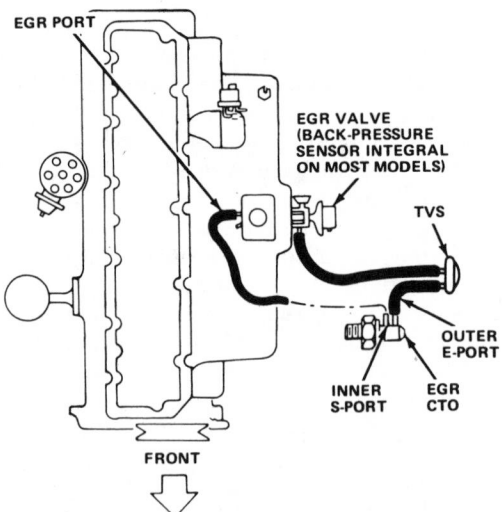

1980–81 6-258 EGR system

valve. When the diaphragm is actuated by vacuum, the valve opens and meters exhaust gas through special passages into the intake manifold below the carburetor.

Coolant Temperature Override Switch

This switch is located in the intake manifold at the coolant passage adjacent to the oil filler tube on V8s and on the left-side of the cylin-der block on the Sixes. The outer port of the switch is open and not used on 1973–74 models, or is connected to either the EGR valve or BPS (when used). The inner port is connected by a hose to the EGR fitting at the carburetor. The center port (1973–74 only) is connected to the EGR valve. When coolant temperature is below 160°F, the center port of the switch is closed and no vacuum signal is applied to the EGR valve, therefore, no exhaust gas will flow through the valve. When the coolant temperature reaches 115°F (160°F in 1973 only), both the center

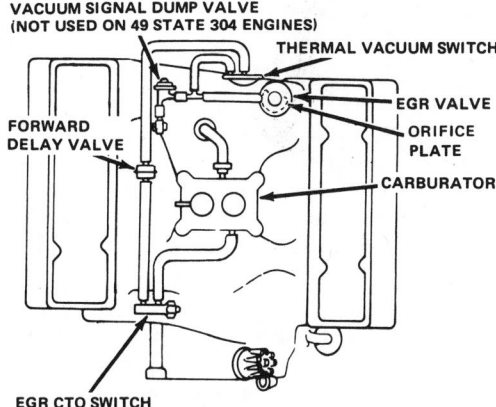

1980–81 8-304 EGR system

port and the inner port of the switch are open and a vacuum signal is applied to the EGR valve. This vacuum signal is, however, subject to regulation by the low and high temperature signal modulators (1973 only) or BPS when used.

LOW TEMPERATURE VACUUM SIGNAL MODULATOR (1973 ONLY)

This unit is located near the center of the radiator behind the grill opening. The low temperature vacuum signal modulator vacuum hose is connected by a plastic T-fitting to the EGR vacuum signal hose. The modulator is open when ambient temperatures are below 60°F. This causes a weakened vacuum signal to the EGR valve and a resultant decrease in the amount of exhaust gas being recirculated.

HIGH TEMPERATURE VACUUM SIGNAL MODULATOR (1973 ONLY)

This unit is located at the firewall just to the right of the battery case. The high temperature vacuum signal modulator is connected to the EGR vacuum signal hose by a plastic T-fitting. The modulator opens when the underhood air temperatures reach 115°F and it causes a weakened vacuum signal to the EGR valve, thus reducing the amount of exhaust gases being recirculated.

THERMAL VACUUM SWITCH (TVS)

The TVS is located in the air cleaner on all 1980 and later engines, and functions as an on/off switch controlled by air cleaner air temperature. The TVS controls the vacuum passage between the EGR CTO valve and the EGR valve. Air temperature in the 40–50°F range cause the TVS to limit the vacuum applied to the EGR valve, thus improving cold engine driveability.

Exhaust Backpressure Sensor (BPS)

This device is used on 1975 California vehicles, on all 1976 models, and on some 1977–81 models in conjunction with the EGR system.

The BPS monitors exhaust backpressure and permits EGR operation only when engine operating conditions are favorable. The BPR units are variously calibrated, are not serviceable, and must be replaced with the identical part as a unit when necessary.

The BPS consists of a diaphragm valve and a spacer connected by a metal tube projecting into an exhaust port in the spacer body. The EGR valve mounts directly on the spacer. On some 1977–81 sixes, the sensor is integral with the EGR valve.

In operation, the metal tube connecting the diaphragm valve to the spacer routes exhaust backpressure from the particular exhaust port to the sensor. When the backpressure reaches a certain level the diaphragm valve spring pressure is overcome, permitting a vacuum signal to the EGR valve, providing that the CTO switch is open.

Thus, EGR operations is only permitted when the engine is warmed up sufficiently and exhaust backpressure relatively high, such as during acceleration and at some cruising speeds. When temperature or backpressure conditions are not met, the vacuum signal is vented to the atmosphere from a vent at the diaphragm valve.

Feedback Systems

Two different feedback systems are used with 1981 and later Jeep vehicles. One, the C4 system is used with 4-151 engines built for sale in California; the other, the Computerized Emission Control (CEC) System is used on 6-258 engines built for sale in California. Each system is designed for the same purpose, to reduce exhaust emission using a Three-Way Catalytic Converter (TWC).

Each system is computerized, utilizing microprocessors, and each is highly complex, requiring professional service. Therefore, no service procedures are given in this book for the diagnosis or repair of these systems.

Catalytic Converter

The catalytic converter is a muffler-like device inserted in the exhaust system. Exhaust gases flow through the converter where a chemical change takes place, reducing carbon monoxide and hydrocarbons to carbon dioxide and water; the latter two elements being harmless. The catalysts promoting this reaction are platinum and palladium-coated beads of alumina.

Because of the chemical reaction which does take place in the converter, the temperature of the converter during operation is higher than the exhaust gases when they leave the engine. However, insulation keeps the outside skin of the converter about the same temperature as the muffler.

An improperly adjusted carburetor or ignition problem which would permit unburned fuel to enter the converter could produce excessive heat. Excessive heat in the converter could result in bulging or other distortion of the converter's shape. If the converter is heat-damaged and must be replaced, the ignition or carburetor problem must be corrected also.

Fuel Tank Vapor Emission Control System

A closed fuel tank system is used to route raw fuel vapor from the fuel tank into the PCV system (1973 Sixes only) or air cleaner snorkle, where it is burned along with the fuel-air mixture. The system prevents raw fuel vapors from entering the atmosphere.

The fuel vapor system consists of internal fuel tank venting, a vacuum-pressure fuel tank filler cap, an expansion tank (1972) or charcoal filled canister, limit fill valve (1972 only), liquid check valve, and internal carburetor venting.

On 1972 models only, fuel vapor pressure in the fuel tank forces the vapor through vent lines to the expansion tank or charcoal filled storage canister. The vapor then travels through a single vent line to the limit fill valve which regulates the vapor flow to the valve cover. The fuel tank vent lines is routed through the limit fill valve to the valve cover on the left side on the 1972 V8. On the 1973 Sixes, it travels to the intake manifold and on the 304 V8 it is routed to the carburetor air cleaner.

On 1973–76 models, the fuel vapor is routed from the fuel tank through vapor vent hoses to the liquid check valve. From the liquid check valve, the fuel vapor is routed to the vapor storage canister which is filled with charcoal. When the engine is not operating the charcoal retains the vapors. When the engine is started vacuum from the air cleaner snorkle routed through a hose leading to the top of the vapor storage canister sucks the vapors from the storage canister. There are three nipples on the top of the canister; one for vapors coming from the fuel tank, one for vapors going to the air cleaner snorkle, and

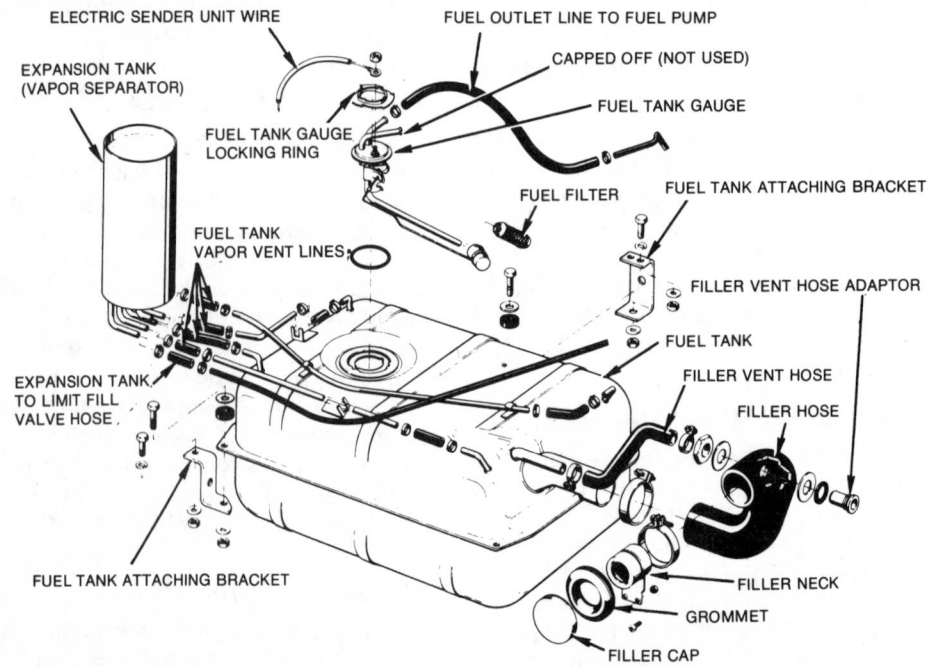

1972–73 fuel tank and vent lines

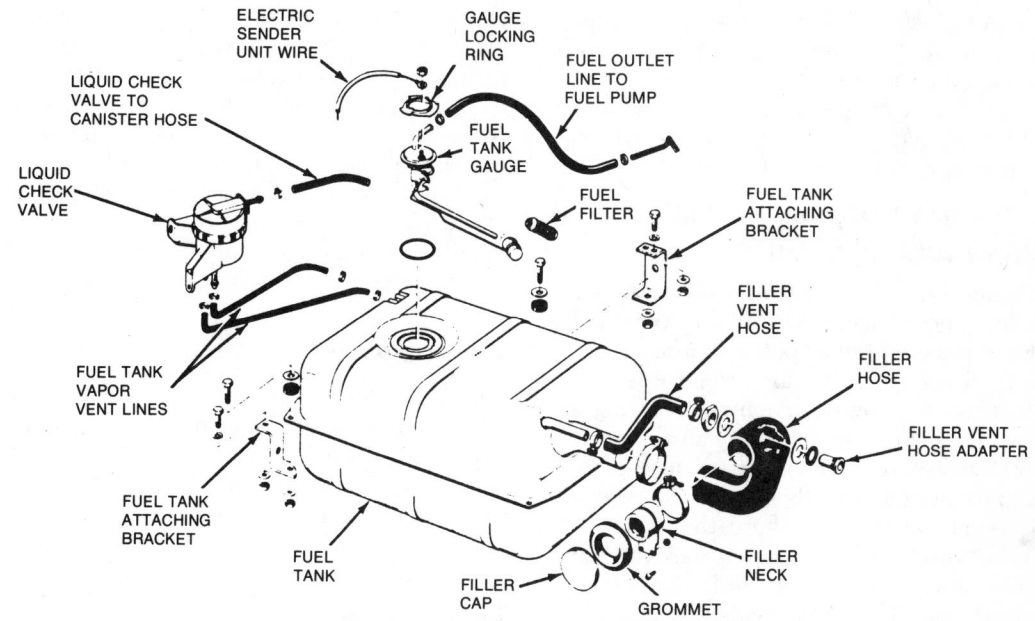

1974–76 fuel tank vapor emission control system

the other nipple is plugged (for use with 4 bbl carburetors on other AMC engines). Fresh air is drawn up through the canister from the bottom through a replaceable filter during operation.

LIMIT FILL VALVE

This valve is essentially a combination vapor flow regulator and pressure relief valve. It regulates vapor flow from the fuel tank vent line into the valve cover. The valve consists of a housing, a spring loaded diaphragm and a diaphragm cover. As tank vent pressure increases, the diaphragm lifts permitting vapor to flow through. The pressure at which this occurs is 4–6 in. of water column. This action regulates the flow of vapors under severe conditions but generally prohibits the flow of vapor during normal temperature operation, thus minimizing driveability problems.

Liquid Check Valve

The liquid check valve prevents liquid fuel from entering the vapor lines leading to the storage canister. The check valve incorporates a float and needle valve assembly. If liquid fuel should enter the check valve, the float will rise and force the needle upward to close the vent passage. With no liquid fuel present in the check valve, fuel vapors pass freely from the tank, through the check valve, and on to the storage canister.

Choke Heat By-Pass Valve (CHBPV) 1976 and later V8

When the engine is first started and begins to warm up, heated air from the exhaust crossover passage in the intake manifold is routed through a heat tube to the choke housing containing the thermostatic spring for regulating the choke flap. A thermostatic by-pass valve, which is integral with the choke heat tube, helps prevent premature choke valve opening during the early part of the warmup period. This is important when ambient temperatures are relatively low and adverse drivability could occur if the choke was opened too soon.

The thermostatic by-pass valve regulates the temperature of the hot airflow to the choke housing by allowing outside unheated air to enter the heat tube. A thermostatic disc in the valve is calibrated to close the valve at 75°F and open it at 55°F.

Fuel Return System

The purpose of the fuel return system is to reduce high temperature fuel vapor problems. The system consists of a fuel return line to the fuel tank and a special fuel filter with an extra outlet nipple to which the return line is connected. During normal operation, a small amount of fuel is returned to the fuel tank. During periods of high underhood temperatures, vaporized fuel in the fuel line is returned to the fuel tank and not passed through the carburetor.

NOTE: *The extra nipple on the special fuel filter should be positioned upward to ensure proper operation of the system.*

Emission Control Checks

ANTI-BACKFIRE DIVERTER VALVE

On the F-head, the anti-backfire valve remains open except when the throttle is closed rapidly from an open position.

To check the valve for proper operation, accelerate the engine in neutral, allowing the throttle to close rapidly. The valve is operating satisfactorily when no exhaust system backfire occurs. A further check can be made by removing the large hose that runs from the anti-backfire valve to the check valve and accelerating the engine and allowing the throttle to close rapidly. If there is an audible momentary interruption of the flow of air then it can be assumed that the vale is working correctly.

To check the valve on a V6, listen for backfire when the throttle is released quickly. If none exists, the valve is doing its job. To check further, remove the large hose that connects the valve with the air pump. Place a finger over the open end of the hose, not the valve, and accelerate the engine, allowing the throttle to close rapidly. The valve is operating satisfactorily if there is a momentary audible rush of air.

To check the diverter valve on American Motors engines, start the engine and let it idle. With the engine idling, there should be little or no air coming out the vents. When the engine is accelerated to 2,000–3,000 rpm, a strong flow of air should be felt at the vents. If the flow of air from the air pump is not diverted through the diverter valve vents when the engine is accelerated to the above mentioned rpm, check and make sure that the vacuum sensing line leading to the valve has vacuum and is not leaking or disconnected. The diverter valve should bleed air when 20 in. Hg or more vacuum is applied to the vacuum sensing line or when the output of the air pump exceeds 5 psi. When the engine is slowly accelerated, the diverter valve should begin to bleed off air between 2,500 and 3,500 rpm.

CHECK VALVE

The check valve in the air distribution manifold prevents the reverse flow of exhaust gases to the pump in the event the pump should become inoperative or should exhaust pressure ever exceed the pump pressure.

To check this valve for proper operation, remove the air supply hose from the pump at the distribution manifold. With the engine running, listen for exhaust leakage where the check valve is connected to the distribution manifold. If leakage is audible, the vale is not operating correctly. A small amount of leakage is normal.

AIR PUMP

Check for the proper drive belt tension and adjust as necessary. Do not pry on the die cast pump housing. Check to see if the pump is discharging air. Remove the air outlet hose at the pump. With the engine running, air should be felt at the pump outlet opening.

EGR Valve

With the engine idling and at normal operating temperature, manually depress the EGR valve diaphragm. This should cause engine speed to drop about 200 rpm. This indicates that the EGR valve had been properly cutting off the flow of exhaust gas at idle and is operating properly.

If the engine speed did not change and the idle is smooth, exhaust gases are not reaching the combustion chambers. The probable cause of this is a plugged passage between the EGR valve and the intake manifold.

If the engine idle is rough and rpm is not affected by depressing the EGR valve diaphragm, the EGR valve is not closing off the flow of exhaust at idle like it's supposed to and there is most likely a fault in the hoses, hose routing, or the EGR valve itself.

NOTE: *The EGR valve can be removed and cleaned with a wire brush and a 9/16 in. drill bit coated with grease (to hold dirt particles) inserted in discharge passage. The drill should be held with a pair of pliers only.*

EGR CTO SWITCH

Before checking the operating of the EGR CTO switch, make sure that the engine coolant is below 100°F.

1. Check the vacuum lines for leaks and proper routing.

2. Disconnect the vacuum line at the backpressure sensor, if so equipped, or at the EGR valve, and connect the line to a vacuum gauge.

3. Operate the engine at 1,500 rpm. No vacuum should be indicated at the gauge. If vacuum is indicated, replace the EGR CTO switch.

4. Allow the engine to idle until the coolant temperature exceeds 115°F.

5. Accelerate the engine to 1,500 rpm. Vacuum should be present at the gauge. If not, replace the EGR CTO switch.

EXHAUST BPS UNIT

1. Make sure that all the EGR vacuum lines are routed correctly and are not leaking.

2. Install a "T" in the vacuum line between the EGR valve and BPS, and attach a vacuum gauge to the "T."

3. Start the engine and allow it to idle. No vacuum should be present.

If vacuum is indicated at idle speed, make sure of correct line connections. Also, be sure that manifold vacuum is not the source. If the carburetor is providing the vacuum, look for a partially open throttle plate which could cause premature ported vacuum to the BPS unit.

4. Accelerate the engine to 2,000 rpm and observe the vacuum gauge for the following:

    a. If the coolant is below 115°F, no vacuum should be present;

    b. With coolant temperature above 115°F, ported vacuum should be indicated;

    c. If no vacuum is indicated at any time, make sure that vacuum is being applied to the inlet side of the BPS. If correct, remove the BPS and either clean it with a wire brush (if blocked) or replace it.

SPARK CTO SWITCH

Before testing the spark CTO switch, make sure that the engine coolant temperature is below 160°F.

1. Remove all the hoses from the CTO switch and plug those which will create a vacuum leak.

2. Connect a vacuum line from a manifold vacuum source to the top port of the CTO switch.

3. Connect a vacuum gauge to the center port.

4. Start the engine. Manifold vacuum should be indicated on the gauge. If not, replace the switch.

5. With the engine still running and the coolant temperature still below 160°F, disconnect the vacuum line from the top port and connect it to the bottom port.

6. No vacuum should be indicated. Replace the switch if there is vacuum.

7. Allow the engine to run until the coolant temperature exceeds 160°F. Manifold vacuum should be indicated. If not, replace the CTO switch.

8. Disconnect the hose from the bottom port and connect ti to the top port again. With the coolant temperature above 160°F, no vacuum should be indicated. If there is, replace the CTO switch.

TVS FUNCTIONAL TEST

1. Allow the air cleaner to cool to between 40 and 50°F.

2. Disconnect the vacuum hoses from the TVS and connect an external vacuum source to one nipple and a vacuum gauge to the other.

3. Apply vacuum to the TVS. Vacuum should not be present when the air temperature is 40–50°F. If vacuum is present, replace the switch.

4. Start the engine and allow the air cleaner to warm above 50°F. Vacuum should be present.

FUEL SYSTEM

Fuel Pump

REMOVAL AND INSTALLATION
All Engines

1. Disconnect the inlet and outlet fuel lines, and any vacuum lines.

2. Remove the two fuel pump body attaching nuts and lockwashers.

3. Pull the pump and gasket free of the engine. Make sure that the mating surfaces of the fuel pump and the engine are clean.

4. Cement a new gasket to the mounting flange of the fuel pump.

5. Position the fuel pump on the engine block so that the lever of the fuel pump rests on the fuel pump cam of the camshaft.

6. Secure the fuel pump to the block with the two cap screws and lock washers.

7. Connect the intake and outlet fuel lines to the fuel pump, and any vacuum lines.

FUEL PUMP TESTING
Volume Check

Disconnect the fuel line from the carburetor. Place the open end in a suitable container. Start the engine and operate it at normal idle

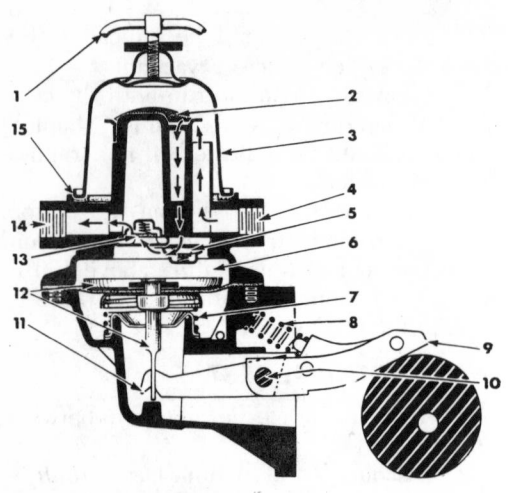

1. Strainer bail and seat
2. Filtering screen
3. Bowl
4. Fuel inlet
5. Inlet valve
6. Pump chamber
7. Diaphragm spring
8. Rocker arm spring
9. Rocker arm
10. Rocker arm pin
11. Rocker arm link
12. Diaphragm and pull rod
13. Outlet valve
14. Fuel outlet
15. Body screw

CJ-2A fuel pump

1. Fuel outlet   2. Vapor return   3. Fuel inlet

Non-serviceable V6 fuel pump

speed. The pump should deliver at least one pin in 30 seconds.

Pressure Check

Disconnect the fuel line at the carburetor. Disconnect the fuel return line from the fuel

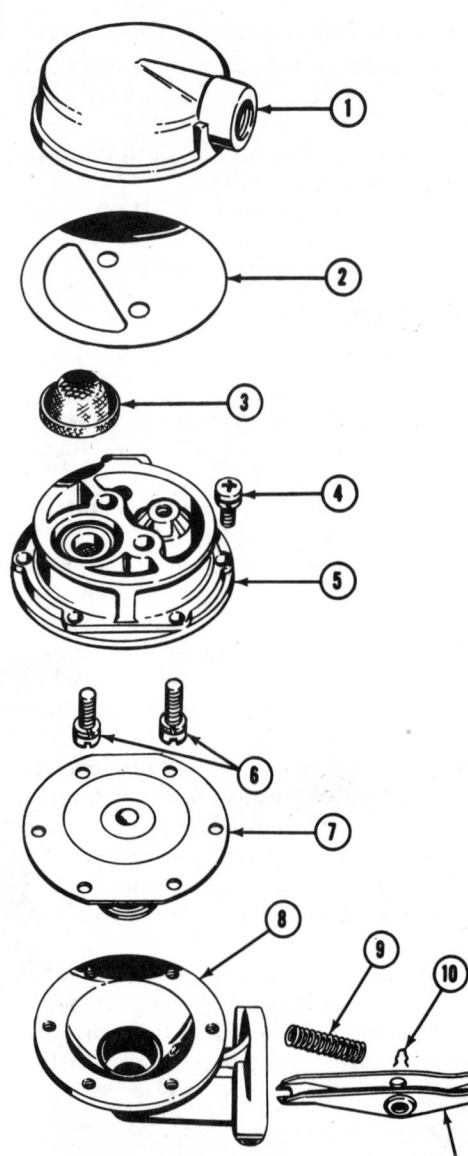

1. Housing cover
2. Air dome diaphragm
3. Strainer
4. Screw and washer
5. Housing
6. Cover screw and lockwashers
7. Main diaphragm
8. Pump body
9. Cam lever return spring
10. Pin retainer
11. Cam lever
12. Cam lever pin
13. Lever seal shaft plug

F-head fuel pump used with electric wipers

filter if so equipped, and plug the nipple on the filter. Install a T-fitting on the open end of the fuel line and refit the line to the carburetor. Plug a pressure gauge into the remaining opening of the T-fitting. The hose leading to the pressure gauge should not be any longer than 6 inches. Start the engine and let it run at idle speed. Bleed any air out of the hose between the gauge and the T-fitting. Pressure readings are given in the Tune-up Specifications Chart.

Carburetors

REMOVAL AND INSTALLATION
All Engines

To remove the carburetor from any engine, first remove the air cleaner from the top of the carburetor. Remove all lines and hoses, noting their positions to facilitate installation. Remove all throttle and choke linkage at the carburetor. Remove the carburetor attaching nuts which hold it to the intake manifold. Lift the carburetor from the engine along with the carburetor base gasket. Discard the gasket. Install the carburetor in the reverse order of removal, using a new base gasket.

OVERHAUL

Efficient carburetion depends greatly on careful cleaning and inspection during overhaul since dirt, gum, water, or varnish in or on the carburetor parts are often responsible for poor performance.

Overhaul your carburetor in a clean, dust-free area. Carefully disassemble the carburetor, referring often to the exploded views. Keep all similar and look-alike parts segre-

1. Cover screw	10. Fuel diaphragm	19. Gasket
2. Lockwasher	11. Oil seal retainer	20. Screw
3. Diaphragm spring	12. Diaphragm and rod	21. Rocker arm spring
4. Spring seat	13. Valve retainer	22. Link spacer
5. Diaphragm and rod	14. Cover	23. Rocker arm
6. Oil seal	15. Gasket	24. Washer
7. Valve assembly	16. Screen	25. Body
8. Body	17. Bowl	
9. Rocker arm pin spring	18. Bail	

4-134 combined fuel and vacuum pump

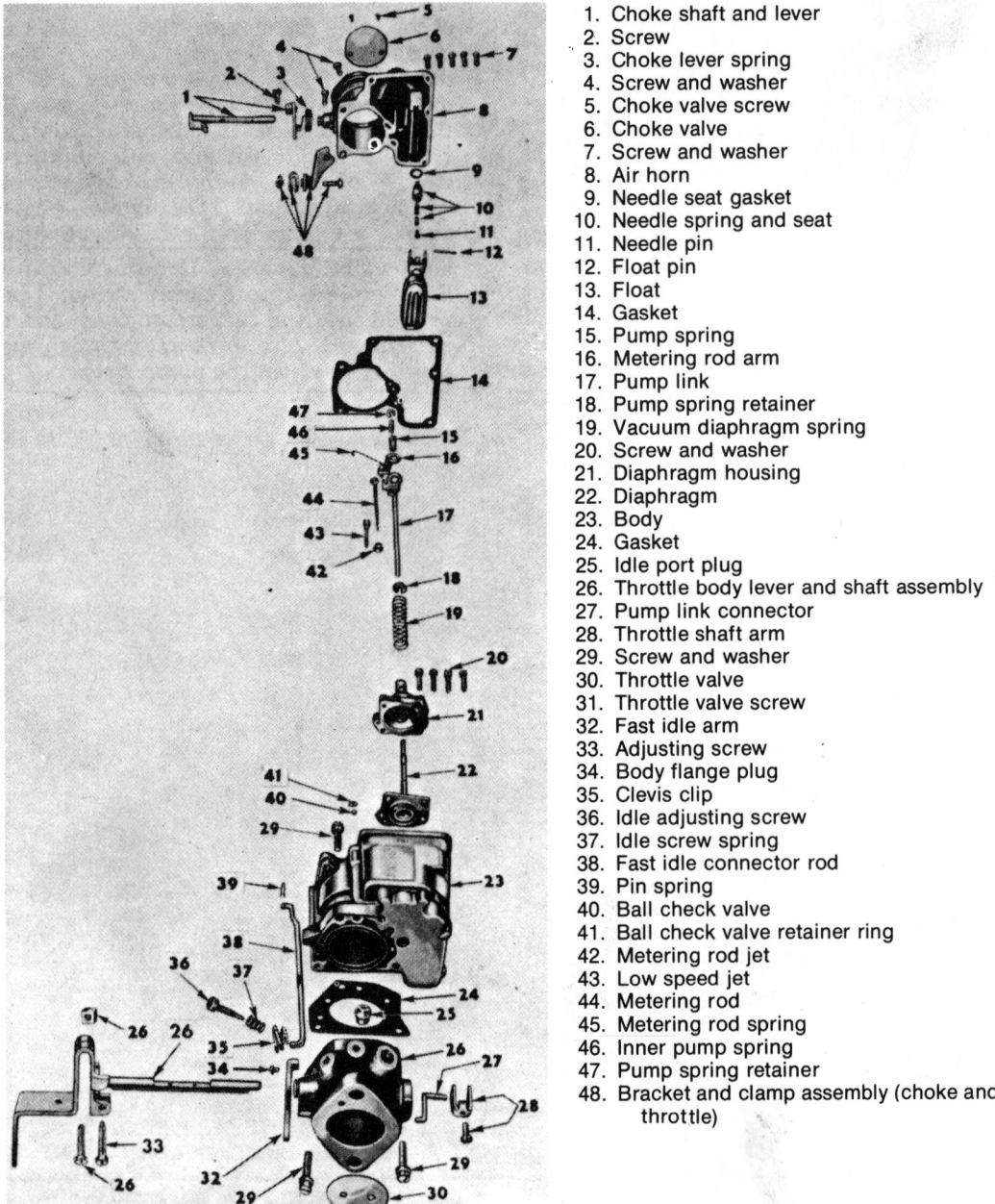

1. Choke shaft and lever
2. Screw
3. Choke lever spring
4. Screw and washer
5. Choke valve screw
6. Choke valve
7. Screw and washer
8. Air horn
9. Needle seat gasket
10. Needle spring and seat
11. Needle pin
12. Float pin
13. Float
14. Gasket
15. Pump spring
16. Metering rod arm
17. Pump link
18. Pump spring retainer
19. Vacuum diaphragm spring
20. Screw and washer
21. Diaphragm housing
22. Diaphragm
23. Body
24. Gasket
25. Idle port plug
26. Throttle body lever and shaft assembly
27. Pump link connector
28. Throttle shaft arm
29. Screw and washer
30. Throttle valve
31. Throttle valve screw
32. Fast idle arm
33. Adjusting screw
34. Body flange plug
35. Clevis clip
36. Idle adjusting screw
37. Idle screw spring
38. Fast idle connector rod
39. Pin spring
40. Ball check valve
41. Ball check valve retainer ring
42. Metering rod jet
43. Low speed jet
44. Metering rod
45. Metering rod spring
46. Inner pump spring
47. Pump spring retainer
48. Bracket and clamp assembly (choke and throttle)

Carter YF carburetor used on the 4-134 engine

gated during disassembly and cleaning to avoid accidental interchange during assembly. Make a note of all jet sizes.

When the carburetor is disassembled, wash all parts (except diaphragms, electric choke units, pump plunger, and any other plastic, leather, fiber, or rubber parts) in clean carburetor solvent. Do not leave parts in the solvent any longer than is necessary to sufficiently loosen the deposits. Excessive

cleaning may remove the special finish from the float bowl and choke valve bodies, leaving these parts unfit for service. Rinse all parts in clean solvent and blow them dry with compressed air or allow them to air dry. Wipe clean all cork, plastic, leather, and fiber parts with a clean, lint-free cloth.

Blow out all passages and jets with compressed air and be sure that there are no restrictions or blockages. Never use wire or

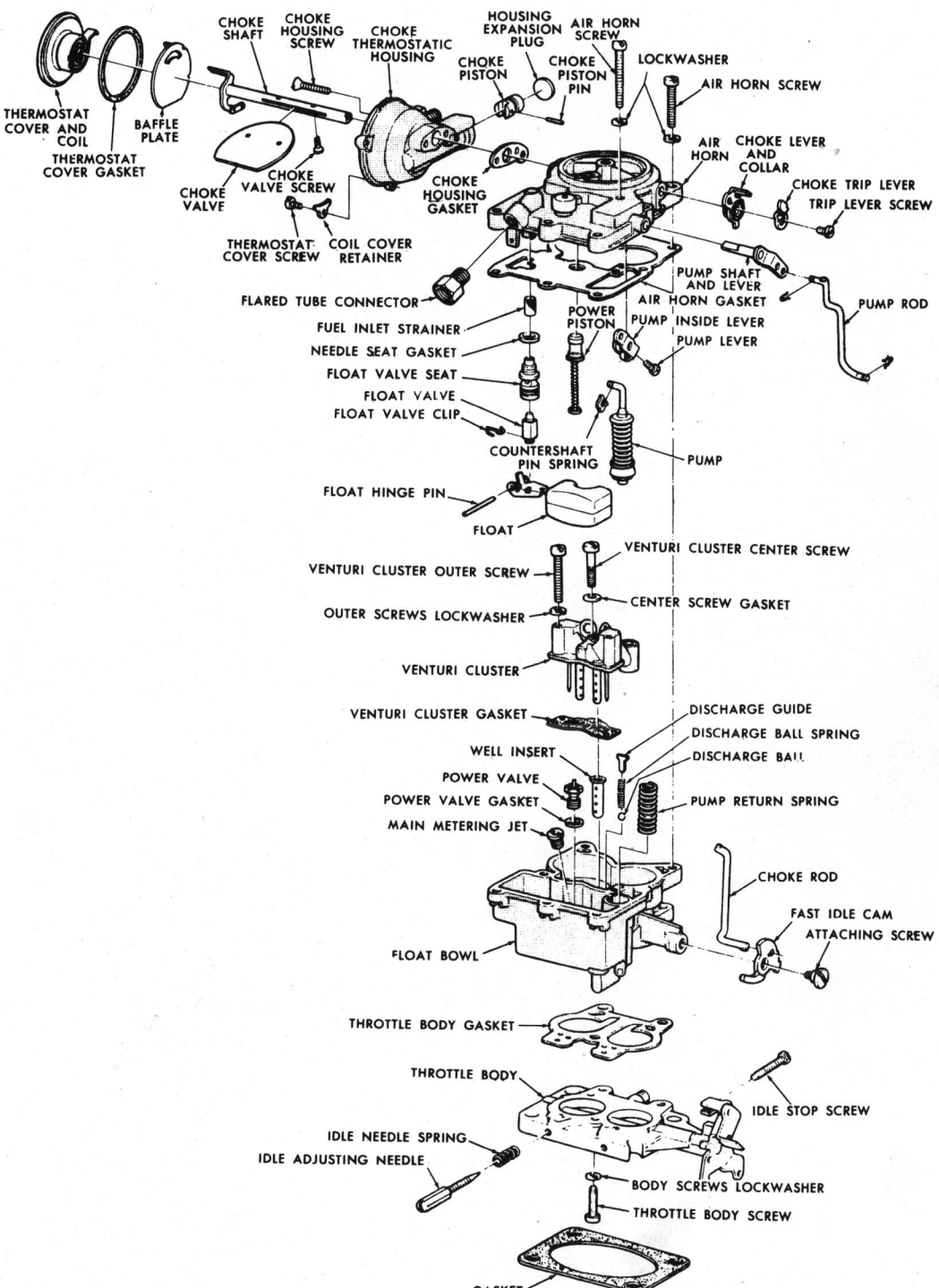

Rochester 2GC carburetor used on V6-225 engines

similar tools to clean jets, fuel passages, or air bleeds. Clean all jets and valves separately to avoid accidental interchange.

Check all parts for wear or damage. If wear or damage is found, replace the defective parts. Especially check the following:

1. Check the float needle and seat for wear. If wear is found, replace the complete assembly.

2. Check the float hinge pin for wear and the float(s) for dents or distortion. Replace the float if fuel has leaked into it.

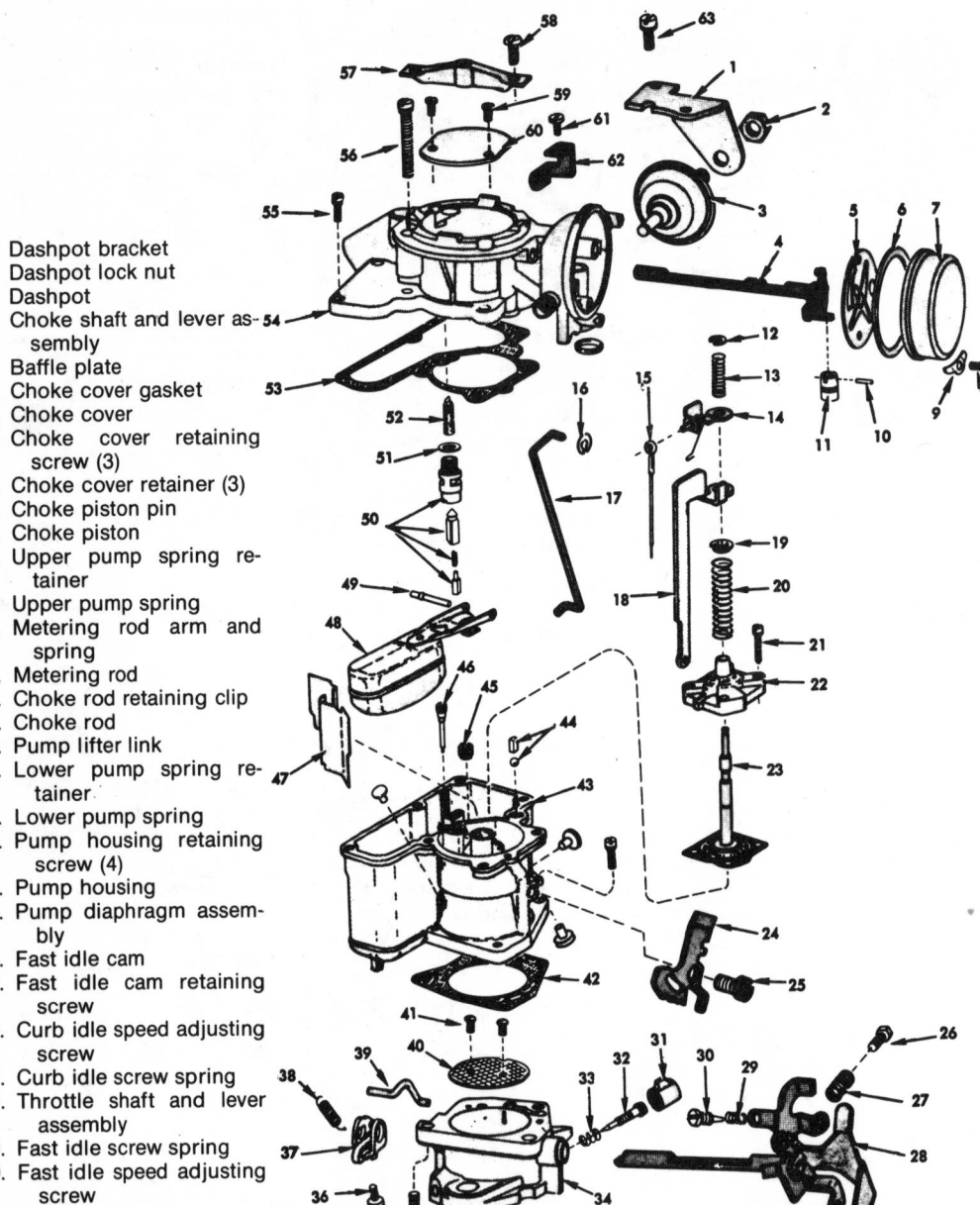

1. Dashpot bracket
2. Dashpot lock nut
3. Dashpot
4. Choke shaft and lever assembly
5. Baffle plate
6. Choke cover gasket
7. Choke cover
8. Choke cover retaining screw (3)
9. Choke cover retainer (3)
10. Choke piston pin
11. Choke piston
12. Upper pump spring retainer
13. Upper pump spring
14. Metering rod arm and spring
15. Metering rod
16. Choke rod retaining clip
17. Choke rod
18. Pump lifter link
19. Lower pump spring retainer
20. Lower pump spring
21. Pump housing retaining screw (4)
22. Pump housing
23. Pump diaphragm assembly
24. Fast idle cam
25. Fast idle cam retaining screw
26. Curb idle speed adjusting screw
27. Curb idle screw spring
28. Throttle shaft and lever assembly
29. Fast idle screw spring
30. Fast idle speed adjusting screw
31. Idle limiter cap
32. Idle mixture screw
33. Idle mixture screw spring
34. Throttle body
35. Throttle body retaining screw (3)
36. Throttle shaft arm set screw
37. Throttle shaft arm
38. Throttle shaft return spring
39. Pump connector link
40. Throttle valve
41. Throttle valve retaining screw (2)
42. Throttle body gasket
43. Main body
44. Pump discharge check ball and weight
45. Metering rod jet
46. Low speed jet
47. Fuel bowl baffle
48. Float and lever assembly
49. Float pin
50. Needle and seat assembly
51. Needle seat gasket
52. Screen
53. Air horn gasket
54. Air horn
55. Short air horn retaining screw (3)
56. Long air horn retaining screw (3)
57. Air cleaner bracket
58. Air cleaner bracket retaining screw (2)
59. Choke valve retaining screw (2)
60. Choke valve
61. Choke lever retaining screw
62. Choke lever
63. Dashpot bracket retaining screw

Carter YF carburetor used on 6-232, 258 engines

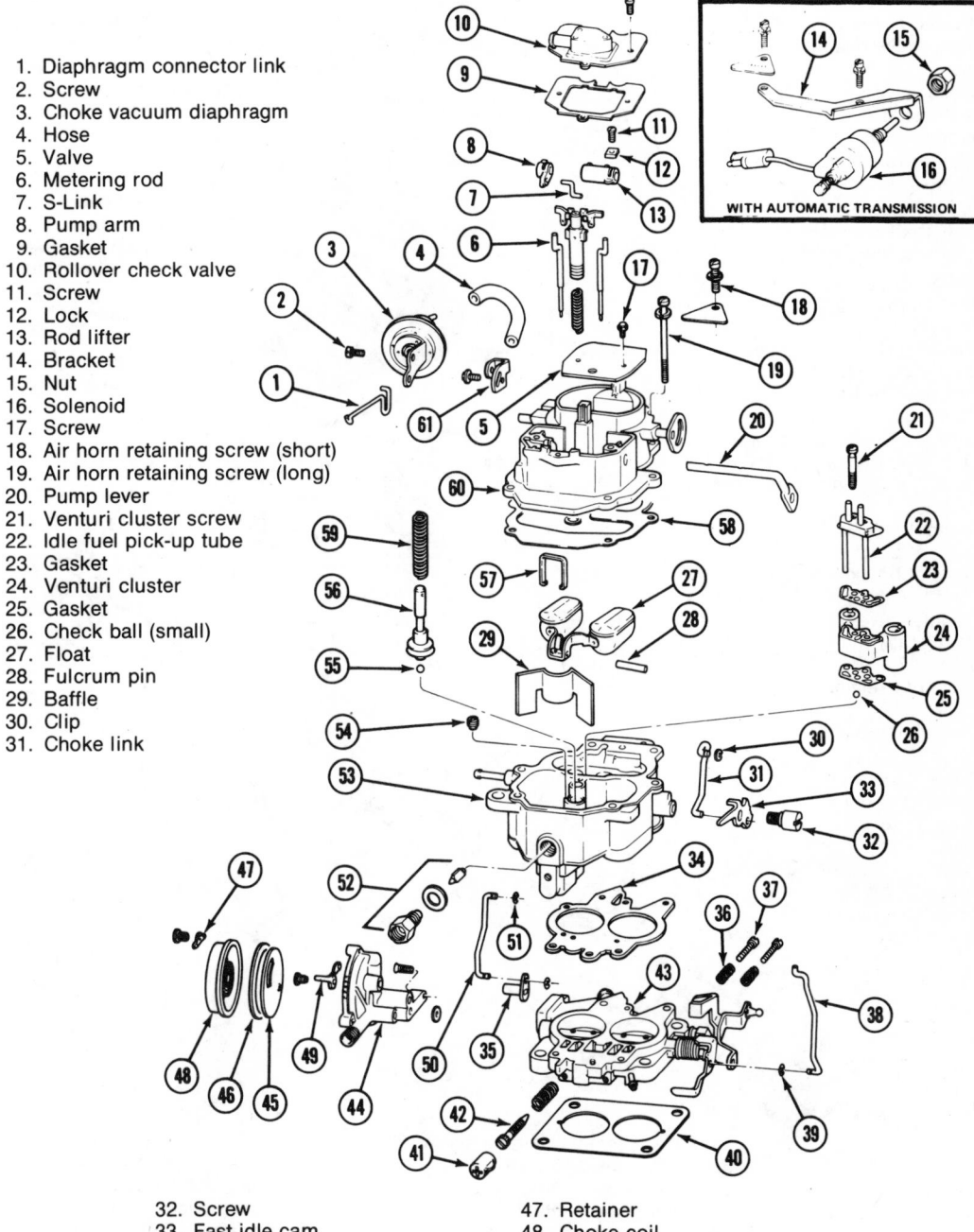

1. Diaphragm connector link
2. Screw
3. Choke vacuum diaphragm
4. Hose
5. Valve
6. Metering rod
7. S-Link
8. Pump arm
9. Gasket
10. Rollover check valve
11. Screw
12. Lock
13. Rod lifter
14. Bracket
15. Nut
16. Solenoid
17. Screw
18. Air horn retaining screw (short)
19. Air horn retaining screw (long)
20. Pump lever
21. Venturi cluster screw
22. Idle fuel pick-up tube
23. Gasket
24. Venturi cluster
25. Gasket
26. Check ball (small)
27. Float
28. Fulcrum pin
29. Baffle
30. Clip
31. Choke link

WITH AUTOMATIC TRANSMISSION

32. Screw	47. Retainer
33. Fast idle cam	48. Choke coil
34. Gasket	49. Lever
35. Thermostatic choke shaft	50. Choke rod
36. Spring	51. Clip
37. Screw	52. Needle and seat assembly
38. Pump link	53. Main body
39. Clip	54. Main metering jet
40. Gasket	55. Check ball (large)
41. Limiter cap	56. Accelerator pump plunger
42. Screw	57. Fulcrum pin retainer
43. Throttle body	58. Gasket
44. Choke housing	59. Spring
45. Baffle	60. Air horn
46. Gasket	61. Lever

Carter BBD carburetor used on 6-258 engines

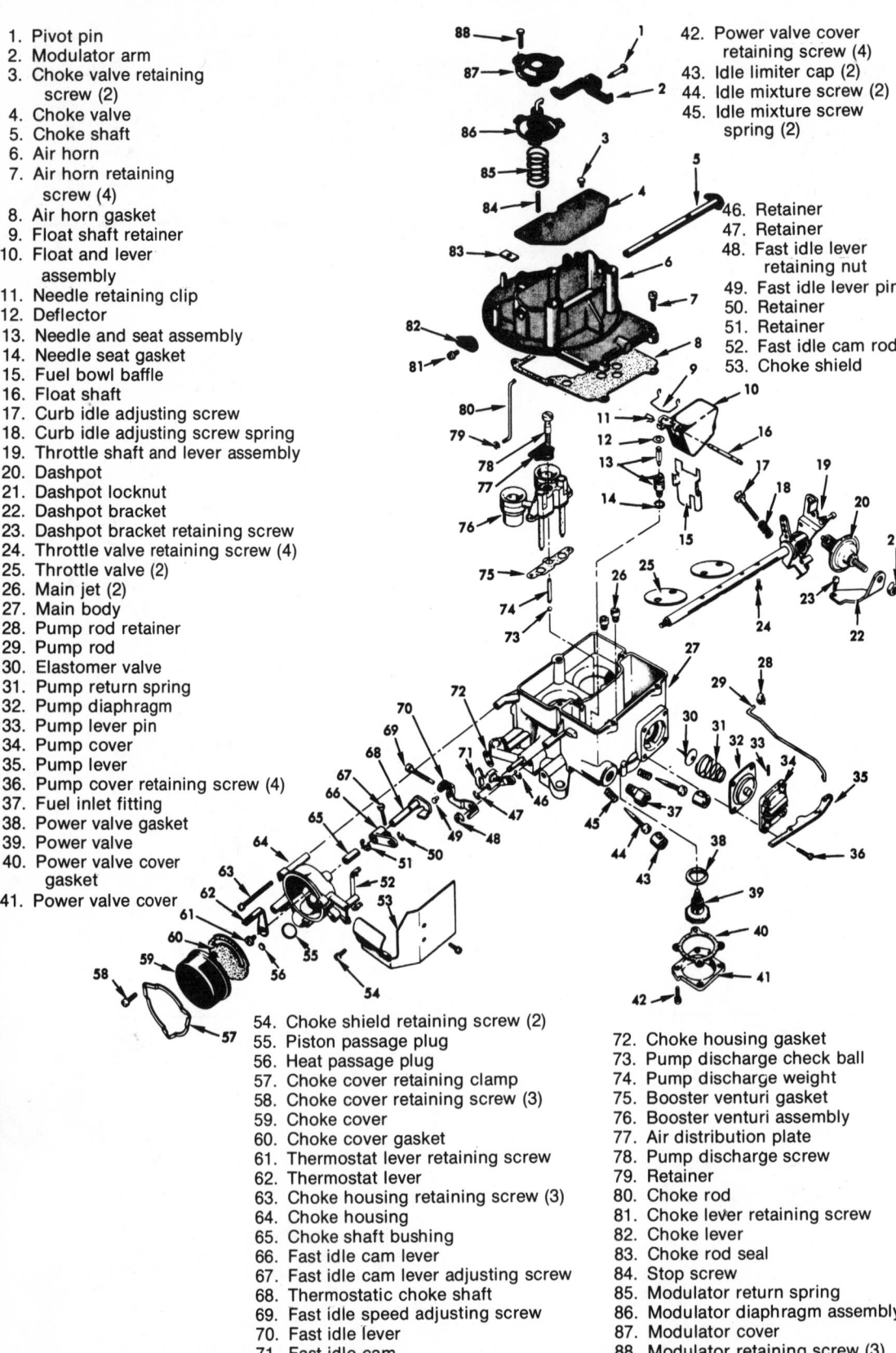

1. Pivot pin
2. Modulator arm
3. Choke valve retaining screw (2)
4. Choke valve
5. Choke shaft
6. Air horn
7. Air horn retaining screw (4)
8. Air horn gasket
9. Float shaft retainer
10. Float and lever assembly
11. Needle retaining clip
12. Deflector
13. Needle and seat assembly
14. Needle seat gasket
15. Fuel bowl baffle
16. Float shaft
17. Curb idle adjusting screw
18. Curb idle adjusting screw spring
19. Throttle shaft and lever assembly
20. Dashpot
21. Dashpot locknut
22. Dashpot bracket
23. Dashpot bracket retaining screw
24. Throttle valve retaining screw (4)
25. Throttle valve (2)
26. Main jet (2)
27. Main body
28. Pump rod retainer
29. Pump rod
30. Elastomer valve
31. Pump return spring
32. Pump diaphragm
33. Pump lever pin
34. Pump cover
35. Pump lever
36. Pump cover retaining screw (4)
37. Fuel inlet fitting
38. Power valve gasket
39. Power valve
40. Power valve cover gasket
41. Power valve cover

42. Power valve cover retaining screw (4)
43. Idle limiter cap (2)
44. Idle mixture screw (2)
45. Idle mixture screw spring (2)
46. Retainer
47. Retainer
48. Fast idle lever retaining nut
49. Fast idle lever pin
50. Retainer
51. Retainer
52. Fast idle cam rod
53. Choke shield

54. Choke shield retaining screw (2)
55. Piston passage plug
56. Heat passage plug
57. Choke cover retaining clamp
58. Choke cover retaining screw (3)
59. Choke cover
60. Choke cover gasket
61. Thermostat lever retaining screw
62. Thermostat lever
63. Choke housing retaining screw (3)
64. Choke housing
65. Choke shaft bushing
66. Fast idle cam lever
67. Fast idle cam lever adjusting screw
68. Thermostatic choke shaft
69. Fast idle speed adjusting screw
70. Fast idle lever
71. Fast idle cam

72. Choke housing gasket
73. Pump discharge check ball
74. Pump discharge weight
75. Booster venturi gasket
76. Booster venturi assembly
77. Air distribution plate
78. Pump discharge screw
79. Retainer
80. Choke rod
81. Choke lever retaining screw
82. Choke lever
83. Choke rod seal
84. Stop screw
85. Modulator return spring
86. Modulator diaphragm assembly
87. Modulator cover
88. Modulator retaining screw (3)

Autolite 2100 carburetor used on 8-304 engines

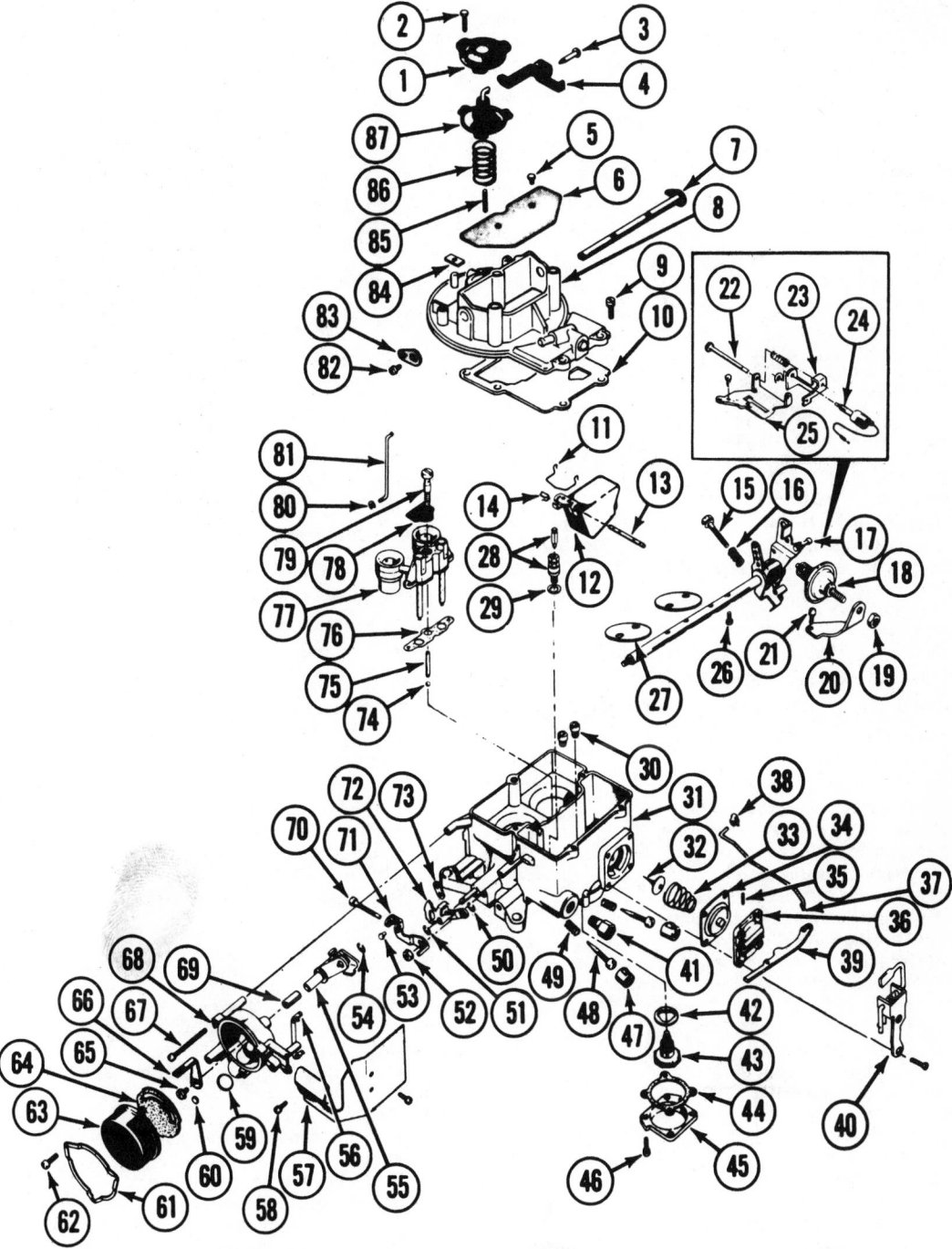

1. Modulator cover (if equipped)
2. Modulator retaining screw (3) (if equipped)
3. Pivot pin
4. Modulator arm
5. Choke valve retaining screw (2)
6. Choke valve
7. Choke shaft
8. Air horn
9. Air horn retaining screw (4)
10. Air horn gasket

11. Float and lever assembly
12. Float shaft retainer
13. Float shaft
14. Needle retaining clip
15. Curb idle adjusting screw
16. Curb idle adjusting screw spring
17. Throttle shaft and lever assembly
18. Dashpot
19. Dashpot locknut
20. Dashpot bracket

Motorcraft 2150 carburetor used on 8-304 engines

3. Check the throttle and choke shaft bores for wear or an out-of-round condition. Damage or wear to the throttle arm, shaft, or shaft bore will often require replacement of the throttle body. These parts require a close tolerance of fit; wear may allow air leakage, which could affect starting and idling.

NOTE: *Throttle shafts and bushings are not included in overhaul kits. They can be purchased separately.*

4. Inspect the idle mixture adjusting needles for burrs or grooves. Any such condition requires replacement of the needle, since you will not be able to obtain a satisfactory idle.

5. Test the accelerator pump check valves. They should pass air one way but not the other. Test for proper seating by blowing and sucking on the valve. Replace the valve if necessary. If the valve is satisfactory, wash the valve again to remove breath moisture.

6. Check the bowl cover for warped surfaces with a straightedge.

7. Closely inspect the valves and seats for wear and damage, replacing as necessary.

8. After the carburetor is assembled, check the choke valve for freedom of operation.

Carburetor overhaul kits are recommended for each overhaul. These kits contain all gaskets and new parts to replace those that deteriorate most rapidly. Failure to replace all parts supplied with the kit (especially gaskets) can result in poor performance later.

After cleaning and checking all components, reassemble the carburetor, using new parts and referring to the exploded view. When reassembling, make sure that all screws and jets are tight in their seats, but do not overtighten, as the tips will be distorted. Tighten all screws gradually, in rotation. Do not tighten needle valves into their seats; uneven jetting will result. Always use new gaskets. Be sure to adjust the float level when reassembling.

FLOAT AND FUEL LEVEL ADJUSTMENT
4-134—Carter YF

1. Remove and invert the bowl cover.
2. Remove the bowl cover gasket.
3. Allow the weight of the float to rest on the needle and spring. Be sure that there is no compression of the spring other than by the weight of the float.
4. Adjust the level by bending the float

21. Dashpot bracket retaining screw
22. Adjusting screw
23. Carriage
24. Electric solenoid
25. Mounting bracket
26. Throttle valve retaining screw (4)
27. Throttle valve (2)
28. Needle and seat assembly
29. Needle seat gasket
30. Main jet (2)
31. Main body
32. Elastomer valve
33. Pump return spring
34. Pump diaphragm
35. Pump lever pin
36. Pump cover
37. Pump rod
38. Pump rod retainer
39. Pump lever
40. Bowl vent bellcrank
41. Fuel inlet fitting
42. Power valve gasket
43. Power valve
44. Power valve cover gasket
45. Power valve cover
46. Power valve cover retaining screw (4)
47. Idle limiter cap (2)
48. Idle mixture screw (2)
49. Idle mixture screw spring (2)
50. Retainer
52. Fast idle lever retaining nut
53. Fast idle lever pin
54. Retainer

55. Lever and shaft
56. Fast idle cam rod
57. Choke shield
58. Choke shield retaining screw (2)
59. Piston passage plug
60. Heat passage plug
61. Choke cover retaining clamp
62. Choke cover retaining screw (3)
63. Choke cover and coil
64. Choke cover gasket
65. Coil lever retaining screw
66. Coil lever
67. Choke housing retaining screw (3)
68. Choke housing
69. Choke shaft bushing
70. Fast idle speed adjusting screw
71. Fast idle lever
72. Fast idle cam
73. Choke housing gasket
74. Pump discharge check ball
75. Pump discharge weight
76. Booster venturi gasket
77. Booster venturi assembly
78. Air distribution plate
79. Pump discharge screw
80. Retainer
81. Choke rod
82. Choke lever retaining screw
83. Choke plate lever
84. Choke rod seal
85. Stop screw
86. Modulator return spring (if equipped)
87. Modulator diaphragm assembly (if equipped)

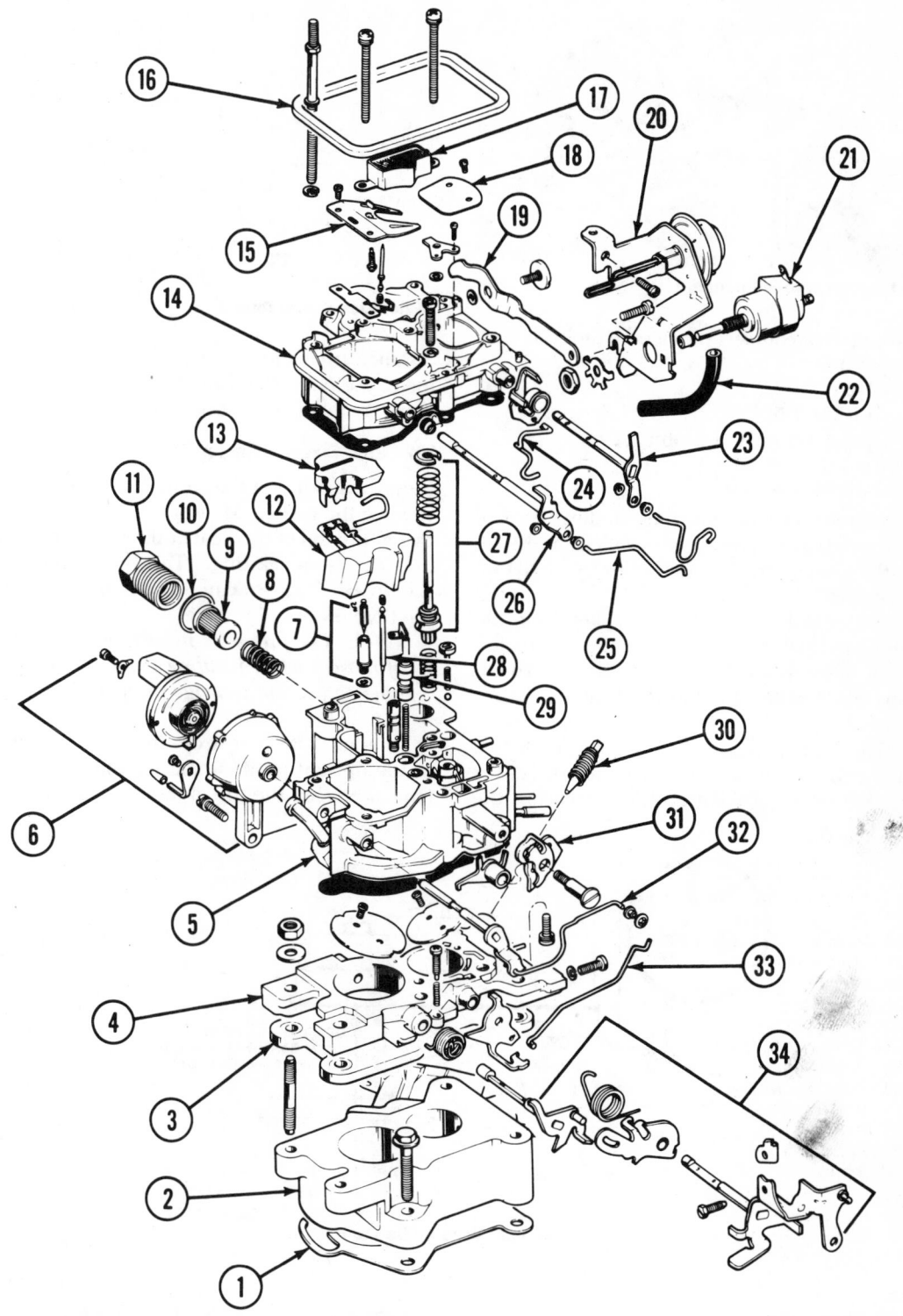

1. Gasket
2. Intake adapter
3. Insulator
4. Throttle body
5. Main body
6. Electric stat cover and coil
7. Needle seat assembly
8. Spring
9. Fuel inlet filter
10. Gasket
11. Fuel inlet fitting
12. Float assembly

Rochester 2SE carburetor used on 49 states 4-151 engines; the E2SE used on California engines is similar

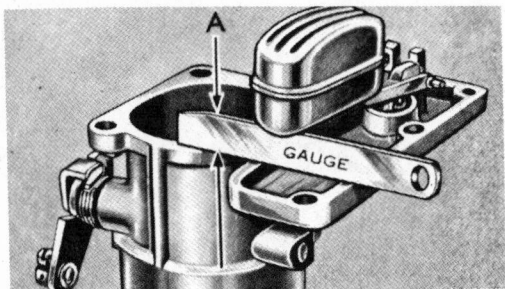

4-134 float level adjustment

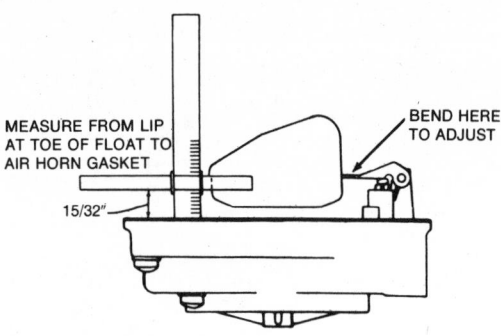

MEASURE FROM LIP
AT TOE OF FLOAT TO
AIR HORN GASKET

BEND HERE
TO ADJUST

15/32"

V6 float level adjustment

arm lip that contacts the needle (not the arm) to provide:

CJ-2A, CJ-3A .... $\frac{3}{8}$"

CJ-3B, CJ-5, CJ-6 prior to 1968 .... $\frac{5}{16}$"

CJ-5, CJ-6 1968 and later .... $\frac{17}{64}$"

V6—Rochester 2G

The procedure for adjusting the float level of the two barrel carburetor installed on the V6 is the same as the procedure for the 4-134 up to step 4.

The actual measurement is taken from the air horn gasket to the lip at the toe of the float. This distance should be $\frac{15}{32}$ in. To adjust the float level, bend the float arm as required.

The float drop adjustment is accomplished in the following manner: With the bowl cover turned in the upright position, measure the distance from the gasket to the notch at the toe of the float. Bend the tang as required to obtain a measurement of $1\frac{7}{32}$ in.

232, 258 Sixes—Carter YF

Remove and invert the air horn assembly and remove the gasket. Measure the distance between the top of the float at the free end, and the air horn casting. The measurement should be $\frac{29}{64}-\frac{31}{64}$ in. Adjust by bending the float lever.

NOTE: *The fuel inlet needle must be held off its seat while bending the float lever in order to prevent damage to the needle and seat.*

To adjust the float drop, hold the air horn in the upright position and measure the distance between the top of the float, at the ex-

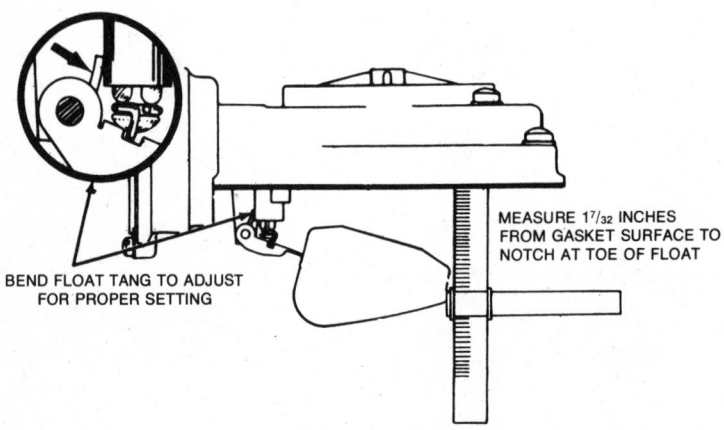

BEND FLOAT TANG TO ADJUST
FOR PROPER SETTING

MEASURE $1\frac{7}{32}$ INCHES
FROM GASKET SURFACE TO
NOTCH AT TOE OF FLOAT

V6 float drop adjustment

13. Float baffle	21. Idle stop solenoid	29. Power piston
14. Air horn	22. Vacuum hose	30. Idle needle and spring
15. Air valve	23. Vacuum break lever	31. Fast idle cam
16. Air horn gasket	24. Choke link	32. Intermediate choke rod
17. Vent screen	25. Air valve rod	33. Pump rod
18. Choke valve	26. Air valve lever	34. Throttle lever assembly
19. Pump lever	27. Accelerator pump	
20. Vacuum break and bracket	28. Metering rod	

CHILTON'S
FUEL ECONOMY
& TUNE-UP TIPS

Tune-Up • Spark Plug Diagnosis • Emission Controls

Fuel System • Cooling System • Tires and Wheels

General Maintenance

CHILTON'S FUEL ECONOMY & TUNE-UP TIPS

Fuel economy is important to everyone, no matter what kind of vehicle you drive. The maintenance-minded motorist can save both money and fuel using these tips and the periodic maintenance and tune-up procedures in this Repair and Tune-Up Guide.

There are more than 130,000,000 cars and trucks registered for private use in the United States. Each travels an average of 10-12,000 miles per year, and, in total they consume close to 70 billion gallons of fuel each year. This represents nearly ⅔ of the oil imported by the United States each year. The Federal government's goal is to reduce consumption 10% by 1985. A variety of methods are either already in use or under serious consideration, and they all affect your driving and the cars you will drive. In addition to "down-sizing", the auto industry is using or investigating the use of electronic fuel delivery, electronic engine controls and alternative engines for use in smaller and lighter vehicles, among other alternatives to meet the federally mandated Corporate Average Fuel Economy (CAFE) of 27.5 mpg by 1985. The government, for its part, is considering rationing, mandatory driving curtailments and tax increases on motor vehicle fuel in an effort to reduce consumption. The government's goal of a 10% reduction could be realized — and further government regulation avoided — if every private vehicle could use just 1 less gallon of fuel per week.

How Much Can You Save?

Tests have proven that almost anyone can make at least a 10% reduction in fuel consumption through regular maintenance and tune-ups. When a major manufacturer of spark plugs sur-

TUNE-UP

1. Check the cylinder compression to be sure the engine will really benefit from a tune-up and that it is capable of producing good fuel economy. A tune-up will be wasted on an engine in poor mechanical condition.

2. Replace spark plugs regularly. New spark plugs alone can increase fuel economy 3%.

3. Be sure the spark plugs are the correct type (heat range) for your vehicle. See the Tune-Up Specifications.

Heat range refers to the spark plug's ability to conduct heat away from the firing end. It must conduct the heat away in an even pattern to avoid becoming a source of pre-ignition, yet it must also operate hot enough to burn off conductive deposits that could cause misfiring.

The heat range is usually indicated by a number on the spark plug, part of the manufacturer's designation for each individual spark plug. The numbers in bold-face indicate the heat range in each manufacturer's identification system.

Manufacturer	Typical Designation
AC	R **45** TS
Bosch (old)	WA **145** T30
Bosch (new)	HR **8** Y
Champion	RBL **15** Y
Fram/Autolite	**4**15
Mopar	P-**62** PR
Motorcraft	BR**F**-42
NGK	BP **5** ES-15
Nippondenso	W **16** EP
Prestolite	14GR **5** 2A

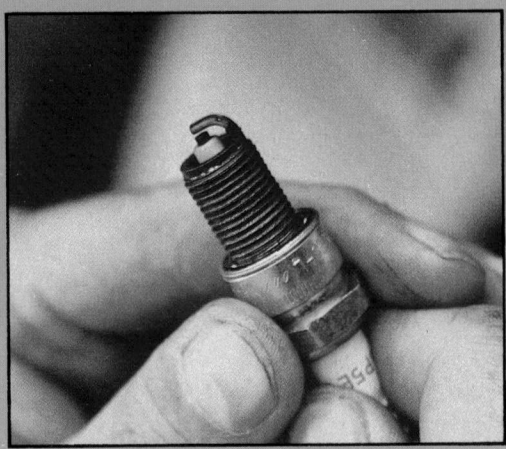

Periodically, check the spark plugs to be sure they are firing efficiently. They are excellent indicators of the internal condition of your engine.

On AC, Bosch (new), Champion, Fram/Autolite, Mopar, Motorcraft and Prestolite, a higher number indicates a hotter plug. On Bosch (old), NGK and Nippondenso, a higher number indicates a colder plug.

4. Make sure the spark plugs are properly gapped. See the Tune-Up Specifications in this book.

5. Be sure the spark plugs are firing efficiently. The illustrations on the next 2 pages show you how to "read" the firing end of the spark plug.

6. Check the ignition timing and set it to specifications. Tests show that almost all cars

veyed over 6,000 cars nationwide, they found that a tune-up, on cars that needed one, increased fuel economy over 11%. Replacing worn plugs alone, accounted for a 3% increase. The same test also revealed that 8 out of every 10 vehicles will have some maintenance deficiency that will directly affect fuel economy, emissions or performance. Most of this mileage-robbing neglect could be prevented with regular maintenance.

Modern engines require that all of the functioning systems operate properly for maximum efficiency. A malfunction anywhere wastes fuel. You can keep your vehicle running as efficiently and economically as possible, by being aware of your vehicles operating and performance characteristics. If your vehicle suddenly develops performance or fuel economy problems it could be due to one or more of the following:

PROBLEM	POSSIBLE CAUSE
Engine Idles Rough	Ignition timing, idle mixture, vacuum leak or something amiss in the emission control system.
Hesitates on Acceleration	Dirty carburetor or fuel filter, improper accelerator pump setting, ignition timing or fouled spark plugs.
Starts Hard or Fails to Start	Worn spark plugs, improperly set automatic choke, ice (or water) in fuel system.
Stalls Frequently	Automatic choke improperly adjusted and possible dirty air filter or fuel filter.
Performs Sluggishly	Worn spark plugs, dirty fuel or air filter, ignition timing or automatic choke out of adjustment.

Check spark plug wires on conventional point type ignition for cracks by bending them in a loop around your finger.

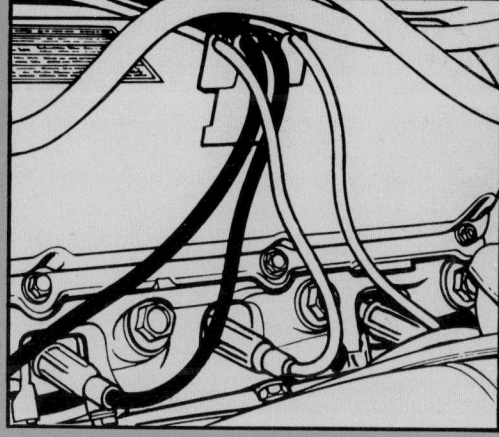

Be sure that spark plug wires leading to adjacent cylinders do not run too close together. (Photo courtesy Champion Spark Plug Co.)

have incorrect ignition timing by more than 2°.

7. If your vehicle does not have electronic ignition, check the points, rotor and cap as specified.

8. Check the spark plug wires (used with conventional point-type ignitions) for cracks and burned or broken insulation by bending them in a loop around your finger. Cracked wires decrease fuel efficiency by failing to deliver full voltage to the spark plugs. One misfiring spark plug can cost you as much as 2 mpg.

9. Check the routing of the plug wires. Misfiring can be the result of spark plug leads to adjacent cylinders running parallel to each other and too close together. One wire tends to pick up voltage from the other causing it to fire "out of time".

10. Check all electrical and ignition circuits for voltage drop and resistance.

11. Check the distributor mechanical and/or vacuum advance mechanisms for proper functioning. The vacuum advance can be checked by twisting the distributor plate in the opposite direction of rotation. It should spring back when released.

12. Check and adjust the valve clearance on engines with mechanical lifters. The clearance should be slightly loose rather than too tight.

SPARK PLUG DIAGNOSIS

Normal

APPEARANCE: This plug is typical of one operating normally. The insulator nose varies from a light tan to grayish color with slight electrode wear. The presence of slight deposits is normal on used plugs and will have no adverse effect on engine performance. The spark plug heat range is correct for the engine and the engine is running normally.

CAUSE: Properly running engine.

RECOMMENDATION: Before reinstalling this plug, the electrodes should be cleaned and filed square. Set the gap to specifications. If the plug has been in service for more than 10-12,000 miles, the entire set should probably be replaced with a fresh set of the same heat range.

Oil Deposits

APPEARANCE: The firing end of the plug is covered with a wet, oily coating.

CAUSE: The problem is poor oil control. On high mileage engines, oil is leaking past the rings or valve guides into the combustion chamber. A common cause is also a plugged PCV valve, and a ruptured fuel pump diaphragm can also cause this condition. Oil fouled plugs such as these are often found in new or recently overhauled engines, before normal oil control is achieved, and can be cleaned and reinstalled.

RECOMMENDATION: A hotter spark plug may temporarily relieve the problem, but the engine is probably in need of work.

Incorrect Heat Range

APPEARANCE: The effects of high temperature on a spark plug are indicated by clean white, often blistered insulator. This can also be accompanied by excessive wear of the electrode, and the absence of deposits.

CAUSE: Check for the correct spark plug heat range. A plug which is too hot for the engine can result in overheating. A car operated mostly at high speeds can require a colder plug. Also check ignition timing, cooling system level, fuel mixture and leaking intake manifold.

RECOMMENDATION: If all ignition and engine adjustments are known to be correct, and no other malfunction exists, install spark plugs one heat range colder.

Photos Courtesy Champion Spark Plug Co.

Carbon Deposits

APPEARANCE: Carbon fouling is easily identified by the presence of dry, soft, black, sooty deposits.

CAUSE: Changing the heat range can often lead to carbon fouling, as can prolonged slow, stop-and-start driving. If the heat range is correct, carbon fouling can be attributed to a rich fuel mixture, sticking choke, clogged air cleaner, worn breaker points, retarded timing or low compression. If only one or two plugs are carbon fouled, check for corroded or cracked wires on the affected plugs. Also look for cracks in the distributor cap between the towers of affected cylinders.

RECOMMENDATION: After the problem is corrected, these plugs can be cleaned and reinstalled if not worn severely.

MMT Fouled

APPEARANCE: Spark plugs fouled by MMT (Methycyclopentadienyl Maganese Tricarbonyl) have reddish, rusty appearance on the insulator and side electrode.

CAUSE: MMT is an anti-knock additive in gasoline used to replace lead. During the combustion process, the MMT leaves a reddish deposit on the insulator and side electrode.

RECOMMENDATION: No engine malfunction is indicated and the deposits will not affect plug performance any more than lead deposits (see Ash Deposits). MMT fouled plugs can be cleaned, regapped and reinstalled.

High Speed Glazing

APPEARANCE: Glazing appears as shiny coating on the plug, either yellow or tan in color.

CAUSE: During hard, fast acceleration, plug temperatures rise suddenly. Deposits from normal combustion have no chance to fluff-off; instead, they melt on the insulator forming an electrically conductive coating which causes misfiring.

RECOMMENDATION: Glazed plugs are not easily cleaned. They should be replaced with a fresh set of plugs of the correct heat range. If the condition recurs, using plugs with a heat range one step colder may cure the problem.

Ash (Lead) Deposits

APPEARANCE: Ash deposits are characterized by light brown or white colored deposits crusted on the side or center electrodes. In some cases it may give the plug a rusty appearance.

CAUSE: Ash deposits are normally derived from oil or fuel additives burned during normal combustion. Normally they are harmless, though excessive amounts can cause misfiring. If deposits are excessive in short mileage, the valve guides may be worn.

RECOMMENDATION: Ash-fouled plugs can be cleaned, gapped and reinstalled.

Detonation

APPEARANCE: Detonation is usually characterized by a broken plug insulator.

CAUSE: A portion of the fuel charge will begin to burn spontaneously, from the increased heat following ignition. The explosion that results applies extreme pressure to engine components, frequently damaging spark plugs and pistons.

Detonation can result by over-advanced ignition timing, inferior gasoline (low octane) lean air/fuel mixture, poor carburetion, engine lugging or an increase in compression ratio due to combustion chamber deposits or engine modification.

RECOMMENDATION: Replace the plugs after correcting the problem.

Photos Courtesy Fram Corporation

EMISSION CONTROLS

13. Be aware of the general condition of the emission control system. It contributes to reduced pollution and should be serviced regularly to maintain efficient engine operation.

14. Check all vacuum lines for dried, cracked or brittle conditions. Something as simple as a leaking vacuum hose can cause poor performance and loss of economy.

15. Avoid tampering with the emission control system. Attempting to improve fuel econ-

FUEL SYSTEM

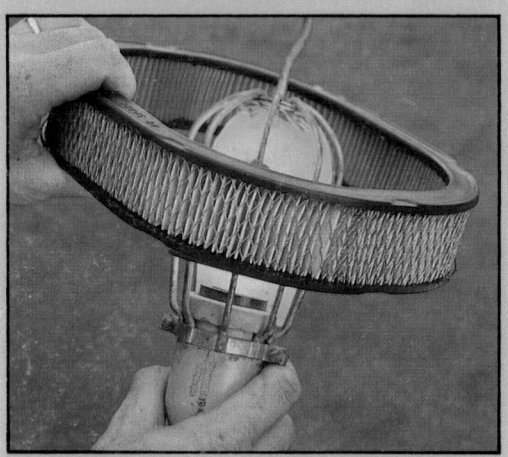

Check the air filter with a light behind it. If you can see light through the filter it can be reused.

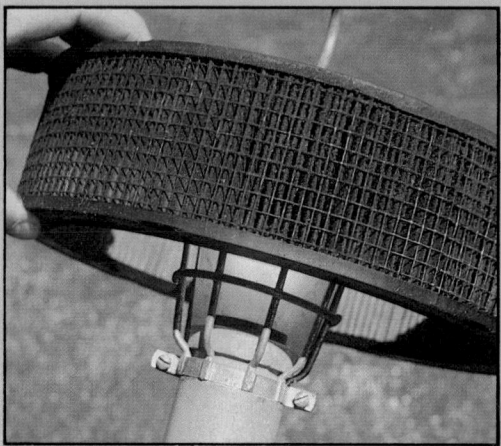

Extremely clogged filters should be discarded and replaced with a new one.

18. Replace the air filter regularly. A dirty air filter richens the air/fuel mixture and can increase fuel consumption as much as 10%. Tests show that ⅓ of all vehicles have air filters in need of replacement.

19. Replace the fuel filter at least as often as recommended.

20. Set the idle speed and carburetor mixture to specifications.

21. Check the automatic choke. A sticking or malfunctioning choke wastes gas.

22. During the summer months, adjust the automatic choke for a leaner mixture which will produce faster engine warm-ups.

COOLING SYSTEM

29. Be sure all accessory drive belts are in good condition. Check for cracks or wear.

30. Adjust all accessory drive belts to proper tension.

31. Check all hoses for swollen areas, worn spots, or loose clamps.

32. Check coolant level in the radiator or expansion tank.

33. Be sure the thermostat is operating properly. A stuck thermostat delays engine warm-up and a cold engine uses nearly twice as much fuel as a warm engine.

34. Drain and replace the engine coolant at least as often as recommended. Rust and scale

TIRES & WHEELS

38. Check the tire pressure often with a pencil type gauge. Tests by a major tire manufacturer show that 90% of all vehicles have at least 1 tire improperly inflated. Better mileage can be achieved by over-inflating tires, but never exceed the maximum inflation pressure on the side of the tire.

39. If possible, install radial tires. Radial tires deliver as much as ½ mpg more than bias belted tires.

40. Avoid installing super-wide tires. They only create extra rolling resistance and decrease fuel mileage. Stick to the manufacturer's recommendations.

41. Have the wheels properly balanced.

omy by tampering with emission controls is more likely to worsen fuel economy than improve it. Emission control changes on modern engines are not readily reversible.

16. Clean (or replace) the EGR valve and lines as recommended.

17. Be sure that all vacuum lines and hoses are reconnected properly after working under the hood. An unconnected or misrouted vacuum line can wreak havoc with engine performance.

---

23. Check for fuel leaks at the carburetor, fuel pump, fuel lines and fuel tank. Be sure all lines and connections are tight.

24. Periodically check the tightness of the carburetor and intake manifold attaching nuts and bolts. These are a common place for vacuum leaks to occur.

25. Clean the carburetor periodically and lubricate the linkage.

26. The condition of the tailpipe can be an excellent indicator of proper engine combustion. After a long drive at highway speeds, the inside of the tailpipe should be a light grey in color. Black or soot on the insides indicates an overly rich mixture.

27. Check the fuel pump pressure. The fuel pump may be supplying more fuel than the engine needs.

28. Use the proper grade of gasoline for your engine. Don't try to compensate for knocking or "pinging" by advancing the ignition timing. This practice will only increase plug temperature and the chances of detonation or pre-ignition with relatively little performance gain.

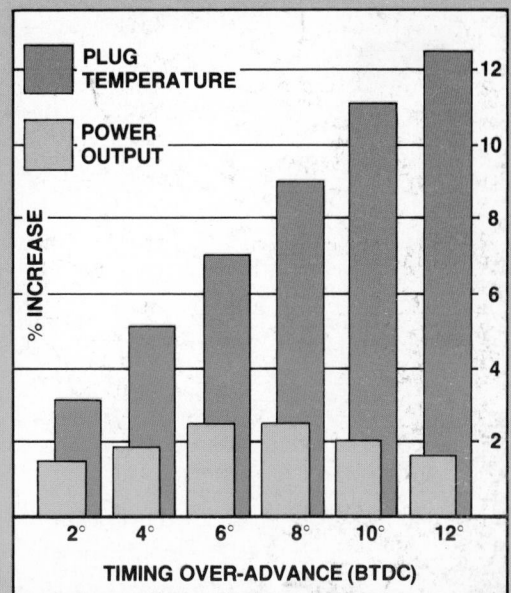

Increasing ignition timing past the specified setting results in a drastic increase in spark plug temperature with increased chance of detonation or preignition. Performance increase is considerably less. (Photo courtesy Champion Spark Plug Co.)

---

that form in the engine should be flushed out to allow the engine to operate at peak efficiency.

35. Clean the radiator of debris that can decrease cooling efficiency.

36. Install a flex-type or electric cooling fan, if you don't have a clutch type fan. Flex fans use curved plastic blades to push more air at low speeds when more cooling is needed; at high speeds the blades flatten out for less resistance. Electric fans only run when the engine temperature reaches a predetermined level.

37. Check the radiator cap for a worn or cracked gasket. If the cap does not seal properly, the cooling system will not function properly.

---

42. Be sure the front end is correctly aligned. A misaligned front end actually has wheels going in different directions. The increased drag can reduce fuel economy by .3 mpg.

43. Correctly adjust the wheel bearings. Wheel bearings that are adjusted too tight increase rolling resistance.

Check tire pressures regularly with a reliable pocket type gauge. Be sure to check the pressure on a cold tire.

GENERAL MAINTENANCE

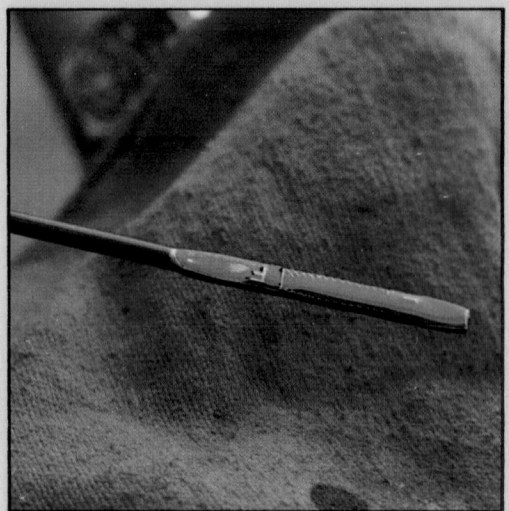

Check the fluid levels (particularly engine oil) on a regular basis. Be sure to check the oil for grit, water or other contamination.

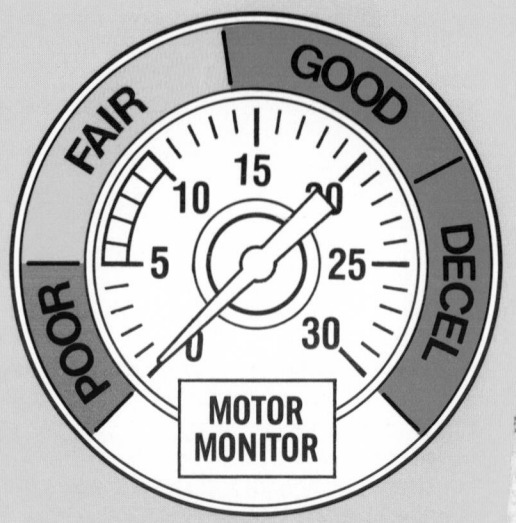

A vacuum gauge is another excellent indicator of internal engine condition and can also be installed in the dash as a mileage indicator.

44. Periodically check the fluid levels in the engine, power steering pump, master cylinder, automatic transmission and drive axle.

45. Change the oil at the recommended interval and change the filter at every oil change. Dirty oil is thick and causes extra friction between moving parts, cutting efficiency and increasing wear. A worn engine requires more frequent tune-ups and gets progressively worse fuel economy. In general, use the lightest viscosity oil for the driving conditions you will encounter.

46. Use the recommended viscosity fluids in the transmission and axle.

47. Be sure the battery is fully charged for fast starts. A slow starting engine wastes fuel.

48. Be sure battery terminals are clean and tight.

49. Check the battery electrolyte level and add distilled water if necessary.

50. Check the exhaust system for crushed pipes, blockages and leaks.

51. Adjust the brakes. Dragging brakes or brakes that are not releasing create increased drag on the engine.

52. Install a vacuum gauge or miles-per-gallon gauge. These gauges visually indicate engine vacuum in the intake manifold. High vacuum = good mileage and low vacuum = poorer mileage. The gauge can also be an excellent indicator of internal engine conditions.

53. Be sure the clutch is properly adjusted. A slipping clutch wastes fuel.

54. Check and periodically lubricate the heat control valve in the exhaust manifold. A sticking or inoperative valve prevents engine warm-up and wastes gas.

55. Keep accurate records to check fuel economy over a period of time. A sudden drop in fuel economy may signal a need for tune-up or other maintenance.

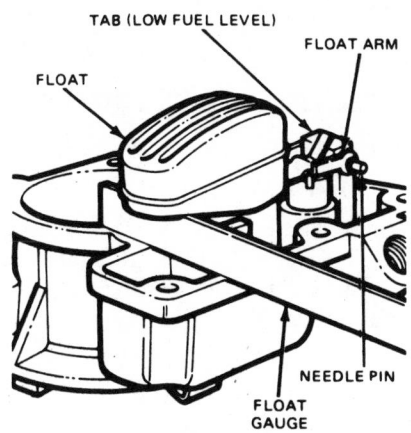

3-232, 258 Carter YF float adjustment

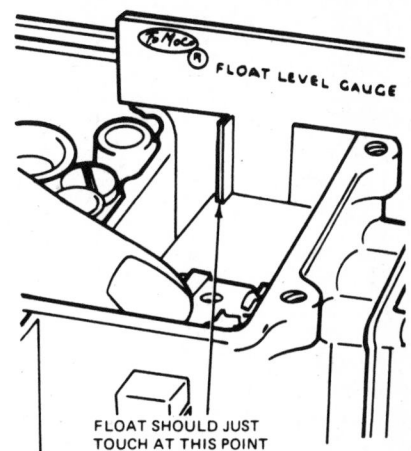

Autolite 2100 and Motorcraft 2150 dry float adjustment

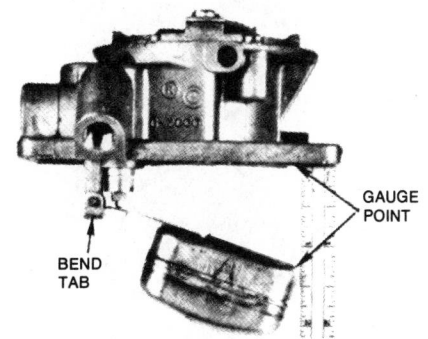

6-232, 258 Carter YF float drop adjustment

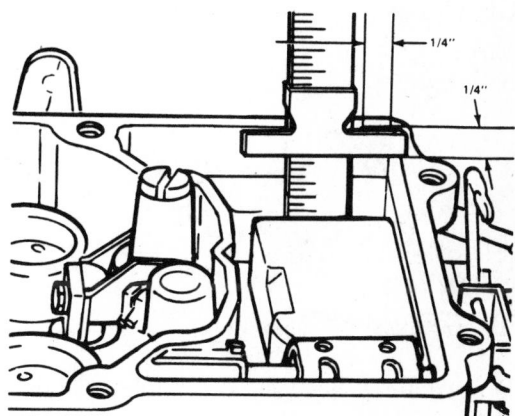

Motorcraft 2150 wet float adjustment

treme outer end, and the air horn casting. The measurement should be 1¼ in. to 1973, 1⅜ in. 1974–78. Adjust by bending the tab at the rear of the float lever.

6-258 Carter BBD 2-bbl

1. Remove the air horn.
2. Apply light finger pressure to the vertical float tab to exert GENTLE pressure against the inlet needle.
3. Lay a straight edge across the float bowl and measure the gap between the straight edge and the top of the float at its highest point. The gap should be ¼ in.
4. To adjust, remove the float and bend the lower tab. Replace the float and check the gap.

8-304 Autolite 2100, Motorcraft 2150 Dry Adjustment

With the air horn assembly and the gasket removed raise the float by pressing down on the float tab until the fuel inlet needle is lightly seated. Using a T-scale, measure the distance from the fuel bowl machined surface

to either corner of the float ⅛" from the free end. The measurement should be ¾ in. through 1975, $3/16$–$15/32$ in. 1976–81. To adjust bend the float tab and hold the fuel inlet needle off its seat in order to prevent damage to the seat and the tip of the needle.

8-304 Motorcraft 2150 Wet Adjustment

CAUTION: *Exercise extreme care when performing this adjustment as fuel vapors and liquid fuel are present!*

1. Place the vehicle on a flat, level surface and run the engine to normal operating temperature. Turn off the engine and remove the air cleaner.
2. Remove the air horn attaching screws, but leave the air horn in place.
3. Start the engine and let it idle for one minute. Shut off the engine and remove the air horn and gasket.
4. Use a T-scale to measure the vertical distance between the machined surface of

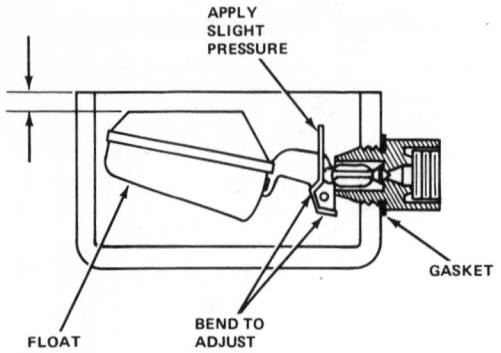

BBD float adjustment

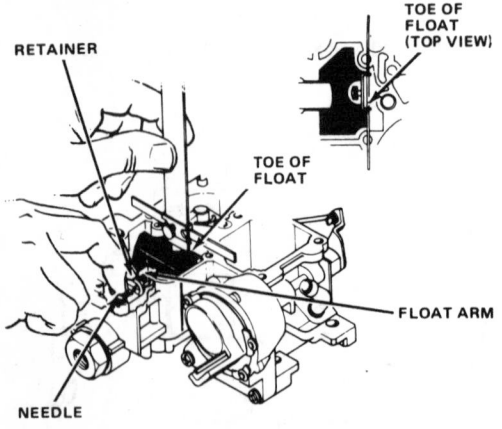

2SE and E2SE float adjustment

the carburetor body and the fuel level in the bowl. Make this measurement as near the center of the bowl as possible. The proper distance is $^{59}/_{64}$ in. To adjust, bend the float tab.

> NOTE: *Every time an adjustment is made, the air horn must be replaced, and the engine started and idled for one minute to stabilize the fuel level.*

5. Install the air horn and gasket when adjustment is completed.

4-151 Rochester 2SE, and E2SE

1. Remove the air horn.
2. Hold the float retainer and push down lightly on the float.
3. Using a T-scale, at a point $^3/_{16}$ in. from the end of the float, measure the distance from the top surface of the float bowl to the top of the float. The distance should be .208 in. with manual trans., .256 in. with automatic trans., and .208 for all Calif. E2SE models.
4. Bend the float arm as necessary to adjust.

5. Replace the air horn and gasket when adjustment is complete.

FAST IDLE LINKAGE ADJUSTMENT

NOTE: *With air cleaner removed.*

4-134 Carter YF

With the choke held in the wide open position, the lip on the fast-idle rod should contact the boss on the body casting. Adjust it by bending the fast idle link at the offset in the link.

1. Fast idle connector rod
2. Fast idle link

4-134 fast idle adjustment

6-225 Rochester 2G

No fast idle speed adjustment is required. Fast idle is controlled by the curb idle speed adjustment screw. If the curb idle speed is set correctly and the choke rod is properly adjusted, fast idle speed will be correct.

6-232, 258 through 1973—Carter YF

Partially open the throttle and close the choke valve to rotate the fast idle cam into the cold start position. While holding the choke valve closed, release the throttle. With the fast idle cam in this position, the fast idle adjusting screw must be aligned with the index mark at the back side of the cam. Adjust by bending the choke rod at its upper angle.

6-232, 258 1974-78—Carter YF

Position the fast idle screw on the second step of the fast idle cam, against the shoulder of the high step on the cam. Adjust by bend-

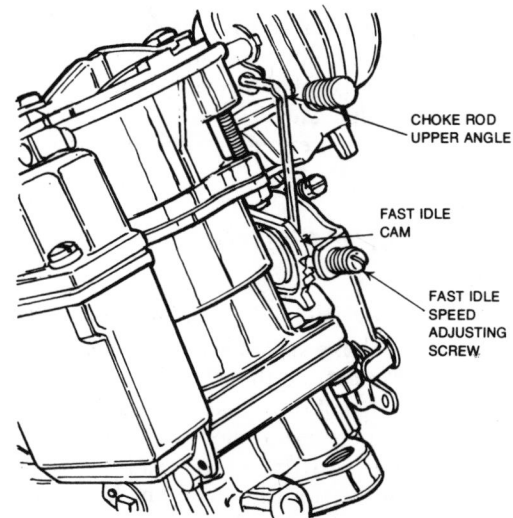

Carter YF fast idle cam linkage adjustment

ing the choke plate connecting rod to obtain $13/64$ in. clearance between the lower edge of the choke plate and the air horn wall.

6-258 Carter BBD 2-bbl

1. Loosen the choke housing cover and turn it one-quarter turn right. Tighten one screw.

2. Slightly open the throttle and place the fast idle screw on the second cam step.

3. Measure the distance between the choke plate and the air horn wall. The gap should be $7/64$ in.

4. If adjustment is necessary, bend the fast idle cam link down to increase and up to decrease the gap.

5. Return the choke cover cap to the original setting.

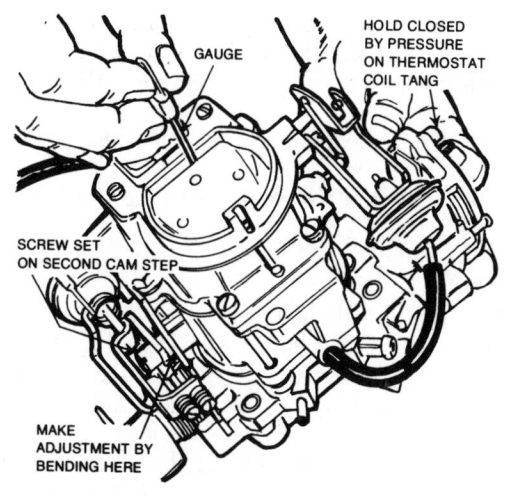

BBD fast idle cam adjustment

8-304 Autolite 2100, Motorcraft 2150

Push down on the fast idle cam lever until the fast idle speed adjusting screw is contacting the second step (index), and against the shoulder of the high step. Measure the clearance between the lower edge of the choke valve and air horn wall. Adjust by turning the fast idle cam lever screw to obtain $19/64$ in. through 1975 and $1/8$ in. 1976–79. Adjust the automatic choke.

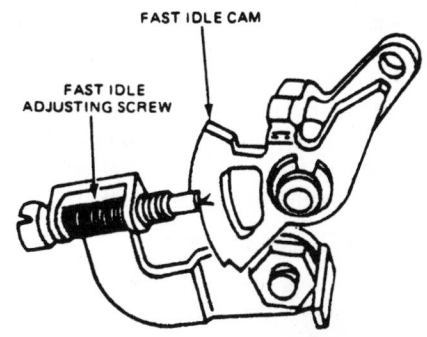

Autolite 2100, Motorcraft 2150 fast idle cam setting

4-151 Rochester 2SE, E2SE

1. Make sure the choke coil adjustment is correct and that the fast idle speed is correct.

2. Obtain a Choke Angle Gauge, tool #J-26701-A. Rotate the degree scale to the zero degree mark opposite the pointer.

3. With the choke valve completely closed, place the magnet on the tool squarely on the choke plate. Rotate the bubble unit until it is centered.

4. Rotate the degree scale until the 25° mark is opposite the pointer. On carburetors with choke cover sticker number 70172, the angle is 18°.

5. Place the fast idle screw on the second step of the cam.

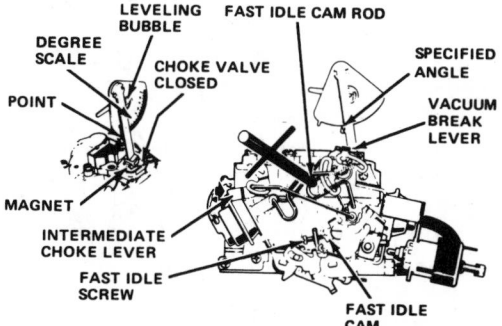

2SE, E2SE fast idle cam position adjustment

6. Close the choke plate by pushing on the intermediate choke lever.

7. Push the vacuum brake lever toward the open choke position until the lever is against the rear tang on the choke lever.

8. Adjust by bending the fast idle cam rod until the bubble is centered.

CHOKE SETTING ADJUSTMENT

4-134 and V6-225

The choke is manually operated by a cable that runs from the dash mounted control pull knob to the set screw on the choke actuating arm. To adjust the choke, loosen the set screw at the choke actuating lever and push in the dash knob as far as it will go. Open the choke plate as far as it will go and hold it with your finger while the set screw is tightened.

6-232, 258 and 8-304

The automatic choke setting is made by loosening the choke cover in the desired direction as indicated by an arrow on the face of the cover. The original setting will be satisfactory for most driving conditions. However, if the engine stumbles or stalls on acceleration during warmup, the choke may be set richer or leaner no more than two graduations from the original setting.

4-151 Rochester 2SE, E2SE

NOTE: *Once the rivets and choke cover are removed, a choke cover retainer kit is necessary for assembly.*

1. Remove the rivets, retainers, choke cover and coil following the instructions found in the cover retainer kit.

2. Position the fast idle adjustment screw on the highest step of the fast idle cam.

3. Push on the intermediate choke lever and close the choke plate.

4. Insert the proper plug gauge, .050–

.080 in. for manual trans. and .85 in. for automatic trans., in the hole adjacent to the coil lever. The edge of the lever should barely contact the plug gauge.

5. Bend the intermediate choke rod to adjust.

UNLOADER ADJUSTMENT

6-232, 258

With the throttle held fully open, apply pressure on the choke valve toward the closed position and measure the clearance between the lower edge of the choke valve and the air horn wall. The measurement should be ¼ in. 1972–73, $9/32$ in. 1974–81. Adjust by bending the tang on the throttle lever which contacts the fast idle cam. Bend toward the cam to increase the clearance.

NOTE: *Do not bend the unloader downward from a horizontal plane. After making the adjustment, make sure the unloader tang does not contact the main body flange when the throttle is fully open. A clearance of .070" must be present. Final unloader adjustment must always be done on the vehicle. The throttle should be fully opened by depressing the accelerator pedal to the floor. This is to assure that full throttle is obtained.*

4-151

1. Obtain a Carburetor Choke Angle Gauge, tool #J-26701-A. Rotate the scale on the gauge until the 0 mark is opposite the pointer.

2. Close the choke plate completely and set the magnet squarely on top of it.

3. Rotate the bubble until it is centered.

4. Rotate the degree scale until the 32° mark is opposite the pointer. On carburetors with choke cover sticker number 70172 the setting is 19°.

5. Hold the primary throttle valve wide open.

6. Bend the throttle lever tang until the bubble is centered.

304 V8

With the throttle held fully open, apply pressure on the choke valve toward the closed position and measure the clearance between the lower edge of the choke valve and the air horn wall. The setting should be ¼ in., $5/16$ for 1979. Adjust by bending the tang on the fast idle lever, which is located on the throttle linkage. Refer to the "Note" under the

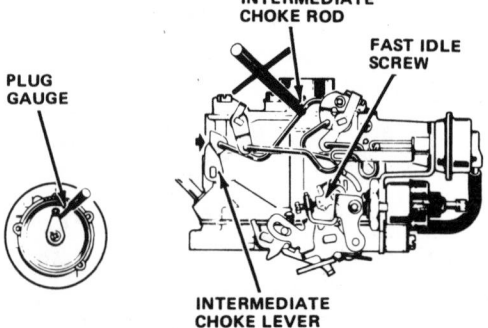

PLUG GAUGE

INTERMEDIATE CHOKE ROD

FAST IDLE SCREW

INTERMEDIATE CHOKE LEVER

2SE, E2SE choke coil lever adjustment

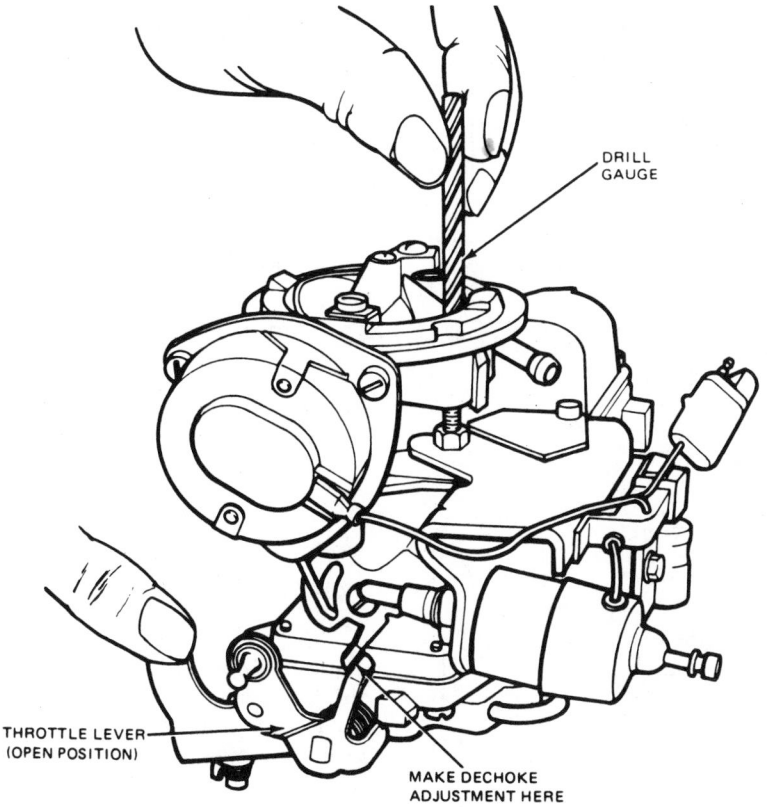

Carter YF choke unloader adjustment

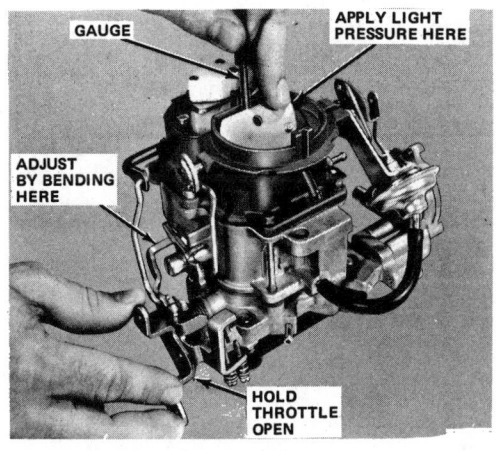

BBD choke unloader adjustment

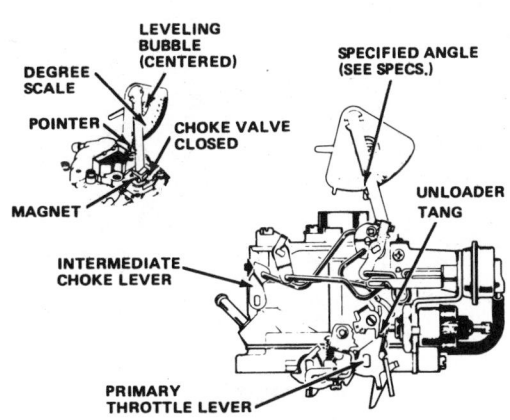

2SE, E2SE choke unloader adjustment

procedure for adjusting the unloader on the Sixes.

DASHPOT ADJUSTMENT

Inline Sixes and V8

With the throttle set at curb idle position fully depress the dashpot stem and measure the clearance between the stem and the throttle lever. Adjust by loosening the lock nut and turning the dashpot.

F-Head and V6

The adjustment is made with the engine idling. Loosen the dashpot locknut and turn the assembly until the plunger contacts the

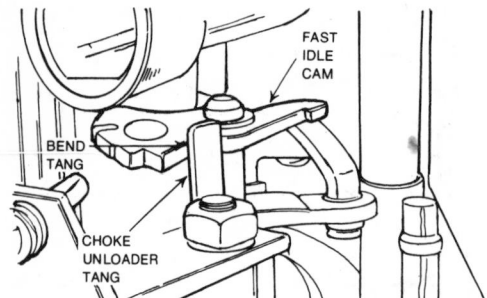

Motorcraft 2150 choke unloader adjustment

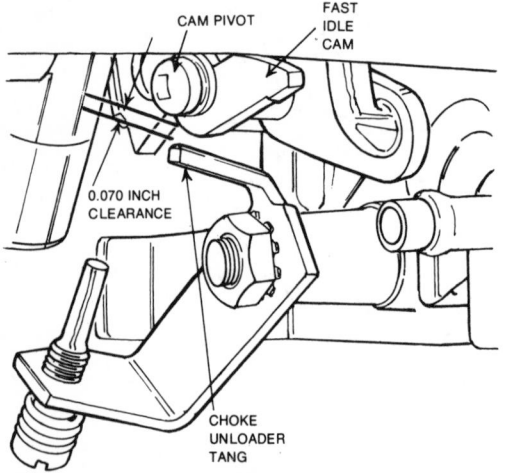

Motorcraft 2150 choke unloader/fast idle cam clearance

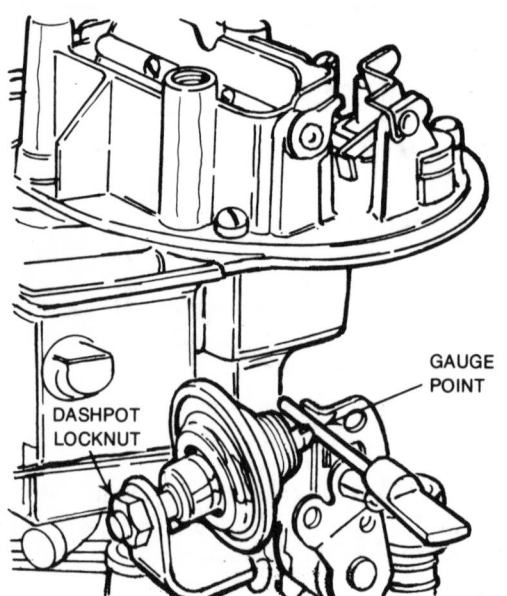

Typical dashpot adjustment

Dashpot Stem-to-Throttle Lever Clearance (in.)

	'72	'73	'74	'75	'76
232	$3/32$	$3/32$	$3/32$	$5/64$	$5/64$
258	$3/32$	$3/32$	$3/32$	$5/64$	$5/64$
304	$7/64$	$9/64$	$9/64$	$3/32$	$5/64$

throttle lever without being depressed. Then, turn the assembly 2½ turns against the lever, depressing the plunger. Tighten the locknut.

Fuel Tank

REMOVAL AND INSTALLATION

Through 1969

To remove the fuel tank, first make sure that the tank is either completely drained or that the level is at least below any of the vent lines or filler openings so that when these lines are disconnected fuel will not run out.

Remove the driver's seat from the vehicle.

Disconnect all of the ventline hoses, the fuel gauge electrical lead, the fill hose and the fuel outlet line at the tank.

Remove the tank hold down screws from the mounting brackets, or the hold down strap, and lift the tank from the vehicle.

If there is still gas in the tank, be careful not to spill any fuel when lifting it out of the vehicle. Also, empty the tank of all fuel and flush it with water before soldering or welding the tank.

Install the tank in the reverse order of removal.

1970–81

The fuel tank is attached to the frame by brackets and bolts. The brackets are attached to the tank at the seam flange or the skid plate.

Before removing the fuel tank, make sure that the level of the fuel inside the tank is at least below any of the various hoses connected. It is best to either drain or siphon the majority of fuel out of the tank to make it easier to handle while removing it.

Carburetor Specifications

All measurements in inches (in.)

Year	Model	Application	Float Level		Float Drop	Fast Idle Linkage	Choke Linkage	Choke Unloader
			Dry	Wet				
1953–67	Carter YF	4—134	5/16	—	—	See Text	Manual	Manual
1968–71	Carter YF	4—134	17/16	—	—	See Text	Manual	Manual
1972–73	Carter YF	6—232,258	15/32	—	1¼	See Text	Index	¼
1974–78	Carter YF	6—232,258	15/32	—	1⅜	13/64	Index	9/32
1979–81	Carter BBD	6—258	¼	—	—	7/64	1 Rich	9/32
1965–71	Rochester 2G	V6—225	15/32	—	1 7/32	See Text	Manual	Manual
1972–75	Autolite/Motorcraft 2100, 2150	8—304	2/5	25/32	—	19/64	2 Rich	¼, 9/32①
1976–78	Autolite/Motorcraft 2100, 2150	8—304	17/32	59/64	—	⅛	1 Rich, 2 Rich②	9/32
1979	Autolite/Motorcraft 2100, 2150	8—304	17/32	59/64	—	⅛	1 Rich, 2 Rich②	9/32
1980–81	Motorcraft 2150	8—304	11/32	59/64	—	⅛	③	⅓
1980–81	Rochester 2SE, E2SE	4—151	④	—	—	25°	TR	32°

NOTE: *Autolite and Motorcraft carburetors are the same products produced under different names.*

① 1974–75

② Non-California manual

③ Manual, 49 states: 2 Rich
Automatic and Calif.: 1 Rich

④ Manual: .208
Automatic and Calif.: .256

Chassis Electrical

HEATER

Blower Motor

REMOVAL AND INSTALLATION

Through 1977

1. Disconnect the battery ground cable. Detach any interfering control cables.
2. Disconnect the electrical connections:
   a. Heater switch
   b. Ground wire
   c. Battery connector
3. Remove the screws that hold the motor to the heater assembly and remove the blower motor housing and motor.
4. Remove fan and blower motor from blower motor housing.
5. Reverse the procedure to install.

1978–81

The heater housing assembly has to be removed to get out the blower motor.

1. Drain about two quarts of coolant.
2. Disconnect the heater hoses at the engine side of the firewall.
3. Detach the heater control cables.
4. Disconnect the motor wiring.
5. Detach the water drain hose and the defroster hose.
6. Remove the nuts from the studs in the engine compartment.

7. Tilt the heater housing assembly down and pull it back toward the inside of the vehicle.
8. Remove the attaching screws and the blower motor.
9. On installation, make sure that the seals around the core tubes and blower motor are in place.

Core

REMOVAL AND INSTALLATION

Through 1974

1. Drain the cooling system.
2. Mark the duct halves to be sure they are reassembled properly.
3. Remove the screws that fasten the two halves of the duct together.
4. Remove the screws that secure the heater core to the duct.
5. Remove the heater core from the vehicle.
6. Install in reverse order of the above procedure.

1975–76

1. Drain about two quarts of coolant from the radiator.
2. Disconnect the battery cables, remove the battery and battery box.
3. Disconnect the heater hoses.

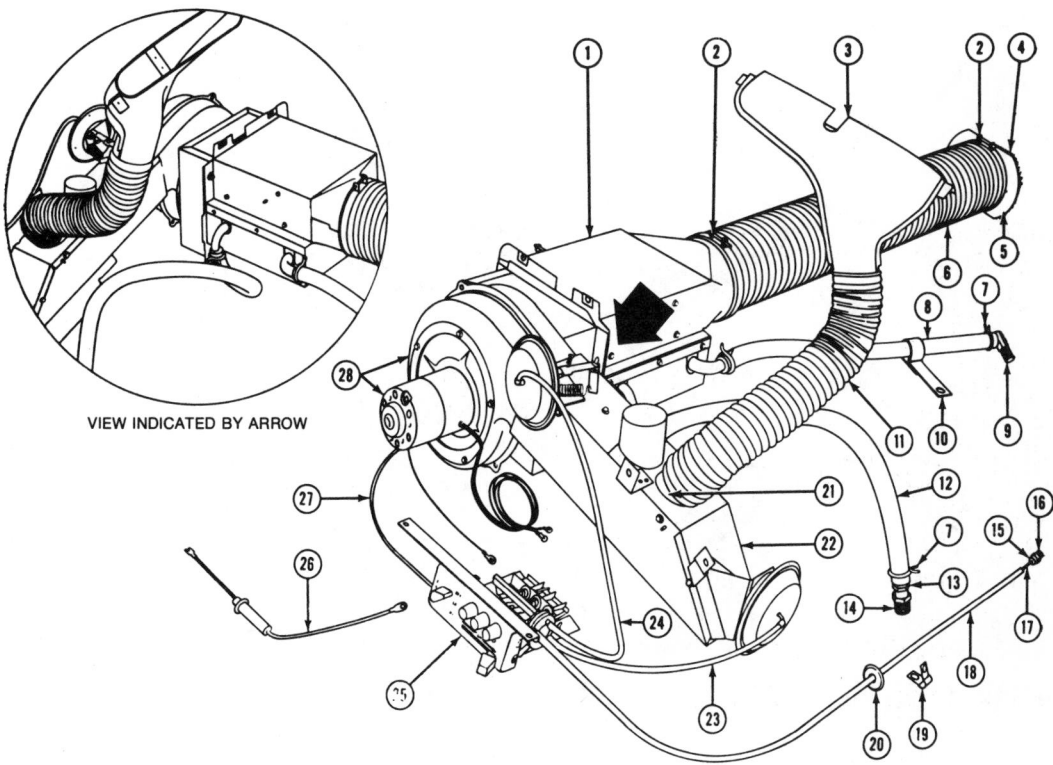

VIEW INDICATED BY ARROW

1. Heater assembly
2. Hose clamp
3. Defroster nozzle
4. Air duct screen
5. Air duct and heater collar
6. Air duct intake tube
7. Hose clamp
8. Straight hot water hose
9. Heater tube elbow
10. Heater hose support bracket
11. Defroster hose
12. Hot water hose
13. Heater nipple
14. Reducing bushing
15. Inverted flared tube nut
16. Inverted flared tube connector
17. Heater vacuum to engine tube
18. Heater control tube
19. Clip
20. Grommet
21. Defroster bushing
22. Heat distributor assembly
23. Heater control tube
24. Heater control tube
25. Heater control assembly
26. Fuse holder assembly
27. Bowden wire (control panel to
    heater)
28. Blower and air inlet assembly

Heater assembly through 1971. Earlier heaters are less complicated

4. Disconnect the damper door control cables.

5. Disconnect the blower motor wiring harness at the switch and ground wire at the instrument panel.

6. Remove the glove box.

7. Disconnect the water drain hose and defroster hose.

8. Disconnect the heater-to-air deflector duct at the heater housing.

9. Remove the nuts from the heater housing studs in the engine compartment and remove the heater housing assembly.

10. Remove the heater core from the heater housing.

11. Install the heater core in the reverse order of removal, refill the radiator, run the engine and check for leaks.

1978–81

The heater housing assembly has to be removed to get out the heater core. The procedure is the same as for blower motor removal and installation.

WINDSHIELD WIPERS

Wiper Blades and Arms
REMOVAL AND INSTALLATION

To remove the blade, pull it away from the windshield. Push against the tip of the wiper arm to compress the locking spring and disengage the retaining pin. Pivot the blade clockwise to unhook it from the arm. To install the blade, just snap it into position.

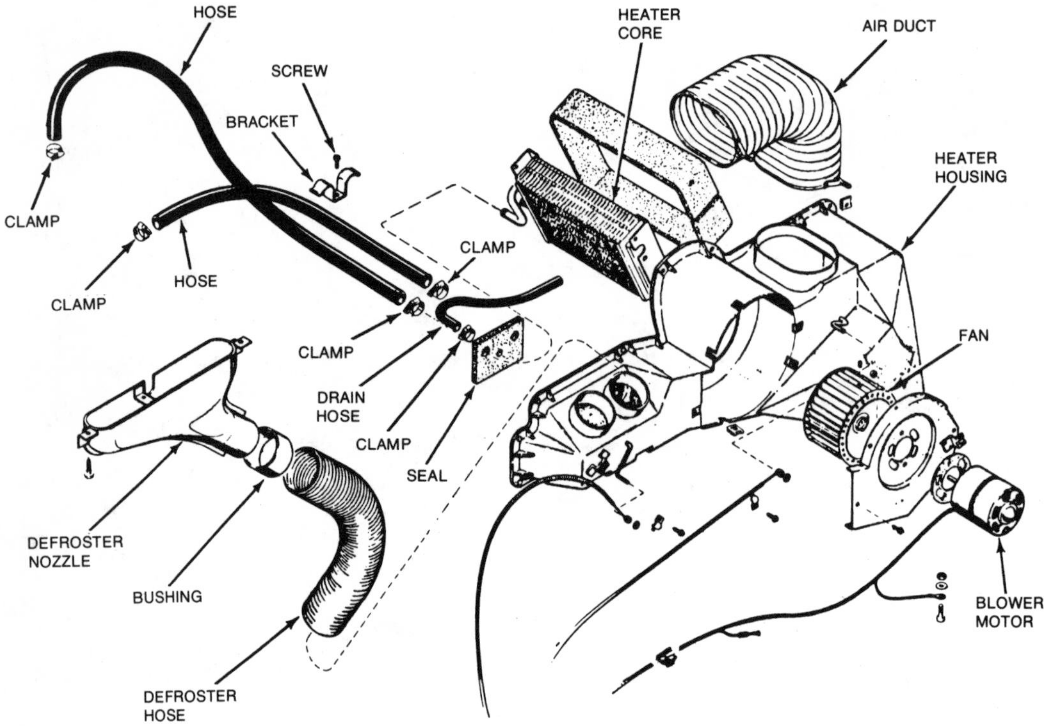

HOSE

SCREW

BRACKET

HEATER CORE

AIR DUCT

CLAMP

HOSE

CLAMP

CLAMP

HEATER HOUSING

CLAMP

DRAIN HOSE

CLAMP

SEAL

FAN

DEFROSTER NOZZLE

BUSHING

DEFROSTER HOSE

BLOWER MOTOR

1972–77 heater assembly

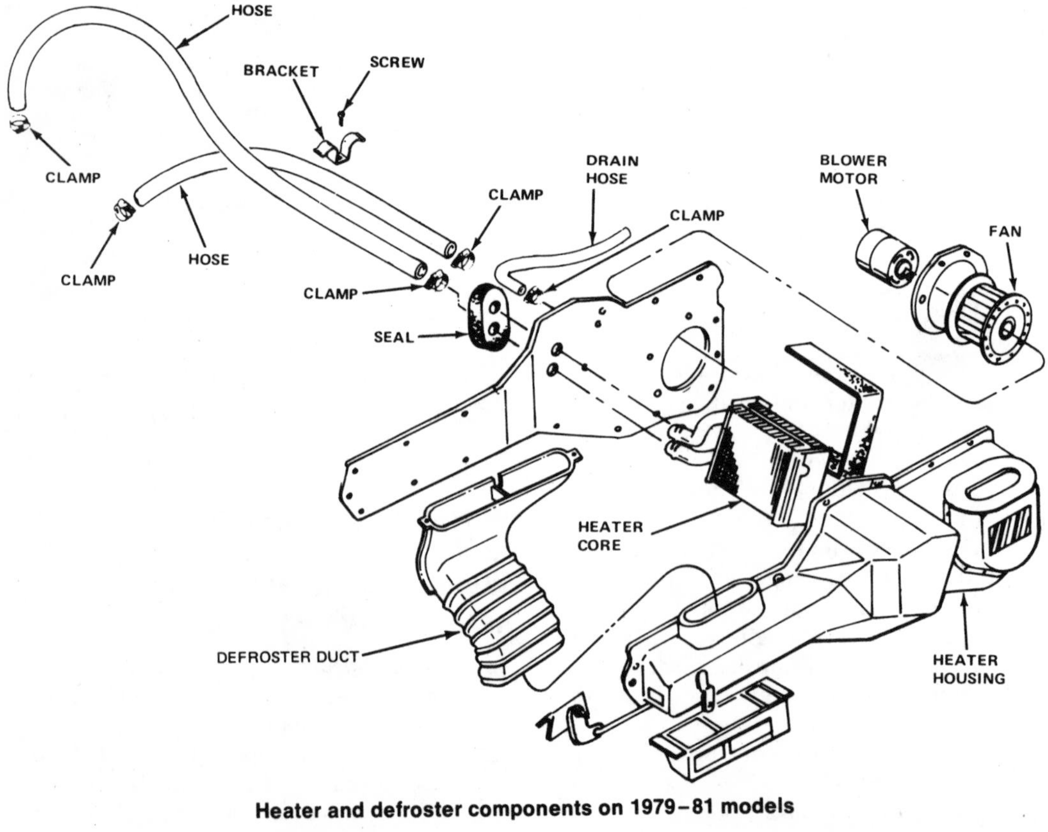

HOSE

BRACKET

SCREW

DRAIN HOSE

BLOWER MOTOR

CLAMP

CLAMP

CLAMP

FAN

CLAMP

CLAMP

HOSE

CLAMP

SEAL

HEATER CORE

DEFROSTER DUCT

HEATER HOUSING

Heater and defroster components on 1979–81 models

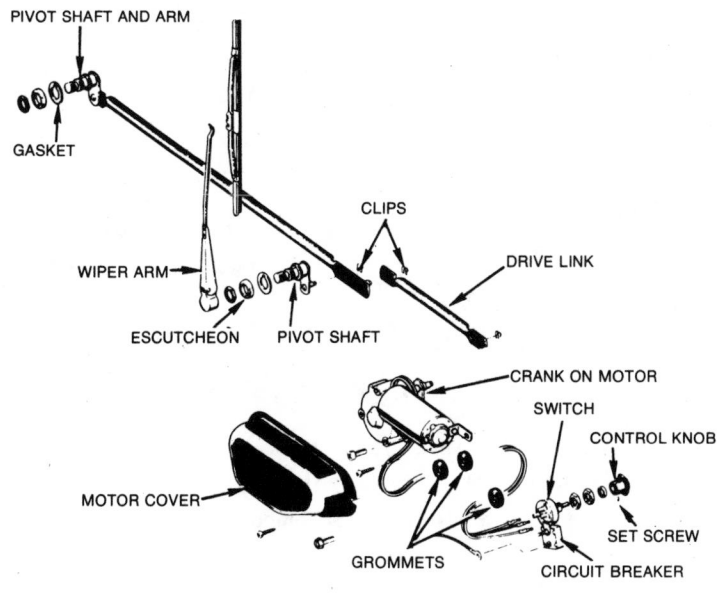

1972-75 wiper assembly

To remove the arm, simply pry it straight off carefully. When you reinstall it, make sure that it doesn't hit the rubber moulding at either edge of the windshield while running.

Motor

REMOVAL AND INSTALLATION

Through 1971

Remove the windshield wiper assembly from the pivot shaft. Remove the vacuum hose or wire from the motor. Remove all attaching screws that hold the motor to the windshield assembly and remove the motor from the vehicle. Install in the reverse order.

1972-75

1. Remove the crash pad, if any. Remove the extreme left plastic hole plug from the bottom of the windshield frame air duct and disconnect the drive link from the motor crank.
2. Loosen the wiper control knob setscrew.
3. Remove the control switch and mark the location of the wires on the switch prior to removing them from the switch.
4. Remove the motor cover and the motor.
5. Install in the reverse order of the above procedure.

NOTE: *The motor cover must be sealed when installing.*

1976-81

1. If your Jeep has crash padding, you have to fold the windshield down for access. Even if you don't have the padding, you can't get the wires out to remove the motor from the vehicle, unless the windshield is down.
2. Remove the wiper motor cover.
3. Remove the left access plug from the bottom of the windshield.
4. Disconnect the drive link from the left wiper pivot by sliding the clip off.

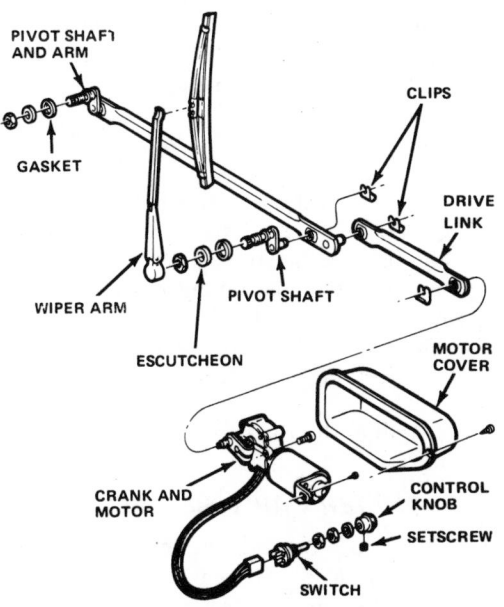

1976-78 windshield wiper components

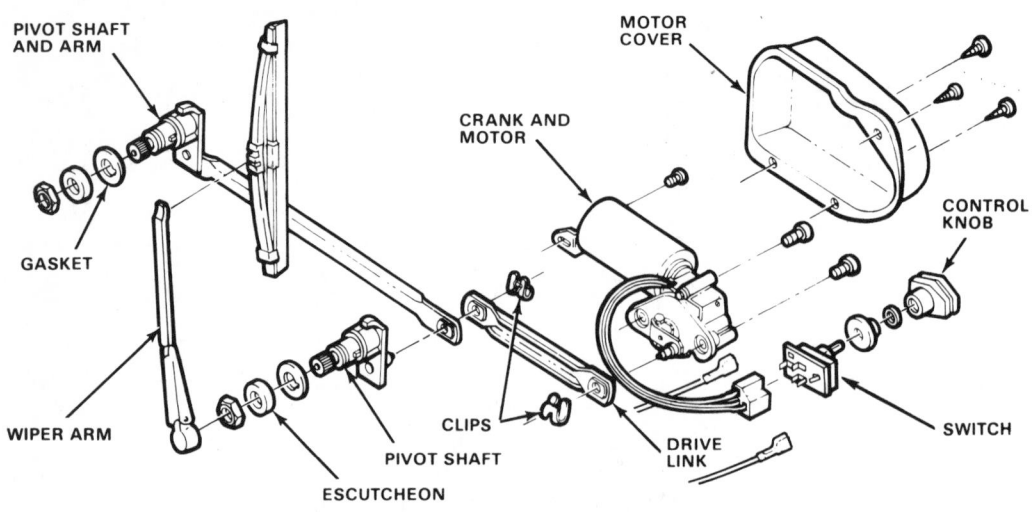

1979–81 windshield wiper components

5. Detach the wiring from the switch.

6. Remove the mounting screws and the wiper motor.

7. Reverse the procedure for installation.

Linkage

REMOVAL AND INSTALLATION

NOTE: *Jeeps through 1971 have no windshield wiper linkage.*

1972–75

1. Remove the wiper arms and pivot shaft nuts, washers, escutcheons and gaskets.

2. Disconnect the drive arm from the motor crank.

3. Remove the individual links where necessary, to remove the pivot shaft bodies without excessive interference.

4. Reverse the procedure for installation.

1976–81

1. Remove the wiper arms.

2. Remove the nuts attaching the pivots to the windshield frame.

3. Remove the necessary components from the top of the windshield frame.

4. Remove the windshield hold-down knobs and fold the windshield forward.

5. Remove the access hole covers on both sides of the windshield.

6. Disconnect the wiper motor drive link from the left wiper pivot.

7. Remove the wiper pivot shafts and linkage from the access hole.

8. Install the linkage in the reverse order.

INSTRUMENT CLUSTER

REMOVAL AND INSTALLATION

Through 1975

1. Disconnect one battery cable.

2. Separate the speedometer cable from the speedometer head.

3. Remove the screws that hold up the heater control bracket. (1972 and later only)

4. Remove the attaching nuts that hold the cluster to the dash.

5. Remove the gauge wires and cluster lamps and remove the cluster assembly.

6. Install in the reverse order. After installing the cluster, connect the battery and check all of the lights and gauges for proper operation.

1976–81

1. Disconnect the negative battery cable.

2. Disconnect the speedometer cable from the back of the speedometer.

3. Remove the instrument cluster attaching nuts and remove the cluster.

4. Disconnect the instrument cluster electrical connectors and remove the cluster from the vehicle.

5. Install in the reverse order.

SPEEDOMETER CABLE REPLACEMENT

1. Reach up behind the center of the speedometer head. The cable is connected by a threaded ring. Unscrew the ring and pull the cable sheath from the head.

2. The cable core can be pulled from the sheath.

3. If the core is broken, detach the other end of the sheath from the transmission. Pull out the broken end.

4. When installing the cable, apply a very small amount of speedometer cable graphite lubricant.

RADIO

REMOVAL AND INSTALLATION

Through 1975

The only factory installed radio available on these models was offered in 1975. It is a simple under-dash unit, similar to those dealer installed in earlier models. Removal and installation are obvious.

1976-81

1. Disconnect the battery ground cable.

2. Remove the control knobs, nuts, and bezel.

3. On 1976 and early 1977 models, you may have to detach the defroster hose. With air conditioning, remove the screws and lower the assembly.

4. Disconnect the radio bracket from the instrument panel.

5. Tilt the radio down and remove it toward the steering wheel.

6. Detach the antenna, speaker, and power wires.

7. Reverse the procedure for installation.

LIGHTING

Headlight

REMOVAL AND INSTALLATION

1. Remove the one lower attaching screw from the headlight trim ring. Pull out slightly at the bottom and push up to disengage the upper retaining tab.

2. Remove the trim ring.

3. Remove the three retaining screws from the retaining ring.

4. Pull the headlamp out and disconnect the wire harness.

When installing the headlamp, the number "2" is placed at the top of the lamp.

5. Install in reverse order of the above procedure. Check for proper seating of the lamp in its mounting ring and check for proper alignment.

FUSIBLE LINKS

Fusible links are sections of wire, with special insulation, designed to melt under elec-

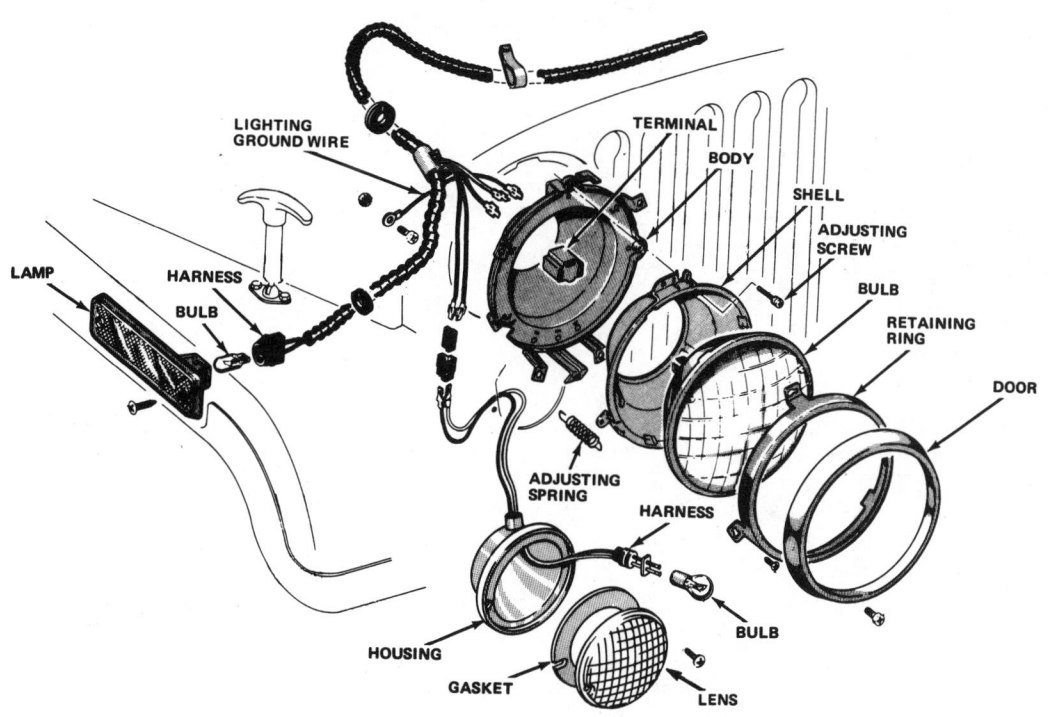

Typical front end lighting arrangement

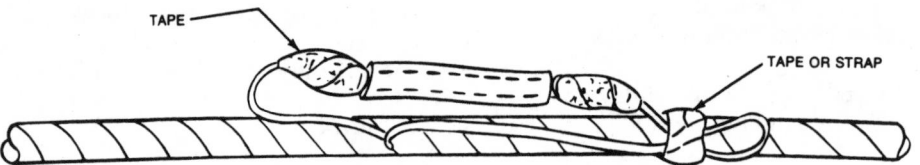

REMOVE EXISTING VINYL TUBE SHIELDING
REINSTALL OVER FUSE LINK BEFORE CRIMPING
FUSE LINK TO WIRE ENDS

TAPE

TAPE OR STRAP

TYPICAL REPAIR USING THE SPECIAL #17 GA. (9.00" LONG-YELLOW) FUSE LINK REQUIRED FOR THE AIR/COND.
CIRCUITS (2) #687E and #261A LOCATED IN THE ENGINE COMPARTMENT

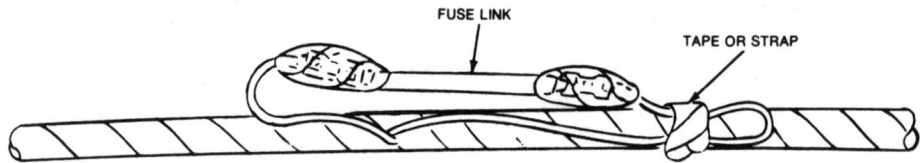

FUSE LINK

TAPE OR STRAP

TYPICAL REPAIR FOR ANY IN-LINE FUSE LINK USING THE SPECIFIED GAUGE FUSE LINK FOR THE SPECIFIC CIRCUIT

TAPE

TYPICAL REPAIR USING THE EYELET TERMINAL FUSE LINK OF THE SPECIFIED GAUGE FOR ATTACHMENT TO A CIRCUIT WIRE END

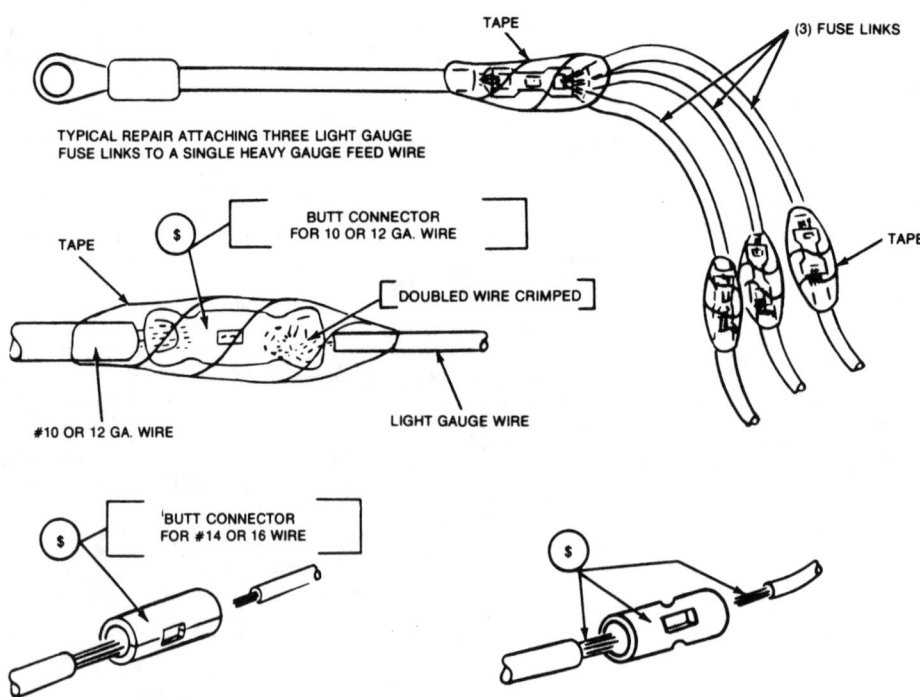

TAPE

(3) FUSE LINKS

TYPICAL REPAIR ATTACHING THREE LIGHT GAUGE
FUSE LINKS TO A SINGLE HEAVY GAUGE FEED WIRE

TAPE

TAPE

BUTT CONNECTOR
FOR 10 OR 12 GA. WIRE

$

DOUBLED WIRE CRIMPED

#10 OR 12 GA. WIRE

LIGHT GAUGE WIRE

BUTT CONNECTOR
FOR #14 OR 16 WIRE

$

$

FUSIBLE LINK REPAIR PROCEDURE

General fuse link repair procedure

VERTICAL ADJUSTMENT   HORIZONTAL ADJUSTMENT

1972–81 headlight adjustment

trical overload. There is usually one in the main wire from the battery, and near the alternator output side. If one melts, it must be replaced with a new link of the correct amperage rating. Never replace a melted link with ordinary wire; you run the risk of melting your entire wiring harness.

Fuse Application Chart

Fuse Application	Fuse (Amp)
Early 4—134 (6 volt)	
Directional Signal	SFE-14
Heater	SFE-14
Early 4—134 (12 volt)	
Directional Signal	SFE-9
Heater	SFE-9
Late 4—134 and V6—225	
Heater	15 amp
Backup Lights	9 amp
Windshield Wiper	14 amp
Directional Signal	14 amp
4-way Flasher	14 amp

Fuse Application Chart (cont.)

Fuse Application	Fuse (Amp)
1972–75	
Backup Lights	9 amp
Brake Failure	9 amp
Cigar Lighter	14 amp
Directional Signal	9 amp
4-way Flasher	14 amp
Head Lights	25 amp circuit breaker
Heater	15 amp
Windshield Wiper/Washer	6 amp circuit breaker
1976–77	
Heater/AC	25 amp
Backup Lights and Lighter	15 amp
Tail and Stop Lights	20 amp
Cluster Feed, Brake Failure and Parking Brake Warning	3 amp
Directional Signal and wipers	10 amp
Headlights	25 amp circuit breaker in switch
Panel Lights	3 amp
Radio	10 amp (5 amp inline)
Hazard warning flasher	15 amp
Windshield washer	4.5 amp circuit breaker in fuse panel
1978–81	
Heater/Air Conditioner	25 amp
Backup Lights, Lighter	10 amp
Tail and Stop Lights	①
Cluster Feed, Parking Brake Warning, Brake Failure	3 amp
Turn Signal, Wipers	10 amp
Headlights	20 amp circuit breaker in switch
Panel Lights	3 amp
Radio	② 10 amp (5 amp inline)
Hazard Warning Flasher	①
Windshield washer	4.5 amp circuit breaker in fuse panel

① Check marking on fuse box. 10, 15, and 20 amp fuses have been used
② Or 3 amp in fuse block

Light Bulb Specifications

Bulb Application	Early Models (6 Volt)	Early F-Head (12 Volt)	Late F-Head and V6	1972 and Later (All Engines)
Headlights	5040-S or 6006	5400-S or 6012	6012	6012③
Parking Lights or Marker Reflector	63	67	1157	194
Park and Directional Signal	1158	1176 or 1034	1157	1157A
Stop, Tail, and Directional Signal	1158	1034	1157	1157
Indicator Lamps:				
Headlight Beam	51	53–57	53–57	57②
Directional Signal	51	53	53	57②
Charge Lamp	51	53–57	53–57	57②
Oil Pressure	51	57	57	57②
Instrument Lamp	55	57	57	57②
License	—	—	1155	1155
Back-up	—	—	1156	1156
Clock	—	—	—	1816①
Steering Column Automatic Transmission Indicator	—	—	—	1816①
Courtesy	—	—	—	89
Hazard Warning Flasher	—	—	—	552
Oil Pressure Gauge	—	—	—	1895
Radio	—	—	—	1893
Tachometer	—	—	—	1895
Voltmeter	—	—	—	1895

① 1892 on 1977–81 models
② 53 on 1973–81 models
③ 6014—1974 and later, 6012 and 6014 are interchangeable

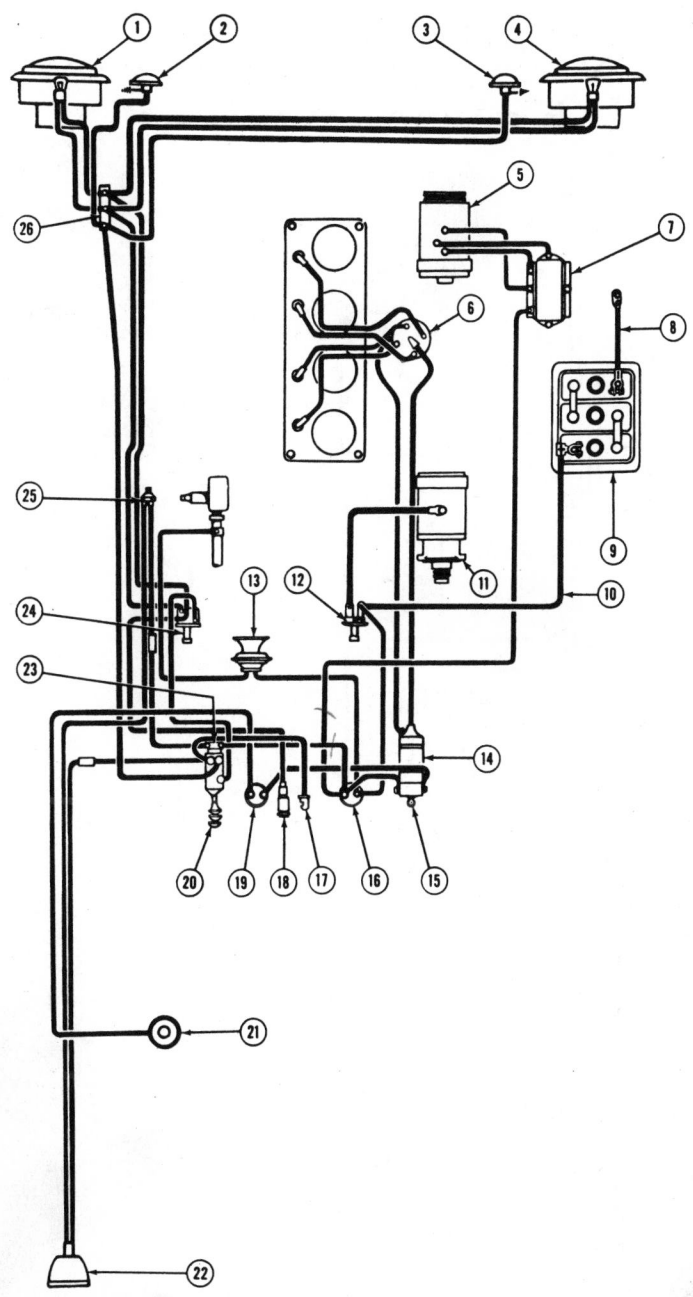

1. Left headlamp
2. Left parking lamp
3. Right parking lamp
4. Right headlamp
5. Generator
6. Distributor
7. Voltage regulator
8. Negative ground cable
9. Battery
10. Positive cable
11. Starting motor
12. Starting switch
13. Horn
14. Ignition coil
15. Ignition switch
16. Ammeter
17. Dash light
18. Tell-tale light
19. Fuel gauge
20. Light switch
21. Fuel gauge sending unit
22. Tail and stop light
23. Light switch circuit breaker
24. Dimmer switch
25. Stop light switch
26. Junction block

CJ-2A wiring diagram (6-volt system)

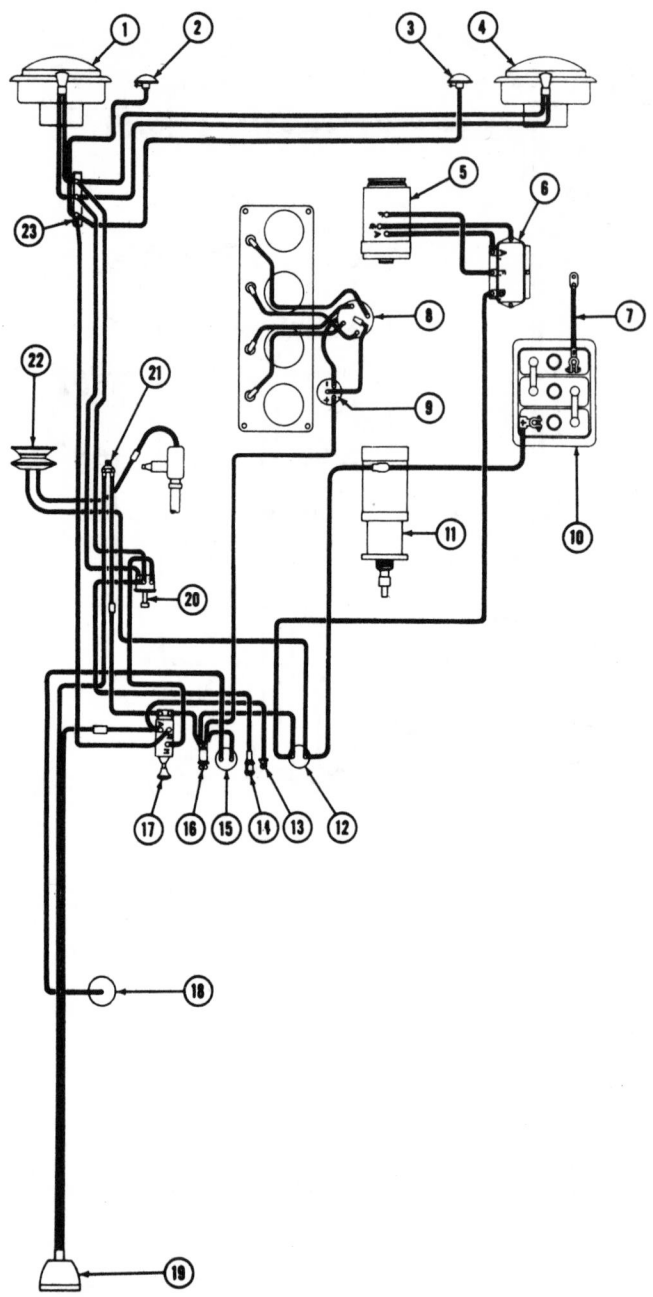

1. Left headlamp	13. Dash light
2. Left parking lamp	14. Tell-tale light
3. Right parking lamp	15. Fuel gauge
4. Right headlamp	16. Ignition switch
5. Generator	17. Light switch
6. Voltage regulator	18. Fuel gauge sending unit
7. Negative ground cable	19. Tail and stop light
8. Distributor	20. Dimmer switch
9. Ignition coil	21. Stop light switch
10. Battery	22. Horn
11. Starting motor	23. Junction block
12. Ammeter	

CJ-3A wiring diagram (6-volt system)

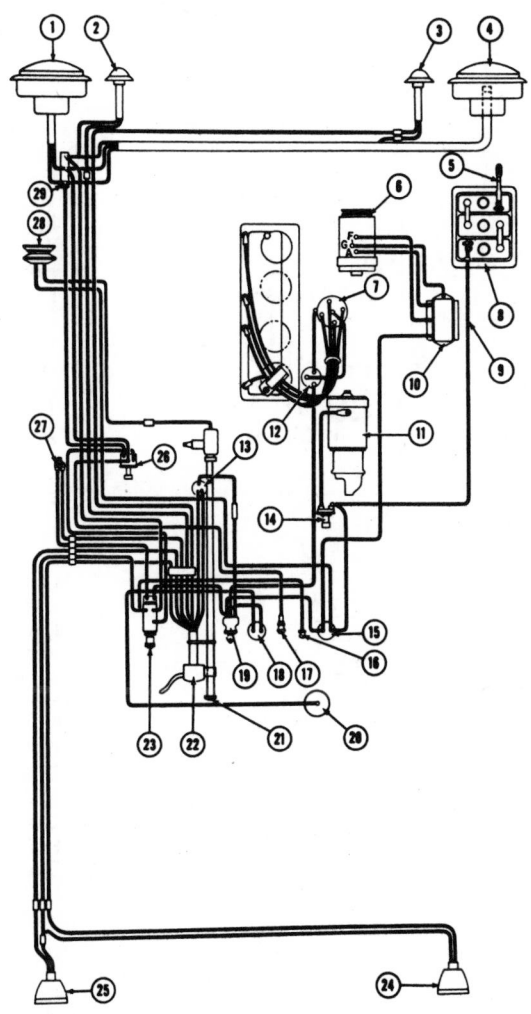

1. Left headlamp
2. Left parking lamp
3. Right parking lamp
4. Right headlamp
5. Negative ground cable
6. Generator
7. Distributor
8. Battery
9. Positive cable
10. Voltage regulator
11. Starting motor
12. Ignition coil
13. Signal flasher
14. Starting switch
15. Ammeter
16. Dash light
17. Tell-tale light
18. Fuel gauge
19. Ignition switch
20. Fuel gauge sending unit
21. Horn button
22. Directional signal switch
23. Light switch
24. Right tail and stop lamp
25. Left tail and stop lamp
26. Dimmer switch
27. Stop light switch
28. Horn
29. Junction block

CJ-3B through serial number 35522

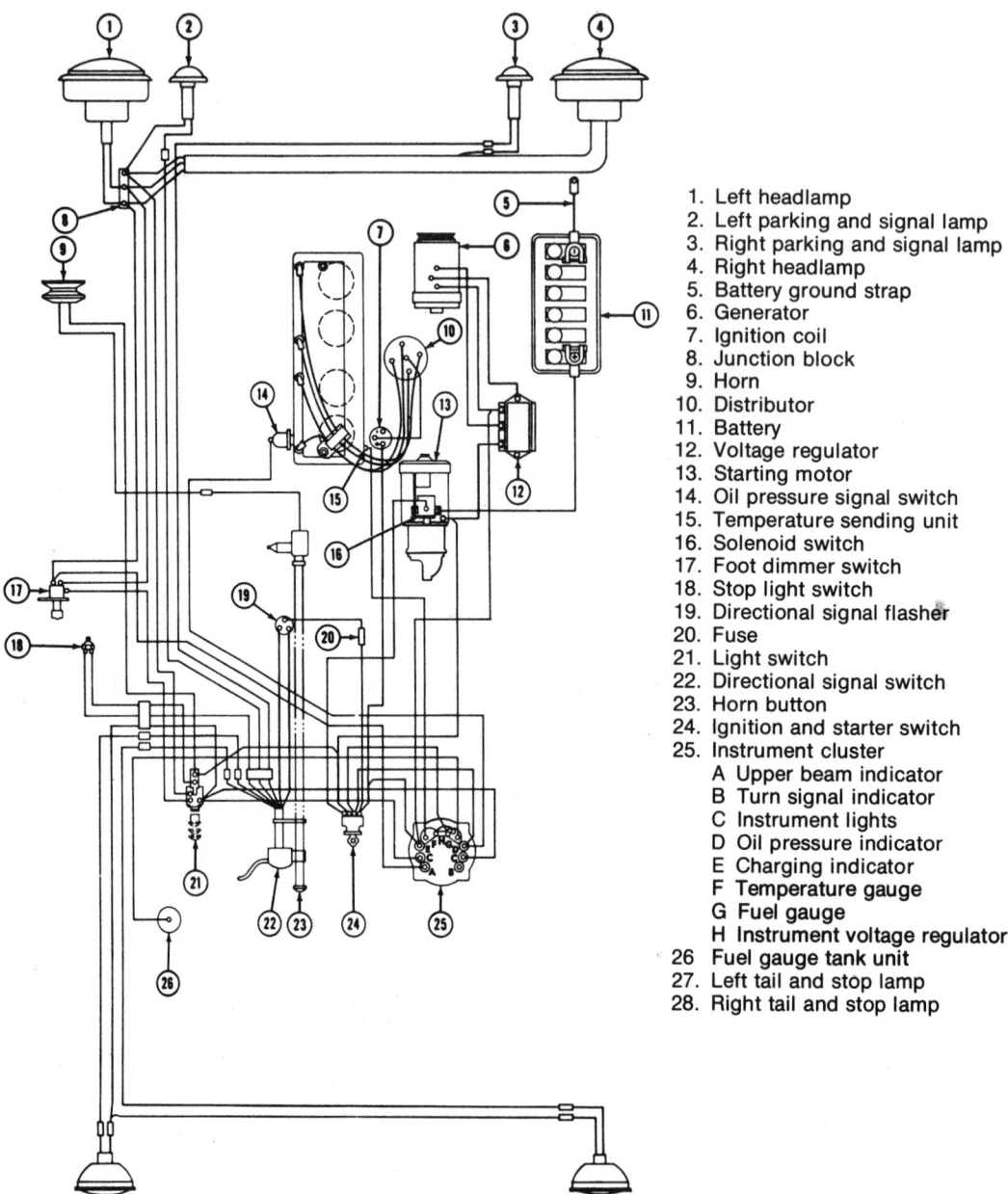

1. Left headlamp
2. Left parking and signal lamp
3. Right parking and signal lamp
4. Right headlamp
5. Battery ground strap
6. Generator
7. Ignition coil
8. Junction block
9. Horn
10. Distributor
11. Battery
12. Voltage regulator
13. Starting motor
14. Oil pressure signal switch
15. Temperature sending unit
16. Solenoid switch
17. Foot dimmer switch
18. Stop light switch
19. Directional signal flasher
20. Fuse
21. Light switch
22. Directional signal switch
23. Horn button
24. Ignition and starter switch
25. Instrument cluster
    A Upper beam indicator
    B Turn signal indicator
    C Instrument lights
    D Oil pressure indicator
    E Charging indicator
    F Temperature gauge
    G Fuel gauge
    H Instrument voltage regulator
26 Fuel gauge tank unit
27. Left tail and stop lamp
28. Right tail and stop lamp

CJ-3B after serial number 35522

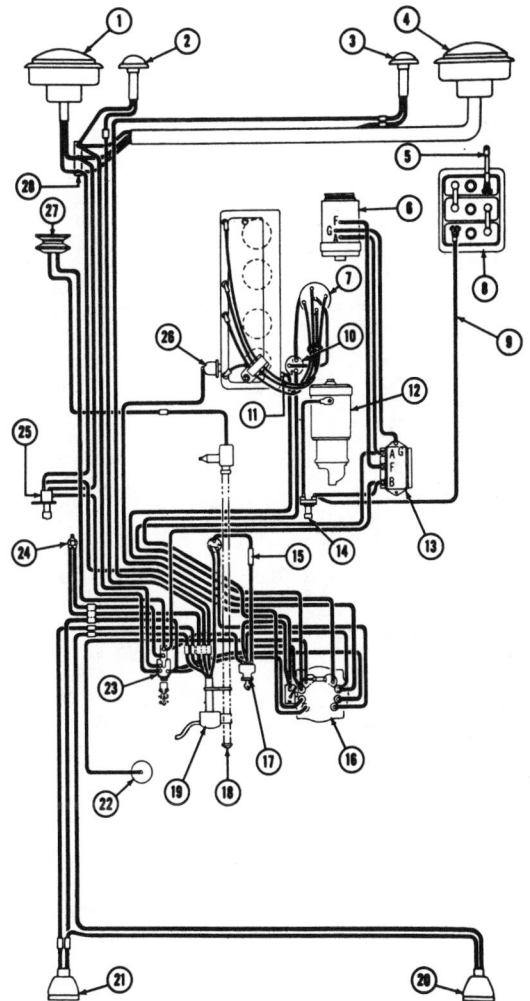

1. Left headlamp
2. Left parking lamp
3. Right parking lamp
4. Right headlamp
5. Negative ground cable
6. Generator
7. Distributor
8. Battery
9. Positive cable
10. Ignition coil
11. Temperature sending unit
12. Starting motor
13. Voltage regulator
14. Starting switch
15. Fuse
16. Instrument switch
17. Ignition switch
18. Horn button
19. Directional signal switch
20. Right tail and stop lamp
21. Left tail and stop lamp
22. Fuel gauge sending unit
23. Light switch
24. Stop light switch
25. Dimmer switch
26. Oil pressure sending unit
27. Horn
28. Junction block

CJ-5 and CJ-6 through 1971 through serial number 49248 CJ-5, and 12577 CJ-6

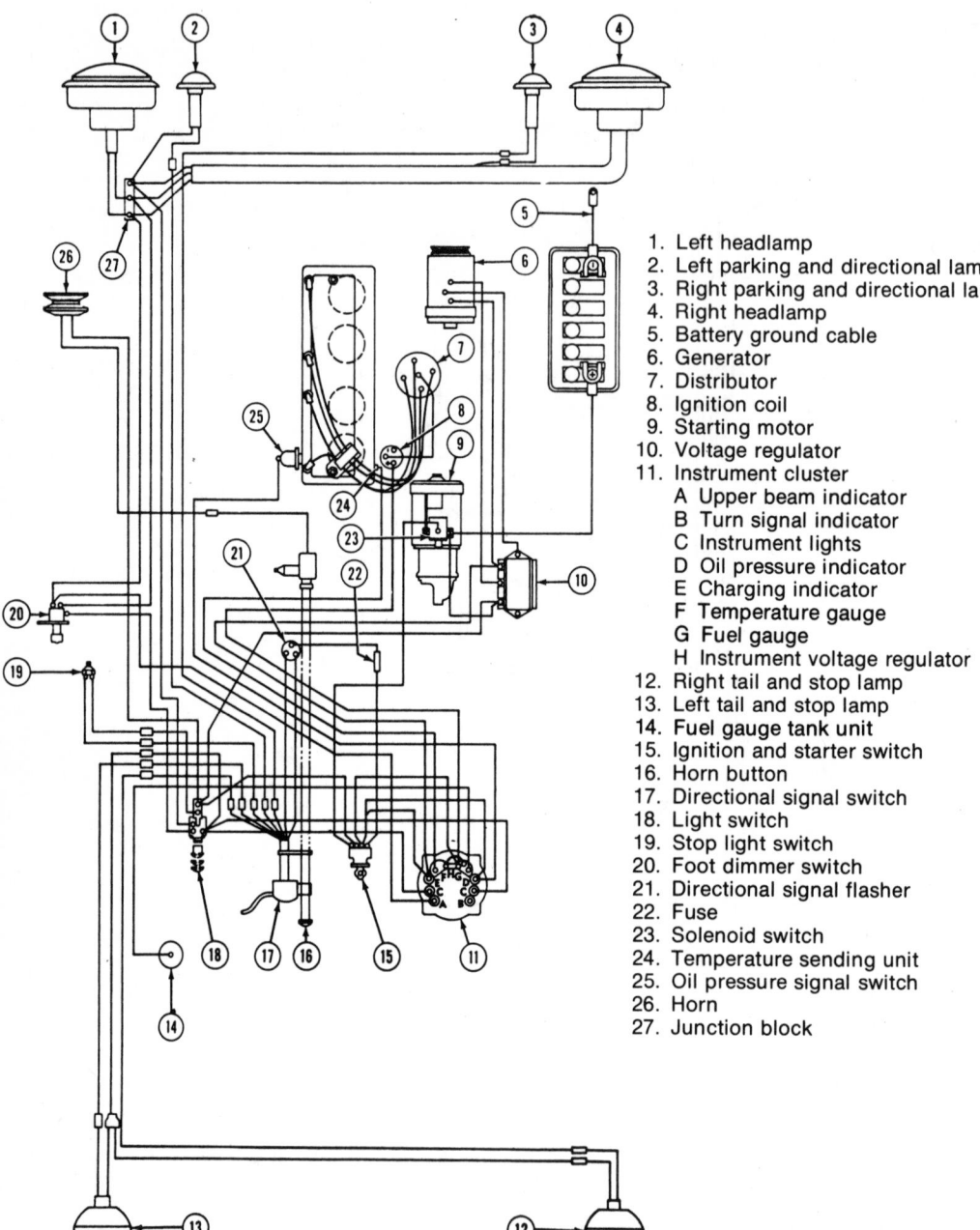

1. Left headlamp
2. Left parking and directional lamp
3. Right parking and directional lamp
4. Right headlamp
5. Battery ground cable
6. Generator
7. Distributor
8. Ignition coil
9. Starting motor
10. Voltage regulator
11. Instrument cluster
    A Upper beam indicator
    B Turn signal indicator
    C Instrument lights
    D Oil pressure indicator
    E Charging indicator
    F Temperature gauge
    G Fuel gauge
    H Instrument voltage regulator
12. Right tail and stop lamp
13. Left tail and stop lamp
14. Fuel gauge tank unit
15. Ignition and starter switch
16. Horn button
17. Directional signal switch
18. Light switch
19. Stop light switch
20. Foot dimmer switch
21. Directional signal flasher
22. Fuse
23. Solenoid switch
24. Temperature sending unit
25. Oil pressure signal switch
26. Horn
27. Junction block

CJ-5 and CJ-6 through 1971 after serial number 49248 CJ-5, and 12577 CJ-6

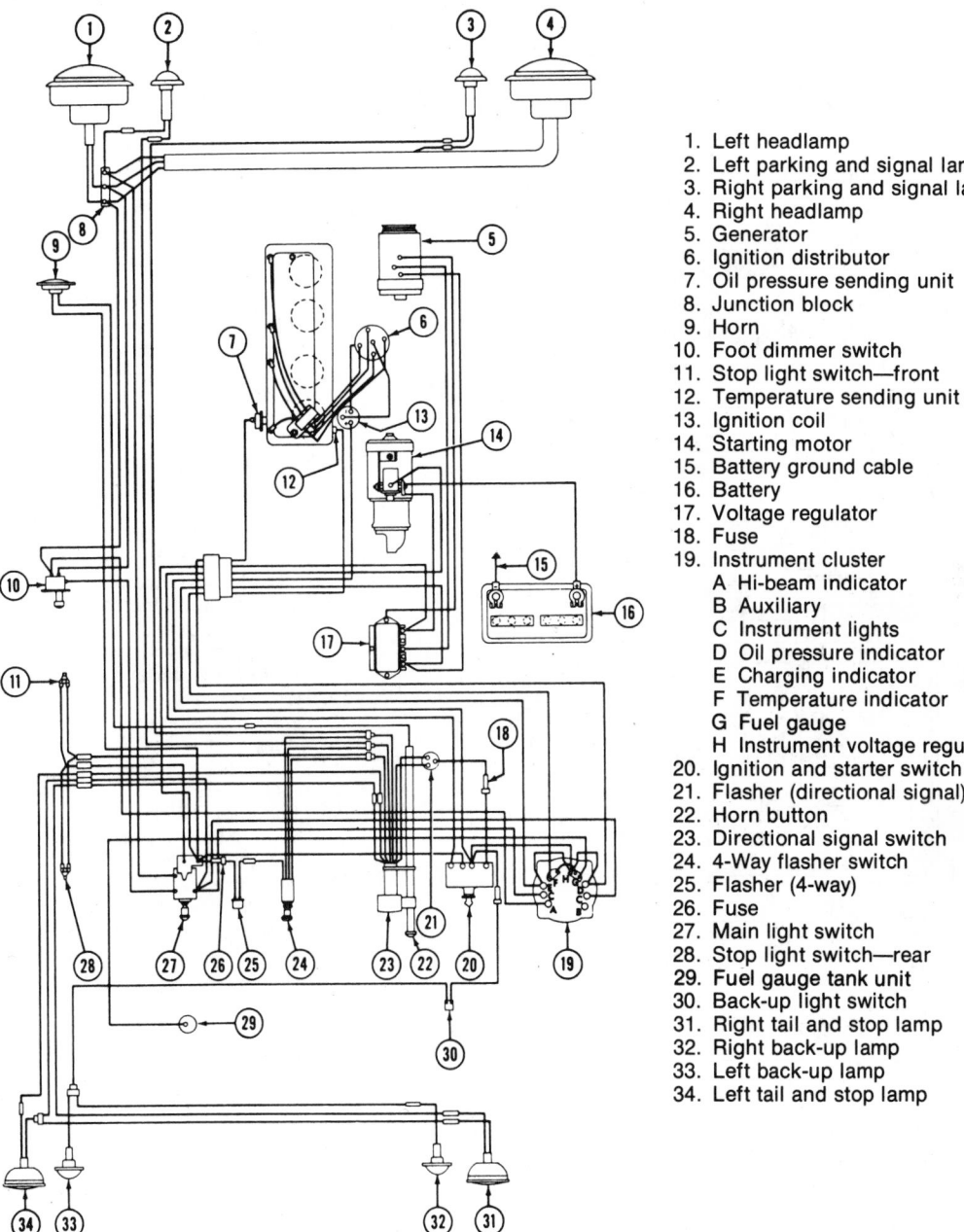

1. Left headlamp
2. Left parking and signal lamp
3. Right parking and signal lamp
4. Right headlamp
5. Generator
6. Ignition distributor
7. Oil pressure sending unit
8. Junction block
9. Horn
10. Foot dimmer switch
11. Stop light switch—front
12. Temperature sending unit
13. Ignition coil
14. Starting motor
15. Battery ground cable
16. Battery
17. Voltage regulator
18. Fuse
19. Instrument cluster
    A Hi-beam indicator
    B Auxiliary
    C Instrument lights
    D Oil pressure indicator
    E Charging indicator
    F Temperature indicator
    G Fuel gauge
    H Instrument voltage regulator
20. Ignition and starter switch
21. Flasher (directional signal)
22. Horn button
23. Directional signal switch
24. 4-Way flasher switch
25. Flasher (4-way)
26. Fuse
27. Main light switch
28. Stop light switch—rear
29. Fuel gauge tank unit
30. Back-up light switch
31. Right tail and stop lamp
32. Right back-up lamp
33. Left back-up lamp
34. Left tail and stop lamp

CJ-5 and CJ-6 with late F-head engine

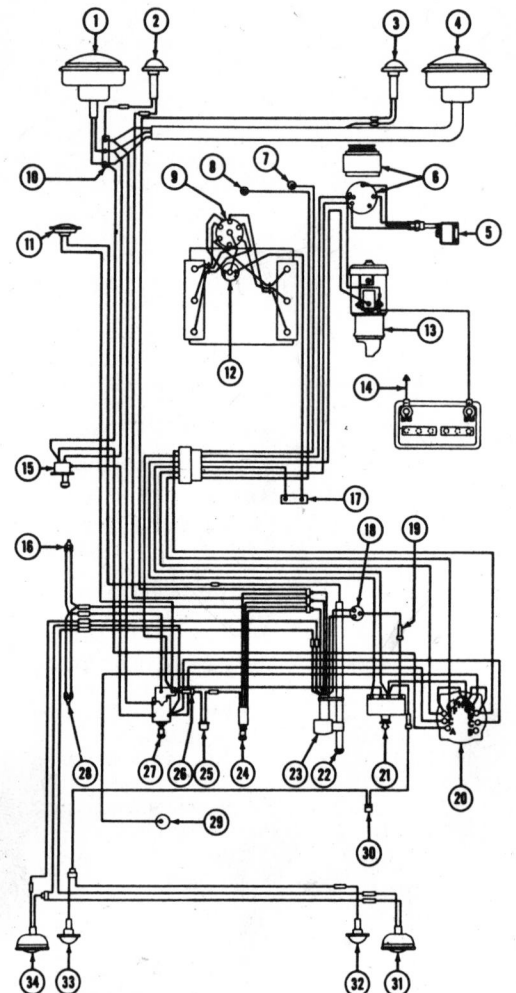

1. Left headlamp
2. Left parking and signal lamp
3. Right parking and signal lamp
4. Right headlamp
5. Voltage regulator
6. Alternator
7. Oil pressure sender
8. Temperature sender
9. Ignition distributor
10. Junction block
11. Horn
12. Ignition coil
13. Starting motor
14. Battery ground cable
15. Foot dimmer switch
16. Stop light switch—front
17. Ballast
18. Flasher (directional signal)
19. Fuse
20. Instrument cluster
   A Hi-beam indicator
   B Auxiliary
   C Instrument lights
   D Oil pressure indicator
   E Charging indicator
   F Temperature indicator
   G Fuel gauge
   H Instrument voltage regulator
21. Ignition and starter switch
22. Horn button
23. Directional signal switch
24. 4-Way flasher switch
25. Flasher (4-way)
26. Fuse
27. Main light switch
28. Stop light switch—rear
29. Fuel gauge tank unit
30. Back-up light switch
31. Right tail and stop lamp
32. Right back-up lamp
33. Left back-up lamp
34. Left tail and stop lamp

CJ-5 and CJ-6 V6

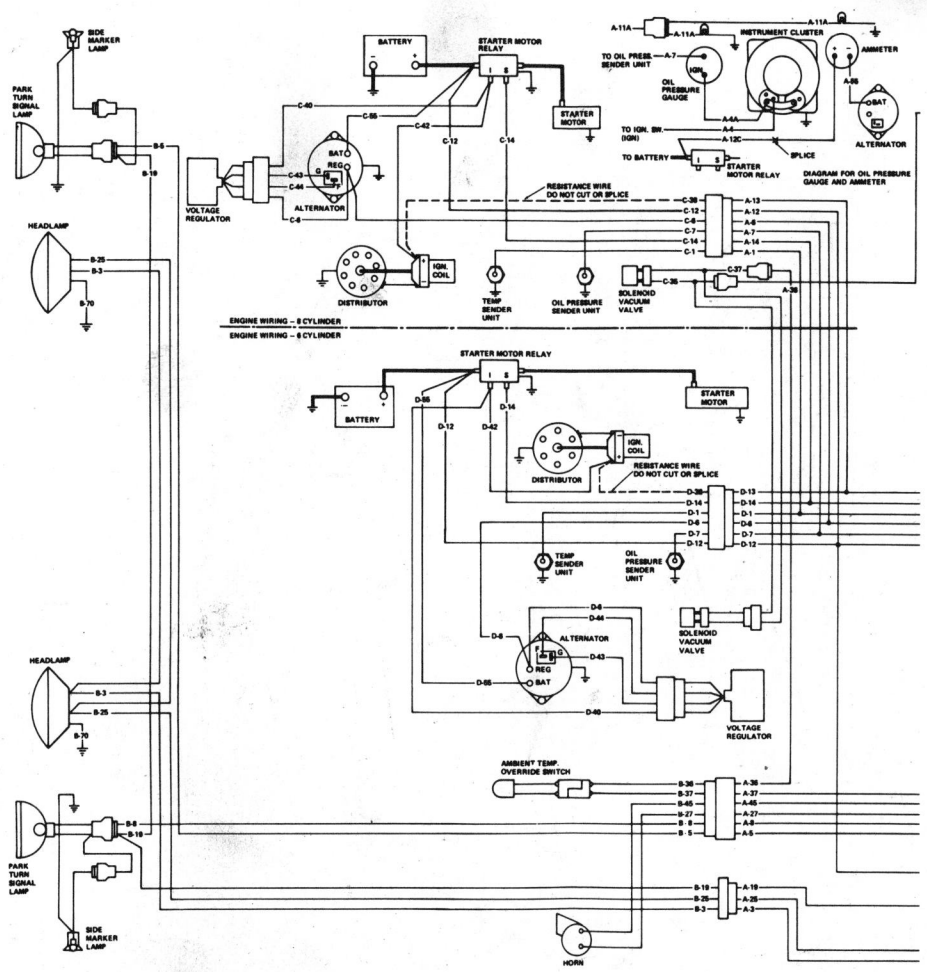

1972–73

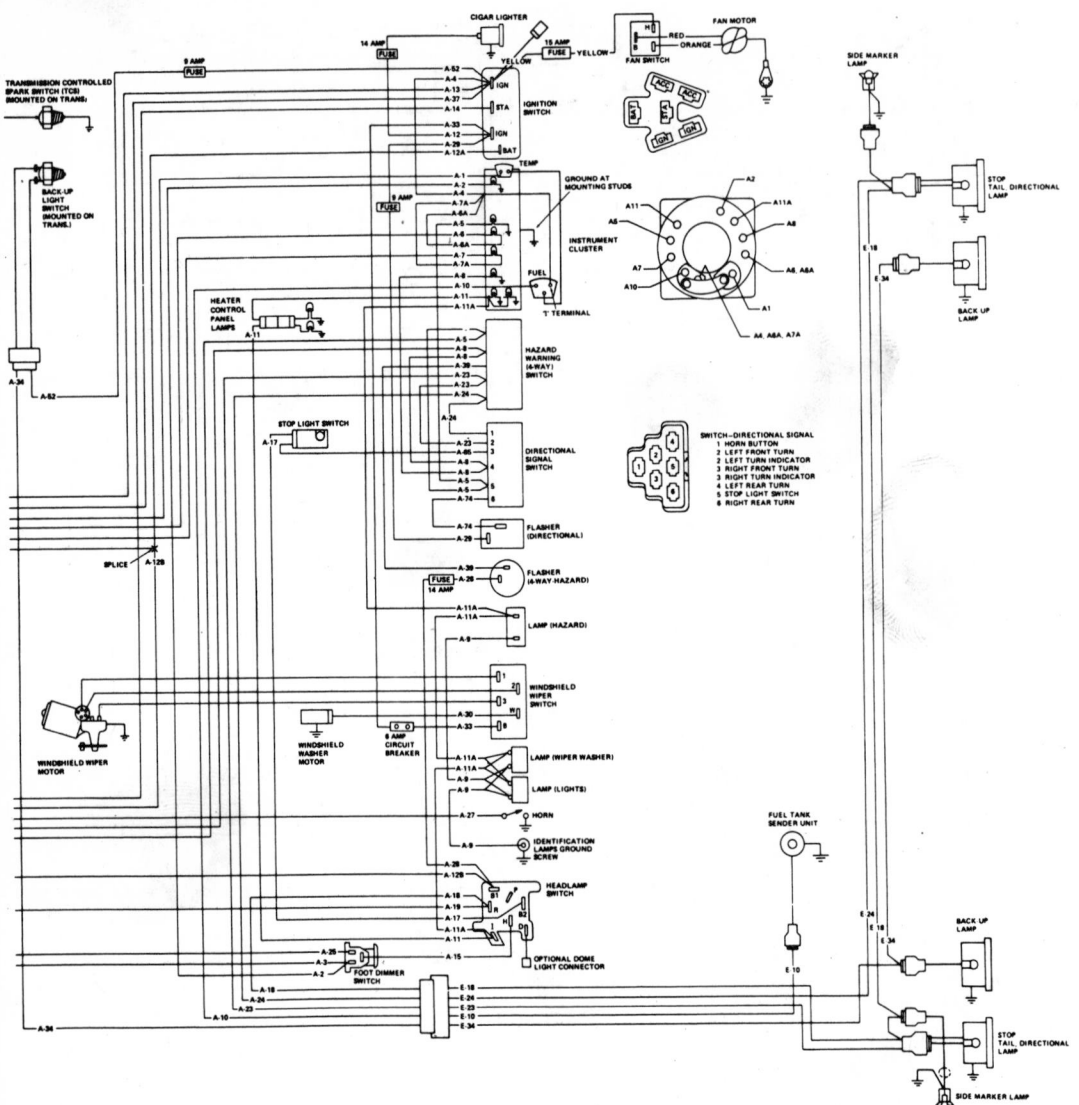

1972–73

Chassis Electrical

No.	GA.	Color	Instrument and Control Harness
A–1	18	Blue-yellow tr.	Cluster "A" temp. to connector (temp. sender)
A–2	18	White-red tr.	Cluster "L" Hi-beam indicator to dimmer switch (hi-beam)
	14	Red-white tr.	Dimmer switch (hi-beam) to headlamp junction block (hi-beam)
A–3	18	Green-white tr.	Cluster "K" ignition to ignition switch (ignition term.)
	18	Black-white tr.	Cluster "J" right turn indicator to directional signal switch (right turn)
A–4	16	Black	Directional signal switch (right turn) to directional signal lamp (right turn)
	18	Gray	Cluster "H" (charge indicator) to connector (alternator auxiliary term.)
A–5	18	Purple	Cluster "G" (oil indicator) to connector (oil pressure sender)
A–6	18	Yellow-black tr.	Cluster "E" left turn indicator to directional signal switch (left turn)
A–7	16	Yellow	Directional signal switch (left turn) to directional signal light (left turn)
A–8	18	Black-yellow tr.	Cluster "D" ground to instrument panel ground (mounting)
A–9	18	White	Cluster "C" gas gauge to connector (frame harness)
A–10	18	Red-blue tr.	Cluster "B" panel lights to dimmer switch to connector (gear selector)
A–11	14	Green	Ignition switch (ignition term.) to resistance wire
A–14	16	Light blue	Connector (ignition switch starter term.) to connector (neutral safety switch)
A–14A	16	Light blue	Connector (neutral safety switch) to connector (starter motor starter term.)
A–15	10	Red	Auxiliary circuit breaker to connector (solenoid "B" term.)
A–16	14	Red-white tr.	Light switch circuit breaker to auxiliary circuit breaker
A–17	14	Red-white tr.	Ignition switch "B" term. to auxiliary circuit breaker
A–18	14	Red-white tr.	Auxiliary circuit breaker to horn relay
A–19	14	Red-white tr.	Cigar lighter to auxiliary circuit
A–20	16	Brown	Auxiliary circuit breaker to stop light switch
A–21	14	Green	Light switch "H" term. to foot dimmer switch "B" term.
A–22	16	Light blue	Light switch (parking term.) to headlamp junction block (parking term.)
A–23	16	Yellow	Light switch (tail light term.) to instrument dimmer switch
A–23	16	Yellow	Instrument dimmer switch to connector (frame harness tail lamps)
A–24	18	Green-white tr.	Connector (ignition switch accessory term.) to connector (backup light switch)
A–25	18	Green-white tr.	Connector (backup light switch—standard) to connector (backup light switch—auto) to connector (frame harness—backup lights)
A–26	16	Black	Foot dimmer switch (low-beam) to headlamp junction block (low-beam)
A–27	16	Brown	Connector (turn signal switch) to connector (stop light switch)
A–28	18	Black-yellow tr.	Connector (steering column horn button) to horn relay
A–29	16	Light blue	Connector (turn signal switch) to connector (signal lamp rear left)
A–30	16	Orange	Connector (turn signal switch) to connector (signal lamp rear right)
A–33	14	Red-white tr.	Auxiliary circuit breaker to flasher (hazard warning)
A–34	18	Red	Ignition switch (accessory term.) (fused) to flasher (directional signal)
A–35	16	Orange	Connector (vacuum solenoid switch) to connector (temp. override switch)
A–36	16	Orange	connector (ignition switch—ignition term.) to connector (temp. override switch)

No.	GA.	Color	Harness Assembly—Headlights, Parking and Signal Lamps
B–1	14	Red-white tr.	Connector (circuit breaker—auxiliary feed) to horn relay (battery)
B–2	18	Black-yellow tr.	Connector (steering column—horn button) to horn relay (horn button)
B–3	16	Yellow	Connector (turn signal switch—left turn) to connector (directional signal lamp—left turn)
B–4	16	Black	Connector (turn signal switch—right turn) to connector (directional signal lamp—right turn)
B–5	16	Light blue	Junction block (parking term.) to connector (parking lamp—left) to connector (parking lamp—right)
B–6	14	Red-white tr.	Junction block (hi-beam) to connector (headlamp hi-beam—left) to connector (headlamp hi-beam—right)
B–7	16	Black	Junction block (low-beam) to connector (headlamp low-beam—left) to connector (headlamp low-beam—right)
B–8	18	Black-white tr.	Headlamp ground to ground mounting (2 cables)
B–9	16	Orange	Connector (vacuum solenoid switch) to connector (temp. override switch)
B–10	16	Orange	Connector ignition switch ignition term. to connector temp. override switch

Chassis Electrical (cont.)

No.	GA.	Color	Engine Harness (V-8)
C–1	14	Green	Resistance wire (ignition) to coil (+) term.
C–2	14	Green	Coil (+) term. to starting solenoid (ignition)
C–3	16	Yellow	Starter solenoid (ignition) to alternator regulator (ignition)
C–4	16	Light blue	Connector (ignition switch—starter term.) to starter solenoid (starter term.)
C–5	18	Purple	Connector (oil pressure indicator) to oil pressure sender
C–6	18	Blue-yellow tr.	Connector (temp. indicator) to temp. sender
C–7	18	Gray	Connector (cluster "H" term.) to alternator (auxiliary term.) to alternator, regulator (auxilary term.)
C–8	18	Green-white tr.	Alternator regulator (field term.) to alternator (fiel term.)
C–9	16	Black	Alternator regulator (ground term.) to alternator (ground)
C–10	10	Red	Starter solenoid ("B" term.) to connector (circuit breaker—feed)
C–11	10	Yellow	Starter solenoid ("B" term.) to alternator (output term.)
C–12	16	Brown	Connector (transistor solenoid) (T.C.S.) vacuum switch
C–13	16	Black	Connector (sensor switch) (T.C.S.) to vacuum switch

No.	GA.	Color	Engine Harness (6 Cyl.)
D–1	14	Green	Resistance wire (ignition) to coil (+) term.
D–2	14	Green	Coil (+) term. to starting solenoid (ignition)
D–3	16	Yellow	Starter solenoid (ignition) to alternator regulator (ignition)
D–4	16	Light blue	Connector (ignition switch—starter term.) to starter solenoid (starter term.)
D–5	18	Purple	Connector (oil pressure indicator) to oil pressure sender
D–6	18	Blue-yellow tr.	Connector (temperature indicator) to temperature sender
D–7	18	Gray	Connector (cluster "H" term.) to alternator (auxiliary term.) to alternator regulator (auxiliary term.)
D–8	18	Green-white tr.	Alternator regulator (field term.) to alternator (field term.)
D–9	16	Black	Alternator regulator (ground term.) to alternator (ground term.)
D–10	10	Red	Starter solenoid ("B" term.) to connector (circuit breaker feed)
D–11	10	Yellow	Starter solenoid ("B"term.) to alternator (output term.)

1972–73

Chassis Electrical (cont.)

No.	GA.	Color	Instrument and Control Harness
1	18	Purple w/tr.	Bulkhead connector (temperature sender) to temperature gauge
2	18	Gray w/tr.	Foot dimmer switch (hi-beam) to instrument cluster (hi-beam indicator)
3	14	Gray w/tr.	Foot dimmer switch (hi-beam) to bulkhead connector (hi-beam)
4	18	Red	Fuse panel (cluster feed) to instrument constant voltage regulator
4A	18	Red	Instrument constant voltage regulator (ignition terminal) to oil pressure gauge (ignition terminal)
5A	18	Green	Bulkhead connector (right turn & hazard front) to hazard switch
5B	18	Green	Hazard switch to steering column connector (right turn & hazard front)
5C	18	Green	Steering column connector to instrument cluster lamp (right turn)
7	18	Purple	Bulkhead connector (oil pressure sender) to oil pressure gauge
8A	18	Green w/tr.	Bulkhead connector (left turn & hazard front) to hazard switch
8B	18	Green w/tr.	Hazard switch to steering column connector (left turn & hazard front)
8C	18	Green w/tr.	Steering column connector to instrument cluster lamp (left turn)
9A	18	Black	Windshield wiper & washer switch light to instrument panel lights ground
9B	18	Black	Windshield wiper & washer light to light switch light
9C	18	Black	Instrument panel lights ground to hazard light
9D	18	Black	Hazard light to voltmeter (−) terminal
10	18	Pink	Bulkhead connector (frame harness-fuel sender unit) to instrument cluster fuel gauge (S-terminal)
11A	18	Orange	Fuse panel (lights—accessories) to splice "D"
11B	18	Orange	Light switch light to windshield wiper & washer switch light
11C	18	Orange	Splice "D" to windshield wiper & washer switch light
11D	18	Orange	Splice "D" to hazard light
11E	18	Orange	Splice "D" to splice "C"
11F	18	Orange	Splice "C" to right instrument panel light
11G	18	Orange	Splice "C" to left instrument panel light connector
11H	18	Orange	Left instrument panel light connector to left instrument panel light
11J	18	Orange	Splice "C" to instrument cluster oil pressure gauge light
11K	18	Orange	Splice "C" to instrument cluster voltmeter light
12A	10	Red	Bulkhead connector (alternator & voltage regulator) to splice "A"
12B	12	Red	Bulkhead connector (horn) to splice "A"
12C	12	Red	Fuse panel (traffic hazard) to splice "A"
12D	12	Red	Splice "A" to light switch (battery feed)
12E	12	Red	Splice "A" to ignition switch
12F	12	Red	Fuse panel (cigar lighter) to splice "A"
13A	14	Red w/tr.	Bulkhead connector (coil) to tachometer connector
13B	14	Red w/tr.	Tachometer connector to ignition switch
14	16	Lt blue	Bulkhead connector (starting motor solenoid) to ignition switch
15	14	Red w/tr.	Light switch (foot dimmer switch feed) to foot dimmer switch
17	14	Red w/tr.	Fuse panel (tail—stop) to stop light switch
18	16	White	Bulkhead connector (chassis harness—tail lamps) to (bulkhead connector—headlamp harness marker lights
19	16	White	Bulkhead connector (marker lamps) to light switch (parking lamps)
23	16	Lt green w/tr	Bulkhead connector (chassis harness left turn & hazard) to hazard switch (left turn & hazard—rear)
23A	16	Lt green w/tr.	Hazard switch to steering column connector (left turn & hazard—rear)
24	16	Lt green	Bulkhead connector (chassis harness right turn & hazard) to hazard switch (right turn & hazard—rear)
24A	16	Lt green	Hazard switch to steering column connector (right turn & hazard—rear)
25	16	Gray	Bulkhead connector (headlamps) to foot dimmer switch (lo-beam)
26	14	Red w/tr.	Fuse panel (heater—battery) to heater blower switch
27	18	Black w/tr.	Bulkhead connector (horn) to horn button
30	16	Yellow	Bulkhead connector (windshield wiper & washer) to windshield wiper & washer switch
33	14	Red w/tr.	Fuse panel (radio) to windshield wiper & washer switch
34	18	White w/tr.	Bulkhead connector (back-up light switch) to bulkhead connector (chassis harness—back-up lights)
39	16	Pink	Fuse panel (traffic hazard flash) to hazard flasher
52	18	Red	Fuse panel (back-up lamps) to bulkhead connector (back-up light switch)
57	18	Black	Bulkhead connector (brake failure switch) to brake warning light (ground)
60	14	Red	Cigar lighter connector to cigar lighter
65	16	Red w/tr.	Stop light switch to steering column connector (brake switch & hazard feed)
66	18	Red w/tr.	Fuse panel (panel lamps) to light switch (panel lights feed)
67A	12	Yellow	Fuse panel lamps to ignition switch

Chassis Electrical (cont.)

No.	GA.	Color	Instrument and Control Harness
67B	18	Yellow	Ignition switch to instrument cluster voltmeter (+) terminal
74	18	Red w/tr.	Fuse panel (flash—directional signal) to steering column connector (flasher & directional signal feed)
75	12	Red w/tr.	Ignition switch to splice "B"
75A	12	Red w/tr	Fuse panel (heater—battery) to splice "B"
75B	12	Red w/tr.	Fuse panel lamps to splice "B"
77	16	Black	Bulkhead connector (brake failure switch) to brake warning light connection
78	16	Red w/tr.	Bulkhead connector (alternator—voltage regulator) to splice "B" in circuit 75
77A	16	Black	Fuse panel (warning light) to brake warning light

No.	GA.	Color	Harness Assembly—Headlamp, Parking and Signal Lamps
3A	14	Gray w/tr.	Bulkhead connector (hi-beam) to left headlamp connector (hi-beam)
3B	14	Gray w/tr.	Left headlamp connector (hi-beam) to right headlamp connector (hi-beam)
5A	16	Green	Bulkhead connector (right turn signal) to right turn signal splice "K"
5B	16	Green	Right turn splice "K" to right side marker lamp assembly
5C	16	Green	Right turn splice"K" to right front park & turn signal lamp assembly
8A	16	Green w/tr.	Bulkhead connector (left turn sgnal) to left turn signal splice "H"
8B	16	Green w/tr.	Left turn splice "H" to left side marker lamp assembly
8C	16	Green w/tr.	Left turn splice "H" to left front park & turn signal lamp assembly
19A	16	White	Bulkhead connector (parking lights) to splice "J"
19B	16	White	Parking lights splice "J" to left side marker lamp assembly
19C	16	White	Parking lights splice "L" to right front park & turn signal lamp assembly
19D	16	White	Parking lights splice "M" to left front park & turn signal lamp assembly
19E	16	White	Parking lights splice "L" to right side marker lamp assembly
19F	16	White	Left parking lamps splice "M" to right parking lamps splice "L"
19G	16	White	Splice "J" to splice "M"
25A	16	Gray	Bulkhead connector (lo-beam) to left headlamp connector (lo-beam)
25B	16	Gray	Left headlamp connector (lo-beam) to right headlamp connector (lo-beam)
27	14	Black w/tr.	Bulkhead connector (horn) to horn assembly
30	16	Yellow	Bulkhead connector (windshield wiper & washer switch) to windshield washer motor
45	14	Red w/tr.	Bulkhead connector (horn) to horn assembly
57	16	Black	Bulkhead connector (brake failure switch) to brake failure switch connector to brake failure switch
70	16	Black	Left and right headlamp ground terminals to ground mounting
77	16	Black w/tr.	Bulkhead connector (brake failure switch) to brake failure swich connector to brake failure switch

W/tr. = With tracer

No.	GA.	Color	Harness Assembly—Engine (Six cylinder)
1	18	Purple w/tr.	Bulkhead connector (temperature gauge) to temperature sender
7	18	Purple	Bulkhead connector (oil pressure gauge) to oil pressure sender
12A	14	Red	$5/16$ stud to splice "E" (fusible link in alternator/regulator circuit)
12B	10	Red	Splice "E" to ¼ stud (alternator/regulator circuit)
12C	10	Red	Bulkhead connector (alternator/regulator) to splice "F" at fusible link
12D	14	Red	Splice "F" to $5/16$ stud (fusible link in alternator/regulator circuit)
12E	14	Red	¼ stud to alternator/regulator assembly
13	14	Red w/tr.	Bulkhead connector (ignition switch) to coil (+) terminal
14	16	Lt blue	Bulkhead connector (ignition switch) to starting motor solenoid (starting terminal)
34	18	White w/tr.	Bulkhead connector (back-up lamps) to back-up light switch connector
34A	18	White w/tr.	Back-up light switch connector to back-up light switch
35	16	Red w/tr.	Back-up light switch connector to vacuum solenoid switch
37	16	Orange	Back-up light switch connector to vacuum solenoid switch
37A	16	Orange	Back-up light switch connector to transmission controlled spark switch (T.C.S.)
52	18	White w/tr.	Bulkhead connector (back-up lamps) to back-up light switch connector

Chassis Electrical (cont.)

No.	GA.	Color	Instrument and Control Harness
52A	18	White w/tr.	Back-up light switch connector to back-up light switch
78	24	Black w/tr.	Bulkhead connector alternator/regulator) to alternator & voltage regulator
79	16	Green	Coil (−) terminal to electronic ignition pack
80	16	Blue	Distributor to electronic ignition pack
81	16	Yellow	Distributor to electronic ignition pack
82	16	Red w/tr.	Coil (+) terminal to electronic ignition pack

No.	GA.	Color	Harness Assembly—Engine (V-8)
1*	18	Purple w/tr.	Bulkhead connector (temperature gauge) to temperature sender
7	18	Purple	Bulkhead connector (oil pressure gauge) to oil pressure sender
12A*	14	Red	5/16 stud to splice "E" (fusible link in alternator circuit)
12B	10	Red	Splice "E" to 1/4 stud (alternator circuit)
12C*	10	Red	Bulkhead connector (alternator) to splice "F" at fusible link
12D*	14	Red	Splice "F" to 5/16 stud (fusible link in alternator circuit)
13	14	Red w/tr.	Bulkhead connector (ignition switch) to splice "G"
13A	14	Red W/TR	Splice "G" to coil (+) terminal
14*	16	Lt blue	Bulkhead connector (ignition switch) to starting motor solenoid (starting terminal)
34*	18	White w/tr.	Bulkhead connector (back-up lights) to back-up light switch connector
34A*	18	White w/tr.	Back-up light switch connector to back-up light switch
40	16	Yellow	Splice "G" (circuit no. 13) to voltage regulator
41	18	Gray	Voltage regulator to alternator
43	16	Black	Voltage regulator to alternator
44	18	Green	Voltage regulator to alternator
52	18	White w/tr.	Bulkhead connector (back-up lights) to back-up light switch connector
52A	18	White w/tr.	Back-up light switch connector to back-up light switch
79	16	Green	Coil (−) terminal to electronic ignition pack
80	16	Blue	Distributor to electronic ignition pack
81	16	Yellow	Distributor to electronic ignition pack
82	16	Red w/tr.	Splice "G" (circuit no. 13) to electronic ignition pack

No.	GA.	Color	Harness Assembly—Chassis
10	16	Pink	Bulkhead connector (fuel gauge—instrument unit) to connector (fuel tank sending unit)
18	16	White	Bulkhead connector (tail lamps) to connector (left tail, stop & license lamp)
18A	16	White	Connector (left tail, stop & license lamp) to connector (left rear marker lamp)
18B	16	White	Connector (left rear marker lamp) to connector (right tail & stop lamp)
18C	16	White	Connector (right tail & stop lamp) to connector (right rear marker lamp)
23	16	Lt green w/tr.	Bulkhead connector (left turn & hazard) to connector (left tail, stop & license lamp)
24	16	Lt green	Bulkhead connector (right turn & hazard) to connector (right tail & stop lamp)
34	18	White w/tr.	Bulkhead connector (back-up lights) to connector (left back-up lamp)
34A	18	White w/tr.	Connector (left back-up lamp) to connector (right back-up lamp)

No.	GA.	Color	Harness Assembly—Directional signal Switch
5B	18	Green	Connector (steering column) to right front position contact
8B	18	Green w/tr.	Connector (steering column) to left front position contact
23A	16	Lt green w/tr.	Connector (steering column) to left rear position contact
24A	16	Lt green	Connector (steering column) to right rear position contact
65	16	Red w/tr.	Connector (steering column) to brake switch position contact
74	18	Red w/tr.	Connector (steering column) to flasher position contact

(*) Combined with 6 cylinder wiring
W/tr. = With tracer

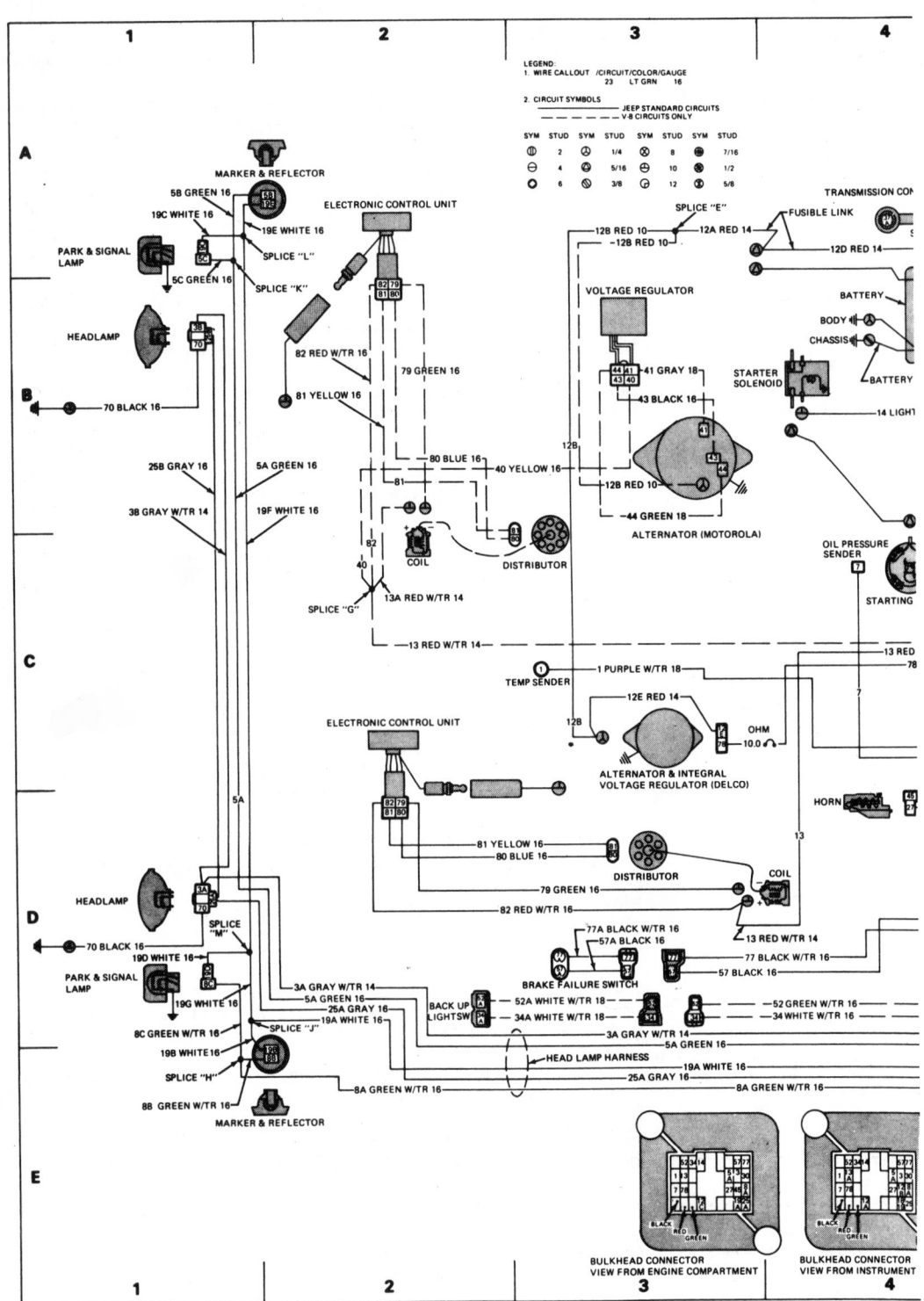

LEGEND:
1. WIRE CALLOUT /CIRCUIT/COLOR/GAUGE
          23   LT GRN   16
2. CIRCUIT SYMBOLS
                                JEEP STANDARD CIRCUITS
                                V-8 CIRCUITS ONLY

MARKER & REFLECTOR

5B GREEN 16
19C WHITE 16
19E WHITE 16
SPLICE "L"
5C GREEN 16
SPLICE "K"

PARK & SIGNAL LAMP

ELECTRONIC CONTROL UNIT

TRANSMISSION CON

SPLICE "E"   FUSIBLE LINK
12B RED 10   12A RED 14
−12B RED 10
                                12D RED 14

BATTERY
BODY
CHASSIS   BATTERY

VOLTAGE REGULATOR

STARTER SOLENOID

HEADLAMP

70 BLACK 16

82 RED W/TR 16
81 YELLOW 16

79 GREEN 16

44 41 GRAY 18
43 40
43 BLACK 16

14 LIGHT

25B GRAY 16   5A GREEN 16
3B GRAY W/TR 14   19F WHITE 16

80 BLUE 16   40 YELLOW 16
81
82
40
COIL
13A RED W/TR 14
SPLICE "G"

12B
−12B RED 10
−44 GREEN 18
ALTERNATOR (MOTOROLA)

OIL PRESSURE SENDER

STARTING

DISTRIBUTOR

13 RED W/TR 14

1 PURPLE W/TR 18
TEMP SENDER

12E RED 14

OHM
10.0

13 RED
78

7

ELECTRONIC CONTROL UNIT

12B
76
ALTERNATOR & INTEGRAL VOLTAGE REGULATOR (DELCO)

HORN

HEADLAMP

81 YELLOW 16
80 BLUE 16
79 GREEN 16
82 RED W/TR 16

DISTRIBUTOR

COIL

13

13 RED W/TR 14

70 BLACK 16
SPLICE "M"
19D WHITE 16

77A BLACK W/TR 16
57A BLACK 16
BRAKE FAILURE SWITCH

77 BLACK W/TR 16
57 BLACK 16

PARK & SIGNAL LAMP

19G WHITE 16
8C GREEN W/TR 16
19B WHITE 16
SPLICE "H"
8B GREEN W/TR 16

3A GRAY W/TR 14
5A GREEN 16
25A GRAY 16
19A WHITE 16
SPLICE "J"

BACK UP LIGHTSW

52A WHITE 18
34A WHITE 18

52 GREEN W/TR 16
34 WHITE W/TR 16

3A GRAY W/TR 14
5A GREEN 16
HEAD LAMP HARNESS
19A WHITE 16
25A GRAY 16
8A GREEN W/TR 16   8A GREEN W/TR 16

MARKER & REFLECTOR

BULKHEAD CONNECTOR
VIEW FROM ENGINE COMPARTMENT

BULKHEAD CONNECTOR
VIEW FROM INSTRUMENT

BLACK
RED
GREEN

BLACK
RED
GREEN

1974−75

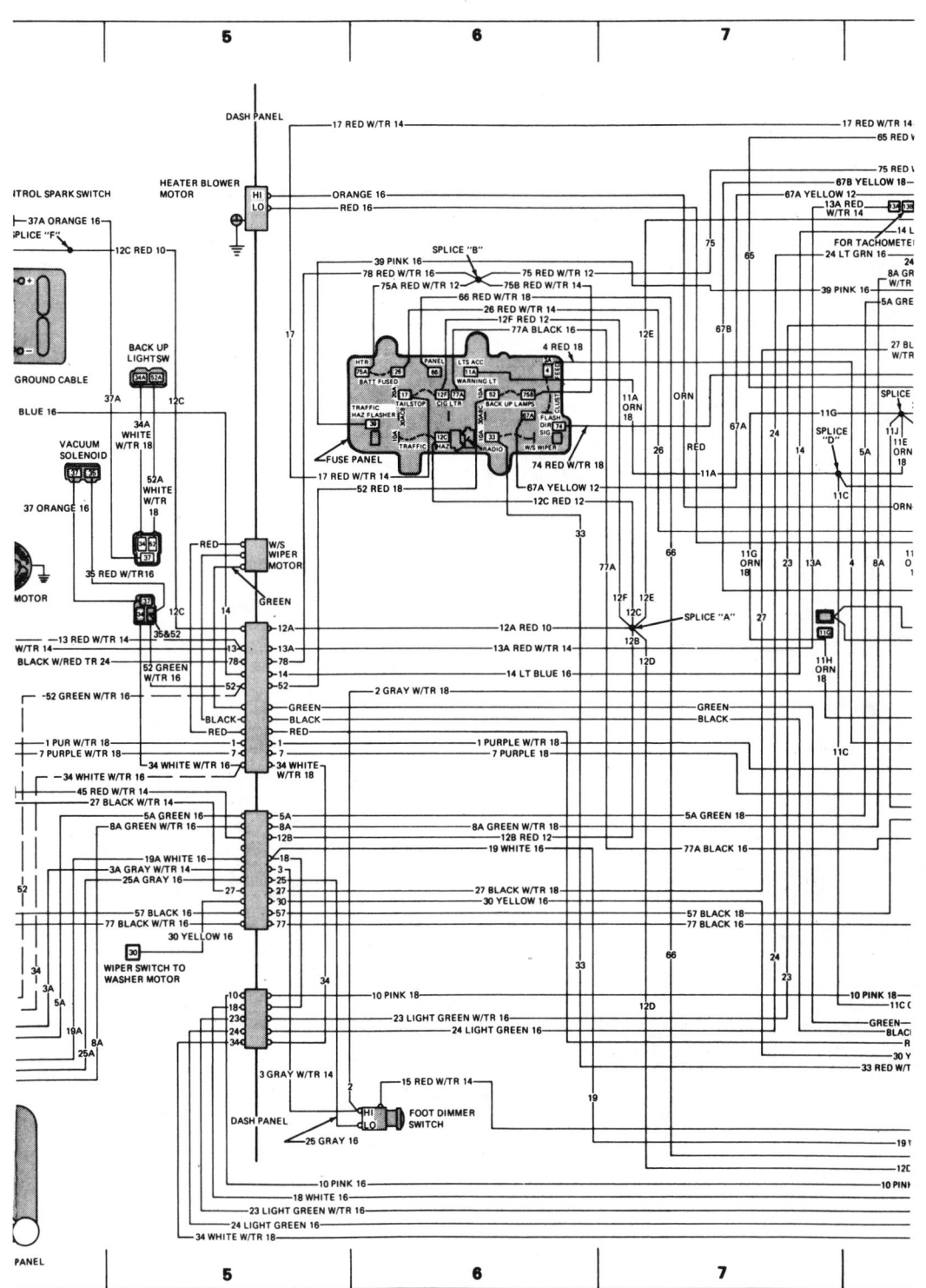

1974–75

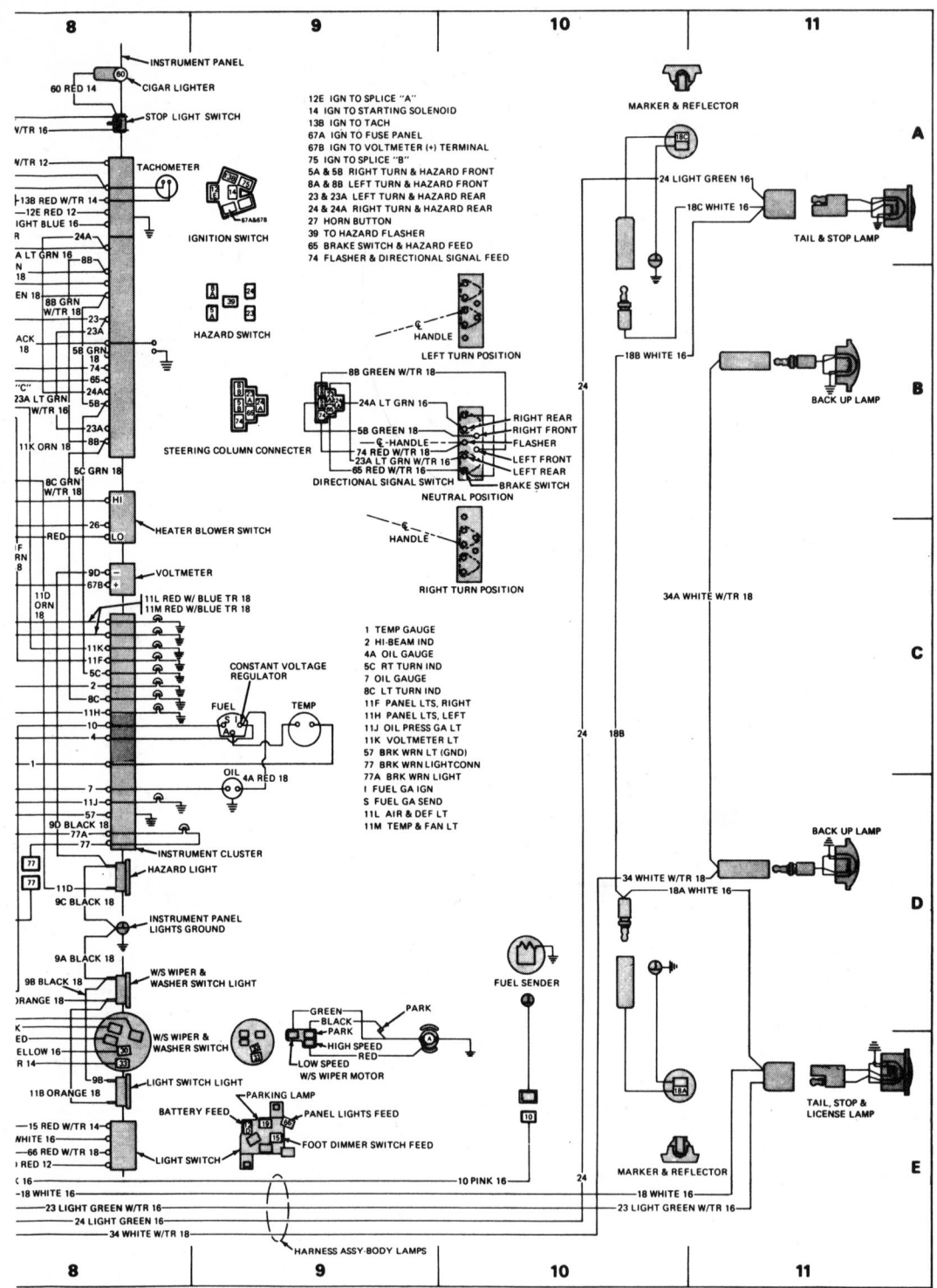

1974–75

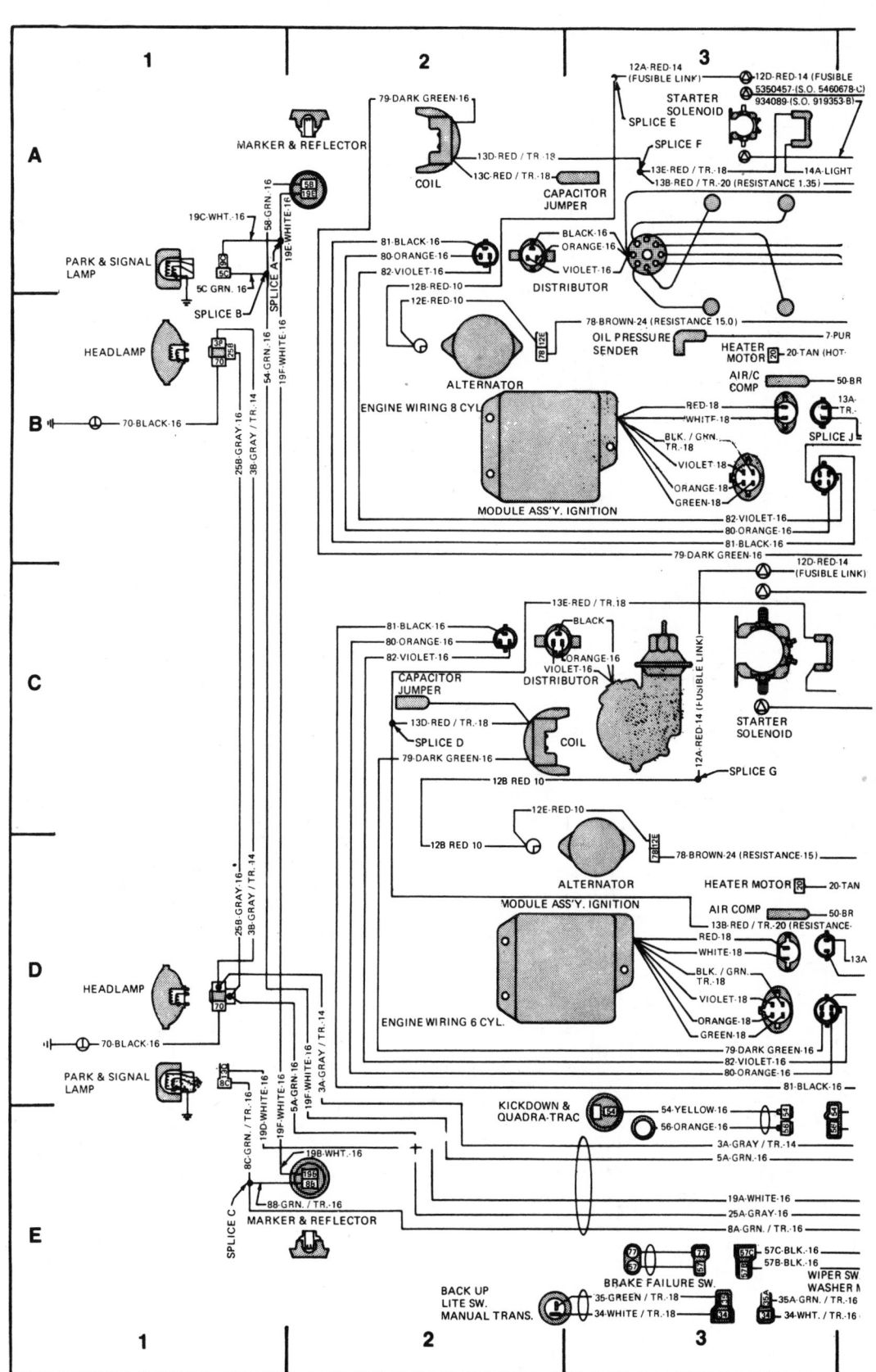

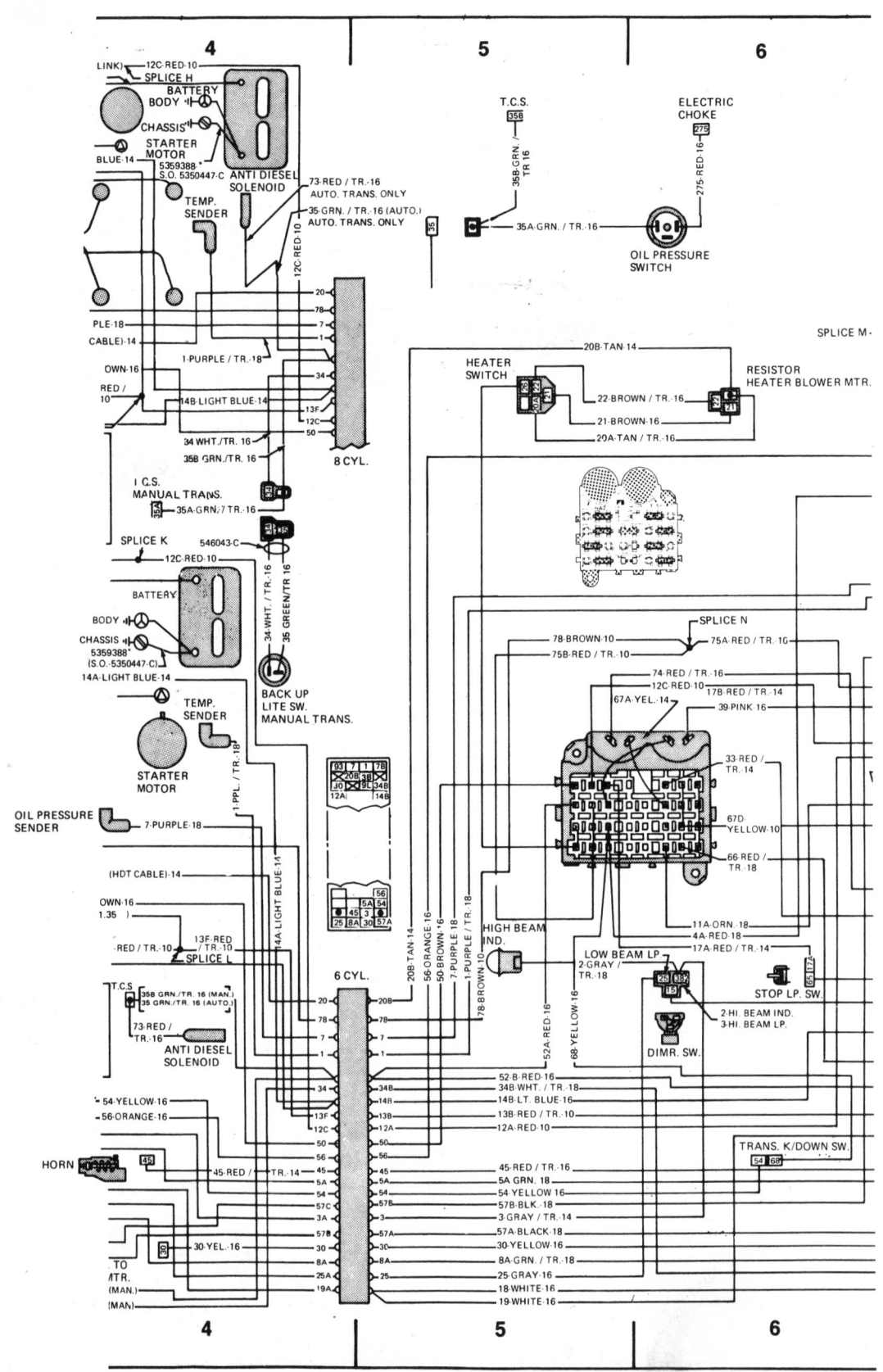

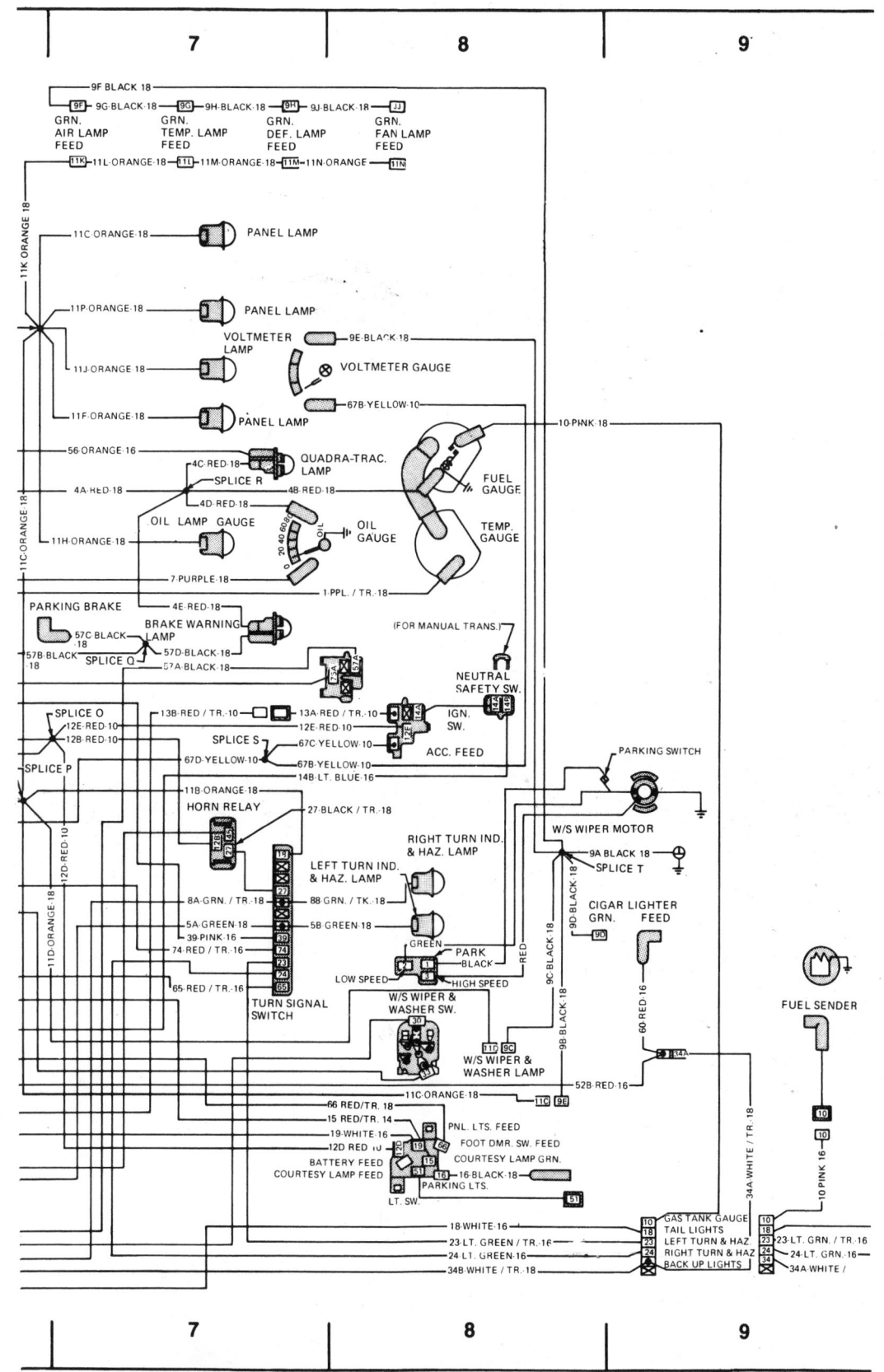

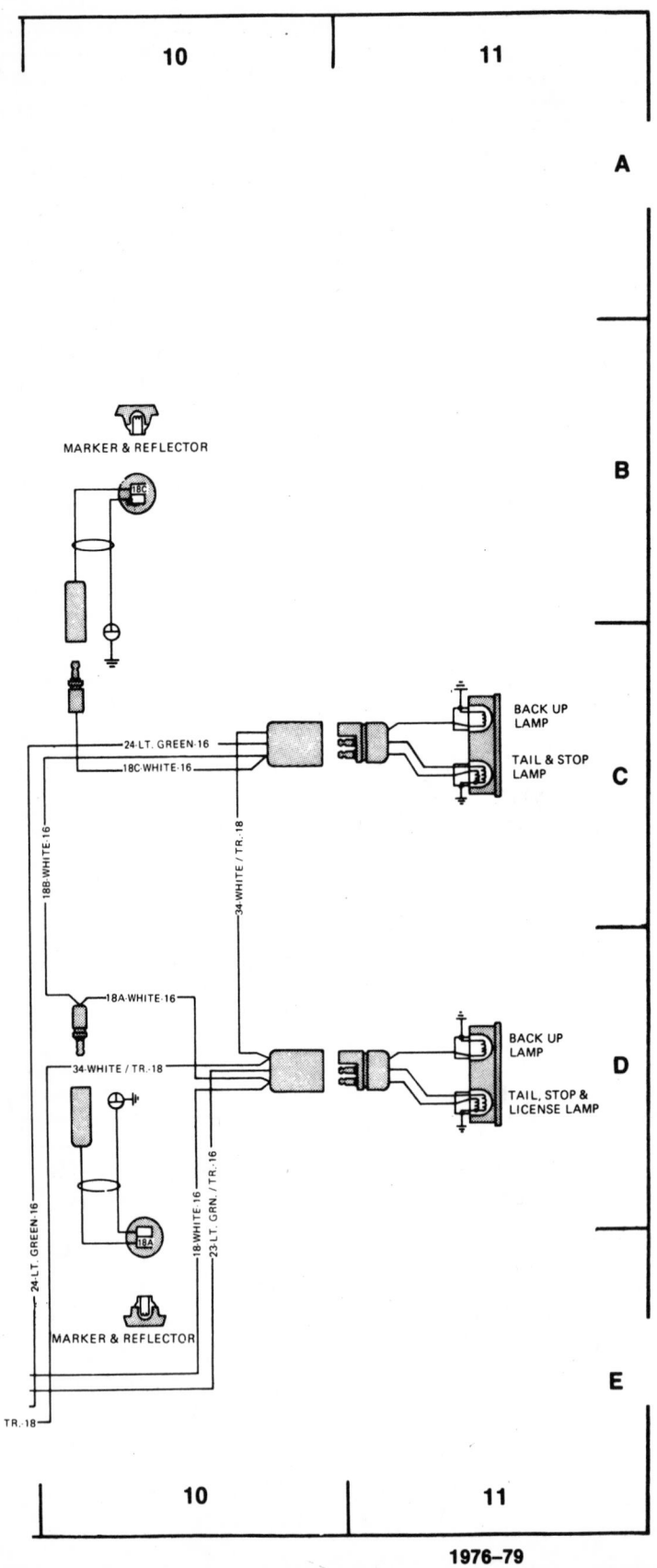

10 | 11

A

B

MARKER & REFLECTOR

BACK UP LAMP

24-LT. GREEN-16

18C-WHITE-16

TAIL & STOP LAMP

C

18B-WHITE-16

34-WHITE / TR.-18

BACK UP LAMP

18A-WHITE-16

34-WHITE / TR.-18

D

TAIL, STOP & LICENSE LAMP

24-LT. GREEN-16

18-WHITE-16

23-LT. GRN. / TR.-16

MARKER & REFLECTOR

E

TR.-18

10 | 11

1976–79

Component Grid Locator

Nomenclature	Location
Accessory Feed	C-8
Air Conditioner Compressor, 8-Cylinder	B-3
Alternator, 8-Cylinder	B-2
Alternator, 6-Cylinder	D-3
Anti-Diesel Solenoid, 8-Cylinder	A-4
Anti-Diesel Solenoid, 6-Cylinder	D-4
Back-up Lamp, Right Side	C-11
Back-up Lamp, Left Side	D-11
Back-up Light Switch	
Manual Transmission	C-4
Back-up Light Switch	
Manual Transmission	E-2
Battery, 8-Cylinder	A-4
Battery, 6-Cylinder	C-4
Body, 8-Cylinder	A-4
Body, 6-Cylinder	C-4
Brake Failure Switch	E-3
Brake Warning Lamp	C-7
Capacitor Jumper, 8-Cylinder	A-3
Capacitor Jumper, 6-Cylinder	C-2
Chassis, 8-Cylinder	A-4
Chassis, 6-Cylinder	C-4
Cigar Lighter Feed	D-9
Coil, 8-Cylinder	A-2
Coil, 6-Cylinder	C-2
Dimmer Switch	D-6
Distributor, 8-Cylinder	A-2
Distributor, 6-Cylinder	C-3
Electric Choke	A-6
Fuel Gauge	B-6
Fuel Sender	D-9
Ground Air Lamp Feed	A-7
Ground Defogger Lamp Feed	A-7
Ground Fan Lamp Feed	A-8
Ground Temperature Lamp Feed	A-7
Headlamp, Right Side	B-1
Headlamp, Left Side	D-1
Heater Motor, 8-Cylinder	B-3
Heater Motor, 6-Cylinder	D-3
Heater Switch	B-5
High Beam Indicator	D-5
Horn	E-4
Horn Relay	D-7
Ignition Switch	C-8
Kickdown & Quadra-Trac, 6-Cylinder	E-3
Left Turn Indicator & Hazard Lamp	D-8
Low Beam L.P.	D-6

Component Grid Locator (cont.)

Nomenclature	Location
Marker & Reflector, Right Side	A-2
Marker & Reflector, Left Side	E-2
Marker & Reflector, Right Side	B-10
Marker & Reflector, Left Side	E-10
Module Assembly Ignition, 8-Cylinder	B-2
Module Assembly Ignition, 6-Cylinder	D-3
Neutral Safety Switch	C-8
Oil Lamp Gauge	B-7
Oil Pressure Sender, 8-Cylinder	B-3
Oil Pressure Sender, 6-Cylinder	C-4
Oil Pressure Switch	A-6
Panel Lamp	A-7
Panel Lamp	B-7
Park & Signal Lamp, Right Side	A-1
Park & Signal Lamp, Left Side	D-1
Parking Brake	C-7
Quadra-Trac Lamp	B-7
Resistor Heater Blower Motor	B-6
Splice, 8-Cylinder	B-4
Splice, 6-Cylinder	A-1
Splice, 6-Cylinder	C-4
Splice, 6-Cylinder	A-1
Splice, 6-Cylinder	C-2
Splice, 6-Cylinder	C-3
Splice	B-6
Splice	C-6
Splice	C-6
Splice	C-7
Splice	C-7
Starting Motor, 8-Cylinder	A-4
Starting Motor, 6-Cylinder	C-4
Starter Solenoid, 8-Cylinder	A-3
Starter Solenoid, 6-Cylinder	C-3
Stop Lamp Switch	D-6
Tail & Stop Lamp, Right Side	C-11
Tail & Stop Lamp, Left Side	D-11
T.C.S. Manual Transmission	B-4
Temperature Gauge	C-8
Temperature Sender, 8-Cylinder	A-4
Temperature Sender, 6-Cylinder	C-4
Transmission Kickdown Switch	E-6
Turn Signal Switch	D-7
Voltmeter Gauge	B-7
Windshield Wiper & Washer Lamp	D-8
Windshield Wiper Motor	C-9
Windshield Wiper & Washer Switch	D-8

1976–79

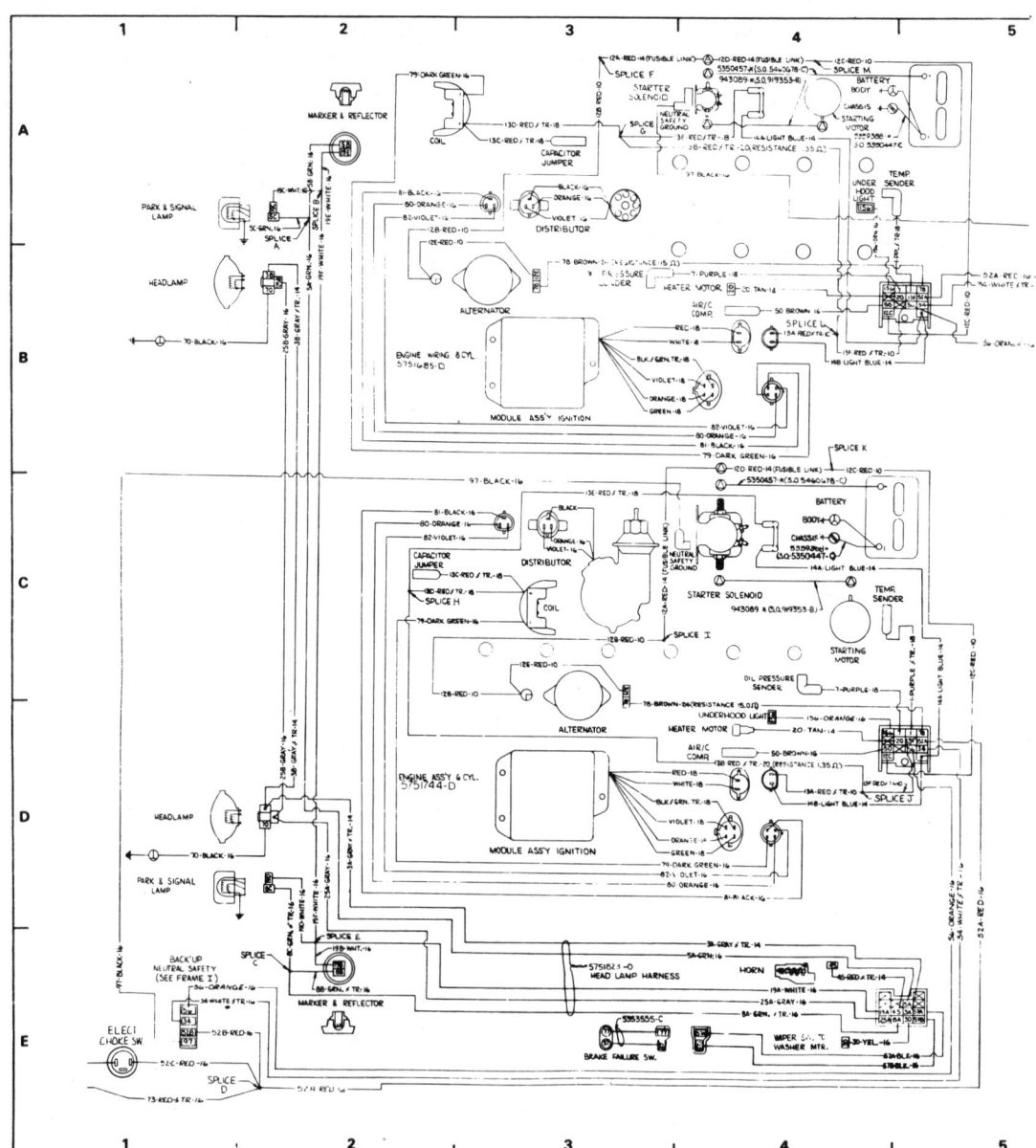

1980 wiring diagram

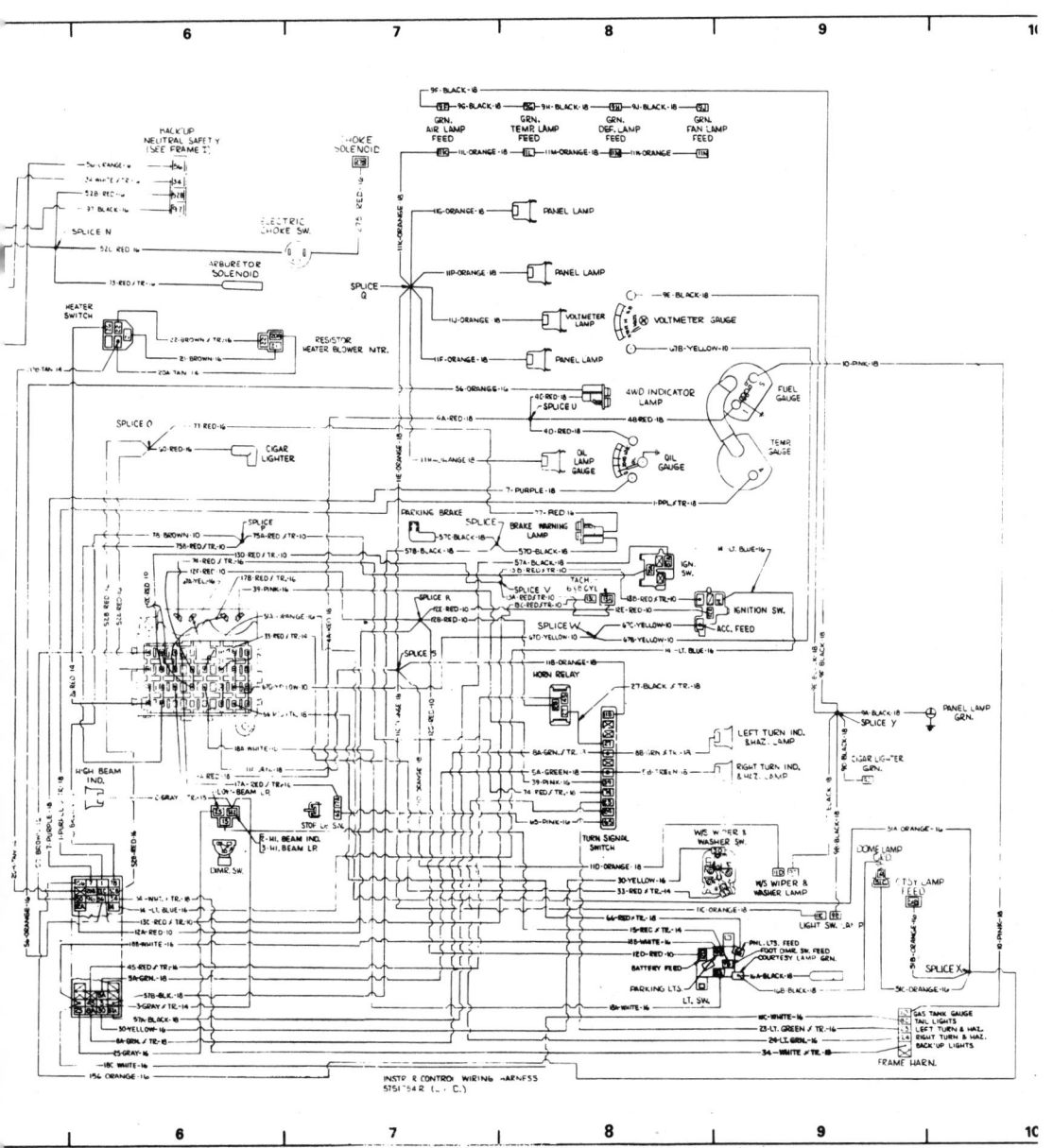

1980 wiring diagram

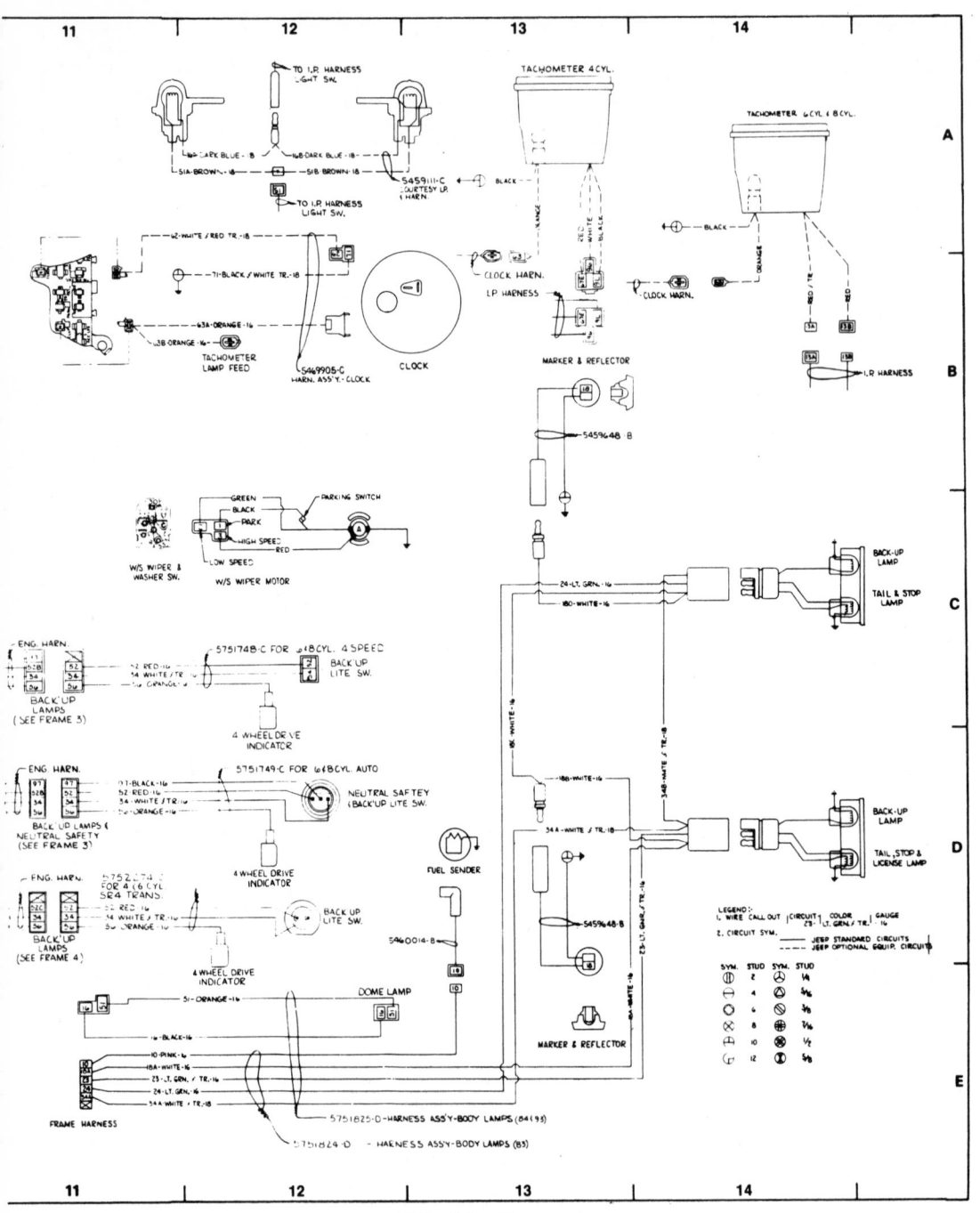

1980 wiring diagram

NOMENCLATURE	LOCATION	NOMENCLATURE	LOCATION
Accessory Feed	C-8	Neutral Safety Switch	D-12
Air Conditioner Compressor, 8-Cylinder	B-4	Oil Lamp Gauge	B-8
Alternator, 8-Cylinder	B-3	Oil Pressure Sender, 8-Cylinder	B-3
Alternator, 6-Cylinder	D-3	Oil Pressure Sender, 6-Cylinder	C-4
Back-up Lamp, Right Side	C-14	Panel Lamp	A-8
Back-up Lamp, Left Side	D-14	Panel Lamp	B-8
Back-up Light Switch		Park & Signal Lamp, Right Side	A-1
Manual Transmission	C-12	Park & Signal Lamp, Left Side	D-1
Back-up Light Switch		Parking Brake	C-7
Automatic Transmission	D-12	Four Wheel Drive Indicator	B-8
Battery, 8-Cylinder	A-4	Resistor, Heater Blower Motor	B-6
Battery, 6-Cylinder	C-4	Splice A	A-2
Body Ground, 8-Cylinder	A-4	Splice B	A-2
Body Ground, 6-Cylinder	C-4	Splice C	E-2
Brake Failure Switch	E-3	Splice D	E-2
Brake Warning Lamp	C-8	Splice E	E-2
Capacitor Jumper, 8-Cylinder	A-3	Splice F, 8-Cylinder	A-3
Capacitor Jumper, 6-Cylinder	C-2	Splice G, 8-Cylinder	A-3
Chassis Ground, 8-Cylinder	A-4	Splice H, 6-Cylinder	C-2
Chassis Ground, 6-Cylinder	C-4	Splice I, 6-Cylinder	C-3
Cigar Lighter Feed	D-9	Splice J, 6-Cylinder	D-4
Coil, 8-Cylinder	A-2	Splice K, 6-Cylinder	B-4
Coil, 6-Cylinder	C-3	Splice L, 8-Cylinder	B-4
Dimmer Switch	D-6	Splice M, 8-Cylinder	A-4
Distributor, 8-Cylinder	A-3	Splice N	A-6
Distributor, 6-Cylinder	C-3	Splice O	B-6
Electric Choke	A-7	Splice P	C-6
Fuel Gauge	B-9	Splice Q	B-7
Fuel Sender	D-12	Splice R	C-7
Ground Air Lamp Feed	A-7	Splice S	C-7
Ground Defogger Lamp Feed	A-8	Splice T	C-7
Ground Fan Lamp Feed	A-8	Splice U	B-8
Ground Temperature Lamp Feed	A-8	Splice V	C-8
Headlamp, Right Side	B-1	Splice W	C-8
Headlamp, Left Side	D-1	Splice X	E-10
Heater Motor, 8-Cylinder	B-4	Splice Y	D-9
Heater Motor, 6-Cylinder	D-4	Starting Motor, 8-Cylinder	A-4
Heater Switch	B-6	Starting Motor, 6-Cylinder	C-4
High Beam Indicator	D-6	Starter Solenoid, 8-Cylinder	A-4
Horn	E-4	Starter Solenoid, 6-Cylinder	C-4
Horn Relay	C-8	Stop Lamp Switch	D-7
Ignition Switch	C-9	Tail & Stop Lamp, Right Side	C-14
Left Turn Indicator &		Tail & Stop Lamp, Left Side	D-14
Hazard Lamp	D-9	Temperature Gauge	B-9
Low Beam L.P.	D-6	Temperature Sender, 8-Cylinder	A-4
Marker & Reflector, Right Side — Front	A-2	Temperature Sender, 6-Cylinder	C-4
Marker & Reflector, Left Side — Front	E-2	Turn Signal Switch	D-8
Marker & Reflector, Right Side — Rear	B-13	Voltmeter Gauge	B-8
Marker & Reflector, Left Side — Rear	E-13	Windshield Wiper & Washer Lamp	D-9
Module Assembly Ignition,		Windshield Wiper Motor	C-11
8-Cylinder	B-3	Windshield Wiper & Washer Switch	D-8
Module Assembly Ignition,			
6-Cylinder	D-3		

1980 wiring diagram

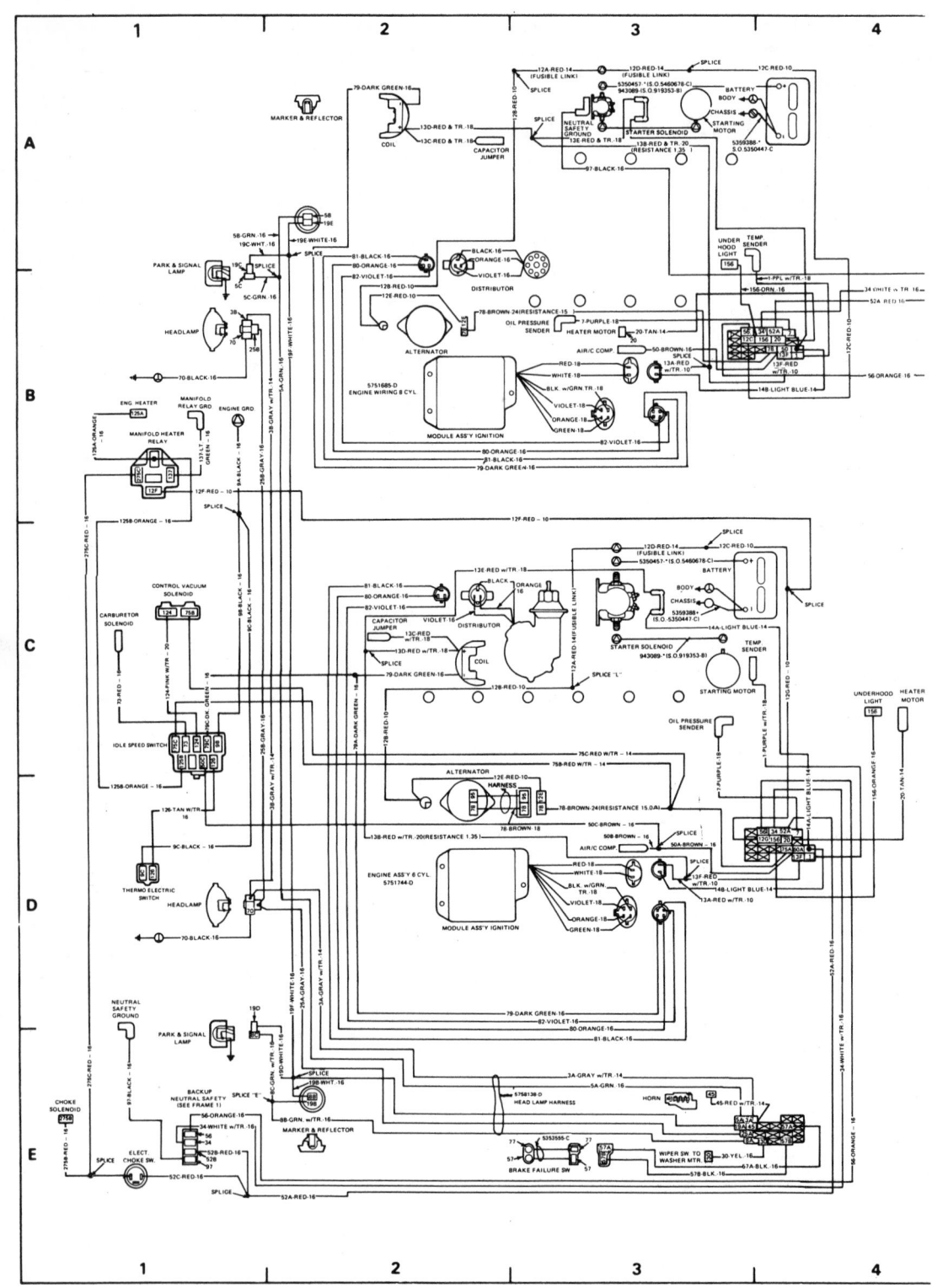

1981 wiring diagram

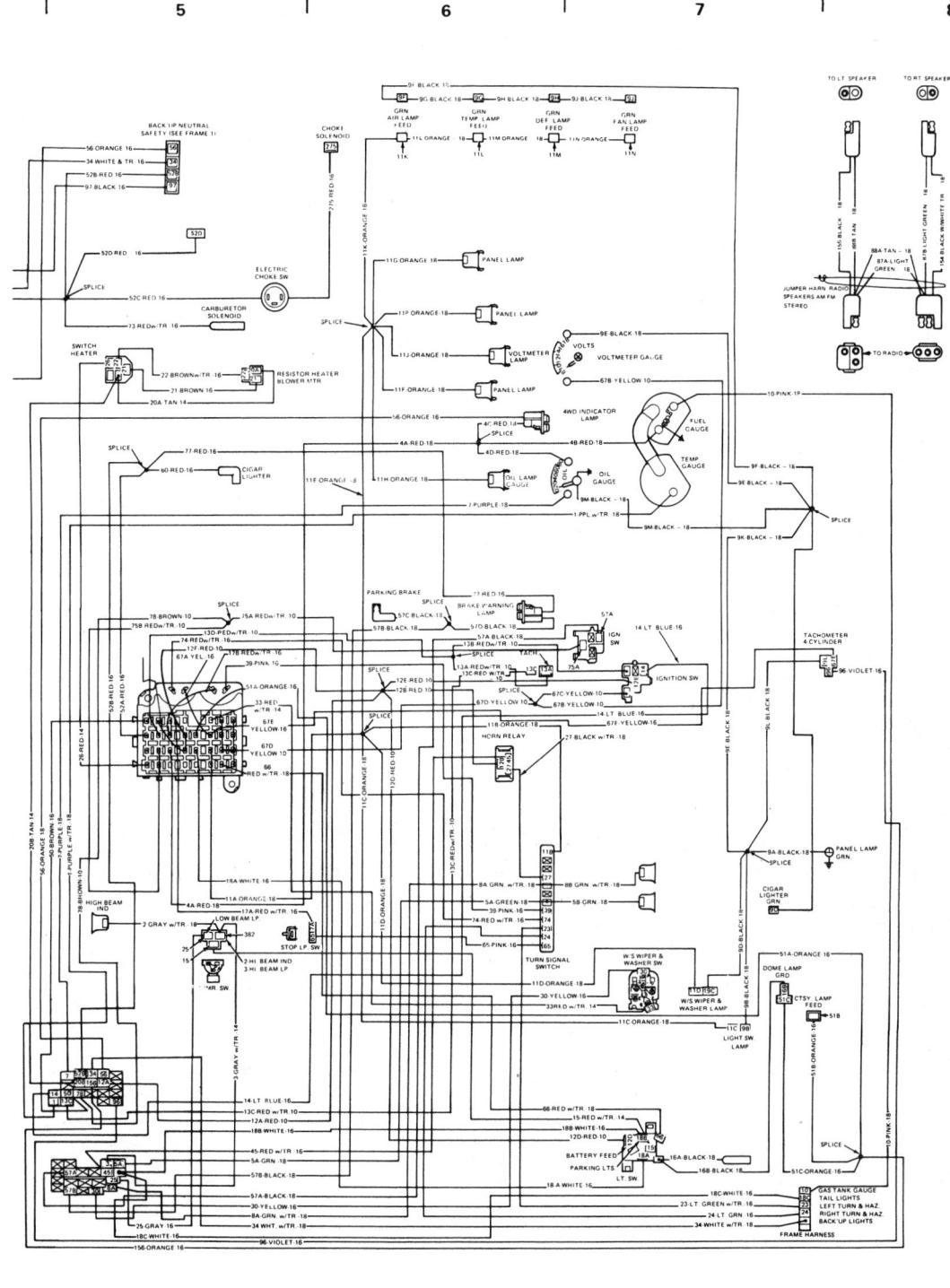

1981 wiring diagram

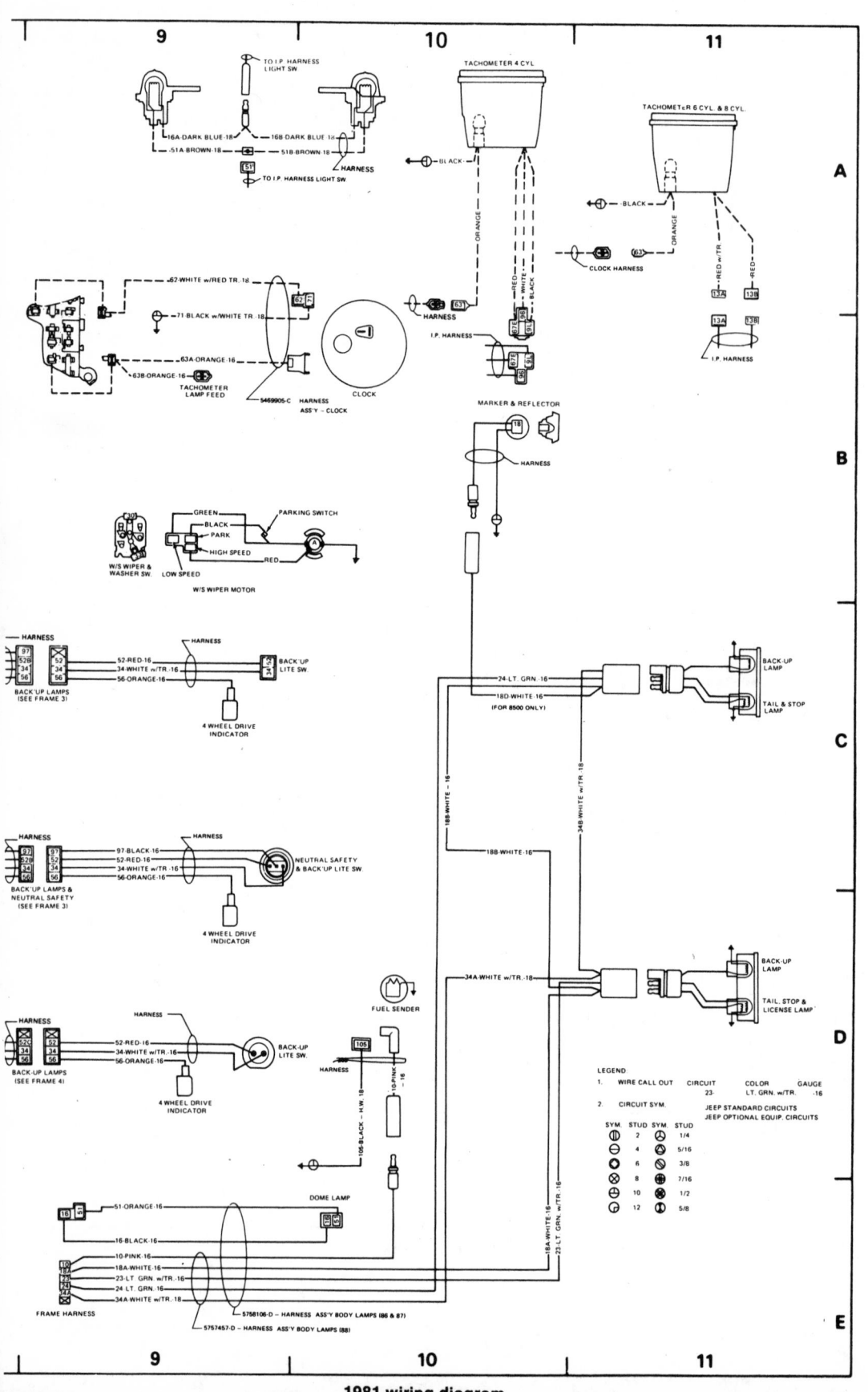

1981 wiring diagram

NOMENCLATURE	LOCATION
Accessory Feed	C-7
Air Conditioner Compressor, 8-Cylinder	B-3
Alternator, 8-Cylinder	B-2
Alternator, 6-Cylinder	D-3
Back-up Lamp, Right Side	C-11
Back-up Lamp, Left Side	D-11
Back-up Light Switch Manual Transmission	C-9, D-9
Back-up Light Switch Automatic Transmission	D-9
Battery, 8-Cylinder	A-4
Battery, 6-Cylinder	C-4
Body Ground, 8-Cylinder	A-4
Body Ground, 6-Cylinder	C-4
Brake Failure Switch	E-3
Brake Warning Lamp	C-6
Capacitor Jumper, 8-Cylinder	A-3
Capacitor Jumper, 6-Cylinder	C-2
Chassis Ground, 8-Cylinder	A-4
Chassis Ground, 6-Cylinder	C-4
Cigar Lighter Feed	D-7
Coil, 8-Cylinder	A-2
Coil, 6-Cylinder	C-3
Dimmer Switch	D-5
Distributor, 8-Cylinder	A-3
Distributor, 6-Cylinder	C-3
Electric Choke	B-5, E-1
Fuel Gauge	B-7
Fuel Sender	D-10
Ground Air Lamp Feed	A-6
Ground Defogger Lamp Feed	A-6
Ground Fan Lamp Feed	A-7
Ground Temperature Lamp Feed	A-6
Headlamp, Right Side	B-1
Headlamp, Left Side	D-1
Heater Motor, 8-Cylinder	B-3
Heater Motor, 6-Cylinder	D-3
Heater Switch	B-5
High Beam Indicator	D-5
Horn	E-3
Horn Relay	C-6
Ignition Switch	C-7
Left Turn Indicator & Hazard Lamp	E-7
Low Beam L.P.	D-5
Marker & Reflector, Right Side — Front	A-2
Marker & Reflector, Left Side — Front	E-2
Marker & Reflector, Right Side — Rear	B-10
Marker & Reflector, Left Side — Rear	E-10
Module Assembly Ignition, 8-Cylinder	B-3
Module Assembly Ignition, 6-Cylinder	D-3

NOMENCLATURE	LOCATION
Neutral Safety Switch	D-9
Oil Lamp Gauge	B-6
Oil Pressure Sender, 8-Cylinder	B-3
Oil Pressure Sender, 6-Cylinder	D-3
Panel Lamp	B-6
Park & Signal Lamp, Right Side	A-1
Park & Signal Lamp, Left Side	D-1
Parking Brake	C-6
Four Wheel Drive Indicator	C-9, D-9
Resistor, Heater Blower Motor	B-5
Splice A	A-2
Splice B	B-2
Splice C	C-2
Splice D	E-2
Splice E	E-2
Splice F	E-2
Splice G	A-3
Splice H	A-3
Splice I	A-3
Splice J	B-3
Splice K	C-3
Splice L	C-3
Splice M	D-4
Splice N	B-5
Splice O	B-5
Splice P	C-5
Splice Q	B-6
Splice R	B-6
Splice S	C-6
Splice T	C-6
Splice U	C-6
Splice V	C-6
Splice W	C-6
Splice X	D-7
Splice Y	E-8
Starting Motor, 8-Cylinder	A-3
Starting Motor, 6-Cylinder	C-4
Starter Solenoid, 8-Cylinder	A-3
Starter Solenoid, 6-Cylinder	C-3
Stop Lamp Switch	D-5
Tail & Stop Lamp, Right Side	C-11
Tail & Stop Lamp, Left Side	D-11
Temperature Gauge	B-7
Temperature Sender, 8-Cylinder	A-4
Temperature Sender, 6-Cylinder	C-4
Turn Signal Switch	D-6
Voltmeter Gauge	B-7
Windshield Wiper & Washer Lamp	D-7
Windshield Wiper Motor	C-9
Windshield Wiper & Washer Switch	D-7

1981 wiring diagram

Clutch and Transmission

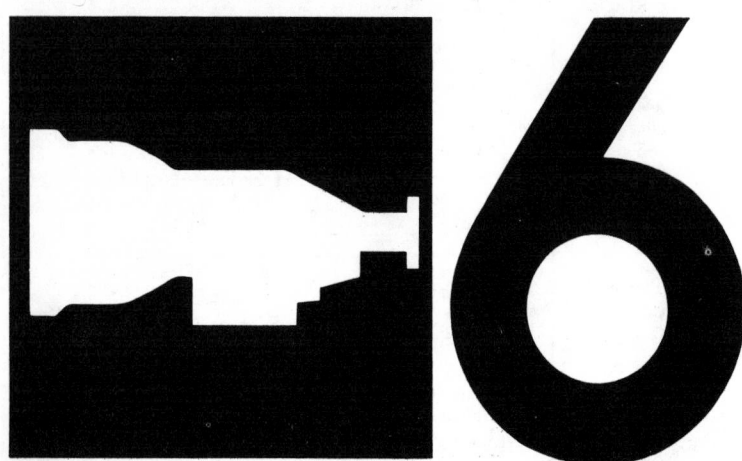

MANUAL TRANSMISSION

REMOVAL AND INSTALLATION

1945–71

CJ-2A after serial #38221, CJ-3A, CJ-3B, CJ-5, and CJ-6 models are equipped with a Warner T90C, 3-speed heavy duty transmission having no external linkage. CJ-2A models up to serial #38221 have the same T90C transmission, but with remote, external linkage. CJ-5 and CJ-6 models are also equipped with a Warner T98A heavy duty 4-speed transmission as an option. This transmission has no external linkage. The following removal and installation procedures are for both the 3- and 4-speed transmissions.

1. Raise and support the vehicle on jack stands.

2. Drain the transmission and transfer case.

3. Remove the shift lever and shift housing. On CJ-2A models up to serial #38221 remove the remote linkage as follows:

    a. Remove the shift rods from the transmission and from the steering remote control clutch levers.

    b. Remove the shift lever fulcrum pin and remove the shift lever.

    c. Remove the toe plates from the floor pan at the steering column.

    d. Remove the two screws holding the linkage housing to the steering column, and lift the housing from the positioning pin.

    e. Remove the shift assembly down through the floor pan.

    f. Remove the lower clutch and shift lever from the housing by turning counterclockwise.

    g. Remove the upper clutch and shift lever in the same manner.

4. Remove the set screw from the transfer case shift lever pivot pin. Remove the pivot pin, shift levers, and shift lever springs.

5. If the vehicle is equipped with a power take-off, remove the shift lever plate screws and lift out the lever.

6. Disconnect the front and rear driveshafts from the transfer case. If the vehicle is equipped with a power take-off, disconnect the transfer case end of the pto drive shaft.

7. Disconnect the speedometer cable at the transfer case.

8. Disconnect the hand brake cable.

9. Disconnect the clutch cable at the bellcrank.

10. Place jacks under the transmission and engine. Protect the oil pan with a wood block.

11. Remove the nuts holding the rear mount to the cross member.

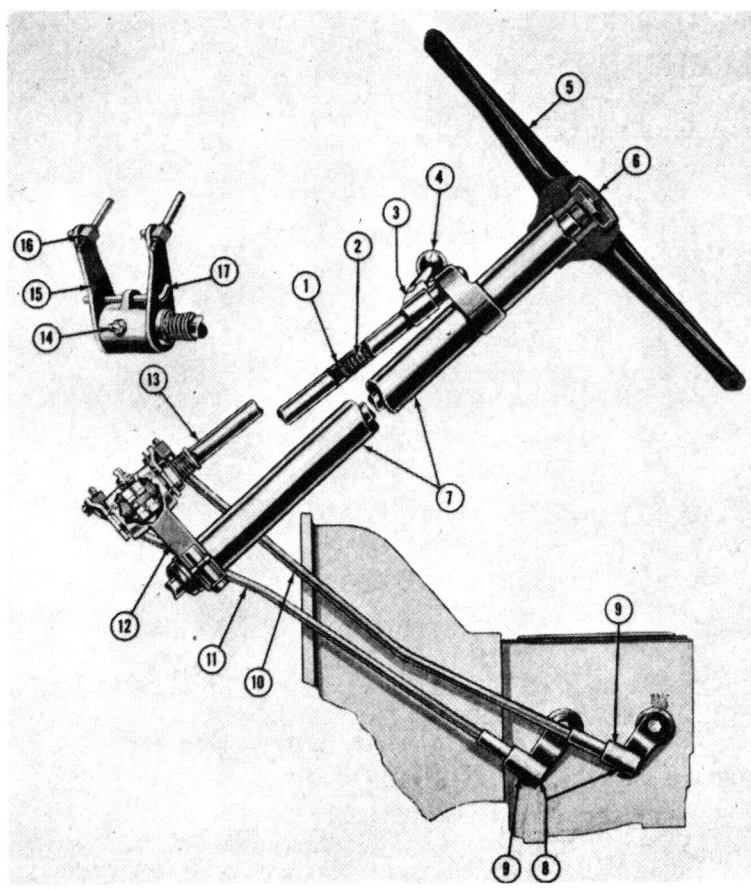

1. Stop screw
2. Bias spring
3. Gearshift lever
4. Lever ball
5. Steering sheel
6. Horn button
7. Column and bearing
8. End nuts
9. Shift rod ends
10. Shift rod
11. Shift rod
12. Cross-shift bracket
13. Control shaft
14. Lubrication fitting
15. Lever and clutch
16. Adjusting yoke
17. Aligning rod

Remote linkage used on CJ-2A models prior to serial number 38221

12. Remove the transfer case-to-cross-member bolt.

13. Remove the frame center cross member-to-frame side rail bolts and remove the cross member. Remove the transmission-to-bellhousing bolts.

14. Force the transmission to the right to disengage the clutch control lever tube ball joint.

15. Lower the engine and transmission. Slide the transmission and transfer case assemblies toward the rear until they clear the clutch.

16. Remove the six screws and lockwashers attaching the transfer case rear cover and remove the cover. If the vehicle is equipped with a power take-off, remove the pto shift unit.

17. Remove the cotter pin, nut, and washer holding the transfer case main drive gear on the rear end of the transmission mainshaft. If possible, remove the main drive gear. If that's not possible, see steps 19 and so.

18. Remove the transmission-to-transfer case bolts.

19. Separate the transfer case from the transmission. When separating, take care to avoid dislodging the transmission mainshaft bearing. Thisbearing should remain in the transmission.

20. Install a transmission mainshaft retaining plate tool #W-194 to prevent the mainshaft from pulling out of the case. If this tool is not available, loop a piece of wire around the mainshaft directly in back of the second speed gear. Install the shift housing right and left bolts part way into the case. Attach each end of the wire to the bolts. Support the transfer case, and with a soft mallet, tap lightly on the end of the mainshaft to loosen the gear and separate the two units.

21. Installation is the reverse of removal.

1972-81

Several different transmission have been used on Jeep vehicles in this period:

- 1972–75: T-14A 3-speed and T-18 4-speed
- 1976–79: T-150 3-speed and T-18A 4-speed
- 1980: T-176 4-speed used on all CJ-5 and on CJ-7 with 8-304 engine
  SR-4 4-speed used on CJ-7 with 6-258 engine
- 1981: T-176 used on some 6-258 engines and all 8-304 engines
  SR-4 4-speed used on all 4-151 engines and some 6-258 engines

1. Remove all floor lever knobs, trim rings and boots.

2. Remove the floor pan section from above the transmission shift control and unbolt the lever assembly from the transmission (early three-speed models). On the four-speed models exc. SR-4 and T-176, and three-speeds starting 1976, unscrew the shift control housing cap, remove the washer, spring, shift lever and pin. On SR-4 models, remove the shift lever housing bolts and remove the shift lever and housing assembly.

3. On T-18A, remove the transfer case shift lever and bracket assembly. On T-176 models, press and turn the lever retainer and remove the shift lever assembly.

4. Raise the vehicle.

5. Index mark the driveshafts for proper alignment at installation.

6. Remove the front driveshaft.

7. Disconnect the front end of the rear driveshaft from the transfer case.

8. Disconnect the clutch cable and remove the cable mounting bracket from the transfer case on 1972 models only.

9. Disconnect the speedometer cable, back-up light switch wires, transmission controlled spark advance, and parking brake cable if connected to the crossmember.

10. If equipped with a V8 engine, disconnect the exhaust pipe at the manifolds and lower them.

Support the engine with a jack. Disconnect the support crossmember from the frame side rail.

11. Remove the bolts that attach the transmission to the clutch housing.

12. Lower the transmission slightly.

13. Move the transmission and transfer case assembly and crossmember backward far enough for the transmission clutch shaft to clear the clutch housing.

14. Remove the assembly from under the vehicle.

15. Install in the reverse order of removal

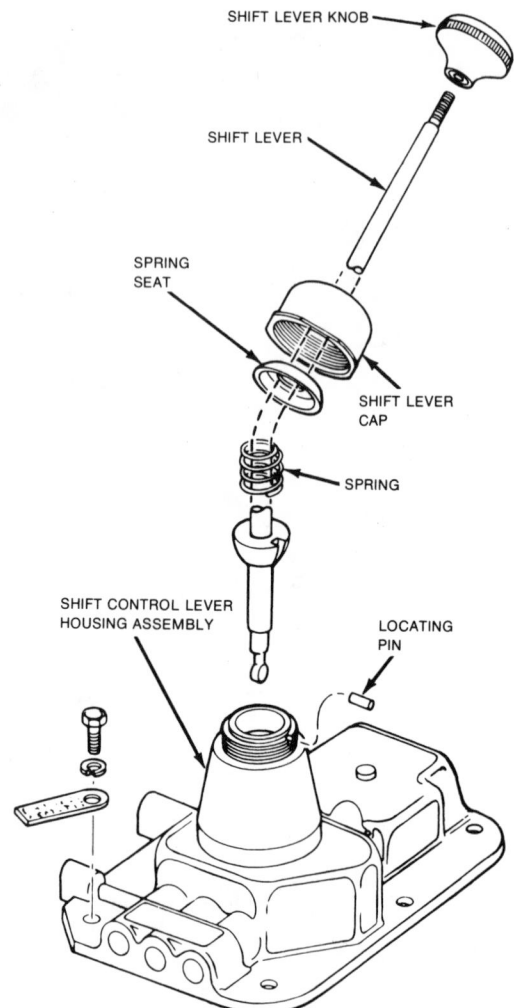

Shift lever removal for T-18A and all 3-speed units starting in 1974

taking note of the following points prior to installing the transmission:

Position the wave washer and the throwout bearing and sleeve assembly in the throwout fork. Center the bearing over the pressure plate release levers.

Protect the splines and throw-out bearing alignment and slowly slide the transmission into position. Some maneuvering may be necessary in order to match the transmission input shaft splines and the clutch driven plate splines.

Observe the following torque values:
- Starter bolts
  4-151 . . . . 54 ft. lb.
  others . . . . 18 ft. lb.
- Transmission-to-clutch housing 54 ft. lb.
- Transfer case-to-transmission . . 30 ft. lb.

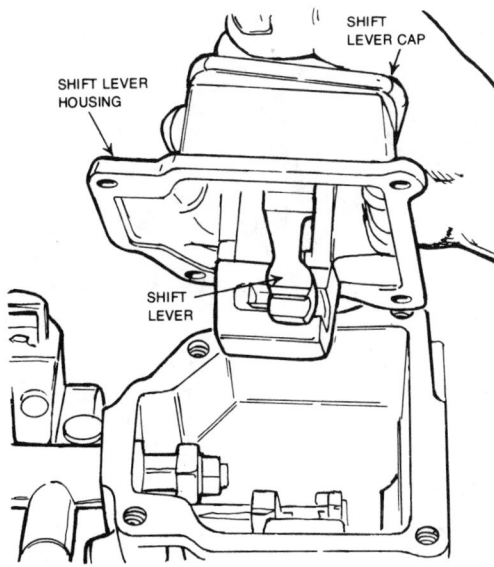

SR-4 shift lever removal

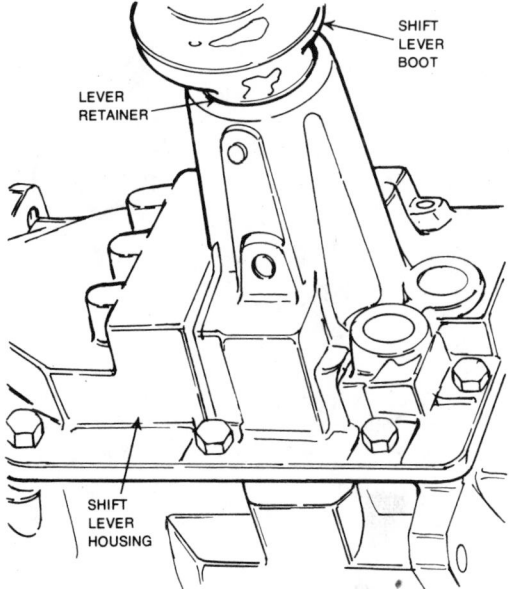

T-176 shift lever removal

- Crossmember bolts . . . . 30 ft. lb.
- U-joint strap bolts . . . . 15 ft. lb.

Shift Linkage Adjustment

CJ-2A

First disconnect the shift rods from the remote control levers. Check for binding of the remote control shaft on the steering column and make the necessary adjustments to eliminate any binding condition.

If the shift is not smooth and positive, first make sure that the transmission is in Neutral and then remove the shift rods at the transmission by removing the clevis pins. Slip a short piece of snug fitting ¼ in. aligning rod through the gearshift levers and housing.

This places the shift lever and clutch assemblies in the Neutral position. Adjust the shift rod yokes at the transmission end so that the clevis pins can be installed freely without moving the shift levers on the transmission. Remove the alignment pin.

If shifting from First to Second is difficult or the transmission hangs up in First gear, shorten the Low and Reverse rod one turn at a time and until the condition is corrected. Usually three turns are required.

Should the fault continue after completing the above adjustment, check further as follows. First, remove the lubricating fitting from the shifter housing.

Use a narrow feeler gauge which will enter the opening for the lubricator and check the clearance between the faces of the shifting clutches. The clearance should be 0.015 in. to 0.031 in. If the clearance is greater, the assembly must be removed for adjustment. The shift dog which engages the clutch slots should not have more than 0.009 in. clearance in the slots. If the clearance between the clutch grooves and cross pins is too great, these parts must be replaced.

To remove the remote control housing from the steering column for repairs, the following procedure is suggested:

1. Remove the shifting rods from the transmission and also from the steering column remote control clutch levers.

2. Remove the gearshift lever fulcrum pin and the gearshift lever.

3. Remove the plates on the toe board at the steering post.

4. Remove the two screws that hold the remote control housing to the steering post and lift the housing from the positioning pin.

5. Remove the assembly down through the floor pan.

6. Remove the lower clutch and shift lever from the housing by turning counterclockwise.

7. Remove the upper clutch and shift lever in the same manner.

8. Wash all of the parts in a suitable clearing solution and replace all worn parts before reassembling.

9. Assemble the upper clutch assembly in the housing making sure that the alignment hole in the housing faces the engine.

Turn the upper lever assembly in as far as it will go and then back off one full turn until the hole in the clutch lever aligns with the hole in the housing.

10. Assemble the lower clutch lever assembly in the housing until the faces of the clutches contact, then back off not more than one-half of a turn which should bring the aligning hole in the lever in line with the hole in the housing. If the one-half turn does not bring the alignment hole into the proper position, it will be necessary to grind off the face of the lower clutch so that it can be backed off one-half turn from contact with the upper clutch. The proper clearance of 0.015 in. is obtained when the lower clutch is backed off one-half turn.

11. Assemble the unit to the steering post in the reverse order of removal and adjust the remote control rods.

12. If, after assembly, the shifter dog catches on the edge of the slot in the clutch when moving the lever up and down, disconnect the shift rod at the transmission end and either lengthen or shorten it slightly to correct this condition.

CLUTCH

Vehicles with the 4-134 engine have a 8½ or 9¼ in. clutch plate. The clutch is either a three pressure spring, three fingered Auburn clutch or a six pressure spring, three fingered Rockford clutch.

Jeeps with the V6 engine have a General Motors diaphragm type clutch.

1972–81 models have a 10½ in. direct spring pressure type clutch, as standard equipment except Scrambler. The Scrambler has a 9⅛ in. clutch standard with the 10½ in. clutch as an option.

REMOVAL AND INSTALLATION

4-134

1. Remove the transmission and transfer case from the vehicle.

2. Remove the flywheel housing.

3. Mark the clutch pressure plate and engine flywheel with a center punch so the clutch assembly may be installed in the same position after adjustments or replacement are complete.

4. Loosen the clutch pressure plate bracket bolts equally, a little at a time, to

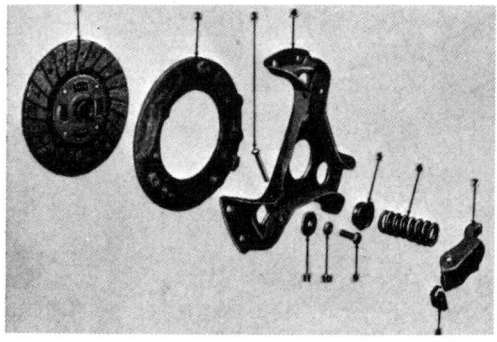

1. Driven plate and hub
2. Pressure plate
3. Pivot pin
4. Bracket
5. Spring cup
6. Pressure spring
7. Release lever
8. Return spring
9. Adjusting screw
10. Jam nut
11. Washer

4-134 Auburn clutch

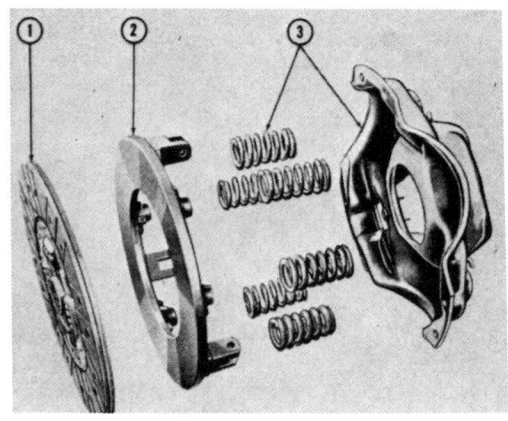

1. Driven plate and hub
2. Pressure plate
3. Backing plate and pressure spring

4-134 Rockford clutch

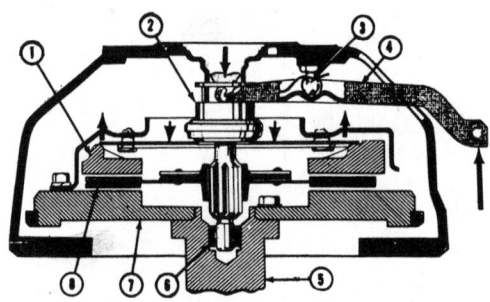

1. Pressure plate
2. Throwout bearing
3. Pivot point
4. Clutch fork
5. Engine crankshaft
6. Pilot bearing
7. Flywheel
8. Driven plate

V6 clutch cutaway

prevent distortion and relieve the clutch springs evenly. Remove the bolts.

5. Remove the pressure plate assembly (bracket and pressure plate) and driven plate from the flywheel. The driven plate will just be resting on the pressure plate housing since it usually is mounted on the input shaft of the transmission, which has been removed. Be careful that it does not fall down and cause injury.

6. Replace the clutch assembly in the reverse order of removal taking note of the following items:

The clutch release bearing (throwout bearing) is lubricated at time of assembly and no attempt should be made to lubricate it. Put a small amount of grease in the pilot bushing. Install the driven plate with the short end of the hub toward the flywheel. Use a spare transmission mainshaft or an aligning arbor to align the pressure plate assembly and the driven plate. Leave the arbor in place while tightening the pressure plate screws evenly a turn or two at a time.

7. Install a reverse order of removal.

V6

1. Remove the transmission and transfer case.

2. Remove the clutch throwout bearing and pedal return spring from the clutch fork.

3. Remove the flywheel housing from the engine.

4. Disconnect the clutch fork from the ball stud by forcing it toward the center of the vehicle.

5. Mark the clutch cover and flywheel with a center punch so that the cover can later be installed in the same position on the flywheel. This is necessary to maintain engine balance.

6. Loosen the clutch attaching bolts alternately, one turn at a time to avoid distorting the clutch cover flange, until the diaphragm spring is released.

7. Support the pressure plate and cover assembly while removing the last of the bolts; remove the pressure plate and driven plate from the flywheel.

8. If it is necessary to disassemble the pressure plate assembly, note the position of the grooves on the edge of the pressure plate and cover. These marks must be aligned during assembly to maintain balance. The clutch diaphragm spring and two pivot rings are riveted to the clutch cover. Inspect the spring, rings and cover for excessive wear or dam-

age. If there is a defect, replace the complete cover assembly.

9. Replace the clutch assembly in reverse order of the removal procedure, taking note of the following:

Use extreme care at all times not to get the clutch driven plate dirty in any way. Lightly lubricate the inside of the clutch driven plate's spline with a coat of wheel bearing grease. Do the same to the input shaft of the transmission. Wipe off all excess grease so that none will fly off and get onto the driven plate. Lubricate the throwout bearing collar, the ball stud and the clutch fork with wheel bearing grease. Use a pilot shaft or a spare transmission main shaft to align the driven shaft and the clutch pressure plate when attaching the assembly to the flywheel. Tighten down on the clutch-to-flywheel attaching bolts alternately so that the clutch is drawn squarely into position on the flywheel. Each bolt must be tightened one turn at a time to avoid bending the clutch cover flange. Torque the bolts to 30–40 ft. lbs.

1972–81 except 4-151

1. Remove the transmission.
2. Remove the starter.
3. Remove the throwout bearing and sleeve assembly.
4. Remove the bell housing.
5. Mark the clutch cover, pressure plate and the flywheel with a center punch so that these parts can be later installed in the same position.
6. Remove the clutch cover-to-flywheel attaching bolts. When removing these bolts, loosen them in rotation, one or two turns at a time, until the spring tension is released. The clutch cover is a steel stamping which could be warped by improper removal procedures, resulting in clutch chatter when reused.
7. Remove the clutch assembly from the flywheel. Install in reverse order of removal referring to the paragraph at the end of the removal and installation procedure for the V6 clutch. Torque pressure plate bolts to 40 ft. lb.

4-151

1. Remove the shift lever boot.
2. Remove the shift lever assembly.
3. Raise the vehicle and support it on jack stands.
4. Remove the transmission and transfer case.

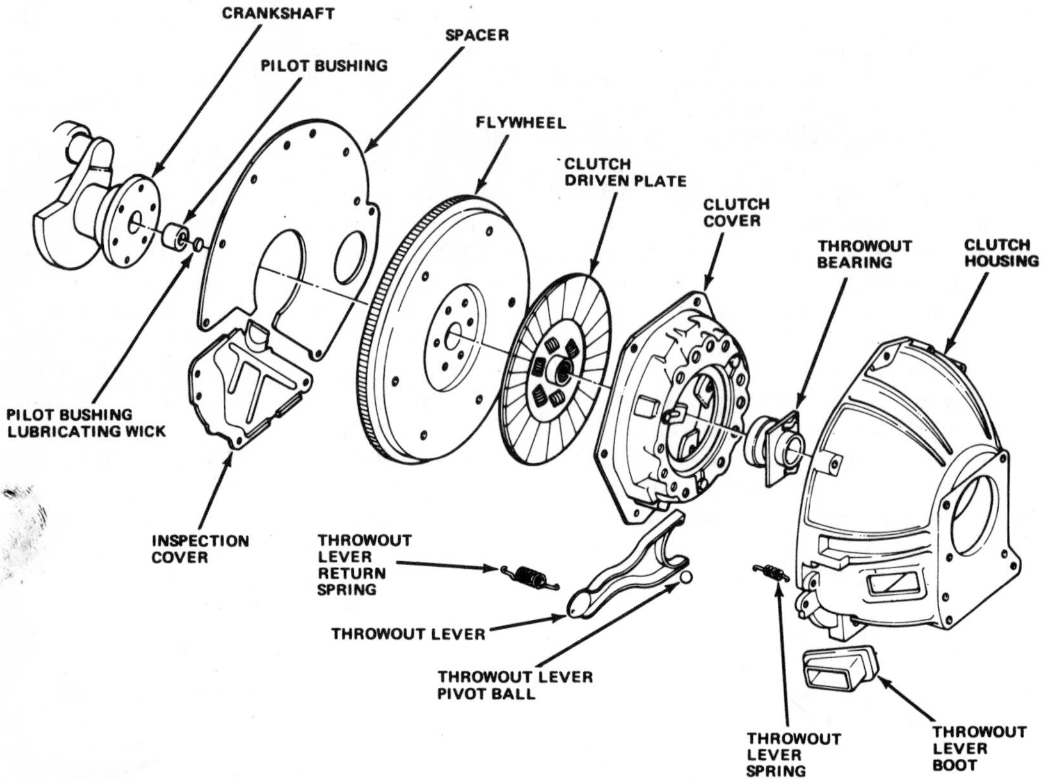

CRANKSHAFT
SPACER
PILOT BUSHING
FLYWHEEL
CLUTCH
DRIVEN PLATE
CLUTCH
COVER
THROWOUT
BEARING
CLUTCH
HOUSING
PILOT BUSHING
LUBRICATING WICK
INSPECTION
COVER
THROWOUT
LEVER
RETURN
SPRING
THROWOUT LEVER
THROWOUT LEVER
PIVOT BALL
THROWOUT
LEVER
SPRING
THROWOUT
LEVER
BOOT

6-232, 258 and 8-304 clutch assembly

5. Remove the slave cylinder-to-clutch housing bolts.

6. Disengage the slave cylinder pushrod from the throwout lever and move the cylinder out of the way.

7. Remove the starter.

8. Remove the throwout bearing.

9. Unbolt and remove the clutch housing.

10. Mark the position of the clutch pressure plate and remove the pressure plate bolts evenly, a little at a time in rotation.

11. Remove the pilot bushing lubricating

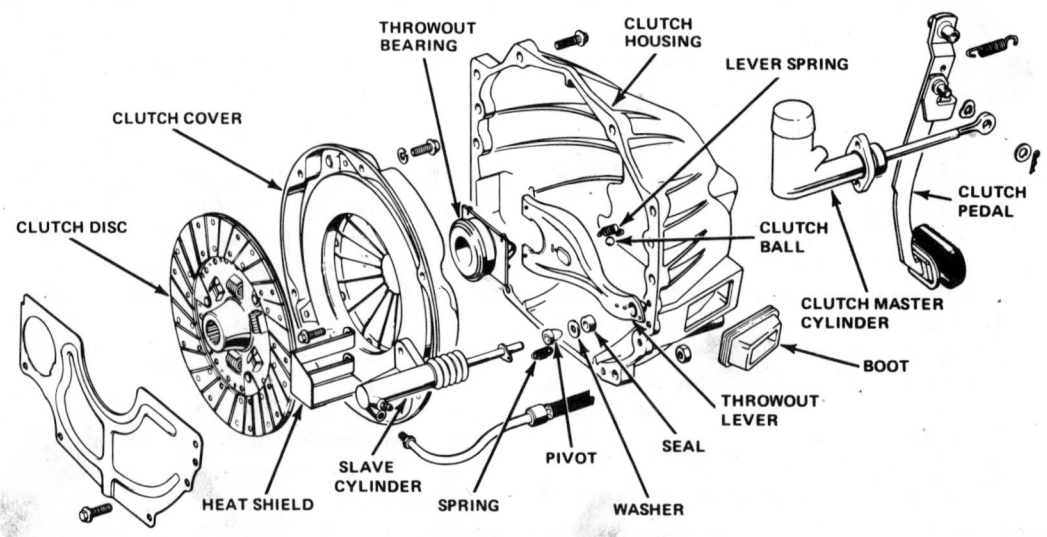

4-151 clutch assembly

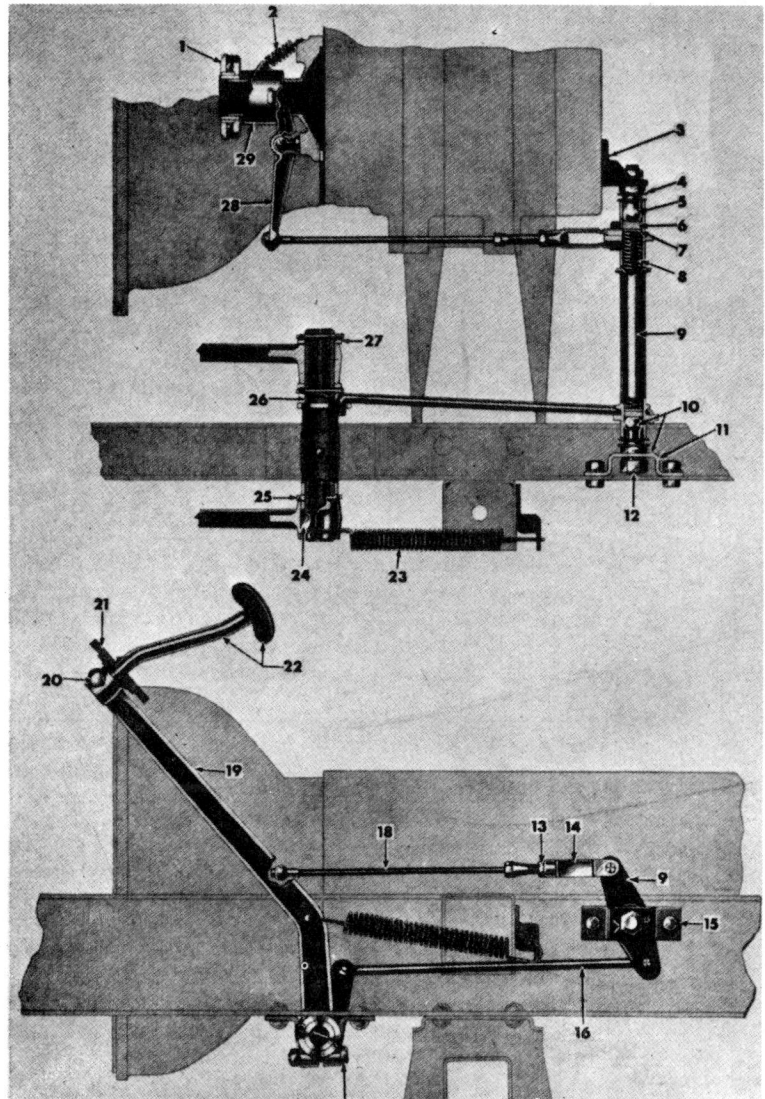

1. Clutch release bearing
2. Carrier spring
3. Bracket
4. Dust seal
5. Ball stud
6. Pad
7. Retainer
8. Control tube spring
9. Control lever and tube
10. Ball stud and bracket
11. Frame bracket
12. Ball stud nut
13. Yoke lock nut
14. Adjusting yoke
15. Bolt
16. Pedal release rod
17. Pedal clamp bolt
18. Control cable
19. Clutch pedal
20. Screw and lockwasher
21. Draft pad
22. Pedal pad and shank
23. Retracting spring
24. Pedal to shaft key
25. Washer
26. Pedal shaft
27. Master cylinder tie bar
28. Control lever
29. Bearing carrier

Clutch linkage used on CJ-3B, CJ-5 and CJ-6 through 1971

wick from its bore in the crankshaft and soak the wick in clean engine oil.

12. Installation is the reverse of removal. Torque the pressure plate bolts to 23 ft. lb., tightening them evenly, a little at a time in rotation. Torque the clutch housing to 54 ft. lb.; the transmission-to-clutch housing bolts to 54 ft. lb.; the transfer case-to-transmission bolts to 30 ft. lb.

CLUTCH LINKAGE ADJUSTMENT
Through 1971

As the clutch facings wear out the free travel of the clutch pedal diminishes. When suffi-cient wear occurs, the pedal clearance must be adjusted to 1–1½ in. The free pedal clearance is adjusted by lengthening or short-ening the clutch fork cable. To make this ad-justment, loosen the jam nut on the cable clevis and lengthen or shorten the cable to obtain the proper clearance at the pedal pad, then tighten the jam nut.

NOTE: *On some older Jeeps, a side move-ment of the clutch and brake pedals may develop. This is the result of wear on the pedals, shafts, and bushings. One way to compensate for this wear is to install a pedal slack adjuster kit.*

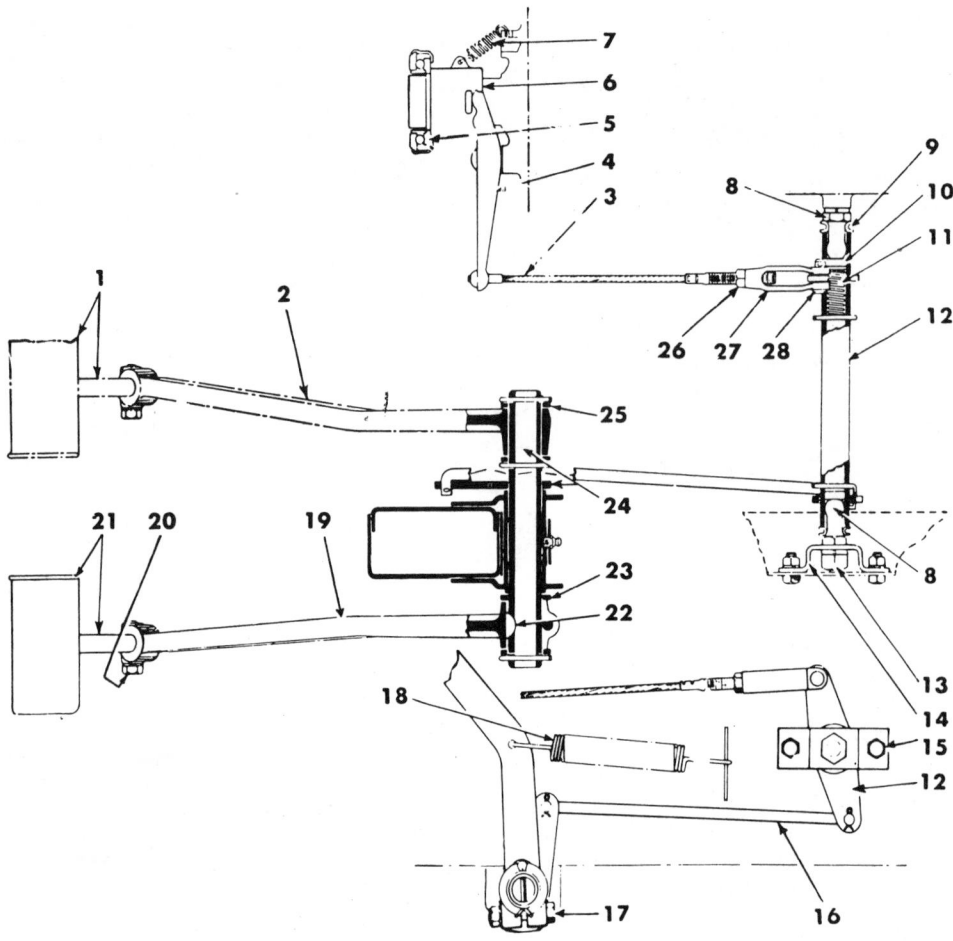

1. Brake pedal pad
2. Brake pedal
3. Control cable
4. Control lever
5. Release bearing
6. Release bearing carrier
7. Bearing carrier spring
8. Ball stud
9. Dust seal
10. Control tube retainer
11. Control tube spring
12. Control tube and lever
13. Ball stud nut
14. Frame bracket
15. Bracket to frame bolt
16. Pedal rod
17. Pedal clamp bolt
18. Pedal retracting spring
19. Clutch pedal
20. Pedal pad clamp bolt
21. Clutch pedal pad
22. Pedal to shaft key
23. Pedal shaft washer
24. Pedal shaft
25. Brake master cylinder tee bar
26. Adjusting yoke lock nut
27. Adjusting yoke
28. Adjusting yoke clevis pin

CJ-2A, CJ-3A clutch linkage

Pedal Height Adjustment—1972 Only

The clutch pedal has an adjustable stop located on the pedal support bracket directly behind the instrument cluster.

Adjust the stop to provide the specified clearance between the top of the pedal pad and the closest point on the bare floor pan. The distance must be 8 in.

Control Cable Adjustment—1972 Only

1. Lift up the clutch pedal against the pedal support bracket stop.

2. Unhook the clutch fork return spring.

3. Loosen the ball adjusting nut until some cable slack exists.

4. Adjust the ball adjusting nut until the slack is removed from the cable and the

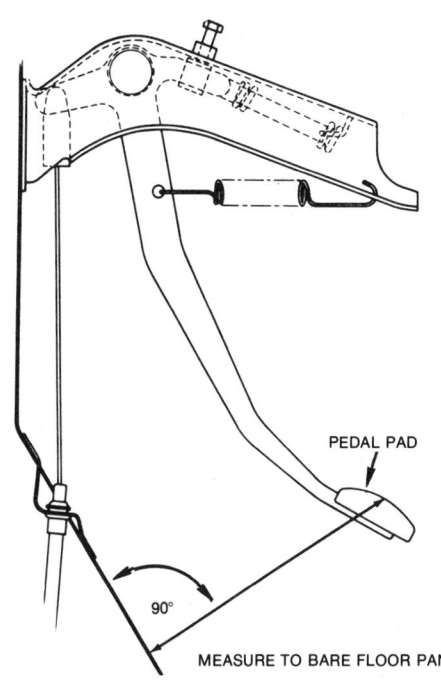

PEDAL PAD

90°

MEASURE TO BARE FLOOR PAN

Clutch pedal height adjustment—1972 only

clutch throwout bearing contacts the pressure plate fingers.

5. Back off the ball adjusting nut ¾ of a turn to provide the proper amount of free play. Tighten the jam nut.

6. Hook the clutch fork return spring.

1973–75

1. Adjust the bellcrank outer support bracket to provide approximately ⅛ in. of bellcrank end play.

2. Lift up the clutch pedal against the pedal stop.

3. On the clutch push rod (pedal to bellcrank) adjust the lower ball pivot assembly onto or off the rod (as required) to position the bellcrank inner lever parallel to the front face of the clutch housing (slightly forward from vertical).

4. Adjust the clutch fork release rod (bellcrank to release fork) to obtain the maximum specified clutch pedal free play of ¾ in. on 1973–74 models and 1 in. on 1975 models.

1976–81

NOTE: *4-151 models have a non-adjustable hydraulic clutch.*

1. Lift the pedal up against the stop.

2. Loosen the release rod adjuster jam nut, under the vehicle.

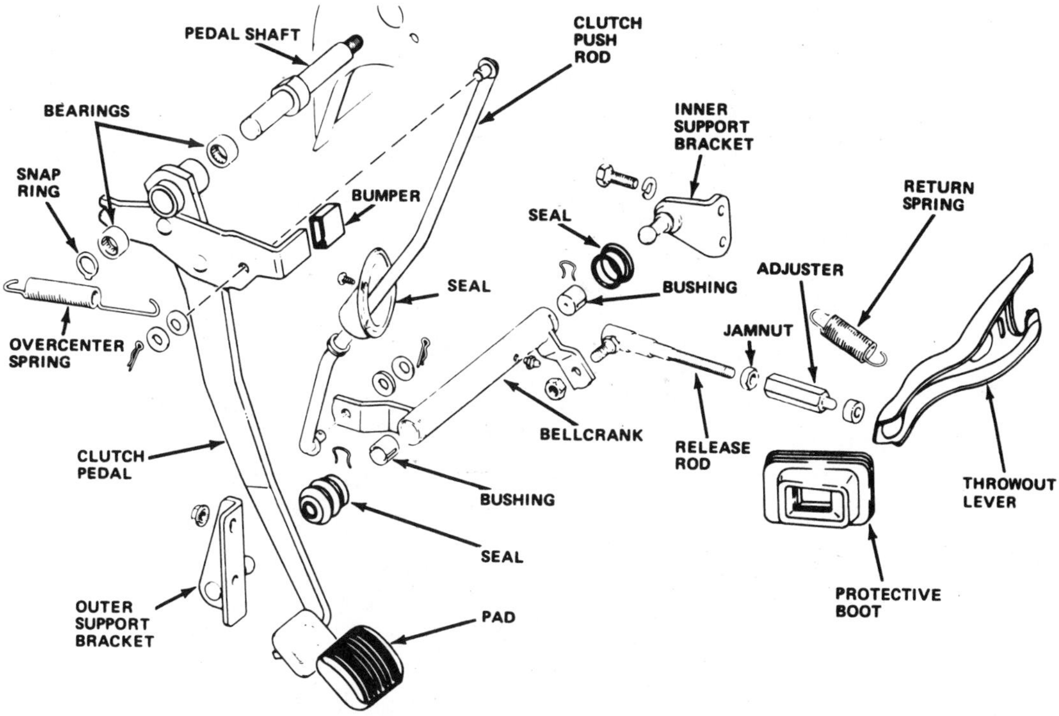

PEDAL SHAFT

CLUTCH
PUSH
ROD

BEARINGS

INNER
SUPPORT
BRACKET

RETURN
SPRING

SNAP
RING

BUMPER

SEAL

ADJUSTER

SEAL

BUSHING

OVERCENTER
SPRING

SEAL

JAMNUT

CLUTCH
PEDAL

BELLCRANK

RELEASE
ROD

THROWOUT
LEVER

BUSHING

OUTER
SUPPORT
BRACKET

SEAL

PAD

PROTECTIVE
BOOT

6-232, 258 and 8-304 clutch linkage

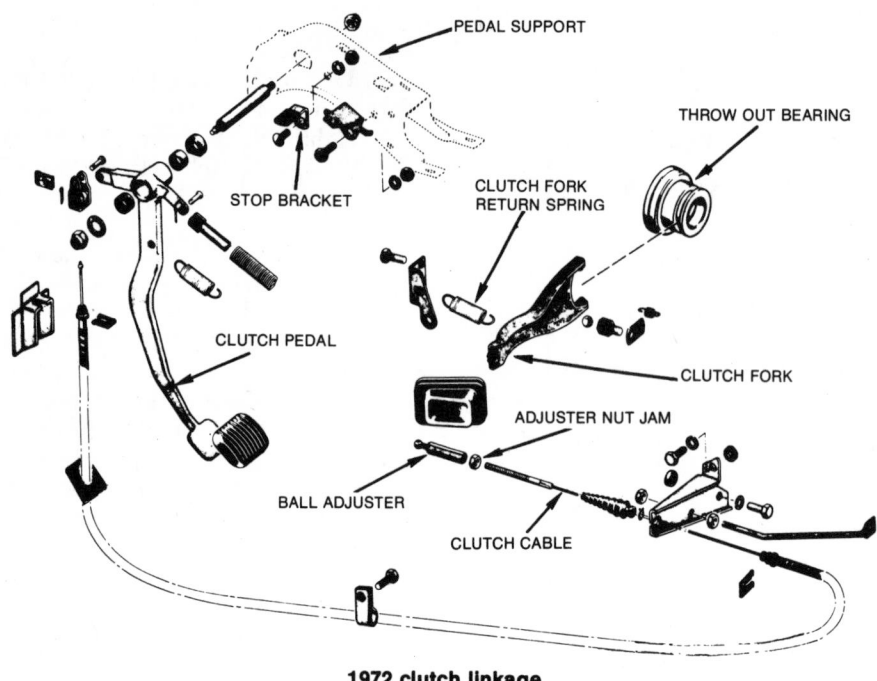

1972 clutch linkage

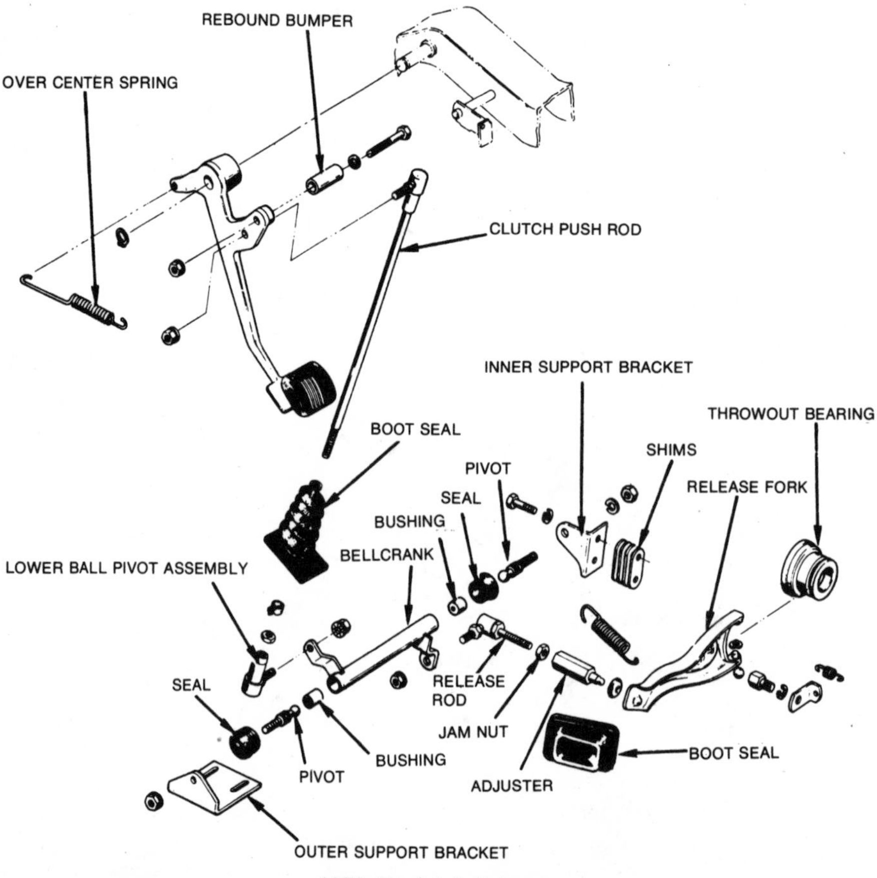

1973–75 clutch linkage

3. Adjust the pedal free-play to about one inch.

4. Tighten the jam nut.

AUTOMATIC TRANSMISSION

Jeep vehicles through 1979 use the General Motors Turbo Hydra-Matic 400 unit. Beginning in 1980, Jeep vehicles use the Chrysler model 904 TorqueFlite unit. See Chapter 1 for oil and filter change.

SHIFT LINKAGE ADJUSTMENT

1976-79

1. Place the column shift lever in Neutral.

2. Loosen the gearshift rod clamp adjustment locknut under the vehicle. Make sure that the lever on the transmission is fully in the Neutral position.

3. Tighten the locknut.

4. Check that the engine can be started only in Park and Neutral and that each gear position is fully engaged.

1980-81

1. Raise and support the vehicle on jack stands.

2. Loosen the shift rod trunnion jamnuts.

3. Remove the lockpin retaining the trunnion to the bell crank and disengage the trunnion at the bell crank.

4. Place the shift lever in Park and lock the column.

5. Move the transmission case lever as far into the Park (rearward) position as possible. Check that the driveshaft will not rotate in this position.

6. Adjust the shift rod trunnion to obtain free pin fit in the bell crank arm and tighten the trunnion jamnuts.

NOTE: *All play must be eliminated for proper adjustment. Eliminate play by pulling downward on the shift rod and pressing on the outer bell crank.*

7. Move the gearshift lever to Park and Neutral and check to see if the engine starts.

8. Road test the vehicle.

BAND ADJUSTMENTS

NOTE: *The GM Turbo Hydra-Matic 400 used in 1976–79 models, does not have any band adjustments. The following apply only to the Chrysler built 904 used in 1980 and later models.*

Front Band

1. Raise and support the vehicle on jack stands.

2. Loosen the adjusting screw locknut and back the locknut off five turns.

3. Mark the adjusting screw location. Check that it turns freely. If not, squirt some Liquid Wrench,® WD-40® or similar substance on it.

4. Tighten the adjusting screw to 36 in. lb. using, if necessary, an adaptor such as the one pictured, and a $5/16''$ square socket.

NOTE: *If the adaptor is not used, and the torque wrench is applied directly to the adjuster, tighten the adjuster to 72 in. lb.*

5. Back off the adjuster two full turns.

6. Hold the adjuster firmly and tighten the locknut to 35 ft. lb.

7. Lower the vehicle.

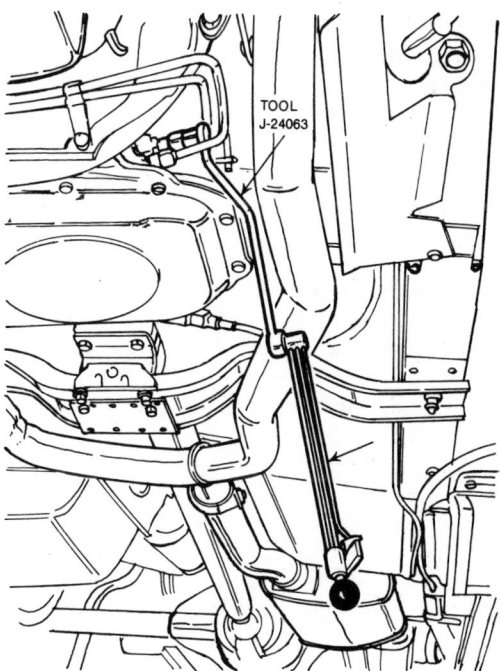

Chrysler 904 front band adjustment

Rear Band

NOTE: *The transmission oil pan must be removed to gain access to the adjusting screw.*

1. Raise and support the vehicle on jack stands.

2. Remove the pan.

3. Remove the adjusting screw locknut.

4. Tighten the adjusting screw to 41 in. lb. using a torque wrench and a $1/4''$ 6-point socket.

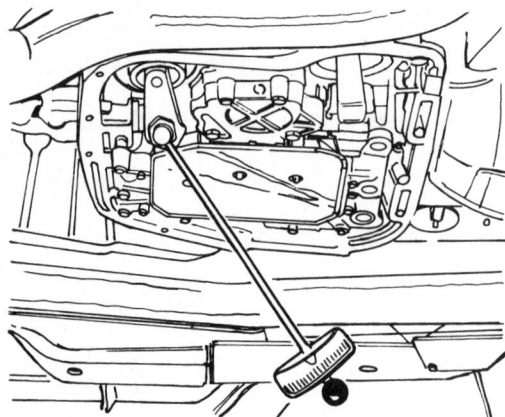

Chrysler 904 rear band adjustment

5. Back off the adjusting screw four full turns.

6. Hold the adjusting screw firmly, install the locknut and tighten it to 35 in. lb.

7. Install the oil pan and new gasket. Torque the bolts to 150 in. lb.

8. Lower the vehicle. Fill the transmission with Dexron II fluid.

THROTTLE LINKAGE ADJUSTMENT 1980–81

4-151

1. Remove the air cleaner.

2. Remove the spark plug wire holder from the throttle cable bracket and move the holder and wires aside.

3. Raise and support the vehicle on jack stands.

4. Hold the throttle control lever rearward against its stop. Hook one end of a spare spring to the lever and hook the opposite end to any convenient point. This will hold the lever in position.

5. Lower the vehicle.

6. Block the choke open and move the carburetor linkage completely off the fast idle cam.

7. On vehicles without air conditioning, turn the ignition to ON to energize the solenoid.

8. Unlock the throttle control cable by releasing the T shaped adjuster clamp on the cable by lifting it upward with a small screwdriver.

9. Grasp the outer sheath of the cable and move the cable and sheath forward to remove any load on the cable bell crank.

10. Adjust the cable by moving the cable and sheath rearward until there is no play at all between the plastic cable and the bell crank ball.

11. When play has been eliminated, lock the cable by pressing the T shaped clamp downward until it snaps into place.

12. Turn the ignition off. Install all parts and remove the spare spring.

6-258

1. Disconnect the throttle control rod spring at the carburetor.

2. Raise and support the vehicle on jack stands.

3. Use the throttle control rod spring to hold the throttle control lever forward against its stop, by hooking one end of the spring on the throttle control lever and the other end on the throttle linkage bell crank

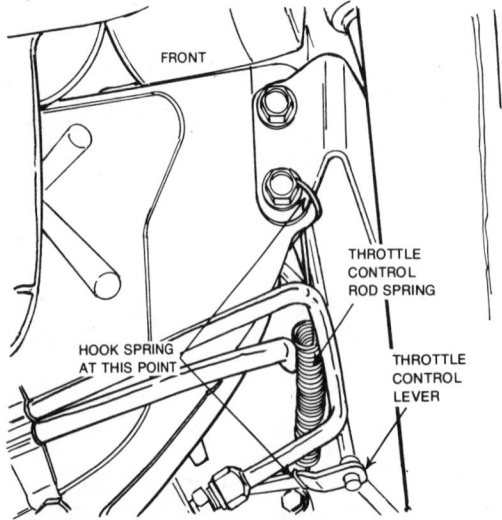

Installing the throttle control lever spring on the 4-151

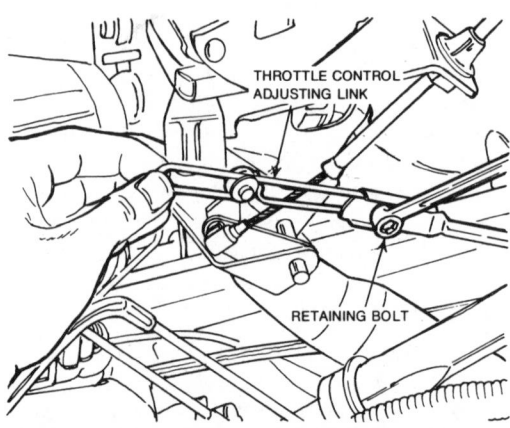

Tightening the link retaining bolt on 1980–81 6-258

bracket which is attached to the transmission housing.

4. Block the choke plate open and move the throttle linkage off the fast idle cam.

5. On carburetors equipped with a throttle operated solenoid valve, turn the ignition ON to energize the solenoid, then open the throttle halfway to allow the solenoid to lock and return the carburetor to the idle position.

6. Loosen the retaining bolt on the throttle control adjusting link. DO NOT REMOVE THE SPRING CLIP AND NYLON WASHER!

7. Pull on the end of the link to eliminate play and tighten the retaining bolt.

8. Remove the throttle control rod spring and install it on the control rod from where it came.

9. Lower the vehicle.

8-304

1. Disconnect the throttle control rod spring at the carburetor.

2. Raise and support the vehicle on jack stands.

3. Use the throttle control rod spring to hold the transmission throttle valve control lever against its stop.

4. Block the choke plate open and make sure the throttle linkage is off the fast idle cam.

NOTE: *On carburetors equipped with a throttle operated solenoid valve, turn the ignition to ON to energize the solenoid. Then turn the throttle half way to allow the solenoid to lock and return the carburetor to idle.*

5. Loosen the retaining bolt on the throttle control rod adjuster link. Remove the

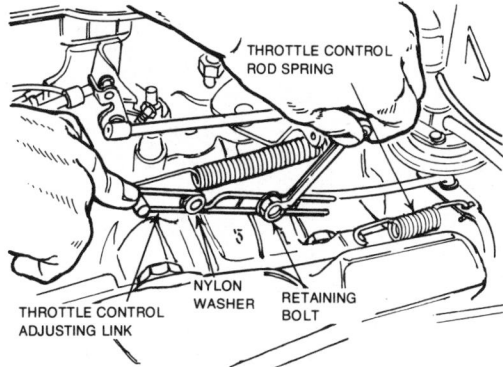

Tightening the link retaining bolt on 1980–81 8-304

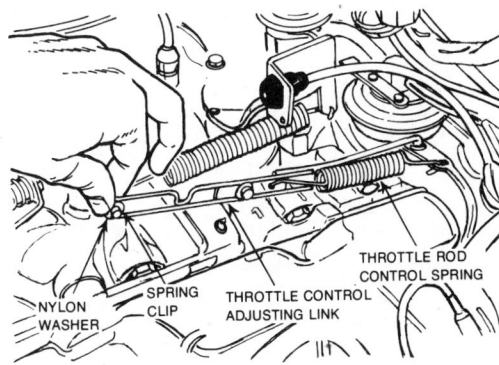

Installing the nylon washer and spring clip on 1980–81 8-304

spring clip and move the nylon washer to the rear of the link.

6. Push on the end of the link to eliminate play and tighten the link retaining bolt.

7. Install the nylon washer and spring clip.

8. Remove the throttle control rod spring and install it in its intended position.

9. Lower the vehicle.

NEUTRAL SAFETY SWITCH ADJUSTMENT

GM Turbo Hydra-Matic

This switch prevents the engine from being started in any position other than Park or Neutral. It also controls the backup lights.

1. Set the parking brake.

2. Make sure the shift linkage is adjusted correctly.

3. Remove the switch from the base of the steering column, inside the vehicle.

4. Shift into Park and lock the column by removing the key.

5. Move the switch lever until it aligns with the letter P on the back of the switch. Insert a $3/32$ in. drill bit in the hole below the letter N on the switch. Move the switch lever till it stops against the drill bit.

6. Install the switch to the column, tighten the screws, and remove the drill bit.

7. Check that the engine will start only in Park and Neutral, and that the backup lights come on only in Reverse.

Chrysler 904

This switch is mounted in the transmission and has no direct adjustment. Proper operation is determined by correct shift linkage adjustment.

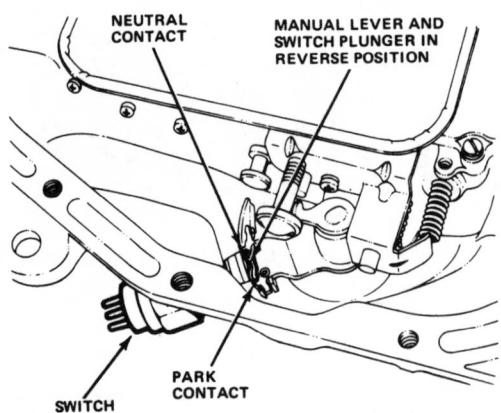

Chrysler 904 neutral start and backup light switch

REMOVAL AND INSTALLATION

1976–79

1. Remove the dipstick.
2. Detach the radiator shroud.
3. Mark the driveshafts for reinstallation.

4. If the vehicle has low range, disconnect the shift linkage and remove the unit.
5. Detach the speedometer cable.
6. Mark and remove the Emergency Drive hoses and wire.
7. Unbolt the vacuum line bracket at the rear of the transfer case.
8. Detach the downshift solenoid wire at the transmission.
9. Remove the starter.
10. Remove the torque converter housing inspection cover.
11. Matchmark the torque converter and drive plate for reassembly. Remove the bolts.
12. Remove the rear support cushion to crossmember nuts.
13. Support the transmission with a transmission jack, using a safety chain.
14. Remove the rear crossmember.
15. Detach the transmission shift linkage. Detach the linkage bracket, bushing, and lever from the frame.

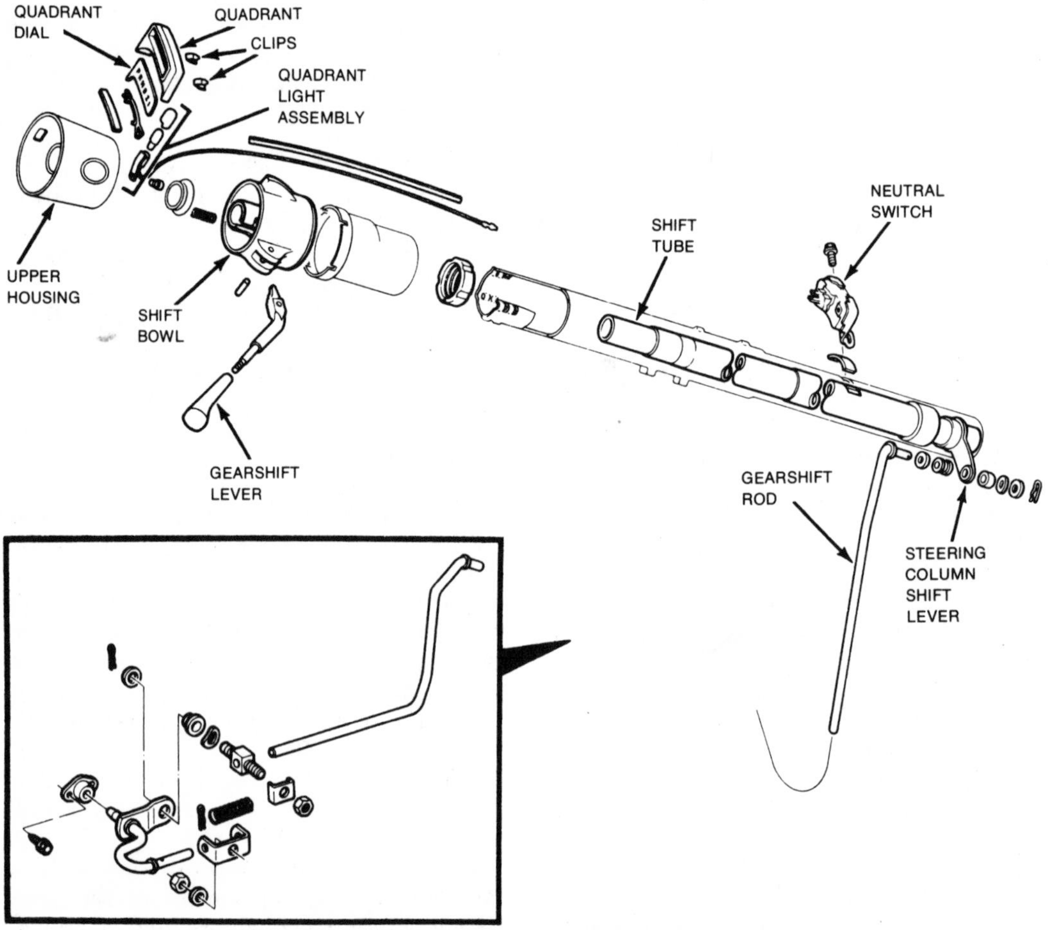

GM Turbo Hydra-Matic 400 shift linkage and neutral start switch

16. Detach and wire up the front drive-shaft.

17. Detach the cooler lines from the transmission.

18. Disconnect the vacuum hose at the modulator.

19. Support the engine.

20. Remove the converter housing to engine bolts.

21. Remove the dipstick tube.

22. Move the transmission back till it clears the engine. Hold the converter in place and lower the transmission.

23. On installation, align the torque converter and drive plate matchmarks. Dowels on the engine must line up with holes in the converter housing. Observe the following torque valves: transmission-to-engine bolts 42 ft. lbs; converter-to-drive plate bolts 30 ft. lb. The rest of the job requires replacing all the items removed in the previous steps. Fill the transmission as explained in Chapter 1.

1980–81

1. Remove the fan shroud.

2. Disconnect the transmission fill tube upper bracket.

3. Raise and support the vehicle on jack stands.

4. Remove the converter housing inspection cover.

5. Remove the fill tube.

6. Remove the starter.

7. Mark the driveshafts for installation.

8. Remove the driveshafts.

9. On 8-304 models, disconnect the exhaust pipes at the manifolds.

10. Disconnect the gearshift and throttle linkages.

11. Disconnect the neutral start switch.

12. Mark the driveplate and converter for realignment.

13. Remove the converter-to-driveplate bolts.

14. Take up the transmission weight with a floor jack. It's a good idea to chain the transmission to the jack.

15. Remove the rear crossmember-to-transmission bolts.

16. Remove the rear crossmember.

17. Lower the transmission slightly and disconnect the fluid cooler lines.

18. Remove the transmission-to-engine bolts.

19. Roll the transmission rearward to clear the crankshaft, lower the jack and remove the unit.

20. Installation is the reverse of removal. Observe the following torque values:
- transmission-to-engine bolts .. 28 ft. lb.
- converter-to-drive plate bolts
     4-151 .... 40 ft. lb.
     6 and 8 .... 26 ft. lb.

MANUAL TRANSFER CASE

Three different manual transfer cases have been used in Jeep vehicles:
- 1945–71 Spicer 18
- 1972–79 Dana 20
- 1980–81 Dana 300

These are all 2-speed units. The Spicer 18 is controlled by 2 floor-mounted levers, while all others are controlled by single floor mounted levers. One important note on CJ-2A models: beginning with serial number 24196, oil circulation was provided between the transmission and the Spicer 18 by the drilling of passages between the units. The rear face of the transmission case is drilled with two $7/16$ inch holes and two ¼ inch holes. The front face of the transfer case is drilled with the $7/16$ inch holes.

REMOVAL AND INSTALLATION
Through 1971

The transfer case can be removed without removing the transmission.

1. Drain the transfer case and transmission and replace the drain plugs.

2. Disconnect the brake cable.

3. Disconnect the front and rear driveshafts at the transfer case.

4. Disconnect the speedometer cable at the transfer case.

5. Disconnect the transfer case shift levers. On vehicles equipped with two shift levers loosen the set screw and remove the pivot pin. Use a prying tool to pry the shift lever springs away from the shift levers. On models equipped with a single shift lever remove the pivot pin cotter key and the adjusting rod attaching nut to remove the shift lever.

6. Remove the cover plate on the rear face of the transfer case or power take-off shift unit. Remove the cotter key, nut and washer from the transmission main shaft.

7. If possible, remove the transfer case main drive gear from the transmission main shaft. If it is not possible, continue on.

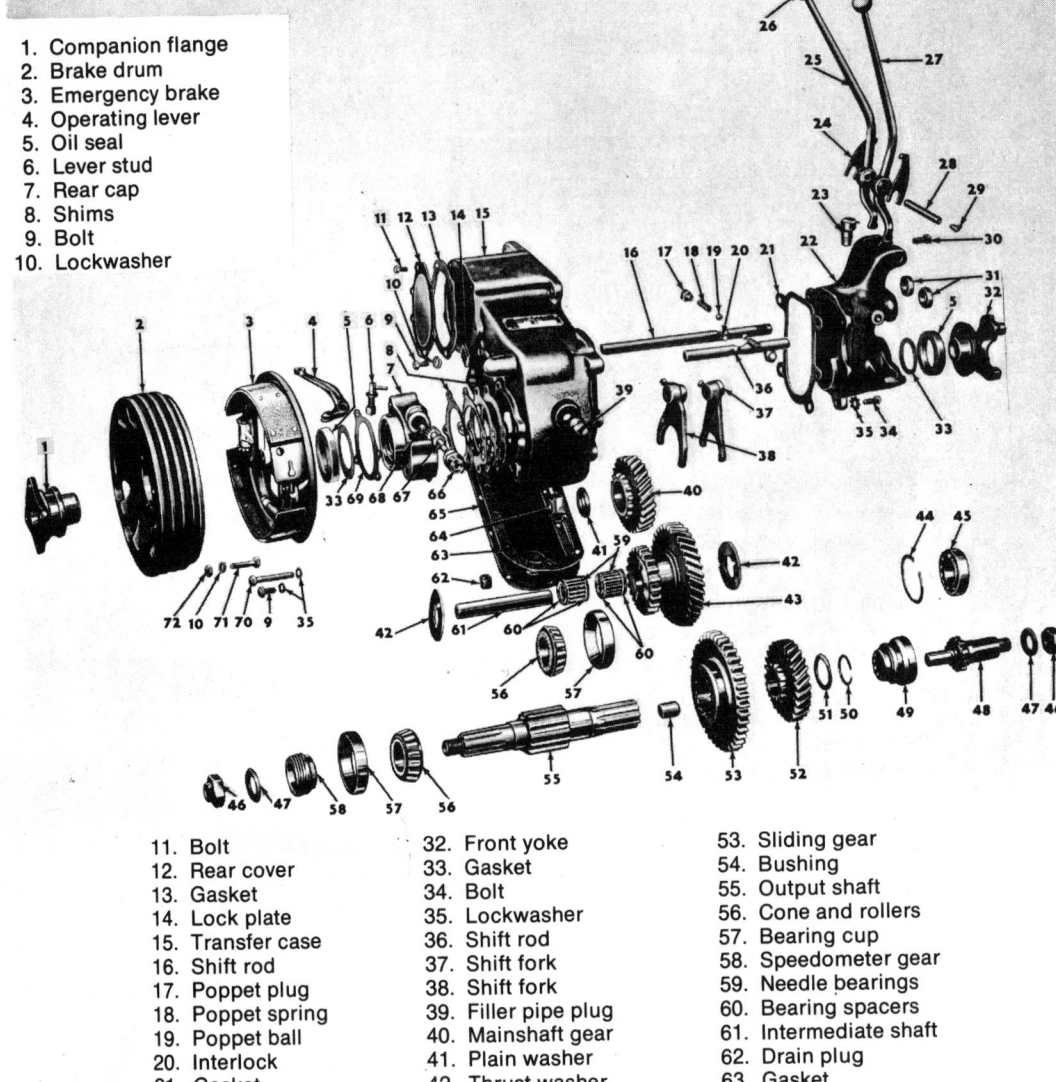

1. Companion flange
2. Brake drum
3. Emergency brake
4. Operating lever
5. Oil seal
6. Lever stud
7. Rear cap
8. Shims
9. Bolt
10. Lockwasher

11. Bolt	32. Front yoke	53. Sliding gear
12. Rear cover	33. Gasket	54. Bushing
13. Gasket	34. Bolt	55. Output shaft
14. Lock plate	35. Lockwasher	56. Cone and rollers
15. Transfer case	36. Shift rod	57. Bearing cup
16. Shift rod	37. Shift fork	58. Speedometer gear
17. Poppet plug	38. Shift fork	59. Needle bearings
18. Poppet spring	39. Filler pipe plug	60. Bearing spacers
19. Poppet ball	40. Mainshaft gear	61. Intermediate shaft
20. Interlock	41. Plain washer	62. Drain plug
21. Gasket	42. Thrust washer	63. Gasket
22. Front cap	43. Intermediate gear	64. Nut
23. Breather	44. Snap ring	65. Bottom cover
24. Shift lever spring	45. Bearing	66. Sleeve
25. Shift lever	46. Nut	67. Speedometer gear
26. Shift lever handle	47. Washer	68. Bushing
27. Shift lever	48. Output clutch shaft	69. Gasket
28. Pivot pin	49. Output clutch gear	70. Bolt
29. Lubrication fitting	50. Snap ring	71. Bolt
30. Set screw	51. Thrust washer	72. Hex nut
31. Oil seal	52. Output shaft gear	

Spicer 18 transfer case used on late CJ-3B and early CJ-5

8. Remove the transmission-to-transfer case mounting bracket bolt and nut.

9. Remove the transmission-to-transfer case attaching bolts.

10. Remove the transfer case. If the transfer case main drive gear has not been removed in step 7, proceed as follows: Brace the end of the transmission main shaft so that it cannot be moved in the transmission, then pull the transfer case to the rear to loosen the gear. Remove the gear. When separating the two housings, be careful that the transmission main shaft bearing, which bears in both housings, remains in the transmission case.

NOTE: *If the transfer case is being removed from the transmission with the two*

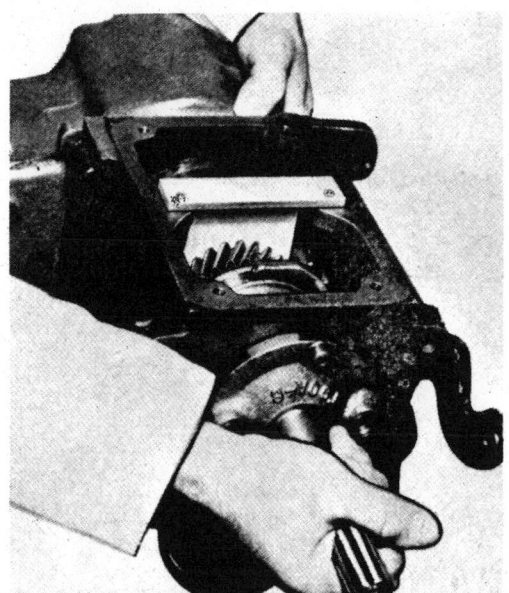

Transmission mainshaft retaining plate installed for removing the Spicer 18 transfer case from the transmission

units out of the vehicle, use the above procedure starting from step 6 and replacing step 10 with the following procedure:

10A. Remove the transmission shift housing. Install a transmission mainshaft retaining plate to prevent the mainshaft from pulling out of the transmission case. Should this tool be unavailable, loop a piece of wire around the mainshaft directly in back of the mainshaft second speed gear. Install the transmission shift housing right and left front attaching bolts part way into the transmission case. Twist the wire and attach each end to one of the screws. Tighten the wire. With the mainshaft securely in place, support the transfer case and with a rawhide mallet or brass drift and hammer, then tap lightly on the end of the mainshaft to loosen the gear and separate the two units.

11. Install in the reverse order of removal taking note of the following: When installing the rear adapter plate on a four-speed transmission, be sure that the cap screw heads do not protrude beyond the adapter plate face and that they do not interfere with the transfer case fitting tightly against the rear adapter plate. Also, when installing the transfer case gear on the transmission rear splined drive shaft, tighten the large gear nut securely and insert the cotter pin. Sink the cotter pin well into the nut slots so it will clear the power take-off drive (if so equipped).

1972–1975

1. Remove the transfer case shift lever knob and trim ring and boot.
2. Remove the transfer case shift lever.
3. Lift and support the vehicle.
4. Drain the transfer case lubricant.
5. Mark the yokes for reference during assembly and disconnect the front and rear driveshafts from the transfer case.
6. Install the transfer case drain plug.
7. Disconnect the parking brake cable at the equalizer and mounting bracket.
8. Disconnect the speedometer cable.
9. Remove the screws which attach the transfer case to the transmission. Install two ⅜ x 4 in. threaded dowel pins, one on each side of the case.
10. Remove the transfer case.
11. Remove the gasket between the transmission and the transfer case.
12. Place a new gasket on the dowel pins in the transmission case before installing the transfer case back onto the transmission.
13. Shift the transfer case to 4WD Low position.
14. Position the transfer case on the dowel pins.
15. Rotate the transfer case output shaft until the gears engage with the output gear on the transmission. Slide the transfer case forward to the transmission.
NOTE: *Be sure that the transfer case fits flush against the transmission. Severe damage will result if the transfer case bolts are tightened while the transfer case is binding.*
16. Install one attaching screw. Remove the dowel pins and install all of the remaining attaching screws.
17. Connect the driveshafts in the same positions from which they were removed.
18. Connect the speedometer cable and parking brake cable.
19. Fill the transfer case with the proper amount of lubricant. See Chapter 1.
20. Lower the vehicle.
21. Install the transfer case lever, trim boot and lever knob.

1976–79

1. Remove the shift lever knob, trim ring, and boot.
2. Remove the transmission access cover from the floorpan.
3. Drain the lubricant from the transfer case and transmission.

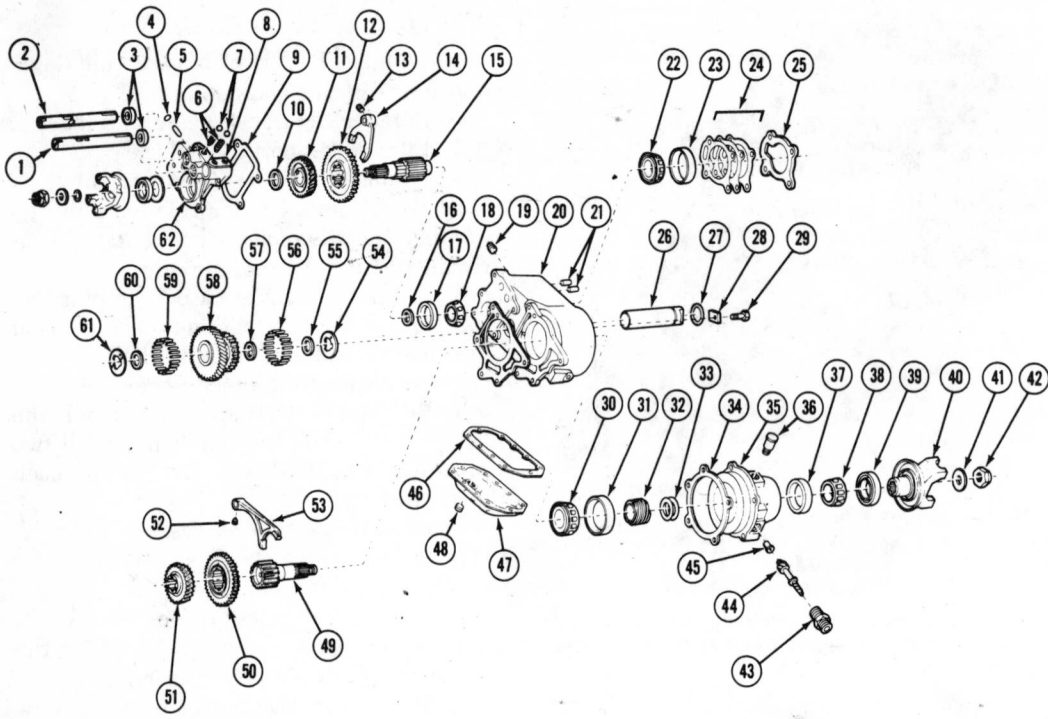

1. Shift rod—rear output shaft shift fork
2. Shift rod—front output shaft shift fork
3. Shift rod oil seal
4. Interlock plug
5. Interlock
6. Poppet ball spring
7. Poppet ball
8. Front bearing cap
9. Front bearing cap gasket
10. Front output shaft thrust washer
11. Front output shaft gear
12. Front output shaft sliding gear
13. Setscrew
14. Front output shaft shift fork
15. Front output shaft
16. Front output shaft spacer
17. Front output shaft front bearing cup
18. Front output shaft front bearing
19. Filler plug
20. Transfer case
21. Thimble cover
22. Front output shaft rear bearing
23. Front output shaft rear bearing cup
24. Front output shaft rear bearing cup shims
25. Cover plate
26. Intermediate shaft
27. Intermediate shaft O-ring
28. Lock plate
29. Lock plate bolt
30. Rear output shaft front bearing
31. Rear output shaft front bearing cup
32. Speedometer drive gear
33. Rear output shaft bearing shim
34. Rear bearing cap gasket
35. Rear bearing cap
36. Breather
37. Rear bearing cap cup
38. Rear bearing cap bearing
39. Rear bearing cap oil seal
40. Rear yoke
41. Rear yoke washer
42. Rear yoke nut
43. Speedometer sleeve
44. Speedometer driven gear
45. Speedometer bushing
46. Bottom cover gasket
47. Bottom cover
48. Drain plug
49. Rear output shaft
50. Rear output shaft sliding gear
51. Mainshaft gear
52. Setscrew
53. Rear output shaft shift fork
54. Intermediate gear thrust washer
55. Intermediate gear bearing spacer
56. Intermediate gear shaft needle bearings
57. Intermediate gear bearing spacer
58. Intermediate gear
59. Intermediate gear shaft needle bearings
60. Intermediate gear bearing spacer
61. Intermediate gear thrust washer
62. Front bearing cap

Dana 20 transfer case components

4. Disconnect the torque reaction bracket from the frame crossmember, if so equipped.

5. Support the engine and transmission by placing a jackstand under the clutch housing.

6. Remove the rear frame crossmember.

7. Mark the driveshaft yokes for refer-

ence during assembly and disconnect the front and rear driveshafts from the transfer case.

8. Disconnect the speedometer cable from the transfer case.

9. Remove the bolts attaching the transfer case to the transmission and remove the transfer case. Remove the gasket which goes between the transmission and transfer case.

NOTE: *There is one transfer case attaching bolt located at the bottom right corner of the transmission that must be removed from the front end of the case.*

10. Install the transmission-to-transfer case gasket on the transmission.

11. Shift the transfer case into the 4WD low position.

12. Install a ⅜-16 x 4 in. dowel pin on each side of the transmission to assist in guiding the transfer case into place during installation.

13. Position the transfer case on the dowel pins and slide the case forward until it seats against the transmission. It may be necessary to rotate the transfer case output shaft until the mainshaft gear on the transmission engages the rear output shaft gear in the transfer case.

NOTE: *Make sure that the transfer case is flush against the transmission. The case could be cracked if the attaching bolts are tightened while the transfer case is cocked or binded.*

14. Install two transfer case attaching bolts, but do not tighten them completely.

15. Remove the dowel pins and install the remaining attaching bolts, tightening them all to 30 ft. lbs.

16. Fill the transfer case with SAE 80W-90 gear lubricant (API GL-4).

17. Assemble the remaining components in the reverse order of removal.

1980–81

1. On models with automatic transmission, remove the shift lever knob, trim ring, and boot from the transfer case shift lever.

2. On models with manual transmission, remove the shift lever knob, trim ring, and boot from the transmission and transfer case levers.

3. Remove the transmission access plate from the floor pan.

4. Raise and support the vehicle on jack stands.

5. Support the engine at the clutch housing and remove the rear cross member.

7. Mark the front and rear driveshaft-to-transfer case position and disconnect them at the transfer case.

8. Disconnect the speedometer cable at the transfer case.

9. Disconnect the parking brake cable at the equalizer.

10. Disconnect the exhaust pipe bracket at the transfer case.

11. Unbolt the transfer case from the transmission and remove it.

12. Install is the reverse of removal. Place the transfer case in the 4L position before installing. Torque the transfer case-to-transmission bolts to 30 ft. lb. Torque the driveshaft strap bolts to 16 ft. lb.

NOTE: *Some 1980–81 Vehicles have experienced difficult transfer case shifting. This may be the result of the transfer case shift lever shaft being bent at the threaded end. To correct this condition, the shift lever shaft and, if necessary, the lever must be replaced. The part numbers are:*
- *Shaft: 5360045*
- *Lever w/4-cyl & SR-4, CJ-5 and CJ-7: 5360044*
- *Lever w/6 or 8 & T-176, CJ-7: 5360044*
- *Lever w/6-cyl & SR-4, CJ-7: 5360129*

1. Remove the transfer case.

2. Remove the defective lever shaft, and lever.

3. Install new lever shaft and lever.

4. Install the transfer case.

TRANSFER CASE SHIFT LINKAGE ADJUSTMENT

The only transfer case linkage that is adjustable is the single lever type on some Spicer 18 models through 1971. This linkage should be adjusted to give ½ in. clearance between the floor pan and the lever when in four wheel drive, low range.

AUTOMATIC TRANSFER CASE

Quadra-Trac®

The Warner Quadra-Trac® full-time, automatic transfer case was offered as optional equipment on CJ-7 models from 1976–79. The option was dropped after the 1979 model year.

NOTE: *Complete assembly removal is normally not required except when the front output shaft, front annular bearing, transmission output shaft seals or the transfer*

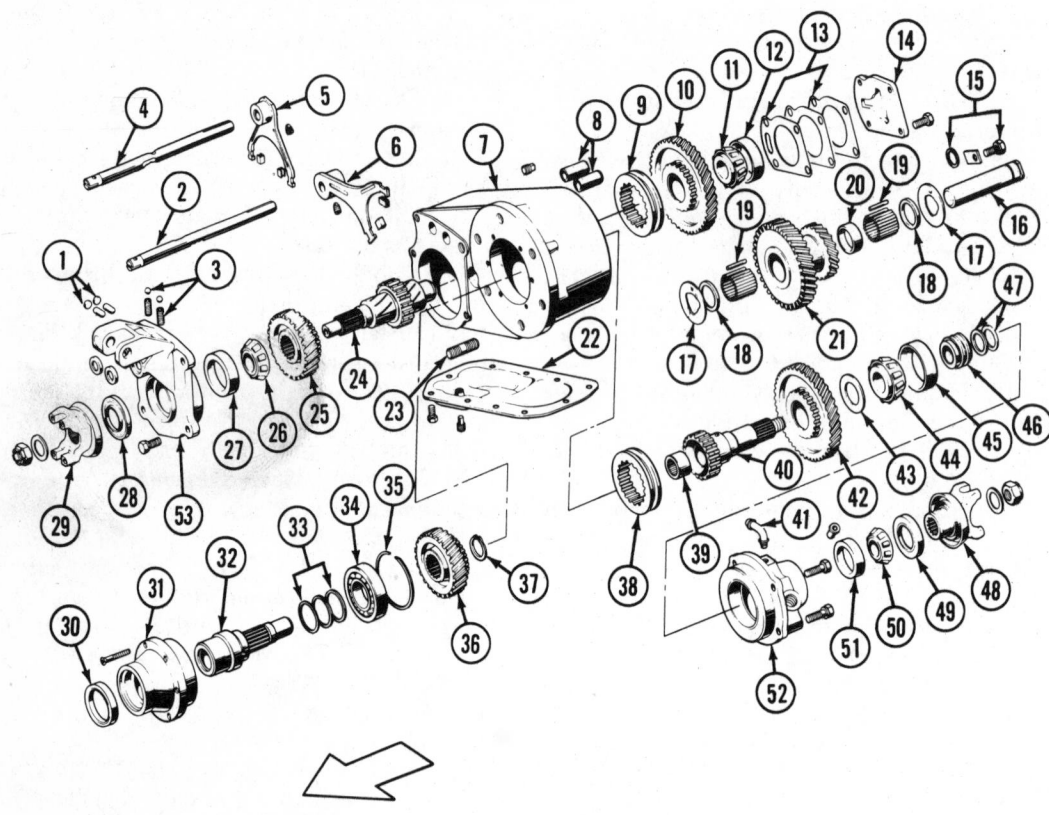

Dana 300 transfer case components

1. Interlock plugs and interlocks
2. Shift rod—rear output shaft fork
3. Poppet balls and springs
4. Shift rod—front output shaft fork
5. Front output shaft shift fork
6. Rear output shaft shift fork
7. Transfer case
8. Thimble covers
9. Clutch sleeve—front output shaft
10. Clutch gear—front output shaft
11. Bearing—front output shaft rear
12. Race—front output shaft bearing
13. End play shims—front output shaft
14. Cover plate
15. Lock plate, bolt and washer
16. Intermediate gear shaft
17. Thrust washer
18. Bearing spacer (thin)
19. Intermediate gear shaft needle bearings
20. Bearing spacer (thick)
21. Intermediate gear
22. Bottom cover
23. Stud (case-to-trans.)
24. Front output shaft
25. Front output shaft gear
26. Front ouput shaft bearing (front)
27. Front output shaft bearing race
28. Oil seal
29. Front yoke
30. Seal
31. Support—input shaft
32. Input shaft
33. Shims
34. Input shaft bearing
35. Input shaft bearing snap ring
36. Rear output shaft gear
37. Snap ring
38. Clutch sleeve—rear output shaft
39. Input shaft rear bearing (needle) (or pilot bearing)
40. Rear output shaft
41. Vent
42. Clutch gear—rear output shaft
43. Thrust washer
44. Bearing—rear output shaft front
45. Race—rear output shaft bearing
46. Speedometer drive gear
47. End play shims
48. Rear yoke
49. Rear output shaft oil seal
50. Bearing—rear output shaft rear
51. Bearing race
52. Rear bearing cap
53. Front bearing cap

case (front housing) require service. To service the chain, drive sprocket, differential unit, diaphragm control system, needle bearing, thrust washer or rear output shaft, the rear half of the Quadra-Trac transfer case can be removed, giving access to these components without removing the unit from the vehicle.

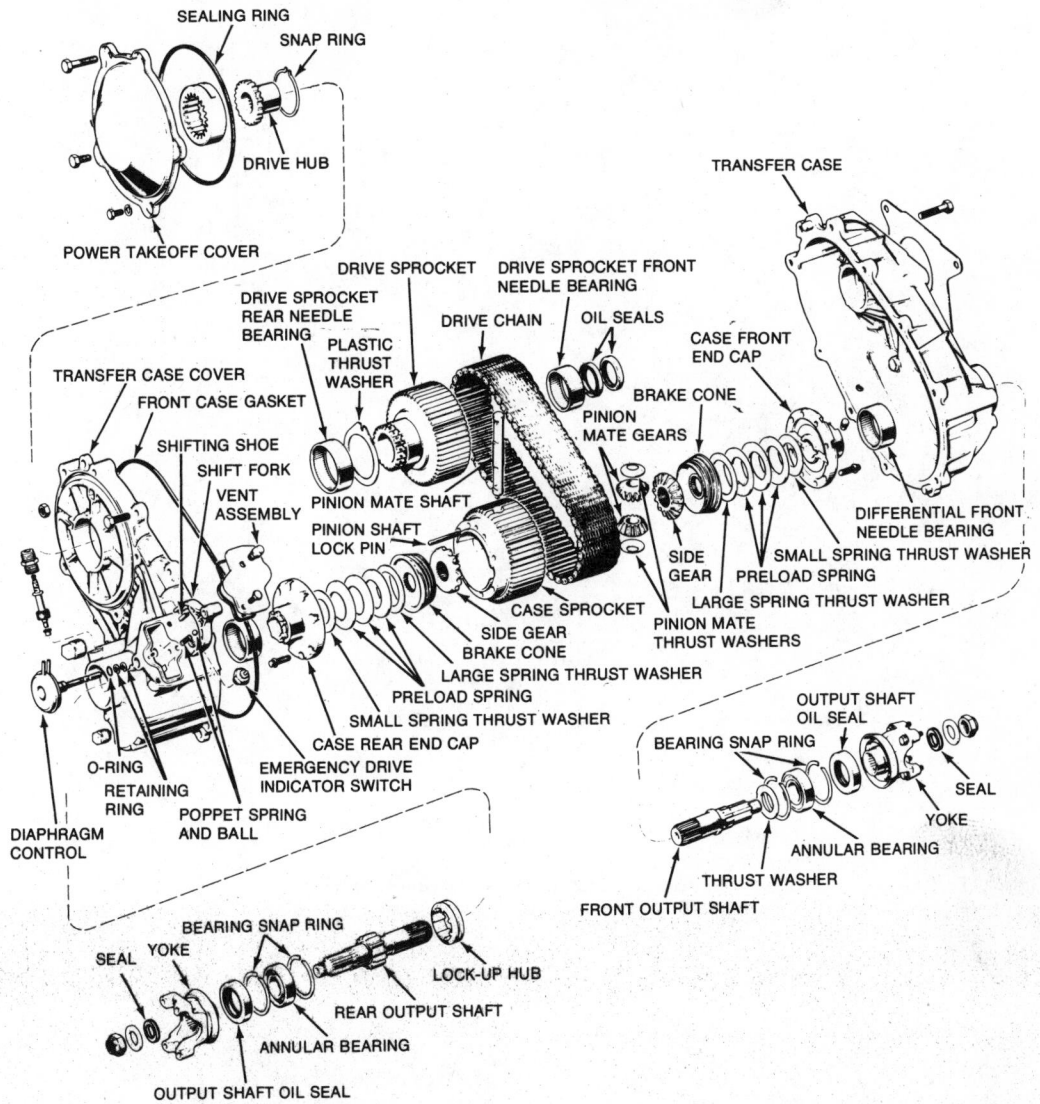

Warner Quadra-Trac® transfer case without low range

REMOVAL AND INSTALLATION

1. Raise and support the vehicle.

2. Mark the front and rear output shaft yokes and universal joints to provide alignment references to be used during assembly.

3. Disconnect the front driveshaft rear universal joint from the transfer case front yoke.

4. Disconnect the rear driveshaft front universal joint from the transfer case rear yoke.

5. Remove the bolts that attach the exhaust pipe support bracket to the transfer case. Support the transmission and remove the rear crossmember.

6. Mark and remove the diaphragm control vacuum hoses, lock-out indicator switch wire and speedometer cable.

7. Disconnect the parking brake cable guide from the pivot on the right frame side.

8. Remove the two transfer case-to-transmission bolts which enter from the front side and the two that enter from the rear side.

9. Move the transfer case assembly backward until the unit is free of the transmission output shaft and lower the assembly from the vehicle.

10. Remove all gasket material from the rear of the transmission and install the Quadra-Trac unit in the reverse order of re-

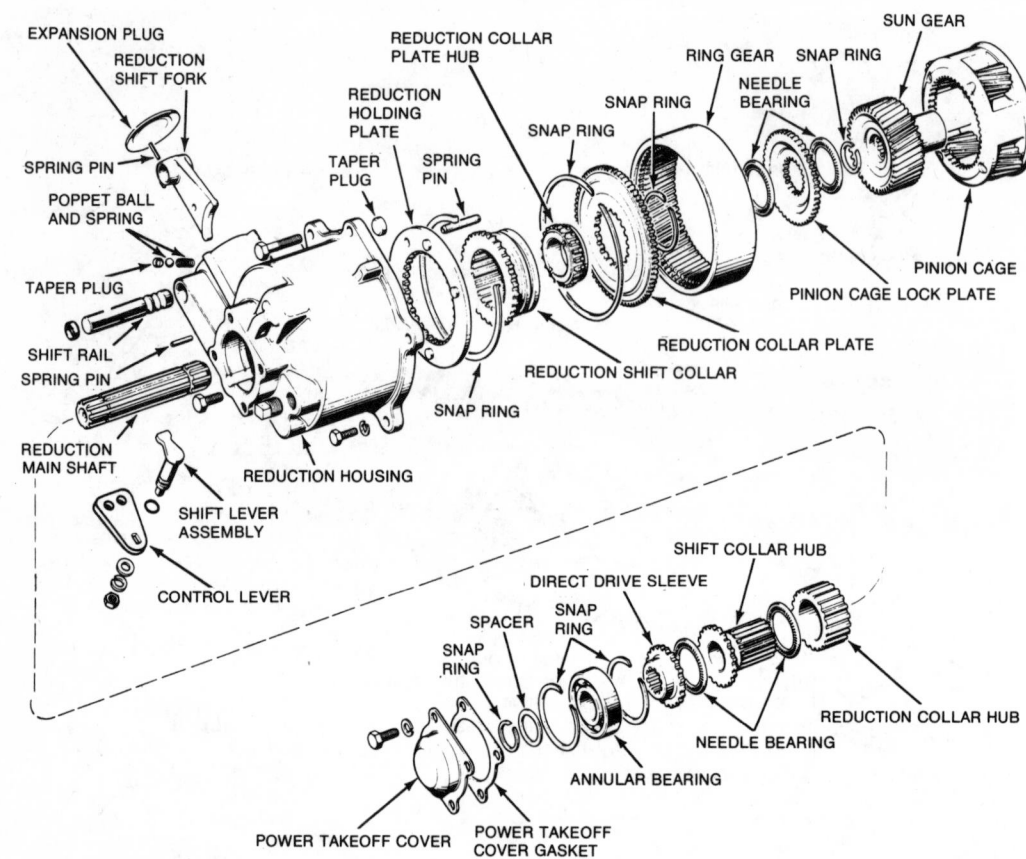

Warner Quadra-Trac® low range unit

moval. Tighten the attaching bolts to 15–25 ft. lbs.

POWER TAKE-OFF

Jeep vehicles were available with an optional power take-off unit. The PTO consists of four assemblies:

1. The shift unit, mounted on the transfer case.
2. The driveshaft and U-joints
3. The shaft drive assembly
4. The pulley drive assembly

The shaft drive exits the rear of the vehicle and is designed to operate trailed equipment. The pulley drive is driven by the shaft drive and is designed to operate stationary equipment by a belt drive. The shaft drive assembly was installed far more frequently than was the pulley drive assembly.

Shift Assembly

REMOVAL AND INSTALLATION

Drive for the PTO is taken from the transfer case main drive gear through an internal sliding gear. The sliding gear is mounted in the shift housing.

1. Remove the bolts in the driveshaft companion flange at the PTO front U-joint.
2. Unbolt and remove the shift lever.
3. Remove the five bolts securing the shift unit to the transfer case and pull it rearward from the case.
4. Installation is the reverse of removal.

DISASSEMBLY AND ASSEMBLY

1. Carefully pry the shift rail and fork forward to clear the poppet ball and spring. Be careful to avoid damaging or losing the ball and spring. Remove the shifting sleeve.

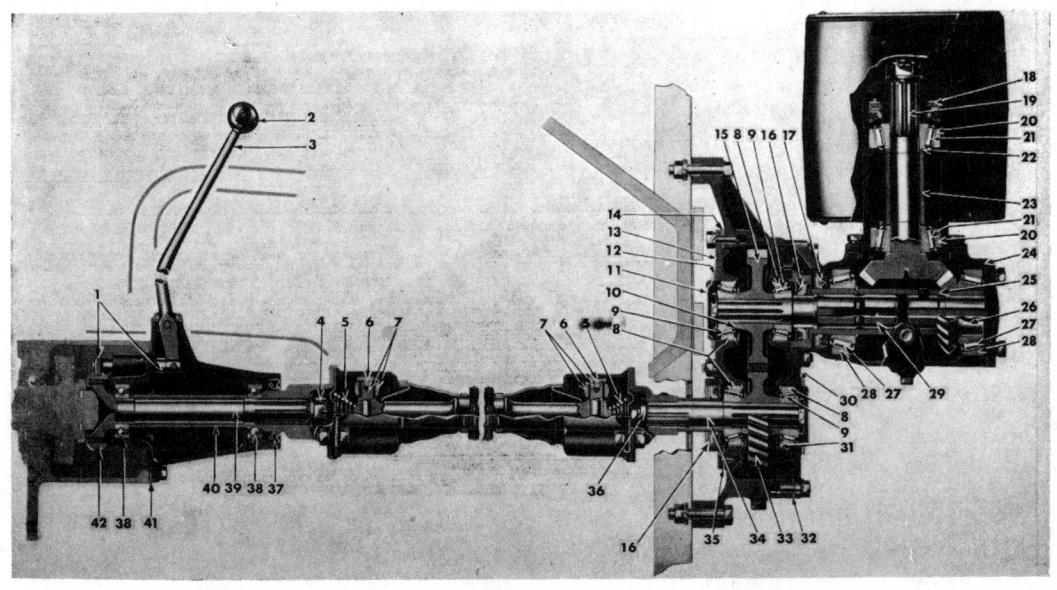

1. Fork and rod	15. Gear	29. Shaft
2. Ball	16. Oil seal	30. Gasket
3. Lever	17. Oil seal	31. Shims
4. Nut	18. Oil seal	32. Gasket
5. Button and spring	19. Gear and shaft	33. Gear
6. Spring	20. Cup	34. Shaft
7. Trunnion and ball	21. Cone and roller	35. Gasket
8. Cup	22. Shims	36. Washer
9. Bearing	23. Spacer	37. Oil seal
10. Snap ring	24. Shims	38. Ball bearing
11. Plate	25. Shims	39. Gear and shaft
12. Gasket	26. Pinion	40. Spacer
13. Retainer	27. Cone and roller	41. Gasket
14. Gasket	28. Cup	42. Sleeve

Power Take-Off assembly

2. Remove the attaching nut and the companion flange.

3. Drive the shaft forward out of the housing.

4. Remove the spacer and bearing from the shaft.

5. Remove the bearing from the housing.

6. Clean and inspect all parts and assemble in reverse of disassembly.

Shaft Drive Unit

REMOVAL AND INSTALLATION

The standard six-splined 1⅜ in. diameter output shaft is driven through two helical cut gears mounted in a housing attached to the vehicle at the center of the frame rear crossmember.

1. Disconnect the rear U-joint at the companion flange.

2. Remove the retaining screw and the flange.

3. Unbolt and remove the assembly from the vehicle.

4. Installation is the reverse of removal.

DISASSEMBLY AND ASSEMBLY

1. Drain the oil from the unit.

2. Remove the rear bearing cover.

3. Remove the nut and lockwasher from the input shaft.

4. Unbolt and remove the input shaft bearing retainer and remove the bearing. Take care not to lose the shims between the gear and the bearing cone.

5. Remove the bearing cone, cup and snap ring.

6. Remove the oil seal retainer and pilot assembly.

7. Press the shaft through the housing, removing the bearing cone, oil seal and retainer as an assembly.

8. Remove the input shaft gear through the rear opening. Push out the bearing cup

and remove the snap ring. Remove the bearing cone and oil seal from the shaft.

9. Remove the output shaft in the same manner as the input shaft.

10. Adjustment of the tapered roller bearings on both shafts is accomplished by shim packs placed between the gear hubs and hearing cones.

11. Assembly is the reverse of disassembly. Fill the unit with 90W gear oil.

Pulley Drive Unit

REMOVAL AND INSTALLATION

This procedure is accomplished simply by unbolting and removing the unit.

DISASSEMBLY AND ASSEMBLY

1. Remove the unit from the vehicle.
2. Drain the oil and clean the unit.

3. Remove the retaining nut and remove the pulley.

4. Unbolt and remove the pulley shaft housing from the gear housing. Don't lose the shims.

5. Press the pulley shaft through the housing, removing the inner bearing cone, spacer and shim pack.

6. Remove the oil seal and outer bearing cone.

7. Remove the bearing retaining cover from the gear housing, then remove the shim pack.

8. Using a brass drift, tap the shaft through the housing; the bearing and gear will come out with it. Be careful not to lose the shim pack.

9. Clean and inspect all parts. Assembly is the reverse of disassembly. Fill the unit with 90W gear oil.

Drive Train

DRIVELINE

Front and Rear Driveshafts

REMOVAL AND INSTALLATION

In order to remove the front and rear driveshafts, unscrew the holding nuts from the universal joint's U-bolts, remove the U-bolts and slide the shaft forward or backward toward the slip joint. The shaft can then be removed from the end yokes and removed from under the vehicle.

Each shaft is equipped with a splined slip joint at one end to allow for variations in length caused by vehicle spring action. Some slip joints are marked with arrows at the spline and sleeve yoke. When installing, align the arrows. If the slip joint is not marked with arrows, align the yokes at the

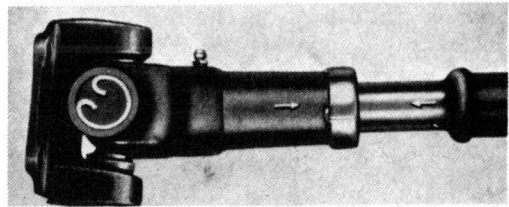

Driveshaft alignment markings

front and rear of the shaft in the same horizontal plane. This is necessary in order to avoid vibration in the drive train.

U-Joints

Most Jeeps use a conventional universal joint at both ends of both driveshafts. The CJ-7 and Scrambler with automatic transmission

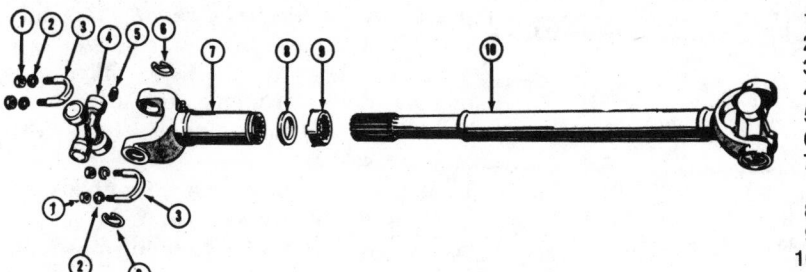

1. U-bolt nut
2. U-bolt washer
3. U-bolt
4. Universal joint journal
5. Lubrication fitting
6. Snap ring
7. Universal joint sleeve yoke
8. Rubber washer
9. Dust cap
10. Propeller shaft tube

1945–71 driveshaft

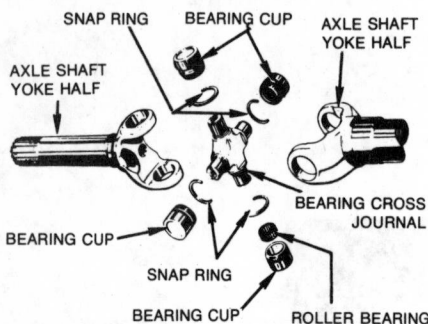

1972–81 single cross cardan U-joint

use a double, or constant velocity, joint at the transfer case end of the front driveshaft. Universal joints through 1971 are held together by snap-rings on the outside of the bearing caps; 1972–79 models have C-type retainer rings on the inside of the bearing caps. The constant velocity joint is also assembled with snap-rings on the outside.

On 1945–71 vehicles, three types of front axle U-joints were used: the Bendix type and the Rzeppa type, used on Axle models 25 and 27, and the more familiar single cross cardan type used on axle model 27AF. All axles after 1972 use the single cross cardan type.

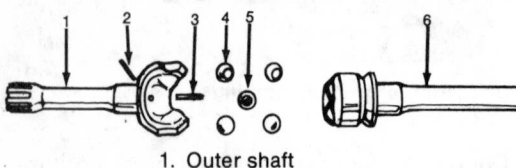

1. Outer shaft
2. Lock pin
3. Center ball pin
4. Universal joint ball
5. Center ball
6. Inner shaft

Bendix front axle U-joint

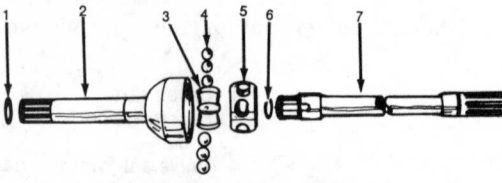

1. Outer axle shaft snap ring
2. Outer shaft
3. Universal joint inner race
4. Ball
5. Cage
6. Axle shaft retainer snap ring
7. Inner shaft

Rzeppa front axle U-joint

OVERHAUL

Through 1971

1. Remove the snap rings by pinching the ends together with a pair of pliers. If the rings do not readily snap out of the groove, tap the end of the bearing lightly to relieve pressure against the rings.

2. After removing the snap rings, press on the end of one bearing until the opposite bearing is pushed from the yoke arm. Turn the joint over and press the first bearing back out of that arm by pressing on the exposed end of the journal shaft. To drive it out, use a soft drift with a flat face, about $1/32$ in. smaller in diameter than the hole in the yoke; otherwise there is danger of damaging the bearing.

3. Repeat this procedure for the other two bearings, then lift out the journal assembly by sliding it to one side.

4. Wash all parts in cleaning solvent and inspect the parts after cleaning. Replace the journal assembly if it is worn extensively. Make sure that the grease channel in each journal trunnion is open.

5. Pack all of the bearing caps ⅓ full of grease and install the rollers (bearings).

6. Press one of the cap/bearing assemblies into one of the yoke arms just far enough so that the cap will remain in position.

7. Place the journal in position in the installed cap, with a cap/bearing assembly placed on the opposite end.

8. Position the free cap so that when it is driven from the opposite end it will be inserted into the opening of the yoke. Repeat this operation for the other two bearings.

9. Install the retaining clips. If the U-joint binds when it is assembled, tap the arms of the yoke slightly to relieve any pressure on the bearings at the end of the journal.

Bendix Joint

With ordinary shop equipment it is nearly impossible to satisfactorily rebuild this unit. For this reason, the factory no longer supplies parts. After considerable mileage, a joint may pull apart upon removal from the vehicle. This does not mean that the joint is no longer useable.

To assemble the axle shaft and universal:

1. Place the differential half of the shaft in a vise with the ground portion above the jaws.

2. Install the center ball (the one with the

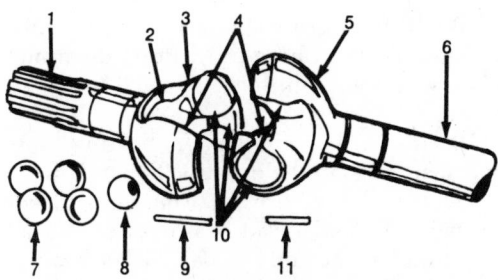

1. Outer shaft
2. Ground faces
3. Outer yoke
4. Flanges
5. Inner yoke
6. Inner shaft
7. Ball
8. Center ball
9. Center ball pin
10. Races
11. Lock pin

Component view of the Bendix joint

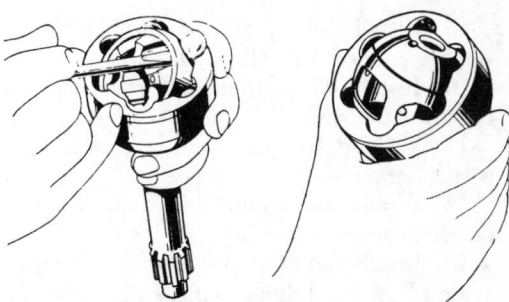

Removing the balls from the Rzeppa joint using a small screwdriver

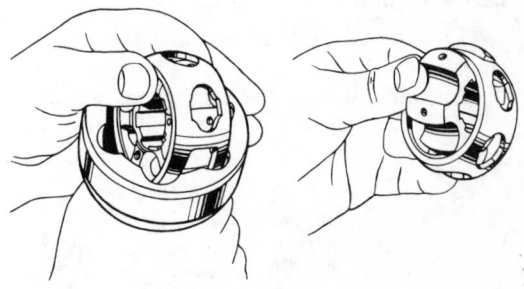

Removing the Rzeppa joint ball cage

drilled hole) in the socket in the shaft, with the hole and groove visible.

3. Drop the center ball pin into the drilled hole in the wheel half of the shaft.

4. Place the wheel half of the shaft on the center ball. Slip the three balls into the races.

5. Turn the center ball until the groove lines up with the race for the remaining ball. Slip the ball into the race and straighten the wheel end of the shaft.

6. Turn the center ball until the pin drops into the hole in the ball.

7. Install the lock pin and center punch both ends to secure it.

Rzeppa Joint

With the joint removed, determine the method of attachment of the axle to the joint. If three bolts are used, use step 1; if there are no screws, skip 1 and proceed to step 2.

1. Remove the three screws securing the front axle to the joint. Pull the shaft free of the splined inner race. Remove the retaining ring and remove the axle shaft retainer.

2. To remove the axle shaft from the joint, use a wooden pry, and exert force in the direction of the axis of the axle shaft. Use a mallet, if necessary, to exert enough force to drive the retaining ring, installed on the end of the shaft, into its groove in the spline, permitting the joint to be slipped off the shaft.

3. Push down on various points of the inner race and cage until the balls can be removed with the help of a small screwdriver.

4. There are two large rectangular holes in the cage as well as four small holes. Turn the cage so that the two bosses in the spindle shaft will drop onto the rectangular holes and lift out the cage.

5. To remove the inner race, turn it so that one of the bosses will drop into a rectangular hole in its cage and shift the race to one side. Lift it out.

6. Assembly is the reverse of disassembly. Take care to keep all parts as clean as possible.

1972–81 Single Cross Cardan Joint

1. Clamp the yoke, not the tube, in a vise.

2. Remove the bearing cap C-retainers. Tap on the bearing caps to relieve pressure as necessary.

3. Support the yoke on the vise jaws.

4. Tap one bearing cap in until the opposite one comes out.

5. Turn the yoke around and tap the exposed end of the spider to drive the remaining bearing cap out.

6. Clean all parts in solvent and dry. Use all the parts in the repair kit, even if some of the old ones seem usable.

7. Lubricate all needle bearings, bearing caps, and bearing surfaces with chassis grease.

8. Place the seals on the spider.

9. Install one cap and needle bearing assembly partway into the shaft yoke.

10. Install the spider and the opposite bearings and cap.

11. Support the yoke and seat both caps with a hammer.

12. Install the retainer C-clips. Tap the bearing caps as necessary.

13. Install the other two cap and bearing assemblies. Hold them in place with tape until the shaft is reinstalled.

1976–81 Constant Velocity (Double cardan) Joint

1. Remove the bearing cap retainer snap-rings.

2. Mark all components for reassembly.

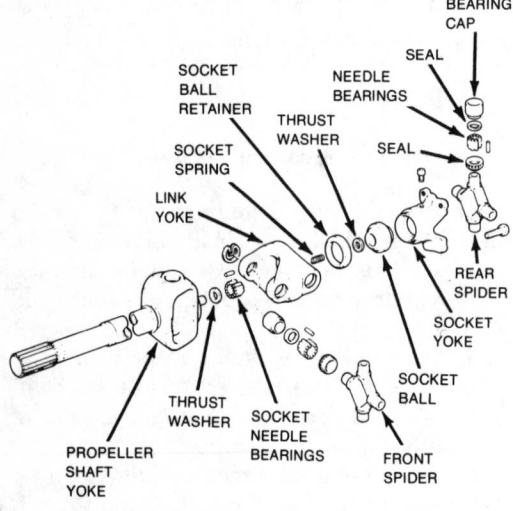

Constant velocity joint

3. Use a ⅝ in. socket as a bearing cap driver and a 1¹/₁₆ in. socket as a bearing cap receiver. Squeeze the assembly in a vise to force out the bearing caps.

4. Repeat the operation of step 3 to remove the bearing caps at the other end of the joint.

5. Clean all parts in solvent and dry.

NOTE: *Do not disassemble the socket yoke, centering ball, spring, needle bearings, retainer, and thrust washers. These parts are sold as an assembly only.*

6. Lubricate all bearings and contact surfaces with chassis grease.

7. Install the bearing caps on the transfer case yoke ends of the rear spider. Tape them in place.

8. Assemble the socket yoke and the rear spider.

9. Place the rear spider in the link yoke and install the bearing caps. Press them into place with the ⅝ in. socket. Install the snap-rings.

10. Install the front spider, bearing caps, and snap-rings in the driveshaft yoke.

11. Install the thrust washer and socket spring in the ball socket bearing bore. Install the thrust washer on the ball socket bearing boss on the driveshaft yoke. Align the ball socket bearing boss with the ball socket bearing bore and insert the boss into the bore.

12. Align the front spider with the link yoke and install the bearing caps and snap-rings.

REAR AXLE

A variety of rear axles have been used:
- 1945–71 CJ-2A before ser. #13453: Spicer 23-2, Ratio 5.38:1.
  CJ-2A after ser. #13453: Spicer 41-2, Ratio 5.38:1
  All others: Spicer 44, Ratio 4.27:1 std; 5.38:1 opt.
- 1972–75 Dana 44, Ratio 3.73:1 std; 4.27:1 opt.
- 1976–78 AMC/Jeep, Ratio 3.54:1 std; 4.09:1 opt.
- 1979–80 AMC/Jeep, Ratio 3.07:1 std; 3.54:1 opt.
- 1981 AMC/Jeep, Ratio 2.73:1, 3.31:1, 3.54:1, 3.73:1

Axle Shaft

REMOVAL AND INSTALLATION

Through 1971

1. Jack up the wheel and remove the hub cap.

2. Remove the axle shaft nut.

3. Use a puller to remove the wheel hub and key.

4. Remove the screws which attach the brake dust shield, grease and bearing retainers, and brake assembly. Remove the shield and retainer.

5. Pull out the axle shaft with a puller, being careful not to lose the adjusting shims. Should the axle shaft be broken, the inner end can usually be drawn out of the housing with a wire loop, after the outer seal is removed. However, if the broken end is less than 8″ long, it will be necessary to remove the differential.

If both shafts are to be removed, keep the

Pulling off the wheel hub

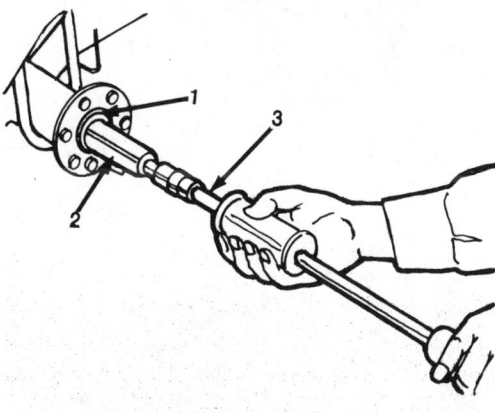

1. Cone and roller
2. Axle
3. Tool

Pulling the axle shaft

shims from each shaft separate and replace them on the shaft from which they were removed in order to maintain the correct bearing adjustment.

6. Install in the reverse order of removal. Use a new grease seal when installing the hub assembly. Install the hub assembly, then the key.

1972–1975

1. Jack up the vehicle and remove the wheels.

2. Remove the brake drum spring lock nuts and remove the drum.

3. Remove the axle shaft flange cup plug by piercing the center with a sharp tool and prying it out.

4. Using the access hole in the axle shaft flange, remove the nuts which attach the backing plate and retainer to the axle tube flange.

5. Remove the axle shaft from the housing with an axle puller.

6. Install in reverse order of removal.

1976–81

1. With the wheel on the ground, remove the axle shaft cotter pin and nut. Loosen the wheel nuts.

2. Raise and support the rear of the vehicle, preferably with jackstands under the axle housing.

3. Remove the wheel.

4. Remove the drum retaining screws, 3 per drum.

5. Remove the drum from the hub. If the brake shoes hold the drum, the brake adjustment will have to be backed off slightly.

6. Attach a puller to the wheel bolts and pull off the hub.

CAUTION: *Don't use a knock-out type puller. It could damage the rear wheel bearings or the differential.*

7. Disconnect the parking brake cable at the equalizer. The equalizer is where the single cable from the parking brake pedal joins the double cable from the rear wheels.

8. Disconnect the brake tube at the wheel cylinder and remove the brake support plate assembly (backing plate), oil seal, and shims (left-side only).

9. Use a puller to remove the axle shaft and bearing.

10. Remove and discard the axle shaft inner oil seal.

11. The bearing cone is pressed onto the shaft. A hydraulic press must be used to remove it.

12. Before installation, pack the axle shaft bearings with high quality grease. Place a

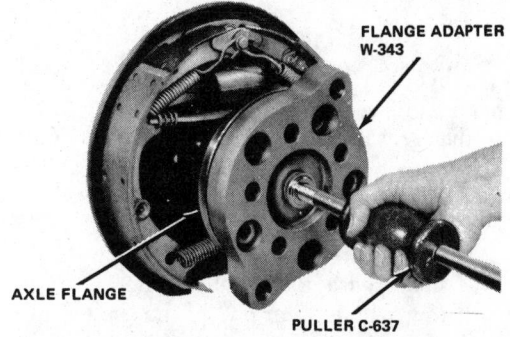

FLANGE ADAPTER W-343

AXLE FLANGE

PULLER C-637

Removing the 1972–75 flanged axle shaft

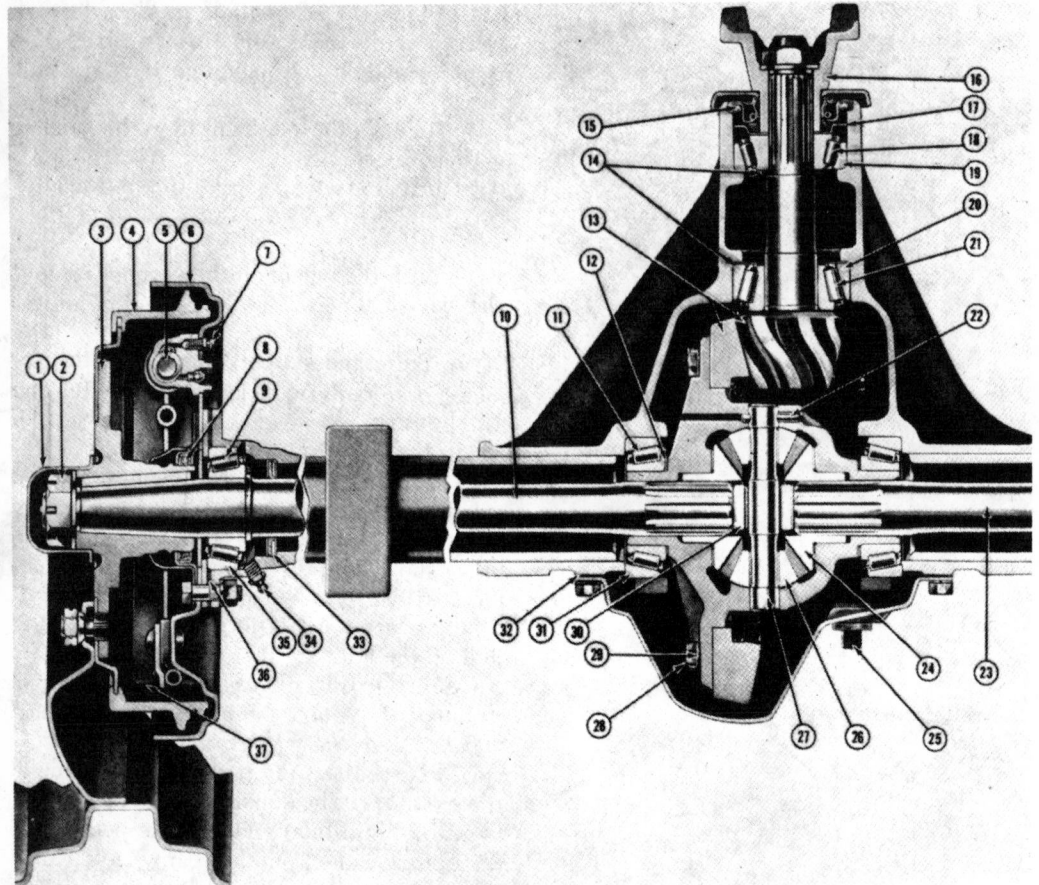

1. Hub cap
2. Hex nut
3. Rear wheel hub
4. Wheel brake drum
5. Brake wheel cylinder
6. Backing plate
7. Brake cylinder bleeder screw
8. Axle shaft outer grease retainer
9. Axle shaft bearing cone and roller
10. Axle shaft—left
11. Differential bearing cone and roller
12. Differential shims
13. Axle drive gear and pinion

14. Pinion bearing shims
15. Drive pinion oil seal
16. Universal joint end yoke
17. Drive pinion oil slinger
18. Drive pinion outer bearing cone and roller
19. Drive pinion outer bearing cup
20. Drive pinion inner bearing cup
21. Drive pinion inner bearing cone and roller
22. Pinion mate shaft pin and lock
23. Axle shaft—right
24. Side gear
25. Pipe plug (filler)

26. Pinion mate
27. Pinion mate shaft
28. Drive gear screw
29. Drive gear screw strap
30. Axle shaft spacer (center block)
31. Differential bearing cup
32. Axle housing cover gasket
33. Axle shaft oil seal (inboard)
34. Lubrication fitting
35. Axle shaft bearing cup
36. Rear axle shaft bearing shims
37. Brake shoe and lining

1945–71 rear axle cutaway

healthy glob of grease in the palm of one hand and force the edge of the bearing into it so that grease fills the bearing. Do this until the whole bearing is packed. Grease packing tools are available which make this task much easier.

13. Press the axle shaft bearings onto the axle shafts with the small diameter of the cone toward the outer end of the shaft.

CAUTION: *Always press on the inner bearing race.*

14. Coat the inner axle shaft seal with light oil.

15. Coat the outer surface of the metal seal retainer with sealant.

16. Use a seal driver to install the inner oil seal in the axle housing.

17. Install the axle shaft(s), turning them as necessary to fit the splines into the differential.

18. Install the outer bearing cup.

19. Apply sealant to the axle housing

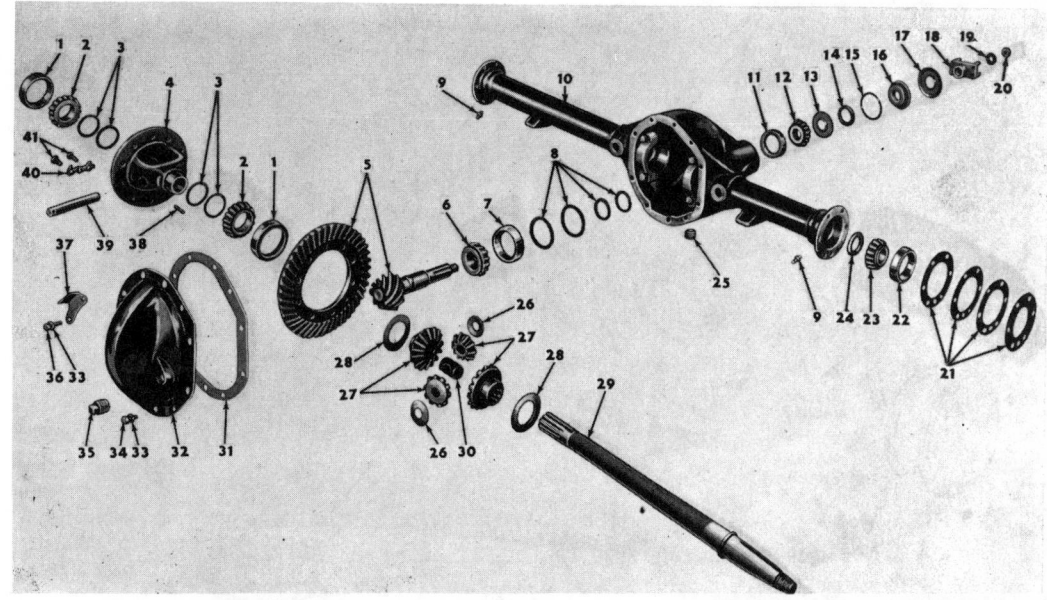

1. Bearing cup	15. Gasket	29. Axle shaft
2. Cone and rollers	16. Oil seal	30. Spacer
3. Shims	17. Dust shield	31. Gasket
4. Differential case	18. End yoke	32. Housing cover
5. Gear and pinion	19. Washer	33. Lockwasher
6. Cone and rollers	20. Pinion nut	34. Screw
7. Cup	21. Shims	35. Filler plug
8. Shims	22. Cup	36. Hex screw
9. Fitting	23. Cone and rollers	37. Tee bracket
10. Housing	24. Oil seal	38. Lock pin
11. Cup	25. Drain plug	39. Pinion shaft
12. Cone and rollers	26. Thrust washer	40. Lock strap
13. Oil slinger	27. Differential gears	41. Screw
14. Felt wick	28. Thrust washer	

1945–71 rear axle components

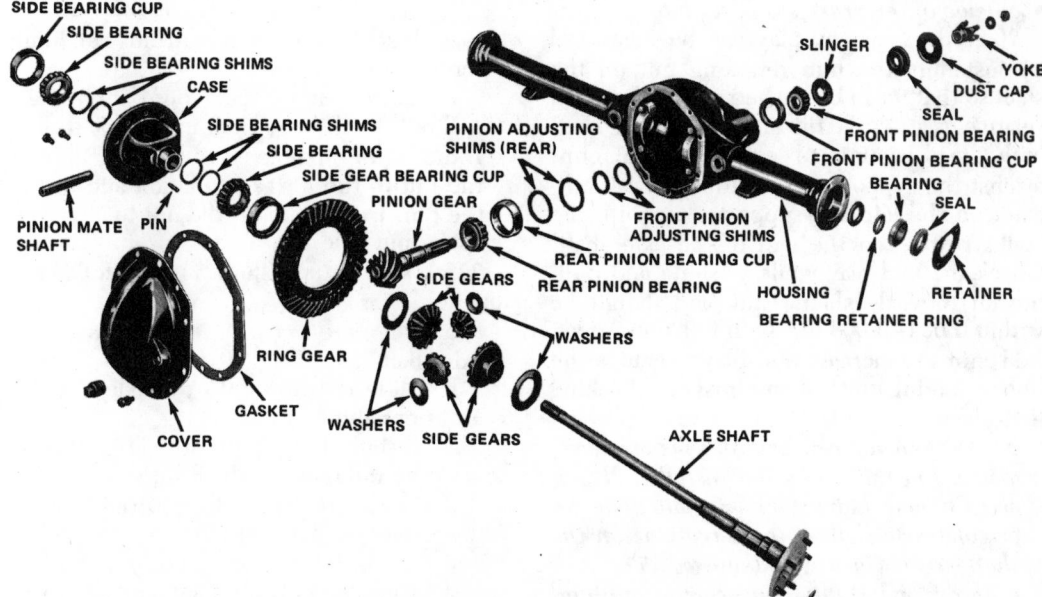

Component view of the 1972–75 flanged rear axle

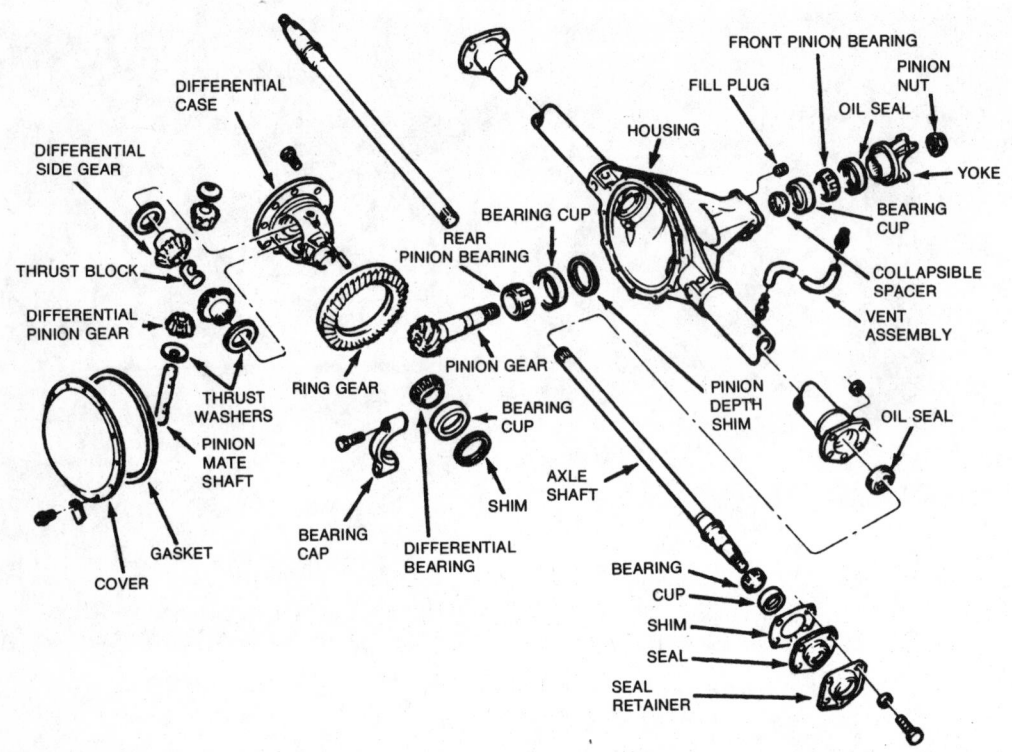

1976–81 rear axle components

flange and brake support plate mounting areas. Install the original shims in their original locations, oil seal assembly, and brake support plate. Tighten the retaining bolts to 35 ft. lbs.

NOTE: *The oil seal and retainer go on the outside of the brake support plate.*

20. Axle shaft end-play can be measured by installing the hub retaining nut on the shaft so that it can be pushed and pulled with relative ease. Strike the end of each axle shaft with a lead hammer to seat the bearing cups against the support plate. Mount a dial indicator on the left-side support plate with the stylus resting on the end of the axle shaft. Check the end-play while pushing and pulling on the axle shaft. End-play should be within 0.004–0.008 in., with 0.006 in. ideal. Add shims to increase end-play. Remove the hub retaining nut when finished checking end-play.

NOTE: *When a new axle shaft is installed, a new hub must also be installed. However, a new hub can be installed on an original axle shaft if the serrations on the shaft are not worn or damaged. The procedures for installing an original hub and a new hub are different.*

21. Install an original hub in the following manner:

a. Align the keyway in the hub with the axle shaft key;

b. Slide the hub onto the axle shaft as far as possible;

c. Install the axle shaft nut and washer;

d. Install the drum, drum retaining screws, and wheel;

e. Lower the vehicle onto its wheels and tighten the axle shaft nut to 250 ft. lbs. If the cotter pin hole is not aligned, tighten the nut to the next castellation and install the pin. Do not loosen the nut to align the cotter pin hole.

22. Install a new hub in the following manner:

a. Align the keyway in the hub with the axle shaft key;

b. Slide the hub onto the axle shaft as far as possible;

c. Install two well-lubricated thrust washers and the axle shaft nut;

d. Install the brake drum, drum retaining screws, and wheel;

e. Lower the vehicle onto its wheels;

f. Tighten the axle shaft nut until the distance from the outer face of the hub to the outer end of the axle shaft is $1^5/_{16}$ in. Pressing the hub onto the axle to the specified distance is necessary to form the hub serrations properly;

g. Remove the axle shaft nut and one thrust washer;

h. Install the axle shaft nut and tighten it to 250 ft. lbs. If the cotter pin hole is not aligned, tighten the nut to the next castellation and install the pin. Do not loosen the nut to install the cotter pin.

23. Connect the brake line to the wheel cylinder and bleed the brake hydraulic system and adjust the brake shoes.

FRONT AXLE

The following front axles have been used:
- 1945–71 Spicer 25, 27, 27A Ratio 4.27:1 std.; 5.38:1 opt.
- 1972–81 Dana 30 with ratios matching the rear axle

Steering knuckle pivot pin or ball joint repairs are covered in the next chapter, under Steering. Locking hubs and front wheel bearings are covered in Chapter 1.

Axle Shaft

REMOVAL AND INSTALLATION

Through 1971

The front axle shaft and universal joint assembly is removed as an assembly.

NOTE: *See the U-Joint section of this chapter for a description of the three types used on these axles.*

1. Remove the wheel.
2. Remove the hub with a puller. If there are locking hubs, remove them as detailed in Chapter 1.

Pulling the front drive hub

Pulling off axle shaft drive flange

3. Remove the axle shaft driving flange bolts.

4. Apply the foot brakes and remove the axle shaft flange with a puller.

5. Release the locking lip on the lockwasher and remove the outer nut, lockwasher, adjusting nut, and bearing lockwasher.

6. Remove the wheel hub and drum assembly with the bearings. Be careful not to damage the oil seal.

7. Remove the hydraulic brake tube and the brake backing plate screws.

8. Remove the spindle.

9. Remove the axle shaft and universal joint assembly.

10. Single cross cardan type installation is the reverse of the removal procedure.

11. **Bendix type** installation is as follows:

a. Enter the U-joint and shaft assembly into the housing. Mesh the splined end of the shaft with the differential and push into place.

b. Install the wheel bearing spindle.

c. Install the brake tube and backing plate.

d. Grease and assemble the wheel bearings and hub and drum on the spindle. Install the bearing washer and adjusting nut. Tighten the nut until a slight drag is felt, then back off $1/_6$ turn. Install remaining parts.

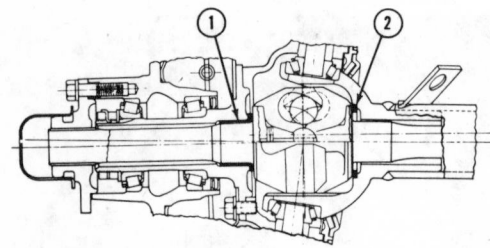

1. Bushing
2. Thrust washer

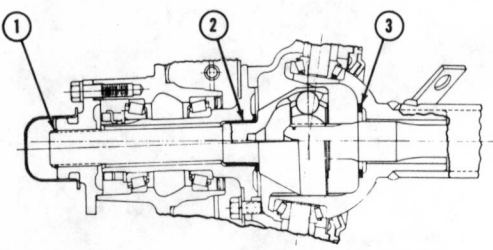

1. Snap ring
2. Bushing
3. Thrust washer

Bendix (top) and Rzeppa joint axle shafts

12. **Early Rzeppa** type requires a shimming procedure. Installation is the same as the Bendix type except that a shim pack must be installed between the driving flange and the wheel hub to determine the proper operating clearance for the U-joint. To do this:

a. Install the drive flange on the axle splines without shims.

b. Install the axle nut and tighten it snugly.

c. Install two opposite flange bolts snugly.

d. Use a feeler gauge to measure the gap between the outer end of the hub and the inner face of the driving flange. This determines the amount of shimming to be used. It is necessary to install shims of a thickness equal to the measured gap plus .15–.050 in. If no gap is found, install a .010 in. shim.

e. Install the correct amount of shims, replace the flange and install the six bolts. Install the axle shaft nut and make sure that the proper end float has been obtained. To do this, back off the shaft nut so that a .050 in. feeler will fit between the nut and driving flange. Tap the end of the shaft with a soft mallet which will force in the shaft the amount of end float. Measure the clearance between the nut and driving flange. Clearance should be .015–.050 in.

13. Late Rzeppa type installation is the same as the Bendix type except that a snap ring is used to secure the outer end of the shaft controlling end float.

1972–81

NOTE: *On models with locking hubs, refer to Chapter 1 for hub removal and installation.*

1. Remove the hub cap. On models with disc brakes, remove the caliper.

2. Remove the drive flange snap-ring.

3. On models with disc brakes, remove the rotor hub bolts, cover and gasket. On models with drum brakes, remove the axle flange bolts, lockwashers, and flatwashers.

4. If the axle is on the vehicle, apply the foot brakes. Remove the axle flange with a puller.

5. Release the locking lip of the lockwasher, and remove the outer nut, lockwasher, adjusting nut, and bearing lockwasher.

6. On models with disc brakes, remove the bearing and rotor. On models with drum brakes, back off on the brake adjusting star wheel adjusters and remove the brake drum assembly with the bearings. Be careful not to damage the oil seal.

7. On models with drum brakes, remove the brake backing plate. If the axle is on the vehicle, it will first be necessary to disconnect the brake hose between the front brake line and the flexible connection. On models with disc brakes, remove the adapter and splash shield.

Wheel bearing nut wrench

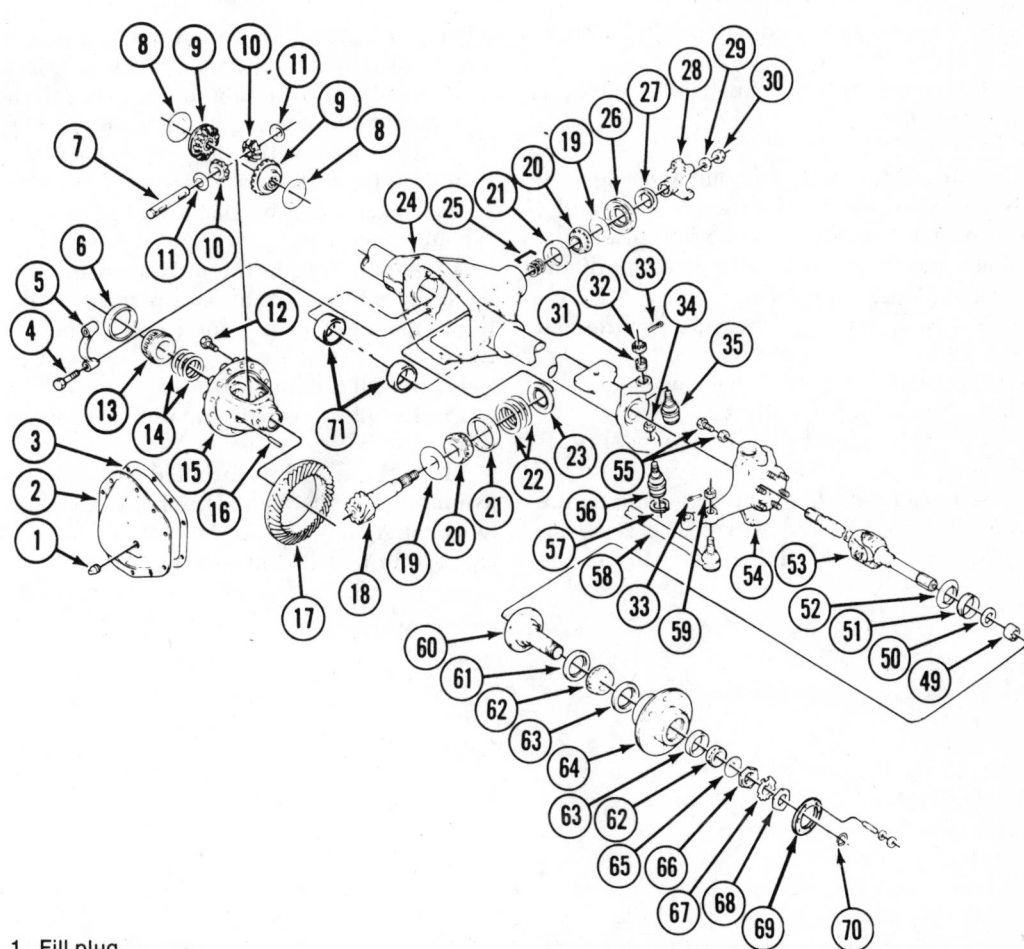

1. Fill plug
2. Axle housing cover
3. Axle housing cover gasket
4. Differential bearing cap bolt
5. Differential bearing cap
6. Differential bearing cup (2)
7. Pinion mate shaft
8. Thrust washer
9. Differential side gear
10. Differential pinion gear
11. Thrust washer
12. Ring gear mounting bolts
13. Differential bearing (2)
14. Differential bearing preload shims
15. Differential case
16. Pinion mate shaft pin
17. Ring gear
18. Pinion gear
19. Slinger
20. Pinion bearing
21. Pinion bearing cup
22. Pinion depth shims
23. Baffle
24. Axle housing
25. Pinion preload shims
26. Oil seal
27. Dust cap
28. Yoke
29. Washer
30. Pinion nut

31. Upper ball stud split ring seat
32. Upper ball stud nut
33. Cotter pin
34. Lower ball stud jamnut
35. Upper ball stud
49. Spindle bearing
50. Washer
51. Seal
52. Seal seat
53. Axle shaft
54. Steering knuckle
55. Steering stop bolt
56. Lower ball stud
57. Snap ring
58. Tie rod
59. Tie rod end nut
60. Spindle
61. Seal
62. Bearing
63. Bearing cup
64. Hub
65. Tabbed washer
66. Inner locknut
67. Lock washer
68. Outer locknut
69. Gasket
70. Snap ring
71. Inner oil seal

Dana 30 front axle assembly

8. Remove the spindle and spindle bushing.

9. Remove the axle shaft and universal joint assembly.

10. Clean all parts.

11. Insert the universal joint and axle shaft assembly into the axle housing, being careful not to knock out the inner seal. Insert the splined end of the axle shaft into the differential and push into place.

12. Install the wheel bearing spindle and bushing.

13. Install the brake backing plate, or adapter and splash shield.

14. Grease and assemble the wheel bearings and oil seal.

15. Install the wheel hub and drum on the wheel bearing spindle. On disc brakes, install the rotor, hub, and caliper. Install the wheel bearing washer and adjusting nut. Tighten the nut to 50 ft. lb., and back if off $1/6$–$1/4$ turn while rotating the hub. Install the lockwasher and nut, tighten the nut to 50 ft. lb. and then bend the lip of the lockwasher over onto the locknut.

16. Install the drive flange and gasket onto the hub and attach with six capscrews and lockwashers. Torque the capscrews to 30 ft. lb. in an alternate and even pattern. Install the snap-ring onto the outer end of the axle shaft.

17. Install the hub cap.

18. Install the wheel, lug nuts, and wheel disc.

19. If the tube was installed with the axle assembly on the vehicle, check the front wheel alignment, bleed the brakes and lubricate the front axle universal joints.

Suspension and Steering

FRONT AND REAR SUSPENSION

All springs should be examined periodically for broken or shifted leaves, loose or missing clips, angle of the spring shackles, and position of the springs on the saddles. Springs with shifted leaves do not retain their normal strength. Missing clips may permit the spirit leaves to fan out or break on rebound. Broken leaves may make the vehicle hard to handle or permit the axle to shift out of line. Weakened springs may break causing difficulty in steering. Spring attaching clips or bolts must be tight. It is suggested that they be checked at each vehicle inspection.

All front springs on models through 1971, except as noted below, have shackles at the front of the springs and pivot bolts at the rear of the springs. Model CJ-5 up to serial number 44437 and Model CJ-6 up to serial number 11981 have shackles at the rear of the front springs, and pivot bolts at the front.

All rear springs have shackles at the rear and pivot bolts at the front.

NOTE: *On 1972 and later models, all spring ends have silent block-type rubber bushings. Never lubricate these rubber bushings.*

Springs
REMOVAL AND INSTALLATION
Through 1971

1. Raise the vehicle with a jack under the axle and place a jackstand under the frame side rail. Then lower the axle jack so that the load is relieved from the spring and the wheels rest on the floor.

2. Remove the nuts which secure the spring clip bolts. Remove the spring plate and clip bolts. Free the spring from the axle by raising the axle jack.

3. Remove the pivot bolt nut and drive out the pivot bolt. Disconnect the shackle either by removing the lower nuts and bolts on the rubber-bushed shackles, or by removing the threaded bushings on the U-shackles.

4. To replace, first install the pivot bolt. Then, connect the shackle using the following procedures.

5. On bronze-bushed pivot bolts, install the bolt and nut and tighten the nut. Then back it off two cotter pin slots and install the cotter pin. The nut must be drawn up tightly but must be sufficiently loose to allow the spring to pivot freely. Otherwise the spring might break.

6. On rubber-bushed pivot bolts and lock-

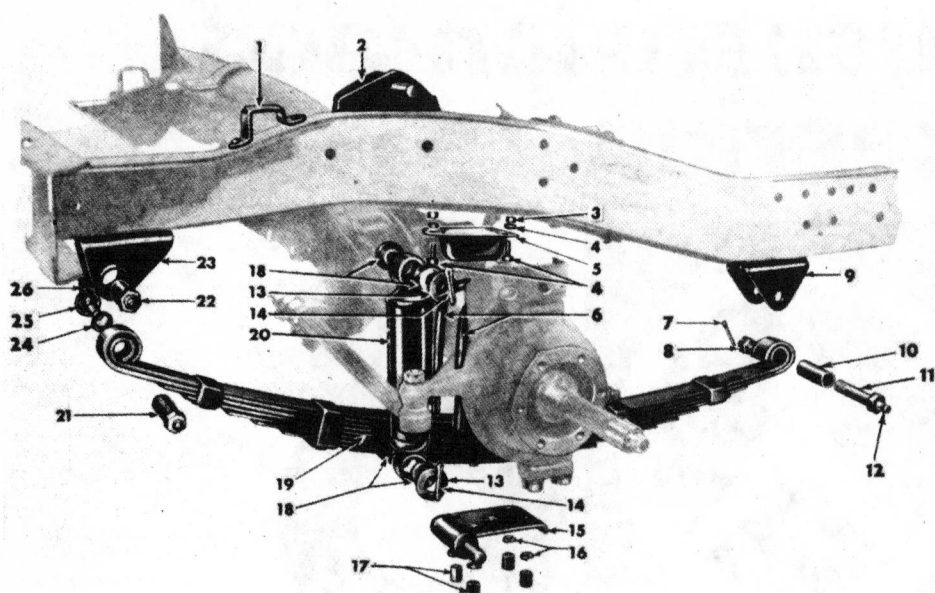

1. Bracket
2. Bracket and shaft
3. Nut
4. Screw and lockwasher
5. Axle bumper
6. Left clip
7. Cotter pin
8. Nut
9. Bracket
10. Eye bushing
11. Pivot bolt
12. Lubrication fitting
13. Washer
14. Cotter pin
15. Plate and shaft
16. Lockwasher
17. Nut
18. Bushing
19. Front spring
20. Shock absorber
21. Lower bushing
22. Upper bushing
23. Bracket
24. Grease seal retainer
25. Grease seal
26. U-bolt

CJ-2A, CJ-3A and early CJ-3B front spring assembly

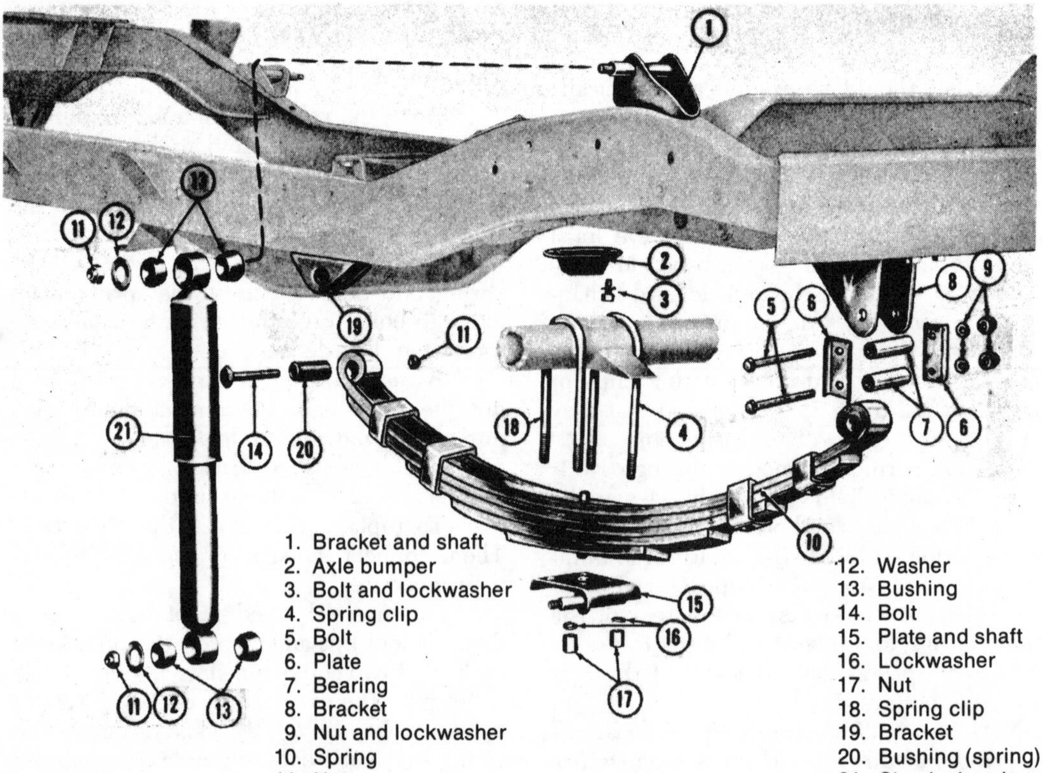

1. Bracket and shaft
2. Axle bumper
3. Bolt and lockwasher
4. Spring clip
5. Bolt
6. Plate
7. Bearing
8. Bracket
9. Nut and lockwasher
10. Spring
11. Nut
12. Washer
13. Bushing
14. Bolt
15. Plate and shaft
16. Lockwasher
17. Nut
18. Spring clip
19. Bracket
20. Bushing (spring)
21. Shock absorber

Front spring and shock absorber, late CJ-3B and early CJ-5 and CJ-6

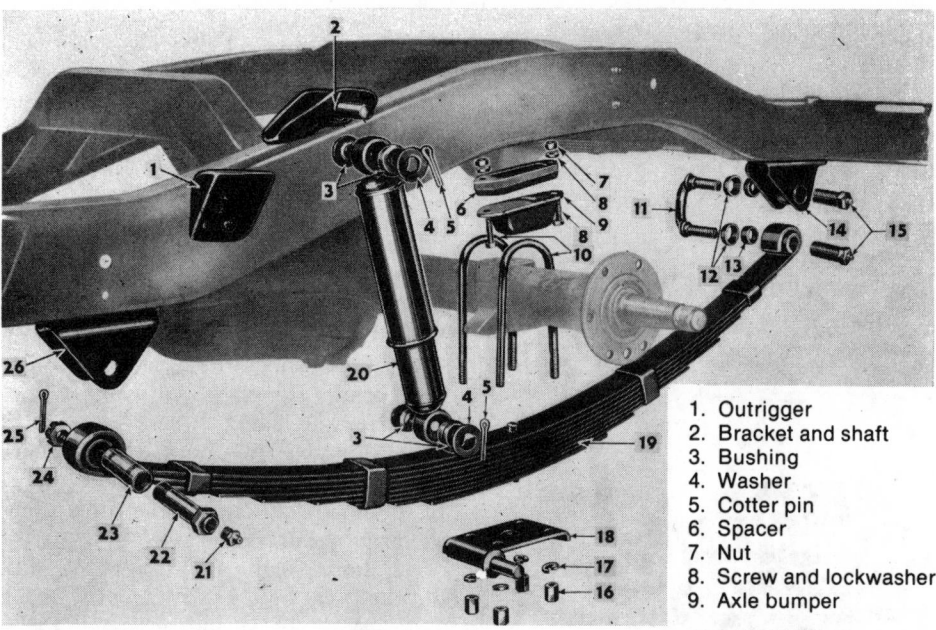

1. Outrigger
2. Bracket and shaft
3. Bushing
4. Washer
5. Cotter pin
6. Spacer
7. Nut
8. Screw and lockwasher
9. Axle bumper

10. Spring clip	16. Nut	22. Pivot bolt
11. Spring shackle "U" bolt	17. Lockwasher	23. Eye bushing
12. Grease seal retainer	18. Plate and shaft	24. Nut
13. Grease seal	19. Rear spring	25. Cotter pin
14. Bracket	20. Shock absorber	26. Bracket
15. Bushing	21. Lubrication fitting	

Rear spring and shock absorber, CJ-2A, CJ-3A and CJ-3B

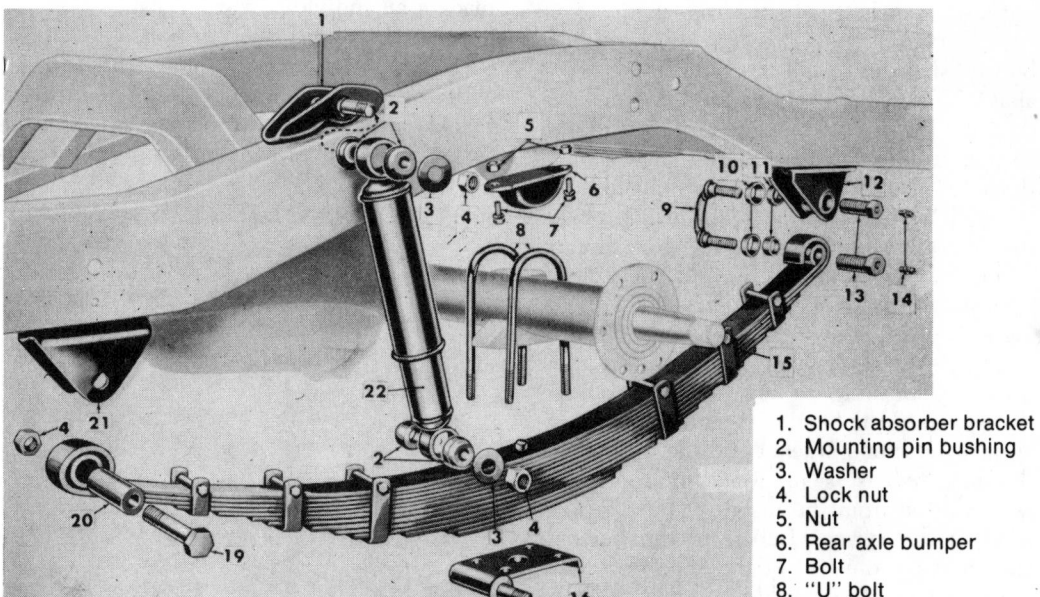

1. Shock absorber bracket
2. Mounting pin bushing
3. Washer
4. Lock nut
5. Nut
6. Rear axle bumper
7. Bolt
8. "U" bolt
9. Shackle
10. Retainer

11. Grease seal	15. Rear spring assembly	19. Pivot bolt
12. Bracket	16. Rear spring clip plate	20. Rubber bushing
13. Threaded shackle bushing	17. Lockwasher	21. Spring pivot bracket
14. Lube fitting	18. "U" bolt nut	22. Shock absorber assembly

Rear spring and shock absorber, CJ-5 and CJ-6 through 1971. Late models had no grease fittings in the shackle

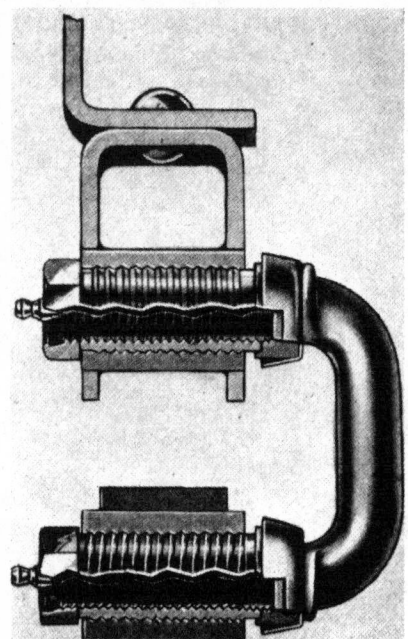

Front spring shackles with grease fittings used through early 1957. Right hand thread bushings have plain, hex heads. Left hand thread bushings have a groove around the heads

nuts (or lockwasher and nut) only tighten the bolt enough to hold the bushings in position until the vehicle is lowered from the jack.

7. Connect the shackle. On rubber-bushed shackles install the bolts as in step 6 above. For U-shackles, insert the shackle through the frame bracket and eye of the spring. Holding the U-shackle tightly against the frame, start the upper bushing on the shackle, taking care that when it enters the thread in the frame it does not crossthread. Screw the bushing on the shackle tightly against the spring eye, and thread the bushing in approximately half way. Then, altering in approximately half way. Then, alternately from top bushing to lower bushing, turn them in until the head of the bushing is snug against the frame bracket and the bushing in the spring eye is $1/32$ in. away from the spring as measured from the inside of the hexagon head in the spring. Lubricate the bushing and then try the flex of the shackle, which must be free. If a shackle is tight, rethread the bushings on the shackle.

8. Move the axle into position on the spring by lowering or raising the axle jack. Install the spring clip bolts, spring plate, lockwashers, and nuts. Torque the nuts to 50–55 ft. lbs. Avoid over-tightening. Be sure the spring is free to move at both ends.

9. Remove both jacks. On rubber gushed shackles and pivot bolts, allow the weight of the vehicle to seat the bushings in their operating positions. Then torque the nuts to 27–30 ft. lbs.

1972–81

1. Raise the vehicle with a jack under the axle. Place a jackstand under the frame side rail. Then lower the axle jack so the load is relieved from the spring and the wheels just touch the floor.

2. Disconnect the shock absorber from the spring clip plate. Disconnect the front stabilizer bar, if any.

3. Remove the nuts which secure the spring clips (U-bolts). Remove the spring plate and spring clips. Free the spring from the axle by raising the axle.

4. Remove the pivot bolt nut and drive out the pivot bolt. Disconnect the shackle.

5. With the spring removed, the spring shackle and/or shackle plate may be removed from the spring.

6. Inspect the bushings in the eye of the main spring leaf and the bushings of the spring shackle for excessive wear. Replace if necessary.

7. The spring can be disassembled for replacing an individual spring leaf, by removing the clips and the center bolts.

8. To install the spring on the vehicle, with the bushings in place and the spring shackle attached to the springs, position the spring in the pivot hanger and install the pi-

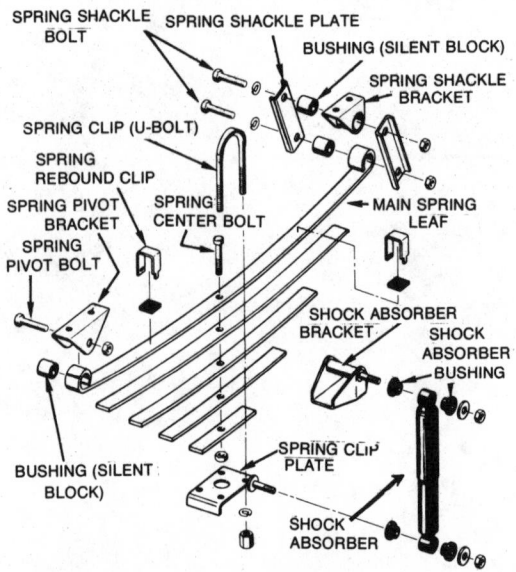

1972–75 front spring assembly

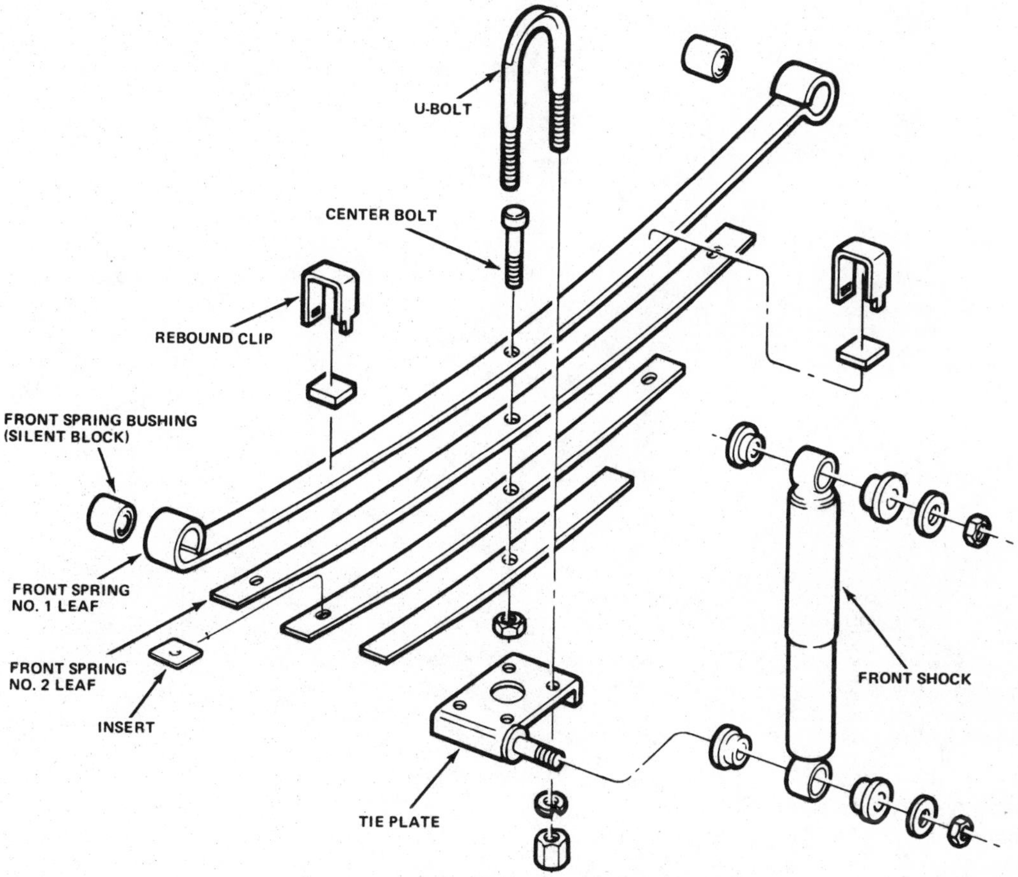

U-BOLT

CENTER BOLT

REBOUND CLIP

FRONT SPRING BUSHING
(SILENT BLOCK)

FRONT SPRING
NO. 1 LEAF

FRONT SPRING
NO. 2 LEAF

INSERT

TIE PLATE

FRONT SHOCK

Front spring and shock absorber, 1976–78 models

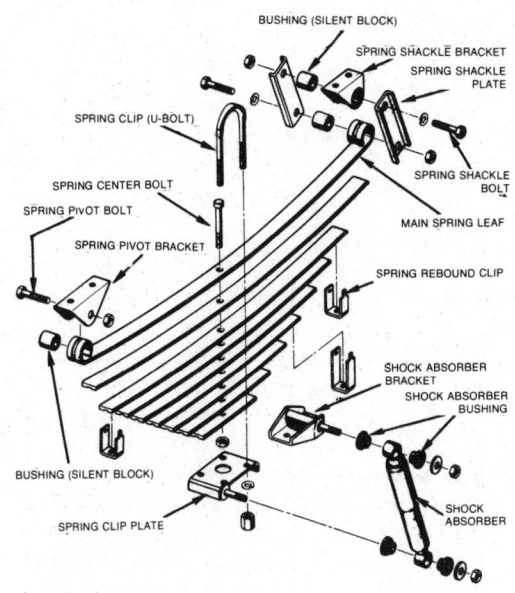

BUSHING (SILENT BLOCK)

SPRING SHACKLE BRACKET

SPRING SHACKLE
PLATE

SPRING CLIP (U-BOLT)

SPRING CENTER BOLT

SPRING PIVOT BOLT

SPRING SHACKLE
BOLT

SPRING PIVOT BRACKET

MAIN SPRING LEAF

SPRING REBOUND CLIP

SHOCK ABSORBER
BRACKET

SHOCK ABSORBER
BUSHING

BUSHING (SILENT BLOCK)

SHOCK
ABSORBER

SPRING CLIP PLATE

1972–75 rear spring assembly

vot bolt and lock nut. Only tighten the lock
nut enough to hold the bushings in position
until the vehicle is lowered from the jack.

9. Position the spring and install the
shackle, shackle bolts, shackle plate if applicable, lockwasher, and nut. Only finger
tighten the nuts at this time.

10. Move the axle into position on the
spring by lowering the axle jack. Place the
spring center bolt in the axle saddle hole. Install the spring clips, spring plate, lockwashers and nuts. Torque the $7/16$ in. nuts to 36–
42 ft. lbs. and the ½ in. nuts to 45–65 ft. lbs.
and the $9/16$ nuts to 100 ft. lb.

NOTE: *Be sure that the center bolt is properly centered in the axle saddle.*

11. Connect the shock absorber.

12. Remove the axle and allow the weight
of the vehicle to seat the bushings in their
operating positions. Then torque the $7/16$ in.
spring pivot bolt nuts and spring shackle nuts

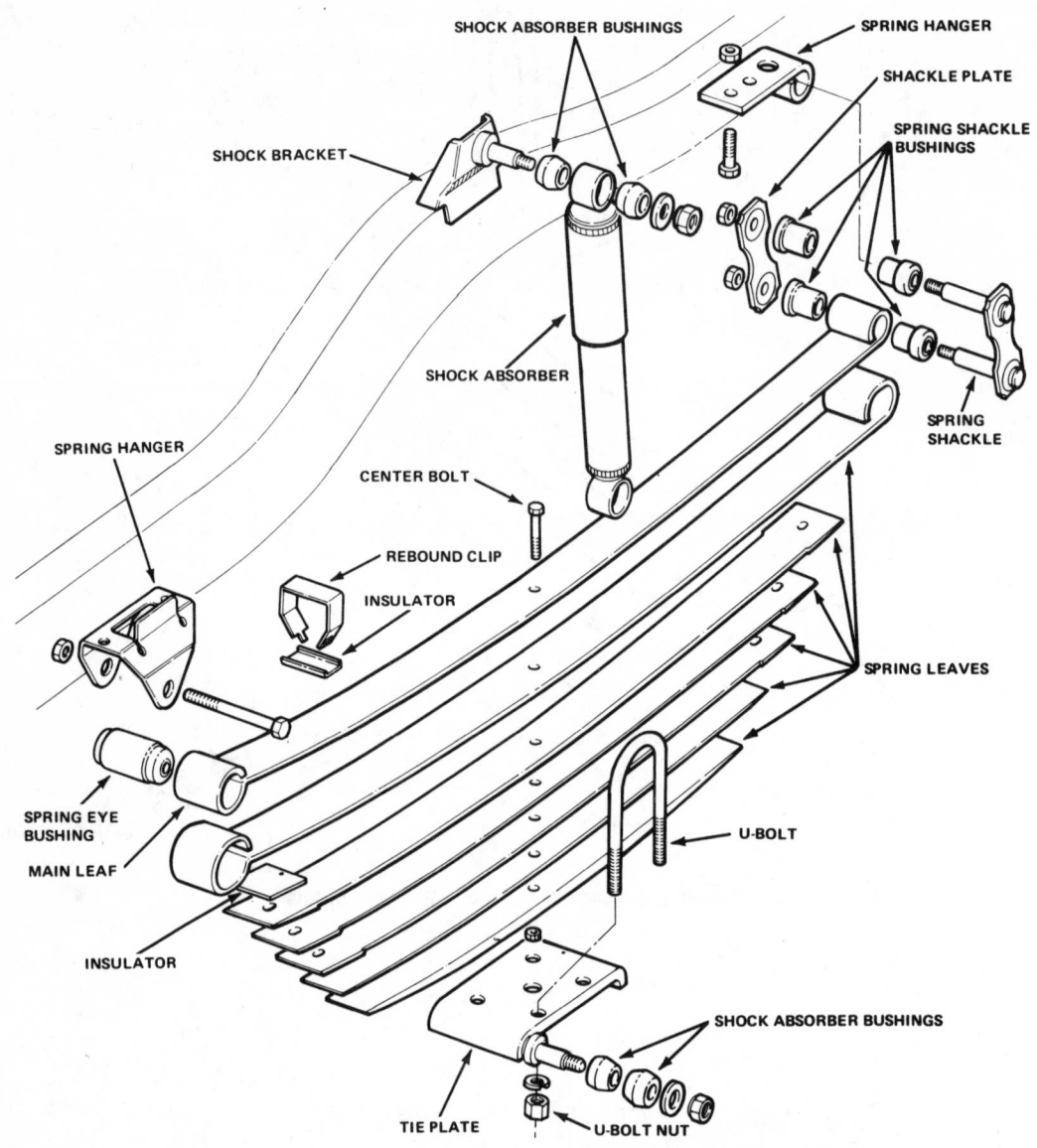

Front spring and shock absorber, 1979–81 models

to 35–50 ft. lbs. Torque the ⅝ in. shackle nuts 55–75 ft. lbs.

NOTE: *Starting 1977, tighten pivot bolts to 100 ft. lbs., and shackle nuts to 24 ft. lbs.*

Shock Absorbers

REMOVAL AND INSTALLATION

1. Remove the locknuts and washers. CJ-2A, CJ-3A and CJ-3B models have cotter pins instead of locknuts. Remove the cotter pins and washers on these models.

2. Pull the shock absorber eyes and rubber bushings from the mounting pins.

3. Install the shocks in reverse order of the removal procedure. Torque the upper bolt to 35 ft. lb. and the lower bolt to 45 ft. lb.

NOTE: *Squeaking usually occurs when movement takes place between the rubber bushings and the metal parts. The squeaking may be eliminated by placing the bushings under great pressure. This is accomplished either by adding additional washers where the cotter pins are used or by tightening the locknuts. Do not use mineral lubricant to stop the squeaking as it will deteriorate the rubber.*

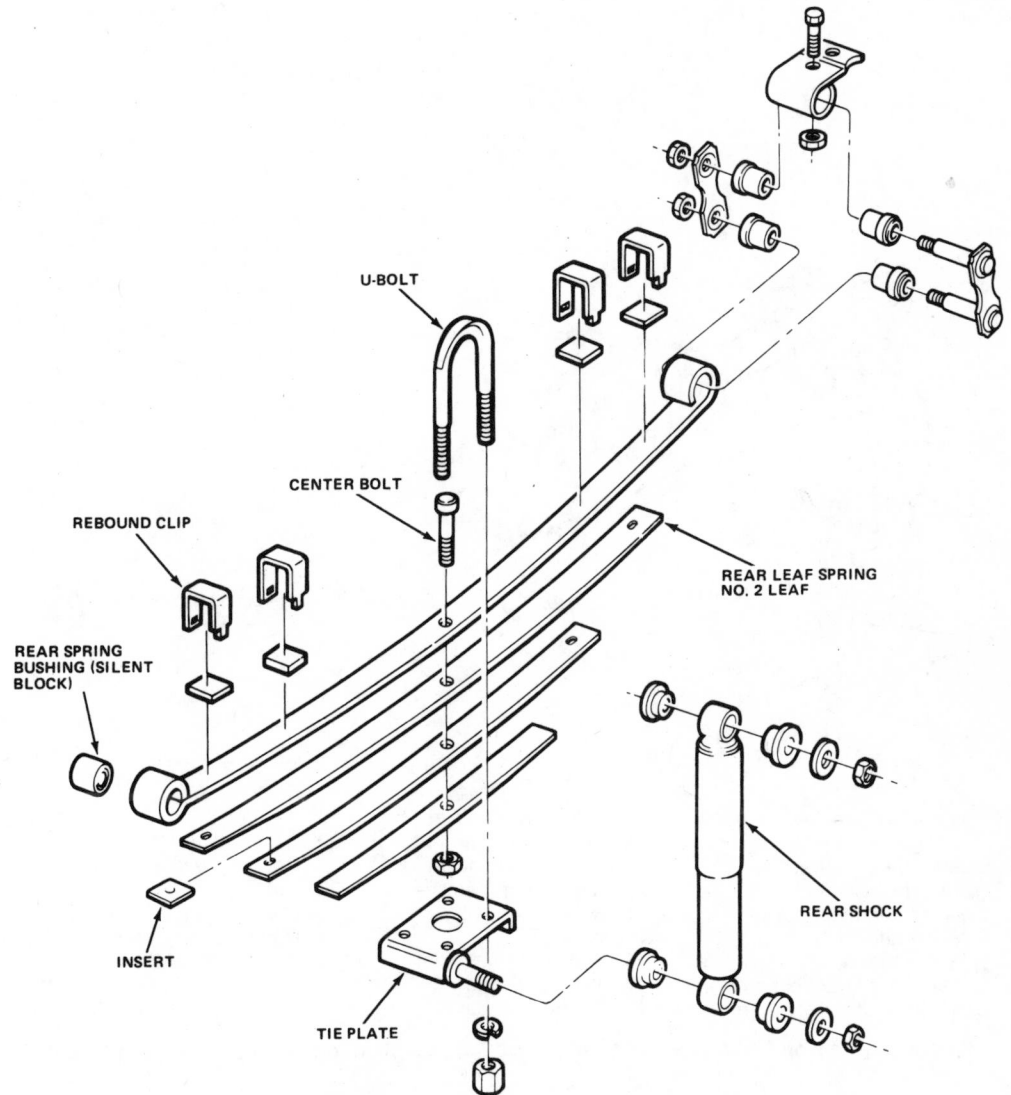

Rear spring and shock absorber, 1976–81 models

Labels in figure:
- U-BOLT
- CENTER BOLT
- REBOUND CLIP
- REAR SPRING BUSHING (SILENT BLOCK)
- INSERT
- TIE PLATE
- REAR LEAF SPRING NO. 2 LEAF
- REAR SHOCK

STEERING

Steering Knuckle and Pivot Pins

Through 1971

The steering knuckle pivot pins take the place of ball joints in a conventional vehicle. The pins pivot on tapered roller bearings located in the axle yoke. Replacement of these bearings requires removal of the hub and brake drum assembly, wheel bearings, axle shaft, spindle, steering tie rod, and steering knuckle. Disassemble the steering knuckle as follows:

REMOVAL AND INSTALLATION

1. Remove the eight screws that hold the oil seal retainer in place.

2. Remove the four screws which secure the lower pivot pin bearig cap.

3. Remove the four screws which hold the upper bearing cap in place. On CJ-2A models before serial number 22972, the nuts also hold the steering arm in place.

4. Remove the bearing cap. On CJ-2A and 3A, remove the brake hose shield.

5. The steering knuckle can now be removed from the axle.

6. Wash all of the parts in cleaning solvent.

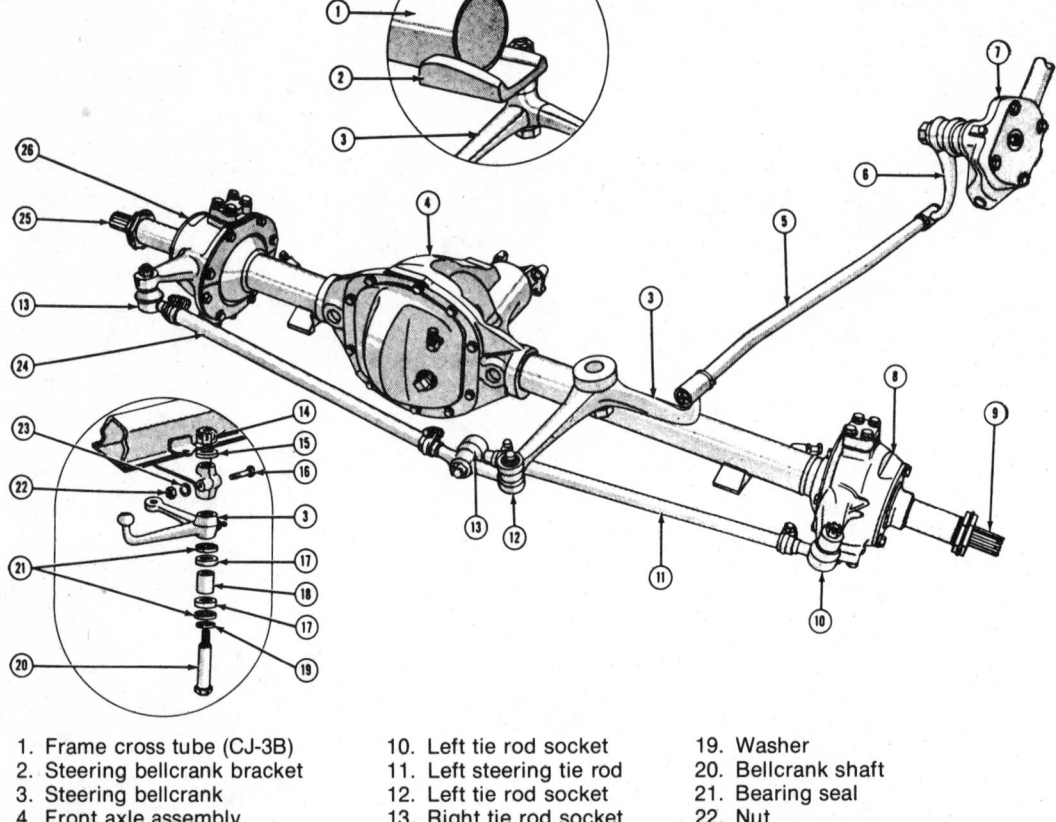

1. Frame cross tube (CJ-3B)
2. Steering bellcrank bracket
3. Steering bellcrank
4. Front axle assembly
5. Steering connecting rod
6. Steering gear arm
7. Steering gear
8. Left steering knuckle and arm
9. Left shaft and universal joint
10. Left tie rod socket
11. Left steering tie rod
12. Left tie rod socket
13. Right tie rod socket
14. Bellcrank nut
15. Washer
16. Bolt
17. Bellcrank bearing
18. Bearing spacer
19. Washer
20. Bellcrank shaft
21. Bearing seal
22. Nut
23. Lockwasher
24. Right steering tie rod
25. Right shaft and universal joint
26. Right steering knuckle and arm

Steering system on CJ-2A (ser. 22972 and up), CJ-3A, CJ-3B, and CJ-5 and CJ-6 through 1971

7. Replace any worn or damaged parts. Inspect the bearings and races for scores, cracks, or chips. Should the bearing cups be damaged, they may be removed and installed with a driver.

8. To install, reverse the removal procedure. When reinstalling the steering knuckle sufficient shims must be installed under the top bearing cap to obtain the correct preload on the bearing. Shims are available in 0.003, 0.005, 0.010, and 0.030 in. thicknesses. Install only one shim of the above thicknesses at the top only. Install the bearing caps, lockwashers, and screws, and tighten securely.

You can check the preload on the bearings by hooking a spring scale in the hole in the knuckle arm for the tie rod sprocket. Take the scale reading when the knuckle has just started its sweep.

The pivot pin bearing preload should be 12–16 lbs with the oil seal removed. Remove or add shims to obtain a preload within these limits. If all shims are removed and adequate preload is still not obtained, a washer may be used under the top bearing cap to increase preload. When a washer is used, shims may have to be reinstalled to obtain proper adjustment.

Open Knuckle and Ball Joints
REMOVAL AND INSTALLATION
1972–81

1. Replacement of the ball joints, or ball stud, as they will be called from here on, requires the removal of the steering knuckle. To remove the steering knuckle, first remove the wheel, brake drum or disc, and hub as an

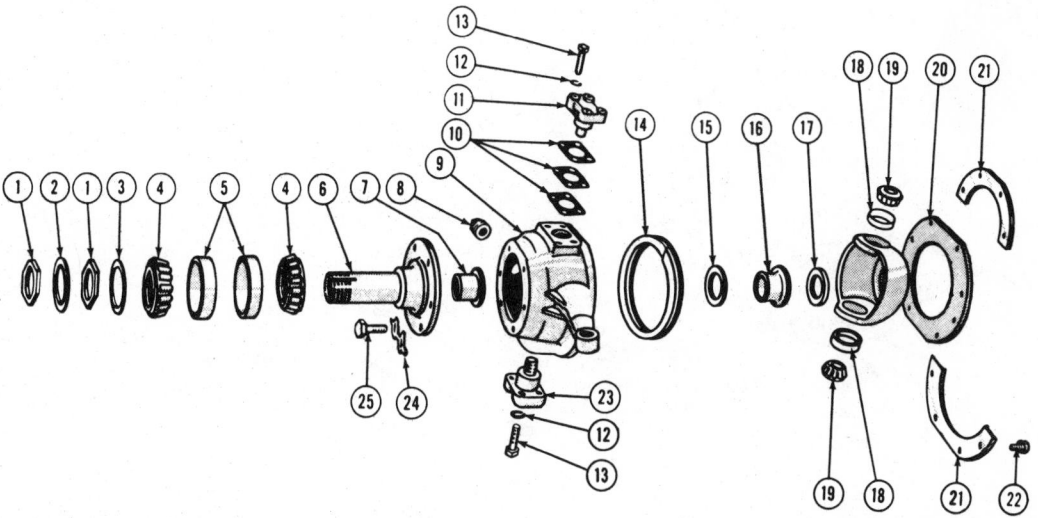

1. Bearing adjusting nut
2. Lockwasher
3. Lockwasher
4. Bearing cone and rollers
5. Bearing cup
6. Spindle
7. Bushing
8. Filler plug
9. Left knuckle and arm

10. Shims
11. Upper bearing cap
12. Lockwasher
13. Bolt
14. Oil seal and backing ring
15. Thrust washer
16. Axle pilot
17. Oil seal
18. Bearing cup

19. Bearing cone and rollers
20. Oil seal
21. Retainer
22. Bolt
23. Lower bearing cap
24. Lock strap
25. Bolt

1945–71 steering knuckle and wheel bearings

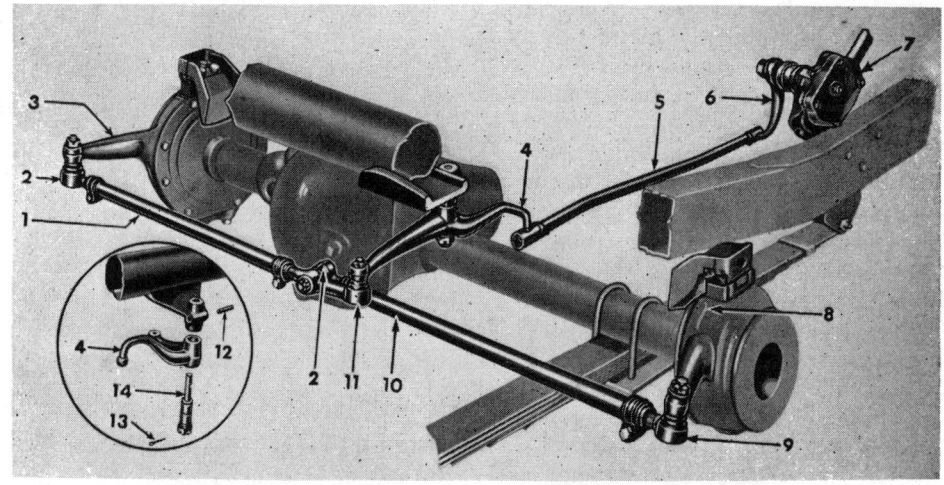

1. Tie rod—right
2. Tie rod socket—right
3. Knuckle and arm—right
4. Steering bell crank
5. Steering connecting rod
6. Steering gear arm
7. Steering gear housing

8. Knuckle and arm—left
9. Tie rod socket—left
10. Tie rod—left
11. Socket assembly
12. Steering bell crank pin
13. Steering bell crank cotter pin
14. Steering bell crank shaft

Steering system, CJ-2A models before serial number 22972

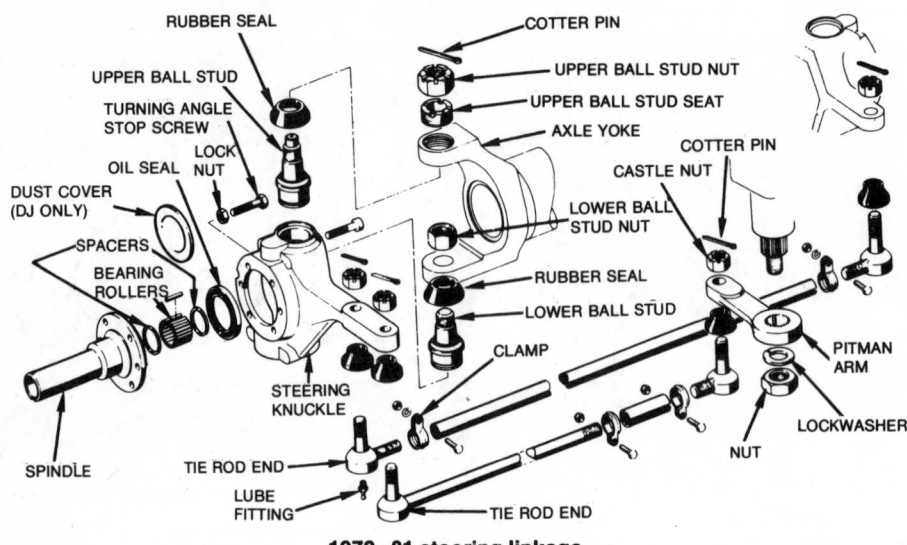

1972–81 steering linkage

assembly. Remove the brake assembly from the spindle. Position the brake assembly on the front axle in a convenient place. Remove the snap ring from the axle shaft.

2. Remove the spindle and bearing assembly. It may be necessary to tap the spindle with a soft mallet to disengage it from the steering knuckle.

3. Slide the axle shaft out through the steering knuckle.

4. Disconnect the steering tie-rods from the knuckle arm.

5. Remove and discard the lower ball stud nut.

6. Remove the cotter pin from the upper stud. Loosen the upper stud until the top edge of the nut is flush with the top end of the stud.

7. Use a lead hammer to unseat the upper and lower studs from the yoke. Remove the upper nut and the knuckle assembly.

8. Remove the ball stud seat from the upper hole in the axle yoke. It is threaded in the hole. There are special wrenches available for removing the seat. Remove the lower ball stud snap ring.

9. Securely clamp the knuckle assembly in a vise with the upper ball stud pointed down.

10. Using a large socket or drift, of approximately the same size as the ball stud, and a mallet, drive the lower stud out of the knuckle.

NOTE: *Throughout this procedure, where a ball stud is either removed or installed, a hydraulic press or a two jawed gear puller can be used and, if at all possible, should*

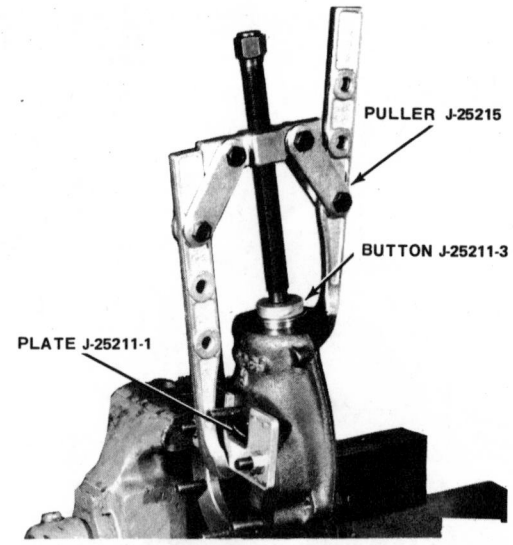

Lower ball stud removal

be used to make the job easier. However it is possible to complete the job using a mallet, drift and a large socket the same size as the ball studs.

11. Place the socket on the bottom surface of the upper ball stud. Place the drift through the hole where the lower ball stud was and place it on the socket. Drive the upper ball stud out of the knuckle with a mallet.

12. Before installing the lower ball stud, run the lower ball stud nut onto the stud just far enough so the head of the stud is flush with the top edge of the nut.

13. Invert the knuckle in the vise. Position the lower ball stud in the knuckle with the nut in place. Place the same size socket

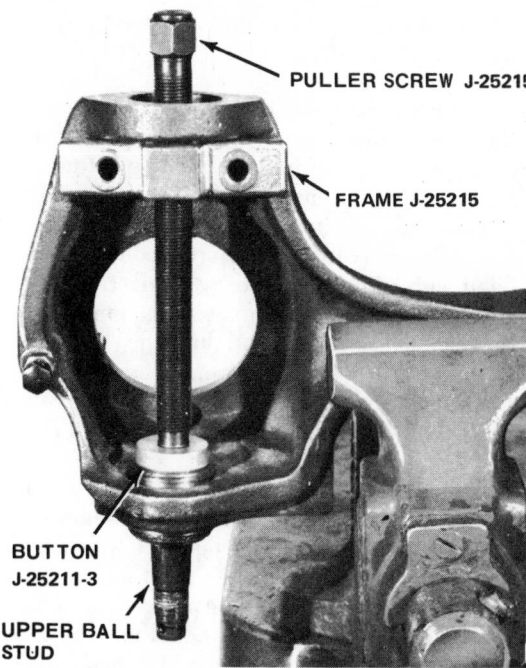

PULLER SCREW J-25215

FRAME J-25215

BUTTON
J-25211-3

UPPER BALL
STUD

Upper ball stud removal

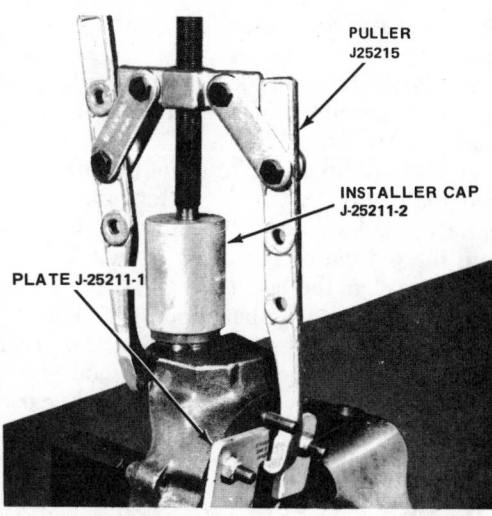

PULLER
J25215

INSTALLER CAP
J-25211-2

PLATE J-25211-1

Upper ball stud installation

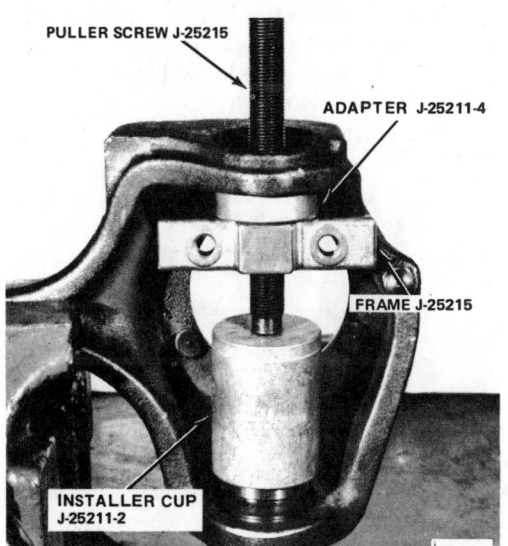

PULLER SCREW J-25215

ADAPTER J-25211-4

FRAME J-25215

INSTALLER CUP
J-25211-2

Lower ball stud installation

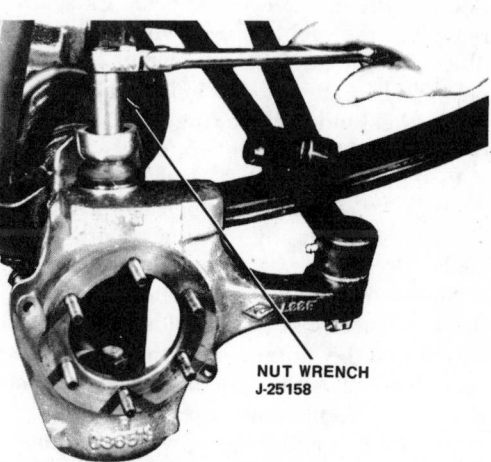

NUT WRENCH
J-25158

Tightening upper ball stud seat

over the nut and drive the ball stud into place with the drift and mallet.

14. Tighten the upper ball stud nut to 10–20 ft. lb. to draw the lower ball stud into the tapered hold in the yoke. Install the upper stud in the same manner as the lower. The drift will not be needed to install the upper ball stud.

15. Install the upper ball stud seat into the axle yoke. Use a new one if the old one shows

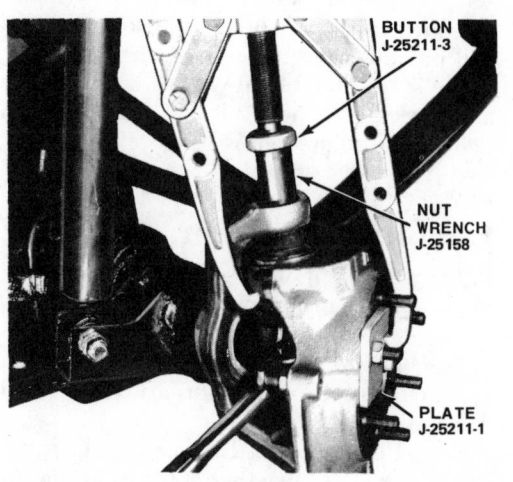

BUTTON
J-25211-3

NUT
WRENCH
J-25158

PLATE
J-25211-1

Steering knuckle installation

evidence of wear. Torque the seat to 50 ft. lb.

16. Install the knuckle assembly onto the axle yoke. Install the lower stud nut. Tighten it to 70–90 ft. lbs.

17. Install the upper stud nut and tighten it to 100 ft. lbs. Install the cotter pin. If the cotter pin holes do not align, tighten the nut until the pin can be installed. Do not loosen the nut to align the holes.

18. Install the axle shaft, spindle and bearing assembly, and brake assembly. Connect the steering rods. Install the drum and hub, and wheel assembly. Adjust the wheel bearings.

Steering Knuckle Oil Seal

Through 1971

Remove the old steering knuckle oil seal by removing the eight screws which hold it in place. Earlier production vehicles have two-piece seals. Later production vehicles have a split oil seal and backing ring assembly, an oil seal felt, and two seal retainer plate halves.

Examine the spherical surface of the axle for scores or scratches which could damage the seal. Smooth any roughness with emery cloth.

Before installing the oil seal felt, make a diagonal cut across the top side of the felt so that it may be slipped over the axle. Install the oil seal assembly in the sequence mentioned above, making sure the backing ring (of the oil seal and backing ring assembly) is toward the wheel.

After driving in wet, freezing weather swing the front wheels from side to side to remove moisture adhering to the oil seal and the spherical surface of the axle housing. This will prevent freezing with resultant damage to the seals. Should the vehicle be stored for any period of time, coat the surfaces with light grease to prevent rusting.

Front End Alignment

Proper alignment of the front wheels must be maintained in order to ensure ease of steering and satisfactory tire life.

The most important factors of front wheel alignment are wheel camber, axle caster, and wheel toe-in.

Wheel toe-in is the distance by which the wheels are closer together at the front than at the rear.

Wheel camber is the amount the top of the wheels incline outward from the vertical.

Front axle caster is the amount in degrees that the steering pivot pins are tilted toward the rear of the vehicle. Positive caster is inclination of the top of the pivot pin toward the rear of the vehicle.

These points should be checked at regular intervals, particularly when the front axle has been subjected to a heavy impact. When checking wheel alignment, it is important that wheel bearings and knuckle bearings (through 1971) be in proper adjustment. Loose bearings will affect instrument readings when checking the camber, pivot pin inclination, and toe-in.

Front wheel camber is preset. Some alignment shops can correct camber to some extent by installing special tapered shims between the steering knuckle and the spindle. Caster is also preset, but can be altered by use of tapered shims between the axle pad and the springs. Wheel toe-in is adjustable.

TURNING ANGLE

To avoid damage to the U-joints, it is advisable to check the turning angle periodically. An adjustment turntable is adviseable for properly determining the angle.

Correct turning angles are:

1. Stop screw

1945–71 turning angle adjusting screw

- 1945–71 All CJ-2A and 3A: 23° max. CJ-3B before ser. #57348-35326, CJ-5 before serial #57548-48284, CJ-6 before ser. #57748-12497: 23° max. All models after the above serial numbers: 27.5° max.
- 1972–75 With standard (F78 x 15) tires: 34–35° With larger optional tires: 31°
- 1976 31°
- 1977 29°
- 1978–81 31–32°

To adjust the turning angle, loosen the locknut (on some early models, a securing weld will have to be broken) and turn the adjusting screw. The adjusting screw is located on the axle tube near the knuckle on early models, and on the knuckle, just below the axle centerline on later models.

CASTER ADJUSTMENT

Caster angle is established in the axle design by tilting the top of the kingpins toward the rear and the bottom of the kingpins forward so that an imaginary line through the center of the kingpins would strike the ground at a point ahead of the point of the contact.

The purpose of caster is to provide steering stability which will keep the front wheels in the straight ahead position and also assist in straightening up the wheels when coming out of a turn.

If the angle of caster, when accurately measured, is found to be incorrect, correct it to the specification given at the end of this section by either installing new parts or installing caster shims between the axle pad and the springs.

If the camber and toe-in are correct and it is known that the axle is not twisted, a satisfactory check may be made by testing the vehicle on the road. Before road testing, make sure all tires are properly inflated, being particularly careful that both front tires are inflated to exactly the same pressure.

If the vehicle turns easily to either side but is hard to straighten out, insufficient caster for easy handling of the vehicle is indicated. If correction is necessary, it can usually be accomplished by installing shims between the springs and axle pads to secure the desired result.

CAMBER ADJUSTMENT

The purpose of camber is to more nearly place the weight of the vehicle over the tire contact patch on the road to facilitate ease of steering. The result of excessive camber is irregular wear of the tires on the outside shoulders and is usually caused by bent axle parts.

The result of excessive negative or reverse camber will be hard steering and possibly a wandering condition. Tires will also wear on the inside shoulders. Negative camber is usually caused by excessive wear or looseness of the front wheel bearings, axle parts or the result of a sagging axle.

Unequal camber may cause any or a combination of the following conditions: unstable steering, wandering, kick-back or road shock, shimmy or excessive tire wear. The cause of unequal camber is usually a bent steering knuckle or axle end.

Correct wheel camber is set in the axle at the time of manufacture. It is important that the camber be the same on both front wheels.

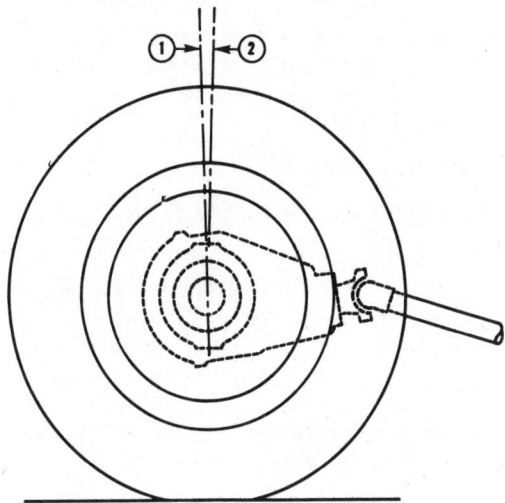

1. Vertical line   2. Caster angle

Caster

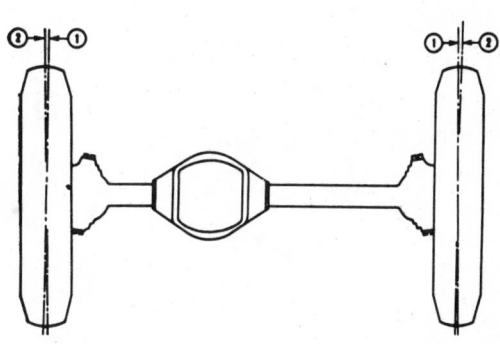

1. Vertical line   2. Camber angle

Camber

Wheel Alignment Specifications

Year	Model	Preferred Caster (deg)	Preferred Camber (deg)	Toe-in (in.)	Steering Axis Inclination (deg)
1945–73	All	3P	1½P	$^3/_{64}$–$^3/_{32}$	7½
1974–80	All	3P	1½P	$^3/_{64}$–$^3/_{32}$	8½
1981	All	6P	1½	$^3/_{64}$–$^3/_{32}$	8½

TOE-IN ADJUSTMENT

Through 1971

The toe-in may be adjusted with a line or straight edge as the vehicle tread is the same in the front and rear. To set the adjustment both tie rods must be adjusted as outlined below:

Set the tie rod end of the steering bell-crank at right angles with the front axle. Place a straight edge or line against the left rear wheel and left front wheel to determine if the wheel is in a straight ahead position. If the front wheel tire does not touch the straight edge at both the front and rear, it will be necessary to adjust the left tie rod by loosening the clamps on each end and turning the rod until the tire touches the straight edge.

Check the right hand side in the same manner, adjusting the tie rod if necessary making sure that the bell-crank remains at right angles to the axle. When it is determined that the front wheels are in the straight ahead position, set the toe-in by shortening each tie rod approximately ½ turn.

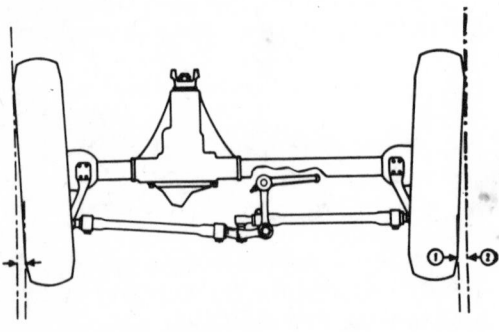

1. Vertical line   2. Toe-in angle

Toe-in

1972–81

First raise the front of the vehicle to free the front wheels. Turn the wheels to the straight ahead position. Use a steadyrest to scribe a pencil line in the center of each tire tread as the wheel is turned by hand. A good way to do this is to first coat a strip with chalk around the circumference of the tread at the center to form a base for a fine pencil line.

Measure the distance between the scribed lines at the front and rear of the wheels using care that both measurements are made at an equal distance from the floor. The distance between the lines should be greater at the rear than at the front by $^3/_{64}$ in. to $^3/_{32}$ in. To adjust, loosen the clamp bolts and turn the tie rod with a small pipe wrench. The tie rod is threaded with right and left hand threads to provide equal adjustment at both wheels. Do not overlook retightening the clamp bolts.

It is common practice to measure between the wheel rims. This is satisfactory providing the wheels run true. By scribing a line on the tire tread, measurement is taken between the road contact points reducing error caused by wheel run-out.

Steering Wheel

REMOVAL AND INSTALLATION

1945–75

1. Disconnect the negative battery cable.
2. Set the front tires in a straight ahead position.
3. Pull the horn button from the steering wheel.
4. Remove the steering wheel nut and horn button contact cup.
5. Scribe a line mark on the steering wheel and steering shaft if there is not one already. Release the turn signal assembly from the steering post and install a puller.

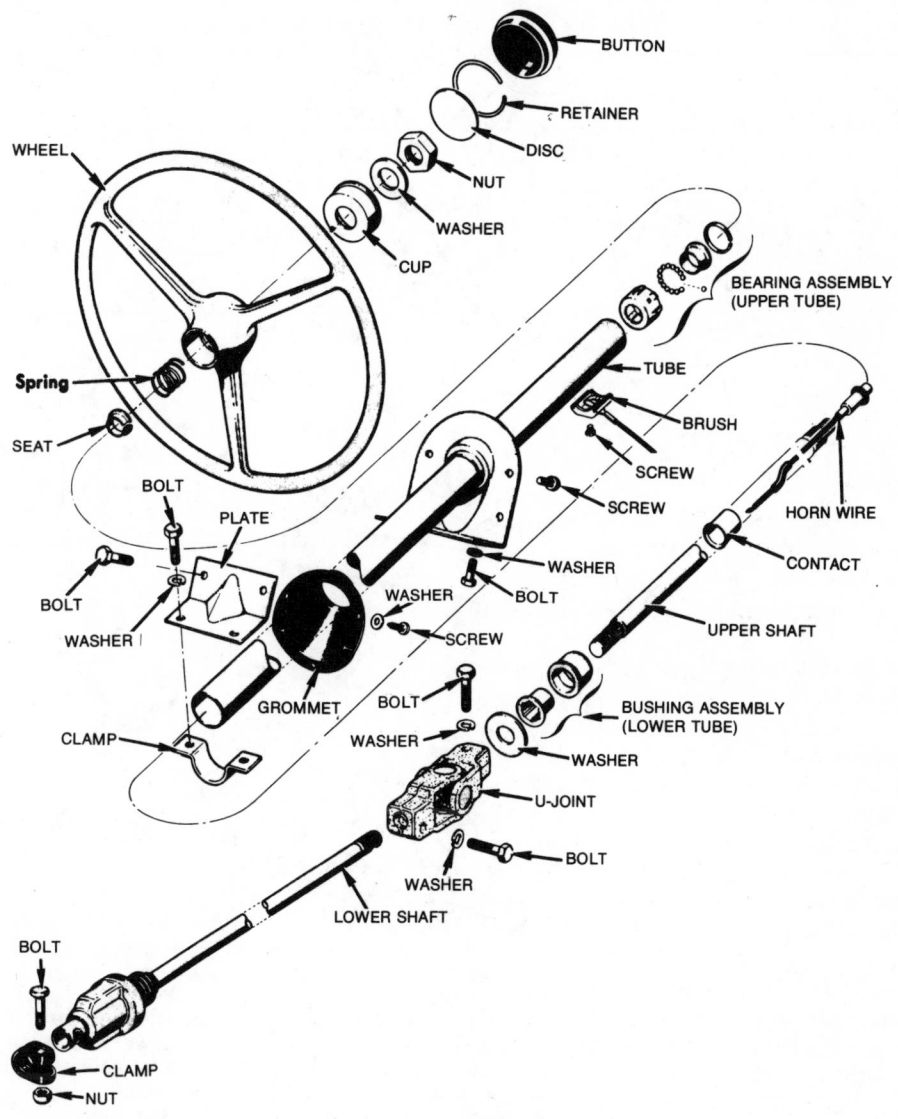

1972–75 steering column assembly

6. Remove the steering wheel and spring.

7. To install, align the scribe marks on the steering shaft with the steering wheel and secure the steering wheel spring, steering wheel, and horn button contact cup with the steering wheel nut.

8. Install the horn button.

9. Connect the battery cable and test the horn.

1976–81

1. Disconnect the negative battery cable.

2. Place the front wheels in the straight-ahead position.

3. Remove the horn button from the steering wheel. Turn the button until the locktabs on the button align with the notches in the contact cup and pull upward to remove it. With the sport wheel, just pull the button up.

4. Remove the steering wheel nut and washer.

5. If the Jeep is equipped with a sport style steering wheel, remove the horn button, nut and washer, bottom retaining ring, and horn contact ring.

6. Remove the plastic horn contact cup retainer and remove the cup and contact plate from the steering wheel.

7. Remove the horn contact pin and bushing from the steering wheel.

8. Paint or scribe alignment marks on the

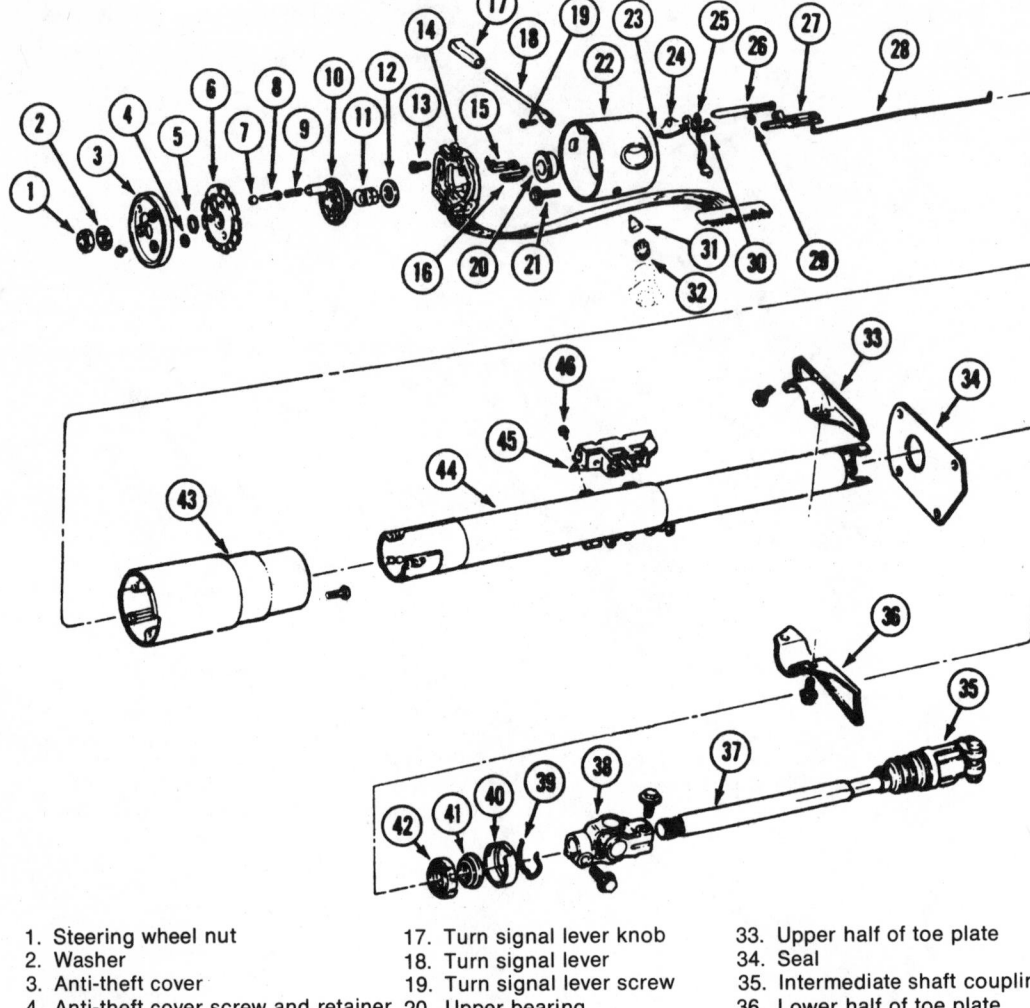

1. Steering wheel nut
2. Washer
3. Anti-theft cover
4. Anti-theft cover screw and retainer
5. Steering shaft snap-ring
6. Lockplate
7. Bushing
8. Horn contact pin
9. Spring
10. Concelling cam
11. Upper bearing preload spring
12. Thrust washer
13. Turn signal switch screw
14. Turn signal switch
15. Buzzer switch
16. Buzzer switch spring
17. Turn signal lever knob
18. Turn signal lever
19. Turn signal lever screw
20. Upper bearing
21. Housing retaining screw
22. Housing
23. Rack preload spring
24. Key release lever spring
25. Wave washer
26. Lockbolt
27. Lock rack
28. Remote rod
29. Spring washer
30. Key release lever
31. Hazard warning switch knob
32. Sector
33. Upper half of toe plate
34. Seal
35. Intermediate shaft coupling
36. Lower half of toe plate
37. Intermediate shaft
38. U-joint
39. Snap-ring
40. Retainer
41. Lower bearing
42. Lower bearing adapter
43. Shroud
44. Jacket
45. Ignition switch
46. Ignition switch screw

1976 steering column. Later models are slightly different in the area of the anti-theft cover

steering wheel and shaft for reference during assembly.

9. Remove the steering wheel using a puller.

10. Install the steering wheel in the reverse order, tightening the nut to 20 ft. lbs. for 1976–77, and 30 ft. lbs. for 1978–81.

Turn Signal Switch Replacement

1945–75

The turn signal switch is attached to the steering column; the whole unit is mounted externally. To remove the switch assembly,

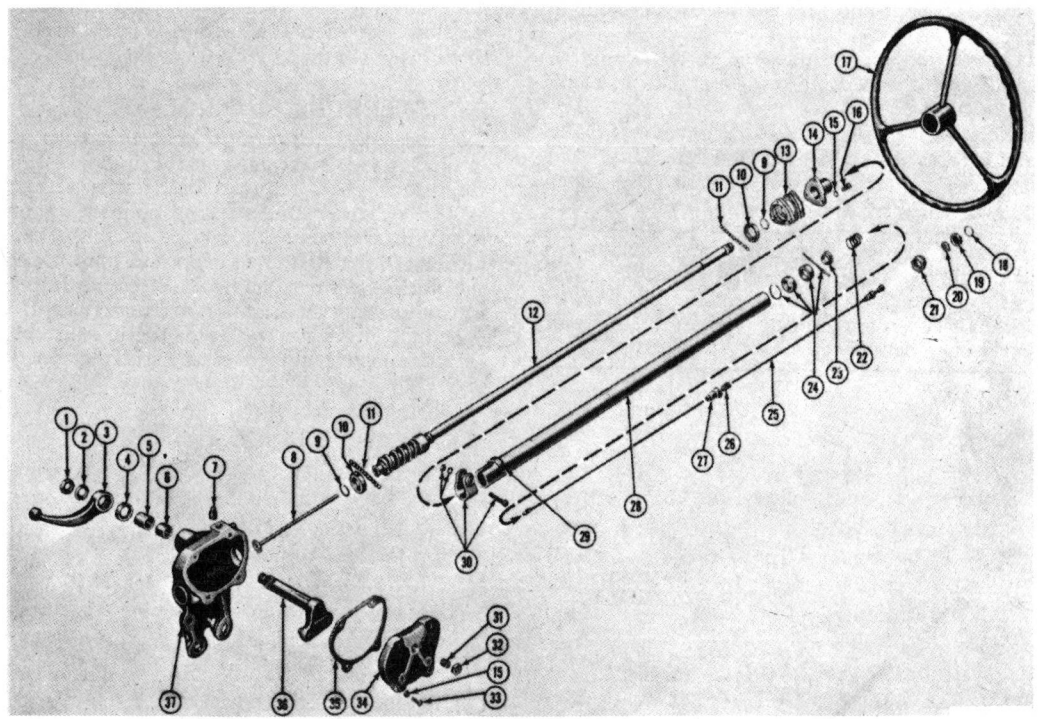

1. Nut	14. Upper cover	27. Spring cap
2. Lockwasher	15. Lockwasher	28. Steering column
3. Steering gear arm	16. Bolt	29. Oil hole cover
4. Lever shaft oil seal	17. Steering wheel	30. Clamp
5. Outer housing bushing	18. Horn button retainer	31. Adjusting screw
6. Inner housing bushing	19. Horn button	32. Nut
7. Filler plug	20. Horn button cap	33. Bolt
8. Cover and tube	21. Nut	34. Side cover
9. Ball retainer ring	22. Spring	35. Gasket
10. Cup	23. Spring seat	36. Shaft and lever
11. Ball (steel)	24. Bearing	37. Housing
12. Tube and cam	25. Horn cable	
13. Shims	26. Horn button spring	

1953–71 steering column and gear

remove the attaching screws, unfasten the wires and remove the unit from the steering column.

The most frequent causes of failure in the directional signal system are loose connections and burned out bulbs. A flashing rate of approximately twice normal usually indicates a burned-out bulb in the circuit.

When trouble in the signal switch is suspected, it is advisable to make a few checks to definitely locate the trouble before going to the effort of removing the signal switch.

First check the fuse. There is an inline fuse located between the ignition switch and the turn signal flasher.

If the fuse checks out OK, next eliminate the flasher unit by substituting a known good flasher. If a new flasher does not cure the trouble, check the signal system wiring connections at the fuse and at the steering column connector.

NOTE: *If the right front parking light and the right rear stop light are inoperative, switch failure is indicated. If the brake lights function properly, the rear signal lights are OK.*

To check the switch on models through 1971, first put the control lever in the neutral position. Then disconnect the wire to the right side circuit and bridge it to the "L" terminal, thus by-passing the signal switch. If the right side circuit lights, the signal switch is inoperative and must be replaced.

To check out the switch on the 1972 and 1973 models, disconnect the switch at the six wire connector. Use a jumper wire from the

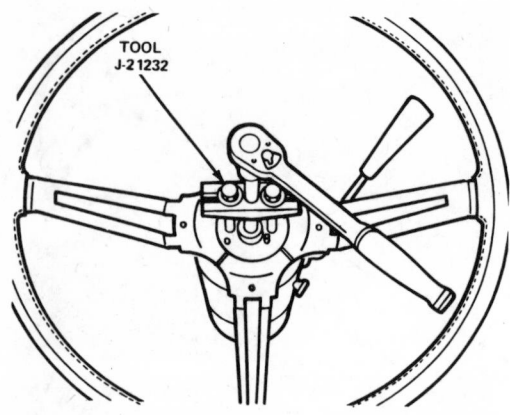

Steering wheel removal

white (battery feed) wire to the other wires. Circuitry is as follows:

- White to Orange—Right rear
- White to Black—Right front
- White to Yellow—Left front
- White to Blue—Left rear

If the lights in any of these circuits light then the switch is bad and must be replaced.

1976–79

1. Disconnect the negative battery cable.
2. Remove the steering wheel.
3. Loosen the anti-theft cover retaining screws on 1976 models and lift the cover from the steering column. It is not necessary to completely remove these screws.
4. Depress the lockplate and pry the round wire snap-ring from the steering shaft groove. A lockplate compressor tool is available for compressing the lockplate.
5. Remove the lockplate, directional signal canceling cam, upper bearing preload spring, and thrust washer from the steering shaft.
6. Move the directional signal actuating lever to the right turn position and remove the lever.
7. Depress the hazard warning light switch and remove the button by turning it counterclockwise.
8. Remove the directional signal wiring harness connector block from its mounting bracket on the right-side of the lower column.
9. On vehicles equipped with an automatic transmission, use a stiff wire, such as a paper clip, to depress the lock tab which retains the shift quadrant light wire in the connector block.
10. Remove the directional signal switch retaining screws and pull the switch and wiring harness from the steering column.
11. Guide the wiring harness of the new switch into position and carefully align the switch assembly. Make sure that the actuating lever pivot is correctly aligned and seated in the upper housing pivot boss prior to installing the retaining screws.
12. Install the directional signal lever and actuate the directional signal switch to assure correct operation.
13. Place the thrust washer, spring, and directional signal canceling cam on the upper end of the steering shaft.
14. Align the lockplate splines with the steering shaft splines and place the lockplate in position with the directional signal canceling cam shaft protruding through the dogleg opening in the lockplate.
15. Install the snap-ring.
16. Install the anti-theft cover.
17. Install the steering wheel and connect the negative battery cable.
18. Check the operation of the turn signal switch.

1980–81

1. Disconnect the battery ground.
2. Cover the painted areas of the column.
3. Remove the column-to-dash bezel.
4. Loosen the toe plate screws.
5. With tilt columns, place the column in the non-tilt position.
6. Remove the steering wheel.
7. Remove the lock plate cover.
8. Compress the lock plate and unseat the steering shaft snap ring as follows:

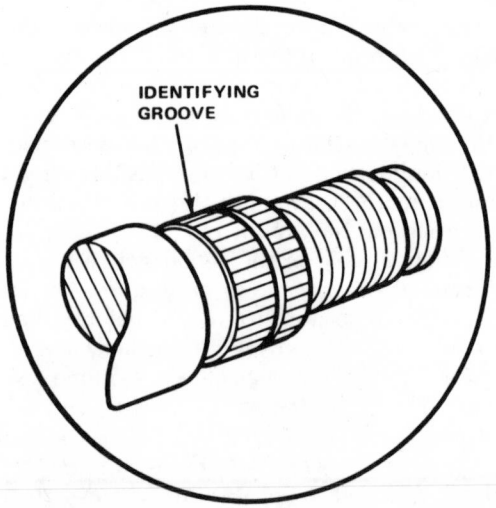

Metric steering shaft identification

a. Check the steering shaft nut threads. Metric threads have an identifying groove in the steering wheel splines. SAE threads do not.

b. With SAE threads use a compressor tool such as tool J-23653 to compress the lock plate and remove the snap ring.

c. If the shaft has metric threads, replace the forcing screw in the compressor with metric forcing screw J-23653-4 before using.

9. Remove the compressor and snap ring.

10. Remove the lock plate, canceling cam and upper bearing preload spring.

11. Place the turn signal lever in the right turn position and remove the lever.

12. Remove the hazard warning knob. Press the knob inward and turn counterclockwise to remove it.

13. Remove the wiring harness protectors.

14. Disconnect the wiring harness connectors.

15. Remove the turn signal switch attaching screws and lift out the switch.

Ignition Switch

REPLACEMENT

1945–75

1. Disconnect the battery ground cable.

2. On models through 1972, unscrew the nut from the front of the instrument panel and remove the switch.

3. On 1973–75 models, reach behind the panel and press the switch in against the spring. Turn the bezel counterclockwise to release.

4. Lower the switch and detach the wiring.

5. Reverse the procedure for installation.

1976–81

The ignition switch is on top of the lower part of the steering column, inside the vehicle.

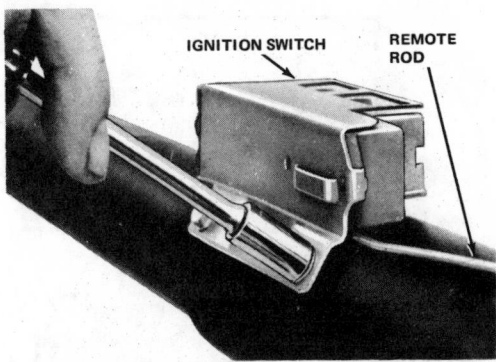

Ignition switch removal or installation, column mounted switches

1. Put the key in the lock and turn to the Off-unlocked position.

2. Disconnect the battery ground cable.

3. Detach the wire connectors at the switch.

4. Remove the switch screws.

5. Disconnect the actuating rod from the switch and remove the switch.

6. Move the switch slider all the way down the column. Move it back toward the steering wheel two clicks to the center Off-unlocked position.

7. Engage the column actuating rod in the switch slider and fasten the switch down.

8. Connect the wire connectors, then the battery ground cable.

Ignition Lock Cylinder

REPLACEMENT

1945–75

1. Remove the ignition switch.

2. Put the key in the lock and turn it to the On position.

3. Insert a heavy paper clip wire or something similar through the release hole in the side of the switch. Push in the retaining ring until the lock cylinder can be pulled out.

4. To install the new lock cylinder, line up

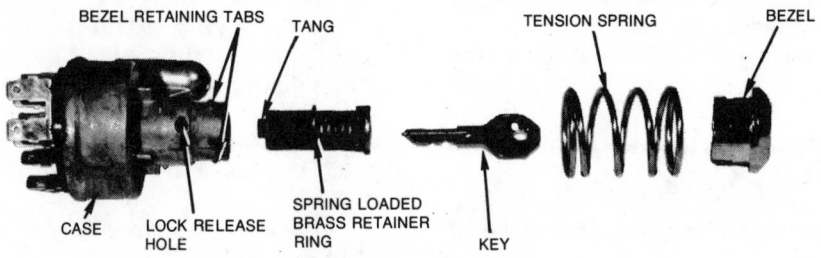

1973–75 ignition switch and lock cylinder details

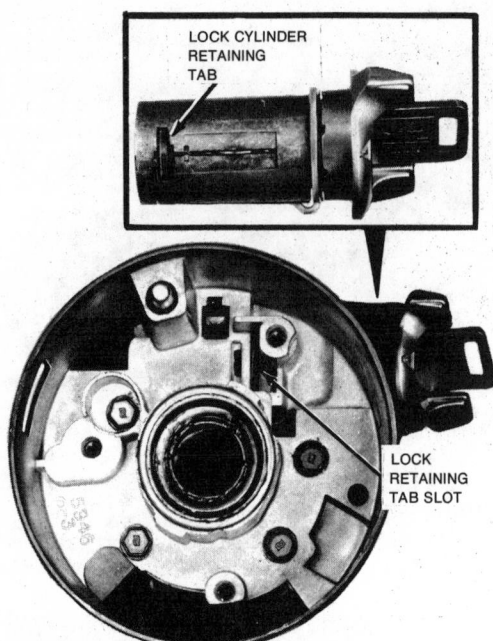

1976–81 ignition lock cylinder removal

the tang on the cylinder with the slot in the case and push the cylinder in.

5. Replace the switch.

1976–81

1. Disconnect the battery ground cable.

2. Remove the turn signal switch as described earlier in this chapter. You don't have to remove the switch completely, just set it aside.

3. Insert the key. With manual transmission, put it in the On position: with automatic, put it in Off-Lock.

4. Working through the slot next to the turn signal switch mounting boss, use a thin screwdriver to release the lock cylinder.

5. To install, insert the key in the new lock cylinder. Hold the sleeve and turn the key clockwise until it stops. Align the cylinder retaining tab with the housing slot and insert the cylinder. Push the cylinder in, rotate to engage, then push in until the retaining tab engages the housing groove.

6. The rest of the procedure is the reverse of removal.

Power Steering Pump

REMOVAL AND INSTALLATION

If the power steering pump has to be removed to service another component, it is not necessary to remove the hoses from the pump. Just disconnect the mounting fixtures and lift the pump away from the engine and lay it out of the way. The only time the power steering hoses have to be removed from the pump is when the pump has to be removed from the vehicle for service or replacement.

1. Remove the pump drive belt tension adjusting bolt. Disconnect the belt from the pump.

2. Disconnect the return and pressure hoses from the pump. Cover the hose connector and union on the pump and open ends of the hoses to avoid the entrance of dirt.

3. On the 304 V8, remove the front bracket from the engine.

4. Remove the two nuts which secure the rear of the pump to the bracket, and the two bolts which secure the front of the pump to the bracket and remove the pump.

5. To install, position the pump in the bracket and install the rear attaching screws. On the 304 V8, install the front bracket.

6. Connect the hydraulic hoses. Adjust the drive belt tension.

7. Fill the pump reservoir to the correct level.

8. Start the engine and wait for at least three minutes before turning the steering wheel. Check the level frequently during this time.

9. Slowly turn the steering wheel through its entire range a few times with the engine running. Recheck the level and inspect for possible leaks.

NOTE: *If air becomes trapped in the fluid, the pump may become noisy until all of the air is out. This may take some time since trapped air does not bleed out rapidly.*

Manual Steering Gear
REMOVAL AND INSTALLATION
1945–71

The steering gear has to be removed down through the floor pan.

1. Remove the left front fender.

2. On early CJ-2A models with remote control steering linkage, disconnect the control rods at the transmission.

3. Remove the steering wheel.

4. Unbolt the steering column bracket from the instrument panel.

5. Disconnect the exhaust pipe at the manifold.

6. Remove the steering column cover plate from the floorboard.

7. On early CJ-2A models, remove the

1. Cotter pin
2. Adjusting plug
3. Ball seat
4. Ball seat spring
5. Plug spring
6. Draglink
7. Adjusting plug
8. Dust cover
9. Dust cover shield
10. Lubricating fitting

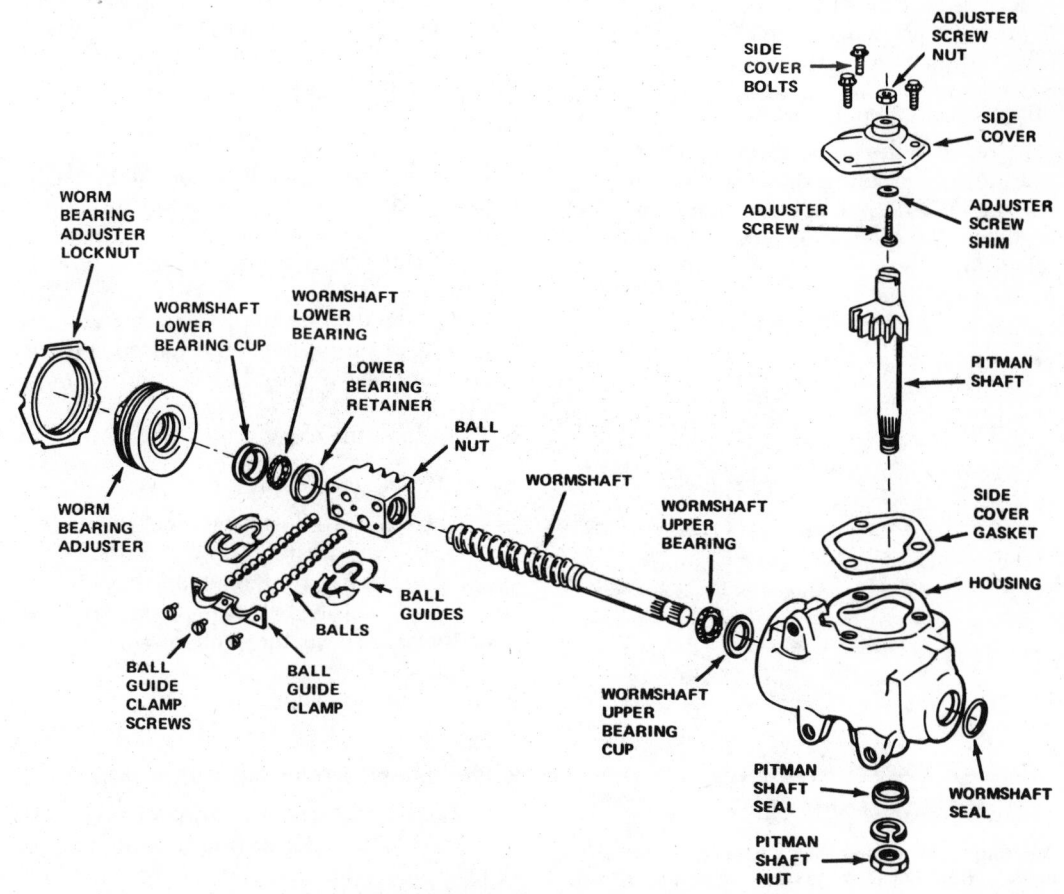

Typical drag link

two screws holding the shift control rods housing to the steering column.

8. On CJ-2A models, remove the horn wire contact. On all other models, disconnect the horn wire.

9. On early CJ-2A models, lower the shift linkage through the floor.

10. Remove the drag link from the steering gear arm ball.

11. Unbolt the steering gear housing from the frame.

12. Lower the steering gear through the floor pan and over the outside of the frame rail.

13. Installation is the reverse of removal. Adjust the shifting linkage on early CJ-2A models.

Typical manual steering gear components

1972–75

1. Disconnect the steering gear from the lower steering shaft by removing the bolt and nut attaching the coupling to the worm shaft.

2. Disconnect the steering arm from the connecting rod.

3. Remove the upper steering gear-to-frame bracket bolt.

4. Remove the two lower steering gear-to-frame bracket bolts and remove the gear.

5. Installation is the reverse of removal. Torque the pitman arm-to-shaft nut to 160–210 ft. lb.; the steering bracket-to-frame ⅜ in. bolt to 35–45 ft. lb.; the steering bracket-to-frame ⁷/₁₆ in. bolt to 60–70 ft. lb.; the steering gear-to-bracket bolts to 60–80 ft. lb.

1976–81

1. Remove the intermediate shaft-to-wormshaft coupling clamp bolt and disconnect the intermediate shaft.

2. Remove the pitman arm nut and lockwasher.

3. Using a puller, remove the Pitman arm from the shaft.

4. Raise the left side of the vehicle slightly to relieve tension on the left front spring and rest the frame on a jack stand.

5. Remove the steering gear lower bracket-to-frame bolts.

6. Remove the bolts attaching the steering gear upper bracket to the crossmember. Beginning in 1979, one of these bolts is a Torx® head bolt. This bolt, and some others may be removed with the aid of a 9 inch extension. Remove the gear.

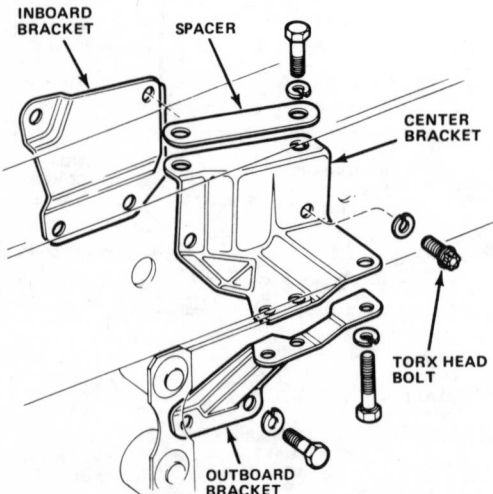

Steering gear mounting brackets, 1972–81 models. Note the Torx® fastener used on 1979–81 models

NOTE: *Loctite 271® or similar material must be applied to all attaching bolt threads prior to installation.*

7. Position the tie plate upper and lower mounting brackets on the gear and install the bolts. Torque the bracket-to-gear bolts to 70 ft. lb. and the bracket-to-tie plate bolt to 55 ft. lb.

8. Align and engage the intermediate shaft coupling with the steering gear wormshaft splines.

9. Position the steering gear on the frame and install the mounting bolts. Torque the bolts to 55 ft. lb. Install the Pitman arm and torque the nut to 185 ft. lb.

NOTE: *The steering gear may produce a slight roughness, this can be eliminated by turning the steering wheel full left and right 10–15 times.*

MANUAL STEERING GEAR ADJUSTMENTS

1945–71

Before adjusting, remove all load from the system by disconnecting the drag link from the steering arm and loosening the instrument panel bracket bolts and the steering gear-to-frame bolts.

STEERING SHAFT PLAY ADJUSTMENT

1. Remove the shims installed between the steering gear housing and the upper cover.

2. Loosen the housing side cover adjusting screw.

3. Loosen the housing cover to cut and remove one or more shims as required. Proper adjustment allows a slight drag and free operation.

4. Tighten the cover.

BACKLASH ADJUSTMENT

1. Loosen the adjusting screw locknut.

2. Turn the adjusting screw in until a very slight drag is felt through the mid-point in steering wheel travel. This procedure is done with the wheels in the straight-ahead position.

3. Tighten the adjusting screw locknut.

1972–75

WORM BEARING PRELOAD ADJUSTMENT

1. Loosen the steering gear end cover.

2. Add to or subtract from the number of shims under the cover to obtain a rolling torque of 2–5 in. lb.

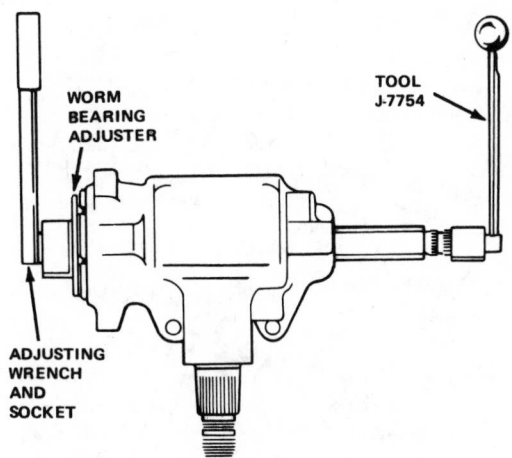

Adjusting worm bearing preload

3. Tighten the cover bolts alternately and evenly to 18–22 ft. lb.

STEERING GEAR CLEARANCE ADJUSTMENT

1. Loosen the locknut and turn the adjusting screw on the side cover, counterclockwise until the worm gear shaft turns freely through its entire range of travel.

2. Count the number of turns necessary to rotate the worm gear shaft through its travel.

3. Turn the shaft to center point.

4. Rotate the shaft back and forth over center, and tighten the adjusting screw until the shaft binds slightly at the center point.

5. Adjust the screw to obtain a rolling torque of 7–12 in. lb. through the center.

6. Hold the adjusting screw and tighten the locknut to 16–20 ft. lb.

1976–81

WORM BEARING PRELOAD ADJUSTMENT

1. Tighten the worm bearing adjuster until it bottoms, then back it off ¼ turn.

2. Install a torque wrench and socket J-7754 or its equivalent on the splined end of the wormshaft.

3. Rotate the wormshaft clockwise until it hits the stop, then back it off ½ turn.

4. Tighten the wormshaft bearing adjuster until the torque required to rotate the shaft is 5–8 in. lb.

NOTE: *The adjustment must be made with the wormshaft no more than ½ turn from the stop.*

5. Tighten the worm bearing adjuster locknut to 23 ft. lb. Check rotating torque. Check and record the worm bearing preload reading.

Adjusting Pitman shaft overcenter torque drag

PITMAN SHAFT OVERCENTER ADJUSTMENT

1. Rotate the wormshaft from stop-to-stop and count the number of turns.

2. Rotate the wormshaft back from the stop, ½ the total number of turns.

3. Install a torque wrench and socket J-7754 on the splined end of the wormshaft.

4. Tighten the pitman shaft adjuster screw, while rotating the shaft back and forth over center, until the torque equals the worm bearing preload setting of 5–8 in. lb. previously recorded.

5. Rotate the shaft over center and continue tightening the adjuster until the drag torque is increased by an additional 4–10 in. lb., but do not exceed 16 in. lb. combined total.

6. Hold the adjuster screw and tighten the locknut to 23 ft. lb. Do not allow the adjuster to turn, or the adjustment will have to be made over again!

Power Steering Gear

REMOVAL AND INSTALLATION

1972–75

1. Disconnect the hoses at the gear and raise them above the pump to prevent fluid loss.

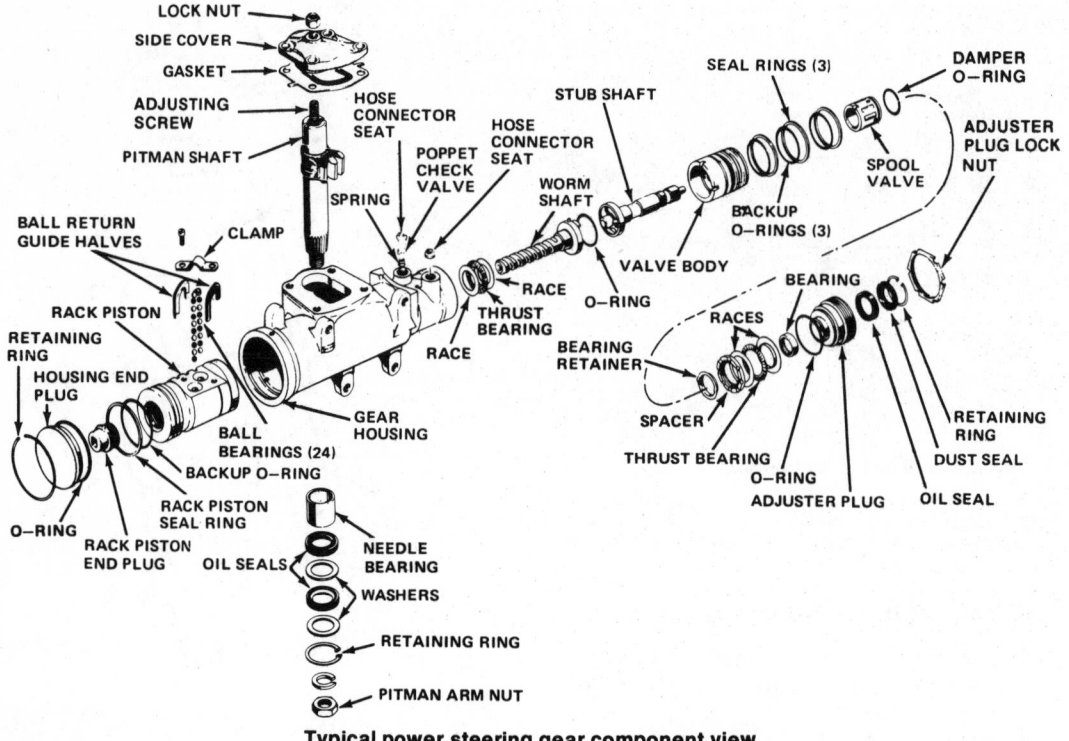

Typical power steering gear component view

2. Remove the pinch bolt from the lower flange.

3. Remove the pitman arm nut and lockwasher, and remove the pitman arm with a puller.

4. Unbolt and remove the pump.

5. Installation is the reverse of removal. Torque the pitman arm nut to 160–210 ft. lb. and the gear-to-frame bolts to 55 ft. lb.

1976–81

1. Disconnect the hoses at the gear and raise them above the pump to prevent fluid loss.

2. Remove the clamp bolt and nut attaching the intermediate shaft coupling to the steering gear stub shaft and disconnect the intermediate shaft.

3. Mark the pitman shaft and arm for alignment. Remove the pitman nut and lockwasher and remove the pitman arm with a puller.

4. Raise the left side of the vehicle slightly to relieve tension from the spring. Support with a jack stand under the frame.

5. Remove the three lower steering gear mounting bracket-to-frame bolts.

6. Remove the two steering gear-to-crossmember upper bolts. Remove the gear and brackets as an assembly.

7. Remove the brackets from the gear. NOTE: *Prior to installation, all bolts must be coated with Loctite 271® or its equivalent.*

8. Position the mounting brackets on the gear and torque the bolts to 70 ft. lb.

9. Align and connect the intermediate shaft coupling to the steering gear stub shaft.

10. Position the steering gear on the frame and crossmember. Install and tighten the bolts to 55 ft. lb.

11. Lower the vehicle.

12. Install the intermediate shaft coupling-to-steering gear stub shaft clamp bolt and nut. Tighten the nut to 45 ft. lb.

13. Align and install the pitman arm, nut and lockwasher. Torque the nut to 185 ft. lb. Stake the nut in two places.

14. Connect the hoses. Torque the hose connections to 25 ft. lb.

POWER STEERING GEAR ADJUSTMENTS

NOTE: *The gear must be adjusted off the vehicle. All adjustments must be made in the sequence described below. Worm bearing preload is always adjusted first!*

Worm Bearing Preload Adjustment

1. Mount the gear assembly in a vise.

2. Torque the adjuster plug to 20 ft. lb.

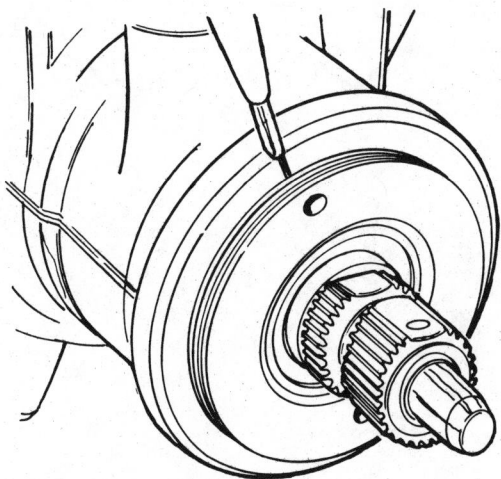

Marking power steering gear housing adjacent to the hole in the adjuster

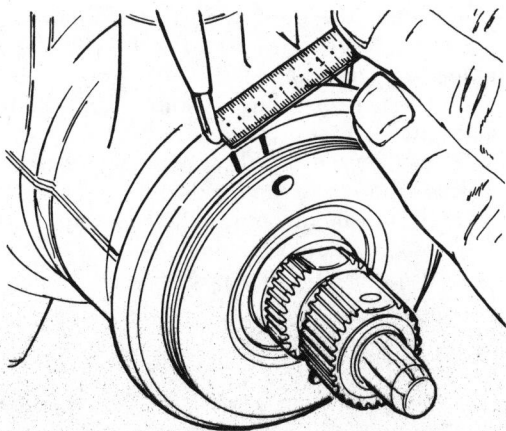

Making a second mark, ³/₁₆ to ¼ inch from the first on models through 1979 and ½ inch from the first, on 1980–81 models

3. Mark the gear housing in line with one of the adjuster plug holes.

4. Measure counterclockwise ³/₁₆–¼ in from the first mark on models through 1979 and ½ inch from the first mark on 1980–81 models, and make another mark.

5. Turn the adjuster plug counterclockwise to align the hole with the second mark.

6. Hold the adjuster plug and torque the locknut to 85 ft. lb. Do not allow the adjuster to turn.

7. Turn the stubshaft clockwise to its stop, then back ¼ turn.

8. Using a torque wrench of no more than 50 in. lb. capacity and a 12 point deep socket, check the rotating torque at the splined end of the stub shaft at or near a vertical position. Torque should be 4–10 in. lb.

Measuring wormshaft bearing preload on power steering gears

9. If the torque cannot be adjusted within these limits, the gear will have to be rebuilt.

Pitman Shaft Overcenter Adjustment

1. Loosen the adjuster screw locknut.

2. Turn the adjuster screw counterclockwise until the screw is fully extended. Turn the screw back in one full turn.

3. Count the number of turns to rotate the stubshaft from stop-to-stop.

4. Turn the shaft back ½ the number of turns. At this point the flat surface of the

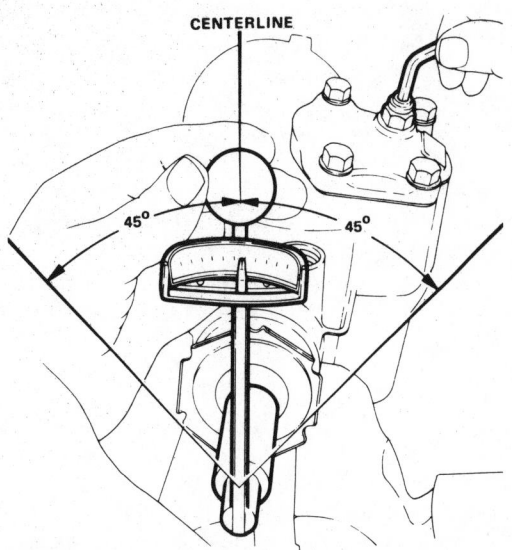

Measuring Pitman shaft overcenter torque drag on power steering gears

stubshaft should be upward and the master spline on the pitman shaft should be aligned with the adjuster screw.

5. Install a 50 in. lb. torque wrench and deep 12 point socket on the splined end of the stub shaft. Place the torque wrench in a vertical position.

6. Rotate the torque wrench 45° to each side and record the highest torque at or near center. Record this reading.

7. Adjust the torque by turning the adjuster screw clockwise. Adjustment is: the recorded reading plus 4–8 in. lb. for new gears, but not exceeding 14 in. lb. total; the previously recorded reading plus 4–5 in. lb. for used gears, but not exceeding 14 in. lb. combined total.

8. Tighten the adjuster screw locknut to 20 ft. lb. while holding the adjuster screw.

9. Install the gear.

Tie Rod End

REMOVAL AND INSTALLATION

1. Remove the cotter pins and retaining nuts at both ends of the tie rod and from the end of the connecting rod where it attaches to the tie rod.

2. Remove the nut attaching the steering

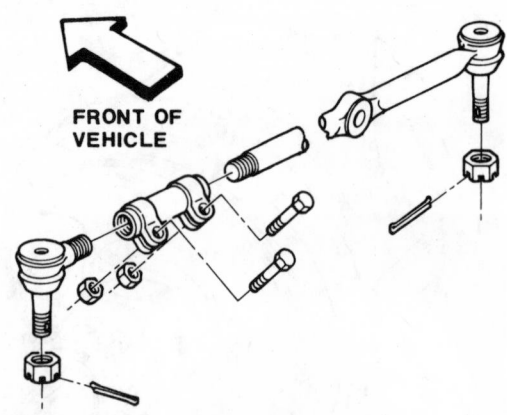

FRONT OF VEHICLE

Typical tie rod assembly

damper push rod to the tie rod bracket and move the damper aside.

3. Remove the tie rod ends from the steering arms and connecting rod with a puller.

4. Count the number of threads showing on the tie rod before removing the ends, as a guide to installation.

5. Loosen the adjusting tube clamp bolts and unthread the ends.

6. Installation is the reverse of removal. Torque the connecting rod-to-tie rod nut to 40 ft. lb. on models through 1971 and to 70 ft. lb. on 1972 and later models.

7. Adjust toe-in, if necessary.

Brakes

BRAKE SYSTEM

Adjustment—Drum Brakes Only

The method of brake adjustment varies depending on whether the vehicle is equipped with cam adjustment brakes or star wheel adjustment brakes with self adjusters. When the brake linings become worn, effective brake pedal travel is reduced. Adjusting the brake shoes will restore the necessary travel.

Before adjusting the brakes, check the spring nuts, brake dust shield to axle flange bolts, and wheel bearing adjustments. Any looseness in these parts will cause erratic brake operation. Also on models through 1971 make sure that the brake pedal has the correct amount of free travel without moving the master cylinder piston (free play). There should be about ½ in. of free play at the master cylinder eye bolt. Turn the eye bolt to adjust free play. On models from 1972 on, the pedal free travel is determined by the pedal pushrod length and is not adjustable. If pedal free travel is less than $1/16$ in., relace the pushrod.

Release the parking brakes and centralize the brake shoes in the drums by depressing the brake pedal hard and then releasing it. It is best to have all four wheels off the ground when the brakes are adjusted so that you can go back to each wheel to double check your adjustments.

INITIAL BRAKE SHOE ADJUSTMENT

If the brake assemblies have been disassembled, an initial adjustment must be made before the drum is installed. It may also be necessary to back off the adjustment to remove the drums.

When the brake parts have been installed in their correct position, adjust the adjusting screw assemblies to a point where approximately ⅜ in. of threads are exposed between the star wheel and the star wheel nut.

CAM ADJUSTMENT BRAKES

1. Jack up the vehicle until all of the wheels, or at least the one to be adjusted first, are off the ground.

2. Turn the forward shoe adjusting cams on the left side of the vehicle clockwise until the shoes are tight against the drums. Then turn the cams in the opposite direction until the wheels rotate freely without brake drag.

3. Turn the rear adjusting cams on the left side counter-clockwise until the shoes are tight against the drums. Then turn the cams in the opposite direction until the wheels rotate freely without brake drag.

4. Repeat the two steps given above on the right side of the vehicle, turning the for-

Brake adjustment points on CJ-2A and CJ-3A models. Note the anchor pin adjusters at the bottom of the backing plate

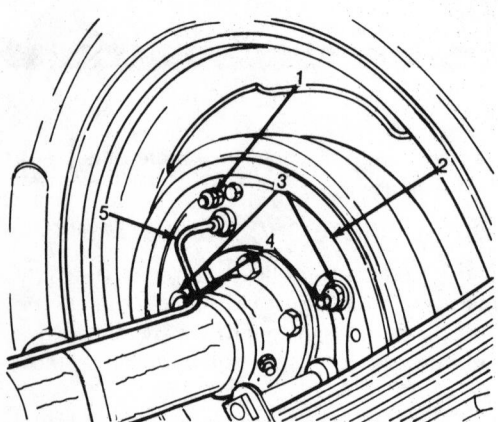

1. Bleeder screw
2. Brake backing plate
3. Eccentric lock nut
4. Eccentric adjusting screw
5. Brake fluid line

Brake adjustments on all CJ-3B models and CJ-5 and CJ-6 models with cam adjusters

ward shoe adjusting cams counterclockwise and the rear shoe adjusting cams clockwise to tighten.

On CJ-2A and CJ-3A models, if additional adjustment is required or when installing new brakes, reset the anchor pins as follows:

a. With the brakes installed and the drum in place, loosen the anchor pin locknuts at the bottom of the backing plate.

b. Turn the anchor pins in toward each other until a brake shoe-to-drum clearance is .005 in. at the lower end of the shoe and .008 in. at the upper end. On early

models, a slot in the brake drum was provided to measure this clearance; the slot was eliminated on later models.

STAR WHEEL ADJUSTING TYPE BRAKES (WITH SELF-ADJUSTERS)

1. Jack up the vehicle.
2. Remove the access slot cover and using a brake adjusting tool or screw driver, rotate the star wheel until the wheel is locked and can't be turned by hand. To tighten, rotate the star wheel in the clockwise direction.
3. Back off the star wheel until the wheel rotates freely. To back off the star wheel on the brake, insert an ice pick or thin screw driver in the adjusting screw slot to hold the automatic adjusting lever away from the star wheel. Do not attempt to back off on the adjusting screw without holding the adjusting lever away from the star wheel as the adjuster will be damaged.

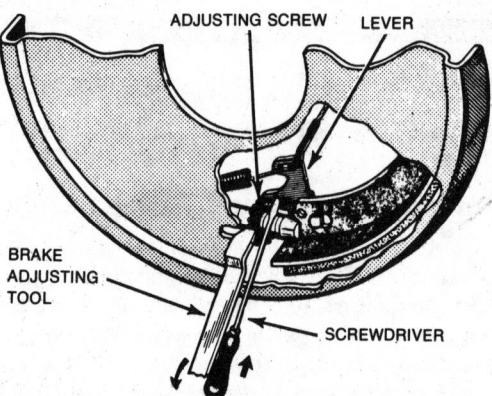

To loosen the self-adjusting drum brake, you have to hold the adjusting lever away from the star wheel

HYDRAULIC SYSTEM

Master Cylinder

REMOVAL AND INSTALLATION

To remove the master cylinder, disconnect and plug the brake lines, disconnect the wires from the stoplight switch, disconnect the master cylinder pushrod at the brake pedal (non-power brakes only—1972–81), remove all attaching bolts and nuts and lift the assembly from the vehicle.

Installation is the reverse of the removal procedure. Torque the mounting bolts to 30 ft. lb. Bleed the hydraulic system.

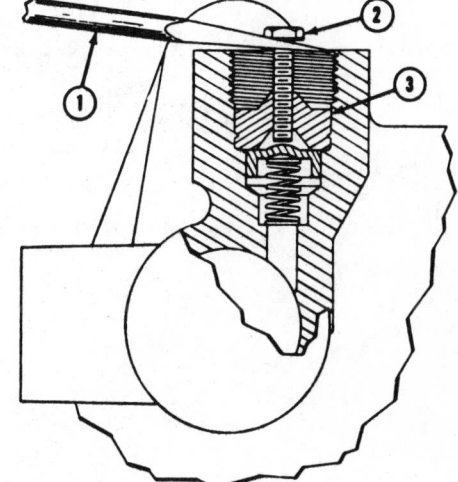

1. Pushrod
2. Boot
3. Piston stop lock wire
4. Stop plate
5. Piston
6. Master cylinder cup
7. Valve spring assembly
8. Valve seat
9. Supply tank
10. Filler cap gasket
11. Filler cap
12. Outlet fitting gasket
13. Outlet fitting
14. Outlet fitting bolt
15. Outlet fitting bolt

Single system master cylinder

OVERHAUL

Single System

1. After the master cylinder has been removed it should be dismantled and washed in alcohol. Never wash any part of the hydraulic braking system in gasoline or kerosene.

2. After all the parts have been thoroughly cleaned with alcohol, make a careful inspection, replacing those parts which show signs of deterioration.

3. Inspect the cylinder bore. If it is rough it should be honed out or a new cylinder installed.

4. Clean out the cylinder with alcohol. Pass a wire through the ports that open from the supply reservoir into the cylinder bore to make sure that these passages are free of any foreign matter.

5. Install a new piston, primary cup, valve, and valve seat when rebuilding the master cylinder.

6. When reassembling the master cylinder, dip all internal parts in clean brake fluid. Install the valve seat in the end of the cylinder with the flat surface toward the valve.

7. Install the valve assembly.

8. Install the return spring and primary cup. The flat side of the cup goes toward the piston.

9. Install the piston and the piston stop snap ring.

10. Install the fitting connection.

11. Fill the reservoir half full with brake fluid and operate the piston with the piston rod until fluid is ejected at the fitting.

12. Install the master cylinder to the firewall or in position under the floor pan. Fill it to a level ½ in. below the top of the fill hole.

1. Screwdriver
2. Self-tapping screw
3. Tube seat

Removing tube seats

13. Make the necessary connections and adjust the pedal clearance.

14. Bleed the brake lines.

15. Recheck the entire hydraulic brake system to make sure there are no leaks.

Dual System—Through 1975

1. Remove the filler cap and empty all the fluid.

2. The stop light switch and primary piston stop, located in the stop light switch outlet hole, must be removed before removing the snap ring from the piston bore. Remove the snap ring, pushrod assembly and the primary and secondary piston assemblies. Air pressure applied in the piston stop hole will help facilitate the removal of the secondary piston assembly.

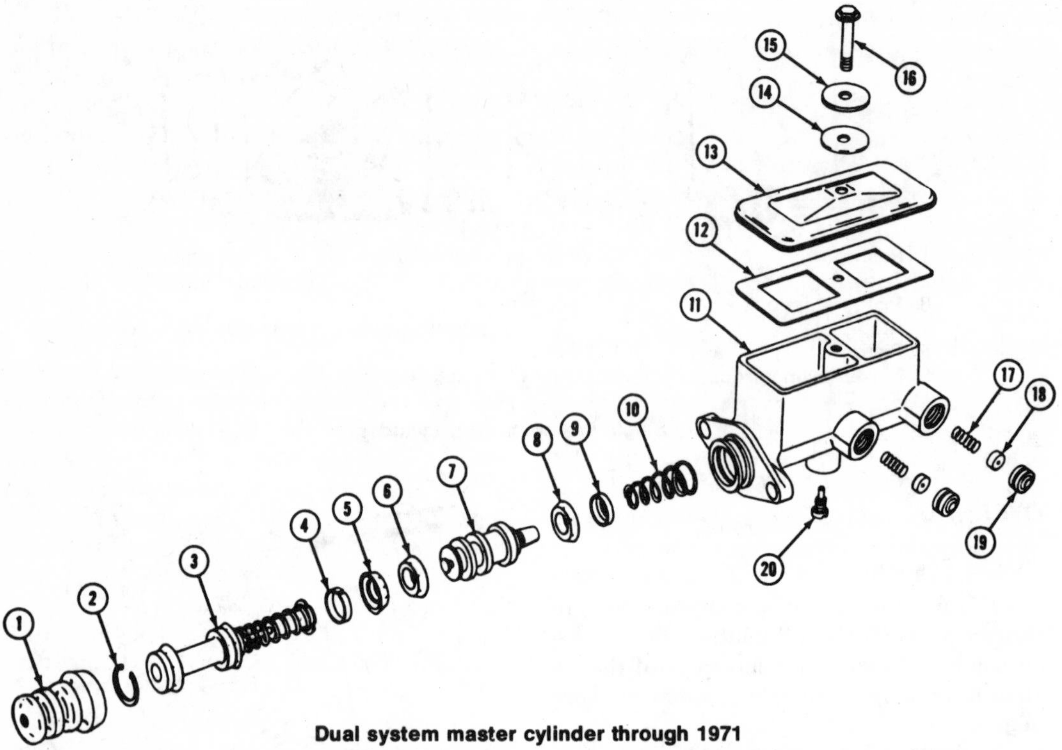

Dual system master cylinder through 1971

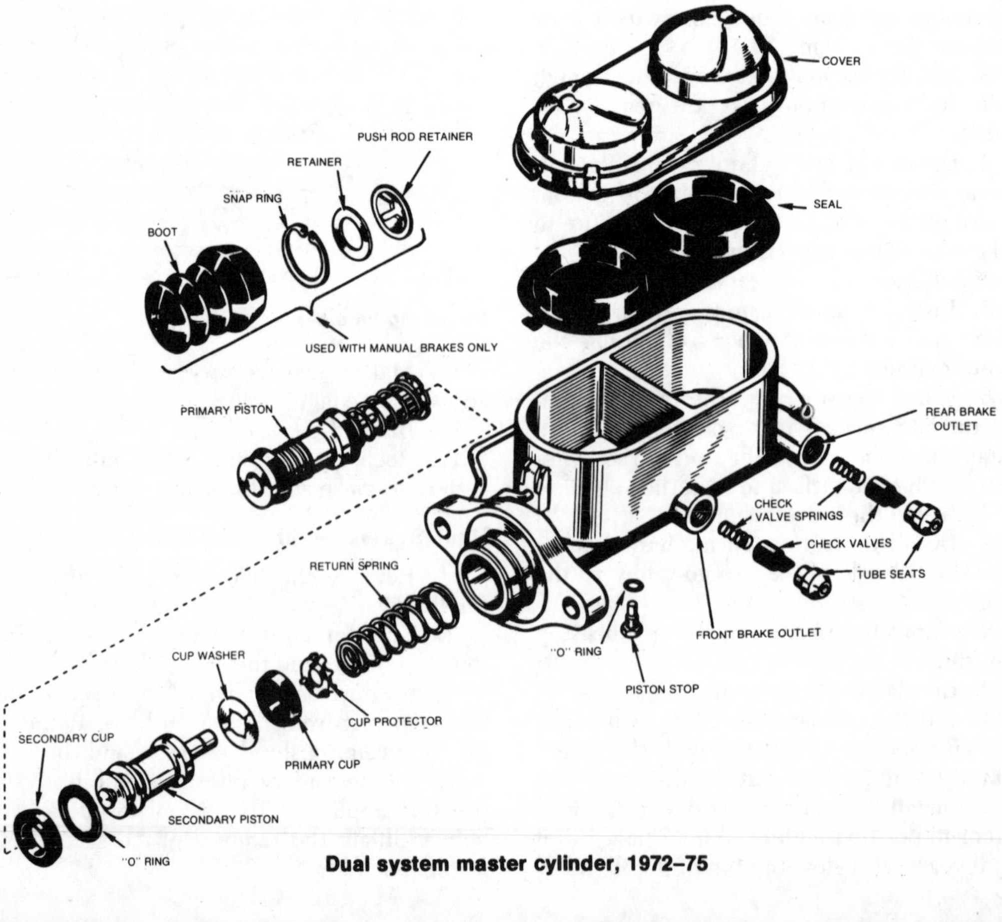

Dual system master cylinder, 1972–75

3. The residual check valves are located under the front and rear fluid outlet tube seats.

4. The tube seats must be removed with self tapping screws to permit the removal of the check valves. Screw the self-tapping screws into the tube seats and place two screw driver tips under the screw head and force the screw upward.

5. Remove the expander in the rear secondary cup, secondary cups, return spring, cup protector, primary cup, and washer from the secondary piston.

6. Immerse all of the metal parts in clean brake fluid and clean them. Use an air hose to blow out dirt and cleaning solvent from recesses and internal passages.

7. After cleaning, place all of the parts on clean paper or in a clean pan.

8. Inspect all parts for damage or excessive wear. Replace any damaged, worn, or chipped parts. Inspect the hydraulic cylinder bore for signs of scoring, rust, pitting, or etching. Any of these will require replacement of the hydraulic cylinder.

9. Prior to assembling the master cylinder, dip all of the components in clean brake fluid and place them on clean paper or in a clean pan.

10. Install the primary cup washer, primary cup, cup protector, and return spring on the secondary piston.

11. Install the piston cups in the double groove end of the secondary piston, so the flat side of the cups face each other (lip of the cups away from each other). Install the cup expander in the lip groove of the end cup.

12. Coat the cylinder bore and piston assemblies with clean brake fluid before installing any parts in the cylinder.

13. Install the secondary piston assembly first and then the primary piston.

14. Install the pushrod assembly, which includes the pushrod, boot, and rod retainer, and secure with the snap ring. Install the primary piston stop and stop light switch.

15. Place new rubber check valves over the check valve springs and install in the outlet holes, spring first.

16. Install the tube seats, flat side toward the check valve, and press in with tube nuts or the master cylinder brake tube nuts.

17. Before the master cylinder is installed on the vehicle it must be bled. Support the cylinder assembly in a vise and fill both fluid reservoirs with brake fluid.

18. Loosely install a plug in each outlet of the cylinder. Depress the push rod several times until air bubbles cease to appear in the brake fluid.

19. Tighten the plugs and attempt to depress the piston. The piston travel should be restricted after all of the air is expelled.

20. Install the master cylinder in the vehicle and bleed all the hydraulic lines at the wheel cylinders.

Dual System—1976-81

1. Remove the master cylinder from the vehicle and remove the cover and diaphragm seal. Drain the brake fluid from the reservoir and mount it in a vise.

2. With non-power brakes, slide the boot back on the pushrod. Push the pushrod in and unseat the primary piston snap-ring. Remove the pushrod, boot, snap-ring, and pushrod retainer as an assembly. With power brakes, push the primary piston in with a wooden dowel and remove the piston snap-ring.

3. Remove the primary and secondary piston assemblies. Air pressure applied through the piston stop hole will help in the removal of the secondary piston.

4. Remove the piston seal and piston cups from the secondary piston. It is not necessary to disassemble the primary piston because a new complete primary piston assembly is supplied in the rebuilding kit.

5. Clean and inspect the master cylinder. Replace the master cylinder body if the bore is severely scored, corroded, or pitted, cracked, porous, or is otherwise damaged. Check the by-pass and compensator ports to make sure that they are open and not plugged or dirty. Use brake fluid and air pressure to open these passages. Do not use wire.

NOTE: *Use only clean brake fluid or an approved cleaning solvent to wash the master cylinder. Do not use any solvent containing mineral oil such as gasoline, kerosene, alcohol, or carbon tetrachloride. Mineral oil harms rubber components.*

6. Check the tube seats in the outlet ports. Replace the seats only if they are cracked, scored, cocked in the bore, or loose. Replace the tube seats as follows:

7. Enlarge the hole in the tube seat with a $^{13}/_{64}$ in. drill. Place a flat washer on each outlet port and thread a ¼-20x¾ in. long screw into the seat. Tighten the screw until the seat is loosened. Remove the seat, screw,

and washer. Flush any metal chips away with brake fluid and compressed air.

8. Install the replacement tube seats, if removed, using spare tube fitting nuts to press the seats into place. Be careful that the seats don't become cocked during installation. Make sure that the seats are bottomed. Remove the tube fitting nuts and check for burrs or chips. Rinse the master cylinder in brake fluid and blow out all passages with compressed air.

9. Install the piston cups on the secondary piston. The piston cup installed in the groove at the end of the piston should have its lip facing away from the piston. Install the next cup so that its lip faces the piston.

10. Install the seal protector, piston seal, spring retainer, and return spring on the secondary piston. Install the piston seal so that its lip faces the interior of the master cylinder

bore when the assembly is installed. Make sure that the return spring seats against the retainer and that the retainer is located inside the lip of the piston seal.

11. Lubricate the master cylinder bore and secondary piston seal and cups with brake fluid and install the secondary piston assembly in the cylinder bore.

12. Lubricate the seals on the primary piston assembly with brake fluid and install the assembly in the master cylinder bore.

13. With power brakes, push the primary piston inward with a wooden dowel and install the retaining snap-ring in the groove of the master cylinder bore.

14. With non-power brakes, install the pushrod, pushrod retainer, and boot. Push in and install the piston snap-ring.

15. Install the diaphragm seal on the master cylinder cover.

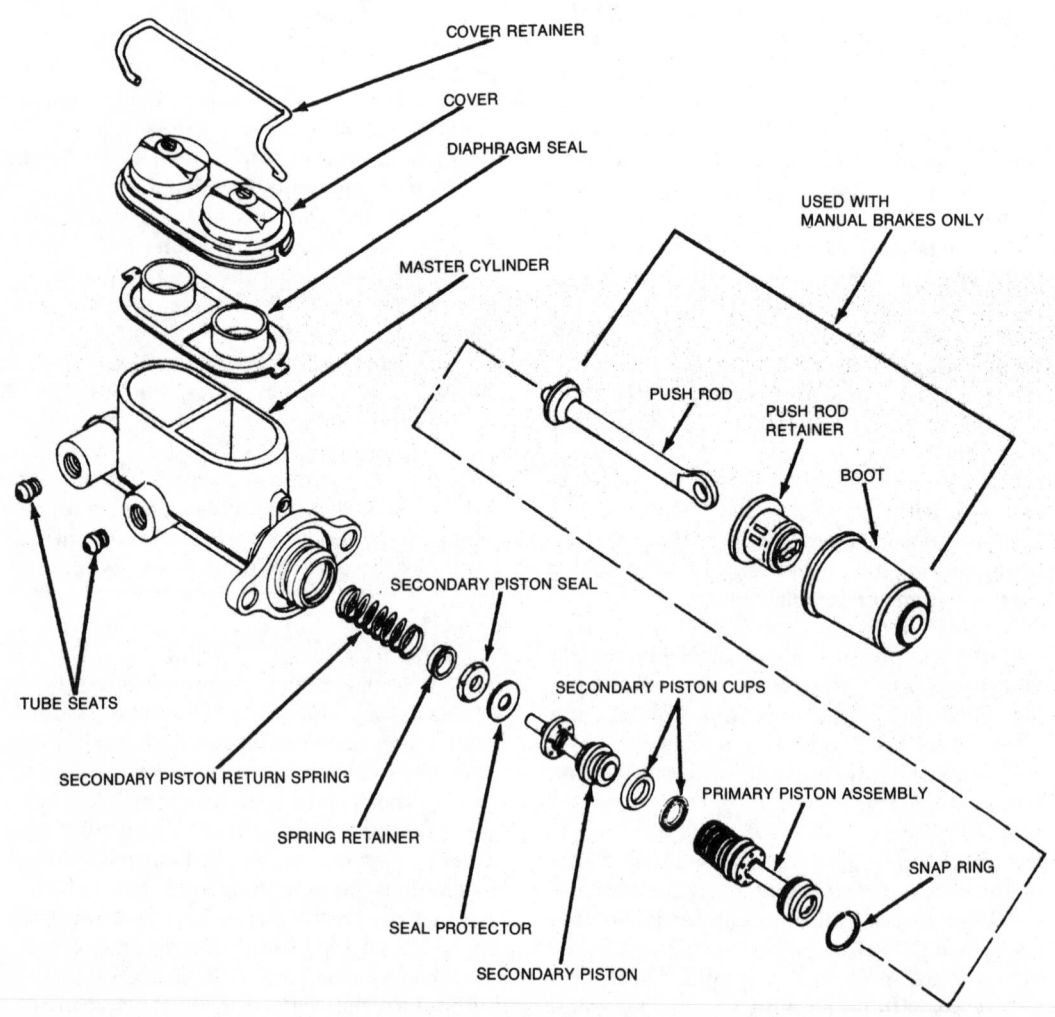

1976–77 master cylinder

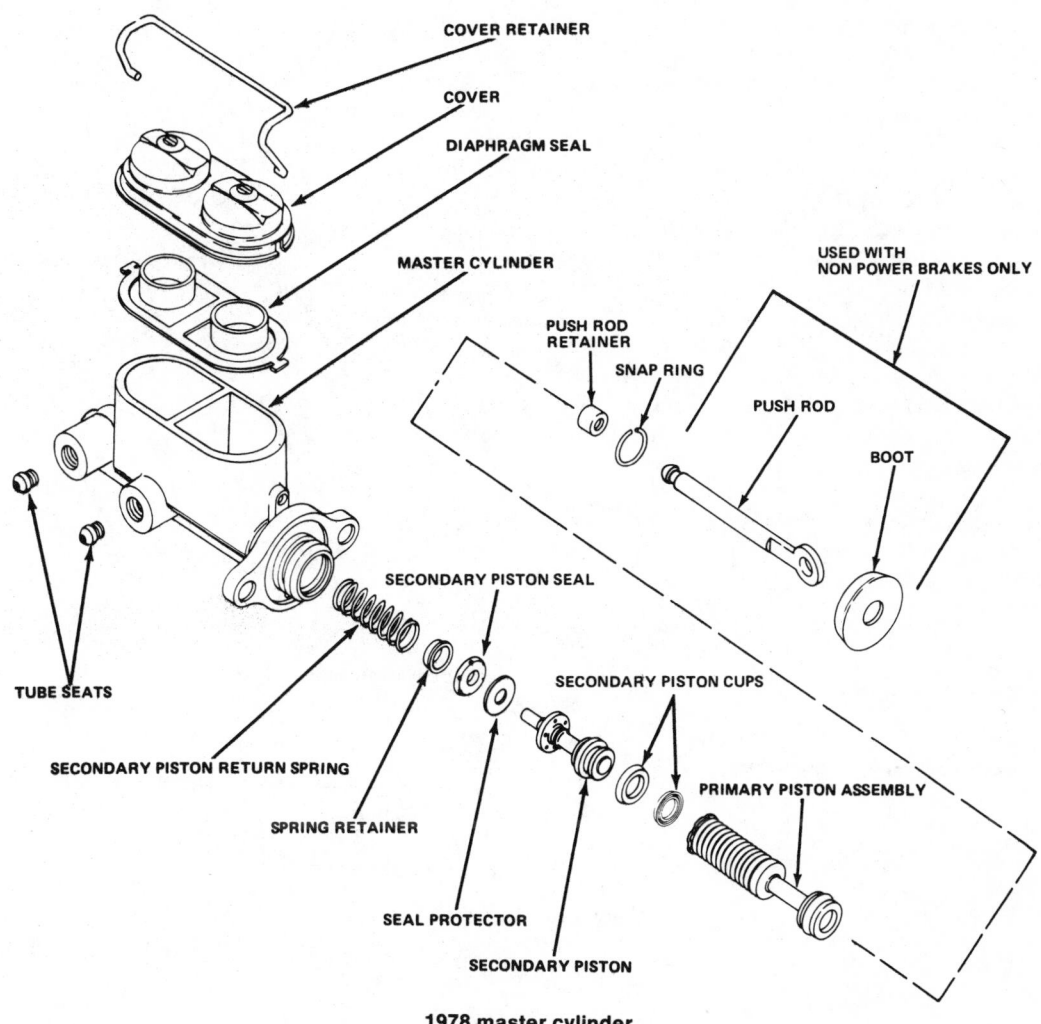

COVER RETAINER

COVER

DIAPHRAGM SEAL

MASTER CYLINDER

USED WITH
NON POWER BRAKES ONLY

PUSH ROD
RETAINER

SNAP RING

PUSH ROD

BOOT

SECONDARY PISTON SEAL

SECONDARY PISTON CUPS

TUBE SEATS

PRIMARY PISTON ASSEMBLY

SECONDARY PISTON RETURN SPRING

SPRING RETAINER

SEAL PROTECTOR

SECONDARY PISTON

1978 master cylinder

16. Install the master cylinder in the vehicle.

Power Brake Booster
REMOVAL AND INSTALLATION

1. Disconnect the power unit pushrod at the pedal.

2. Disconnect the vacuum line at the power unit check valve.

3. Unbolt the master cylinder from the power unit and push the master cylinder aside carefully.

4. Unbolt the power unit bellcrank at the dash panel and remove the power unit and bellcrank as an assembly. If the power unit is being discarded, save the bellcrank for the new unit.

5. Installation is the reverse of removal. Torque the bellcrank-to-dash panel bolts to 35 ft. lb.; the master cylinder-to-power unit bolts to 30 ft. lb.; the pushrod-to-pedal bolt and nut to 35 ft. lb.

Bleeding the Brakes

The hydraulic brake system must be bled whenever a fluid line has been disconnected because air gets into the system. A leak in the system may sometimes be indicated by a spongy brake pedal. Air trapped in the system is compressible and does not permit the pressure applied to the brake pedal to be transmitted solidly through the brakes. The system must be absolutely free from air at all times. When bleeding brakes, bleed at the wheel most distant from the master cylinder first, the next most distant second, and so on. During the bleeding operation the master

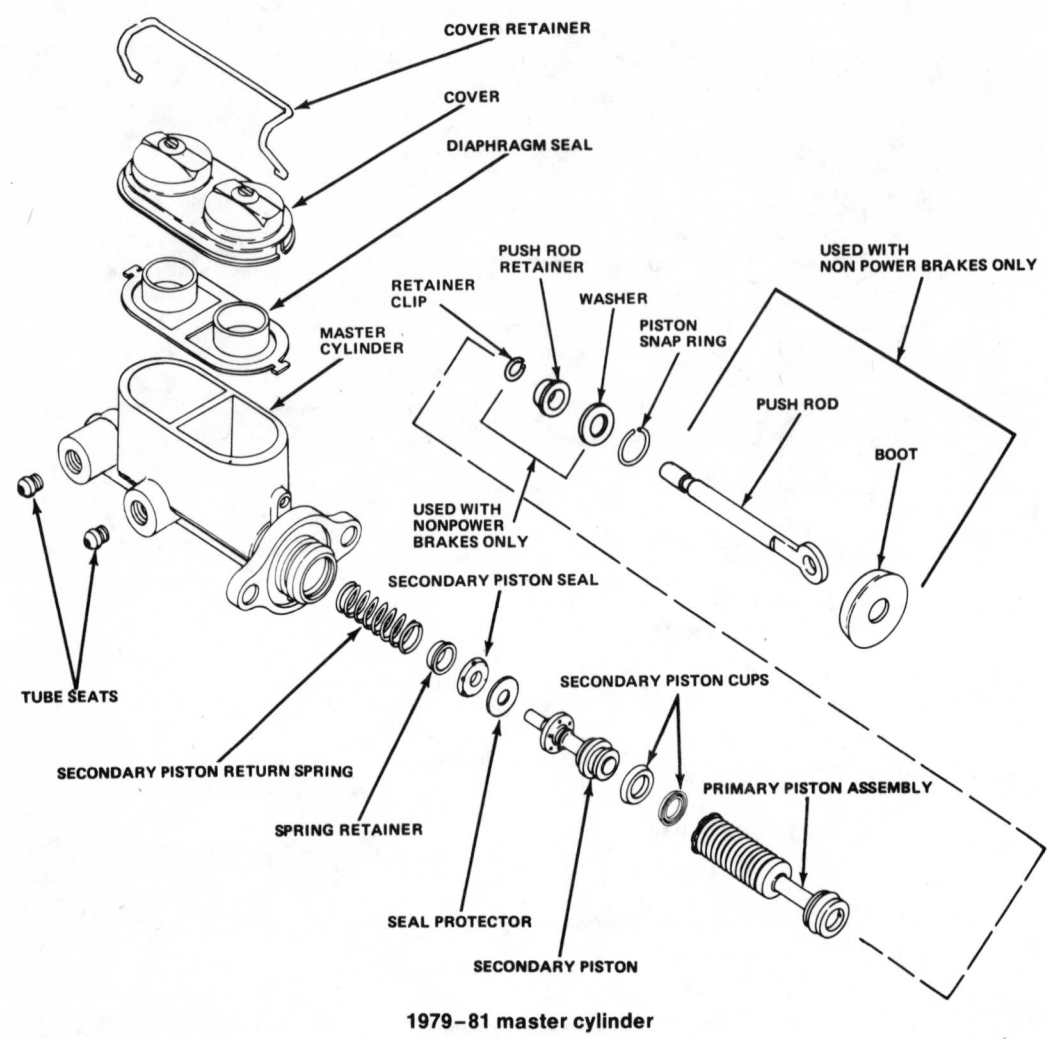

1979–81 master cylinder

cylinder must be kept at least ¾ full of brake fluid.

NOTE: *On 1974 and later models, there is a combination pressure differential (failure warning) and proportioning valve in the hydraulic system. It is in the engine compartment on the inner side of the left frame rail. When bleeding the brake system, the metering section of the valve must be held open. On 1974–76 models, remove the warning switch wire, switch terminal, plunger, and spring from the valve. On all 1977 models and 1978–79 models using a valve assembly with a flat exterior surface, remove the plastic dust cover at the end of the valve and hold the valve stem OUT. On 1978–79 models using a valve assembly with a rounded exterior surface, hold the valve stem IN by pressing against the dust cover boot. Tools are available to hold the valve stem in the proper location or can be fabricated.*

To bleed the brakes, first carefully clean all dirt from around the master cylinder filler cap. If a bleeder tank is used follow the manufacturer's instructions. Remove the filler cap and fill the master cylinder to the lower edge of the filler neck. Clean off the bleeder connections at all four wheel cylinders. Attach the bleeder hose to the right rear wheel cylinder bleeder screw and place the end of the tube in a glass jar, submerged in brake fluid. Open the bleeder valve ½–¾ of a turn.

Have an assistant depress the brake pedal slowly and allow it to return. Continue this pumping action to force any air out of the system. When bubbles cease to appear at the end of the bleeder hose, close the bleeder valve and remove the hose.

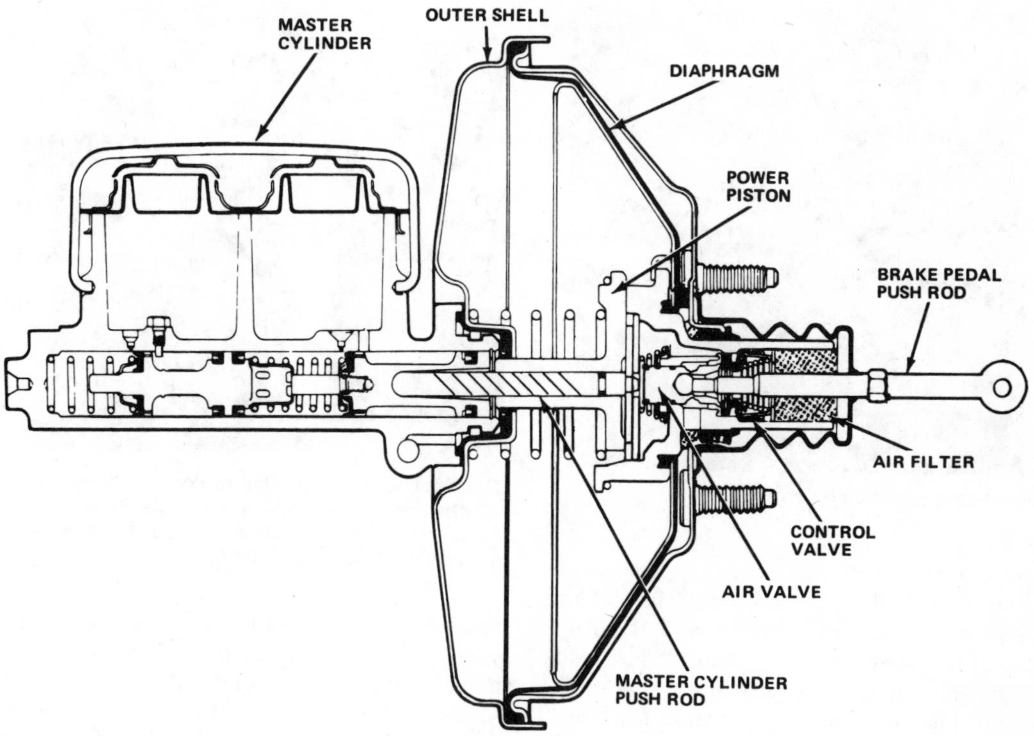

MASTER
CYLINDER

OUTER SHELL

DIAPHRAGM

POWER
PISTON

BRAKE PEDAL
PUSH ROD

AIR FILTER

CONTROL
VALVE

AIR VALVE

MASTER CYLINDER
PUSH ROD

Power brake booster

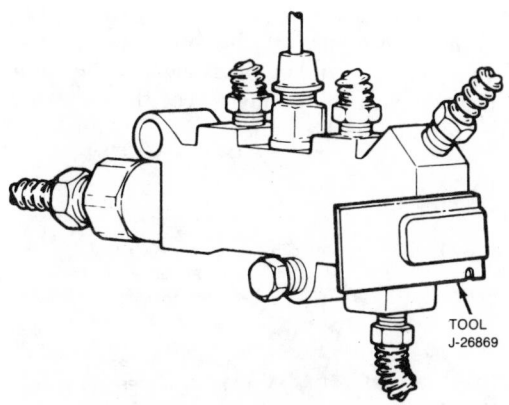

TOOL
J-26869

On the flat surfaced combination valve, the valve stem must be held out when bleeding the brakes. A substitute for the special tool shown can be fabricated

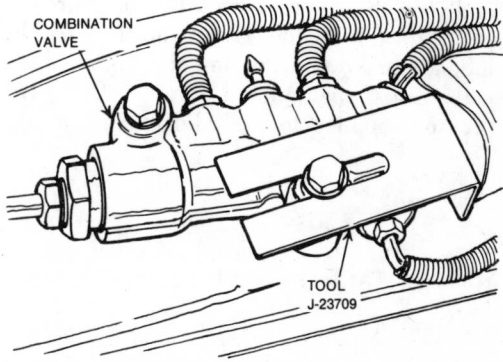

COMBINATION
VALVE

TOOL
J-23709

Metering valve tool installation on round-surfaced combination valve

Check the level of fluid in the master cylinder reservoir and replenish as necessary.

After the bleeding operation at each wheel cylinder has been completed, fill the master cylinder reservoir and replace the filler plug.

Do not reuse the fluid which has been removed from the lines through the bleeding process because it contains air bubbles and dirt.

DISC BRAKES

The front disc brake consists of 3 assemblies: the caliper assembly, the hub and rotor assembly, and the support and shield assembly.

The caliper is a single-piston sliding type, of one-piece casting construction with the inboard side containing the single-piston, piston bore and the bleeder screw and fluid inlet holes. There are two brake pads within

Bleeding the brakes on early models

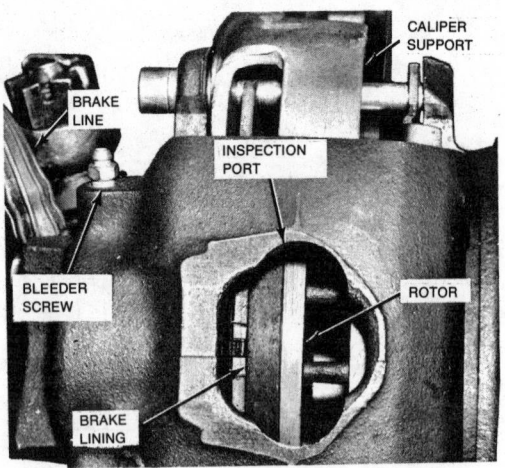

The thickness of the disc brake pad linings can be checked visually. Minimum safe thickness is $1/16$ in. with bonded linings and $1/32$ in. above the rivet heads with riveted lining

the caliper, positioned on either side of the rotor. The brake pads take the place of the brake shoes on drum brakes and the rotor takes the place of brake drums. The pads themselves actually consist of two parts: the metal shoe and the composition lining which is bonded or riveted to the shoe.

The significant operating feature of the single-piston caliper is that it is free to slide laterally on the anchor plate. The pressure applied to the piston is transmitted to the inboard brake pad, forcing the lining of the pad against the inboard rotor surface. The pressure applied to the inboard end or bottom of the piston bore forces the caliper to slide toward the inboard side. This inward movement of the caliper causes the outboard section of the caliper to apply pressure against the lining of the outboard pad, forcing the lining against the outboard surface of the rotor. As hydraulic pressure builds within the brake lines, due to the increased application of pressure at the brake pedal, the brake pad assemblies press against the rotor surfaces with increasing force, thus slowing the rotation of the rotor.

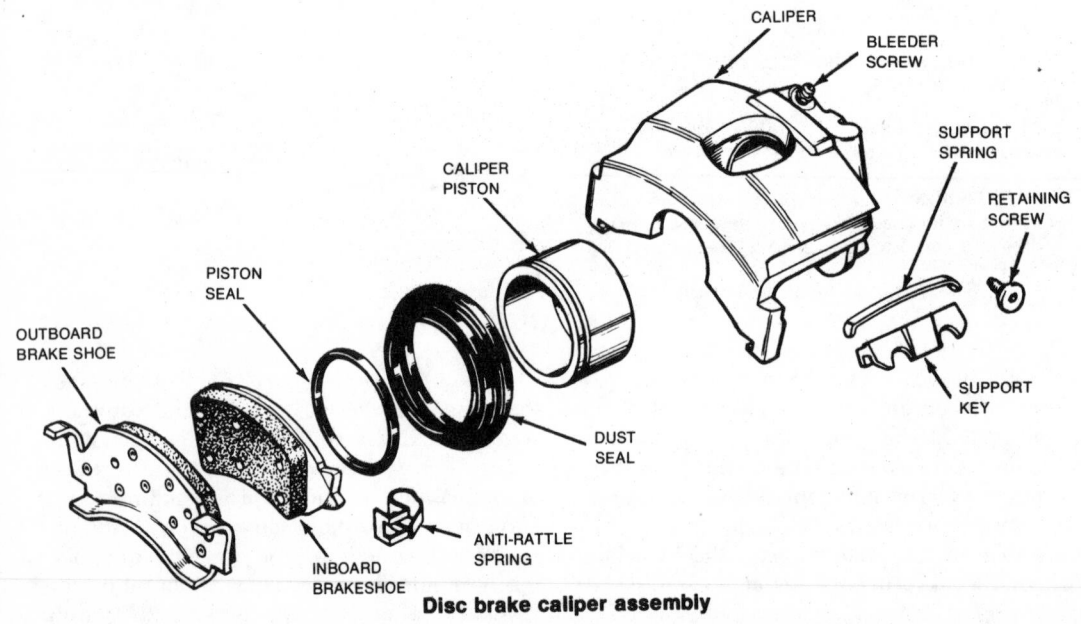

Disc brake caliper assembly

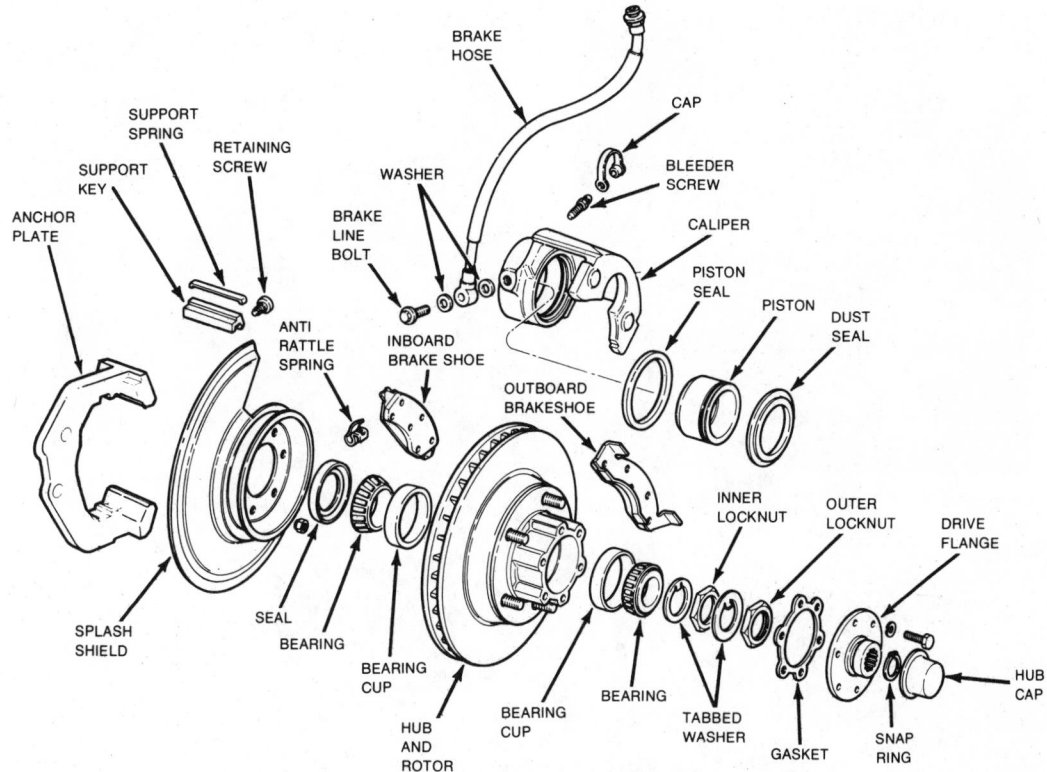

Disc brake components on vehicles without locking hubs

Caliper

REMOVAL AND INSTALLATION

1. Remove ⅔ of the brake fluid from the front reservoir.

2. Raise the vehicle so that the wheel to be worked on is off the ground. Support the vehicle with jack stands.

3. Remove the front wheels.

4. Place a C-clamp on the caliper so that the solid end contacts the back of the caliper and the screw end contacts the metal part of the outboard brake pad.

5. Tighten the clamp until the caliper moves far enough to force the piston to the bottom of the piston bore. This will back the brake pads off the rotor surface to facilitate the removal and installation of the caliper assembly.

6. Remove the C-clamp.

NOTE: *Do not push down on the brake pedal or the piston and brake pads will return to their original positions up against the rotor.*

7. Remove the caliper support key retaining screw with a ¼ in. Allen wrench. Drive the support key and spring out with a punch.

NOTE: *If just the brake pads are being replaced, it is not necessary to remove the caliper assembly entirely from the vehicle. Do not remove the brake line. Rest the caliper on the front spring or other suitable support. Do not allow the brake hose to support the weight of the caliper.*

8. If the caliper is being removed in order to be rebuilt, then it is necessary to disconnect the brake fluid hose. Clean the brake fluid hose-to-caliper connection thoroughly. Remove the hose-to-caliper bolt. Cap or tape the open ends to keep dirt out. Discard the copper gaskets.

9. Install the caliper in the reverse order of removal.

NOTE: *If the brake fluid hose was disconnected, it will be necessary to bleed the hydraulic system.*

OVERHAUL

1. Remove the caliper assembly and remove the brake pads. If the pads are to be reused, mark their location in the caliper.

2. Clean the caliper exterior with clean brake fluid. Drain any residual fluid from the caliper and place it on a clean work surface.

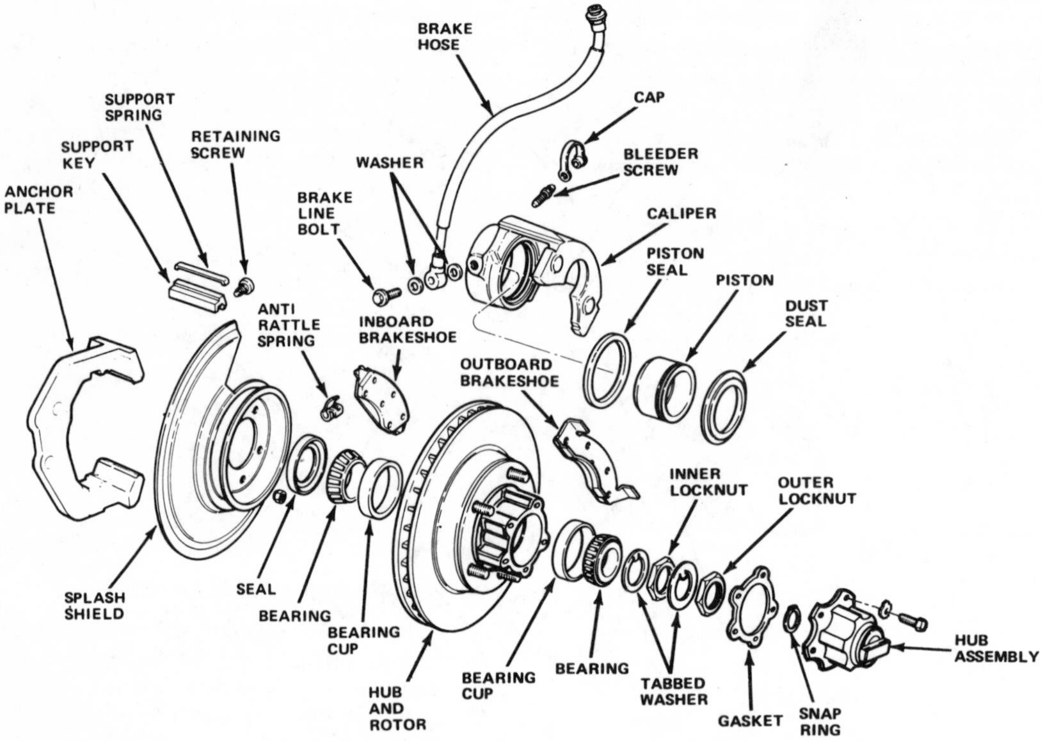

BRAKE
HOSE

CAP

SUPPORT
SPRING

RETAINING
SCREW

WASHER

BLEEDER
SCREW

SUPPORT
KEY

CALIPER

ANCHOR
PLATE

BRAKE
LINE
BOLT

PISTON
SEAL

PISTON

DUST
SEAL

ANTI
RATTLE
SPRING

INBOARD
BRAKESHOE

OUTBOARD
BRAKESHOE

INNER
LOCKNUT

OUTER
LOCKNUT

SPLASH
SHIELD

SEAL

BEARING

BEARING
CUP

HUB
AND
ROTOR

BEARING
CUP

BEARING

TABBED
WASHER

GASKET

SNAP
RING

HUB
ASSEMBLY

Disc brake details on models with locking hubs

NOTE: *Removal of the caliper piston requires the use of compressed air. Do not, under any circumstances, place your fingers in front of the piston in an attempt to catch or protect it when applying compressed air to remove the piston.*

3. Pad the interior of the caliper with clean cloths. Use several cloths and pad the interior well to avoid damaging the piston when it comes out of the bore.

4. Insert an air nozzle into the inlet hole in the caliper and gently apply air pressure on the piston to push it out of the bore. Use only enough air pressure to ease the piston out of the bore.

5. Pry the dust boot out of the bore with a screwdriver. Use caution during this operation to prevent scratching the bore. Discard the dust boot.

6. Remove the piston seal from the piston bore and discard the seal. Use only non-scratching implements such as a wooden stick or a piece of plastic to remove the seal. Do not use a metal tool as it could very easily scratch the bore.

7. Remove the bleeder screw. Remove and discard the sleeves and rubber bushings from the mounting ears.

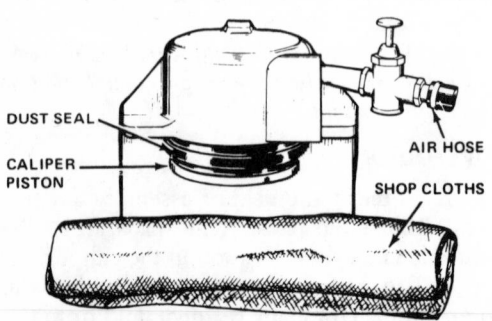

DUST SEAL

CALIPER
PISTON

AIR HOSE

SHOP CLOTHS

Caliper piston removal

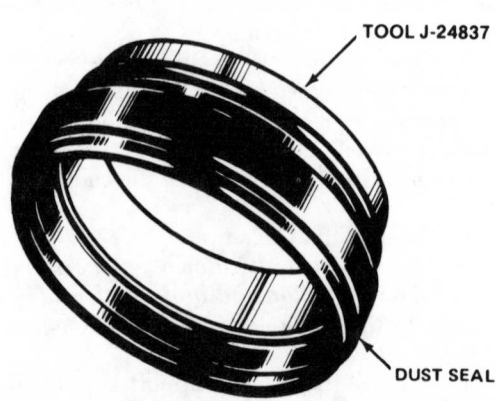

TOOL J-24837

DUST SEAL

Positioning caliper piston dust seal on installation tool

8. Clean all parts with clean brake fluid. Blow out all of the passages in the caliper and bleeder valve. Use only dry and filtered compressed air.

9. Examine the piston for defects. Replace the piston if it is nicked, scratched, corroded.

Examine the caliper piston bore for the same defects as the piston. Minor stains or corrosion can be polished with a fiber brush.

10. Lubricate the bore and new seal with brake fluid and install the seal in the groove in the bore.

11. Lubricate the piston with brake fluid and install the new dust boot into the piston groove so that the fold in the boot faces the

open end of the piston. Slide the metal portion of the dust boot over the open end of the piston and push the retainer toward the back of the piston until the lip on the fold seats in the piston groove. Then push the retainer portion of the boot forward until the boot is flush with the rim at the open end of the piston and snaps into place.

12. Insert the piston in the bore, being careful not to unseat the piston seal. Push the piston to the bottom of the bore.

13. Install the bleeder screw.

14. Connect the brake line to the caliper using new copper gaskets.

15. Install the brake pads.

16. Install the caliper. Bleed the hydraulic system.

Pads

REMOVAL AND INSTALLATION

1. Raise and support the vehicle with jack stands and remove the wheel(s) on the side to be worked on.

2. Remove the caliper assembly as previously outlined in this Chapter under "Caliper Removal and Installation." Take heed of the note given after Step 7 of that procedure.

3. Remove the brake pad assemblies. Remove the anti-rattle spring from the inboard pad. Note the position of the spring before removing it for correct installation later.

4. Wipe the inside of the caliper clean, including the exterior of the dust boot. Inspect the dust boot for cuts or cracks and for proper seating in the piston bore. If evidence of fluid leakage is noted, the caliper should be rebuilt.

NOTE: *You should not use compressed air to clean the inside of the caliper as it may unseat the dust boot seal.*

5. Check the sliding surface of the caliper and anchor plate for rust or corrosion. Clean them with a wire brush and fine sandpaper; lubricate with molydisulphide grease.

6. Install the inboard pad anti-rattle spring on the rear flange of the pad. Make sure the looped section of the spring is away from the rotor.

7. Install the inboard pad with spring attached in the caliper anchor plate.

8. Install the outboard pad in the caliper.

9. Place the caliper over the rotor and on the anchor plate.

NOTE: *Be careful not to damage or dislodge the dust boot.*

10. Insert the support key and spring be-

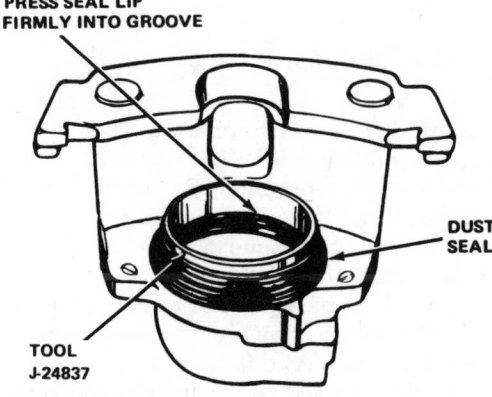

PRESS SEAL LIP FIRMLY INTO GROOVE

DUST SEAL

TOOL J-24837

Caliper piston dust seal installation

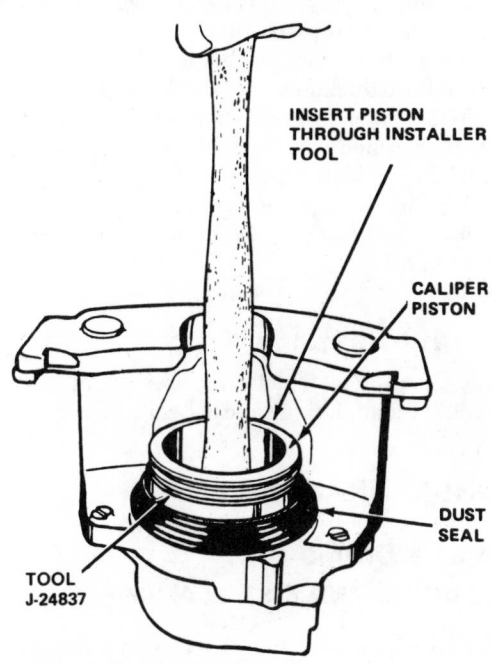

INSERT PISTON THROUGH INSTALLER TOOL

CALIPER PISTON

DUST SEAL

TOOL J-24837

Caliper piston installation

tween the sliding surfaces at the rear of the caliper. Drive them into place with a punch.

11. Install the key retaining screw.

12. Fill the master cylinder to within ¼ in. of the rim.

13. Press firmly on the brake pedal several times till the pedal is firm.

14. Recheck the master cylinder level.

Rotor (Disc)

REMOVAL AND INSTALLATION

The hub and rotor assembly is removed and installed in the same manner as a conventional drum brake hub.

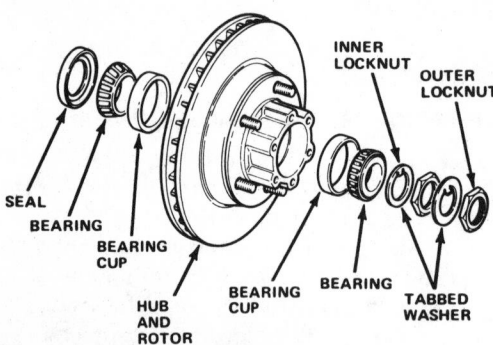

SEAL
BEARING
BEARING CUP
HUB AND ROTOR
BEARING CUP
BEARING
INNER LOCKNUT
OUTER LOCKNUT
TABBED WASHER

Rotor and wheel bearings

INSPECTION AND MEASUREMENT

Check the rotor for surface cracks, nicks, broken cooling fins and scoring of both contact surfaces. Some scoring of the surfaces may occur during normal use. Scoring that is 0.009 in. deep or less is not detrimental to the operation of the brakes.

If the rotor surface is heavily rusted or scaled, clean both surfaces on a disc brake lathe using flat sanding discs before attempting any measurements.

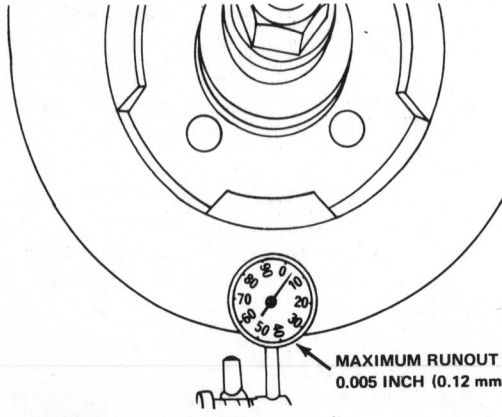

MAXIMUM RUNOUT 0.005 INCH (0.12 mm)

Checking rotor lateral runout

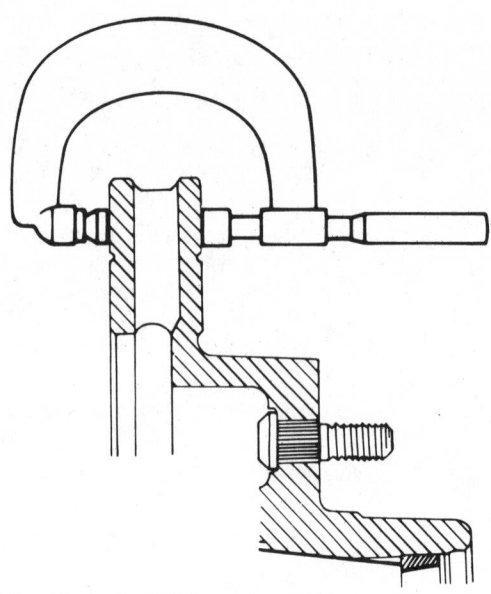

Checking rotor thickness variation

With the hub and rotor assembly mounted on the spindle of the vehicle or a disc brake lathe and all play removed from the wheel bearings, assemble a dial indicator so that the stem contacts the center of the rotor braking surface. Zero the dial indicator before taking any measurements. Lateral runout must not exceed 0.005 in. with a maximum rate of change not to exceed 0.001 in. in 30 degrees of rotation. Excessive runout will cause the rotor to wobble and knock the piston back into the caliper causing increased pedal travel, noise and vibration.

After the rotor has been refinished, the minimum thickness of 1.1207 in. is acceptable for models through 1978; .815 in. for 1979–81 models. Discard the rotor if the thickness is less.

NOTE: *Remember to adjust the wheel bearings after the runout measurement has been taken.*

Wheel Bearings

See Chapter 1 for details on removing, servicing, and adjusting front wheel bearings.

DRUM BRAKES

Brake Drums

REMOVAL AND INSTALLATION

Front

The front brake drums are attached to the wheel hubs by five bolts. These bolts are also used for mounting the wheels on the hub. Press or drive out the bolts to remove the drum from the hub.

When placing the drum on the hub, make sure that the contacting surfaces are clean and flat. Line up the holes in the drum with those in the hub and put the drum over the shoulder on the hub. Insert five new bolts through the drum and hub and drive the bolts into place solidly. Place a round piece of stock approximately the diameter of the head of the bolt, in a vise; next place the hub and drum assembly over it so that the bolt head rests on it. Then flatten the bolt head into the countersunk section of the hub with a punch.

The runout of the drum face should be within 0.030 in. If the runout is found to be greater than 0.030 in., it will be necessary to reset the bolts to correct the condition.

The left hand hub bolts have an L stamped on the head of the bolt.

The left hand threaded nuts may have a groove cut around the hexagon faces, or the word LEFT stamped on the face.

Hubs with left hand threaded hub bolts are installed on the left hand side of the vehicle. Late production vehicles are equipped with right hand bolts and nuts on all four hubs.

Rear

The rear brake drums are held in position by spring clip-type locknuts on models through 1975 and by three drum-to-hub retaining screws on 1976–81 models. After the spring-type locknuts or retaining screws are removed, the drum can be slid off the axle shaft or hub and brake shoes. It may be necessary to back off the brake shoe adjustment so that any lip on the inside of the brake drum clears the brake shoes.

INSPECTION

Using a brake drum micrometer, check all drums. Should a brake drum be scored or rough, it may be reconditioned by grinding

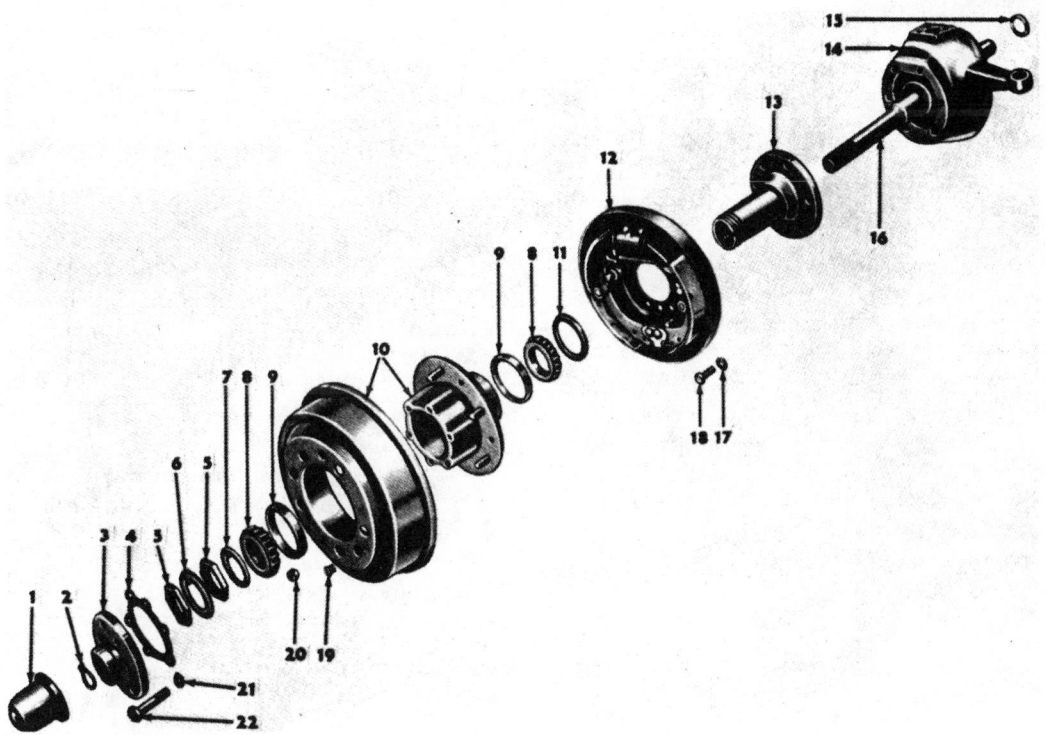

1. Hub cap	9. Cup	17. Lockwasher
2. Snap ring	10. Hub and drum	18. Bolt
3. Drive flange	11. Oil seal	19. Screw
4. Gasket	12. Left front brake	20. Nut
5. Nut	13. Spindle and bushing	21. Lockwasher
6. Lockwasher	14. Left knuckle and arm	22. Bolt
7. Lockwasher	15. Thrust washer	
8. Cone and rollers	16. Universal joint shaft	

1945–71 front hub, drum and brake assembly

1. Oil seal
2. Cone and rollers
3. Cup
4. Shims
5. Bearing retainer
6. Brake
7. Gasket
8. Grease retainer
9. Grease protecter
10. Bolt
11. Hub and drum
12. Shaft key
13. Oil seal
14. Nut
15. Cotter pin
16. Hub cap
17. Nut
18. Lockwasher
19. Bolt

1945–71 rear brake and axle assembly

or turning on a lathe. Do not remove more than 0.030 in. thickness of metal.

Use a clean cloth to clean dirt from the brake drums. If further cleaning is required, use soap and water. Do not use brake fluid, gasoline, kerosene or any other similar solvents.

Brake Shoes

REMOVAL AND INSTALLATION

1. Jack up the vehicle so that all four wheels are off the ground.

2. On vehicles equipped with cam adjustment brakes, turn all eccentrics to the lower side of the cam. On vehicles equipped with star wheel adjustment, turn the star adjuster all the way in.

3. Remove the wheels and the hubs and drums to give access to the brake shoes.

4. Install wheel cylinder clamps to retain the wheel cylinder pistons in place and prevent leakage of brake fluid while replacing the shoes.

5. Remove the return springs with a brake spring removed tool.

6. On models with self adjusters, remove the adjuster cable, cable guide, adjuster lever and adjuster springs.

7. Remove the hold down clips or springs and remove the brake shoes.

8. Before installing the new shoes, now would be a good time to inspect the oil seals in the hubs. If the condition of the seals is doubtful, replace them. Also check the wheel cylinders for leakage. Pull back the dust covers. If there is fluid present behind the dust cover the wheel cylinder must be rebuilt or replaced.

9. Clean the backing plate with a brush or cloth. Place a dab of molydisulphide grease on each spot where the shoes rub the backing plate.

CAUTION: *Never clean brake surfaces with compressed air. The deposits on the brakes contain asbestos which may cause cancer if inhaled.*

NOTE: *Always replace brake lining in axle sets. Never replace linings on one side or just on one wheel.*

10. Install the brakes in the reverse order of removal.

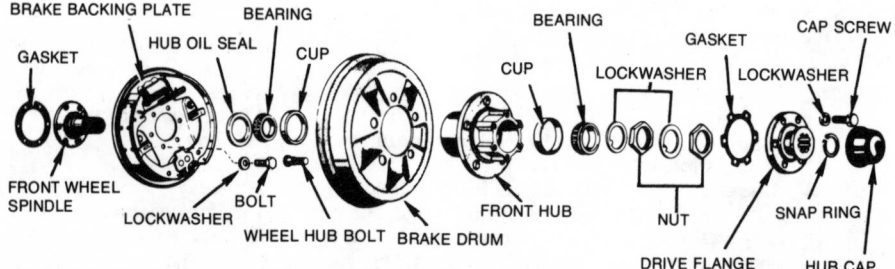

1972 and later front hub and drum brake assembly

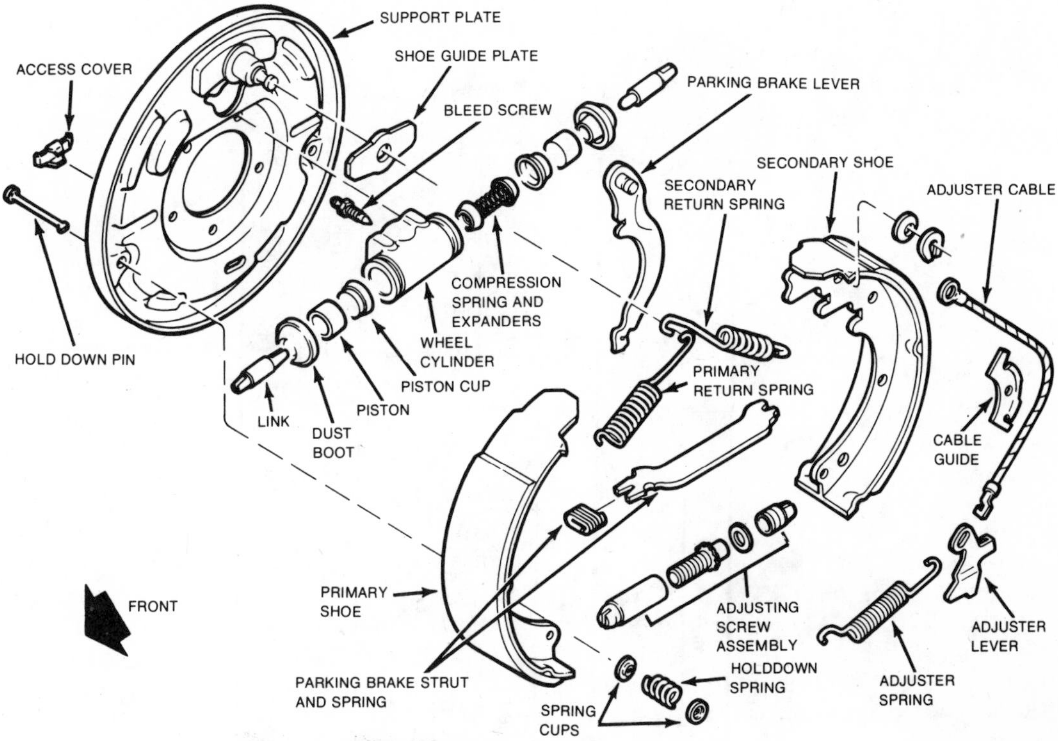

Diagram labels:

ACCESS COVER

SUPPORT PLATE

SHOE GUIDE PLATE

BLEED SCREW

PARKING BRAKE LEVER

SECONDARY SHOE

SECONDARY RETURN SPRING

ADJUSTER CABLE

HOLD DOWN PIN

COMPRESSION SPRING AND EXPANDERS

WHEEL CYLINDER

PISTON CUP

PISTON

LINK

DUST BOOT

PRIMARY RETURN SPRING

ADJUSTER CABLE

CABLE GUIDE

PRIMARY SHOE

PARKING BRAKE STRUT AND SPRING

SPRING CUPS

ADJUSTING SCREW ASSEMBLY

HOLDDOWN SPRING

ADJUSTER SPRING

ADJUSTER LEVER

FRONT

1972–81 self-adjusting rear drum brake components

Wheel Cylinders

OVERHAUL

Wheel cylinder rebuilding kits are available reconditioning wheel cylinders. The kits usually contain new cup springs, cylinder cups and in some, new boots. The most important factor to keep in mind when rebuilding wheel cylinders is cleanliness. Keep all dirt away from the wheel cylinders when you are reassembling them.

1. To remove the wheel cylinder, jack up the vehicle and remove the wheel, hub, and drum.

2. Disconnect the brake line at the fitting on the brake backing plate.

3. Remove the brake assemblies.

4. Remove the screws or nuts that hold the wheel cylinder to the backing plate and remove the wheel cylinder from the vehicle.

5. Remove the rubber dust covers on the ends of the cylinder. Remove the pistons and piston cups and the spring. Remove the bleeder screw and make sure it is not plugged.

6. Discard all of the parts that the rebuilding kit will replace.

7. Examine the inside of the cylinder. If it is severely rusted, pitted or scratched,

then the cylinder must be replaced as the piston cups won't be able to seal against the walls of the cylinder.

8. Using emery cloth or crocus cloth, polish the inside of the cylinder. Do not polish in a lengthwise direction; polish by rotating the wheel cylinder around the polishing cloth supported on your fingers. The purpose of this is to put a new surface on the inside of the cylinder. Keep the inside of the cylinder coated with brake fluid while polishing.

NOTE: *Honing the wheel cylinders is not recommended due to the possibility of removing too much material from the bore, making it too large to seal.*

9. Wash out the cylinder with clean brake fluid after polishing.

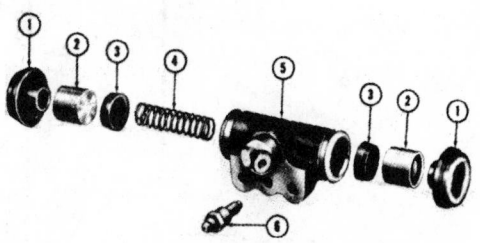

1. Boot	3. Cylinder cup	5. Cylinder
2. Piston	4. Cup spring	6. Bleeder screw

1945–71 wheel cylinder

Brake Specifications

All specifications in inches (in.) unless noted

Year	Model	Wheel Lug Nut Torque (ft. lbs.)	Brake Disc			Brake Drum			Master Cyl. Bore	Wheel Cyl. or Caliper Bore	
			Original Thickness	Minimum Thickness	Maximum Run-out	Original Inside Dia.	Maximum Wear Limit	Maximum Machine o/s		F	R
1945–71	All	60–75	—	—	—	9.00	9.060	—	1.00	1.000	.750
1972–73	All	60–75	—	—	—	11.00	11.030	11.060	1.00	1.125	.975
1974–76①	All	65–90	—	—	—	11.00	11.030	11.060	1.00	1.125	.975
1977	All	65–90	1.200	1.120	.005	11.00	11.030	11.060	1.00	3.100	.975
1978	All	65–90	1.200	1.120	.005	11.00	11.030	11.060	1.00	3.100	.875
1979–81	All	75	1.000	.815	.005	10.00	10.030	10.060	1.00	2.600	.875

① and 1977 models with drum brakes

10. When reassembling the cylinder dip all of the parts in clean brake fluid. Reassemble in the reverse order of removal.

Front Wheel Bearings

See Chapter 1 for full details on front wheel bearing removal, service, and adjustment.

PARKING BRAKE

Adjustment

Through 1971, Transmission Brake

Make sure that the brake handle on the instrument panel is fully released. Check the operating linkage and the cable to make sure that they don't bind. If necessary, free the cable and lubricate it. Rotate the brake drum until one pair of the three sets of holes are over the shoe adjusting screw wheels in the brake drum. Use the edge of the holes in the brake drum as a fulcrum for the brake adjusting tool or a screwdriver. Rotate each notched adjusting screw by moving the handle of the tool away from the center of the drive shaft until the shoes are snug against the drum. Back off seven notches on the adjusting screw wheels to secure the proper running clearance between the shoes and the drum.

1972–81

1. Make sure that the hydraulic brakes are in satisfactory adjustment.

2. Raise the rear wheels off the ground and disengage the parking brake.

3. Loosen the locknut on the brake cable adjusting rod, located directly behind the frame center crossmember.

4. Spin the wheels and tighten the adjustment until the rear wheels drag slightly. Loosen the adjustment until there is no drag and the wheels spin freely.

5. Tighten the locknut to lock the adjusting nut.

1. Cable and conduit	9. Backing plate	17. Yoke
2. Tube fastener	10. Shoe and lining	18. Yoke and plug
3. Spring	11. Return spring	19. Adjusting spring
4. Bracket	12. Drum	20. Bracket
5. Rear cap	13. Hex bolt	21. Operating lever
6. Bushing	14. Rear flange	22. Adjusting clevis
7. Driven gear	15. Plain washer	23. Spring clip
8. Sleeve	16. Nut	24. spring link

Driveshaft mounted hand brake

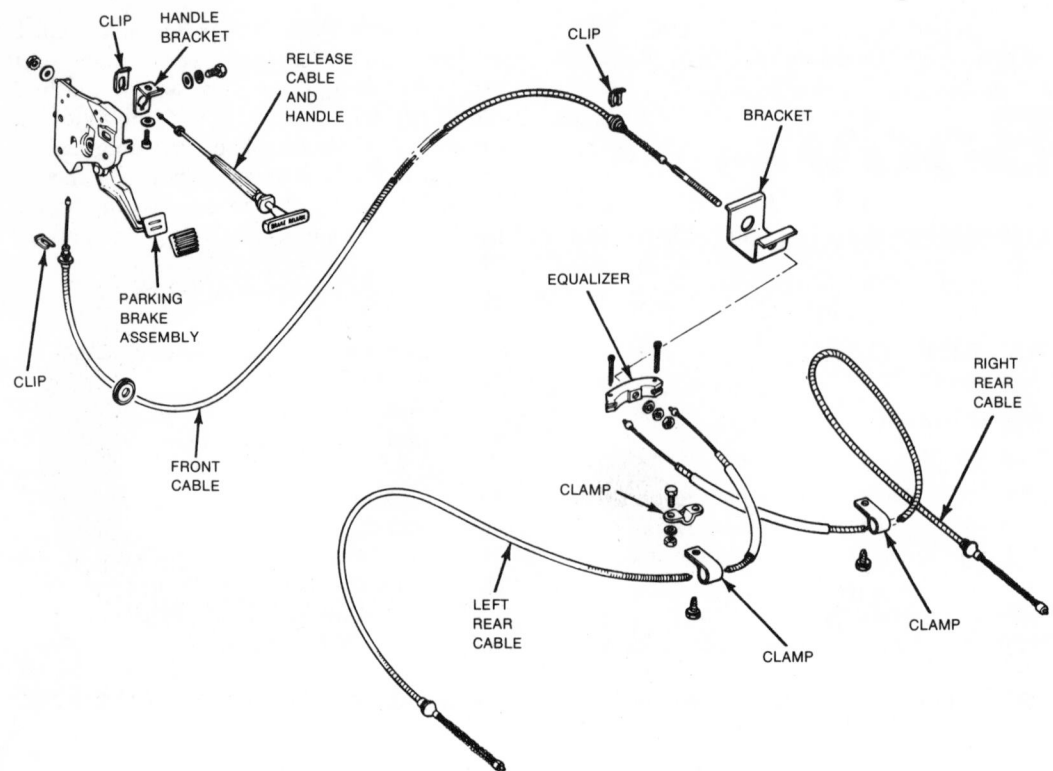

1972–81 parking brake system components

Body

10

You can repair most minor auto body damage yourself. Minor damage usually falls into one of several categories: (1) small scratches and dings in the paint that can be repaired without the use of body filler, (2) deep scratches and dents that require body filler, but do not require pulling, or hammering metal back into shape and (3) rust-out repairs. The repair sequences illustrated in this chapter are typical of these types of repairs. If you want to get involved in more complicated repairs including pulling or hammering sheet metal back into shape, you will probably need more detailed instructions. Chilton's *Minor Auto Body Repair, 2nd Edition* is a comprehensive guide to repairing auto body damage yourself.

TOOLS AND SUPPLIES

The list of tools and equipment you may need to fix minor body damage ranges from very basic hand tools to a wide assortment of specialized body tools. Most minor scratches, dings and rust holes can be fixed using an electric drill, wire wheel or grinder attachment, half-round plastic file, sanding block, various grades of sandpaper (#36, which is coarse through #600, which is fine) in both wet and dry types, auto body plastic,

primer, touch-up paint, spreaders, newspaper and masking tape.

Most manufacturers of auto body repair products began supplying materials to professionals. Their knowledge of the best, most-used products has been translated into body repair kits for the do-it-yourselfer. Kits are available from a number of manufacturers and contain the necessary materials in the required amounts for the repair identified on the package.

Kits are available for a wide variety of uses, including:

- Rusted out metal
- All purpose kit for dents and holes
- Dents and deep scratches
- Fiberglass repair kit
- Epoxy kit for restyling.

Kits offer the advantage of buying what you need for the job. There is little waste and little chance of materials going bad from not being used. The same manufacturers also merchandise all of the individual products used—spreaders, dent pullers, fiberglass cloth, polyester resin, cream hardener, body filler, body files, sandpaper, sanding discs and holders, primer, spray paint, etc.

CAUTION: *Most of the products you will be using contain harmful chemicals, so be extremely careful. Always read the complete label before opening the containers. When* *you put them away for future use, be sure they are out of children's reach!*

Most auto body repair kits contain all the materials you need to do the job right in the kit. So, if you have a small rust spot or dent you want to fix, check the contents of the kit before you run out and buy any additional tools.

ALIGNING BODY PANELS

Doors

There are several methods of adjusting doors. Your vehicle will probably use one of those illustrated.

Whenever a door is removed and is to be reinstalled, you should matchmark the position of the hinges on the door pillars. The holes of the hinges and/or the hinge attaching points are usually oversize to permit alignment of doors. The striker plate is also moveable, through oversize holes, permitting up-and-down, in-and-out and fore-and-aft movement. Fore-and-aft movement is made by adding or subtracting shims from behind the striker and pillar post. The striker should be adjusted so that the door closes fully and remains closed, yet enters the lock freely.

DOOR HINGES

Don't try to cover up poor door adjustment with a striker plate adjustment. The gap on each side of the door should be equal and uniform and there should be no metal-to-metal contact as the door is opened or closed.

1. Determine which hinge bolts must be loosened to move the door in the desired direction.

2. Loosen the hinge bolt(s) just enough to allow the door to be moved with a padded pry bar.

3. Move the door a small amount and check the fit, after tightening the bolts. Be sure that there is no bind or interference with adjacent panels.

4. Repeat this until the door is properly positioned, and tighten all the bolts securely.

Hood, Trunk or Tailgate

As with doors, the outline of hinges should be scribed before removal. The hood and trunk can be aligned by loosening the hinge bolts in their slotted mounting holes and moving the hood or trunk lid as necessary.

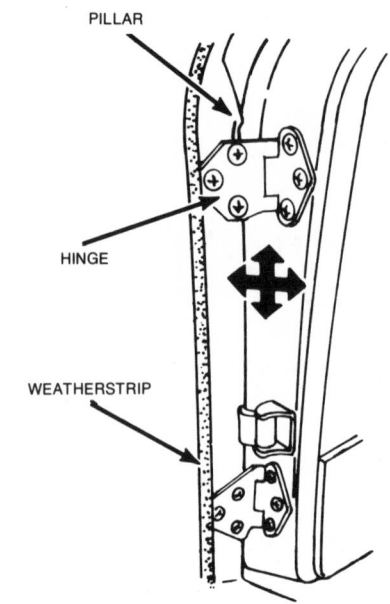

Door hinge adjustment

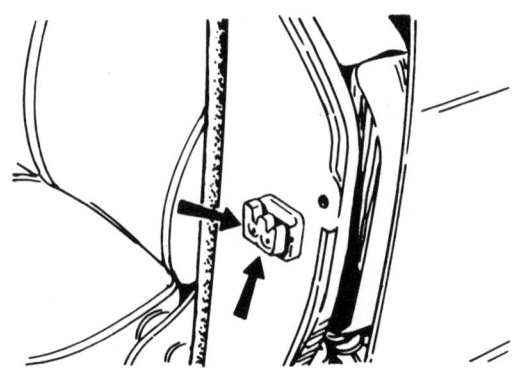

Move the door striker as indicated by arrows

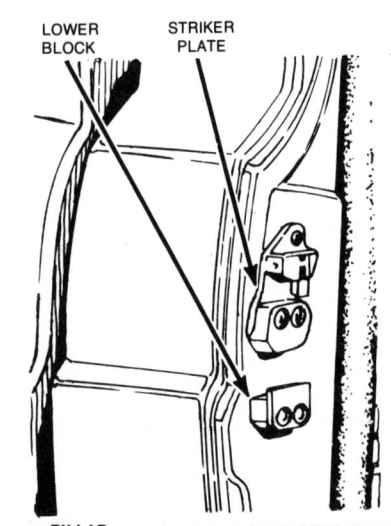

Striker plate and lower block

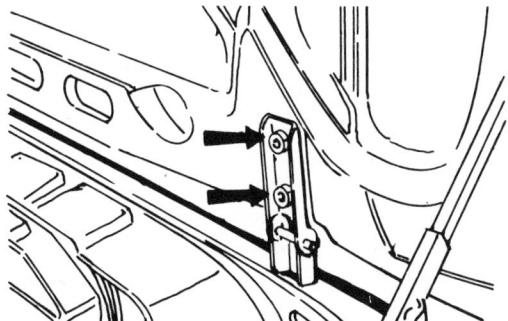

Loosen the hinge boots to permit fore-and-aft and horizontal adjustment

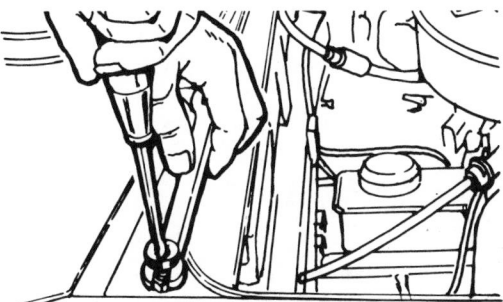

The hood is adjusted vertically by stop-screws at the front and/or rear

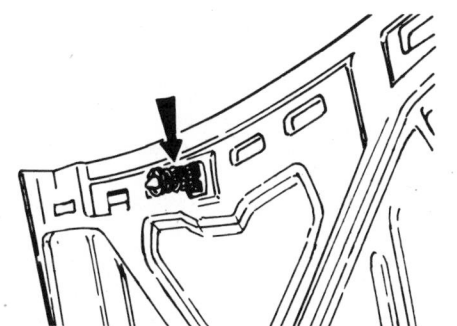

The hood pin can be adjusted for proper lock engagement

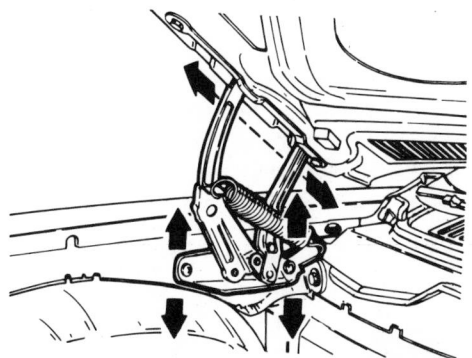

The height of the hood at the rear is adjusted by loosening the bolts that attach the hinge to the body and moving the hood up or down

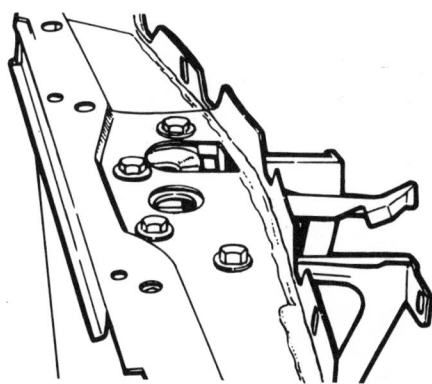

The base of the hood lock can also be repositioned slightly to give more positive lock engagement

The hood and trunk have adjustable catch locations to regulate lock engagement. Bumpers at the front and/or rear of the hood provide a vertical adjustment and the hood lockpin can be adjusted for proper engagement.

The tailgate on the station wagon can be adjusted by loosening the hinge bolts in their slotted mounting holes and moving the tailgate on its hinges. The latchplate and latch striker at the bottom of the tailgate opening can be adjusted to stop rattle. An adjustable bumper is located on each side.

RUST, UNDERCOATING, AND RUSTPROOFING

Rust

Rust is an electrochemical process. It works on ferrous metals (iron and steel) from the inside out due to exposure of unprotected surfaces to air and moisture. The possibility of rust exists practically nationwide—anywhere humidity, industrial pollution or chemical salts are present, rust can form. In coastal areas, the problem is high humidity and salt air; in snowy areas, the problem is chemical salt (de-icer) used to keep the roads clear, and in industrial areas, sulphur dioxide is present in the air from industrial pollution and is changed to sulphuric acid when it rains. The rusting process is accelerated by high temperatures, especially in snowy areas, when vehicles are driven over slushy roads and then left overnight in a heated garage.

Automotive styling also can be a contributor to rust formation. Spot welding of panels creates small pockets that trap moisture and form an environment for rust formation. Fortunately, auto manufacturers have been working hard to increase the corrosion protection of their products. Galvanized sheet metal enjoys much wider use, along with the increased use of plastic and various rust retardant coatings. Manufacturers are also designing out areas in the body where rust-forming moisture can collect.

To prevent rust, you must stop it before it gets started. On new vehicles, there are two ways to accomplish this.

First, the car or truck should be treated with a commercial rustproofing compound. There are many different brands of franchised rustproofers, but most processes involve spraying a waxy "self-healing" compound under the chassis, inside rocker panels, inside doors and fender liners and similar places where rust is likely to form. Prices for a quality rustproofing job range from $100–$250, depending on the area, the brand name and the size of the vehicle.

Ideally, the vehicle should be rustproofed as soon as possible following the purchase. The surfaces of the car or truck have begun to oxidize and deteriorate during shipping. In addition, the car may have sat on a dealer's lot or on a lot at the factory, and once the rust has progressed past the stage of light, powdery surface oxidation rustproofing is not likely to be worthwhile. Professional rustproofers feel that once rust has formed, rustproofing will simply seal in moisture already present. Most franchised rustproofing operations offer a 3–5 year warranty against rust-through, but will not support that warranty if the rustproofing is not applied within three months of the date of manufacture.

Undercoating should not be mistaken for rustproofing. Undercoating is a black, tarlike substance that is applied to the underside of a vehicle. Its basic function is to deaden noises that are transmitted from under the car. It simply cannot get into the crevices and seams where moisture tends to collect. In fact, it may clog up drainage holes and ventilation passages. Some undercoatings also tend to crack or peel with age and only create more moisture and corrosion attracting pockets.

The second thing you should do immediately after purchasing the car is apply a paint sealant. A sealant is a petroleum based product marketed under a wide variety of brand names. It has the same protective properties as a good wax, but bonds to the paint with a chemically inert layer that seals it from the air. If air can't get at the surface, oxidation cannot start.

The paint sealant kit consists of a base coat and a conditioning coat that should be applied every 6–8 months, depending on the manufacturer. The base coat must be applied before waxing, or the wax must first be removed.

Third, keep a garden hose handy for your car in winter. Use it a few times on nice days during the winter for underneath areas, and it will pay big dividends when spring arrives. Spraying under the fenders and other areas which even car washes don't reach will help remove road salt, dirt and other build-ups which help breed rust. Adjust the nozzle to a high-force spray. An old brush will help break up residue, permitting it to be washed away more easily.

It's a somewhat messy job, but worth it in the long run because rust often starts in those hidden areas.

At the same time, wash grime off the door sills and, more importantly, the under portions of the doors, plus the tailgate if you have a station wagon or truck. Applying a coat of wax to those areas at least once before and once during winter will help fend off rust.

When applying the wax to the under parts of the doors, you will note small drain holes. These holes often are plugged with undercoating or dirt. Make sure they are cleaned out to prevent water build-up inside the doors. A small punch or penknife will do the job.

Water from the high-pressure sprays in car washes sometimes can get into the housings for parking and taillights, so take a close look. If they contain water merely loosen the retaining screws and the water should run out.

Repairing Scratches and Small Dents

Step 1. This dent (arrow) is typical of a deep scratch or minor dent. If deep enough, the dent or scratch can be pulled out or hammered out from behind. In this case no straightening is necessary

Step 2. Using an 80-grit grinding disc on an electric drill grind the paint from the surrounding area down to bare metal. This will provide a rough surface for the body filler to grab

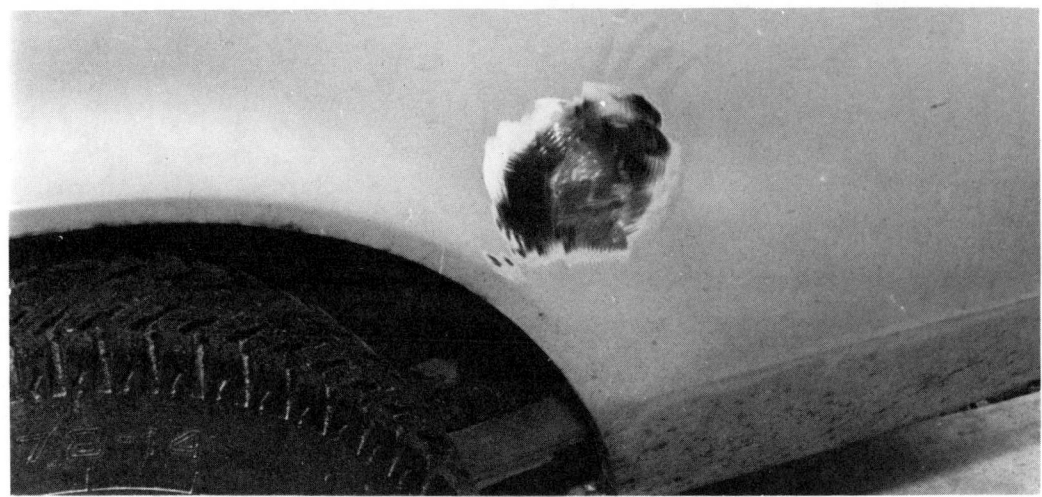

Step 3. The area should look like this when you're finished grinding

Step 4. Mix the body filler and cream hardener according to the directions

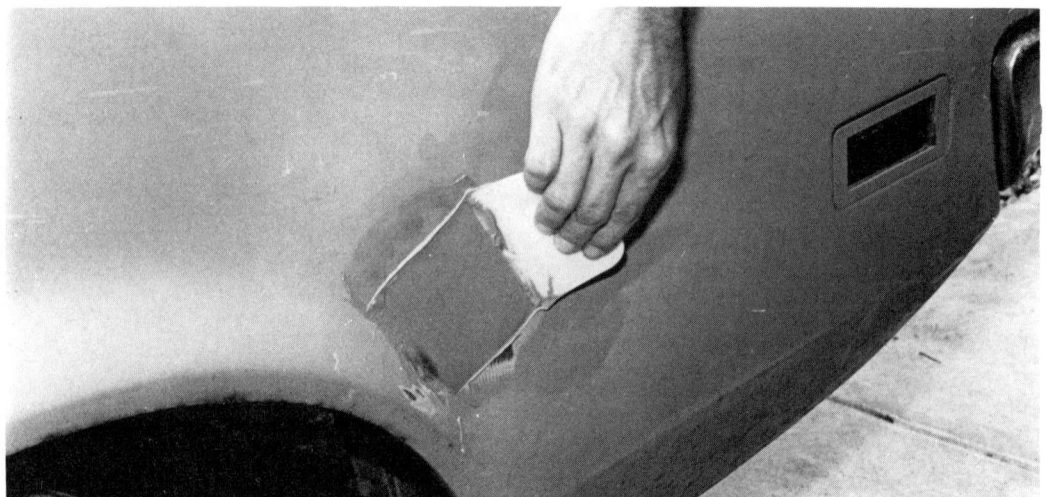

Step 5. Spread the body filler evenly over the entire area. Be sure to cover the area completely

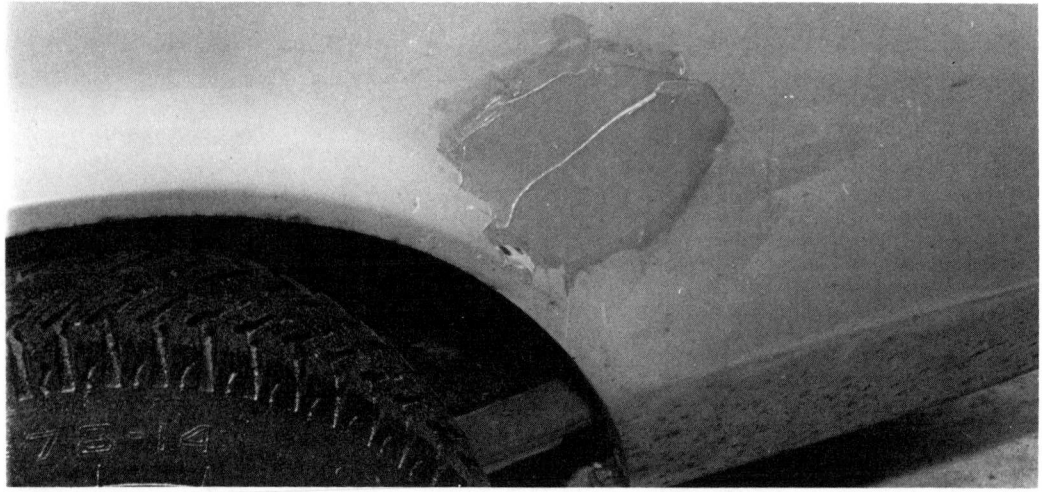

Step 6. Let the body filler dry until the surface can just be scratched with your fingernail

Step 7. Knock the high spots from the body filler with a body file

Step 8. Check frequently with the palm of your hand for high and low spots. If you wind up with low spots, you may have to apply another layer of filler

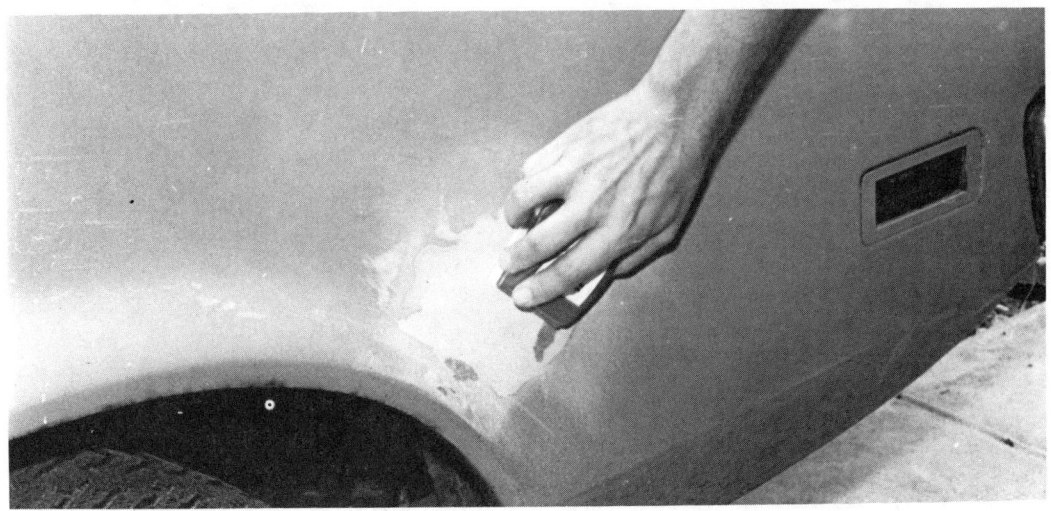

Step 9. Block sand the entire area with 320 grit paper

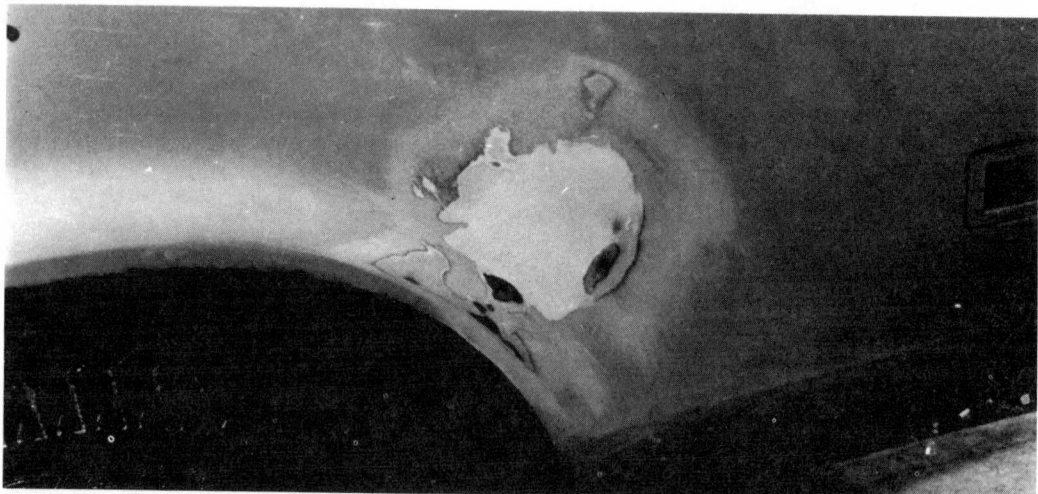

Step 10. When you're finished, the repair should look like this. Note the sand marks extending 2—3 inches out from the repaired area

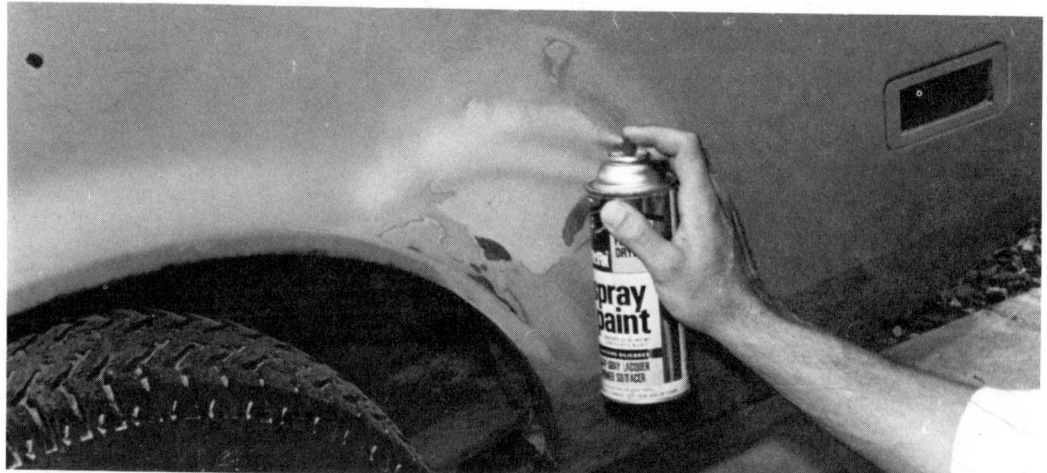

Step 11. Prime the entire area with automotive primer

Step 12. The finished repair ready for the final paint coat. Note that the primer has covered the sanding marks (see Step 10). A repair of this size should be able to be spotpainted with good results

REPAIRING RUST HOLES

One thing you have to remember about rust: even if you grind away all the rusted metal in a panel, and repair the area with any of the kits available, *eventually* the rust will return. There are two reasons for this. One, rust is a chemical reaction that causes pressure under the repair from the inside out. That's how the blisters form. Two, the back side of the panel (and the repair) is wide open to moisture, and unpainted body filler acts like a sponge. That's why the best solution to rust problems is to remove the rusted panel and install a new one or have the rusted area cut out and a new piece of sheet metal welded in its place. The trouble with welding is the expense; sometimes it will cost more than the car or truck is worth.

One of the better solutions to do-it-yourself rust repair is the process using a fiberglass cloth repair kit (shown here). This will give a strong repair that resists cracking and moisture and is relatively easy to use. It can be used on large or small holes and also can be applied over contoured surfaces.

Step 1. Rust areas such as this are common and are easily fixed

Step 2. Grind away all traces of rust with a 24-grit grinding disc. Be sure to grind back 3—4 inches from the edge of the hole down to bare metal and be sure all traces of rust are removed

Step 3. Be sure all rust is removed from the edges of the metal. The edges must be ground back to un-rusted metal

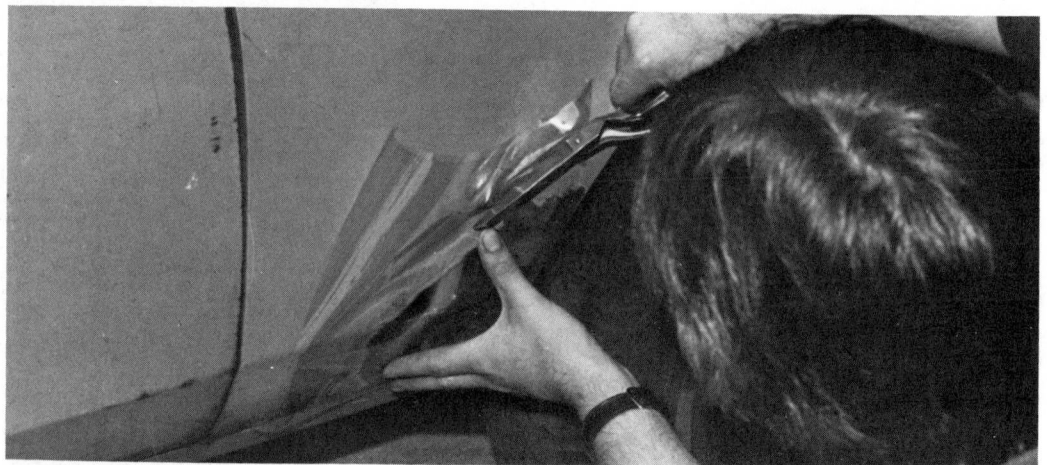

Step 4. If you are going to use release film, cut a piece about 2″ larger than the area you have sanded. Place the film over the repair and mark the sanded area on the film. Avoid any unnecessary wrinkling of the film

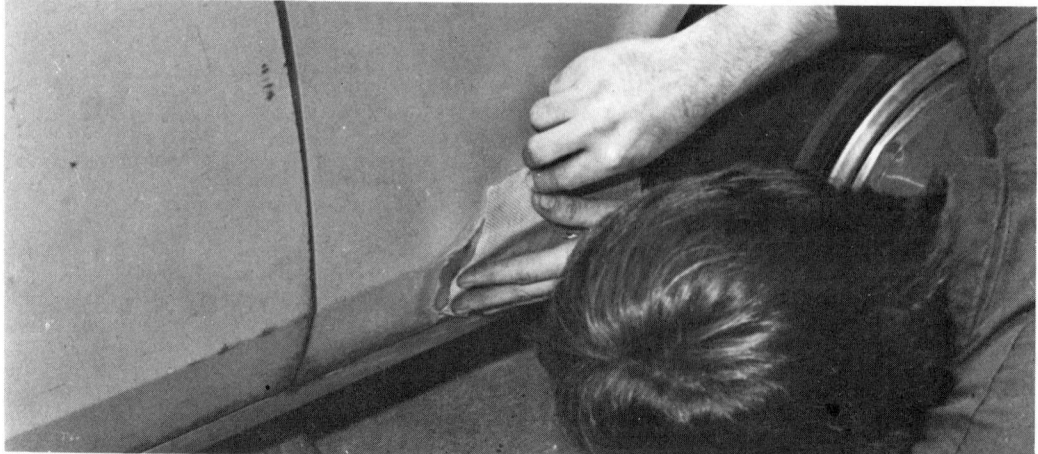

Step 5. Cut 2 pieces of fiberglass matte. One piece should be about 1″ smaller than the sanded area and the second piece should be 1″ smaller than the first. Use sharp scissors to avoid loose ends

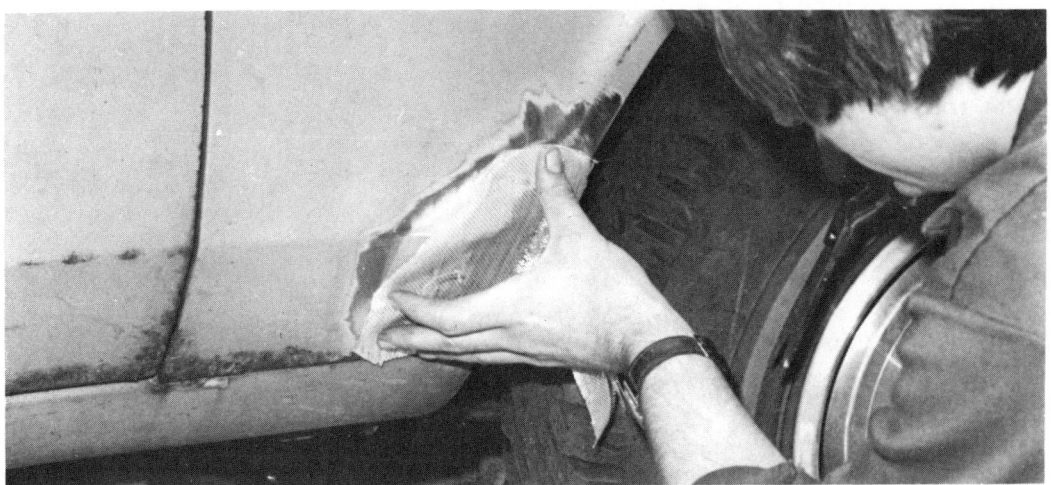

Step 6. Check the dimensions of the release film and cloth by holding them up to the repair area

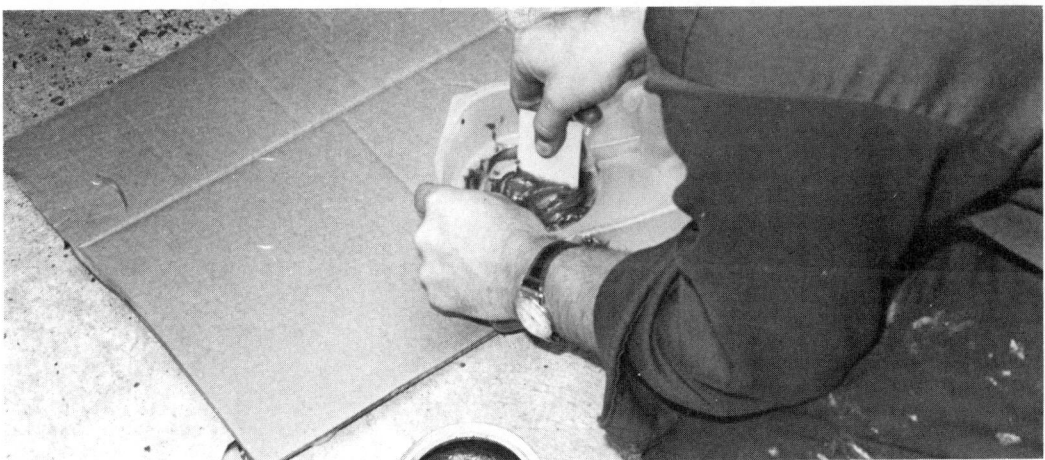

Step 7. Mix enough repair jelly and cream hardener in the mixing tray to saturate the fiberglass material or fill the repair area. Follow the directions on the container

Step 8. Lay the release sheet on a flat surface and spread an even layer of filler, large enough to cover the repair. Lay the smaller piece of fiberglass cloth in the center of the sheet and spread another layer of repair jelly over the fiberglass cloth. Repeat the operation for the larger piece of cloth. If the fiberglass cloth is not used, spread the repair jelly on the release film, concentrated in the middle of the repair

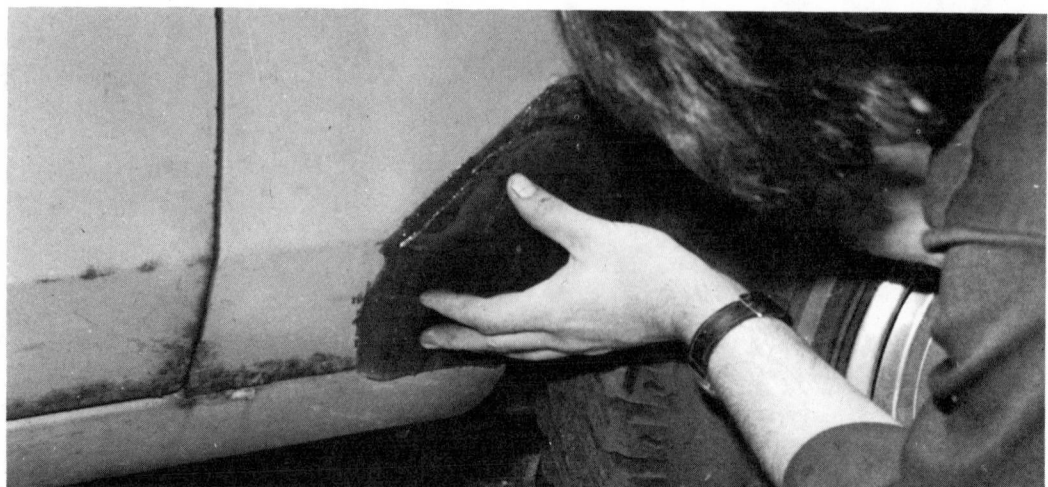

Step 9. Place the repair material over the repair area, with the release film facing outward

Step 10. Use a spreader and work from the center outward to smooth the material, following the body contours. Be sure to remove all air bubbles

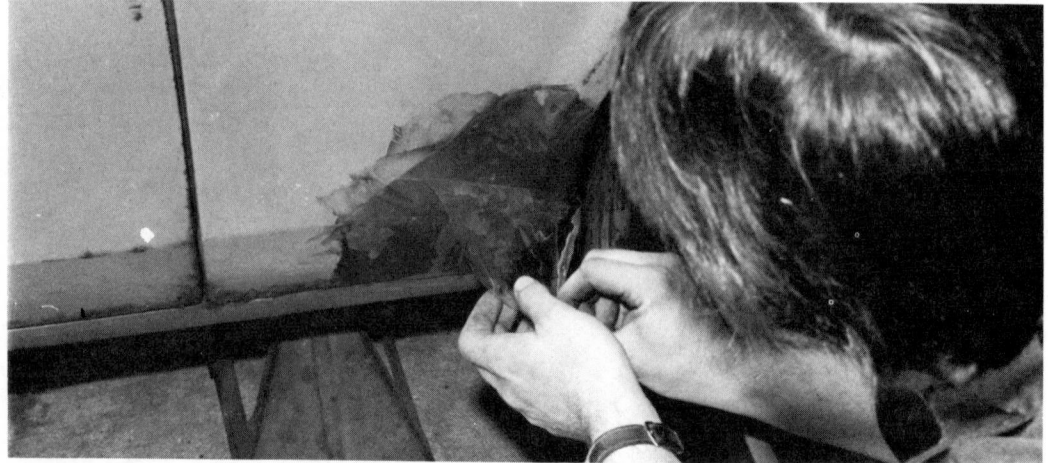

Step 11. Wait until the repair has dried tack-free and peel off the release sheet. The ideal working temperature is 65—90° F. Cooler or warmer temperatures or high humidity may require additional curing time

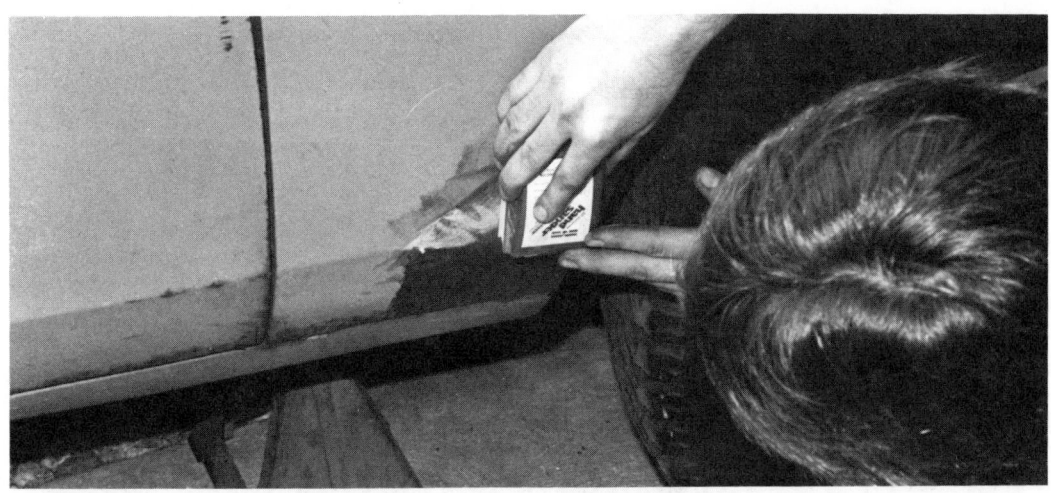

Step 12. Sand and feather-edge the entire area. The initial sanding can be done with a sanding disc on an electric drill if care is used. Finish the sanding with a block sander

Step 13. When the area is sanded smooth, mix some topcoat and hardener and apply it directly with a spreader. This will give a smooth finish and prevent the glass matte from showing through the paint

Step 14. Block sand the topcoat with finishing sandpaper

Step 15. To finish this repair, grind out the surface rust along the top edge of the rocker panel

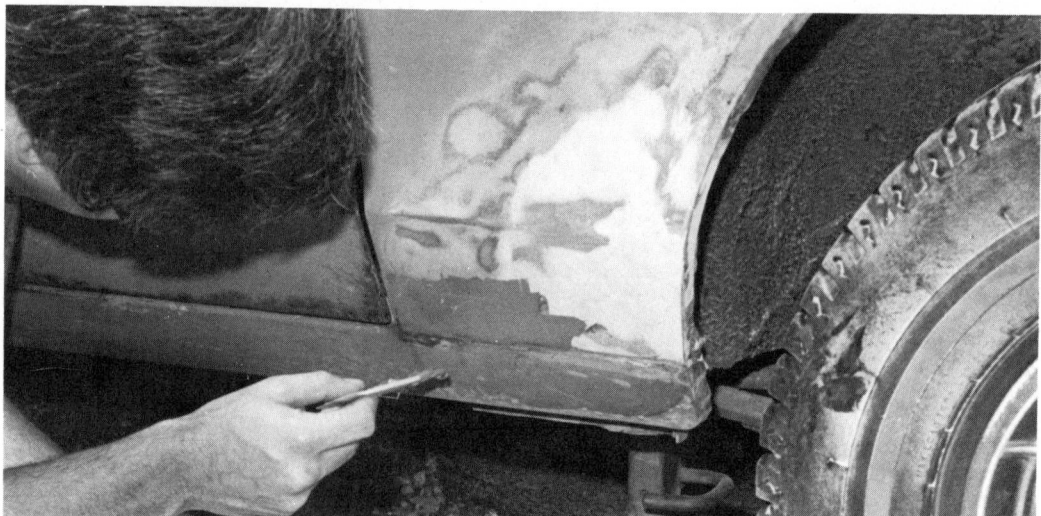

Step 16. Mix some more repair jelly and cream hardener and apply it directly over the surface

Step 17. When it dries tack-free, block sand the surface smooth

Step 18. If necessary, mask off adjacent panels and spray the entire repair with primer. You are now ready for a color coat

AUTO BODY CARE

There are hundreds—maybe thousands—of products on the market, all designed to protect or aid your car's finish in some manner. There are as many different products as there are ways to use them, but they all have one thing in common—the surface must be clean.

Washing

The primary ingredient for washing your car is water, preferably "soft" water. In many areas of the country, the local water supply is "hard" containing many minerals. The little rings or film that is left on your car's surface after it has dried is the result of "hard" water.

Since you usually can't change the local water supply, the next best thing is to dry the surface before it has a chance to dry itself.

Into the water you usually add soap. Don't use detergents or common, coarse soaps. Your car's paint never truly dries out, but is always evaporating residual oils into the air. Harsh detergents will remove these oils, causing the paint to dry faster than normal. Instead use warm water and a non-detergent soap made especially for waxed surfaces or a liquid soap made for waxed surfaces or a liquid soap made for washing dishes by hand.

Other products that can be used on painted surfaces include baking soda or plain soda water for stubborn dirt.

Wash the car completely, starting at the top, and rinse it completely clean. Abrasive grit should be loaded off under water pressure; scrubbing grit off will scratch the finish. The best washing tool is a sponge, cleaning mitt or soft towel. Whichever you choose, replace it often as each tends to absorb grease and dirt.

Other ways to get a better wash include:

• Don't wash your car in the sun or when the finish is hot.

• Use water pressure to remove caked-on dirt.

• Remove tree-sap and bird effluence immediately. Such substances will eat through wax, polish and paint.

One of the best implements to dry your car is a turkish towel or an old, soft bath towel. Anything with a deep nap will hold any dirt in suspension and not grind it into the paint.

Harder cloths will only grind the grit into the paint making more scratches. Always start drying at the top, followed by the hood and trunk and sides. You'll find there's always more dirt near the rocker panels and wheelwells which will wind up on the rest of the car if you dry these areas first.

Cleaners, Waxes and Polishes

Before going any farther you should know the function of various products.

Cleaners—remove the top layer of dead pigment or paint.

Rubbing or polishing compounds—used to remove stubborn dirt, get rid of minor scratches, smooth away imperfections and partially restore badly weathered paint.

Polishes—contain no abrasives or waxes; they shine the paint by adding oils to the paint.

Waxes—are a protective coating for the polish.

CLEANERS AND COMPOUNDS

Before you apply any wax, you'll have to remove oxidation, road film and other types of pollutants that washing alone will not remove.

The paint on your car never dries completely. There are always residual oils evaporating from the paint into the air. When enough oils are present in the paint, it has a healthy shine (gloss). When too many oils evaporate the paint takes on a whitish cast known as oxidation. The idea of polishing and waxing is to keep enough oil present in the painted surface to prevent oxidation; but when it occurs, the only recourse is to remove the top layer of "dead" paint, exposing the healthy paint underneath.

Products to remove oxidation and road film are sold under a variety of generic names—polishes, cleaner, rubbing compound, cleaner/polish, polish/cleaner, self-polishing wax, pre-wax cleaner, finish restorer and many more. Regardless of name there are two types of cleaners—abrasive cleaners (sometimes called polishing or rubbing compounds) that remove oxidation by grinding away the top layer of "dead" paint, or chemical cleaners that dissolve the "dead" pigment, allowing it to be wiped away.

Abrasive cleaners, by their nature, leave thousands of minute scratches in the finish, which must be polished out later. These should only be used in extreme cases, but are usually the only thing to use on badly oxidized paint finishes. Chemical cleaners are much milder but are not strong enough for severe cases of oxidation or weathered paint.

The most popular cleaners are liquid or paste abrasive polishing and rubbing compounds. Polishing compounds have a finer abrasive grit for medium duty work. Rubbing compounds are a coarser abrasive and for heavy duty work. Unless you are familiar with how to use compounds, be very careful. Excessive rubbing with any type of compound or cleaner can grind right through the paint to primer or bare metal. Follow the directions on the container—depending on type, the cleaner may or may not be OK for your paint. For example, some cleaners are not formulated for acrylic lacquer finishes.

When a small area needs compounding or heavy polishing, it's best to do the job by hand. Some people prefer a powered buffer for large areas. Avoid cutting through the paint along styling edges on the body. Small, hand operations where the compound is applied and rubbed using cloth folded into a thick ball allow you to work in straight lines along such edges.

To avoid cutting through on the edges when using a power buffer, try masking tape. Just cover the edge with tape while using power. Then finish the job by hand with the tape removed. Even then work carefully. The paint tends to be a lot thinner along the sharp ridges stamped into the panels.

Whether compounding by machine or by hand, only work on a small area and apply the compound sparingly. If the materials are spread too thin, or allowed to sit too long, they dry out. Once dry they lose the ability to deliver a smooth, clean finish. Also, dried out polish tends to cause the buffer to stick in one spot. This in turn can burn or cut through the finish.

WAXES AND POLISHES

Your car's finish can be protected in a number of ways. A cleaner/wax or polish/cleaner followed by wax or variations of each all provide good results. The two-step approach (polish followed by wax) is probably slightly better but consumes more time and effort. Properly fed with oils, your paint should never need cleaning, but despite the best polishing job, it won't last unless it's protected with wax. Without wax, polish must be renewed at least once a month to prevent oxidation. Years ago (some still swear by it today), the best wax was made from the Brazilian palm, the Carnuba, favored for its vegetable base and high melting point. However, modern synthetic waxes are harder, which means they protect against moisture better, and chemically inert silicone is used for a long lasting protection. The only problem with silicone wax is that it penetrates all layers of paint. To repaint or touch up a panel or car protected by silicone wax, you have to completely strip the finish to avoid "fisheyes."

Under normal conditions, silicone waxes will last 4–6 months, but you have to be careful of wax build-up from too much waxing. Too thick a coat of wax is just as bad as no wax at all; it stops the paint from breathing.

Combination cleaners/waxes have become popular lately because they remove the old layer of wax plus light oxidation, while putting on a fresh coat of wax at the same time. Some cleaners/waxes contain abrasive cleaners which require caution, although many cleaner/waxes use a chemical cleaner.

Applying Wax or Polish

You may view polishing and waxing your car as a pleasant way to spend an afternoon, or as a boring chore, but it has to be done to keep the paint on your car. Caring for the paint doesn't require special tools, but you should follow a few rules.

1. Use a good quality wax.

2. Before applying any wax or polish, be sure the surface is completely clean. Just because the car looks clean, doesn't mean it's ready for polish or wax.

3. If the finish on your car is weathered, dull, or oxidized, it will probably have to be compounded to remove the old or oxidized paint. If the paint is simply dulled from lack of care, one of the non-abrasive cleaners known as polishing compounds will do the trick. If the paint is severely scratched or really dull, you'll probably have to use a rubbing compound to prepare the finish for waxing. If you're not sure which one to use, use the polishing compound, since you can easily ruin the finish by using too strong a compound.

4. Don't apply wax, polish or compound in direct sunlight, even if the directions on the can say you can. Most waxes will not cure properly in bright sunlight and you'll probably end up with a blotchy looking finish.

5. Don't rub the wax off too soon. The result will be a wet, dull looking finish. Let the wax dry thoroughly before buffing it off.

6. A constant debate among car enthusiasts is how wax should be applied. Some maintain pastes or liquids should be applied in a circular motion, but body shop experts have long thought that this approach results in barely detectable circular abrasions, especially on cars that are waxed frequently. They advise rubbing in straight lines, especially if any kind of cleaner is involved.

7. If an applicator is not supplied with the wax, use a piece of soft cheesecloth or very soft lint-free material. The same applies to buffing the surface.

SPECIAL SURFACES

One-step combination cleaner and wax formulas shouldn't be used on many of the special surfaces which abound on cars. The one-step materials contain abrasives to achieve a clean surface under the wax top coat. The abrasives are so mild that you could clean a car every week for a couple of years without fear of rubbing through the paint. But this same level of abrasiveness might, through repeated use, damage decals used for special trim effects. This includes wide stripes, wood-grain trim and other appliques.

Painted plastics must be cleaned with care. If a cleaner is too aggressive it will cut through the paint and expose the primer. If bright trim such as polished aluminum or chrome is painted, cleaning must be performed with even greater care. If rubbing compound is being used, it will cut faster than polish.

Abrasive cleaners will dull an acrylic finish. The best way to clean these newer finishes is with a non-abrasive liquid polish. Only dirt and oxidation, not paint, will be removed.

Taking a few minutes to read the instructions on the can of polish or wax will help prevent making serious mistakes. Not all preparations will work on all surfaces. And some are intended for power application while others will only work when applied by hand.

Don't get the idea that just pouring on some polish and then hitting it with a buffer will suffice. Power equipment speeds the operation. But it also adds a measure of risk. It's very easy to damage the finish if you use the wrong methods or materials.

Caring for Chrome

Read the label on the container. Many products are formulated specifically for chrome, but others contain abrasives that will scratch the chrome finish. If it isn't recommended for chrome, don't use it.

Never use steel wool or kitchen soap pads to clean chrome. Be careful not to get chrome cleaner on paint or interior vinyl surfaces. If you do, get it off immediately.

Troubleshooting

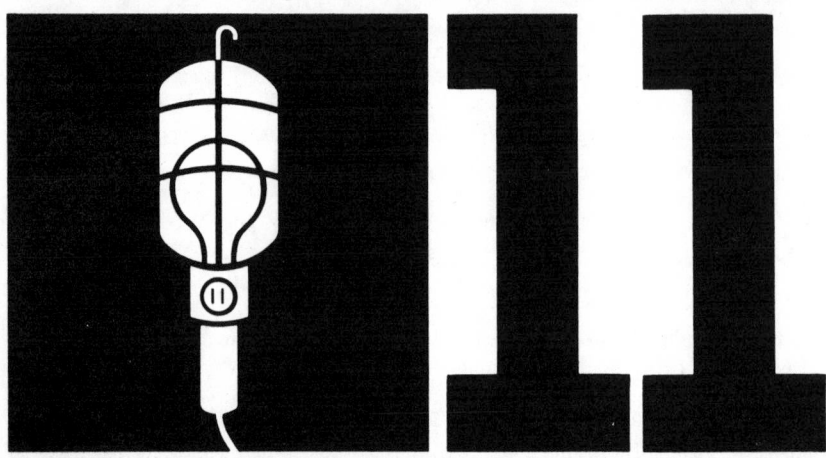

This section is designed to aid in the quick, accurate diagnosis of automotive problems. While automotive repairs can be made by many people, accurate troubleshooting is a rare skill for the amateur and professional alike.

In its simplest state, troubleshooting is an exercise in logic. It is essential to realize that an automobile is really composed of a series of systems. Some of these systems are interrelated; others are not. Automobiles operate within a framework of logical rules and physical laws, and the key to troubleshooting is a good understanding of all the automotive systems.

This section breaks the car or truck down into its component systems, allowing the problem to be isolated. The charts and diagnostic road maps list the most common problems and the most probable causes of trouble. Obviously it would be impossible to list every possible problem that could happen along with every possible cause, but it will locate MOST problems and eliminate a lot of unnecessary guesswork. The systematic format will locate problems within a given system, but, because many automotive systems are interrelated, the solution to your particular problem may be found in a number of systems on the car or truck.

USING THE TROUBLESHOOTING CHARTS

This book contains all of the specific information that the average do-it-yourself mechanic needs to repair and maintain his or her car or truck. The troubleshooting charts are designed to be used in conjunction with the specific procedures and information in the text. For instance, troubleshooting a point-type ignition system is fairly standard for all models, but you may be directed to the text to find procedures for troubleshooting an individual type of electronic ignition. You will also have to refer to the specification charts throughout the book for specifications applicable to your car or truck.

TOOLS AND EQUIPMENT

The tools illustrated in Chapter 1 (plus two more diagnostic pieces) will be adequate to troubleshoot most problems. The two other tools needed are a voltmeter and an ohmmeter. These can be purchased separately or in combination, known as a VOM meter.

In the event that other tools are required, they will be noted in the procedures.

Troubleshooting Engine Problems

See Chapters 2, 3, 4 for more information and service procedures.

Index to Systems

System	To Test	Group
Battery	Engine need not be running	1
Starting system	Engine need not be running	2
Primary electrical system	Engine need not be running	3
Secondary electrical system	Engine need not be running	4
Fuel system	Engine need not be running	5
Engine compression	Engine need not be running	6
Engine vacuum	Engine must be running	7
Secondary electrical system	Engine must be running	8
Valve train	Engine must be running	9
Exhaust system	Engine must be running	10
Cooling system	Engine must be running	11
Engine lubrication	Engine must be running	12

Index to Problems

Problem: Symptom	Begin at Specific Diagnosis, Number
Engine Won't Start:	
Starter doesn't turn	1.1, 2.1
Starter turns, engine doesn't	2.1
Starter turns engine very slowly	1.1, 2.4
Starter turns engine normally	3.1, 4.1
Starter turns engine very quickly	6.1
Engine fires intermittently	4.1
Engine fires consistently	5.1, 6.1
Engine Runs Poorly:	
Hard starting	3.1, 4.1, 5.1, 8.1
Rough idle	4.1, 5.1, 8.1
Stalling	3.1, 4.1, 5.1, 8.1
Engine dies at high speeds	4.1, 5.1
Hesitation (on acceleration from standing stop)	5.1, 8.1
Poor pickup	4.1, 5.1, 8.1
Lack of power	3.1, 4.1, 5.1, 8.1
Backfire through the carburetor	4.1, 8.1, 9.1
Backfire through the exhaust	4.1, 8.1, 9.1
Blue exhaust gases	6.1, 7.1
Black exhaust gases	5.1
Running on (after the ignition is shut off)	3.1, 8.1
Susceptible to moisture	4.1
Engine misfires under load	4.1, 7.1, 8.4, 9.1
Engine misfires at speed	4.1, 8.4
Engine misfires at idle	3.1, 4.1, 5.1, 7.1, 8.4

Sample Section

Test and Procedure	Results and Indications	Proceed to
4.1—Check for spark: Hold each spark plug wire approximately ¼″ from ground with gloves or a heavy, dry rag. Crank the engine and observe the spark.	→ If no spark is evident:	→ 4.2
	→ If spark is good in some cases:	→ 4.3
	→ If spark is good in all cases:	→ 4.6

Specific Diagnosis

This section is arranged so that following each test, instructions are given to proceed to another, until a problem is diagnosed.

Section 1—Battery

Test and Procedure	Results and Indications	Proceed to
1.1—Inspect the battery visually for case condition (corrosion, cracks) and water level.	If case is cracked, replace battery:	**1.4**
	If the case is intact, remove corrosion with a solution of baking soda and water (**CAUTION**: *do not get the solution into the battery*), and fill with water:	**1.2**

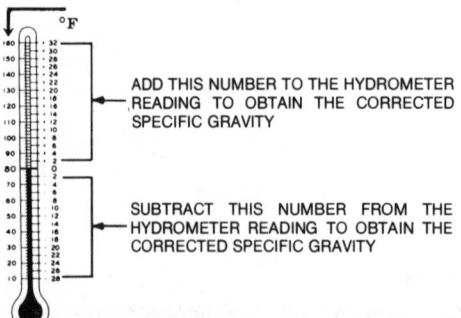

DIRT ON TOP OF BATTERY
CORROSION
PLUGGED VENT
LOOSE CABLE OR POSTS
CRACKS
LOW WATER LEVEL

Inspect the battery case

Test and Procedure	Results and Indications	Proceed to
1.2—Check the battery cable connections: Insert a screwdriver between the battery post and the cable clamp. Turn the headlights on high beam, and observe them as the screwdriver is gently twisted to ensure good metal to metal contact.	If the lights brighten, remove and clean the clamp and post; coat the post with petroleum jelly, install and tighten the clamp:	**1.4**
	If no improvement is noted:	**1.3**

TESTING BATTERY CABLE CONNECTIONS USING A SCREWDRIVER

Test and Procedure	Results and Indications	Proceed to
1.3—Test the state of charge of the battery using an individual cell tester or hydrometer.	If indicated, charge the battery. **NOTE:** *If no obvious reason exists for the low state of charge (i.e., battery age, prolonged storage),* *proceed to:*	**1.4**

°F

ADD THIS NUMBER TO THE HYDROMETER READING TO OBTAIN THE CORRECTED SPECIFIC GRAVITY

SUBTRACT THIS NUMBER FROM THE HYDROMETER READING TO OBTAIN THE CORRECTED SPECIFIC GRAVITY

Specific Gravity (@ 80° F.)

Minimum	Battery Charge
1.260	100% Charged
1.230	75% Charged
1.200	50% Charged
1.170	25% Charged
1.140	Very Little Power Left
1.110	Completely Discharged

The effects of temperature on battery specific gravity (left) and amount of battery charge in relation to specific gravity (right)

Test and Procedure	Results and Indications	Proceed to
1.4—Visually inspect battery cables for cracking, bad connection to ground, or bad connection to starter.	If necessary, tighten connections or replace the cables:	**2.1**

Section 2—Starting System
See Chapter 3 for service procedures

Test and Procedure	Results and Indications	Proceed to
Note: Tests in Group 2 are performed with coil high tension lead disconnected to prevent accidental starting.		
2.1—Test the starter motor and solenoid: Connect a jumper from the battery post of the solenoid (or relay) to the starter post of the solenoid (or relay).	If starter turns the engine normally:	**2.2**
	If the starter buzzes, or turns the engine very slowly:	**2.4**
	If no response, replace the solenoid (or relay).	**3.1**
	If the starter turns, but the engine doesn't, ensure that the flywheel ring gear is intact. If the gear is undamaged, replace the starter drive.	**3.1**
2.2—Determine whether ignition override switches are functioning properly (clutch start switch, neutral safety switch), by connecting a jumper across the switch(es), and turning the ignition switch to "start".	If starter operates, adjust or replace switch:	**3.1**
	If the starter doesn't operate:	**2.3**
2.3—Check the ignition switch "start" position: Connect a 12V test lamp or voltmeter between the starter post of the solenoid (or relay) and ground. Turn the ignition switch to the "start" position, and jiggle the key.	If the lamp doesn't light or the meter needle doesn't move when the switch is turned, check the ignition switch for loose connections, cracked insulation, or broken wires. Repair or replace as necessary:	**3.1**
	If the lamp flickers or needle moves when the key is jiggled, replace the ignition switch.	**3.3**

Checking the ignition switch "start" position

STARTER RELAY
(IF EQUIPPED)

Test and Procedure	Results and Indications	Proceed to
2.4—Remove and bench test the starter, according to specifications in the engine electrical section.	If the starter does not meet specifications, repair or replace as needed:	**3.1**
	If the starter is operating properly:	**2.5**
2.5—Determine whether the engine can turn freely: Remove the spark plugs, and check for water in the cylinders. Check for water on the dipstick, or oil in the radiator. Attempt to turn the engine using an 18″ flex drive and socket on the crankshaft pulley nut or bolt.	If the engine will turn freely only with the spark plugs out, and hydrostatic lock (water in the cylinders) is ruled out, check valve timing:	**9.2**
	If engine will not turn freely, and it is known that the clutch and transmission are free, the engine must be disassembled for further evaluation:	**Chapter 3**

Section 3—Primary Electrical System

Test and Procedure	Results and Indications	Proceed to
3.1—Check the ignition switch "on" position: Connect a jumper wire between the distributor side of the coil and ground, and a 12V test lamp between the switch side of the coil and ground. Remove the high tension lead from the coil. Turn the ignition switch on and jiggle the key.	If the lamp lights:	**3.2**
	If the lamp flickers when the key is jiggled, replace the ignition switch:	**3.3**
	If the lamp doesn't light, check for loose or open connections. If none are found, remove the ignition switch and check for continuity. If the switch is faulty, replace it:	**3.3**

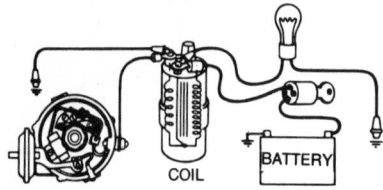

Checking the ignition switch "on" position

3.2—Check the ballast resistor or resistance wire for an open circuit, using an ohmmeter. See Chapter 3 for specific tests.	Replace the resistor or resistance wire if the resistance is zero. **NOTE: *Some ignition systems have no ballast resistor.***	**3.3**

 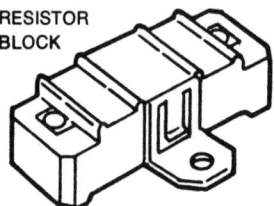

CALIBRATED
RESISTANCE
LEAD

RESISTOR
BLOCK

Two types of resistors

3.3—On point-type ignition systems, visually inspect the breaker points for burning, pitting or excessive wear. Gray coloring of the point contact surfaces is normal. Rotate the crankshaft until the contact heel rests on a high point of the distributor cam and adjust the point gap to specifications. On electronic ignition models, remove the distributor cap and visually inspect the armature. Ensure that the armature pin is in place, and that the armature is on tight and rotates when the engine is cranked. Make sure there are no cracks, chips or rounded edges on the armature.	If the breaker points are intact, clean the contact surfaces with fine emery cloth, and adjust the point gap to specifications. If the points are worn, replace them. On electronic systems, replace any parts which appear defective. If condition persists:	**3.4**

Test and Procedure	Results and Indications	Proceed to
3.4—On point-type ignition systems, connect a dwell-meter between the distributor primary lead and ground. Crank the engine and observe the point dwell angle. On electronic ignition systems, conduct a stator (magnetic pickup assembly) test. See Chapter 3.	On point-type systems, adjust the dwell angle if necessary. **NOTE:** *Increasing the point gap decreases the dwell angle and vice-versa.* If the dwell meter shows little or no reading; On electronic ignition systems, if the stator is bad, replace the stator. If the stator is good, proceed to the other tests in Chapter 3.	**3.6** **3.5**

Dwell is a function of point gap

3.5—On the point-type ignition systems, check the condenser for short: connect an ohmeter across the condenser body and the pigtail lead.	If any reading other than infinite is noted, replace the condenser	**3.6**

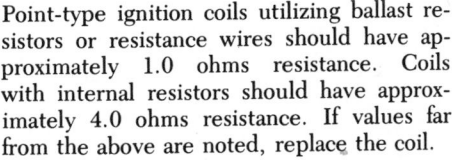

Checking the condenser for short

3.6—Test the coil primary resistance: On point-type ignition systems, connect an ohmmeter across the coil primary terminals, and read the resistance on the low scale. Note whether an external ballast resistor or resistance wire is used. On electronic ignition systems, test the coil primary resistance as in Chapter 3.	Point-type ignition coils utilizing ballast resistors or resistance wires should have approximately 1.0 ohms resistance. Coils with internal resistors should have approximately 4.0 ohms resistance. If values far from the above are noted, replace the coil.	**4.1**

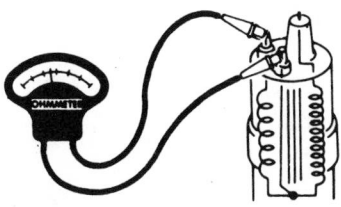

Check the coil primary resistance

Section 4—Secondary Electrical System
See Chapters 2–3 for service procedures

Test and Procedure	Results and Indications	Proceed to
4.1—Check for spark: Hold each spark plug wire approximately ¼″ from ground with gloves or a heavy, dry rag. Crank the engine, and observe the spark.	If no spark is evident:	**4.2**
	If spark is good in some cylinders:	**4.3**
	If spark is good in all cylinders:	**4.6**

Check for spark at the plugs

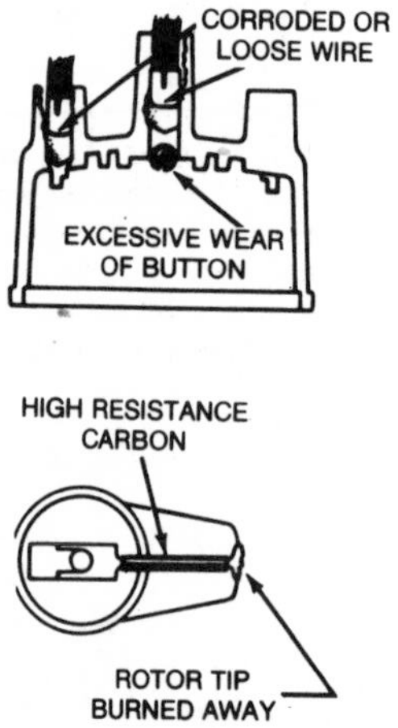

Test and Procedure	Results and Indications	Proceed to
4.2—Check for spark at the coil high tension lead: Remove the coil high tension lead from the distributor and position it approximately ¼″ from ground. Crank the engine and observe spark. **CAUTION: This test should not be performed on engines equipped with electronic ignition.**	If the spark is good and consistent:	**4.3**
	If the spark is good but intermittent, test the primary electrical system starting at 3.3:	**3.3**
	If the spark is weak or non-existent, replace the coil high tension lead, clean and tighten all connections and retest. If no improvement is noted:	**4.4**
4.3—Visually inspect the distributor cap and rotor for burned or corroded contacts, cracks, carbon tracks, or moisture. Also check the fit of the rotor on the distributor shaft (where applicable).	If moisture is present, dry thoroughly, and retest per 4.1:	**4.1**
	If burned or excessively corroded contacts, cracks, or carbon tracks are noted, replace the defective part(s) and retest per 4.1:	**4.1**
	If the rotor and cap appear intact, or are only slightly corroded, clean the contacts thoroughly (including the cap towers and spark plug wire ends) and retest per 4.1: If the spark is good in all cases:	**4.6**
	If the spark is poor in all cases:	**4.5**

CORRODED OR LOOSE WIRE

EXCESSIVE WEAR OF BUTTON

HIGH RESISTANCE CARBON

ROTOR TIP BURNED AWAY

Inspect the distributor cap and rotor

Test and Procedure	Results and Indications	Proceed to
4.4—Check the coil secondary resistance: On point-type systems connect an ohmmeter across the distributor side of the coil and the coil tower. Read the resistance on the high scale of the ohmmeter. On electronic ignition systems, see Chapter 3 for specific tests.	The resistance of a satisfactory coil should be between 4,000 and 10,000 ohms. If resistance is considerably higher (i.e., 40,000 ohms) replace the coil and retest per 4.1. **NOTE:** *This does not apply to high performance coils.*	

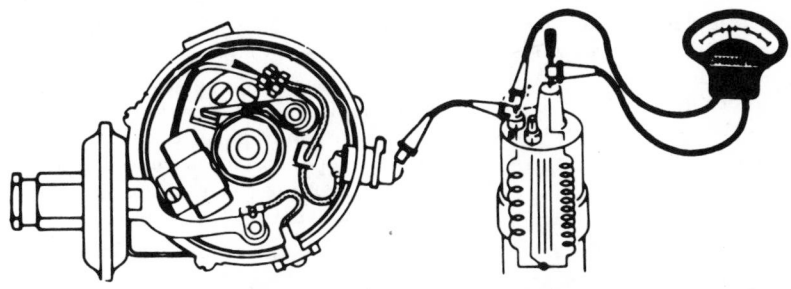

Testing the coil secondary resistance

4.5—Visually inspect the spark plug wires for cracking or brittleness. Ensure that no two wires are positioned so as to cause induction firing (adjacent and parallel). Remove each wire, one by one, and check resistance with an ohmmeter.	Replace any cracked or brittle wires. If any of the wires are defective, replace the entire set. Replace any wires with excessive resistance (over $8000\,\Omega$ per foot for suppression wire), and separate any wires that might cause induction firing.	**4.6**

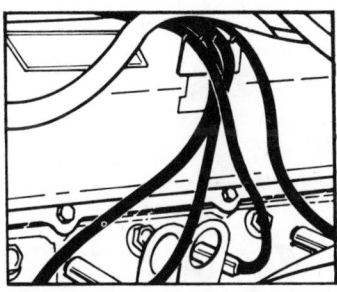

Misfiring can be the result of spark plug leads to adjacent, consecutively firing cylinders running parallel and too close together

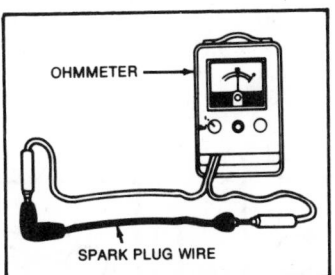

On point-type ignition systems, check the spark plug wires as shown. On electronic ignitions, do not remove the wire from the distributor cap terminal; instead, test through the cap

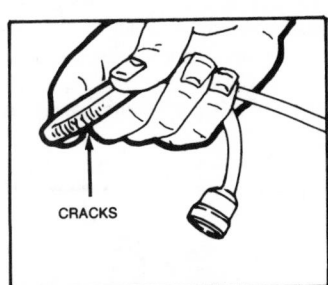

Spark plug wires can be checked visually by bending them in a loop over your finger. This will reveal any cracks, burned or broken insulation. Any wire with cracked insulation should be replaced

4.6—Remove the spark plugs, noting the cylinders from which they were removed, and evaluate according to the color photos in the middle of this book.	See following.	**See following.**

Test and Procedure	Results and Indications	Proceed to
4.7—Examine the location of all the plugs.	The following diagrams illustrate some of the conditions that the location of plugs will reveal.	**4.8**

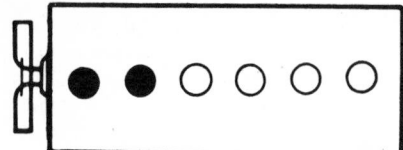

Two adjacent plugs are fouled in a 6-cylinder engine, 4-cylinder engine or either bank of a V-8. This is probably due to a blown head gasket between the two cylinders

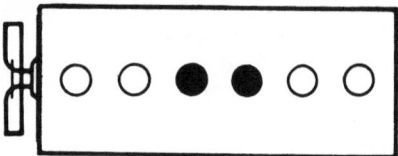

The two center plugs in a 6-cylinder engine are fouled. Raw fuel may be "boiled" out of the carburetor into the intake manifold after the engine is shut-off. Stop-start driving can also foul the center plugs, due to overly rich mixture. Proper float level, a new float needle and seat or use of an insulating spacer may help this problem

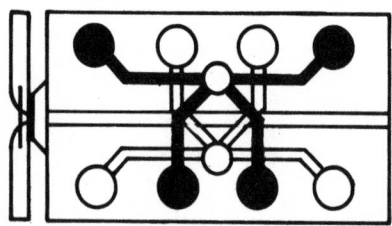

An unbalanced carburetor is indicated. Following the fuel flow on this particular design shows that the cylinders fed by the right-hand barrel are fouled from overly rich mixture, while the cylinders fed by the left-hand barrel are normal

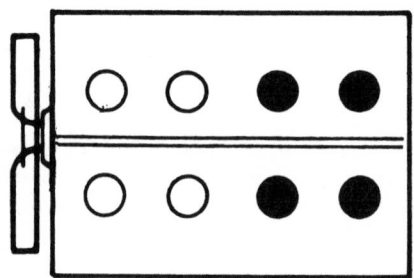

If the four rear plugs are overheated, a cooling system problem is suggested. A thorough cleaning of the cooling system may restore coolant circulation and cure the problem

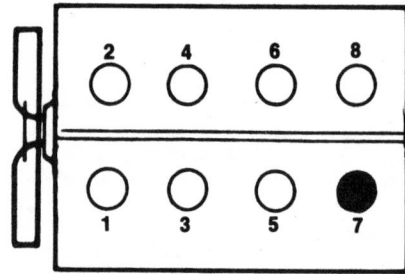

Finding one plug overheated may indicate an intake manifold leak near the affected cylinder. If the overheated plug is the second of two adjacent, consecutively firing plugs, it could be the result of ignition cross-firing. Separating the leads to these two plugs will eliminate cross-fire

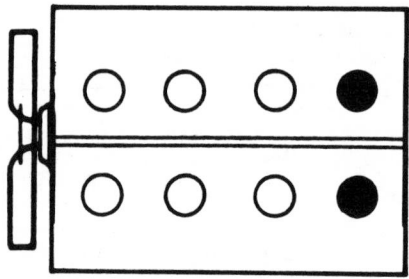

Occasionally, the two rear plugs in large, lightly used V-8's will become oil fouled. High oil consumption and smoky exhaust may also be noticed. It is probably due to plugged oil drain holes in the rear of the cylinder head, causing oil to be sucked in around the valve stems. This usually occurs in the rear cylinders first, because the engine slants that way

Test and Procedure	Results and Indications	Proceed to
4.8—Determine the static ignition timing. Using the crankshaft pulley timing marks as a guide, locate top dead center on the compression stroke of the number one cylinder.	The rotor should be pointing toward the No. 1 tower in the distributor cap, and, on electronic ignitions, the armature spoke for that cylinder should be lined up with the stator.	**4.8**
4.9—Check coil polarity: Connect a voltmeter negative lead to the coil high tension lead, and the positive lead to ground (**NOTE:** *Reverse the hook-up for positive ground systems*). Crank the engine momentarily.	If the voltmeter reads up-scale, the polarity is correct:	**5.1**
	If the voltmeter reads down-scale, reverse the coil polarity (switch the primary leads):	**5.1**
	Checking coil polarity	

Section 5—Fuel System
See Chapter 4 for service procedures

Test and Procedure	Results and Indications	Proceed to
5.1—Determine that the air filter is functioning efficiently: Hold paper elements up to a strong light, and attempt to see light through the filter.	Clean permanent air filters in solvent (or manufacturer's recommendation), and allow to dry. Replace paper elements through which light cannot be seen:	**5.2**
5.2—Determine whether a flooding condition exists: Flooding is identified by a strong gasoline odor, and excessive gasoline present in the throttle bore(s) of the carburetor.	If flooding is not evident:	**5.3**
	If flooding is evident, permit the gasoline to dry for a few moments and restart.	
	If flooding doesn't recur:	**5.7**
	If flooding is persistent:	**5.5**
	If the engine floods repeatedly, check the choke butterfly flap	
5.3—Check that fuel is reaching the carburetor: Detach the fuel line at the carburetor inlet. Hold the end of the line in a cup (not styrofoam), and crank the engine.	If fuel flows smoothly:	**5.7**
	If fuel doesn't flow (**NOTE:** *Make sure that there is fuel in the tank*), or flows erratically:	**5.4**
	Check the fuel pump by disconnecting the output line (fuel pump-to-carburetor) at the carburetor and operating the starter briefly	

Test and Procedure	Results and Indications	Proceed to
5.4—Test the fuel pump: Disconnect all fuel lines from the fuel pump. Hold a finger over the input fitting, crank the engine (with electric pump, turn the ignition or pump on); and feel for suction.	If suction is evident, blow out the fuel line to the tank with low pressure compressed air until bubbling is heard from the fuel filler neck. Also blow out the carburetor fuel line (both ends disconnected):	5.7
	If no suction is evident, replace or repair the fuel pump: **NOTE:** *Repeated oil fouling of the spark plugs, or a no-start condition, could be the result of a ruptured vacuum booster pump diaphragm, through which oil or gasoline is being drawn into the intake manifold (where applicable).*	5.7
5.5—Occasionally, small specks of dirt will clog the small jets and orifices in the carburetor. With the engine cold, hold a flat piece of wood or similar material over the carburetor, where possible, and crank the engine.	If the engine starts, but runs roughly the engine is probably not run enough. If the engine won't start:	5.9
5.6—Check the needle and seat: Tap the carburetor in the area of the needle and seat.	If flooding stops, a gasoline additive (e.g., Gumout) will often cure the problem:	5.7
	If flooding continues, check the fuel pump for excessive pressure at the carburetor (according to specifications). If the pressure is normal, the needle and seat must be removed and checked, and/or the float level adjusted:	5.7
5.7—Test the accelerator pump by looking into the throttle bores while operating the throttle.	If the accelerator pump appears to be operating normally:	5.8
	If the accelerator pump is not operating, the pump must be reconditioned. Where possible, service the pump with the carburetor(s) installed on the engine. If necessary, remove the carburetor. Prior to removal:	5.8
Check for gas at the carburetor by looking down the carburetor throat while someone moves the accelerator		
5.8—Determine whether the carburetor main fuel system is functioning: Spray a commercial starting fluid into the carburetor while attempting to start the engine.	If the engine starts, runs for a few seconds, and dies:	5.9
	If the engine doesn't start:	6.1

Test and Procedure	Results and Indications	Proceed to
5.9—Uncommon fuel system malfunctions: See below:	If the problem is solved: If the problem remains, remove and recondition the carburetor.	6.1

Condition	Indication	Test	Prevailing Weather Conditions	Remedy
Vapor lock	Engine will not restart shortly after running.	Cool the components of the fuel system until the engine starts. Vapor lock can be cured faster by draping a wet cloth over a mechanical fuel pump.	Hot to very hot	Ensure that the exhaust manifold heat control valve is operating. Check with the vehicle manufacturer for the recommended solution to vapor lock on the model in question.
Carburetor icing	Engine will not idle, stalls at low speeds.	Visually inspect the throttle plate area of the throttle bores for frost.	High humidity, 32–40° F.	Ensure that the exhaust manifold heat control valve is operating, and that the intake manifold heat riser is not blocked.
Water in the fuel	Engine sputters and stalls; may not start.	Pump a small amount of fuel into a glass jar. Allow to stand, and inspect for droplets or a layer of water.	High humidity, extreme temperature changes.	For droplets, use one or two cans of commercial gas line anti-freeze. For a layer of water, the tank must be drained, and the fuel lines blown out with compressed air.

Section 6—Engine Compression
See Chapter 3 for service procedures

6.1—Test engine compression: Remove all spark plugs. Block the throttle wide open. Insert a compression gauge into a spark plug port, crank the engine to obtain the maximum reading, and record.	If compression is within limits on all cylinders:	7.1
	If gauge reading is extremely low on all cylinders:	6.2
	If gauge reading is low on one or two cylinders: (If gauge readings are identical and low on two or more adjacent cylinders, the head gasket must be replaced.)	6.2

Checking compression

6.2—Test engine compression (wet): Squirt approximately 30 cc. of engine oil into each cylinder, and retest per 6.1.	If the readings improve, worn or cracked rings or broken pistons are indicated:	**See Chapter 3**
	If the readings do not improve, burned or excessively carboned valves or a jumped timing chain are indicated: **NOTE:** *A jumped timing chain is often indicated by difficult cranking.*	7.1

Section 7—Engine Vacuum
See Chapter 3 for service procedures

Test and Procedure	Results and Indications	Proceed to
7.1—Attach a vacuum gauge to the intake manifold beyond the throttle plate. Start the engine, and observe the action of the needle over the range of engine speeds.	See below.	**See below**

INDICATION: normal engine in good condition

Proceed to: 8.1

Normal engine
Gauge reading: steady, from 17–22 in./Hg.

INDICATION: sticking valves or ignition miss

Proceed to: 9.1, 8.3

Sticking valves
Gauge reading: intermittent fluctuation at idle

INDICATION: late ignition or valve timing, low compression, stuck throttle valve, leaking carburetor or manifold gasket

Proceed to: 6.1

Incorrect valve timing
Gauge reading: low (10–15 in./Hg) but steady

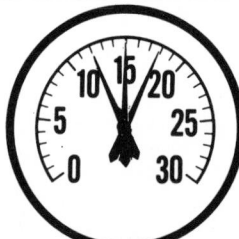

INDICATION: improper carburetor adjustment or minor intake leak.

Proceed to: 7.2

Carburetor requires adjustment
Gauge reading: drifting needle

INDICATION: ignition miss, blown cylinder head gasket, leaking valve or weak valve spring

Proceed to: 8.3, 6.1

Blown head gasket
Gauge reading: needle fluctuates as engine speed increases

INDICATION: burnt valve or faulty valve clearance. Needle will fall when defective valve operates

Proceed to: 9.1

Burnt or leaking valves
Gauge reading: steady needle, but drops regularly

INDICATION: choked muffler, excessive back pressure in system

Proceed to: 10.1

Clogged exhaust system
Gauge reading: gradual drop in reading at idle

INDICATION: worn valve guides

Proceed to: 9.1

Worn valve guides
Gauge reading: needle vibrates excessively at idle, but steadies as engine speed increases

White pointer = steady gauge hand

Black pointer = fluctuating gauge hand

Test and Procedure	*Results and Indications*	*Proceed to*
7.2—Attach a vacuum gauge per 7.1, and test for an intake manifold leak. Squirt a small amount of oil around the intake manifold gaskets, carburetor gaskets, plugs and fittings. Observe the action of the vacuum gauge.	If the reading improves, replace the indicated gasket, or seal the indicated fitting or plug: If the reading remains low:	**8.1** **7.3**
7.3—Test all vacuum hoses and accessories for leaks as described in 7.2. Also check the carburetor body (dashpots, automatic choke mechanism, throttle shafts) for leaks in the same manner.	If the reading improves, service or replace the offending part(s): If the reading remains low:	**8.1** **6.1**

Section 8—Secondary Electrical System
See Chapter 2 for service procedures

Test and Procedure	*Results and Indications*	*Proceed to*
8.1—Remove the distributor cap and check to make sure that the rotor turns when the engine is cranked. Visually inspect the distributor components.	Clean, tighten or replace any components which appear defective.	**8.2**
8.2—Connect a timing light (per manufacturer's recommendation) and check the dynamic ignition timing. Disconnect and plug the vacuum hose(s) to the distributor if specified, start the engine, and observe the timing marks at the specified engine speed.	If the timing is not correct, adjust to specifications by rotating the distributor in the engine: (Advance timing by rotating distributor opposite normal direction of rotor rotation, retard timing by rotating distributor in same direction as rotor rotation.)	**8.3**
8.3—Check the operation of the distributor advance mechanism(s): To test the mechanical advance, disconnect the vacuum lines from the distributor advance unit and observe the timing marks with a timing light as the engine speed is increased from idle. If the mark moves smoothly, without hesitation, it may be assumed that the mechanical advance is functioning properly. To test vacuum advance and/or retard systems, alternately crimp and release the vacuum line, and observe the timing mark for movement. If movement is noted, the system is operating.	If the systems are functioning: If the systems are not functioning, remove the distributor, and test on a distributor tester:	**8.4** **8.4**
8.4—Locate an ignition miss: With the engine running, remove each spark plug wire, one at a time, until one is found that doesn't cause the engine to roughen and slow down.	When the missing cylinder is identified:	**4.1**

Section 9—Valve Train
See Chapter 3 for service procedures

Test and Procedure	Results and Indications	Proceed to
9.1—Evaluate the valve train: Remove the valve cover, and ensure that the valves are adjusted to specifications. A mechanic's stethoscope may be used to aid in the diagnosis of the valve train. By pushing the probe on or near push rods or rockers, valve noise often can be isolated. A timing light also may be used to diagnose valve problems. Connect the light according to manufacturer's recommendations, and start the engine. Vary the firing moment of the light by increasing the engine speed (and therefore the ignition advance), and moving the trigger from cylinder to cylinder. Observe the movement of each valve.	Sticking valves or erratic valve train motion can be observed with the timing light. The cylinder head must be disassembled for repairs.	**See Chapter 3**
9.2—Check the valve timing: Locate top dead center of the No. 1 piston, and install a degree wheel or tape on the crankshaft pulley or damper with zero corresponding to an index mark on the engine. Rotate the crankshaft in its direction of rotation, and observe the opening of the No. 1 cylinder intake valve. The opening should correspond with the correct mark on the degree wheel according to specifications.	If the timing is not correct, the timing cover must be removed for further investigation.	**See Chapter 3**

Section 10—Exhaust System

Test and Procedure	Results and Indications	Proceed to
10.1—Determine whether the exhaust manifold heat control valve is operating: Operate the valve by hand to determine whether it is free to move. If the valve is free, run the engine to operating temperature and observe the action of the valve, to ensure that it is opening.	If the valve sticks, spray it with a suitable solvent, open and close the valve to free it, and retest. If the valve functions properly: If the valve does not free, or does not operate, replace the valve:	 10.2 10.2
10.2—Ensure that there are no exhaust restrictions: Visually inspect the exhaust system for kinks, dents, or crushing. Also note that gases are flowing freely from the tailpipe at all engine speeds, indicating no restriction in the muffler or resonator.	Replace any damaged portion of the system:	11.1

Section 11—Cooling System
See Chapter 3 for service procedures

Test and Procedure	Results and Indications	Proceed to
11.1—Visually inspect the fan belt for glazing, cracks, and fraying, and replace if necessary. Tighten the belt so that the longest span has approximately ½″ play at its mid-point under thumb pressure (see Chapter 1).	Replace or tighten the fan belt as necessary:	**11.2**

Checking belt tension

Test and Procedure	Results and Indications	Proceed to
11.2—Check the fluid level of the cooling system.	If full or slightly low, fill as necessary:	**11.5**
	If extremely low:	**11.3**
11.3—Visually inspect the external portions of the cooling system (radiator, radiator hoses, thermostat elbow, water pump seals, heater hoses, etc.) for leaks. If none are found, pressurize the cooling system to 14–15 psi.	If cooling system holds the pressure:	**11.5**
	If cooling system loses pressure rapidly, reinspect external parts of the system for leaks under pressure. If none are found, check dipstick for coolant in crankcase. If no coolant is present, but pressure loss continues:	**11.4**
	If coolant is evident in crankcase, remove cylinder head(s), and check gasket(s). If gaskets are intact, block and cylinder head(s) should be checked for cracks or holes.	
	If the gasket(s) is blown, replace, and purge the crankcase of coolant: **NOTE:** *Occasionally, due to atmospheric and driving conditions, condensation of water can occur in the crankcase. This causes the oil to appear milky white. To remedy, run the engine until hot, and change the oil and oil filter.*	**12.6**
11.4—Check for combustion leaks into the cooling system: Pressurize the cooling system as above. Start the engine, and observe the pressure gauge. If the needle fluctuates, remove each spark plug wire, one at a time, noting which cylinder(s) reduce or eliminate the fluctuation.	Cylinders which reduce or eliminate the fluctuation, when the spark plug wire is removed, are leaking into the cooling system. Replace the head gasket on the affected cylinder bank(s).	

Pressurizing the cooling system

Test and Procedure	Results and Indications	Proceed to
11.5—Check the radiator pressure cap: Attach a radiator pressure tester to the radiator cap (wet the seal prior to installation). Quickly pump up the pressure, noting the point at which the cap releases.	If the cap releases within ± 1 psi of the specified rating, it is operating properly:	**11.6**
	If the cap releases at more than ± 1 psi of the specified rating, it should be replaced:	**11.6**

Checking radiator pressure cap

Test and Procedure	Results and Indications	Proceed to
11.6—Test the thermostat: Start the engine cold, remove the radiator cap, and insert a thermometer into the radiator. Allow the engine to idle. After a short while, there will be a sudden, rapid increase in coolant temperature. The temperature at which this sharp rise stops is the thermostat opening temperature.	If the thermostat opens at or about the specified temperature:	**11.7**
	If the temperature doesn't increase: (If the temperature increases slowly and gradually, replace the thermostat.)	**11.7**
11.7—Check the water pump: Remove the thermostat elbow and the thermostat, disconnect the coil high tension lead (to prevent starting), and crank the engine momentarily.	If coolant flows, replace the thermostat and retest per 11.6:	**11.6**
	If coolant doesn't flow, reverse flush the cooling system to alleviate any blockage that might exist. If system is not blocked, and coolant will not flow, replace the water pump.	

Section 12—Lubrication
See Chapter 3 for service procedures

Test and Procedure	Results and Indications	Proceed to
12.1—Check the oil pressure gauge or warning light: If the gauge shows low pressure, or the light is on for no obvious reason, remove the oil pressure sender. Install an accurate oil pressure gauge and run the engine momentarily.	If oil pressure builds normally, run engine for a few moments to determine that it is functioning normally, and replace the sender.	—
	If the pressure remains low:	**12.2**
	If the pressure surges:	**12.3**
	If the oil pressure is zero:	**12.3**
12.2—Visually inspect the oil: If the oil is watery or very thin, milky, or foamy, replace the oil and oil filter.	If the oil is normal:	**12.3**
	If after replacing oil the pressure remains low:	**12.3**
	If after replacing oil the pressure becomes normal:	—

Test and Procedure	Results and Indications	Proceed to
12.3—Inspect the oil pressure relief valve and spring, to ensure that it is not sticking or stuck. Remove and thoroughly clean the valve, spring, and the valve body.	If the oil pressure improves: If no improvement is noted:	— **12.4**
12.4—Check to ensure that the oil pump is not cavitating (sucking air instead of oil): See that the crankcase is neither over nor underfull, and that the pickup in the sump is in the proper position and free from sludge.	Fill or drain the crankcase to the proper capacity, and clean the pickup screen in solvent if necessary. If no improvement is noted:	**12.5**
12.5—Inspect the oil pump drive and the oil pump:	If the pump drive or the oil pump appear to be defective, service as necessary and retest per 12.1: If the pump drive and pump appear to be operating normally, the engine should be disassembled to determine where blockage exists:	**12.1** **See Chapter 3**
12.6—Purge the engine of ethylene glycol coolant: Completely drain the crankcase and the oil filter. Obtain a commercial butyl cellosolve base solvent, designated for this purpose, and follow the instructions precisely. Following this, install a new oil filter and refill the crankcase with the proper weight oil. The next oil and filter change should follow shortly thereafter (1000 miles).		

TROUBLESHOOTING EMISSION CONTROL SYSTEMS

See Chapter 4 for procedures applicable to individual emission control systems used on specific combinations of engine/transmission/model.

TROUBLESHOOTING THE CARBURETOR

See Chapter 4 for service procedures

Carburetor problems cannot be effectively isolated unless all other engine systems (particularly ignition and emission) are functioning properly and the engine is properly tuned.

Condition	Possible Cause
Engine cranks, but does not start	1. Improper starting procedure 2. No fuel in tank 3. Clogged fuel line or filter 4. Defective fuel pump 5. Choke valve not closing properly 6. Engine flooded 7. Choke valve not unloading 8. Throttle linkage not making full travel 9. Stuck needle or float 10. Leaking float needle or seat 11. Improper float adjustment
Engine stalls	1. Improperly adjusted idle speed or mixture **Engine hot** 2. Improperly adjusted dashpot 3. Defective or improperly adjusted solenoid 4. Incorrect fuel level in fuel bowl 5. Fuel pump pressure too high 6. Leaking float needle seat 7. Secondary throttle valve stuck open 8. Air or fuel leaks 9. Idle air bleeds plugged or missing 10. Idle passages plugged **Engine Cold** 11. Incorrectly adjusted choke 12. Improperly adjusted fast idle speed 13. Air leaks 14. Plugged idle or idle air passages 15. Stuck choke valve or binding linkage 16. Stuck secondary throttle valves 17. Engine flooding—high fuel level 18. Leaking or misaligned float
Engine hesitates on acceleration	1. Clogged fuel filter 2. Leaking fuel pump diaphragm 3. Low fuel pump pressure 4. Secondary throttle valves stuck, bent or misadjusted 5. Sticking or binding air valve 6. Defective accelerator pump 7. Vacuum leaks 8. Clogged air filter 9. Incorrect choke adjustment (engine cold)
Engine feels sluggish or flat on acceleration	1. Improperly adjusted idle speed or mixture 2. Clogged fuel filter 3. Defective accelerator pump 4. Dirty, plugged or incorrect main metering jets 5. Bent or sticking main metering rods 6. Sticking throttle valves 7. Stuck heat riser 8. Binding or stuck air valve 9. Dirty, plugged or incorrect secondary jets 10. Bent or sticking secondary metering rods. 11. Throttle body or manifold heat passages plugged 12. Improperly adjusted choke or choke vacuum break.
Carburetor floods	1. Defective fuel pump. Pressure too high. 2. Stuck choke valve 3. Dirty, worn or damaged float or needle valve/seat 4. Incorrect float/fuel level 5. Leaking float bowl

Condition	Possible Cause
Engine idles roughly and stalls	1. Incorrect idle speed 2. Clogged fuel filter 3. Dirt in fuel system or carburetor 4. Loose carburetor screws or attaching bolts 5. Broken carburetor gaskets 6. Air leaks 7. Dirty carburetor 8. Worn idle mixture needles 9. Throttle valves stuck open 10. Incorrectly adjusted float or fuel level 11. Clogged air filter
Engine runs unevenly or surges	1. Defective fuel pump 2. Dirty or clogged fuel filter 3. Plugged, loose or incorrect main metering jets or rods 4. Air leaks 5. Bent or sticking main metering rods 6. Stuck power piston 7. Incorrect float adjustment 8. Incorrect idle speed or mixture 9. Dirty or plugged idle system passages 10. Hard, brittle or broken gaskets 11. Loose attaching or mounting screws 12. Stuck or misaligned secondary throttle valves
Poor fuel economy	1. Poor driving habits 2. Stuck choke valve 3. Binding choke linkage 4. Stuck heat riser 5. Incorrect idle mixture 6. Defective accelerator pump 7. Air leaks 8. Plugged, loose or incorrect main metering jets 9. Improperly adjusted float or fuel level 10. Bent, misaligned or fuel-clogged float 11. Leaking float needle seat 12. Fuel leak 13. Accelerator pump discharge ball not seating properly 14. Incorrect main jets
Engine lacks high speed performance or power	1. Incorrect throttle linkage adjustment 2. Stuck or binding power piston 3. Defective accelerator pump 4. Air leaks 5. Incorrect float setting or fuel level 6. Dirty, plugged, worn or incorrect main metering jets or rods 7. Binding or sticking air valve 8. Brittle or cracked gaskets 9. Bent, incorrect or improperly adjusted secondary metering rods 10. Clogged fuel filter 11. Clogged air filter 12. Defective fuel pump

TROUBLESHOOTING FUEL INJECTION PROBLEMS

Each fuel injection system has its own unique components and test procedures, for which it is impossible to generalize. Refer to Chapter 4 of this Repair & Tune-Up Guide for specific test and repair procedures, if the vehicle is equipped with fuel injection.

TROUBLESHOOTING ELECTRICAL PROBLEMS

See Chapter 5 for service procedures

For any electrical system to operate, it must make a complete circuit. This simply means that the power flow from the battery must make a complete circle. When an electrical component is operating, power flows from the battery to the component, passes through the component causing it to perform its function (lighting a light bulb), and then returns to the battery through the ground of the circuit. This ground is usually (but not always) the metal part of the car or truck on which the electrical component is mounted.

Perhaps the easiest way to visualize this is to think of connecting a light bulb with two wires attached to it to the battery. If one of the two wires attached to the light bulb were attached to the negative post of the battery and the other were attached to the positive post of the battery, you would have a complete circuit. Current from the battery would flow to the light bulb, causing it to light, and return to the negative post of the battery.

The normal automotive circuit differs from this simple example in two ways. First, instead of having a return wire from the bulb to the battery, the light bulb returns the current to the battery through the chassis of the vehicle. Since the negative battery cable is attached to the chassis and the chassis is made of electrically conductive metal, the chassis of the vehicle can serve as a ground wire to complete the circuit. Secondly, most automotive circuits contain switches to turn components on and off as required.

Every complete circuit from a power source must include a component which is using the power from the power source. If you were to disconnect the light bulb from the wires and touch the two wires together (don't do this) the power supply wire to the component would be grounded before the normal ground connection for the circuit.

Because grounding a wire from a power source makes a complete circuit—less the required component to use the power—this phenomenon is called a short circuit. Common causes are: broken insulation (exposing the metal wire to a metal part of the car or truck), or a shorted switch.

Some electrical components which require a large amount of current to operate also have a relay in their circuit. Since these circuits carry a large amount of current, the thickness of the wire in the circuit (gauge size) is also greater. If this large wire were connected from the component to the control switch on the instrument panel, and then back to the component, a voltage drop would occur in the circuit. To prevent this potential drop in voltage, an electromagnetic switch (relay) is used. The large wires in the circuit are connected from the battery to one side of the relay, and from the opposite side of the relay to the component. The relay is normally open, preventing current from passing through the circuit. An additional, smaller, wire is connected from the relay to the control switch for the circuit. When the control switch is turned on, it grounds the smaller wire from the relay and completes the circuit. This closes the relay and allows current to flow from the battery to the component. The horn, headlight, and starter circuits are three which use relays.

It is possible for larger surges of current to pass through the electrical system of your car or truck. If this surge of current were to reach an electrical component, it could burn it out. To prevent this, fuses, circuit breakers or fusible links are connected into the current supply wires of most of the major electrical systems. When an electrical current of excessive power passes through the component's fuse, the fuse blows out and breaks the circuit, saving the component from destruction.

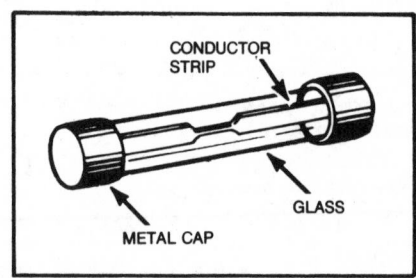

Typical automotive fuse

A circuit breaker is basically a self-repairing fuse. The circuit breaker opens the circuit the same way a fuse does. However, when either the short is removed from the circuit or the surge subsides, the circuit breaker resets itself and does not have to be replaced as a fuse does.

A fuse link is a wire that acts as a fuse. It is normally connected between the starter relay and the main wiring harness. This connection is usually under the hood. The fuse link (if installed) protects all the

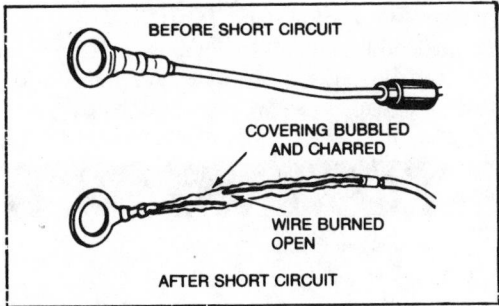

Most fusible links show a charred, melted insulation when they burn out

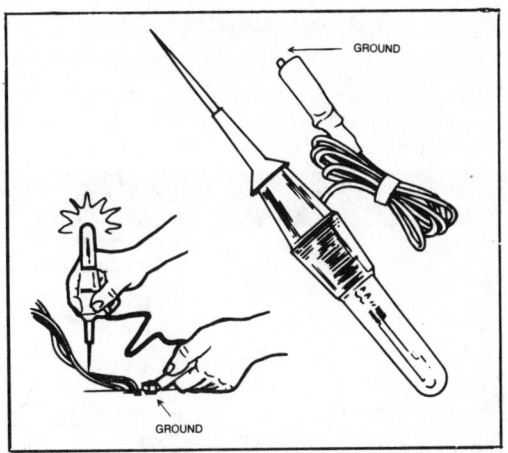

The test light will show the presence of current when touched to a hot wire and grounded at the other end

chassis electrical components, and is the probable cause of trouble when none of the electrical components function, unless the battery is disconnected or dead.

Electrical problems generally fall into one of three areas:

1. The component that is not functioning is not receiving current.

2. The component itself is not functioning.

3. The component is not properly grounded.

The electrical system can be checked with a test light and a jumper wire. A test light is a device that looks like a pointed screwdriver with a wire attached to it and has a light bulb in its handle. A jumper wire is a piece of insulated wire with an alligator clip attached to each end.

If a component is not working, you must follow a systematic plan to determine which of the three causes is the villain.

1. Turn on the switch that controls the inoperable component.

2. Disconnect the power supply wire from the component.

3. Attach the ground wire on the test light to a good metal ground.

4. Touch the probe end of the test light to the end of the power supply wire that was disconnected from the component. If the component is receiving current, the test light will go on.

NOTE: *Some components work only when the ignition switch is turned on.*

If the test light does not go on, then the problem is in the circuit between the battery and the component. This includes all the switches, fuses, and relays in the system. Follow the wire that runs back to the battery. The problem is an open circuit between the

battery and the component. If the fuse is blown and, when replaced, immediately blows again, there is a short circuit in the system which must be located and repaired. If there is a switch in the system, bypass it with a jumper wire. This is done by connecting one end of the jumper wire to the power supply wire into the switch and the other end of the jumper wire to the wire coming out of the switch. If the test light lights with the jumper wire installed, the switch or whatever was bypassed is defective.

NOTE: *Never substitute the jumper wire for the component, since it is required to use the power from the power source.*

5. If the bulb in the test light goes on, then the current is getting to the component that is not working. This eliminates the first of the three possible causes. Connect the power supply wire and connect a jumper wire from the component to a good metal ground. Do this with the switch which controls the component turned on, and also the ignition switch turned on if it is required for the component to work. If the component works with the jumper wire installed, then it has a bad ground. This is usually caused by the metal area on which the component mounts to the chassis being coated with some type of foreign matter.

6. If neither test located the source of the trouble, then the component itself is defective. Remember that for any electrical system to work, all connections must be clean and tight.

Troubleshooting Basic Turn Signal and Flasher Problems

See Chapter 5 for service procedures

Most problems in the turn signals or flasher system can be reduced to defective flashers or bulbs, which are easily replaced. Occasionally, the turn signal switch will prove defective.

F = Front   R = Rear   ● = Lights off   ○ = Lights on

Condition	Possible Cause
Turn signals light, but do not flash 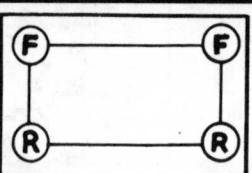	Defective flasher
No turn signals light on either side 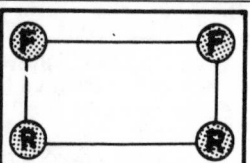	Blown fuse. Replace if defective. Defective flasher. Check by substitution. Open circuit, short circuit or poor ground.
Both turn signals on one side don't work 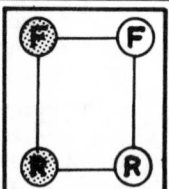	Bad bulbs. Bad ground in both (or either) housings.
One turn signal light on one side doesn't work 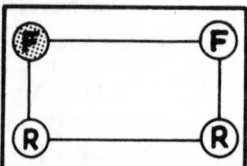	Defective bulb. Corrosion in socket. Clean contacts. Poor ground at socket.
Turn signal flashes too fast or too slowly 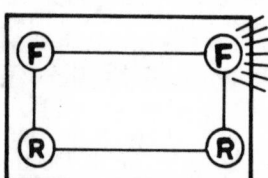	Check any bulb on the side flashing too fast. A heavy-duty bulb is probably installed in place of a regular bulb. Check the bulb flashing too slowly. A standard bulb was probably installed in place of a heavy-duty bulb. Loose connections or corrosion at the bulb socket.
Indicator lights don't work in either direction 	Check if the turn signals are working. Check the dash indicator lights. Check the flasher by substitution.
One indicator light doesn't light 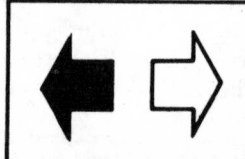	On systems with one dash indicator: See if the lights work on the same side. Often the filaments have been reversed in systems combining stoplights with taillights and turn signals. Check the flasher by substitution. On systems with two indicators: Check the bulbs on the same side. Check the indicator light bulb. Check the flasher by substitution.

Troubleshooting Lighting Problems

See Chapter 5 for service procedures

Condition	Possible Cause
One or more lights don't work, but others do	1. Defective bulb(s) 2. Blown fuse(s) 3. Dirty fuse clips or light sockets 4. Poor ground circuit
Lights burn out quickly	1. Incorrect voltage regulator setting or defective regulator 2. Poor battery/alternator connections
Lights go dim	1. Low/discharged battery 2. Alternator not charging 3. Corroded sockets or connections 4. Low voltage output
Lights flicker	1. Loose connection 2. Poor ground. (Run ground wire from light housing to frame) 3. Circuit breaker operating (short circuit)
Lights "flare"—Some flare is normal on acceleration—If excessive, see "Lights Burn Out Quickly"	High voltage setting
Lights glare—approaching drivers are blinded	1. Lights adjusted too high 2. Rear springs or shocks sagging 3. Rear tires soft

Troubleshooting Dash Gauge Problems

Most problems can be traced to a defective sending unit or faulty wiring. Occasionally, the gauge itself is at fault. See Chapter 5 for service procedures.

Condition	Possible Cause
COOLANT TEMPERATURE GAUGE	
Gauge reads erratically or not at all	1. Loose or dirty connections 2. Defective sending unit. 3. Defective gauge. To test a bi-metal gauge, remove the wire from the sending unit. Ground the wire for an instant. If the gauge registers, replace the sending unit. To test a magnetic gauge, disconnect the wire at the sending unit. With ignition ON gauge should register COLD. Ground the wire; gauge should register HOT.
AMMETER GAUGE—TURN HEADLIGHTS ON (DO NOT START ENGINE). NOTE REACTION	
Ammeter shows charge Ammeter shows discharge Ammeter does not move	1. Connections reversed on gauge 2. Ammeter is OK 3. Loose connections or faulty wiring 4. Defective gauge

Condition	Possible Cause

OIL PRESSURE GAUGE

Condition	Possible Cause
Gauge does not register or is inaccurate	1. On mechanical gauge, Bourdon tube may be bent or kinked. 2. Low oil pressure. Remove sending unit. Idle the engine briefly. If no oil flows from sending unit hole, problem is in engine. 3. Defective gauge. Remove the wire from the sending unit and ground it for an instant with the ignition ON. A good gauge will go to the top of the scale. 4. Defective wiring. Check the wiring to the gauge. If it's OK and the gauge doesn't register when grounded, replace the gauge. 5. Defective sending unit.

ALL GAUGES

Condition	Possible Cause
All gauges do not operate All gauges read low or erratically All gauges pegged	1. Blown fuse 2. Defective instrument regulator 3. Defective or dirty instrument voltage regulator 4. Loss of ground between instrument voltage regulator and frame 5. Defective instrument regulator

WARNING LIGHTS

Condition	Possible Cause
Light(s) do not come on when ignition is ON, but engine is not started Light comes on with engine running	1. Defective bulb 2. Defective wire 3. Defective sending unit. Disconnect the wire from the sending unit and ground it. Replace the sending unit if the light comes on with the ignition ON. 4. Problem in individual system 5. Defective sending unit

Troubleshooting Clutch Problems

It is false economy to replace individual clutch components. The pressure plate, clutch plate and throwout bearing should be replaced as a set, and the flywheel face inspected, whenever the clutch is overhauled. See Chapter 6 for service procedures.

Condition	Possible Cause
Clutch chatter	1. Grease on driven plate (disc) facing 2. Binding clutch linkage or cable 3. Loose, damaged facings on driven plate (disc) 4. Engine mounts loose 5. Incorrect height adjustment of pressure plate release levers 6. Clutch housing or housing to transmission adapter misalignment 7. Loose driven plate hub
Clutch grabbing	1. Oil, grease on driven plate (disc) facing 2. Broken pressure plate 3. Warped or binding driven plate. Driven plate binding on clutch shaft
Clutch slips	1. Lack of lubrication in clutch linkage or cable (linkage or cable binds, causes incomplete engagement) 2. Incorrect pedal, or linkage adjustment 3. Broken pressure plate springs 4. Weak pressure plate springs 5. Grease on driven plate facings (disc)

Troubleshooting Clutch Problems (cont.)

Condition	Possible Cause
Incomplete clutch release	1. Incorrect pedal or linkage adjustment or linkage or cable binding 2. Incorrect height adjustment on pressure plate release levers 3. Loose, broken facings on driven plate (disc) 4. Bent, dished, warped driven plate caused by overheating
Grinding, whirring grating noise when pedal is depressed	1. Worn or defective throwout bearing 2. Starter drive teeth contacting flywheel ring gear teeth. Look for milled or polished teeth on ring gear.
Squeal, howl, trumpeting noise when pedal is being released (occurs during first inch to inch and one-half of pedal travel)	Pilot bushing worn or lack of lubricant. If bushing appears OK, polish bushing with emery cloth, soak lube wick in oil, lube bushing with oil, apply film of chassis grease to clutch shaft pilot hub, reassemble. NOTE: Bushing wear may be due to misalignment of clutch housing or housing to transmission adapter
Vibration or clutch pedal pulsation with clutch disengaged (pedal fully depressed)	1. Worn or defective engine transmission mounts 2. Flywheel run out. (Flywheel run out at face not to exceed 0.005") 3. Damaged or defective clutch components

Troubleshooting Manual Transmission Problems
See Chapter 6 for service procedures

Condition	Possible Cause
Transmission jumps out of gear	1. Misalignment of transmission case or clutch housing. 2. Worn pilot bearing in crankshaft. 3. Bent transmission shaft. 4. Worn high speed sliding gear. 5. Worn teeth or end-play in clutch shaft. 6. Insufficient spring tension on shifter rail plunger. 7. Bent or loose shifter fork. 8. Gears not engaging completely. 9. Loose or worn bearings on clutch shaft or mainshaft. 10. Worn gear teeth. 11. Worn or damaged detent balls.
Transmission sticks in gear	1. Clutch not releasing fully. 2. Burred or battered teeth on clutch shaft, or sliding sleeve. 3. Burred or battered transmission mainshaft. 4. Frozen synchronizing clutch. 5. Stuck shifter rail plunger. 6. Gearshift lever twisting and binding shifter rail. 7. Battered teeth on high speed sliding gear or on sleeve. 8. Improper lubrication, or lack of lubrication. 9. Corroded transmission parts. 10. Defective mainshaft pilot bearing. 11. Locked gear bearings will give same effect as stuck in gear.
Transmission gears will not synchronize	1. Binding pilot bearing on mainshaft, will synchronize in high gear only. 2. Clutch not releasing fully. 3. Detent spring weak or broken. 4. Weak or broken springs under balls in sliding gear sleeve. 5. Binding bearing on clutch shaft, or binding countershaft. 6. Binding pilot bearing in crankshaft. 7. Badly worn gear teeth. 8. Improper lubrication. 9. Constant mesh gear not turning freely on transmission mainshaft. Will synchronize in that gear only.

Condition	Possible Cause
Gears spinning when shifting into gear from neutral	1. Clutch not releasing fully. 2. In some cases an extremely light lubricant in transmission will cause gears to continue to spin for a short time after clutch is released. 3. Binding pilot bearing in crankshaft.
Transmission noisy in all gears	1. Insufficient lubricant, or improper lubricant. 2. Worn countergear bearings. 3. Worn or damaged main drive gear or countergear. 4. Damaged main drive gear or mainshaft bearings. 5. Worn or damaged countergear anti-lash plate.
Transmission noisy in neutral only	1. Damaged main drive gear bearing. 2. Damaged or loose mainshaft pilot bearing. 3. Worn or damaged countergear anti-lash plate. 4. Worn countergear bearings.
Transmission noisy in one gear only	1. Damaged or worn constant mesh gears. 2. Worn or damaged countergear bearings. 3. Damaged or worn synchronizer.
Transmission noisy in reverse only	1. Worn or damaged reverse idler gear or idler bushing. 2. Worn or damaged mainshaft reverse gear. 3. Worn or damaged reverse countergear. 4. Damaged shift mechanism.

TROUBLESHOOTING AUTOMATIC TRANSMISSION PROBLEMS

Keeping alert to changes in the operating characteristics of the transmission (changing shift points, noises, etc.) can prevent small problems from becoming large ones. If the problem cannot be traced to loose bolts, fluid level, misadjusted linkage, clogged filters or similar problems, you should probably seek professional service.

Transmission Fluid Indications

The appearance and odor of the transmission fluid can give valuable clues to the overall condition of the transmission. Always note the appearance of the fluid when you check the fluid level or change the fluid. Rub a small amount of fluid between your fingers to feel for grit and smell the fluid on the dipstick.

If the fluid appears:	It indicates:
Clear and red colored	Normal operation
Discolored (extremely dark red or brownish) or smells burned	Band or clutch pack failure, usually caused by an overheated transmission. Hauling very heavy loads with insufficient power or failure to change the fluid often result in overheating. Do not confuse this appearance with newer fluids that have a darker red color and a strong odor (though not a burned odor).
Foamy or aerated (light in color and full of bubbles)	1. The level is too high (gear train is churning oil) 2. An internal air leak (air is mixing with the fluid). Have the transmission checked professionally.
Solid residue in the fluid	Defective bands, clutch pack or bearings. Bits of band material or metal abrasives are clinging to the dipstick. Have the transmission checked professionally.
Varnish coating on the dipstick	The transmission fluid is overheating

·TROUBLESHOOTING DRIVE AXLE PROBLEMS

First, determine when the noise is most noticeable.

Drive Noise: Produced under vehicle acceleration.

Coast Noise: Produced while coasting with a closed throttle.

Float Noise: Occurs while maintaining constant speed (just enough to keep speed constant) on a level road.

External Noise Elimination

It is advisable to make a thorough road test to determine whether the noise originates in the rear axle or whether it originates from the tires, engine, transmission, wheel bearings or road surface. Noise originating from other places cannot be corrected by servicing the rear axle.

ROAD NOISE

Brick or rough surfaced concrete roads produce noises that seem to come from the rear axle. Road noise is usually identical in Drive or Coast and driving on a different type of road will tell whether the road is the problem.

TIRE NOISE

Tire noise can be mistaken as rear axle noise, even though the tires on the front are at fault. Snow tread and mud tread tires or tires worn unevenly will frequently cause vibrations which seem to originate elsewhere; *temporarily, and for test purposes only,* inflate the tires to 40–50 lbs. This will significantly alter the noise produced by the tires, but will not alter noise from the rear axle. Noises from the rear axle will normally cease at speeds below 30 mph on coast, while tire noise will continue at lower tone as speed is decreased. The rear axle noise will usually change from drive conditions to coast conditions, while tire noise will not. Do not forget to lower the tire pressure to normal after the test is complete.

ENGINE/TRANSMISSION NOISE

Determine at what speed the noise is most pronounced, then stop in a quiet place. With the transmission in Neutral, run the engine through speeds corresponding to road speeds where the noise was noticed. Noises produced with the vehicle standing still are coming from the engine or transmission.

FRONT WHEEL BEARINGS

Front wheel bearing noises, sometimes confused with rear axle noises, will not change when comparing drive and coast conditions. While holding the speed steady, lightly apply the footbrake. This will often cause wheel bearing noise to lessen, as some of the weight is taken off the bearing. Front wheel bearings are easily checked by jacking up the wheels and spinning the wheels. Shaking the wheels will also determine if the wheel bearings are excessively loose.

REAR AXLE NOISES

Eliminating other possible sources can narrow the cause to the rear axle, which normally produces noise from worn gears or bearings. Gear noises tend to peak in a narrow speed range, while bearing noises will usually vary in pitch with engine speeds.

Noise Diagnosis

The Noise Is:	Most Probably Produced By:
1. Identical under Drive or Coast	Road surface, tires or front wheel bearings
2. Different depending on road surface	Road surface or tires
3. Lower as speed is lowered	Tires
4. Similar when standing or moving	Engine or transmission
5. A vibration	Unbalanced tires, rear wheel bearing, unbalanced driveshaft or worn U-joint
6. A knock or click about every two tire revolutions	Rear wheel bearing
7. Most pronounced on turns	Damaged differential gears
8. A steady low-pitched whirring or scraping, starting at low speeds	Damaged or worn pinion bearing
9. A chattering vibration on turns	Wrong differential lubricant or worn clutch plates (limited slip rear axle)
10. Noticed only in Drive, Coast or Float conditions	Worn ring gear and/or pinion gear

Troubleshooting Steering & Suspension Problems

Condition	Possible Cause
Hard steering (wheel is hard to turn)	1. Improper tire pressure 2. Loose or glazed pump drive belt 3. Low or incorrect fluid 4. Loose, bent or poorly lubricated front end parts 5. Improper front end alignment (excessive caster) 6. Bind in steering column or linkage 7. Kinked hydraulic hose 8. Air in hydraulic system 9. Low pump output or leaks in system 10. Obstruction in lines 11. Pump valves sticking or out of adjustment 12. Incorrect wheel alignment
Loose steering (too much play in steering wheel)	1. Loose wheel bearings 2. Faulty shocks 3. Worn linkage or suspension components 4. Loose steering gear mounting or linkage points 5. Steering mechanism worn or improperly adjusted 6. Valve spool improperly adjusted 7. Worn ball joints, tie-rod ends, etc.
Veers or wanders (pulls to one side with hands off steering wheel)	1. Improper tire pressure 2. Improper front end alignment 3. Dragging or improperly adjusted brakes 4. Bent frame 5. Improper rear end alignment 6. Faulty shocks or springs 7. Loose or bent front end components 8. Play in Pitman arm 9. Steering gear mountings loose 10. Loose wheel bearings 11. Binding Pitman arm 12. Spool valve sticking or improperly adjusted 13. Worn ball joints
Wheel oscillation or vibration transmitted through steering wheel	1. Low or uneven tire pressure 2. Loose wheel bearings 3. Improper front end alignment 4. Bent spindle 5. Worn, bent or broken front end components 6. Tires out of round or out of balance 7. Excessive lateral runout in disc brake rotor 8. Loose or bent shock absorber or strut
Noises (see also "Troubleshooting Drive Axle Problems")	1. Loose belts 2. Low fluid, air in system 3. Foreign matter in system 4. Improper lubrication 5. Interference or chafing in linkage 6. Steering gear mountings loose 7. Incorrect adjustment or wear in gear box 8. Faulty valves or wear in pump 9. Kinked hydraulic lines 10. Worn wheel bearings
Poor return of steering	1. Over-inflated tires 2. Improperly aligned front end (excessive caster) 3. Binding in steering column 4. No lubrication in front end 5. Steering gear adjusted too tight
Uneven tire wear (see "How To Read Tire Wear")	1. Incorrect tire pressure 2. Improperly aligned front end 3. Tires out-of-balance 4. Bent or worn suspension parts

HOW TO READ TIRE WEAR

The way your tires wear is a good indicator of other parts of the suspension. Abnormal wear patterns are often caused by the need for simple tire maintenance, or for front end alignment.

Excessive wear at the center of the tread indicates that the air pressure in the tire is consistently too high. The tire is riding on the center of the tread and wearing it prematurely. Occasionally, this wear pattern can result from outrageously wide tires on narrow rims. The cure for this is to replace either the tires or the wheels.

This type of wear usually results from consistent under-inflation. When a tire is under-inflated, there is too much contact with the road by the outer treads, which wear prematurely. When this type of wear occurs, and the tire pressure is known to be consistently correct, a bent or worn steering component or the need for wheel alignment could be indicated.

Feathering is a condition when the edge of each tread rib develops a slightly rounded edge on one side and a sharp edge on the other. By running your hand over the tire, you can usually feel the sharper edges before you'll be able to see them. The most common causes of feathering are incorrect toe-in setting or deteriorated bushings in the front suspension.

When an inner or outer rib wears faster than the rest of the tire, the need for wheel alignment is indicated. There is excessive camber in the front suspension, causing the wheel to lean too much putting excessive load on one side of the tire. Misalignment could also be due to sagging springs, worn ball joints, or worn control arm bushings. Be sure the vehicle is loaded the way it's normally driven when you have the wheels aligned.

Cups or scalloped dips appearing around the edge of the tread almost always indicate worn (sometimes bent) suspension parts. Adjustment of wheel alignment alone will seldom cure the problem. Any worn component that connects the wheel to the suspension can cause this type of wear. Occasionally, wheels that are out of balance will wear like this, but wheel imbalance usually shows up as bald spots between the outside edges and center of the tread.

Second-rib wear is usually found only in radial tires, and appears where the steel belts end in relation to the tread. It can be kept to a minimum by paying careful attention to tire pressure and frequently rotating the tires. This is often considered normal wear but excessive amounts indicate that the tires are too wide for the wheels.

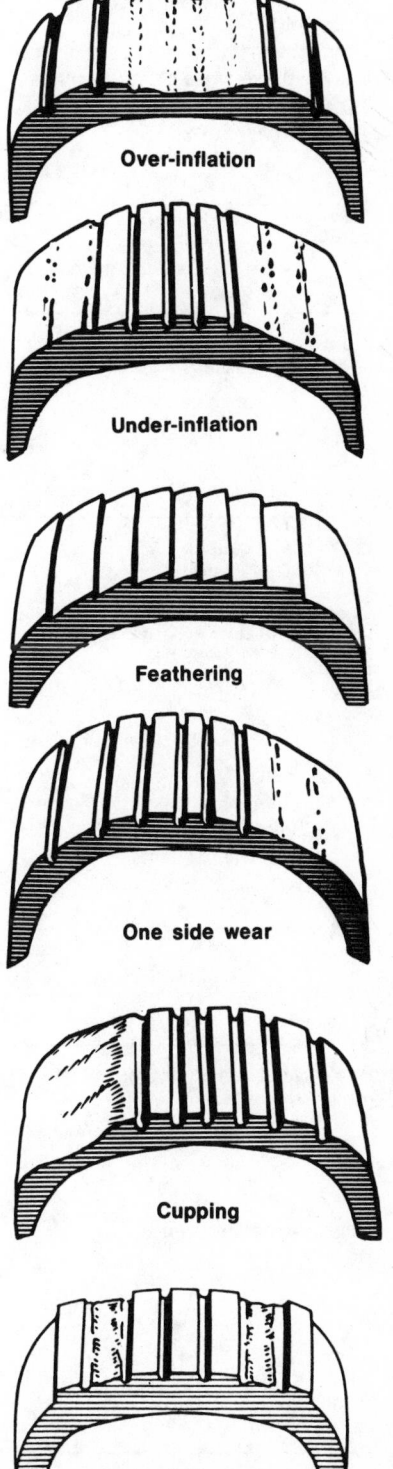

Over-inflation

Under-inflation

Feathering

One side wear

Cupping

Second-rib wear

Troubleshooting Disc Brake Problems

Condition	Possible Cause
Noise—groan—brake noise emanating when slowly releasing brakes (creep-groan)	Not detrimental to function of disc brakes—no corrective action required. (This noise may be eliminated by slightly increasing or decreasing brake pedal efforts.)
Rattle—brake noise or rattle emanating at low speeds on rough roads, (front wheels only).	1. Shoe anti-rattle spring missing or not properly positioned. 2. Excessive clearance between shoe and caliper. 3. Soft or broken caliper seals. 4. Deformed or misaligned disc. 5. Loose caliper.
Scraping	1. Mounting bolts too long. 2. Loose wheel bearings. 3. Bent, loose, or misaligned splash shield.
Front brakes heat up during driving and fail to release	1. Operator riding brake pedal. 2. Stop light switch improperly adjusted. 3. Sticking pedal linkage. 4. Frozen or seized piston. 5. Residual pressure valve in master cylinder. 6. Power brake malfunction. 7. Proportioning valve malfunction.
Leaky brake caliper	1. Damaged or worn caliper piston seal. 2. Scores or corrosion on surface of cylinder bore.
Grabbing or uneven brake action—Brakes pull to one side	1. Causes listed under "Brakes Pull". 2. Power brake malfunction. 3. Low fluid level in master cylinder. 4. Air in hydraulic system. 5. Brake fluid, oil or grease on linings. 6. Unmatched linings. 7. Distorted brake pads. 8. Frozen or seized pistons. 9. Incorrect tire pressure. 10. Front end out of alignment. 11. Broken rear spring. 12. Brake caliper pistons sticking. 13. Restricted hose or line. 14. Caliper not in proper alignment to braking disc. 15. Stuck or malfunctioning metering valve. 16. Soft or broken caliper seals. 17. Loose caliper.
Brake pedal can be depressed without braking effect	1. Air in hydraulic system or improper bleeding procedure. 2. Leak past primary cup in master cylinder. 3. Leak in system. 4. Rear brakes out of adjustment. 5. Bleeder screw open.
Excessive pedal travel	1. Air, leak, or insufficient fluid in system or caliper. 2. Warped or excessively tapered shoe and lining assembly. 3. Excessive disc runout. 4. Rear brake adjustment required. 5. Loose wheel bearing adjustment. 6. Damaged caliper piston seal. 7. Improper brake fluid (boil). 8. Power brake malfunction. 9. Weak or soft hoses.

Troubleshooting Disc Brake Problems (cont.)

Condition	Possible Cause
Brake roughness or chatter (pedal pumping)	1. Excessive thickness variation of braking disc. 2. Excessive lateral runout of braking disc. 3. Rear brake drums out-of-round. 4. Excessive front bearing clearance.
Excessive pedal effort	1. Brake fluid, oil or grease on linings. 2. Incorrect lining. 3. Frozen or seized pistons. 4. Power brake malfunction. 5. Kinked or collapsed hose or line. 6. Stuck metering valve. 7. Scored caliper or master cylinder bore. 8. Seized caliper pistons.
Brake pedal fades (pedal travel increases with foot on brake)	1. Rough master cylinder or caliper bore. 2. Loose or broken hydraulic lines/connections. 3. Air in hydraulic system. 4. Fluid level low. 5. Weak or soft hoses. 6. Inferior quality brake shoes or fluid. 7. Worn master cylinder piston cups or seals.

Troubleshooting Drum Brakes

Condition	Possible Cause
Pedal goes to floor	1. Fluid low in reservoir. 2. Air in hydraulic system. 3. Improperly adjusted brake. 4. Leaking wheel cylinders. 5. Loose or broken brake lines. 6. Leaking or worn master cylinder. 7. Excessively worn brake lining.
Spongy brake pedal	1. Air in hydraulic system. 2. Improper brake fluid (low boiling point). 3. Excessively worn or cracked brake drums. 4. Broken pedal pivot bushing.
Brakes pulling	1. Contaminated lining. 2. Front end out of alignment. 3. Incorrect brake adjustment. 4. Unmatched brake lining. 5. Brake drums out of round. 6. Brake shoes distorted. 7. Restricted brake hose or line. 8. Broken rear spring. 9. Worn brake linings. 10. Uneven lining wear. 11. Glazed brake lining. 12. Excessive brake lining dust. 13. Heat spotted brake drums. 14. Weak brake return springs. 15. Faulty automatic adjusters. 16. Low or incorrect tire pressure.

Condition	Possible Cause
Squealing brakes	1. Glazed brake lining.
	2. Saturated brake lining.
	3. Weak or broken brake shoe retaining spring.
	4. Broken or weak brake shoe return spring.
	5. Incorrect brake lining.
	6. Distorted brake shoes.
	7. Bent support plate.
	8. Dust in brakes or scored brake drums.
	9. Linings worn below limit.
	10. Uneven brake lining wear.
	11. Heat spotted brake drums.
Chirping brakes	1. Out of round drum or eccentric axle flange pilot.
Dragging brakes	1. Incorrect wheel or parking brake adjustment.
	2. Parking brakes engaged or improperly adjusted.
	3. Weak or broken brake shoe return spring.
	4. Brake pedal binding.
	5. Master cylinder cup sticking.
	6. Obstructed master cylinder relief port.
	7. Saturated brake lining.
	8. Bent or out of round brake drum.
	9. Contaminated or improper brake fluid.
	10. Sticking wheel cylinder pistons.
	11. Driver riding brake pedal.
	12. Defective proportioning valve.
	13. Insufficient brake shoe lubricant.
Hard pedal	1. Brake booster inoperative.
	2. Incorrect brake lining.
	3. Restricted brake line or hose.
	4. Frozen brake pedal linkage.
	5. Stuck wheel cylinder.
	6. Binding pedal linkage.
	7. Faulty proportioning valve.
Wheel locks	1. Contaminated brake lining.
	2. Loose or torn brake lining.
	3. Wheel cylinder cups sticking.
	4. Incorrect wheel bearing adjustment.
	5. Faulty proportioning valve.
Brakes fade (high speed)	1. Incorrect lining.
	2. Overheated brake drums.
	3. Incorrect brake fluid (low boiling temperature).
	4. Saturated brake lining.
	5. Leak in hydraulic system.
	6. Faulty automatic adjusters.
Pedal pulsates	1. Bent or out of round brake drum.
Brake chatter and shoe knock	1. Out of round brake drum.
	2. Loose support plate.
	3. Bent support plate.
	4. Distorted brake shoes.
	5. Machine grooves in contact face of brake drum (Shoe Knock).
	6. Contaminated brake lining.
	7. Missing or loose components.
	8. Incorrect lining material.
	9. Out-of-round brake drums.
	10. Heat spotted or scored brake drums.
	11. Out-of-balance wheels.

Troubleshooting Drum Brakes (cont.)

Condition	Possible Cause
Brakes do not self adjust	1. Adjuster screw frozen in thread. 2. Adjuster screw corroded at thrust washer. 3. Adjuster lever does not engage star wheel. 4. Adjuster installed on wrong wheel.
Brake light glows	1. Leak in the hydraulic system. 2. Air in the system. 3. Improperly adjusted master cylinder pushrod. 4. Uneven lining wear. 5. Failure to center combination valve or proportioning valve.

Appendix

General Conversion Table

Multiply by	To convert	To	
2.54	Inches	Centimeters	.3937
30.48	Feet	Centimeters	.0328
.914	Yards	Meters	1.094
1.609	Miles	Kilometers	.621
.645	Square inches	Square cm.	.155
.836	Square yards	Square meters	1.196
16.39	Cubic inches	Cubic cm.	.061
28.3	Cubic feet	Liters	.0353
.4536	Pounds	Kilograms	2.2045
4.226	Gallons	Liters	.264
.068	Lbs./sq. in. (psi)	Atmospheres	14.7
.138	Foot pounds	Kg. m.	7.23
1.014	H.P. (DIN)	H.P. (SAE)	.9861
—	To obtain	From	Multiply by

Note: 1 cm. equals 10 mm.; 1 mm. equals .0394".

Conversion—Common Fractions to Decimals and Millimeters

Common Fractions	Decimal Fractions	Millimeters (approx.)	Common Fractions	Decimal Fractions	Millimeters (approx.)	Common Fractions	Decimal Fractions	Millimeters (approx.)
1/128	.008	0.20	11/32	.344	8.73	43/64	.672	17.07
1/64	.016	0.40	23/64	.359	9.13	11/16	.688	17.46
1/32	.031	0.79	3/8	.375	9.53	45/64	.703	17.86
3/64	.047	1.19	25/64	.391	9.92	23/32	.719	18.26
1/16	.063	1.59	13/32	.406	10.32	47/64	.734	18.65
5/64	.078	1.98	27/64	.422	10.72	3/4	.750	19.05
3/32	.094	2.38	7/16	.438	11.11	49/64	.766	19.45
7/64	.109	2.78	29/64	.453	11.51	25/32	.781	19.84
1/8	.125	3.18	15/32	.469	11.91	51/64	.797	20.24
9/64	.141	3.57	31/64	.484	12.30	13/16	.813	20.64
5/32	.156	3.97	1/2	.500	12.70	53/64	.828	21.03
11/64	.172	4.37	33/64	.516	13.10	27/32	.844	21.43
3/16	.188	4.76	17/32	.531	13.49	55/64	.859	21.83
13/64	.203	5.16	35/64	.547	13.89	7/8	.875	22.23
7/32	.219	5.56	9/16	.563	14.29	57/64	.891	22.62
15/64	.234	5.95	37/64	.578	14.68	29/32	.906	23.02
1/4	.250	6.35	19/32	.594	15.08	59/64	.922	23.42
17/64	.266	6.75	39/64	.609	15.48	15/16	.938	23.81
9/32	.281	7.14	5/8	.625	15.88	61/64	.953	24.21
19/64	.297	7.54	41/64	.641	16.27	31/32	.969	24.61
5/16	.313	7.94	21/32	.656	16.67	63/64	.984	25.00
21/64	.328	8.33						

Conversion—Millimeters to Decimal Inches

mm	inches	mm	inches	mm	inches	mm	inches	mm	inches
1	.039 370	31	1.220 470	61	2.401 570	91	3.582 670	210	8.267 700
2	.078 740	32	1.259 840	62	2.440 940	92	3.622 040	220	8.661 400
3	.118 110	33	1.299 210	63	2.480 310	93	3.661 410	230	9.055 100
4	.157 480	34	1.338 580	64	2.519 680	94	3.700 780	240	9.448 800
5	.196 850	35	1.377 949	65	2.559 050	95	3.740 150	250	9.842 500
6	.236 220	36	1.417 319	66	2.598 420	96	3.779 520	260	10.236 200
7	.275 590	37	1.456 689	67	2.637 790	97	3.818 890	270	10.629 900
8	.314 960	38	1.496 050	68	2.677 160	98	3.858 260	280	11.032 600
9	.354 330	39	1.535 430	69	2.716 530	99	3.897 630	290	11.417 300
10	.393 700	40	1.574 800	70	2.755 900	100	3.937 000	300	11.811 000
11	.433 070	41	1.614 170	71	2.795 270	105	4.133 848	310	12.204 700
12	.472 440	42	1.653 540	72	2.834 640	110	4.330 700	320	12.598 400
13	.511 810	43	1.692 910	73	2.874 010	115	4.527 550	330	12.992 100
14	.551 180	44	1.732 280	74	2.913 380	120	4.724 400	340	13.385 800
15	.590 550	45	1.771 650	75	2.952 750	125	4.921 250	350	13.779 500
16	.629 920	46	1.811 020	76	2.992 120	130	5.118 100	360	14.173 200
17	.669 290	47	1.850 390	77	3.031 490	135	5.314 950	370	14.566 900
18	.708 660	48	1.889 760	78	3.070 860	140	5.511 800	380	14.960 600
19	.748 030	49	1.929 130	79	3.110 230	145	5.708 650	390	15.354 300
20	.787 400	50	1.968 500	80	3.149 600	150	5.905 500	400	15.748 000
21	.826 770	51	2.007 870	81	3.188 970	155	6.102 350	500	19.685 000
22	.866 140	52	2.047 240	82	3.228 340	160	6.299 200	600	23.622 000
23	.905 510	53	2.086 610	83	3.267 710	165	6.496 050	700	27.559 000
24	.944 880	54	2.125 980	84	3.307 080	170	6.692 900	800	31.496 000
25	.984 250	55	2.165 350	85	3.346 450	175	6.889 750	900	35.433 000
26	1.023 620	56	2.204 720	86	3.385 820	180	7.086 600	1000	39.370 000
27	1.062 990	57	2.244 090	87	3.425 190	185	7.283 450	2000	78.740 000
28	1.102 360	58	2.283 460	88	3.464 560	190	7.480 300	3000	118.110 000
29	1.141 730	59	2.322 830	89	3.503 903	195	7.677 150	4000	157.480 000
30	1.181 100	60	2.362 200	90	3.543 300	200	7.874 000	5000	196.850 000

To change decimal millimeters to decimal inches, position the decimal point where desired on either side of the millimeter measurement shown and reset the inches decimal by the same number of digits in the same direction. For example, to convert 0.001 mm to decimal inches, reset the decimal behind the 1 mm (shown on the chart) to 0.001; change the decimal inch equivalent (0.039″ shown) to 0.000039″.

Tap Drill Sizes

National Fine or S.A.E.

Screw & Tap Size	Threads Per Inch	Use Drill Number
No. 5	44	37
No. 6	40	33
No. 8	36	29
No. 10	32	21
No. 12	28	15
1/4	28	3
5/16	24	1
3/8	24	Q
7/16	20	W
1/2	20	29/64
9/16	18	33/64
5/8	18	37/64
3/4	16	11/16
7/8	14	13/16
1 1/8	12	1 3/64
1 1/4	12	1 11/64
1 1/2	12	1 27/64

Tap Drill Sizes

National Coarse or U.S.S.

Screw & Tap Size	Threads Per Inch	Use Drill Number
No. 5	40	39
No. 6	32	36
No. 8	32	29
No. 10	24	25
No. 12	24	17
1/4	20	8
5/16	18	F
3/8	16	5/16
7/16	14	U
1/2	13	27/64
9/16	12	31/64
5/8	11	17/32
3/4	10	21/32
7/8	9	49/64
1	8	7/8
1 1/8	7	63/64
1 1/4	7	1 7/64
1 1/2	6	1 11/32

Decimal Equivalent Size of the Number Drills

Drill No.	Decimal Equivalent	Drill No.	Decimal Equivalent	Drill No.	Decimal Equivalent
80	.0135	53	.0595	26	.1470
79	.0145	52	.0635	25	.1495
78	.0160	51	.0670	24	.1520
77	.0180	50	.0700	23	.1540
76	.0200	49	.0730	22	.1570
75	.0210	48	.0760	21	.1590
74	.0225	47	.0785	20	.1610
73	.0240	46	.0810	19	.1660
72	.0250	45	.0820	18	.1695
71	.0260	44	.0860	17	.1730
70	.0280	43	.0890	16	.1770
69	.0292	42	.0935	15	.1800
68	.0310	41	.0960	14	.1820
67	.0320	40	.0980	13	.1850
66	.0330	39	.0995	12	.1890
65	.0350	38	.1015	11	.1910
64	.0360	37	.1040	10	.1935
63	.0370	36	.1065	9	.1960
62	.0380	35	.1100	8	.1990
61	.0390	34	.1110	7	.2010
60	.0400	33	.1130	6	.2040
59	.0410	32	.1160	5	.2055
58	.0420	31	.1200	4	.2090
57	.0430	30	.1285	3	.2130
56	.0465	29	.1360	2	.2210
55	.0520	28	.1405	1	.2280
54	.0550	27	.1440		

Decimal Equivalent Size of the Letter Drills

Letter Drill	Decimal Equivalent	Letter Drill	Decimal Equivalent	Letter Drill	Decimal Equivalent
A	.234	J	.277	S	.348
B	.238	K	.281	T	.358
C	.242	L	.290	U	.368
D	.246	M	.295	V	.377
E	.250	N	.302	W	.386
F	.257	O	.316	X	.397
G	.261	P	.323	Y	.404
H	.266	Q	.332	Z	.413
I	.272	R	.339		

Anti-Freeze Chart

Temperatures Shown in Degrees Fahrenheit +32 is Freezing

Cooling System Capacity Quarts	Quarts of ETHYLENE GLYCOL Needed for Protection to Temperatures Shown Below													
	1	2	3	4	5	6	7	8	9	10	11	12	13	14
10	+24°	+16°	+ 4°	−12°	−34°	−62°								
11	+25	+18	+ 8	− 6	−23	−47								
12	+26	+19	+10	0	−15	−34	−57°							
13	+27	+21	+13	+ 3	− 9	−25	−45							
14			+15	+ 6	− 5	−18	−34							
15			+16	+ 8	0	−12	−26							
16			+17	+10	+ 2	− 8	−19	−34	−52°					
17				+18	+12	+ 5	− 4	−14	−27	−42				
18				+19	+14	+ 7	0	−10	−21	−34	−50°			
19				+20	+15	+ 9	+ 2	− 7	−16	−28	−42			
20					+16	+10	+ 4	− 3	−12	−22	−34	−48°		
21					+17	+12	+ 6	0	− 9	−17	−28	−41		
22					+18	+13	+ 8	+ 2	− 6	−14	−23	−34	−47°	
23					+19	+14	+ 9	+ 4	− 3	−10	−19	−29	−40	
24					+19	+15	+10	+ 5	0	− 8	−15	−23	−34	−46°
25					+20	+16	+12	+ 7	+ 1	− 5	−12	−20	−29	−40
26						+17	+13	+ 8	+ 3	− 3	− 9	−16	−25	−34
27						+18	+14	+ 9	+ 5	− 1	− 7	−13	−21	−29
28						+18	+15	+10	+ 6	+ 1	− 5	−11	−18	−25
29						+19	+16	+12	+ 7	+ 2	− 3	− 8	−15	−22
30						+20	+17	+13	+ 8	+ 4	− 1	− 6	−12	−18

For capacities over 30 quarts divide true capacity by 3. Find quarts Anti-Freeze for the ⅓ and multiply by 3 for quarts to add.

Row 25 column 14: −50°

Row 26 column 14: −44

Row 27 column 14: −39

Row 28 column 14: −34

Row 29 column 14: −29

Row 30 column 14: −25

For capacities under 10 quarts multiply true capacity by 3. Find quarts Anti-Freeze for the tripled volume and divide by 3 for quarts to add.

To Increase the Freezing Protection of Anti-Freeze Solutions Already Installed

Cooling System Capacity Quarts	Number of Quarts of ETHYLENE GLYCOL Anti-Freeze Required to Increase Protection													
	From +20° F. to					From +10° F. to					From 0° F. to			
	0°	−10°	−20°	−30°	−40°	0°	−10°	−20°	−30°	−40°	−10°	−20°	−30°	−40°
10	1¾	2¼	3	3½	3¾	¾	1½	2¼	2¾	3¼	¾	1½	2	2½
12	2	2¾	3½	4	4½	1	1¾	2½	3¼	3¾	1	1¾	2½	3¼
14	2¼	3¼	4	4¾	5½	1¼	2	3	3¾	4½	1	2	3	3½
16	2½	3½	4½	5¼	6	1¼	2½	3½	4¼	5¼	1¼	2¼	3¼	4
18	3	4	5	6	7	1½	2¾	4	5	5¾	1½	2½	3¾	4¾
20	3¼	4½	5¾	6¾	7½	1¾	3	4¼	5½	6½	1½	2¾	4¼	5¼
22	3½	5	6¼	7¼	8¼	1¾	3¼	4¾	6	7¼	1¾	3¼	4½	5½
24	4	5½	7	8	9	2	3½	5	6½	7½	1¾	3½	5	6
26	4¼	6	7½	8¾	10	2	4	5½	7	8¼	2	3¾	5½	6¾
28	4½	6¼	8	9½	10½	2¼	4¼	6	7½	9	2	4	5¾	7¼
30	5	6¾	8½	10	11½	2½	4½	6½	8	9½	2¼	4¼	6¼	7¾

Test radiator solution with proper hydrometer. Determine from the table the number of quarts of solution to be drawn off from a full cooling system and replace with undiluted anti-freeze, to give the desired increased protection. For example, to increase protection of a 22-quart cooling system containing Ethylene Glycol (permanent type) anti-freeze, from +20° F. to −20° F. will require the replacement of 6¼ quarts of solution with undiluted anti-freeze.

Index

Chilton's Repair & Tune-Up Guides

The complete line covers domestic cars, imports, trucks, vans, RV's and 4-wheel drive vehicles.

BOOK CODE	TITLE
#7032	Arrow & D-50 Pick-Ups 79-81
#6637	Aspen & Volare 76-78
#5902	Audi 70-73
#7028	Audi 4000 & 5000 77-81
#6337	Audi Fox 73-75
#5807	Barracuda and Challenger 65-72
#6931	Blazer & Jimmy 69-80
#6844	BMW 70-79
#7045	Camaro 67-81
#6695	Capri 70-77
#7041	Champ/Arrow/Sapporo 77-81
#6316	Charger, Coronet 71-75
#6836	Chevette 76-80
#6840	Chevrolet Mid Size 64-79 Covers Chevelle, Laguna, El Camino, Monte Carlo & Malibu
#7135	Chevrolet 68-81 All Full-Size Chevrolet Models
#6936	Chevrolet & GMC Pick-Ups 70-80
#6930	Chevrolet & GMC Vans 67-80
#7051	Chevrolet LUV 72-81 Inc. 4 x 4 Models
#6841	Chevy II, Nova 62-79
#7037	Colt & Challenger 71-80
#6691	Corvair 60-69 All Models and Engines, Inc. Turbo.
#6576	Corvette 53-62
#6843	Corvette 63-79
#6933	Cutlass 70-80
#6962	Dasher, Rabbit, Scirocco, Jetta 74-80
#5790	Datsun 61-72
#6960	Datsun 73-80
#7050	Datsun Pick-Ups 70-81
#6932	Datsun Z and ZX 70-80
#6554	Dodge 68-77
#6486	Dodge Charger 67-70
#6934	Dodge & Plymouth Vans 67-80
#6320	Fairlane and Torino 62-75
#6965	Fairmont & Zephyr 78-80
#6485	Fiat 64-70
#7042	Fiat 69-81
#6846	Fiesta 78-80
#5996	Firebird 67-74
#7140	Ford Bronco 66-81
#6983	Ford Courier 72-80
#6842	Ford and Mercury 68-79 All Full-Size Models
#6696	Ford and Mercury Mid-Size 71-78 Covers Torino, Gran Torino, Ranchero, Elite, LTD II, Thunderbird, Montego, and Cougar
#6913	Ford Pick-Ups 65-80
#6849	Ford Vans 61-80
#6935	GM Subcompact 71-80 Covers Vega, Monza, Astre, Sunbird, Starfire, Skyhawk
#7049	GM X-Body 80-81 Covers Citation, Omega, Phoenix and Skylark
#6937	Granada/Monarch 75-80

BOOK CODE	TITLE
#6980	Honda 73-80
#5912	International Scout 67-73
#5998	Jaguar 69-74
#7136	Jeep CJ 45-81
#6739	Jeep Wagoneer, Commando, and Cherokee 66-79
#6634	Maverick/Comet 70-77
#6981	Mazda 71-80
#7031	Mazda RX-7 78-81
#6065	Mercedes-Benz 59-70
#5907	Mercedes-Benz 68-73
#6809	Mercedes-Benz 74-79
#6780	MG 61-79
#6542	Mustang 65-73
#6812	Mustang II 74-78
#6963	Mustang & Capri 79-80 Inc. Turbo.
#6845	Omni/Horizon 78-80
#5792	Opel 64-70
#6575	Opel 71-75
#6473	Pacer 75-76
#5982	Peugeot 70-74
#7027	Pinto & Bobcat 71-80
#6552	Plymouth 68-76
#5822	Porsche 69-73
#6331	Ramcharger & Trail Duster 74-75
#5985	Rebel/Matador 67-74
#5821	Road Runner, Satellite, Belvedere, GTX 68-73
#5988	Saab 99 69-75
#6978	Snowmobiles 76-80
#6982	Subaru 70-80
#5905	Tempest, GTO and Le Mans 68-73
#5795	Toyota 66-70
#7036	Toyota Corolla/Carina/Tercel/Starlet 70-81
#7043	Toyota Celica & Supra 71-81
#7044	Toyota Corona/Cressida/Crown/Mk II 70-81
#6276	Toyota Land Cruiser 66-74
#7035	Toyota Pick-Ups 70-81
#5910	Triumph 69-73
#6326	Valiant and Duster 68-76
#5796	Volkswagen 49-71
#6837	Volkswagen 70-81
#6529	Volvo 56-69
#7040	Volvo 70-81

AUTOMOTIVE SPECIALITY BOOKS

BOOK CODE	TITLE
#6754	Chilton's Diesel Guide
#6942	Chilton's Guide to Consumers' Auto Repairs and Prices
#6940	Chilton's Minor Auto Body Repair
#6908	Chilton's More Miles Per Gallon
#6867	Chilton's Motorcycle Owner's Handbook
#6727	Chilton's Off-Roading Guide
#6811	Chilton's Repair Guide for Small Engines - Covers 2 and 4-stroke air cooled gasoline engines up to 20 hp.

Chilton's Repair & Tune-Up Guides are available at your local retailer or by mailing a check or money order for **$9.95** plus **$1.00** to cover postage and handling to:

**Chilton Book Company
Dept. DM,
Radnor, PA 19089**

NOTE: When ordering be sure to include name & address, book code & title.